Understanding Nonprofit Organizations

# Understanding Nonprofit Organizations

## *Governance, Leadership, and Management*

**Third Edition**

*Edited by*
J. STEVEN OTT
AND LISA A. DICKE

*With case studies by*
C. KENNETH MEYER

**WESTVIEW PRESS**

A Member of the Perseus Books Group

Westview Press was founded in 1975 in Boulder, Colorado, by notable publisher and intellectual Fred Praeger. Westview Press continues to publish scholarly titles and high-quality undergraduate- and graduate-level textbooks in core social science disciplines. With books developed, written, and edited with the needs of serious nonfiction readers, professors, and students in mind, Westview Press honors its long history of publishing books that matter.

Westview Press books are available at special discounts for bulk purchases in the United States by corporations, institutions, and other organizations. For more information, please contact the Special Markets Department at the Perseus Books Group, 2300 Chestnut Street, Suite 200, Philadelphia, PA 19103, or call (800) 810-4145, ext. 5000, or e-mail special.markets@perseusbooks.com.

Library of Congress Cataloging-in-Publication Data

Understanding nonprofit organizations : governance, leadership and management / edited by J. Steven Ott, Lisa A. Dicke ; contributions by C. Kenneth Meyer.—Third edition.
     pages cm
   Includes bibliographical references.
   ISBN 978-0-8133-4961-9 (paperback)
1.  Nonprofit organizations—United States. 2.  Voluntarism—United States.  I. Ott, J. Steven. II. Dicke, Lisa A., 1960–
   HD2769.2.U6U53 2015
   658'.0480973—dc23
                                                                              2015004074

10 9 8 7 6 5 4 3 2 1

# Contents

## I     Governance of Nonprofit Organizations     1

## II     The Legal Framework (Jared C. Bennett)     33

## VII     Contracts, Partners, and Collaborations                      225

## VIII    Budgets, Financial Reports, and Management Control           267

## IX      Managing Volunteers                                          293

## X    Accountability and Evaluation                                       327

# Tables and Figures

## Figures

## Tables

# Foreword

Leaders and communities across the globe are asking more and more of nonprofit organizations—more with regard to creativity, more with regard to responsiveness, more with regard to impact and results. These are exciting and challenging times for those who lead and manage nonprofit organizations, and the sector's capacity to deliver on its promises and to serve our communities and citizens well hinges directly on the effectiveness of its leaders and managers. Nonprofits serve in roles of pivotal significance in the shared-power global environment of today, and their leaders and managers must be adept at assessing and addressing the needs and challenges posed by an environment characterized by greater variation and complexity, coupled with cycles of change that are deeper and faster than we traditionally have known. The pace of change and the extent of that change are demanding a greater level of knowledge, sophistication, and skill from those who lead and manage these organizations.

Thus, I am delighted that Steve Ott, Lisa Dicke, and their colleagues have prepared the third edition of this valuable book, *Understanding Nonprofit Organizations,* as a resource to help inform and educate those who lead and manage nonprofit organizations. An undertaking of this magnitude is very demanding, so we are fortunate that Steve, Lisa, and their colleagues have chosen to invest their energies in creating the next generation of this important volume.

This third edition arrives at a very interesting and important time. Although the recession that gripped the economies of the world at the end of the 2000s has to a large degree disappeared, it has left in its wake a very different environment for nonprofit organizations. Some

have recovered from the stresses of the recession relatively well, yet for the leaders and managers of the majority of nonprofit organizations, conditions remain exceptionally challenging. Many nonprofits, especially health and human services organizations, continue to be challenged by the residual effects of the recession's "triple whammy"—the intersection of exceptional growth in demand for critical services; a very different resource environment reflective of significant changes in the nature and form of both philanthropic and governmental financial support; and organizations' limited recovery from the decline in internal resources (to the extent that they existed) as investments, endowments, and other assets diminished in value owing to the same economic dynamics. Even as the economy has improved, the financial state of the sector appears to be nearly as precarious as it was at the height of the recession. The Nonprofit Finance Fund, in the summary report of its 2014 survey of nonprofits, reports that 80 percent of "lifeline" nonprofits continue to report growth in demand for services, and more than half of the surveyed organizations report that they have been unable to meet this demand. These organizations are financially challenged as well: 56 percent report that they have less than three months' worth of cash on hand (including the 12 percent that report less than one month's worth of cash on hand at survey time). These statistics remain very similar to the numbers reported at the height of the recession in 2010! To this day, our safety nets are fraying, the level of stress throughout the sector is significant, and the potential for relief appears to be very spotty. Many of the organizations in this vital sector are in very fragile condition, and it is going to take a strong new generation of leadership and management to sustain and develop them.

Most concur that these trends affirm that the nonprofit world is changing (and being changed) in relatively fundamental ways. Nonprofit sector scholar Lester Salamon (2010), who has lauded the sector's resilience, also has written that the context of nonprofit leadership and management has changed so much that it is not at all the same work as in the past. Some aspects have become easier, yet much has become significantly more complex and difficult. Salamon identifies four key types of challenges confronting the sector:

- The challenges of *finance,* ranging from governmental retrenchment to the changing nature of public support to a decline in the share of private giving relative to nonprofit need
- The challenges of more and different kinds of *competition,* ranging from intra-sector competition among nonprofits for time, talent, and treasure to inter-sector competition among nonprofits and for-profits for attention, credibility, and business as they jockey for the opportunity to provide services in an increasingly ambivalent marketplace
- The challenges of *effectiveness,* which arise from the increased demands that nonprofits demonstrate and prove their performance, results, and accountability
- The challenges of *technology* as new and increasingly sophisticated digital technologies and social media become available to both the sector and a good share of its constituents, leading to heightened expectations for new levels of communication, engagement, and responsiveness—and to new definitions of effectiveness (Salamon 2010, 97)

Many others have issued studies and reports that chronicle in similar ways the changes and challenges confronting sector leaders and managers. The Alliance for Children and Families, in its 2011 report on its assessment of the changing nonprofit human services environment, describes a set of six "disruptive forces" that are driving what it terms a "human services revolution." The Alliance states that, in an environment characterized by the forces of purposeful experimentation, information liberation, integration of science, an uncompromising demand for impact, branding causes rather than organizations, and the need to attract investors rather than donors, the success of a nonprofit organization will hinge on its ability to capitalize on the opportunities that these forces enable (Alliance for Children and Families 2011, 31).

Similarly, Heather Gowdy and her associates (2009), in an earlier assessment prepared for the James Irvine Foundation, assert that the nonprofit sector is at a unique point in time, "an inflection point" that is driving fundamental reshaping of the sector. They argue that successful nonprofit leaders and managers must build their capacity to be attuned to rapid and continual shifts such as these as they prepare to manage strategically in the fundamentally new operating environment that is emerging from the *convergence* of five central trends (and especially, they stress, from the interaction of these five converging trends):

- Demographic shifts that redefine participation, including the emergence of increasingly intergenerational and multicultural workplaces that must effectively address issues of engagement, inclusion, and equity
- Technological advances, including the rise of social media and new ways of communicating, that demand greater openness and transparency and both enable and require nonprofits to strategically leverage and facilitate collaborative engagement
- Growing networks (technological as well as social) that allow dialogue, work, and even decision making to be organized in multiple new and relatively more fluid ways
- Rising interest in civic engagement and volunteerism, reflecting both growing expectations for

new levels and multiple forms of engagement and heightened expectations of nonprofits that they will create opportunities better tailored to the times and ways that participants wish to become involved

- A blurring of sectoral boundaries as nonprofits, for-profits, and even governmental agencies compete and collaborate in increasingly diverse ways that both enhance and sometimes confuse opportunities for the creation of private wealth and social capital

These dynamics are challenging, yet they are not necessarily negative. Effective nonprofit leaders and managers are being both innovative and strategic as they explore ways to navigate these changes. For example:

- The realization that it is impossible to operate as they have in the past has led many nonprofit organizations and their leaders to fundamentally rethink what they do and how they do it. At best, nonprofits achieve greater focus as they clarify the core of their mission and then seek innovative ways to address it.
- Many nonprofit organizations, as they experience the problems posed by their traditional revenue strategies, are rethinking their business and revenue models. The exceptional growth in interest in nonprofit social entrepreneurship reflects a new level of creativity as many nonprofits employ different and more diverse ways to fund and finance their work.
- New forms of organizing are being explored and tested, particularly via the expanded use of creative forms of alliances and networks. There is expanded involvement in service-delivery networks as nonprofits recognize that they cannot achieve their results alone.
- There is growing use of hybrid forms of organization that extend across and blur traditional sector boundaries. Such organizations blend the practices of business, government, and nonprofits to achieve results that cannot be achieved in any single sector.

- New and richer ways of understanding and ensuring accountability are being developed at both the organizational and system levels to complement those that operate within programs. Systems are being developed in ways that more effectively gather and employ data to document and enhance performance and effectiveness at both the organizational and program levels of operation.
- Smaller nonprofits are investing in increasingly sophisticated yet lower-cost software that makes it feasible to become more effective in strategy and planning, decision making, constituent relations, and financial and performance management processes.
- Nonprofits are taking marketing more seriously and bringing more sophisticated practices to marketing and branding (which is no longer just a euphemism for fundraising and selling). These practices include adapting and employing social media and other emerging approaches and technologies to enhance constituent relations, communications, alliance and relationship building, and transparency and accountability at relatively low cost.
- Savvy nonprofits also are proactively addressing the human resources facets of nonprofit leadership and management, from developing new leadership talent to succession planning to changing how they engage new generations in their work—for example, by tapping the strong interest of many young people in community-building activities. These agencies are creating new ways for young adults from all types of backgrounds to become more engaged in service in the sector.
- Increasing numbers are taking advantage of the phenomenal growth in the number and scope of programs in nonprofit leadership and management—both formal degree programs at the bachelor's and master's degree levels and various certificate and other nondegree programs—to build the capacity of both current and aspiring leaders.
- New forms of leadership and governance are being explored and developed as nonprofit

organizations and their leaders work to capitalize on all of these trends and dynamics.

Needless to say, these conditions demand the best of even the most experienced nonprofit executives and boards. This is not an easy time to run a nonprofit, and this third edition offers important knowledge and insights to those who choose to lead and manage in this new era of nonprofit service.

Some question whether there is any substantive difference between "nonprofit management" and management in other types of organizations. After all, most of the nonprofit management functions explained in this volume are germane to the successful management of any organization. So is there a difference? At core, whether in nonprofit or for-profit organizations, the central purpose of management is the same. However, there are unique dimensions to *nonprofit* management that are important to recognize because they have a distinct impact on the success of those who do this work (Renz 2010, 800–801).

- *The unique legal context:* To state the obvious, the nonprofit sector in the United States and most other nations of the world is legally distinct from the other sectors. It is neither for-profit business nor government, even as it carries certain characteristics of each, and this difference in legal context is significant to the practice of management. (Most notably, it limits the range of strategic options available to the leadership team.)
- *The unique ownership structure:* One of the legal differences that becomes significant to management is that of organizational ownership. In the United States and many other nations, it is generally not possible to own (that is, to have an equity stake in, such as stock) a nonprofit charitable organization. In practical terms, the typical US charity is "owned" by the community or segment of the community that it exists

to serve. Thus, its governing board and management must act as stewards of the assets of the organization on behalf of the community, even as there is no singular clear external source of accountability or control over the affairs of the organization. Such diffusion of control and accountability creates both unique opportunities and complications for nonprofit management.

- *The unique financial and capital structure:* Further complicating the unique work of nonprofit management is the financial context for a typical nonprofit organization, which often will be much more complex than it is for for-profit businesses of similar size. The typical nonprofit's complicated mix of clients and markets, which correlates directly to complicated business models grounded in diverse and inconsistent funding and financing models, makes the work of nonprofit management distinctive. The typical for-profit business gets its financial support from a relatively uncomplicated set of sources; nonprofits increasingly must fund and finance their operations with a mix of philanthropic resources and earned income derived from a relatively diverse set of sources. Each source imposes its own expectations for operations, management performance, and organizational accountability. Among the most demanding are the governmental sources, since acceptance of funds from government typically intensifies the demands for procedural as well as performance accountability.
- *The unique accountability context:* Legal and ownership differences blend with the unique political and cultural context of the nonprofit sector to further complicate the work of nonprofit management. One characteristic of the nonprofit organization's diffuse and unclear accountability is that the typical organization has multiple significant stakeholders, most of whom think that they are, or should be, "in charge." These stakeholders bring diverse and conflicting performance expectations to bear on the organization, and therefore on its

management team. In today's environment of heightened concern for accountability and performance, the management team cannot afford to overtly ignore most such expectations, even when they are inconsistent. Thus, one of the most challenging tasks of *nonprofit* management is to craft a course of action that strikes a reasonable balance among the divergent and shifting expectations and demands of the organization's multiple stakeholders. To meet this challenge management must have exceptional political sophistication and sensitivity to the external environment. Further, efficiency in the social sector cannot be assessed as it is in business. A sector that serves to address the expressive and artistic needs of a community cannot legitimately be judged by the same criteria brought to bear on those that serve instrumental functions. Indeed, this is where part of the accountability paradox of the sector arises—because many seek to turn the sector into a purely instrumental form. (In its own way, government has done more to create this dynamic than any other part of society.) For many communities, the important value of the sector extends far beyond that of a service provider.

These distinctions are relatively subtle, yet they are very real and very significant, and the failure to understand and address their implications is potentially disabling to the unprepared nonprofit leader or manager.

Some worry, as we continue to develop the professional capacity of the sector's management, that the distinctive character of nonprofits in civil society will be lost. Indeed, there can be some rather dark sides to the professionalization of the management of the nonprofit sector. But there is no reason to believe that this must be the case. Indeed, drawing on a key marketing concept, we can and must remember to regularly and clearly articulate the key differentiators that distinguish nonprofit organizations from all oth-

ers. If professionalization and education are implemented appropriately, the sector will not lose its way because, at core, effective management must be grounded in and defined by mission accomplishment. So the challenge in difficult times is to never forget why we do what we do. I am optimistic that we are very unlikely to forget our mission—our volunteers and donors and community leaders will not let this happen. Although the sector's public trust ratings are less than I'd like, it remains true that the average citizen values the nonprofit sector and considers it an essential part of a viable society. We know this in no small part because year after year we continue to see people across the globe coming together to invest their time and resources to advance the work and impact of the millions of nonprofits (a good share of them all-volunteer organizations) that exist to address their community's needs, interests, and aspirations.

It is through the effective practice of leadership and management that the organizations of the third sector will continue to grow and develop in their capacity to successfully address the needs of a diverse and complicated world. Fortunately, the new generation of nonprofit managers preparing to lead these important organizations understands the increasingly complex nature of the work of nonprofit management.

Steve Ott, Lisa Dicke, and their colleagues are to be congratulated for preparing this new edition. It is a welcome contribution to the literature of the nonprofit sector because it explains in useful terms what we need to know about nonprofit organizations, how they function, and how they can effectively be led and managed. This new edition has been revised to help leaders and managers understand and address the trends, needs, and dynamics described in this foreword, with new chapters on innovation, networked organizations, social entrepreneurship, and the changing philanthropic and resource environments. These chapters are written by leading scholars and professionals, people who know their topics very well, and they are organized and presented in a way that brings important clarity to the management of this new generation of nonprofit organizations. We are fortunate to have this valuable resource to inform our work in these exciting and promising times.

*David O. Renz*
Midwest Center for Nonprofit Leadership
Henry W. Bloch School of Management
University of Missouri–Kansas City
September 2014

# References

Alliance for Children and Families. 2011. *Disruptive Forces: Driving a Human Services Revolution.* Milwaukee, WI: Alliance for Children and Families.

Gowdy, Heather, Alex Hildebrand, David La Piana, and Melissa Mendes Campos. 2009. "Convergence: How Five Trends Will Reshape the Social Sector." San Francisco: James Irvine Foundation.

Nonprofit Finance Fund. 2014. *Nonprofit Finance Fund 2014 State of the Sector Survey.* New York: Nonprofit Finance Fund.

Renz, David. 2010. "Conclusion." In *The Jossey-Bass Handbook of Nonprofit Leadership and Management,* 3rd ed., edited by David O. Renz, 794–805. San Francisco: Jossey-Bass.

Salamon, Lester. 2010. "The Changing Context of Nonprofit Leadership and Management." In *The Jossey-Bass Handbook of Nonprofit Leadership and Management,* 3rd ed., edited by David O. Renz, 77–100. San Francisco: Jossey-Bass.

# Preface

Understanding Nonprofit Organizations is a collection of twenty-two of the most important and informative articles, chapters, and essays written about the workings of nonprofit organizations in the United States. This third edition also includes twenty cases that can be used to illustrate many of the complex managerial issues raised in the readings and to encourage critical thinking.

There are no easy solutions to the problems and complexities faced by nonprofit managers. Together, the introductions to each part, the chapter readings, and the case studies provide an opportunity for readers to learn, reflect, and analyze circumstances, grapple with solutions, and provide solid rationales for the decisions they make and the positions they take.

The book speaks to the governance, leadership, and management functions of the thousands of organizations in the nonprofit sector that engage in a surprisingly wide array of activities and provide an enormous range of services—mostly for the purpose of either improving aspects of the quality of life in the United States or preventing its deterioration. In our opinion, this volume includes much of the most insightful and interesting literature that can be found about nonprofit organizations. We hope that you will agree.

*Understanding Nonprofit Organizations* does not just tell the reader what these authors have written; it presents their works in their own words. It is designed for individuals who are hoping or planning to move into paid or voluntary leadership and management positions in nonprofit organizations—as well as for those who are already involved with nonprofits and want to learn more about their workings. This book provides a cohesive set of readings for a course on nonprofit organizations and management. Instructors and students will also appreciate the array of cases that parallel the major themes presented. The book will most likely be used as a supplement to other texts in courses at the upper-division undergraduate and graduate levels, but it also can stand on its own.

All the introductory essays and reprinted readings attempt to answer two defining questions:

- What is distinctive about the governance, leadership, and management of nonprofit organizations?
- What has caused nonprofit leadership and management to be distinctive?

Each part of the volume attempts to provide rich answers to these two defining questions by addressing a set of long-standing, historic functions and issues from a variety of contemporary perspectives. The essays that open each of the ten parts introduce important issues and concepts, place them in the context of their environment, and explain what students should be looking for as they read the reprinted chapters. To reflect shifts in managerial concerns, the parts in the third edition have been adjusted to address current movements in the nonprofit field, including innovations and advances in communications and social media.

*Understanding Nonprofit Organizations* focuses on internal organizational issues and the environmental forces that affect them. Theories and concepts of the nonprofit sector are the topics of a companion book, *The Nature of the Nonprofit Sector,* now also in its third edition and also edited by us with Westview Press.

A listing of the part titles and the authors and dates of the readings reveals the scope, depth, and currency of the book's coverage—and its usefulness for graduate and upper-division undergraduate courses in nonprofit organizations and management. (See the table of contents for a complete listing of authors and titles.)

## Contents by Part

Although we fully expect to be criticized for excluding other excellent articles and writers, it will be more difficult to criticize the inclusions. We selected those readings that are among the best readings or that best "fit" each of the parts. The authors selected are thoughtful and perceptive, and many have written in this field for many years.

As the book editors, our goals have been to:

- create a clear vision of what this collection of readings will accomplish;
- select previously published articles and chapters that tell the story well;
- edit and condense reprinted readings to make them more readable and to help students focus on the central ideas that make these readings worthwhile;
- provide frameworks in our introductory essays for the topic addressed in each part; and
- let the authors speak for themselves.

The nonprofit sector as we know it is a unique democratic phenomenon, and the governance, management, and leadership of its organizations have differed from business and government. In the past three decades, however, a blurring of the lines between organizations in the nonprofit, government, and business sectors has eroded some of the distinctiveness of nonprofit organizations and thus also some aspects of governing, leading, and managing nonprofits. Most nonprofit organizations are becoming more business-like and/or more government-like in important ways. Change is often beneficial, of course, and there is no doubt that the array of challenges facing the nonprofit sector may be of a magnitude beyond any in the sector's history.[1] To remain robust, the governance, leadership, and management of nonprofit organizations must rise to these challenges and also address the need for strong collaborations, professionalism, and entrepreneurship. Success in the nonprofit sector, however, requires more than this of its leaders. As those familiar with the field have come to recognize, governing boards and executives must also respect the distinctiveness of the nonprofit sector's history and traditions. Those at the helm of nonprofits are expected to contribute to their communities and guide their organizations with care and altruistic hearts.

## Criteria for Selection

Several criteria were used to make final selections about readings to include in this book. The first "test" that any reading had to pass was a "yes" answer to two questions: Should the serious student of the nonprofit sector be expected to be able to identify the authors and their basic themes—the crux of their arguments? Does the reading provide a reason or reasons why the governance, leadership, or management of nonprofit organizations is distinctive?

The second criterion was related to the first: each reading had to make a statement. This criterion did not eliminate controversial readings; quite the contrary, it simply required that a reading not be ignored. Third, the chapter had to be readable. Students who have already had reason to peruse the literature of nonprofit organizations will appreciate the importance of this criterion.

Last, the reading had to fit within this volume: it had to address issues or ideas that are important to the governance, leadership, or management of nonprofit organizations. This book is about the internal structures and workings of nonprofit organizations, not macro issues and macro theories, which are represented in the many interesting readings about the nonprofit sector that can be found in the companion book, *The Nature of the Nonprofit Sector*.[2] Most of the readings that we reviewed fit cleanly into either *Understanding Nonprofit Organizations* or *The Nature of the Nonprofit Sector*. Most decisions as to where they belonged also were easy to make; decisions about readings on intersectoral relations and international nonprofit organizations were the most difficult. The case studies that appear in the third edition of *Understanding Nonprofit Organizations* complement the topics raised in each part of the book. Students will develop a deeper appreciation for dilemmas that arise in the management of nonprofit organizations through the scenarios depicted in the cases. Instructors are encouraged to use the cases to stimulate discussion and to help students recognize and engage with managerial challenges, as well as to hone and strengthen their critical thinking skills. Although the names and places identified in the cases are fictitious, we believe that those with experience in the field will recognize many of the dilemmas as "all too familiar." Yet familiarity does not equal prescription! Such is the challenge and excitement of managing and understanding nonprofit organizations.

We hope that you will enjoy this book!

*J. Steven Ott*
*Lisa A. Dicke*

## Notes

1. Lester M. Salamon, Stephanie L. Geller, and Kasey Spence, "Impact of the 2007–09 Economic Recession on Nonprofit Organizations," Listening Post Project Communique 14 (Baltimore, MD: Johns Hopkins Center for Civil Society Studies, 2009), 5.

2. J. Steven Ott and Lisa A. Dicke, eds., *The Nature of the Nonprofit Sector*, 3rd ed. (Boulder, CO: Westview Press, 2016).

# Acknowledgments

We recognize that space and propriety limit our statements of appreciation, but intellectual contributions that absolutely must be acknowledged include: Stephen Block, University of Colorado–Denver; Kirsten Grønbjerg, Indiana University–Bloomington; David O. Renz, University of Missouri–Kansas City; Patricia Bromley, University of Utah; Russ Cargo, Helena, Montana; and Dr. Hee Soun Jang and Robert L. Bland, University of North Texas.

We also wish to acknowledge and thank C. Kenneth Meyer at Drake University for his collaboration on this third edition of *Understanding Nonprofit Organizations*. His generous contributions of the case study exercises and thoughtful suggestions have improved the volume and helped make the project a joy to undertake and complete.

We also extend special appreciation to Jared Bennett, who updated his introduction to Part II, "The Legal Framework," and Michele Cole, who wrote an original chapter, "Capacity-Building: Strategies for Successful Fundraising," included in Part V. Carolyn Chavez, Carolyn Williamson, Hannah Nickel, and Ashley E. English, at the University of North Texas, Dr. Marina Saitgalina, Oakland University, and Floyd Rosenkranz also provided exceptional support throughout the project.

Our two Perseus Books/Westview Press representatives have been wonderful. Krista Anderson was thorough and persistent in securing permissions to reprint previously published articles and chapters, and Ada Fung artfully steered us through the production of this book, from the first days after the decision was made to publish a third edition to the completion of all editorial processes. Finally, we owe a special debt of gratitude to David Gies and Jay Shafritz, co-collaborators in editing the 1990 book *The Nonprofit Organization: Essential Readings*.[1] Their ahead-of-the-times ideas and insights helped shape our thinking about the nonprofit sector and its organizations—and thus also the concept of this book.

## Note

1. David L. Gies, J. Steven Ott, and Jay M. Shafritz, eds., *The Nonprofit Organization: Essential Readings* (Fort Worth, TX: Harcourt Brace, 1990; originally published by Brooks/Cole, Pacific Grove, CA). This book is now out of print.

# PART I

# GOVERNANCE OF NONPROFIT ORGANIZATIONS

*Governance* is an umbrella term that includes the ultimate authority, accountability, and responsibility for an organization. Nonprofit organizations are governed through complex sets of functional roles and procedures that are defined in laws and tax codes, influenced by numerous external constituencies, and shaped to fit their own missions, structures, activities, personalities, policies, and procedures.[1] The governance of a nonprofit organization is a product of its purposes, people, resources, contracts, clients, boundaries, community coalitions and networks, and actions as prescribed (or prohibited) in its articles of incorporation and bylaws, state laws and codes, and the US Internal Revenue Service (IRS) codes and rules.[2]

A nonprofit organization that incorporates becomes a *corporation* and therefore is similar in many ways, "in the eyes of the law," to a for-profit business.[3] Corporations are *artificial persons*, groups of individuals who obtain legal identities and legal standing through the act of incorporation—or in some cases through the act of legally associating, that is, forming and filing with a state as *associations*. The statutes of nonprofit incorporation differ somewhat from state to state, but all specify that the *board of trustees* (also referred to as the *board of directors*) is the ultimate point of responsibility and accountability for a nonprofit organization.[4] In some states, the laws are even more detailed and define specific responsibilities of boards. The courts have also been active in defining the basic responsibilities of boards. In the landmark 1974 *Sibley Hospital* case, for example, the Federal District Court for the District of Columbia held (among other things) that the board of trustees is responsible for active supervision of a nonprofit corporation's managers and for overseeing its financial management.[5] In 2002, the American Competitiveness and Corporate Accountability Act (commonly known as the Sarbanes-Oxley Act), was signed into law. The purpose of the act was to rebuild trust in America's corporate sector after a series of high-profile accounting scandals. Although very few provisions of Sarbanes-Oxley are directly applicable to nonprofit boards of trustees, it has served as a warning to all boards: "If nonprofit leaders do not ensure effective governance of their organizations, the government may step forward and also regulate nonprofit governance."[6]

By statute, a nonprofit organization's articles of incorporation and bylaws must specify the composition of the board, its responsibilities, and the rules and procedures under which the board will govern. The legal objective is to ensure that the board of trustees abides by applicable laws, makes certain that the organization's activities are directed toward the purposes stated in the articles of incorporation, and protects the organization and its assets through oversight activities.

Most statutes of nonprofit incorporation deal with boards of trustees as legal entities (as "artificial persons"), not as individual persons. When directors are acting in their capacities as members of a board, for the most part they are not "persons" in the eyes of the law, but rather parts of a corporation board—unless they individually violate provisions of laws, bylaws, or articles. The *corporate veil* is the legal assumption that the actions of a corporation are not the actions of its owners and directors and thus its owners and directors usually cannot be held responsible for corporate actions; also, a nonprofit board of trustees and its members are protected from undue personal liability when the nonprofit is incorporated under the laws of a state.[7] In the past few decades, however, the courts have been more inclined to hold individual board members co-responsible for the collective actions of a board; thus, service on a board of trustees involves a degree of exposure to legal liability.

## Governance Defined

*Merriam-Webster's Dictionary* defines *govern* as:

> 1. To direct and control; rule. 2. To regulate; restrain. 3. To be a rule of law for; to determine. Syn. Govern, rule means to exercise power or authority in controlling others. Govern connotes as its end a keeping in a straight course or smooth operation for the good of the individual and the whole.

*Governance* is the function of oversight that a group of people assume when they incorporate under the laws of a state for an organizational purpose that qualifies for nonprofit status. For most observers of nonprofit organizations, governance is "a general term referring to the collective actions of a board of directors or board of trustees in its governing of a tax-exempt organization."[8] Governance includes serving on a board of trustees and exercising and expressing one's attitudes, beliefs, and values on matters pertaining to the organization. Some writers disagree with this narrow construction of governance and believe that the definition should be broader: for example, the term *governance* may be defined to mean the strategic leadership of nonprofit organizations. In current parlance, the term has taken on a more specific meaning as a process for making certain types of management decisions. These are commonly referred to as *strategic decisions*.[9]

The scope and depth of the influence of the board of directors for a nonprofit organization is, to say the least, substantial:

> Most people would agree with these ideals: boards should know who they work for; they should require their organizations to be effective and efficient; they should be in control of their organization; the control they exercise should be of a type that empowers, not strangles; they should be fair in judging but unafraid to judge, rigorously holding delegates accountable; they should be disciplined as to their roles and their behavior; they should require discipline with regard to the role and behavior of their individual members; as the highest authority in enterprise, they should be predictable and trustworthy.[10]

## Who Governs?

Virtually everyone agrees that a nonprofit organization's board of trustees is—and should be—the final authority on governance decisions.[11] The term *board of directors*, or *board of trustees*, refers to a governing board. A *governing board* is a group of individuals who have assumed a legal responsibility for an organization's existence. These individuals make policy and are responsible for how money is generated and spent toward the accomplishment of a mission that can be beneficial to the general public or to a segment of the population.[12]

Not all boards of directors, however, live up to their potential. "Many nonprofit boards, probably the great majority, do not come close to realizing their leadership potential in practice and as a consequence have become increasingly frustrated, dissatisfied, and often angry."[13] In practice, many boards pay more attention to nongoverning activities than to their primary mission.[14]

Most discussions of governance in nonprofit organizations emphasize the roles and functions not only of the board but also of the executive director—usually the top-paid staff person responsible for the day-to-day operations of the organization.[15] "In the voluntary sector context, *governance* generally refers to the arena of action in which boards of directors *and* executive staff are key players. . . . In most nonprofit organizations supported in part by public funds . . . the governance challenge is met by both executive staff and board members."[16] Governing as a set of shared functions also extends to the consideration of input from client and stakeholder groups.[17] Nonprofit governance has also been conceptualized as *traditional* or *contemporary*. "The traditional framework views nonprofit governance at the organizational level where the board of directors and trustees are considered responsible for higher-level policy decisions, the accomplishment of the agency's goals, and conformance to all the legal requirements. In contrast, the contemporary framework views nonprofit governance as moving beyond the internal scope of responsibility to addressing the community or public interest."[18] An organizational life cycle approach to governing has also been proposed.[19]

## Why Governance Is Needed

Nonprofit governance may sound like an unnecessary complication. After all, the presence of multiple actors practically guarantees that there will be multiple headaches. Why is governance even needed in nonprofit organizations, which provide services or engage in other activities that are not for the personal gain of the people who volunteer with, are employed by, or serve on their boards? Only in modern times have legal structures and formal rules seriously affected the efforts of people to help their neighbors. The complexities of our society, the force of law (notably laws that involve licensure and tax-exempt status), and citizens' growing concerns about potential abuses, fraud, and violations of expectations (implied social contracts) by nonprofit organizations, government, small businesses, and communities have all changed the environment for nonprofits, and with it the "ground rules."[20]

A well-functioning, mission-focused, informed, and perhaps influential board of trustees is essential for long-term organizational effectiveness and survival. Networks of information, interorganizational linkages, and knowledge come together through the connections between executive directors and boards of trustees.[21]

Nonprofit organizations also need the benefit of free (or nearly free) advice. Executive directors must be able to turn to board members for counsel and support. The day-to-day time and energy needed to manage the dynamics of a nonprofit's mission, goals, programs, personnel, volunteers, board officers, and external constituencies do not permit an executive director to stay current on all important laws, court rulings, and regulations. Without rapid access to accurate information from experts who are sympathetic board members, and who therefore also know the organization and its programs, a nonprofit organization may sometimes be at considerable risk. This *advice and counsel* function of trustees is only one vital piece, however, of their larger set of responsibilities and accountabilities. Not only do board members have responsibilities as part of the organization's formal internal control and oversight mechanism, but they also fill important boundary-spanning roles that connect the organization with segments of its environment.[22]

Board members are the primary links between a nonprofit organization and its community. Trustees thus function as information channels, interorganizational intermediaries, and sources of legitimacy who buffer an organization from pressures in its environment.[23] They also seek and attract external resources and information through their established networks of relationships.

Thus, governance is both the "steering" and the overseeing of organizational activities, assets, and relationships by boards of trustees and executives, within a framework of law and ethics. From this perspective, governing is a form of philanthropy: "voluntary giving, voluntary serving, and voluntary association to achieve some vision of the public good."[24] Governing is a form of philanthropy because it represents individuals giving their time, effort, and influence to help improve an aspect of the quality of life, or to prevent it from deteriorating.[25]

The challenges facing the nonprofit sector related to governance and boards of trustees are great. The findings from a 2007 survey conducted by Francie Ostrower of over 5,100 public charities in the United States showed that a large percentage of nonprofit boards were racially and ethnically homogeneous, raising questions about their ability to be responsive to a diverse public. The Ostrower report, *Nonprofit Governance in the United States,* also showed that a substantial percentage of nonprofit board members were not actively engaged in basic governance activities such as fundraising, monitoring of programs, and community relations. Likewise, 70 percent of nonprofit organizations reported having some difficulty finding board members.[26]

## Readings Reprinted in Part I

In the classic "Board of Directors," Stephen Block emphasizes the unequivocal governance responsibilities of boards. "Accountability for any nonprofit organization ultimately rests with its board of directors. . . . Although the board may delegate management authority to a paid staff person, . . . the board can never be relieved of its legal and fiduciary responsibilities. Governing board members are stewards of the public interest."[27]

Block addresses many board-related issues, including board purposes, relationships between a board and an executive director, important board responsibilities, the functions of specific board officers, the board's role in development, board diversity, the desirable size of a board, board liability, the dismissal of board members who are not performing, and fundamental differences between governing, advisory, and honorary boards.

Also reprinted in this section is "Applying Sarbanes-Oxley Governance Principles to Nonprofits Organizations," from "Guide to Nonprofit Corporate Governance in the Wake of Sarbanes-Oxley," a report prepared by the American Bar Association (ABA). As noted earlier, governing and accountability rest with the board of directors, and these responsibilities may not be delegated. The ABA report provides an overview of the major provisions of the 2002 act and fashions them to the governing environment of nonprofits, with specific application to the legal, fiduciary, and accountability concerns relevant to the composition of a nonprofit's board of directors and the activities and responsibilities under their purview.

Ten general principles are discussed that have emerged from Sarbanes-Oxley and have implications for nonprofits including the: role of boards, importance of independent directors, audit committees, governance and nominating committees, compensation committees, disclosure and integrity of institutional information, ethics and business conduct codes, executive and director compensation, monitoring compliance and investigating complaints, and document destruction and retention. Each of these principles is a matter of concern for the board of directors who collectively and, more recently, individually are responsible for ensuring the health and fiscal integrity of the organization and compliance with legal directives. Although only two provisions of Sarbanes-Oxley pertain directly to nonprofits, all of the provisions are worthy of consideration. "Board members are supposed to know what the organizations they oversee are actually doing; fiduciary responsibility has meaning and consequences for board members; there is a relationship between good governance and organizational effectiveness; and . . . institutional funders and individual donors should be legitimately concerned with and attentive to nonprofit governance."[28]

## Case Studies in Part I

The case studies in Part I, "Welcome to the Board of Directors" and "Unwelcome News: Nonprofit Scandal," provide readers with an opportunity to consider the decisions and activities that fall under the purview of a member of a board of directors. In "Welcome to the Board of Directors," a new member of a national board is elated to become a part of the governing body. As often happens, however, she must soon confront a preexisting board culture that creates a less-than-ideal state of affairs.

In "Unwelcome News," a scandal involving the founder and CEO of a long-established nonprofit organization hits the front pages. In this case, the actions and inactions of a board of directors with regard to their oversight responsibilities are front and center. Readers are asked at the end of the case to consider the role of a board of directors and its obligations prior to and after an incident of alleged wrongdoing.

## Notes

1. Robert D. Herman and David O. Renz, "Multiple Constituencies and the Social Construction of Nonprofit Organization Effectiveness" (reprinted in Part X of *Understanding Nonprofit Organizations*, 2nd ed., 2012).

2. In some states the terms *charter* or *articles of association* are used instead of *articles of incorporation*.

3. Although nonprofit organizations and for-profit corporations share many similarities, they also have important differences. From a legal perspective, however, both may be corporations.

4. For a more detailed discussion, see Part II, "The Legal Framework."

5. *"Sibley Hospital"* is the popular name for *Stern v. Lucy Webb Hayes National Training School* (381 F. Supp. 1003 [D. DC, 1974]).

6. BoardSource and Independent Sector, "The Sarbanes-Oxley Act and Implications for Nonprofit Organizations," 2003 (revised January 2006), https://www.independentsector.org/uploads/Accountability_Documents /sarbanes_oxley_implications.pdf.

7. Statutes vary widely among states, however, and court interpretations of liability statutes have changed considerably in recent decades. Staying abreast of legal rulings and interpretations is an ongoing responsibility for nonprofit boards.

8. J. Steven Ott and Jay M. Shafritz, "Governance," in J. Steven Ott and Jay M. Shafritz, *The Facts on File Dictionary of Nonprofit Organization Management* (New York: Facts on File, 1986), 172.

9. Vic Murray, "Governance of Nonprofit Organizations," in *The International Encyclopedia of Public Policy and Administration*, edited by Jay M. Shafritz (Boulder, CO: Westview Press, 1998), 993.

10. John Carver and Miriam Carver, *The Policy Governance Model and the Role of the Board Member* (San Francisco: Jossey-Bass/Wiley, 2009), 2.

11. See, for example, John Carver, *Boards That Make a Difference*, 3rd ed. (San Francisco: Jossey-Bass/Wiley, 2006); and Cyril O. Houle, *Governing Boards*, 2nd ed. (San Francisco: Jossey-Bass, 1997).

12. Stephen R. Block, *Perfect Nonprofit Boards: Myths, Paradoxes, and Paradigms* (Needham Heights, MA: Simon & Schuster Custom Publishing, 1998), 30.

13. Doug Eadie, *Extraordinary Board Leadership: The Keys to High-Impact Governing,* 2nd ed. (Sudbury, MA: Jones and Bartlett, 2009), 9.

14. See, for example, ibid., 1–34.

15. See Murray, "Governance of Nonprofit Organizations," 993–997; and Judith R. Saidel, "Expanding the Governance Construct: Functions and Contributions of Nonprofit Advisory Groups," *Nonprofit and Voluntary Sector Quarterly* 27, no. 4 (December 1998): 421, 422.

16. Saidel, "Expanding the Governance Construct," 421, 422. Saidel argues that advisory groups and committees also fill important governance roles in many nonprofit organizations with government grants or contracts.

17. Kelly LeRoux, "Paternalistic or Participatory Governance? Examining Opportunities for Client Participation in Nonprofit Social Service Organizations," *Public Administration Review* (May-June 2009): 504–517.

18. Shamima Ahmed, "Nonprofit Governance," in Shamima Ahmed, *Effective Non-Profit Management: Context, Concepts, and Competencies* (Boca Raton, FL: CRC Press, 2012), 95–131, 95.

19. Mike Burns, *Act Your Age! Organizational Life Cycles: How They Impact Your Board* (Branford, CT: BWB Solutions, 2010).

20. See Part IX in our companion book *The Nature of the Nonprofit Sector,* 3rd ed., edited by J. Steven Ott and Lisa A. Dicke (Boulder, CO: Perseus/Westview Press, 2016).

21. Melissa Middleton-Stone, "Nonprofit Boards of Directors: Beyond the Governance Function," in *The Nonprofit Sector: A Research Handbook,* edited by W. W. Powell (New Haven, CT: Yale University Press, 1987), 141–153.

22. See Part VI, "Community Theories of the Nonprofit Sector," in Ott and Dicke, *The Nature of the Nonprofit Sector,* 3rd ed.

23. Pamela A. Popielarz and J. Miller McPherson, "On the Edge or in Between: Niche Position, Niche Overlap, and the Duration of Voluntary Association Memberships," *American Journal of Sociology* 101, no. 3 (November 1995): 698–720.

24. Warren F. Ilchman, "Philanthropy," in Shafritz, *The International Encyclopedia of Public Policy and Administration,* 1654–1661.

25. See Part VIII, "Theories of Giving and Philanthropy," in Ott and Dicke, *The Nature of the Nonprofit Sector,* 3rd ed.

26. Francie Ostrower, "Nonprofit Governance in the United States: Findings on Performance and Accountability from the First National Representative Study," Urban Institute, 2007, http://www.urban.org/UploadedPDF/411479_Nonprofit_Governance.pdf; see also "Five Questions for Francie Ostrower," Urban Institute: Elevate the Debate, July 19, 2007, www.urban.org/toolkit/fivequestions/FOstrower.cfm?renderforprint=1.

27. Stephen R. Block, "Board of Directors," in Shafritz, *The International Encyclopedia of Public Policy and Administration,* 201–209, 201.

28. Rick Cohen, "Sarbanes-Oxley: Ten Years After," *Nonprofit Quarterly* (December, 30 2012), https://nonprofitquarterly.org/governancevoice/21563-sarbanes-oxley-ten-years-later.html.

## CHAPTER 1

# Board of Directors

## Stephen R. Block

[B]oards of directors are] vested with the legal responsibility to govern and control the affairs of organizations. Accountability for any nonprofit organization ultimately rests with its board of directors (sometimes called board of trustees). Although the board may delegate management authority to a paid staff person, known as the executive director, the board can never be relieved of its legal and fiduciary responsibilities. Governing board members are stewards of the public interest and have a burden of responsibility to use and preserve the organization's assets for advancing a beneficial mission.

Board membership is an admirable act of citizenship for those who are willing to accept a significant amount of volunteering. These special people are generally not compensated for their board service, and they must balance their board obligations with personal demands of work, family responsibilities, and other community activities. This commitment to community service is tied to a long history of voluntary action, with roots that precede the founding of the United States. The innate desire to help is said to be a unique quality in America, a democratic attribute that influences the modern nonprofit board of directors.

Because of the board's legal responsibilities, personal limitations on directors' time, and the daily involvement of the executive director, there is often confusion between the board and staff over roles, responsibilities, turf, and expectations for performance. The board and executive director must clearly understand their mutual expectations if they are to develop a healthy governing body.

## Why Have a Board?

Of the many reasons for having a board of directors, legal necessity is primary. In some states, only one board member is required for incorporating an organization, but most states require at least three or more individuals to serve as directors of a governing board. The Internal Revenue Service also requires nonprofit organizations seeking or maintaining recognition for tax-exempt purposes to have governing boards of directors. Members of governing boards are expected to engage willingly in board activities, without receiving any benefit of the organization's assets or earnings.

Aside from the legal necessities, the most practical reasons for having a board of directors

---

Originally published in *The International Encyclopedia of Public Policy and Administration,* edited by Jay M. Shafritz, copyright © 1998. Reprinted by permission of Westview Press, a member of The Perseus Books Group.

are to ensure that the organization is effectively managed and is working toward the achievement of a mission that has a public purpose. Few nonprofit organizations have the resources to employ the personnel with the expertise that is necessary to accomplish their organizational activities. The collective wisdom of the board of directors can serve as a bank of skilled and knowledgeable resources to provide support, advice, and counsel. It has been widely proposed that board members should comprise the three Ws; individuals who are willing to "work," some with "wisdom," and others with "wealth."

## Why Would Someone Want to Serve on a Board?

Each person has his or her own reason for voluntary board service; however, one of the most often-stated is to serve one's community. Volunteering as a board member is an honor and a fundamental privilege of a free people.

There are many reasons for joining or for staying on a board. For example, board participation may be an expectation of one's employer. It may provide an opportunity for gaining or maintaining social status in the community, satisfy socializing needs, lead to new knowledge and skills, and enhance one's résumé. For some people, voluntary board service satisfies religious convictions based on a belief in the organization's cause or mission; or is based on personal experience of a problem (such as a disease or tragedy) that is addressed by the work and mission of the organization.

## The Board's Relationship with Its Executive Director

Various authors have described their ideas about the ideal working relationship between the board and executive director. Two governance models prevail. One model builds on the traditional view

that the executive director is employed as a subordinate to the board. The working relationship is characterized by distinct and separate roles for the board and executive director, with the board directing, supervising, and limiting the director's activities as the board sees fit.

The other governance model builds on ideas of partnership and collegiality between the executive director and board of directors. This model acknowledges that the board of directors has clearly defined legal responsibilities. However, the model differs from traditional approaches in a fundamental way: The executive director takes an active role in assisting with or coordinating the participation of board members in fulfilling their governance commitment. This form of board management makes full use of the executive director's distinctive management and leadership skills. Consequently, the quality of the board's performance is a direct result of the executive director's ability to steer and promote productive interaction among board members. The executive director can call upon board managers to intervene when necessary in either the internal or external environment of the organization.

## Who Is in Charge of Making Policy?

Prescriptions for effective board practice often state that the board is legally responsible for making policy and the staff is responsible for carrying it out. Though this division of labor is technically correct, it is inaccurate in its practice. The staffs of nonprofit organizations have a significant level of influence on the creation of policy. Since they are closest to the operations and programs of the agency, they may know when a new policy would provide the guidance needed to get the job done. Thus, staff input is almost always required to create new policies. In addition, the staff often shapes the policy by drafting proposed policy statements.

In effective nonprofit organizations, the staff's point of view on matters of policy development is considered an integral part of governance. Often, effective organizations are those in which the board adopts policy with input of the staff, and the staff implement policy with the advice, counsel, and support of the board.

## What Are the Major Areas of Board Responsibility?

There are at least nine major areas of board responsibility; namely, to

1. determine the organization's mission;
2. set policies and adopt plans for the organization's operations;
3. approve the budget, establish fiscal policies and financial controls, and monitor the financial position of the organization;
4. provide adequate resources for the organization through establishment of resource-development goals and commitment to fundraising through giving and soliciting;
5. develop organizational visibility through networking and linkage to the community;
6. ensure that the organization's corporate and governance documents are updated and secured, and all reports are filed as required;
7. recruit and select new board members and provide them with an orientation to the board's business;
8. recruit, hire, evaluate, reward, or terminate, if necessary, the executive director of the organization; and
9. protect and preserve the organization's nonprofit tax-exempt status.

## The Role of Board Officers

The officers of the board of directors have a responsibility to set the tone for organizational leadership. The duties of the president (chairperson), vice president, treasurer, and secretary are described in the organization's bylaws.

### President

In most nonprofit organizations the title and position of president refers to the highest-level volunteer who also serves as chairperson of the organization. However, in some nonprofit organizations a corporate model of governance is followed; therefore, the title of "president" replaces the more commonly used title of "executive director." If the president is also the paid chief executive, the position usually allows for participation as a board member. In this instance, the role of chairperson is handled by the chief volunteer.

The volunteer president or chairperson is responsible for the activities of the board and for assigning board committee chairs, unless assignments are automatically spelled out in the bylaws. The chair is responsible for monitoring the work of the board and evaluating the board's performance. The chair presides at and calls special meetings of the board and sets the direction for organizational goal setting. This volunteer position requires a great deal of time commitment and responsibility.

### Vice President

In the absence of the volunteer president, the vice president usually assumes the duties of president and the responsibility for chairing board meetings. Often, the role of vice president entails chairing a major committee of the board. In some organizations, the vice president automatically becomes president-elect, a succession plan that may not be effective in all organizations.

### Secretary

The board secretary has the obligation to protect the organization's corporate documents, such as the bylaws, the articles of incorporation, board and committee minutes, and important correspondence.

Many individuals try to avoid election to the office of secretary because of the myth that the board secretary must take the minutes of the board and executive committee meetings. The board secretary does not have to write the minutes, but he or she is responsible for ensuring that the minutes are taken and accurately reflect the business meetings of the board and executive committee. Upon becoming official annals of the organization, the board minutes should be signed and dated by the board secretary. In organizations that rely on parliamentary rules and procedures (such as *Robert's Rules of Order Newly Revised*), the board secretary is required to become familiar with the meeting procedures and may have to make procedural rulings.

### Treasurer

The treasurer should not be expected to do the bookkeeping and accounting for the organization. Instead, the treasurer is responsible for making sure that the organization's finances are properly accounted for and excess revenues are wisely invested. If a finance committee exists, the treasurer often serves as its chairperson. On behalf of the board, the treasurer ensures that financial controls are in place and tested on a periodic basis. The treasurer also participates in the selection and recommendation of an auditing firm. The treasurer reports on the financial statements at board meetings, executive committee meetings, and, if applicable, at annual meetings of the organization.

## The Board's Role in Fundraising

The board must play a fundamental role in raising money and resources. Board members also have the personal responsibility of making financial contributions in addition to giving their voluntary time to the organization. Instituting a policy that requires board members to contribute is sometimes employed.

Unanimous giving among the board sets the right tone for fundraising. It enhances the credibility of the organization when it seeks contributions from others. Unanimous-board-giving

practices have even become an expectation among many funders.

Giving is only one part of the board member's obligation; the other part is to assist in planning and solicitation activities. Collectively, the board can identify a pool of potential contributors. Friends, business associates, relatives, and vendors are among likely prospects. Some board members shy away from verbally asking for money, but they may be able to write letters or at least sign letters that have been drafted for them by staff.

## Board Composition

Determining the composition of a board of directors is claimed by some to be a blend of science and art.

Board composition should not be the result of opening the door to just anyone who is willing to serve but should result from purposeful recruitment strategies. Prospective board members, for example, should be familiarized with the organization's purpose, mission, vision, goals, and objectives, as well as board duties, responsibilities, and the organization's expectations.

The task of filling vacancies on the board should be approached carefully and should result in a board composition that is able to advance the organization's mission. There are two preparatory steps to actively recruiting the right person. The initial step is to acknowledge that organizations go through different stages of development similar to the various life cycles experienced by individuals. Various maturational stages lead to differing organizational issues and needs. Assessing which phase an organization is in is useful not only to prepare the organization for change but also to determine the leadership qualities required of potential board members. Matching an organization's life cycle to the requisite skills of a board member could lead to more effective and purposeful organizational outcomes.

A second step is to conduct a thorough demographic inventory of board composition, which will reveal the board's weakest representational areas. Inventory results will show a compositional balance or imbalance in such variables as gender, age range, ethnicity, socioeconomic status, political party affiliation, educational level, professional or vocational interests, knowledge of consumer issues, and location of primary residence. Information of this type can be valuable to organizations especially seeking to create a diverse board.

As suggested, the composition of a board can contribute to the level of ease or difficulty with which an organization is governed and managed. A board composed of individuals with similar socioeconomic backgrounds or other familiar traits may reach consensus more often, but it is less likely to formulate challenging ideas or seek out policy reforms. Compared to homogeneous boards, those that reflect diversity among their members are likely to experience greater participatory challenges. Even though diversity is an enriching quality in a board, its members must contend with differing values, mores, and interpretations of community information and beliefs.

## The Executive Director as Board Member

Some nonprofit organizations use a corporate model of governance structure in which the position of executive director is transformed from staff to member of the board as its president–chief executive officer (CEO).

The model of corporate governance may not be an appropriate structure for all nonprofit organizations. It is used by larger and more complex institutions that rely on a strong CEO. Regardless of size, the CEO as staff and board member must be wary of conflicts of interest and must avoid participating in discussions or decisionmaking that will lead to personal ben-

efits. Critics of nonprofit organizations using corporate models suggest that the CEOs have no choice but to use the knowledge they have acquired in managing the day-to-day operations. This knowledge is often used to influence the direction of the board and organization. . . .

## Board Recruitment and Orientation

Preconditions of board recruitment include identifying the governance needs of organizations in (life-cycle) transition and discovering the characteristics and qualities to be found in new board members. There are many variables to consider in sizing up a board prospect, including:

1. an individual's ability to create a vision, problem-solve, and facilitate conflict resolution;
2. an individual's commitment of time to participate fully;
3. enthusiasm for the organization's mission, vision, goals, and values;
4. a person's skills and experience in such areas as public policy analysis and fundraising, or expertise in program service delivery; and
5. diversity factors.

Once a profile is developed that describes the ideal board member, the recruitment task can formally begin. On the basis of expediency, many nonprofit organizations make the mistake of ignoring the profile and recruiting the friends of board members. Sometimes, individuals are invited to become prospective board members for the simple reason that they are alive and seem agreeable to serving! Serious problems may occur when attempts have not been made to match the needs of the organization with the ideal board member. Locating someone who matches the profile and agrees to serve, however, is not a guarantee of board success. In fact, most governance problems seem to stem from the recruitment process. Though using a profile can increase the likelihood of finding the right person, a perfect match does not guarantee that problems will not arise, such as, nonattendance at board meetings, lack of participation in board committees, an unwillingness to contribute financially, or interfering with or trying to micromanage the day-to-day operations of the organization.

Finding a board prospect who fits the profile is, indeed, a critical part of the assignment, as is fully informing the prospect about specific board duties. The lack of knowledge about the expectations for board member role and governance responsibilities will directly contribute to organizational confusion, ineffectiveness, and a breach in a board member's commitment. Since each organization's board of directors has a different mission and focus for its work, even the seasoned board member who joins a new board should receive a briefing on the organization, its expectations of board members, and board responsibilities. It is imperative to seek an agreement to serve only after the board prospect understands the parameters of board service.

Organizations sometimes give prospects a board-prospecting packet, which may contain some or all of the following: a history of the organization; board job descriptions; a copy of the articles of incorporation and bylaws; a copy of the organization's purpose or mission statement; an organizational chart; and a description of program services, with a list of committees and duties of each. This packet may also include a roster of the current board, with work affiliations, addresses, and phone numbers; dates of future meetings and special events; an annual report and organization brochures, newsletters, or related materials; and a copy of a recent auditor's financial report, annual budget, and financial statements.

It may also be helpful for the organization's board to assign a veteran member to assist the prospect in "learning the ropes." The availability of a support person may encourage the board prospect to join a concerned board of direc-

tors. The veteran could serve as a resource person during the recruitment phase and then as a mentor or helper during the transition period following induction.

## How Many Board Members?

There is no formula for determining the appropriate size of an organization's board of directors. The size of the board must be tailored to suit the needs of the organization.

One helpful way to determine board size is an organizational life-cycle analysis, referred to previously as a prerequisite to board recruitment. Organizations and their boards experience various developmental stages, all of which can influence the number and type of skilled board members that are needed.

Large- and small-sized boards have both advantages and disadvantages. The number of people on a board can be a factor that influences how board members comport themselves. Large boards are generally unwieldy because it is difficult to pay attention to so many people. Because the larger group will find it more difficult to become cohesive and familiar with the cohort, it may tend to be more formal in its board conduct and meetings. Organizations that are just starting out, or those in need of a boost in financial resources, may be better served by a larger board of 20 to 25 individuals. In this case, the larger the number of board members the greater the chances of reaching out to potential donors.

On one hand, smaller boards are limited in accomplishing supportive activities such as fundraising. On the other hand, a smaller group may have to rely on its creativity, such as developing a fundraising plan for implementation by a committee of staff, board members, and other community volunteers. Organizations that do not rely heavily on the board alone for fundraising or other supportive activities might be better served by a board of no more than ten members. The smaller group would have more of an opportunity to become cohesive; learn experientially how to mesh effectively their collective wisdom, advice, and counsel; reach decisions through consensus; and it would have no need to use controlling, parliamentary procedures for conducting board meetings.

## Board Liability

Though nonprofit boards of directors are infrequently sued, the risk of liability is nevertheless a legitimate concern for volunteer board members. Financial losses associated with a lawsuit can be devastating to an organization and its board members. The quality and manner in which boards make decisions or fail to make decisions can result in a legal challenge that tests whether they have met or failed in their responsibilities as stewards of the public interest.

Board members and prospective members are often comforted by the knowledge that the nonprofit organization has purchased a director's and officers' (D&O) liability insurance policy. Concerns about lawsuits have caused a rising demand for this type of insurance, and consequently, premium costs vary widely.

A factor that affects the cost of D&O insurance is the nature of the organization's work, whether it is, for example, a direct service health care agency or an organization that promotes the arts. Features and exclusions may also differ greatly from one policy to another and affect the price and value of the policy.

Indemnification refers to the organization ensuring that it will pay the reasonable costs associated with liability suits, such as judgments and settlements against its board members. This practice is sometimes compelled by state law. In other situations it may be an optional practice of the board. In either event, the organization's bylaws outline the extent of indemnification. Indemnification cannot, however, be exercised when the organization brings a suit

against its own board members. In practice, indemnification is a form of self-insurance and assumes that the organization has the funds to pay legal costs. Given the resources of some nonprofit organizations, this assumption may not be valid.

In addition to indemnification and D&O liability insurance coverage, a board of directors can purchase various liability insurance policies, including, but not limited to, the following specialty policies: general liability, employees' liability, malpractice, automobile, and fiduciary.

To encourage board and other voluntary service in community organizations, all 50 states have passed volunteer protection laws. The extent of protection varies among the states, and this form of legislation has largely been untested in the courts.[1]

Volunteer protection laws and the varieties of liability insurance premiums are not the only ways boards can protect themselves. The most effective form of protection is limiting risk by adhering to effective governance practices. There are three standards of conduct that should guide the board member, as follows:

- *Duty of care:* Imposes an obligation that all board members discharge their duties with the care that an ordinarily prudent person would exercise under similar circumstances. This includes being diligent, attending meetings, and becoming acquainted with issues before reaching a decision.
- *Duty of loyalty:* Requires that each board member act primarily in the best interest of the organization and not in his or her own personal best interest or in the interest of individuals at the expense of the organization.
- *Duty of obedience:* Imposes an obligation that board members will act in conformity with all laws in addition to acting in accordance with the organization's mission.

For the voluntary members of boards of directors, acting prudently, lawfully, and in the best interests of the organization can, in part, be achieved by adhering to the following six responsible board practices:

1. *Becoming an active board member:* Board members who are familiar with the organization's mission and purpose are generally able to make better decisions for the organization. Members may wish to review the mission annually to serve as a reminder that the board uses the mission statement as its guide in decisionmaking.

2. *Attending all meetings:* Being absent from meetings will not necessarily excuse a board member from responsibilities for decisions reached by those in attendance. In fact, a member's absence from meetings increases potential risks for the entire board because it is making decisions without the benefit of the views of all of its members.

3. *Insisting on having sound financial management tools and control systems:* Board members need to learn how to read and use financial statements and audit reports to understand and monitor the organization's fiscal health. They also need to understand that their decisions have a financial impact on the organization.

4. *Speaking up:* Members should not remain silent when they disagree with a decision or an opinion expressed by others. Additionally, board members should ask questions when the organization's goals and objectives are not being met.

5. *Identifying conflicts of interest:* Board members need to avoid participating in discussions or decisionmaking when they have conflicts of interest. Even the perception of a conflict of interest must be avoided, if possible. If they are faced with an actual conflict or even the perception of one, board members must inform the other directors of the situation and excuse themselves from participation in related areas of decisionmaking or transactions.

6. *Staffing:* In addition to its having personnel policy guidelines for the executive director, the board must be certain that these personnel policies are adequate and updated to reflect all applicable mandates of law.

In summary, minimizing the risk of board liability requires an active and involved board of directors.

## Dismissal of Board Members

Terminating a member from the board of directors for nonattendance at board meetings or lack of follow-through on assignments that are required for the board's decisionmaking purposes, for example, is a delicate procedure. Unfortunately, there are times when it becomes necessary to discharge board members because their actions create liability risks.

The chairperson of the board has the responsibility to request resignations from board members. The executive director plays a supportive role to the board chair and board member in what for all can be emotionally trying and embarrassing.

Confidence and sensitivity should be used when approaching the board member with the idea of resignation. A board member should be given every consideration to effect a smooth departure. Ultimately, the member's "saving face" is important for maintaining relationships at this level of community involvement.

To prevent the need for board dismissals or to support the actions of the board chair when a dismissal is called for, the board should adopt a principle stating that its work and organizational mission are too important to allow for unnecessary liability risks associated with uncommitted board members. The board can do some prevention work by adopting a bylaw passage and job description that reflect standards for board member conduct and participation. Of course, some organizations have rules of this type but choose not to enforce them. For a member to violate or ignore such bylaw provisions suggests poor judgment and raises the liability risks of the board.

## How Often Should the Board Meet?

A board is generally required to meet at least once a year. In practice, some hold meetings once a month, every other month, or once each calendar quarter. Frequency of board meetings and the duration of each meeting should reflect the culture of the organization and the type of strategic issues requiring board attention. Dealing with planning and policy issues, threats of litigation or bad publicity, and concerns of financial obligations are reasons for a board to meet more frequently. Organizations that are new in their development, or in process of managing significant changes, as compared with an organization in a steady state, would also benefit from meeting more frequently.

Effective meetings are focused, to the point, and stick to the agenda. Meetings can be effective when board members come prepared, having studied the agenda and the issues prior to the meeting. The agenda should be mailed out at least a week to ten days in advance. Agenda items should be allocated realistic time frames for discussion and taking action, in addition to time designated for the routine review of minutes, financial reports, and progress reports on the implementation of the organization's strategic plans.

Newly identified obstacles are not always solved during board meetings. Instead of reacting to unfinished issues and business with more board meetings, attempts should first be made to streamline the review of issues by assigning the task to an appropriate standing or ad hoc committee. In this way, the committees can try to remedy issues or bring their findings and recommendations back to the board or executive committee without monopolizing the board's time and agenda.

## How Long Should a Board Member Serve?

The solution to a member's length of service that is practiced by many organizations is to stagger the expiring terms of office. Rotations of three-year terms, for example, would mean that each member serves for three years, but, at the end of each year, obligations would end for one-third of the members. This system gives the board ample time to evaluate the performance of board members, to determine whether they should be invited back for another term. Additionally, the experience base accumulated by outgoing board members is information these members use to decide whether they would like to be reelected for another three-year term.

Some organizations also place a limit on the number of consecutive terms a person may serve. After reaching the maximum number of consecutive terms of service, the board member would automatically leave the board. A board member who rotated off could be elected again after a year or more, when consecutive service would not be an issue. After reaching the allowable service limit, an individual could also continue to support the organization's cause in some other capacity, such as on a committee or advisory board.

It is important that all board member terms do not expire at the same time. Without some overlapping representation from members of the board, the organization would lose its important history and continuity of policy development and strategic direction. Veteran board members bring a maturity and depth of understanding about the issues the organization faces, and when the board adds a group of newer members it brings enthusiasm and fresh ideas to the board's governing role.

## How Are Governing Boards, Advisory Boards, and Honorary Boards Different?

When one is referring to the term "board of directors" or "board of trustees," the reference is to a *governing board,* a grouping of individuals who have assumed a legal responsibility for an organization's existence. These people make policy and are responsible for how money is generated and spent, toward the accomplishment of a mission that can be beneficial to the general public or to a segment of the population.

*Advisory boards,* however, do not bear the legal burdens of governing boards. An advisory board exists to assist the governing board or the executive director in examining issues and recommendations. Recommendations that result from the work of an advisory board do not have to be accepted or followed by the governing board.

*Honorary boards* are usually composed of individuals who are well known because of some measure of celebrity or prominence in the community. Honorary boards do not necessarily meet. In fact, some individuals agree to serve as honorary members because they do not have the time or inclination to attend meetings. Individuals serving in this honorary capacity lend credibility to an organization by allowing the use of their prominent names in brochures and on letterheads.

Sometimes, members of honorary boards and advisory boards are enlisted to assist in organizational fundraising activities. The visibility and credibility of the honorary or advisory member sends a signal to the community that the organization is worthy of financial support.

## Types of Committees

Committees are categorized as either standing committees or ad hoc committees. *Ad hoc (or special) committees,* on one hand, have a life span equal to the completion of the committee's assignment. *Standing committees,* on the other hand, are part of the permanent governance structure of an organization with duties and responsibilities described in bylaws. Standing committees may include executive, finance, bylaws, fundraising, public relations, nominating, personnel, planning, and policy committees,

or any other committee that the organization believes should exist indefinitely to aid in governance. Seven of the most common standing committees are described as follows:

1. The *executive committee* functions in place of the full board and handles routine and crisis matters between full board meetings. Empowered to make decisions for the organization, the executive committee is usually composed of the organization's officers. Depending on the size of the organization's board of directors, composition of the executive committee could include committee chairs or other selected leaders among the board. The executive committee is usually chaired by the board's volunteer president or chairperson.

2. The *finance committee* is responsible for monitoring the organization's finances and financial controls and attending to audit requirements. Typical functions for the finance committee are to oversee organizational investments and to work with the executive director to develop an annual budget.

3. The *nominations committee* is responsible for identifying and recruiting appropriate candidates for board positions and bringing forward its recommendations to the full board. This committee sometimes has the responsibility for planning board development activities and board retreats.

4. The *personnel committee* is usually responsible for recommending policies to guide the supervision of staff. In some organizations, this committee may have the responsibility for overseeing the search for an executive director and then for her or his performance evaluation. Members of this committee may need to acquaint themselves with personnel laws and regulations that regulate labor practices.

5. The *program committee* is responsible for monitoring the organization's service delivery system and may assist in evaluating client services. This committee is often responsible for keeping track of community trends that might

affect the organization's short-term and long-term objectives. In complex organizations with multiple services, there may be subcommittees that are responsible for monitoring each of the organization's program services.

6. The *resource development committee* is responsible for examining alternate methods of fundraising and for establishing annual fundraising goals. This committee often is active in the solicitation of gifts or participation in special events. In addition to raising money, it may solicit in-kind contributions.

7. The *public relations* or *community relations committee* has the responsibility for developing good relations with the larger community and with important community groups. The committee examines opportunities to participate in community events that will bring visibility to the organization. It may oversee the writing of press releases and may develop relationships with media professionals.

Participants appointed to standing or ad hoc committees do not need to be members of the board of directors. Committee members may include staff, volunteers, representatives from community agencies, and consumers of services. Committee chairs are usually appointed by the board's chairperson.

## Notes

1. *Note from the editors:* State laws and court decisions may change over time. Consultation is recommended to assess changes in any particular situation.

## References

Block, Stephen R., and Jeffrey W. Pryor. 1991. *Improving Nonprofit Management Practice: A Handbook for Community-Based Organizations.* Rockville, MD: OSAP/Public Health Service, US Department of Health and Human Services.

Carver, John. 1990. *Boards That Make a Difference.* San Francisco: Jossey-Bass.

Chait, Richard P., and Barbara E. Taylor. 1989. "Charting the Territory of Nonprofit Boards." *Harvard Business Review* (January–February): 44–54.

Conrad, William, and William E. Glenn. 1976. *The Effective Voluntary Board of Directors.* Chicago: Swallow Press.

Drucker, Peter F. 1989. "What Business Can Learn from Nonprofits." *Harvard Business Review* (September–October): 88–93.

———. 1990. "Lessons for Successful Nonprofit Governance." *Nonprofit Management and Leadership* 1, no. 1 (Fall): 7–14.

Hadden, Elaine M., and Blaire A. French. 1987. *Nonprofit Organizations: Rights and Liabilities for Members, Directors and Officers.* Wilmette, IL: Callaghan & Co.

Herman, Robert Dean, and Stephen R. Block. 1990. "The Board's Crucial Role in Fund Raising," in Jon Van Til et al., *Critical Issues in American Philanthropy,* 222–241. San Francisco: Jossey-Bass.

Herman, Robert Dean, and Richard D. Heimovics, 1991. *Executive Leadership in Nonprofit Organizations.* San Francisco: Jossey-Bass.

Herman, Robert Dean, and Jon Van Til, eds. 1989. *Nonprofit Boards of Directors: Analyses and Applications.* New Brunswick, NJ: Transaction Publishers.

Houle, Cyril O. 1989. *Governing Boards.* San Francisco: Jossey-Bass.

Kurtz, Daniel L. 1988. *Board Liability.* New York: Moyer Bell.

Middleton, Melissa. 1987. "Nonprofit Boards of Directors: Beyond the Governance Function," in Walter W. Powell, ed., *The Nonprofit Sector: A Research Handbook,* 141–153. New Haven, CT: Yale University Press.

O'Connell, Brian. 1985. *The Board Members Book.* New York: The Foundation Center.

Saidel, Judith R. 1993. "The Board Role in Relation to Government: Alternative Models," in Dennis R. Young, Robert M. Hollister, and Virginia A. Hodgkinson, eds., *Governing, Leading, and Managing Nonprofit Organizations,* 32–51. San Francisco: Jossey-Bass.

## CHAPTER 2

# Applying Sarbanes-Oxley Governance Principles to Nonprofit Organizations

AMERICAN BAR ASSOCIATION COORDINATING COMMITTEE ON NONPROFIT GOVERNANCE

## How Sarbanes-Oxley Impacts the Governance of Profit and Nonprofit Entities

The Sarbanes-Oxley Act (or the "Act") was enacted into law in the summer of 2002. The Act was created largely in response to the serious financial scandals involving Enron, WorldCom, Global Crossing, and other corporations with publicly held stock. The Act directly mandated, or required the SEC or other bodies to enact, a large number of corporate governance reforms. These reforms principally relate to the financial auditing of public companies, compensation of senior executives, disclosures regarding material financial and other information, and the composition and operation of boards of directors responsible for the oversight of public companies.

Most provisions of the Act do not apply to nonprofit organizations. Even nonprofit organizations that have issued securities, such as tax-exempt bonds, are not treated as "issuers" subject to the Act, due to exemptions from federal securities law registration and reporting requirements. *However, the Act's provisions relating to penalties for obstruction of justice, including through document destruction or retaliation against whistleblowers, apply equally to nonprofit organizations.* In addition, many of the principles of the Act may be applied to nonprofit corporations, either voluntarily by organizations wishing to adopt what many now perceive to be "good governance practices," or in response to external forces—whether through governmental regulation or pressure from members, donors, grant-makers, current and prospective board members, creditors, competitors, or organizational accreditation or rating agencies.[1] There are 10 general principles of corporate governance emerging from the Sarbanes-Oxley reforms that may be worthy of consideration for the governance of nonprofit organizations:

**Principle 1, Role of Board:** The organization's governing board should oversee the operations of the organization in such manner as will assure effective and ethical management.

**Principle 2, Importance of Independent Directors:** The independent and non-management board members are an organizational resource that should be used to assure the exercise of independent judgment in key committees and general board decision-making.

**Principle 3, Audit Committee:** An organization with significant financial resources should have an audit committee composed solely of independent directors that should assure the independence of the organization's financial auditors, review the organization's critical accounting policies and decisions and the adequacy of its internal control systems, and oversee the accuracy of its financial statements and reports.

**Principle 4, Governance and Nominating Committees:** An organization should have one or more committees, composed solely of independent directors, that focus on core governance and board composition issues, including the governing documents of the organization and the board; the criteria, evaluation, and nomination of directors; the appropriateness of board size, leadership, composition, and committee structure; and codes of ethical conduct.

**Principle 5, Compensation Committee:** An organization should have a committee composed of independent directors that determines the compensation of the chief executive officer and determines or reviews the compensation of the other executive officers and assures that compensation decisions are tied to the executives' actual performance in meeting predetermined goals and objectives.

**Principle 6, Disclosure and Integrity of Institutional Information:** Disclosures made by an organization regarding its assets, activities, liabilities, and results of operations should be accurate and complete and include all material information. Financial and other information should fairly reflect the condition of the organization and be presented in a manner that promotes rather than obscures understanding. CEOs and CFOs should be able to certify the accuracy of financial and other disclosures and the adequacy of their organizations' internal controls.

**Principle 7, Ethics and Business Conduct Codes:** An organization should adopt and implement ethics and business conduct codes applicable to directors, senior management, agents, and employees that reflect a commitment to operating in the best interests of the organization and in compliance with applicable law, ethical business standards, and the organization's governing documents.

**Principle 8, Executive and Director Compensation:** Executives (and directors if appropriate) should be compensated fairly and in a manner that reflects their contribution to the organization. Such compensation should not include loans, but may include incentives that correspond to success or failure in meeting performance goals.

**Principle 9, Monitoring Compliance and Investigating Complaints:** An organization should have procedures for receiving, investigating, and taking appropriate action regarding fraud or noncompliance with law or organization policy and should protect "whistleblowers" against retaliation.

**Principle 10, Document Destruction and Retention:** An organization should have document retention policies that comply with applicable laws and are implemented in a manner that does not result in the destruction of documents that may be relevant to an actual or anticipated legal proceeding or governmental investigation.

## Applying Sarbanes-Oxley Governance Principles to Nonprofit Organizations

### *Principle 1: Role of the Board*

The organization's governing board should oversee the operations of the organization in such manner as will assure effective and ethical management.

**Application to Nonprofits**

1. *Governance Failures in the Nonprofit Sector.* Like their for-profit counterparts, nonprofit organizations have not been immune to high-profile scandals in which management appeared to have "run amok," and the board seemed either to have acquiesced or been shockingly ignorant of illegal or highly questionable activities. For example, financial improprieties led to the bankruptcy of the Pittsburgh-based Allegheny Health, Education and Research Foundation (AHERF); excessive perks and personal use of corporate assets were issues for the United Way of America parent organization; the accounting practices of the Washington, DC, United Way organization led to allegations of improper revenue recognition; and the US Olympic Committee has been buffeted with continued scandals involving organization leadership. In some cases, conflicts of interest and other improprieties were found at the board level, such as in allegations of excessive compensation and financial mismanagement in the Bishop Estate organization in Hawaii and conflicts of interest charges involving trustees of Adelphi University.

2. *Review of Board Structure and Operations.* In addition to considering reforms involving independent and non-management directors as discussed in Principle 2 below, most nonprofit organizations would benefit from a thorough review of their board structure and operations. The chief aim of such review would be for the organization to determine the optimal size, composition, and operating procedures that would assist the board in fulfilling its oversight duties. . . .

## Principle 2: Importance of Independent Directors

The independent and non-management board members are an organizational resource that should be used to assure the exercise of indepen-

dent judgment in key committees and general board decision making.

**Application to Nonprofits**

1. *Deference to Management.* Like their for-profit counterparts, many nonprofit organizations have over the years slipped into a habitual deference to management, even on major issues. Management often sets the agenda for the board and may even pick, or exercise strong influence over the choice of, board members. Even when a nonprofit board has a majority of unaffiliated, "independent" directors, the board may give a high degree of deference to management. Thus, the "independence" concern here is that all directors understand and fulfill their obligations to independently evaluate the materials and information provided to them, rather than unduly relying on management.

   Another nonprofit-specific independence issue arises from the fact that some nonprofit directors also are substantial contributors and/or fundraisers. That status may give them a proprietary-type interest in the corporation and lead to close scrutiny of management performance. Alternatively, it may lead them to view their board role as primarily a source of financial support rather than an independent overseer. . . .

2. *Application of Independent Director Principles.* Nonprofit boards also may be prone to an "interpersonal" lack of independence, in which some board members may have difficulty disagreeing with other board members, such as a strong-willed board chair or a director whose status as a significant donor, service provider, governmental official, or community representative makes other board members reluctant to present opposing views. To best evaluate whether directors are capable of making independent decisions in the best interests of the organization, the board (or a designated committee or consultant) should carefully scrutinize what factors could adversely affect

board and board member objectivity for the particular organization.

A nonprofit board also may consider whether it would be useful for the board chair to observe board meetings of other (noncompetitive) nonprofit organizations, or work with an organization dynamics consultant to devise strategies for more focused discussion of material issues at board and committee meetings. Such questions may yield answers that respond to the good governance aims of the independent director principles, even if the nonprofit determines it is not appropriate to implement some of such principles at this time.

## Principle 3: Audit Committee

An organization with significant financial resources should have an audit committee composed solely of independent directors that should assure the independence of the organization's financial auditors, review the organization's critical accounting policies and decisions and the adequacy of its internal control systems, and oversee the accuracy of its financial statements and reports.

### Application to Nonprofits

1. *Application of Audit Committee Reforms to Nonprofit Organizations.* Many smaller nonprofit organizations do not have their financial statements audited, although they may use independent accountants to "review" or "compile" their statements. Nonprofit organizations that do have audited financials may have a committee that is responsible for working with auditors and reviewing draft financial statements, but such committee also may perform other tasks (such as exercising responsibility for finance and/or compliance matters) and be comprised of management as well as non-management representatives.

   Certain governance standards for organizations and proposed legislation applicable to nonprofit corporations suggest that any non-

profit organization with gross revenues of as little as $250,000 to $300,000 should have audited financial statements. Many others in the nonprofit sector believe that that target is too low, and suggest that $1 million in gross revenues is a more appropriate threshold level for when a nonprofit organization should have audited financial statements. For small nonprofits with limited resources, the decision whether or not to obtain an audit should be based not only on gross revenue amounts but on the degree of complexity of the organization's financial structure; the experience of those persons who prepare the organization's financials and the underlying documents on which such unaudited financials are based; any history of inaccuracy of financial reports; and the expectations of donors, grant-makers, members, or others.

## Principle 4: Governance/Nominating Committees

An organization should have one or more committees, composed solely of independent directors, that focus on core governance and board composition issues, including the governing documents of the organization and the board; the criteria, evaluation, and nomination of directors; the appropriateness of board size, leadership, composition, and committee structure; and codes of ethical conduct.

### Application to Nonprofits

1. *Governance/Nominating Committees in Nonprofit Organizations.* Many nonprofits have nominating committees, although nominations may be strongly "suggested" or vetted by senior management. It is not as common for nonprofits to have a corporate governance committee, although many have a "bylaws" committee that may or may not also be involved in making recommendations regarding broader corporate governance issues. For nonprofits that do not have any committee that

regularly looks at corporate governance issues, the idea of combining such function with a nominating committee may be useful.

## Principle 5: Compensation Committee

An organization should have a committee composed of independent directors that determines the compensation of the chief executive officer and determines or reviews the compensation of the other executive officers and assures that compensation decisions are tied to the executives' actual performance in meeting predetermined goals and objectives.

### Application to Nonprofits

1. *Excess Benefits Rules and Use of Comparability Data.* While some nonprofits have separate compensation committees, in many nonprofits compensation decisions are made by the board as a whole (with affected management-directors recusing themselves from voting on their own compensation). Nonprofits that are exempt under Section 501(c)(3) or 501(c)(4) of the Code should already be making compensation decisions for senior officers based on objective, documented comparable information and otherwise complying with the procedures under the intermediate sanctions excess benefits rules.[2]

## Principle 6: Disclosure and Integrity of Institutional Information

Disclosures made by an organization regarding its assets, activities, liabilities, and results of operations should be accurate and complete and include all material information. Financial and other information should fairly reflect the condition of the organization and be presented in a manner that promotes rather than obscures understanding. CEOs and CFOs should be able to certify the accuracy of financial and other disclosures and the adequacy of their organizations' internal controls.

### Application to Nonprofits

1. *Executive Certification.* Many nonprofits, particularly those of a substantial size, have begun to consider whether they should require the organization's most senior paid staff members to provide certifications on financial and internal control matters, similar to those required of public companies. As of the date of this Guidebook, there have been proposals in three states to impose Sarbanes-Oxley type requirements on nonprofit organizations.

In addition to such proposed legislation, senior officers of nonprofits can expect that other entities or bodies with whom they deal may find the idea of certification attractive. For example, creditors, grant-makers, donors, regulatory lending authorities, association members, and boards of directors may all find merit, in specific circumstances, to asking the senior officers of a nonprofit to certify regarding the corporation's financial statements and controls or other aspects of the nonprofit's operations.

Large nonprofits, particularly those operating in a highly regulated environment or those subject to significant outside scrutiny by the media, significant donors, grant-makers, public officials, or others, may wish to adopt procedures that generate more detailed information regarding the organization's operations and financial position. Such information may be provided solely to the board and its committees, or portions may be made available to members, prospective donors, the general public, or other interested parties.

## Principle 7: Ethics and Business Conduct Codes

An organization should adopt and implement ethics and business conduct codes applicable to directors, senior management, agents, and employees that reflect a commitment to operating in the best interests of the organization and in compliance with applicable law, ethical business standards, and the organization's governing documents.

## Application to Nonprofits

1. *Conflict of Interest Policies and Procedures.* All nonprofit organizations should have written conflict of interest policies for officers, directors, employees, and, in some cases, volunteers. Such policies should cover "self-dealing" transactions with the organization (i.e., when the officer, director, employee, a family member, or affiliated corporation is "on the other side" of a transaction with the corporation), as well as prohibitions against personal use of corporate assets, such as appropriating empty office space to run a personal business without payment to the organization, use or disclosure of confidential information, and taking advantage of opportunities that rightly belong to the organization.

2. *Ethics and Business Conduct Codes.* In addition to conflict of interest policies, every nonprofit organization should have an ethics or business conduct code. Models of such codes are available on the websites of many public companies and elsewhere. Management should monitor compliance with such codes closely. Organizations can and should also require those who do business with the organization (i.e., independent contractors and vendors) to comply with such codes in their dealings with the corporation.

that compensation (salary, bonuses, and other payments made to executives) are based on an analysis of compensation received by executives at comparable organizations (including applicable for-profit corporations) and are reasonable with respect to the organization's revenues, assets, and complexity, and that any incentive portions of executive compensation are tied to the accomplishment of organizational or executive performance goals. Unlike for-profit businesses, the goals set for a nonprofit executive may focus more on mission-related accomplishments than financial results. However, goals related to financial stability and attracting additional funds for use in the organization's mission also are appropriate. It is critical that all compensation be properly reported for tax purposes.

Some of the scandals in the nonprofit sector have involved excessive executive and/or director perks, such as expensive modes of travel, payment for a spouse's travel expenses, and retreats or meetings at exotic locations. As the national mood becomes less tolerant of such practices in the public and company sectors, it can be expected that perks will be increasingly questioned in the nonprofit sector. In addition, for nonprofits that are tax-exempt, excessive perks could be seen as "private inurement" or "private benefits" inconsistent with the organization's tax-exempt status.

## Principle 8: Executive and Director Compensation

Executives (and directors if appropriate) should be compensated fairly and in a manner that reflects their contribution to the organization. Such compensation should not include loans, but may include incentives that correspond to success or failure in meeting performance goals.

## Application to Nonprofits

1. *Executive Compensation.* Nonprofit boards or their compensation committees should verify

## Principle 9: Monitoring Compliance and Investigating Complaints

An organization should have procedures for receiving, investigating, and taking appropriate action regarding fraud or noncompliance with law or organization policy and should protect "whistleblowers" against retaliation.

## Application to Nonprofits

1. *Complaint and Response Procedure in Nonprofit Organizations.* All nonprofit organizations should have some written policy or program

for the communication of concerns regarding possible financial, accounting, or other legal and ethical violations to senior officers and members of the board of directors, as appropriate under the circumstances. Depending on the nonprofit organization's activities, compliance issues may be of great or modest concern. However, there should always be some mechanism for concerned employees, volunteers, or outside individuals to effectively communicate compliance concerns to the board or a nonaffected officer. In addition, nonprofit organizations should have written policies prohibiting retaliation against employees who raise concerns regarding actual or potential wrongdoing in the organization. **Because the whistleblower-protection provisions of the Act apply to all organizations, every nonprofit organization should carefully review its current policies and procedures in this area and assure that, at a minimum, it complies with the whistleblower provisions of the Act, as well as whistleblower provisions in other federal and state laws.**

### Principle 10: Document Destruction and Retention

An organization should have document retention policies that comply with applicable laws and are implemented in a manner that does not result in the destruction of documents that may be relevant to an actual or anticipated legal proceeding or governmental investigation.

**Application to Nonprofits**

1. *Review of Document Destruction and Retention Policies.* The increased criminal sanctions for

obstruction of justice by destruction of documents apply to all persons and entities, not just publicly traded corporations, and to any kind of official federal proceeding or federal agency investigation. **Thus, now is a good time for nonprofit organizations to review their existing document retention/destruction policies, update them to make it clear that routine destruction should be curtailed for any documents that are identified as potentially subject to a known or reasonably anticipated investigation by a governmental entity, and assure that these policies otherwise conform to regulations applicable to the particular nonprofit organization.**

## Notes

1. "Good governance practices" is the term used here to refer to practices and procedures that are viewed as evidencing or tending to result in good governance. These practices and procedures have many sources, including federal laws such as the Act; stock exchange rules; SEC regulations; state law requirements; recommendations by institutional investors, corporate governance commentators, business organizations, associations of lawyers, corporate executives, and rating standards organizations; and actual practice by leading corporations. Many of the standards and principles articulated by these sources then come to be reflected in practices and procedures adopted by boards over a period of time. Although notions of what constitutes "good" governance practices generally evolve slowly over time, one or more important events, such as a significant court decision or the passage of a law such as the Sarbanes-Oxley Act, periodically "raise the bar" and accelerate the evolution of good governance practices.

2. Internal Revenue Code Section 4958.

# WELCOME TO THE BOARD OF DIRECTORS

*C. Kenneth Meyer and Alison Lemke*

Bethany Brown was elated when she learned that, by popular vote of other members of her professional health care society, she was elected to its board of directors at the national level. It had been a long road to navigate. Since she had become a member of the society nearly twenty years earlier, she had held several positions on the executive committee of the association at the state level and had volunteered extensively with the national association.

Over the years she had never refused to lend a helping hand, even if the committee assignment was more "work horse" than "show horse." She had contributed her energies and talents to the association because she agreed with its mission and value statements and felt that it had done a respectable job in meeting what she later termed "the needs, wants, desires, expectations, and demands of its nearly 50,000 state, national and international members." She could clearly recall her graduate studies adviser, and major professor, insisting that all graduate students become members of their professional associations because it would be an excellent way to pursue continual lifelong learning and professional development. And if they met the academic qualifications for membership, they should also respond positively, he suggested, to any invitation to join their discipline's national honorary society. Minimally, such memberships would look great, he said, on the "office bragging wall."

Bethany started her term on the national board of directors with zeal and optimism. She looked forward to the challenge and felt well prepared for the responsibility she knew she would be given. She had many years of experience in her health-related profession, having worked as a practitioner/provider and also in various management roles. She also had a lengthy history of volunteer service with the association at both the state and national levels. The various capacities in which she had worked and volunteered had prepared her well, she hoped, to be an effective board member and leader at the national level.

Bethany was not naive about the presence of some tension and divisiveness within the national association: there had been a history over the years of many troublesome turf battles between management and volunteer governance members. These skirmishes seemed to focus on issues of power and control between members of the board of directors and the executive director (both past and current) and national office staff. There had also been a protracted history of governance changes within the association. For a number of years, the requirement that major policy decisions be passed by a legislative body composed of representatives from every state in the nation had led to policy gridlock. Important motions and policy decisions died amid debate and disagreement in the legislative body, and confidence had diminished in the ability of the national board to act resolutely on anything, especially any important national problem.

Several years earlier, a governance restructure movement had succeeded, perhaps against all odds, and the legislative body had voted to eliminate itself. Many in the association thought that this was a move in the right direction. Now the association was governed by a single, twenty-member board of directors, with members elected by vote of all association members from a national slate of candidates. As a student of organizational theory, Bethany knew the pros and cons associated with the size of this board. Larger boards give voice to a wider range of constituent interests, but they can also lead to "grandstanding" by some members and result, literally, in a "runaway" board of directors.

After the governance restructuring had been implemented, many volunteer association leaders, including Bethany, assumed that the turf battles and tension between the elected volunteer leadership and the association management staff would end. Unfortunately, Bethany discovered during her first year on the board of directors that a great deal of tension and distrust persisted. To Bethany, a newly elected board member, it appeared that both sides were culpable. During board meetings, she observed an insatiable pursuit of power plays that were identifiable even to the most inexperienced board member. As she told another board member in confidence at a luncheon meeting, the power exuded by the executive director and "Mahogany Row" was palpable!

To better understand the working relations that evolved between the board of directors and the executive suite, a historical note is in order. As is common for most national boards of directors associated with academic disciplines, whether in the health sciences, business, public administration, or the arts and natural sciences, the elected board members were often professionals who had extensive managerial and/or academic teaching and research backgrounds. They were accomplished and often came from work settings in which they had wielded considerable influence, if not power. If they came to the board with extensive management experience, they were accustomed to being in charge of staff, managing day-to-day operations, dealing with budgets and financial accountings, and leading work units. If they came from academic teaching and research positions, they were accustomed to being immersed in the study of the clinical or subject areas pertinent to the profession, thereby earning great respect and enhancing the reputation of their department and parent university, but they often had little formal knowledge of association management and of the pedestrian, but salient, issues that regularly appeared on the board of directors' agenda.

After a year of being on the board of directors, Bethany saw that those from either background faced significant challenges in becoming effective board members. Those from managerial backgrounds tended to delve deeply into how policies and objectives would be implemented within the association's office, and they often became preoccupied with budget questions related to how much money should be allotted to particular activities. On the other hand, those from academic backgrounds tended, in Bethany's view, to debate various aspects of issues and policy decisions endlessly without ever reaching conclusions about how to move forward on them. The academics were used to reaching decisions by consensus—after lengthy, tedious debates.

On the other hand, Bethany could see that the paid management staff of the association also, and quite often, raised the tensions between board and staff. The association was large enough that it employed a staff of more than 175 people. For the past five years its executive director had been Henry Gray, who had risen through the ranks and was a veteran of previous governance structures and turf battles between staff and association leaders. Some members felt that he personally benefited from the "bar stool syndrome" and that it served his rise to a position of national prominence. He had great name recognition, was a person of some presence when he addressed the board, and could "wine and dine," "lift a few," and tell stories with the best of them. He was no stranger to conflict, but he was a weak leader in the area of conflict resolution and compromise.

Bethany's impression was that Henry, although personable and competent in many areas of management, was highly selective of the information he chose to share with members of the board; as a result, not all relevant or pertinent information was available to the board regarding the progress being made on some of the association's strategic objectives. Board members, particularly when they were new to the board of directors, did not always feel comfortable asking for information because, through word and deed, he seemed to convey the message that questions and concerns were unwelcome.

As Bethany often stated under her breath, "Yours is not to question why; yours is but to do or die." She knew her expected place, but as a seasoned professional, she was not ready to accept her newly assigned status and role—at least not as envisioned by Henry.

Although Bethany could understand why the executive director tended to erect a wall between the board of directors and the paid staff, it also seemed that his lack of openness and candor exacerbated the tensions that bubbled up and served as a barrier between board members and staff that impeded effective and constructive communication.

After one of the national meetings, she spoke briefly with her old graduate studies adviser about her board experience, and to her surprise, he shared with her a similar set of recollections. Years earlier, he too had been nominated and then elected by the organization membership to a prestigious executive board that also turned out to have several undesirable attributes. He had observed a "clique" mentality among the board members from prestigious colleges and universities. This group often succeeded in setting the guidelines and standards of the organization to mirror their own curricular direction—but not the national direction. Successive executive directors did not come from the academic discipline represented by the association, but instead were drawn from the ranks of career public appointees in Washington, DC. These people developed a network of friends, especially among nonprofit professional organizations, and prospered professionally because of the "entitlements of cronyism."

Year after year, the agenda for this association was developed by the executive director with only limited and highly selective input from those board members who were most compliant with the executive's lead. Important issues within the association related to ethics, discrimination, environmental and global trends, and civil and human rights received scant consideration or attention by the largely older, white, male executive board. Finally, Bethany's professor recalled, precious little input was solicited from the rank-and-file practitioners on the board or in the field.

Bethany's professor went on to say that, in his opinion, the main problem had rested in an elitism in the national office, coupled with the arrogance of a seemingly "untouchable and unaccountable" management cadre who had never distinguished themselves as practitioners or academics but were able to survive on "K Street" as sycophant bureaucrats. He chuckled as he recalled that the executive board meetings were largely centered on accepting the financial and budgetary audit reports prepared by one or another of the "Big Six" accounting firms, approving the two-year budget recommendations that would ensure the continuity of administrative services and making sure the association was actuarially sound insofar as it covered executive salaries, pensions and retirements, health benefits, and other perks. This board gave little attention to expanding the membership rostrum or providing meaningful technical, professional, and curriculum advice to its membership institutions and individual members.

Bethany left this conversation in a state of renewed perplexity: was she dealing with a similar set of issues? She wondered if she would be able to carve out a legacy of service that truly met the needs of the nearly 50,000 academic and practitioner members in her health field niche. Or would she end up disgruntled and alienated instead, like her mentor, after her service to the national board had been rendered?

Bethany reminisced about her many years of volunteer service and how she had prepared herself to meet earlier challenges. She had delved into the existing literature on association governance, issues with boards of directors, strategic planning, and collaborative leadership. After reflecting on her study of these topics, she had felt that it served her well in her various roles at the state level of the association. Now, she wondered, would her knowledge and leadership skills be enough to improve the working relationship between the national association staff and the board of directors as well? She remembered that she had often been a voice of moderation and reason on the state board of directors, and she was also aware that she was increasingly being looked to as a source of knowledge concerning association governance. Bethany could see, without being too vain, that she had the knowledge to make a difference in how the board of directors conducted its business. How could she communicate that, she wondered, and start to make a difference?

## Questions and Instructions

1.  What information should be available to new members of a board of directors? How might some of the issues discussed in the case have been handled through information supplied at a board orientation for new members? Should seasoned board members be expected to attend orientations for new members? Offer justifications for your responses.

2.  Should an executive director get involved in board-of-directors relationship dynamics including any cliques that may form or elitism that may develop? Should the views of the organization's staff members or the views of practitioners outside of the organization affect the decisions of members of a board of directors? Please explain your answers.

3.  Bethany Brown appears to be a thoughtful new recruit to her professional association's board of directors. What is she doing well to prepare herself to serve in this role? What strategies might she also wish to consider?

# UNWELCOME NEWS: NONPROFIT SCANDAL

*Benjamin S. Bingle, Scot Schraufnagel, Micki Chulick, and C. Kenneth Meyer*

## Unwelcome News

The large, bold words jumped off the front page of the daily newspaper on November 8, "Scandal Rocks Local Nonprofit." Alex Jeffries could hardly believe how quickly word had spread. After all, staff members had been made aware of their founder's indiscretions only a day earlier. Staring blankly at the newspaper in his hands, Alex allowed his mind to drift back to the previous day's staff meeting, which might have changed his professional career—if not his life—forever.

## Flashback: "I Don't Believe It"

"Welcome everyone, and thank you for joining us today," said an uncomfortable-looking Jason Richmond, chief operating officer of the Children's Connection, a nonprofit organization serving several counties throughout the Ohio River Valley. "I'm sure you're all wondering why this meeting was called. Unfortunately, I'm the bearer of bad news today. It has come to the attention of our board of directors that the founder and chief executive officer of Children's Connection, Charles Mitchell, is facing some very serious allegations and has been apprehended by the police."

The news hung in the air of the conference room where nearly all of the forty-five Children's Connection employees sat nervously shifting in their seats. Uncertain looks were shared across the room as Jason Richmond continued.

"For those of you who know Charles Mitchell, you're probably wondering how he could ever find himself in this position. He's a kind and caring man who has always put the interests of the children we serve, the community, our partners, and all of you in front of his own personal interests. Keep in mind that Charles has not been found guilty; these are only allegations at this time."

From the back of the room someone finally asked the question on everyone's mind: "So what are the allegations?"

The rest of the executive staff, including the vice presidents and the chief financial officer, exchanged looks that ranged from anger to embarrassment.

"Again, these allegations are currently unfounded, but Charles has been accused of several counts of child abuse dating back to 2010. A former client of Children's Connection has come forward and claimed that Charles fostered an inappropriate relationship with him. We don't have much more information than that right now, but we will be sure to keep you all abreast of developments as they come in."

The air seemed to thicken as Jason's words escaped and hung like a toxic cloud over the room.

All the staff members sat silently. Then one lone voice stammered out loud, "I don't believe it."

## Background

Charles Mitchell had been born and raised in Ohio. After graduating with bachelor's and master's degrees from a large Ohio university, he entered the working world and quickly found success in the banking industry. Charles's business acumen and prominent position within the community opened many doors for him personally and professionally. He became a well-respected civic leader who held positions on many nonprofit boards and seats on various statewide commissions.

Eventually, Charles wanted to help address a cause near and dear to his heart: child foster care. He never openly shared where his passion for children came from, but his commitment soon became obvious through the energy and the money he gave to various organizations with children-focused missions.

Citing a need for more coordinated child foster care services in the Ohio River Valley, Charles took the steps necessary to legally establish Children's Connection in 1995. He was able to secure much of the start-up funding from personal connections, family members, and partnerships he had formed during his banking career. Charles also relied on his extensive professional network to hand-pick the board of directors for Children's Connection. They were personal friends of his, and they held high-status positions throughout the Ohio River Valley.

Children's Connection quickly grew into a respected and well-known institution that generated results and offered reliable services to the region's youth. Foster care placement and retention increased substantially with the involvement of Children's Connection, and its services branched out to include after-school programming, summer camps, and recreational opportunities for children under the age of eighteen.

As time passed Charles transitioned out of banking and stepped into a role as CEO of Children's Connection. This move formalized the nonprofit's reputation as a businesslike and orderly institution with sterling service delivery. Charles selected a few of his closest allies to assume upper-level administration positions—chief financial officer, chief operating officer, and a handful of vice presidents. This elite group could often be seen together on the golf course, at civic events, and at the same table at black-tie fundraisers. Some viewed Charles's approach to hiring as inequitable and unfair, yet it was difficult to argue with it considering the success enjoyed by Children's Connection.

The board of directors—who were responsible for organizational governance, oversight, and formulation of the strategic direction of Children's Connection—was a "who's who" of well-known, upstanding citizens. Charles maintained tight control over who was invited to join the board, and it was clear to many within the organization that Charles, not the board, was in charge. In fact, he had never been evaluated by the board of directors during his entire twelve-year tenure as CEO. He, and the board, viewed performance evaluation as a formality that need not be addressed. Indeed, the board members were ill prepared to handle any major—or perhaps even any minor—organizational challenge because they were held at arm's length by Charles. It was Charles who started Children's Connection, and it was his organization. The board served its purpose by attending events, bringing in money, and taking part in the occasional photo opportunity for the annual report or a news story. Since the board members were personal friends of Charles Mitchell's, he saw no need for term limits, and the organizational bylaws reflected this sentiment.

# Scandal

Since its inception, Children's Connection had served thousands of children. Frontline staff who interacted or worked with the kids in any manner had to receive rigorous training and pass annual examinations in order to maintain their credentials. Although policy on these matters—and on what constituted inappropriate relationships with the children—were distinctly laid out, not all members of the organization abided by the guidelines.

Charles Mitchell, for instance, was regularly seen interacting with Children's Connection clients. Staff thought nothing of his presence as he randomly stopped by after-school events or played catch with young summer campers. Indeed, many often said, "He's the face of the organization—he should be visible!"

This sentiment began to lose favor among some staff as they began to suspect inappropriate relations between their CEO and a few of the children they were serving. No one openly talked about these too-close-for-comfort relationships, but there were those who worried about his intentions. In particular, Charles cultivated very close relationships with members of "Club Mitchell," which was his name for a select group of kids from extremely troubled backgrounds whom he took under his wing. These children—typically between the ages of seven and fifteen—could regularly be seen with Charles at the local ice cream shop, at the mall, at sporting events, and at community functions. The members of Club Mitchell rotated as kids would move away from the region or gain secure living conditions, but there was always a steady rotation of five or six children who were showered with gifts and attention from Charles. In fact, when these kids were between foster homes, he would often invite them to stay at his home.

It was a child who had stayed at Charles's home who came forward to local law enforcement with allegations of the inappropriate relationship imposed by the CEO of Children's Connection.

# Back to Reality

It had only been a week since the news hit the press, and already Alex Jeffries could hardly handle hearing another word about the scandal. Two more children had contacted police about Charles Mitchell, and rumors began circulating about countless others who were poised to join their fellow Club Mitchell members by levying accusations.

Alex and his coworkers had diligently kept up Children's Connection's daily operations, but as public attention to the scandal increased, funding streams were rapidly diminishing. Indeed, when the scandal first broke, the local community foundation as well as numerous banks had notified the organization that its funding would cease at the end of the month.

"While we value the long-standing relationship you have built with us, recent events have made necessary the reevaluation of Commerce Bank's donation to Children's Connection. It has been determined that the activities of Children's Connection no longer align with our strategic objectives," said one such notification from a particularly close ally.

Worse yet, it had been revealed that the foster parents of one of the abused children had reported the misconduct to Children's Connection board members years earlier. The media reports claimed that board members did nothing, although conflicting reports suggested that some board members had tried to remove Charles Mitchell as CEO after learning of the allegations.

Upon hearing this news from a coworker, Alex simply muttered, "It doesn't really matter if the board tried . . . they obviously didn't get anywhere, and the abuse continued for more than a decade. Mr. Mitchell ran that board."

Amid the countless rumors, it was also revealed that two vice presidents and the COO had previously been made aware on multiple occasions of allegations against Charles Mitchell. Nightly news programs reported that administrators at Children's Connection had encouraged a policy of "discretion" on the matter and were not interested in sullying the good name of the organization or its CEO.

With so much uncertainty surrounding the organization, Alex and some of his colleagues began searching for other employment in the area. The writing was on the wall for Children's Connection, and the message was not optimistic.

## Questions and Instructions

1.  What role did Charles Mitchell's personal relationships play in how the scandal unfolded? Please elaborate.
2.  What would you have done differently if you were a Children's Connection board member?
3.  Was the Children's Connection's organizational culture and governance enabling Charles Mitchell's actions in any way? Please explain.
4.  Assuming financial resources could be secured and the organization would be able to continue to operate, what steps would you take as the new CEO to improve the internal controls, human resources approach, and governance of Children's Connection?
5.  The Children's Connection COO and other members of the executive staff were aware of Charles Mitchell's indiscretions before the scandal emerged, yet they did nothing and lied about their knowledge of the situation during the staff meeting. From a human resources perspective, is it ever acceptable to withhold pertinent information or otherwise mislead the employees you manage? Please justify your response.

# PART II

# The Legal Framework

## Jared C. Bennett

For three days, the executive director of a nonprofit organization could not sleep, eat, or focus at work. Her acute agitation stemmed from knowing that, for those three days, a jury of twelve strangers had been deliberating about her future and that of the nonprofit organization that she had founded and worked so hard to build for the past decade.

As she was yet again allowing her mind to wander to what the jurors might be thinking, she received the call that she desperately wanted but also greatly feared. The voice of her attorney—with which she had become all too familiar over the past three years of litigation—somberly said: "The court just called. The jury has finally reached a verdict. I need you to meet me at the courthouse right away."

A nervous "Okay, I'll be right there" was all that she could stammer in response.

From the moment she hung up the phone until she arrived at the courthouse parking lot, the executive director's mind replayed the three years of litigation, starting from the time she was served with the board of trustees' civil complaint alleging that she had breached her fiduciary duties. Her mind first pondered the extensive amount of time she had spent responding to seemingly endless document requests from the board's attorneys, seeking her personal financial records as well as those of the nonprofit. As if having to provide this information to her adversaries wasn't bad enough, she thought, the board had also communicated its accusations against her to the Internal Revenue Service (IRS) and to the state's attorney general. In response to the board's accusations, the IRS issued an administrative summons that required the executive director to produce her financial documents and answer questions under oath about them to an IRS revenue officer. Likewise, investigators from the attorney general's office issued grand jury subpoenas requiring her to produce her financial documents so that the grand jury could review them to see if she had violated any criminal laws.

She thought back over the grueling hours she had spent in depositions, during which her adversaries' attorney peppered her with questions about her private life and her personal finances. She remembered the insinuation in every question from their attorney that she had been both dishonest and incompetent. Although these memories made her blood simmer, it came to a full boil when she recalled the several hours of depositions that she had attended with trustees who repeatedly accused her of wrongdoing. She fumed as she remembered how helpless she had felt having to silently observe as her attorney asked questions to which her adversaries gave their accusatory answers.

"How could the trustees think I would do such a thing when I am the one who started this operation and sacrificed so much to make this place what it is today?" she muttered to herself while driving.

Her anger quickly changed to bewilderment as she recalled the seemingly endless stream of letters that the attorneys had exchanged, the numerous motions the attorneys had drafted and argued before the court, the court hearings and scheduling conferences that had preceded the trial, the attempted settlement negotiations, and finally, the hard-fought three-week trial that had required her to relive all of these events of the past three years. After all this, she hated litigation.

Her bewilderment then changed to tears as she thought about the cost of producing all those documents, the $200 an hour that the nonprofit had been paying her attorney for his work, and the incalculable amount of time that she wanted to spend fulfilling the mission of the nonprofit but instead was wasting on litigation. "How could it have come to this?" she asked herself as she exited the car and walked toward the courthouse doors. After going through security, she saw the all-too-familiar face of her attorney in the hallway.

"Are you nervous?" the attorney asked.

"What do you think?" she curtly replied. "What if the jury comes back finding me liable?"

"Well, we can always appeal," the attorney replied.

"How much does that cost, and how long does that take?" the executive director inquired.

"For my firm to prepare an appellate brief for a case this complicated and to argue it before an appellate court, you can expect the cost to be around $10,000, and the case may last another year or two," the attorney dryly replied. "Even then, you may not win. In fact, if we prevail on appeal, the appellate court may simply order a new trial."

"But what if I win the trial?" the executive director asked, trying to sound positive.

"Then the board of trustees can appeal, and we would have to respond by filing an appellate brief and by arguing the matter before the appellate court," the attorney said.

"So, no matter what, I may be in this for another two years and $10,000? And even after all of that, we may be back here for more proceedings and possibly *another* trial?" the executive director asked incredulously.

"I'm afraid so," the attorney said. "We had better get into the courtroom. I see that the other side has arrived."

A few minutes after they entered the courtroom, the bailiff entered and declared, "All rise for the judge and the jury." As the jury entered, some jurors looked right at the executive director, but others looked elsewhere and avoided eye contact with her. Without any preliminary comments, the judge cut to the chase: "Please be seated. Has the jury reached a verdict?"

"Yes, your honor," the jury foreperson replied.

"Then let's hear it," said the judge.

"As to the first cause of action, whether the defendant breached her fiduciary duties, we the jury find . . . "

The sad fact is that regardless of the verdict reached by this jury, the executive director, the board of trustees, and the nonprofit organization have all lost. Litigation is extremely costly in time and money, neither of which is an abundant resource for most nonprofit organizations. Moreover, litigation permanently damages trust and the interpersonal relationships on which all nonprofit organizations rely to effectively fund and accomplish their important societal missions. Therefore, those who lead and manage nonprofit organizations simply cannot afford to be unaware of or indifferent to the many laws that govern the activities of such organizations and those who lead them.

For example, nonprofit organization managers and trustees need to be aware of the laws governing taxes, torts (i.e., personal injury), contracts, securities, antitrust, property, labor, employment discrimination, and bankruptcy, to name only a few areas. Since we cannot present an exhaustive analysis of all the laws that apply to nonprofit organizations, this part introduction and the two reprinted readings will seek to familiarize nonprofit leaders with only three basic areas of law that are universal to nonprofit organizations: (1) tax exemption, (2) the duties imposed on decision-making, and (3) tort liability.

## Tax Exemption

The tax exemptions that federal and state governments provide to qualifying nonprofit organizations recognize the vital role that nonprofits play in society. Without these tax advantages, few, if any, organizations would be able to survive the financial burden of providing the services on which so many vulnerable people rely. After all, who could possibly make a successful for-profit business when the business model is to distribute as much food as possible to the homeless without receiving anything in return?

Nevertheless, recent fraud scandals—too numerous and notorious to discuss here—have shown that these tax incentives can be abused. Thus, federal and most state governments have passed laws that attempt to ensure that organizations availing themselves of the favorable tax treatment are actually engaging in the types of activities that society has deemed worthy of special tax concessions. To achieve the dual purpose of incentivizing worthy nonprofit activities while protecting against waste, fraud, and abuse, Congress has enacted Internal Revenue Code provisions that apply specifically to nonprofit organizations (Title 26 of the United States Code). For example, 26 USC § 501(c)(3) provides that the following types of organizations are exempt from federal taxation:

> Corporations, and any community chest, fund, or foundation, organized and operated exclusively for religious, charitable, scientific, testing for public safety, literary, or educational purposes, or to foster national or international amateur sports competition (but only if no part of its activities involve the provision of athletic facilities or equipment), or for the prevention of cruelty to children or animals, no part of the net earnings of which inures to the benefit of any private shareholder or individual, no substantial part of the activities of which is carrying on propaganda, or otherwise attempting, to influence legislation (except as otherwise provided in subsection (h)), and which does not participate in, or intervene in (including the publishing or distributing of statements), any political campaign on behalf of (or in opposition to) any candidate for public office.

In addition to exempting these organizations from federal taxation, section 501(c)(3) allows individuals and other entities that donate to qualifying 501(c)(3) organizations to deduct these donations from their own tax liability. Consequently, Congress has provided many attractive incentives for organizations that qualify for preferential tax treatment under section 501(c)(3).

Even though Congress created these incentives for qualifying organizations, it did not enact the requirements or tests that an organization would have to meet to qualify for 501(c)(3) status. It delegated the promulgation of the 501(c)(3) qualification rules to the Secretary of the Treasury through the Administrative Procedure Act.[1] The IRS promulgated rules mandating that every would-be 501(c)(3) organization must meet the organizational test and the operational test.[2] "If an organization fails to meet either the organizational test or the operational test, it is not exempt."[3] The US Supreme Court and the IRS also apply a third test that is not expressly stated in IRS regulations or Section 501(c)(3), the community conscience test. Because all three of these tests are necessary to attain and maintain tax-exempt status, each is briefly discussed here.

### The Organizational Test

For a would-be 501(c)(3) entity to meet the organizational test, the IRS must determine that the entity is "organized exclusively for one or more exempt purposes" as listed in section 501(c)(3).[4] To make this determination, the IRS relies primarily on two sources: the *statement of purpose* in the documents creating the organization (usually called "articles of organization" or something similar) and the organization's *plan to dispose of its assets when it eventually dissolves*.[5]

### Statement of Purpose

An entity's *articles of organization* must contain a statement of purpose that shows the entity will engage in the activities exempted from taxation in section 501(c)(3). The statement of purpose in the articles of organization does not have to be highly detailed or elaborate to pass muster. As an illustration, if the statement of purpose in the articles of organization simply says that the entity "is formed for charitable purposes," then, according to the IRS, "such articles ordinarily shall be sufficient for purposes of the organizational test."[6] Even though the statement-of-purpose portion of the organizational test tolerates great generality (e.g., "for charitable purposes"), it also accommodates more specific statements of purpose.[7] However, the organizational test will not accommodate statements of purpose that authorize the entity (1) to devote anything more than an insubstantial part of its operations to purposes that are not exempt under section 501(c)(3)[8]; (2) to engage in political activities in which the organization devotes more than an insubstantial part of its activities to influence legislation "by propaganda or otherwise"[9]; or (3) to wage a political campaign for or against any particular candidate for election.[10] Thus, if the articles of organization contain a 501(c)(3)-compliant statement of purpose, the IRS will determine that the organization has cleared this portion of the organizational test.

### Dissolution

To ensure that the statement of purpose in the articles of organization does more than pay mere lip service to the exempt purposes in section 501(c)(3), the IRS has included a requirement in the organizational test compelling entities to show that their assets will continue to be used for 501(c)(3)-exempt purposes even after the entity is dissolved.[11] For example, the articles of incorporation could say that if the entity should dissolve, all of its assets will be distributed by court order to either a government agency for a public purpose or another organization with an exempt primary purpose under 501(c)(3). "However, an organization does not meet the organizational test if its articles [of organization] or *the law of the State* in which it was created provide that its assets would, upon dissolution, be distributed to its members or shareholders."[12] Indeed, knowledge of state law is very important when it comes to the organizational test. If the entity satisfies the statement of purpose and the dissolution portions of the organizational test, the IRS will determine that the entity has met the first requirement for 501(c)(3) status.

## The Operational Test

Even if the entity passes the organizational test, the IRS will not grant 501(c)(3) status unless its *operations* are also consistent with section 501(c)(3)'s purposes. To make this determination, the IRS relies on three criteria: (1) the entity's primary activities, (2) the entity's distribution of earnings, and (3) whether the entity is an *action organization*.[13]

### Primary Activities

To meet the operational test, the entity must demonstrate that its primary activities fall within an exempt purpose mentioned in section 501(c)(3). Recall that section 501(c)(3) applies only to organizations that are "operated exclusively" for the purposes mentioned therein. However, if this phrase were interpreted literally, then no organization could engage in any business activity outside of the section 501(c)(3) boundaries. Indeed, if nonprofit organizations were not allowed to engage in at least *some* activities that are outside of section 501(c)(3), many nonprofits would lose significant revenue sources on which they have come to rely over recent decades. Given the high cost of a literal interpretation of section 501(c)(3), the IRS has interpreted "exclusively" to mean "primarily." For example, IRS regulations state:

> An organization will be regarded as *operated exclusively* for one or more exempt purposes only if it engages primarily in activities which accomplish one or more of such exempt purposes specified in section 501(c)(3). An organization will not be so regarded if more than an insubstantial part of its activities is not in furtherance of an exempt purpose.[14]

Thus, an organization can engage in profit-making enterprises and still comply with the Operational Test as long as it can demonstrate that its profit-making enterprises are only "an insubstantial part of its activities" and advance "an exempt purpose."[15]

Unfortunately (or fortunately, depending on your point of view), neither the IRS nor the courts have defined what percentage of an organization's activities is considered "insubstantial." Whether nonexempt activities under 501(c)(3) constitute a "substantial" or an "insubstantial" portion of an organization's operations is decided on a case-by-case basis. Because judicial approaches on this issue differ throughout the country, leaders of a nonprofit organization must become familiar with court rulings in the jurisdiction(s) where their organization operates.

### Distribution of Earnings

Many people believe that nonprofit organizations are precluded from earning more than their total expenditures (i.e., generating a profit). This belief is mistaken. Nonprofit organizations may indeed earn profits. What they may not do, however, is distribute profits to trustees or directors for their personal benefit and still pass the operational test.[16] To this end, IRS regulations state that an organization will not meet the operational test if "its net earnings inure in whole or in part to the benefit of private shareholders or individuals."[17] Instead, the organization must show that its earnings are distributed in ways that further its 501(c)(3)-exempt purposes.

### Action Organizations

Designation as an action organization means that an entity has failed to meet the operational test and consequently has failed to attain 501(c)(3) status.[18] An *action organization* devotes more than an "insubstantial" portion of its activities to "attempting to influence legislation by propaganda or otherwise."[19] The IRS will deem an entity to be in the business of influencing legislation—and therefore designate it as an action organization—if it engages in at least one of three activities.

First, an organization that "(a) contacts, or urges the public to contact, members of the legislative body for the purpose of proposing, supporting, or opposing legislation; or (b) advocates the adoption or rejection of legislation," will be deemed an action organization.[20] The IRS defines *legislation* as "action by the Congress, by any State legislature, by any local council or similar governing body, or by the public in a referendum, initiative, constitutional amendment, or similar procedure."[21] Thus, if an organization spends a "substantial part" of its time, effort, and money advocating for or against legislation, then the IRS will deem it an action organization that fails the operational test and consequently will not be afforded 501(c)(3) status.[22]

Second, if an entity "participates or intervenes, directly or indirectly, in any political campaign on behalf of or in opposition to any candidate for public office," then it is an action organization.[23] The IRS has defined the phrase *candidate for public office* to mean "an individual who offers himself, or is proposed by others, as a contestant for an elective public office, whether such office be national, state, or local."[24]

Finally, the IRS will deem an entity to be an action organization if its primary objectives could only be achieved through the adoption or failure of proposed legislation, *and* if the entity advocates or campaigns more than an insubstantial amount for its political ends.[25] Note that the entity must advocate or campaign for a cause. Merely providing information about candidates or an analysis of specific legislation does not constitute "advocacy" or "campaigning" and therefore does not make an entity an action organization.[26]

If the IRS determines that an entity is an action organization, its tax-exempt status is not necessarily in jeopardy because it may still qualify for tax-exempt status under 501(c)(4).[27] Entities that are tax-exempt under 501(c)(4) are known as *civic* or *social welfare organizations*.[28] However, donors to 501(c)(4) organizations cannot write off their donations from their personal or corporate income taxes, which takes away a significant revenue-generating incentive.

Once the IRS is satisfied that a nonprofit organization's primary activities are truly devoted to an exempt purpose under section 501(c)(3), its earnings are properly distributed, and it is not a national organization, then it is deemed to have passed the operational test.

### The Community Conscience Test

Organizations that satisfy the organizational and operational tests still may not qualify for 501(c)(3) status if their primary purpose is *contrary to the community conscience*. Although this requirement is not expressly stated in section 501(c)(3) or other IRS regulations, the IRS introduced it in 1971 through revenue ruling 71-447.[29] An IRS revenue ruling notifies the public about how the IRS will interpret and apply laws, rules, and regulations. Revenue ruling 71-447 provides that organizations that discriminate based on race are not the types of "charities" that section 501(c)(3) was intended to foster, and therefore they cannot receive 501(c)(3) status.[30]

The best-known community conscience case occurred in 1974, when Bob Jones University, a private, nonprofit religious university in South Carolina that openly engaged in racial discrimination, challenged revenue ruling 71-447. The plaintiff claimed that its discriminatory policies were an integral part of its religious beliefs.[31] Because of these racially discriminatory policies, the IRS revoked the university's 501(c)(3) status that it had previously enjoyed.[32] The university sought judicial review of the IRS's determination, which eventually reached the US Supreme Court. The Court affirmed the IRS's determination:

> When the Government grants exemptions or allows deductions all taxpayers are affected; the very fact of the exemption or deduction for the donor means that other taxpayers can be said to be indirect and vicarious "donors." Charitable exemptions are justified on the basis that the exempt entity confers a public benefit—a benefit which the society or the community may not itself choose or be able to provide, or which supplements and advances the work of public institutions already supported by tax revenues. History buttresses logic to make clear that, to warrant exemption under § 501(c)(3), an institution must fall within a category specified in that section and must demonstrably serve and be in harmony with the public interest. The institution's purpose must not be so at odds with the common community conscience as to undermine any public benefit that might otherwise be conferred.[33]

As the IRS's revenue ruling and the Supreme Court's endorsement thereof show, 501(c)(3) status is a symbol of public support for what a nonprofit organization does. Consequently, the IRS will not grant 501(c)(3) status to an organization whose conduct is repugnant to the community conscience.[34]

Many questions surround the community conscience doctrine, however. How does the IRS or a court determine what the community conscience is? How large is the "community" whose conscience the IRS will attempt to determine? If, for example, a charitable nonprofit organization provides condoms and other informational materials on safe sex for teens in an area in which the vast majority of voters would like to shut down the nonprofit and run it out of town, is the nonprofit's activity so contrary to the community conscience as to warrant revocation of 501(c)(3) status? Surely the community conscience test will be litigated. Be that as it may, a nonprofit organization that meets the organizational test and the operational test and works within the community conscience—whatever that means—will be eligible for 501(c)(3) status.

## The Liability of Nonprofit Leaders

Recent scandals involving the nonprofit sector have brought increased scrutiny of the leaders of nonprofit organizations. Accordingly, nonprofit leaders may face criminal and civil liability under federal and state law for the decisions they make. Here in Part II we do not focus on the criminal sanctions that may be imposed against leaders of nonprofits—a topic addressed in Part I in the discussion of the Sarbanes-Oxley Act of 2002[35]—but instead briefly present the civil aspects of liability that will help nonprofit leaders know how to avoid difficult litigation situations like the one presented at the beginning of this introduction.

The executive directors and governing boards of nonprofit organizations may be subject to civil liability under federal and state law. On the federal side, Congress prohibits any person from engaging in *excess benefit transactions* with a 501(c)(3) organization. If a person runs afoul of this prohibition, the IRS may impose heavy penalties against that person, including, among other things, a tax of 200 percent of the improper benefit the person obtained from the prohibited transaction with the nonprofit organization.[36]

As further evidence of how seriously the IRS takes self-dealing, it now requires nonprofit directors and boards to submit disclosure Form 990 regarding their compensation.[37] In 2011 the IRS published a list of over 275,000 nonprofits that lost their nonprofit tax-exempt status for failing to file Form 990.[38] Thus, nonprofit leaders who engage in self-dealing or refuse to disclose their interest in the nonprofit may pay dearly.

In addition to facing federal civil liability for their actions, nonprofit leaders must also protect themselves from civil liability under state law. Although state laws governing nonprofit organizations vary, there are certain *fiduciary duties* that every state imposes on nonprofit directors and their governing boards. For example, courts in many states require nonprofit leaders to abide by a *duty of care*, a *duty of loyalty*, and a *duty of obedience*.[39] Because state laws regarding the duties imposed on nonprofit directors vary somewhat, we rely here on the American Bar Association's "Revised Model Nonprofit Corporation Act," which concisely sums up the duties that nonprofit leaders must perform. The Model Act stipulates that:

> An officer with discretionary authority shall discharge his or her duties under that authority:
> 1. in good faith;
> 2. with the care an ordinarily prudent person in a like position would exercise under similar circumstances; and
> 3. in a manner the officer reasonably believes to be in the best interests of the corporation and its members, if any.[40]

Under the Model Act, *good faith* means that directors rely on the competent advice of others, such as staff, legal counsel, and other professionals, in making decisions that they reasonably believe to be in the best interest of the organization.[41] The Model Act also provides a liability shield for leaders who comply with their duty of good faith.[42] Conversely, the breach of any of these duties may subject nonprofit leaders to civil litigation, which can ruin careers, reputations, the organization itself, and priceless personal relationships no matter who "wins" the litigation.

## General Tort Liability

Besides facing legal liability for their decisions, leaders of nonprofit organizations may also be subject to suit for personal injuries that are allegedly caused by the nonprofit's actions or that occur on the nonprofit's property. Historically, courts developed the *doctrine of charitable immunity*, which barred all suits against nonprofit organizations.[43] The reasons for according nonprofit organizations favored treatment for tort liability are self-evident. Nonprofit organizations provide benefits to the public and often rely heavily on volunteers. If legislatures and courts impose too much liability on nonprofit organizations, their leaders, and their volunteers, nonprofits would be reluctant to provide the services on which so many rely, for fear of being sued. The burden of providing these services would thus shift to the government, thereby increasing the size and cost of governing or resulting in the loss of services that vulnerable individuals need. Thus, courts and legislatures historically have either exempted nonprofits from suits or greatly limited their liability.

Over time, however, that immunity has eroded. Now nonprofits and their leaders are exposed to more potential liability, even though they are still accorded more favorable treatment than for-profit corporations.[44] Many scholars would like to see nonprofit liability expand even further because they do not believe that the historic policy reasons for according nonprofits greater protection from tort litigation are valid in the twenty-first century. For example, some scholars argue that in a modern world where some nonprofit organizations are extremely wealthy and liability insurance is readily available, they should not continue to receive heightened protection from tort liability.[45] Given this debate, nonprofit leaders should carefully watch for future legislation and litigation regarding nonprofit tort immunity in their state.

## Readings Reprinted in Part II

In "Organizational, Operational, and Related Tests and Doctrines" from *The Law of Tax-Exempt Organizations,* nonprofit law expert Bruce R. Hopkins outlines the legal framework and public policy reasons behind the tests governing the formation and operation of 501(c)(3) nonprofit organizations. Hopkins describes the organizational and operational tests in considerable detail and provides examples of how these tests can be met. In addition to describing the current state of this portion of the law governing 501(c)(3) organizations, Hopkins also highlights the questions that courts have yet to face in this important area of the law.

In "Evaluating the Charitable Deduction and Proposed Reforms," Roger Colinvaux, Brian Galle, and Eugene Steuerle provide a policy analysis on tax exemptions generally, their purpose, and their drawbacks. The authors also discuss alternatives and reforms to the charitable deductions.

Finally, in "Punctilios and Nonprofit Corporate Governance: A Comprehensive Look at Nonprofit Directors' Fiduciary Duties," law professor Thomas Lee Hazen and nonprofit board member Lisa Love Hazen discuss the civil liability that nonprofit directors have for their decisions under federal and state law. For example, the Hazens describe the duties imposed on board members, the consequences for breaching them, and best practices for avoiding problems.

## Case Studies in Part II

Two cases are presented in Part II, "Daughter Dearest: Nonprofit Nepotism" and "Conflicting Values." In the first case, the age-old issues of self-dealing and conflicts of interest are brought to light. How should a staff member react when the executive director makes hiring decisions based on personal considerations? At what point do failures to comply with policy (written or otherwise) lead to legal headaches for the nonprofit organization?

In "Conflicting Values," the question is asked: should an ethical concern rise to the level of a legal obligation? Here a member of the board of directors of a local chapter of a national organization finds himself grappling with a national policy directive that is opposed to his personal beliefs. What should be the position of a local organization when organizational values collide with those of a member of the board of directors? The case provides readers with an opportunity to consider the implications of policy mandates that are imposed by parent organizations and the responses to these by potential and existing officers of a local chapter of an organization.

## Notes

1. 5 U.S.C. § 556 (2012).
2. 26 C.F.R. § 1.501(c)(3)-1(a) (2013), amended by 79 Fed. Reg. 37, 631 (July 2, 2014).
3. *Id.*
4. *Id.* § 1.501(c)(3)-(1)(b).
5. *Id.* § 1.501(c)(3)-(1)(b)(1), (4).
6. *Id.* § 1.501(c)(3)-(1)(b)(1)(ii).
7. *Id.*
8. *Id.* § 1.501(c)(3)-(1)(b)(1)(i).
9. *Id.* § 1.501(c)(3)-(1)(b)(3)(i).
10. *Id.* § 1.501(c)(3)-(1)(b)(3)(ii).
11. *Id.* § 1.501(c)(3)-(1)(b)(4).
12. *Id.*
13. *Id.* § 1.501(c)(3)-(1)(c).
14. *Id.* § 1.501(c)(3)-(1)(c)(1) (emphasis in original).
15. *Id.*
16. *Id.* § 1.501(c)(3)-(1)(c)(2).
17. *Id.*
18. *Id.* § 1.501(c)(3)-(1)(c)(3)(i).
19. *Id.* § 1.501(c)(3)-(1)(c)(3)(ii).
20. *Id.* § 1.501(c)(3)-(1)(c)(3)(ii)(a), (b).
21. *Id.* § 1.501(c)(3)-(1)(c)(3)(ii).
22. *Id.*
23. *Id.* § 1.501(c)(3)-1(c)(3)(iii).
24. *Id.*
25. *Id.* § 1.501(c)(3)-1(c)(3)(iv).
26. *Id.*
27. 26 U.S.C. § 501(c)(4).
28. 26 C.F.R. § 501(c)(4)-1(a) (2013).
29. Rev. Rul. 71-447, 1971-2 C.B. 230 (January 1, 1971); Bob Jones Univ. v. United States, 461 US 574, 592 (1974).
30. Bob Jones Univ., 461 U.S. at 579.
31. *Id.* at 580–581 (discussing the university's racially discriminatory policies).
32. *Id.* at 581.
33. *Id.* at 591–592 (footnotes omitted).
34. *Id.* at 592.
35. Pub. L. No. 107–204.

36. 26 U.S.C. § 4958(b).

37. Thomas Lee Hazen and Lisa Love Hazen, "Punctilios and Nonprofit Corporate Governance—A Comprehensive Look at Nonprofit Directors' Fiduciary Duties," 14 *University of Pennsylvania Journal of Business Law* 347, 366–368 (2012).

38. *Id.* at 397.

39. See, e.g., Jaclyn A. Cherry, "Update: The Current State of Nonprofit Director Liability," 37 *Duquesne Law Review* 557, 560–562 (1999).

40. Revised Model Nonprofit Corporation Act § 8.42(a).

41. *Id.* § 8.42(b).

42. *Id.* § 8.42(d).

43. "Developments in the Law—Nonprofit Corporations," 105 *Harvard Law Review* 1578, 1679–1680 (1992).

44. *Id.* at 1680.

45. *Id.* at 1680–1699.

## ▶ CHAPTER 3

# Organizational, Operational, and Related Tests and Doctrines

BRUCE R. HOPKINS

## Forms of Tax-Exempt Organizations

Generally, the Internal Revenue Code does not prescribe a specific organizational form for entities to qualify for tax exemption. Basically, a tax-exempt organization will be a nonprofit corporation, trust (inter vivos or testamentary), or unincorporated association.[1] The IRS is of the view that tax-exempt charitable and social welfare organizations may be formed as limited liability companies;[2] the agency has suggested that this form of entity may be inappropriate for exempt social clubs.[3] Some provisions of the Code, however, mandate, in whole or in part, the corporate form,[4] and other Code provisions (particularly in the employee plan context[5]) mandate the trust form for exempt organizations.[6] Throughout the categories of exempt organizations are additional terms such as clubs, associations, societies, foundations, leagues, companies, boards, orders, posts, and units, which are not terms referencing legal forms. For tax purposes, an organization may

be deemed a corporation even though it is not formally incorporated.[7]

The federal tax provision that describes charitable organizations provides that an organization described in that provision must be a corporation, community chest, fund, or foundation; only the first of these terms has any efficacy in law. An unincorporated association or trust can qualify under this provision, presumably as a fund or foundation or perhaps, as noted, as a corporation.[8] A partnership cannot, however, be tax-exempt as a charitable organization.[9]

An organization already exempt from federal taxation may establish a separate fund or like entity that is itself an exempt organization.[10] The attributes of this type of a fund include a separate category of exemption (for example, an educational research and scholarship fund established by a bar association[11]), a separate governing body, and separate books and accounts.[12] A mere bank deposit cannot, however, amount to a requisite fund; thus, a contribution to it would be considered a nondeductible gift to an individual rather than a possibly deductible gift to a qualified organization.[13]

The formalities of organization of an entity may have a bearing on the tax exemption. This is the case not only in connection with the sufficiency of the governing instruments,[14] but also, and more fundamentally, with regard to whether there is a separate organization in the first instance. An individual may perform worthwhile activities, such as providing financial assistance to needy students, but will receive no tax benefits from his or her beneficence unless he or she establishes and funds a qualified organization that in turn renders the charitable works, such as scholarship grants. One court observed, in the process of denying a charitable contribution deduction, that the federal tax law makes no provision for a charitable deduction in the context of personal ventures, however praiseworthy in character. The court noted that "[t]here is no evidence of such enterprise being a corporation, community chest, fund, or foundation and little information, if any, as to its organization or activities."[15] Assuming the organization is not operated to benefit private interests, its tax exemption will not be endangered because its creator serves as the sole trustee and exercises complete control,[16] although state law may limit or preclude close control.

A "formless aggregation of individuals" cannot be tax-exempt as a charitable entity.[17] At a minimum, the entity—to be exempt—must have an organizing instrument, some governing rules, and regularly chosen officers.[18] These rules have been amply illustrated in the cases concerning so-called personal churches.[19]

Among the nontax factors to be considered in selecting an organizational form are legal liabilities in relation to the individuals involved (the corporate form can limit certain personal liabilities), local law requirements, necessities of governing instruments, local annual reporting requirements, organizational expenses, and any membership requirements.[20] Federal law, other than the tax laws, may also have a bearing on

the choice, such as the organization's comparable status under the postal laws.[21]

A change in form may require a tax-exempt organization to reapply for recognition of exempt status. For example, an unincorporated organization that has been recognized by the IRS as an exempt charitable entity must commence the application process anew if it incorporates.[22]

## Governing Instruments

An organization must have governing instruments to qualify for tax exemption, if only to satisfy the appropriate organizational test. This is particularly the case for charitable organizations, as to which the federal tax law imposes specific organizational requirements.[23] These rules are more stringent if the charitable organization is a private foundation.[24]

If the corporate form is used, the governing instruments will be articles of incorporation and bylaws. An unincorporated organization will have articles of organization, perhaps in the form of a constitution, and, undoubtedly, also bylaws. If a trust, the basic document will be a declaration of trust or trust agreement.

The articles of organization should contain provisions stating the organization's purposes; whether there will be members and, if so, their qualifications and classes; the initial board of directors or trustee(s); the registered agent and incorporators (if a corporation); the dissolution or liquidation procedure; and the required language referencing the appropriate tax law (federal and state) requirements and prohibitions. If the organization is a corporation, particular attention should be given to the appropriate state nonprofit corporation statute, which will contain requirements that may supersede the provisions of the articles of incorporation and bylaws or may apply where the governing instruments are silent.

The bylaws may also contain the provisions of the articles of organization and, in addition, should contain provisions amplifying or stating the purposes of the organization; the terms and conditions of membership (if any); the manner of selection and duties of the directors or trustees and officers; the voting requirements; the procedure for forming committees; the accounting period; any indemnification provisions; the appropriate tax provisions; and the procedure for amendment of the bylaws.

## Organizational Test

An organization, to be tax-exempt as a charitable entity, must be both organized and operated exclusively for one or more of the permissible exempt purposes. This requirement has given rise to an *organizational test* and an *operational test*[25] for charitable organizations. If an organization fails to meet either the organizational test or the operational test, it cannot qualify for exemption from federal income taxation as a charitable entity.[26]

The income tax regulations contemplate two types of governing instruments for a charitable organization: the instrument by which the organization is created (*articles of organization*) and the instrument stating the rules pursuant to which the organization is operated (*bylaws*).[27] For the incorporated organization, the articles of organization are articles of incorporation. For the unincorporated entity, the articles of organization may be so termed or may be termed otherwise, such as a *constitution, agreement of trust,* or *declaration of trust.* Occasionally an unincorporated organization will combine these two types of instruments in one document; while this is technically inappropriate, the IRS is unlikely to find the practice a violation of the organizational test.

An organization is organized exclusively for one or more tax-exempt, charitable purposes only if its articles of organization limit its purposes to one or more exempt purposes[28] and do not expressly empower it to engage, other-

wise than as an insubstantial part of its activities, in activities that in themselves are not in furtherance of one or more exempt purposes.[29] Additional requirements are imposed for the governing instruments of supporting organizations[30] and private foundations.[31] The fact that an organization's organizational documents are not properly executed can be viewed by the IRS as a violation of the organizational test.[32]

### (a) Statement of Purposes

In meeting the organizational test, the charitable organization's purposes, as stated in its articles of organization, may be as broad as, or more specific than, the particular exempt purposes, such as religious, charitable, or educational ends. Therefore, an organization that, by the terms of its articles of organization, is formed for "literary and scientific purposes within the meaning of section 501(c)(3) of the Internal Revenue Code" shall, if it otherwise meets the requirements of the organizational test, be considered to have met the test. Similarly, articles of organization stating that the organization is created solely to "receive contributions and pay them over to organizations which are described in section 501(c)(3) and exempt from taxation under section 501(a) of the Internal Revenue Code" are sufficient for purposes of the organizational test. If the articles of organization state that the organization is formed for "charitable purposes," the articles ordinarily will be adequate for purposes of the organizational test.[33]

Articles of organization of charitable entities may not authorize the carrying on of nonexempt activities (unless they are insubstantial), even though the organization is, by the terms of its articles, created for a purpose that is no broader than the specified charitable purposes.[34] Thus, an organization that is empowered by its articles to "engage in a manufacturing business" or to "engage in the operation of a social club" does not meet the organizational test, regardless of the fact that its articles of organization may state that the organization is created for "charitable purposes within the meaning of section 501(c)(3) of the Internal Revenue Code."[35]

In no case will an organization be considered to be organized exclusively for one or more tax-exempt charitable purposes if, by the terms of its articles of organization, the purposes for which the organization is created are broader than the specified charitable purposes. The fact that the actual operations of the organization have been exclusively in furtherance of one or more exempt purposes is not sufficient to permit the organization to meet the organizational test. An organization wishing to qualify as a charitable entity should not provide in its articles of organization that it has all of the powers accorded under the particular state's nonprofit corporation act, since those powers are likely to be broader than those allowable under federal tax law.[36] Similarly, an organization will not meet the organizational test as a result of statements or other evidence that its members intend to operate only in furtherance of one or more exempt purposes.[37]

An organization is not considered organized exclusively for one or more exempt charitable purposes if its articles of organization expressly authorize it to (1) devote more than an insubstantial part of its activities to attempting to influence legislation by propaganda or otherwise;[38] (2) directly or indirectly participate in, or intervene in (including the publishing or distributing of statements), any political campaign on behalf of or in opposition to any candidate for public office;[39] or (3) have objectives and engage in activities that characterize it as an action organization.[40] The organizational test is not violated, however, where an organization's articles empower it to make the expenditure test election (relating to expenditures for legislative activities)[41] and, only if it so elects, to make direct lobbying or grassroots lobbying expenditures that are not in excess of the ceiling amounts prescribed by that test.[42]

The organizational test requires that the articles of organization limit the purposes of the entity to one or more exempt purposes. Exempt purposes are described in the statute,[43] and include purposes such as charitable, educational, religious, and scientific ones. These purposes are also enumerated in the tax regulations in explication of the term *charitable*,[44] and include purposes such as advancement of religion, lessening the burdens of government, and promotion of social welfare. There is no requirement in the law that the statement of purposes, when exempt purposes are referenced, expressly refer to IRC § 501(c)(3).

There are many other permissible functions of a charitable organization that are not formally recognized as exempt purposes in the Code or the regulations that nonetheless have been recognized as exempt functions (generically) in IRS revenue rulings and court decisions (and thus satisfy the operational test[45]). Purposes of this nature include promotion of health, promotion of the arts, operation of a school, and protection of the environment. Inasmuch as functions of this nature are not exempt functions (as technically defined), they cannot stand alone in a statement of purposes. That is, for the organizational test to be satisfied, one of two statements must be in the articles of organization: (1) if the document contains a purpose that is not an exempt purpose, it should expressly limit the organization's purposes to those described in IRC § 501(c)(3); or (2) if the document contains a purpose that is not an exempt purpose, and that purpose is not contrary to exempt purposes, the document should include a notwithstanding clause.[46]

An overly broad statement of purposes cannot be cured by a provision stating that the organization's activities will be confined to those described in IRC 501(c)(3). Again, this is because activities are considered in connection with the operational test, while the organizational test is concerned with purposes. Also, despite the rules of law governing charitable entities, there is nothing in the organizational test that requires reference to the private inurement doctrine,[47] limitation on attempts to influence legislation,[48] or the prohibition on political campaign activities in the articles of organization.[49]

It is the position of the IRS that only a *creating document* may be looked to in meeting the organizational test.

The law of the state in which an organization is created is controlling in construing the terms of its articles of organization.[50]

## (b) Dissolution Requirements

An organization is not organized exclusively for one or more exempt charitable purposes unless its assets are dedicated to an exempt purpose. An organization's assets will be considered dedicated to an exempt purpose, for example, if, upon dissolution, the assets would, by reason of a provision in the organization's articles of organization or by operation of law, be distributed for one or more exempt purposes, or to the federal government, or to a state or local government, for a public purpose, or would be distributed by a court to another organization to be used in a manner as in the judgment of the court will best accomplish the general purposes for which the dissolved organization was organized. A charitable organization does not, however, meet the organizational test if its articles of organization or the laws of the state in which it was created provide that its assets would, upon dissolution, be distributed to its members or shareholders.[51] Consequently, federal income tax exemption as a charitable organization will be denied where, upon dissolution of the organization, its assets would revert to the individual founders rather than to one or more qualifying charities.[52] A charitable organization's assets may, upon dissolution, be transferred for charitable purposes without necessarily being transferred to a charitable organization.[53]

## (c) Mission Statements

As part of the redesign of the Form 990,[54] the IRS is placing considerable emphasis on mission statements, particularly those of public charities. Thus, the return requests, in two instances, a description of the filing organization's *mission*.[55] An organization may thus have a mission statement in addition to a statement of purpose. A mission statement should not, of course, be inconsistent with the purposes statement.[56]

## Primary Purpose Test

A basic concept of the law of tax-exempt organizations is the *primary purpose rule*. The rule is one of the fundamental bases for determination of the appropriate category of tax exemption (if any) for an organization. The principle is formally explicated, by use of the word *exclusively*,[57] in the context of exempt charitable organizations,[58] exempt social welfare organizations,[59] exempt cemetery companies,[60] exempt health care coverage organizations,[61] and exempt workers' compensation coverage organizations,[62] and by use of the word *substantially* in the case of exempt social clubs.[63] The terms *exclusive* and *substantial* are generally subsumed, in this context, in the word *primary*.[64] This principle of the federal tax law is generally applicable to all categories of exempt organizations.[65]

Consequently, the definition of the word *exclusively*, in the law of tax-exempt organizations, is different from the meaning normally associated with the word. As one court nicely stated, the term *exclusively* "in this statutory context is a term of art and does not mean 'solely.'"[66] The law could not reasonably be interpreted in any other way. That is, if *exclusively* truly meant *exclusively* (as in solely), there would not be an opportunity for the conduct of unrelated business activity. Since that interpretation would render the entire law of unrelated business income taxation[67] meaningless, the interpretation would not be reasonable. Consequently, by treating the word *exclusively* as if it meant *primarily*, the law accommodates the coexistence of some unrelated activities with related ones.

The primary purpose test looks—in a rule frequently honored in its breach—to an organization's purposes rather than its activities.[68] The focus should not be on an organization's primary activities as the test of tax exemption, but on whether the activities accomplish one or more tax-exempt purposes.[69] This is why, for example, an organization may engage in nonexempt or profit-making activities and nonetheless qualify for exemption.[70]

The general rule, as stated by the US Supreme Court in the context of charitable organizations, is that the "presence of a single . . . [nonexempt] purpose, if substantial in nature, will destroy the exemption regardless of the number or importance of truly . . . [exempt] purposes."[71] In the words of the IRS, the rules applicable to charitable organizations in general have been "construed as requiring all the resources of the organization [other than an insubstantial part] to be applied to the pursuit of one or more of the exempt purposes therein specified."[72] Consequently, the existence of one or more authentic exempt purposes of an organization will not be productive of tax exemption as a charitable (or other) entity if a substantial nonexempt purpose is present in its operations.[73]

There is no formal definition of the term *insubstantial* in this setting. Thus, application of the primary purpose test entails an issue of fact to be determined under the facts and circumstances of each case.[74] A court opinion suggested that, where a function represents less than 10 percent of total efforts, the primary purpose test will not be applied to prevent exemption.[75] Another court opinion stated that an organization that received approximately one-third of its revenue from an unrelated business could not qualify for tax-exempt status, in that the level of nonexempt activity "exceed[ed] the benchmark of insubstantiality."[76] Yet the

IRS allowed a charitable organization to remain exempt where it derived two-thirds of its income from unrelated businesses, inasmuch as the net income from these businesses was used to further exempt purposes.[77]

The proper approach to be taken, therefore, when determining whether an organization qualifies as a tax-exempt entity, is to assume arguendo one or more exempt purposes and then endeavor to ascertain whether the organization has a commercial or other nonexempt purpose. On finding a nonexempt purpose, an inquiry should be made as to whether it is primary or incidental to the exempt purposes.[78] Then, if there is a nonexempt purpose that is substantial in nature, the exemption would be precluded.

The primary purpose of an organization is not taken into account only when determining whether it qualifies for tax-exempt status. This purpose can also be a critical factor in application of the unrelated business rules.[79]

## Operational Test

The operational test, as its name indicates, is concerned with how an organization functions in relation to the applicable requirements for tax-exempt status. Thus, in a generic sense, every type of exempt organization is subject to an operational test. Nonetheless, the only operational test to be found in the tax regulations is the test pertaining to exempt charitable organizations.

### (a) Basic Rules

An organization, to qualify as a charitable entity, is regarded as operated exclusively for one or more tax-exempt purposes only if it engages primarily in activities that accomplish one or more of its exempt purposes.[80] The IRS observed that, to satisfy this operational test, the organization's "resources must be devoted to purposes that qualify as exclusively charitable within the meaning of section 501(c)(3) of the

Code and the applicable regulations."[81] An organization will not be so regarded if more than an insubstantial part of its activities is not in furtherance of an exempt purpose.[82] An organization is not considered as operated exclusively for one or more exempt purposes if its net earnings inure in whole or in part to the benefit of private shareholders or individuals.[83] An organization can be substantially dominated by its founder without, for that reason alone, failing to satisfy the operational test.[84] A court concluded, however, that an organization cannot qualify for tax exemption where one individual controls all aspects of the organization's operations and "is not checked" by any governing body.[85]

An organization may meet the federal tax law requirements for charitable entities even though it operates a trade or business as a substantial part of its activities.[86] If the organization has as its primary purpose the carrying on of a trade or business, however, it may not be tax-exempt.[87] The core issue is whether the substantial business activity accomplishes or is in furtherance of an exempt purpose.[88] (The existence of an operating profit is not conclusive as to a business purpose.)[89] Even though the operation of a business does not deprive an organization of classification as a charitable entity, there may be unrelated trade or business tax consequences.[90]

The operational test focuses on the actual purposes the organization advances by means of its activities, rather than on the organization's statement of purposes or the nature of its activities, in recognition of the fact that an organization may conduct a business in furtherance of a tax-exempt purpose and qualify as a charitable entity:

> Under the operational test, the purpose towards which an organization's activities are directed, and not the nature of the activities themselves, is ultimately dispositive of the organization's right to be classified as a section 501(c)(3) organization exempt from tax under section 501(a). . . . [I]t is possible for . . . an activity to be carried on for more than one purpose. . . . The fact that . . . [an] activity may constitute a trade or business does not, of course, disqualify it from classification under section 501(c)(3), provided the activity furthers or accomplishes an exempt purpose. . . . Rather, the critical inquiry is whether . . . [an organization's] primary purpose for engaging in its . . . activity is an exempt purpose, or whether its primary purpose is the nonexempt one of operating a commercial business producing net profits for . . . [the organization]. . . . Factors such as the particular manner in which an organization's activities are conducted, the commercial hue of those activities and the existence and amount of annual or accumulated profits are relevant evidence of a forbidden predominant purpose.[91]

This important distinction between activities and purpose is sometimes overlooked by the IRS and the courts. For example, in one case a court concluded that the operational test was not satisfied because the organization failed to describe its activities in sufficient detail in its application for recognition of tax exemption.[92]

Although an organization might be engaged in only a single activity, that activity may be directed toward multiple purposes, both exempt and nonexempt. If the nonexempt purpose is substantial in nature, the organization will not satisfy the operational test.[93]

Whether an organization has a substantial nonexempt purpose is a question of fact, to be resolved on the basis of all the appropriate evidence.[94]

### (b) Action Organizations

An organization is not operated exclusively for one or more exempt charitable purposes if it is an action organization.[95]

An organization is an *action organization* if a substantial part of its activities is attempting to influence legislation.[96] For this purpose, an organization is regarded as attempting to influence legislation if the organization contacts, or urges the public to contact, members of a legislative body for the purpose of proposing, supporting, or opposing legislation or if it advocates the adoption or rejection of legislation. The term *legislation* includes action by the US Congress, a state legislature, a local council or similar governing body, or the public in a referendum, initiative, constitutional amendment, or similar procedure. An organization will not fail to meet the operational test merely because it advocates, as an insubstantial part of its activities, the adoption or rejection of legislation.[97] Also, an organization for which the expenditure test election (relating to expenditures for legislative activities)[98] is in effect for a tax year is not considered an action organization for the year if it avoids loss of tax exemption by reason of that test.[99]

An organization is an action organization if it participates or intervenes, directly or indirectly, in any political campaign on behalf of or in opposition to any candidate for public office. The phrase *candidate for public office* means an individual who offers himself or herself, or is proposed by others, as a contestant for an elective public office, whether the office is national, state, or local. Activities that constitute participation or intervention in a political campaign on behalf of or in opposition to a candidate include, but are not limited to, the publication or distribution of written or printed statements or the making of oral statements on behalf of or in opposition to the candidate.[100]

An organization is an action organization if it has the following two characteristics: (1) its main or primary objective or objectives (as distinguished from its incidental or secondary objectives) may be attained only by legislation or a defeat of proposed legislation; and (2) it advocates or campaigns for the attainment of this main or primary objective or objectives as distinguished from engaging in nonpartisan

analysis, study, or research, and making the results thereof available to the public. In determining whether an organization has these characteristics, all the surrounding facts and circumstances, including one or more provisions in the articles of organization and all activities of the organization, are considered.[101]

## Exclusively Standard

To be tax-exempt as a charitable organization, an entity must be organized and operated *exclusively* for exempt purposes. As noted,[102] this rule is a term of art that is reflected in the primary purpose test. There is, however, additional law pertaining to the *exclusivity* rule.

A controversial opinion in this regard was authored by a federal court of appeals, which accorded tax exemption to a public parking facility as a charitable organization.[103] The organization was formed by several private businesses and professional persons to construct and operate the facility, utilizing a validation stamp system in an effort to attract shoppers to a city center. The government contended that the operation of a commercial parking facility is not an exempt activity[104] and that a substantial objective of the organization was to encourage the general public to patronize the businesses that participated in the validation stamp system, which constituted private inurement and only incidental public benefit.[105] Concluding that the city involved was the primary beneficiary of the organization's activities, the district court had held that the "business activity itself is similar to that which others engage in for profit, but it is not carried on in the same manner; it is carried on only because it is necessary for the attainment of an undeniably public end."[106] On appeal, the appellate court observed that the lower court "made a quantitative comparison of the private versus the public benefits derived from the organization and operation of the plaintiff corporation" and determined that the requirements for exemption were "adequately fulfilled."[107] The opinion is not illustrative of blind adherence to the exclusively doctrine.

The IRS does not subscribe to the principles of the public parking corporation case and announced that it does not follow the decision.[108] The IRS asserts that this type of a public parking corporation does not operate exclusively for charitable purposes and carries on a business with the general public in a manner similar to organizations that are operated for profit. This position was made clear earlier when the IRS ruled that an organization formed to revive retail sales in an area suffering from continued economic decline by constructing a shopping center that would complement the area's existing retail facilities could not qualify for tax exemption as a charitable entity. The IRS, then taking no notice of the appellate court decision, said that the activities of the organization "result in major benefits accruing to the stores that will locate within the shopping center," thereby precluding the exemption.[109] (An organization that provided free parking to persons visiting a downtown area can, however, qualify as an exempt social welfare organization.)[110]

Application of the concept of *exclusively* may require even more flexibility than has been previously displayed. This may be particularly unavoidable as respects organizations performing services that are considered necessary in today's society, even where the services are parallel with those rendered in commercial settings. For example, the provision of medical services can obviously be an enterprise for profit, yet the IRS was able to rule that an organization formed to attract a physician to a medically underserved rural area, by providing the doctor with a building and facilities at a reasonable rent, qualified as a charitable organization.[111] "In these circumstances," said the IRS, any "personal benefit derived by the physician (the use of the building in which to practice medicine) does not detract from the public purpose of the organization nor lessen the public benefit flowing from its activ-

ities."[112] Similarly, an organization formed to provide legal services for residents of economically depressed communities was ruled to be engaged in charitable activities.[113] Even though those providing the services were subsidized by the organization, the IRS minimized this personal gain by the rationale that they were merely the instruments by which the charitable purposes were accomplished.[114]

## Commensurate Test

Somewhat related to the operational test is another test that the IRS has developed, originally termed the *commensurate test*. This test, historically sparingly applied by the IRS, may be in the process of greater application, at least as to public charities, as the IRS launches a *charitable spending initiative*.

### (a) Application of the Commensurate Test

The commensurate test was first articulated in 1964.[115] Under this test, the IRS is empowered to assess whether a charitable organization is maintaining program activities that are commensurate in scope with its financial resources. In the facts underlying the 1964 ruling, the organization derived most of its income from rents, yet was successful in preserving its tax-exempt status because it satisfied the test, in that it was engaging in an adequate amount of charitable functions notwithstanding the extent of its rental activities.

In 1990, the IRS revoked the tax-exempt status of a charitable organization on a variety of rationales, including the ground that its fund-raising costs were too high and thus violated the *commensurate* test. In a technical advice memorandum,[116] the IRS concluded that the test was transgressed because of its finding that the charity involved expended, during the two years examined, only about 1 percent of its revenue for charitable purposes; the rest was allegedly spent for fund-raising and administration. (The matter of the organization's tax-exempt status was ultimately resolved in court, albeit without application of the commensurate test; the case turned out to be one involving private inurement.[117])

Wrote the IRS:

> The "commensurate test" does not lend itself to a rigid numerical distribution formula—there is no fixed percentage of income that an organization must pay out for charitable purposes. The financial resources of any organization may be affected by such factors as startup costs, overhead, scale of operations, whether labor is voluntary or salaried, phone or postal costs, etc. In each case, therefore, the particular facts and circumstances of the organization must be considered. Accordingly, a specific payout percentage does not automatically mandate the conclusion that the organization under consideration has a primary purpose that is not charitable. In each case, it should be ascertained whether the failure to make real and substantial contributions for charitable purposes is due to reasonable cause.

The IRS added:

> While there is no specified payout percentage, and while special facts and circumstances may control the conclusion, distribution levels that are low invite close scrutiny. The "commensurate" test requires that organizations have a charitable program that is both real and, taking the organization's circumstances and financial resources into account, substantial. Therefore, an organization that raises funds for charitable purposes but consistently uses virtually all its income for administrative and promotional expenses with little or no direct charitable accomplishments cannot reasonably argue that its charitable program is com-

mensurate with its financial resources and capabilities.

The commensurate test and the primary purpose test have an awkward coexistence. For example, a charitable organization was allowed to retain its tax-exempt status while receiving 98 percent of its support from unrelated business income, since 41 percent of the organization's activities were charitable programs.[118] Yet a public charity had its tax exemption revoked, by application of the commensurate test, because in the two years under examination, although bingo gross income was 73 percent and 92 percent of total gross income, only a small amount of this income was distributed for charitable purposes.[119]

### (b) Charitable Spending Initiative

Over the ensuing decades, the IRS has infrequently applied the commensurate test. Nonetheless, in 2009, the IRS announced, as one of its new compliance projects,[120] a charitable spending initiative, which is a "long-range study to learn more about sources and uses of funds in the charitable sector and their impact on the accomplishment of charitable purposes."[121] The IRS said it will be looking at fund-raising, contributions, grants, revenue from related and unrelated businesses, types and amounts of direct and indirect unrelated business expenses, and officer compensation, and the effect each of these elements has on funds available for charitable activities. The first stage of this initiative will focus on "organizations with unusual fund-raising levels and organizations that report unrelated trade or business activity and relatively low levels of program service expenditures."[122]

## Operations for Profit

The IRS, when alleging that an organization is not operated exclusively for an exempt purpose, may base its contention on a finding that the organization's operation is similar to a commercial enterprise operated for profit. As one court observed, however, the "presence of profitmaking activities is not *per se* a bar to qualification of an organization as exempt if the activities further or accomplish an exempt purpose."[123] Similarly, the IRS acknowledged that a charitable organization can have a qualified[124] profit-sharing plan for its employees without endangering its tax exemption.[125]

In one instance, a plan was designed by a hospital as an employee incentive plan, with "profits" defined in the general accounting sense of excess of receipts over expenses.[126] Plan distributions must be reasonable; the distributions were held to not be "dividends" and to not constitute private inurement.[127]

The question as to whether, and if so to what extent, a tax-exempt organization (particularly one that is classified as a charitable entity) can earn a profit is at once difficult and easy to answer. The question is easy to answer in the sense that it is clear that the mere showing of a profit (excess of revenue over expenses) for one or more tax years will not bar tax exemption. If the profit is from what is perceived as a business activity, and the fact of a profit is used to show the commercial hue of the activity, the answer to the question will depend upon the facts and circumstances of the particular case. That is, the decisive factor is likely to be the nature of the activities that give rise to the profits.[128]

An illustrative body of law is that concerning organizations that prepare and sell publications at a profit.[129] In one case, an organization sold religious publications to students attending classes it sponsored and to members of its religious following, for a relatively small profit.[130] In rejecting the government's argument that the receipt of the income indicated that the organization was not operated exclusively for religious purposes, a court held that the sale of religious literature was an activity "closely associated with, and incidental to" the organi-

zation's tax-exempt purposes and bore "an intimate relationship to the proper functioning" of it, and thus that the receipt of the income did not prevent the organization from being an organization organized and operated exclusively for religious purposes.[131]

By contrast, a court denied status as a tax-exempt charitable entity to an organization that prepared and sold religious literature on a nondenominational basis. Because the organization's materials were competitively priced and the sales over a seven-year period yielded substantial accumulated profits that greatly exceeded the amount expended for its activities, the court concluded that the sales activities were the organization's primary concern and that it was engaging in the conduct of a trade or business for profit.[132] Another organization was denied exemption for publishing on a for-profit basis, with the court observing that, were the law otherwise, "every publishing house would be entitled to an exemption on the ground that it furthers the education of the public."[133] Likewise, an organization could not achieve exemption because its primary activity—the publication and sale of books that are religiously inspired and oriented and written by its founder—was conducted in a commercial manner, at a profit.[134]

Each case on this point, therefore, must reflect one of these two analyses. In one case, a court accepted the contention by an organization that its publishing activities furthered its religious purpose of improving the preaching skills and sermons of the clergy of the Protestant, Roman Catholic, and Jewish faiths. Subscriptions for the publications were obtained by advertising and direct mail solicitation, and the publications were sold at a modest profit. The court found that the organization was not in competition with any commercial enterprise and that the sale of religious literature was an integral part of the organization's religious purposes. Said the court: "The fact that . . . [the organization] intended to make a profit, alone, does not negate [the fact] that . . . [it] was operated exclusively for charitable purposes."[135]

By contrast, an organization was denied tax exemption as a charitable entity because it was directly engaged in the conduct of a commercial leasing enterprise for the principal purpose of realizing profits. The enterprise was regarded as its principal activity (measured by total gross income), in which it was an active participant, and not related to an exempt purpose. Further, its charitable activities were deemed to be of relatively minimal consequence.[136] Similarly, a court reflected upon a nonprofit organization's accumulated profits and decided that this was evidence that the primary function of the organization was commercial in nature.[137]

Yet, given an appropriate set of circumstances, the greater the extent of profits, the greater the likelihood that the revenue-producing activity may be considered to be in furtherance of tax-exempt purposes. In one case, an activity—which the organization regarded as fundraising and the IRS considered a business—was held to not be a business because the activity generated a "staggering amount of money" and "astounding profitability" in a manner that could not be replicated in a commercial context.[138] Also, the organization was much more candid with its supporters than would be the case in a commercial setting, leading the court to note that, "[b]y any standard, an enterprise that depends on the consent of its customers for its profits is not operating in a commercial manner and is not a trade or business."[139]

A federal court of appeals, in considering this latter case, took that occasion to strongly state that "[u]nlike what some other courts may do, this court does not find 'profits,' or the maximization of revenue, to be the controlling basis for a determination" as to whether the activity involved is a "business."[140]

Thus, the mere fact of profit-making activities should not, as a matter of law, adversely affect an organization's tax-exempt status. As another federal court of appeals has noted, the "pertinent inquiry" is "whether the [organization's] exempt purpose transcends the profit motive rather than the other way around."[141]

The IRS may use the existence of a profit, however, to characterize the activity as being commercial in nature, thus placing at issue the question as to whether the organization's activities are devoted exclusively to tax-exempt purposes. This approach is sometimes also taken by the courts, such as in a case where the publications of an organization were held to produce an unwarranted profit, thereby depriving it of qualification as an educational organization.[142]

## Notes

1. Rev. Proc. 82-2, 1982-1 C.B. 367.

2. See 3.3(d) in Bruce R. Hopkins, *The Law of Tax-Exempt Organizations,* 10th ed.

3. Priv. Ltr. Rul. 200450041.

4. IRC §§ 501(c)(1), 501(c)(2), 501(c)(3), 501(c)(14), 501(c)(16).

5. See Chapter 19 in Hopkins, *The Law of Tax-Exempt Organizations.*

6. IRC §§ 501(c)(17), 501(c)(18), 501(c)(19), 501(c)(20), 401(a).

7. IRC § 7701(a)(3). See § 4.1(b). The IRS ruled that a tax-exempt organization that had its corporate status irrevocably terminated by a state because of failure to file state annual reports, yet continued to operate, was deemed to have elected to be classified as an association taxable as a corporation pursuant to the check-the-box rules (see § 4.3(d) in Hopkins, *The Law of Tax-Exempt Organizations*) (Priv. Ltr. Rul. 200607027).

8. Fifth-Third Union Trust Co. v. Comm'r, 56 F.2d 767 (6th Cir. 1932).

9. IRS Exempt Organizations Handbook (IRM 7751) § 315.1. Also Emerson Inst. v. United States, 356 F.2d 824 (D.C. Cir. 1966), cert. den., 385 U.S. 822 (1966). In one opinion, a court, in deciding that an organization could not qualify for tax-exempt status because of its role as a general partner in a limited partnership (see § 30.1(a)), placed emphasis on the fact that the partnerships involved "are admittedly for-profit entities" and that none of these partnerships is "intended to be nonprofit" (Housing

Pioneers, Inc. v. Comm'r, 65 T.C.M. 2191, 2195 (1993)); however, the law does not make provision for an entity such as a nonprofit partnership.

10. See Chapter 28 in Hopkins, *The Law of Tax-Exempt Organizations.*

11. American Bar Ass'n v. United States, 84-1 U.S.T.C. ¶ 9179 (N.D. Ill. 1984); Rev. Rul. 58-293, 1958-1 C.B. 146.

12. Rev. Rul. 54-243, 1954-1 C.B. 92.

13. E.g., Pusch v. Comm'r, 39 T.C.M. 838 (1980).

14. Cone v. McGinnes, 63-2 U.S.T.C. ¶ 9551 (E.D. Pa. 1963). See § 4.2.

15. Hewitt v. Comm'r, 16 T.C.M. 468, 471 (1957). Also Doty, Jr. v. Comm'r, 6 T.C. 587 (1974); Walker v. Comm'r, 37 T.C.M. 1851 (1978).

16. Rev. Rul. 66-219, 1966-2 C.B. 208.

17. IRS Exempt Organizations Handbook (IRM 7751) §§ 315.1, 315.2(3), 315.4(2).

18. Kessler v. Comm'r, 87 T.C. 1285 (1986); Trippe v. Comm'r, 9 T.C.M. 622 (1950). Cf. Morey v. Riddell, 205 F. Supp. 918 (S.D. Cal. 1962). A claim that it is unconstitutional not to permit individuals to be tax-exempt was dismissed (Fields v. United States, Civ. No. 96-317 (D.D.C. 1998)).

19. E.g., United States v. Jeffries, 88-2 U.S.T.C. ¶ 9459 (7th Cir. 1988). In general, see § 10.2(c).

20. A separate form (even the corporate form), however, is not always respected. For example, courts find charitable organizations to be the "alter ego" of their founders or others in close control and operating proximity, so that IRS levies against the organizations for their income and assets to satisfy the individuals' tax obligations are upheld (e.g., Towe Antique Ford Found. v. Internal Revenue Serv., 999 F.2d 1387 (9th Cir. 1993); United States v. Kitsos, 770 F. Supp. 1230 (N.D. Ill. 1991), aff'd, 968 F.2d 1219 (7th Cir. 1992); Zahra Spiritual Trust v. United States, 910 F.2d 240 (5th Cir. 1990); Loving Savior Church v. United States, 556 F. Supp. 688 (D.S.D. 1983), aff'd, 728 F.2d 1085 (8th Cir. 1984); Faith Missionary Baptist Church v. Internal Revenue Serv., 174 B.R. 454 (U.S. Bankr. Ct. E.D. Tex. 1994); Church of Hakeem v. United States, 79-2 U.S.T.C. ¶ 9651 (N.D. Cal. 1979)). In general, Henn & Pfeifer, "Nonprofit Groups: Factors Influencing Choice of Form," 11 *Wake Forest L. Rev.* 181 (1975).

21. 39 C.F.R. Part 132 (second class), Part 134 (third class).

22. See § 27.1(b).

23. See § 4.3 in Hopkins, *The Law of Tax-Exempt Organizations.*

24. See § 12.1(g) in Hopkins, *The Law of Tax-Exempt Organizations.*

25. See § 4.5 in Hopkins, *The Law of Tax-Exempt Organizations.*

26. Reg. § 1.501(c)(3)-l(a); Levy Family Tribe Found. v. Comm'r, 69 T.C. 615, 618 (1978).

27. Reg. § 1.501(c)(3)-l(b)(2).

28. See Reg. § 1.501(c)(3)-1(d).

29. Reg.§ 1.501(c)(3)-l(b)(l)(i).

30. See § 12.3(c) in Hopkins, *The Law of Tax-exempt Organizations.*

31. IRC § 508(e). See § 12.1(g).

32. E.g., Priv. Ltr. Rul. 200508019.

33. Reg. § 1.501(c)(3)-l(b)(l)(ii).

34. Rev. Rul. 69-279, 1969-1 C.B. 152; Rev. Rul. 69-256, 1969-1 C.B. 151.

35. Reg. § 1.501(c)(3)-l(b)(iii). Also Interneighborhood Housing Corp. v. Comm'r, 45 T.C.M. 115 (1982); Santa Cruz Bldg. Ass'n v. United States, 411 F. Supp. 871 (E. D. Mo. 1976).

36. E.g., Gen. Couns. Mem. 39633.

37. Reg. § 1.501(c)(3)-l(b)(l)(iv).

38. An organization organized and operated to reform, repeal and decriminalize laws meant to protect children from sexual abuse and sexual predators failed to achieve tax-exempt status as a charitable entity in part because its articles of incorporation mandated substantial legislative activity. (Mysteryboy Incorporation v. Comm'r T.C. Memo, 2010-13 (2010)). See Chapter 22 in Hopkins, *The Law of Tax-Exempt Organizations.*

39. See Chapter 23 in Hopkins, *The Law of Tax-Exempt Organizations.*

40. Reg. § 1.501 (c)(3)-l(b)(3). See § 4.5(b).

41. See § 22.3(d)(iv) in Hopkins, *The Law of Tax-Exempt Organizations.*

42. Reg. § 1.501(c)(3)-l(b)(3)

43. IRC § 501(c)(3).

44. Reg. § 1.501(c)(3)-l(d)(2). See Chapter 7 in Hopkins, *The Law of Tax-Exempt Organizations.*

45. See § 4.5 in Hopkins, *The Law of Tax-Exempt Organizations.*

46. This provision may read as follows: "Notwithstanding other language (or provisions) in the creating document, the purposes will be limited exclusively to exempt purposes within the meaning of

IRC [§] 501(c)(3)." This is from Ardoin, "Organizational Test—IRC 501(c)(3)," prepared as part of the IRS's continuing professional education text for the government's fiscal year 2004.

47. See Chapter 20 in Hopkins, *The Law of Tax-Exempt Organizations*.

48. See Chapter 22 in Hopkins, *The Law of Tax-Exempt Organizations*.

49. See Chapter 23 in Hopkins, *The Law of Tax-Exempt Organizations*.

50. Estate of Sharf v. Comm'r, 38 T.C. 15 (1962), aff'd, 316 F.2d 625 (7th Cir. 1963); Holden Hosp. Corp. v. Southern Ill. Hosp. Corp., 174 N.E. 2d 793 (Ill. 1961).

51. Reg. § 1.501(c)(3)-l(b)(4). E.g., Chief Steward of the Ecumenical Temples & the Worldwide Peace Movement & His Successors v. Comm'r, 49 T.C.M. 640 (1985). Cf. Bethel Conservative Mennonite Church v. Comm'r, 746 F.2d 388 (7th Cir. 1984).

52. Church of Nature in Man v. Comm'r, 49 T.C.M. 1393 (1985); Stephenson v. Comm'r, 79 T.C. 995 (1982); Truth Tabernacle v. Comm'r, 41 T.C.M. 1405 (1981); Calvin K. of Oakknoll v. Comm'r, 69 T.C. 770 (1978), aff'd, 603 F.2d 211 (2d Cir. 1979); General Conference of the Free Church of Am. v. Comm'r, 71 T.C. 920 (1979).

53. Gen. Couns. Mem. 37126, clarifying Gen. Couns. Mem. 33207. Moreover, the absence of a dissolution clause has been held to not be fatal to IRC § 501(c)(3) status, in Universal Church of Scientific Truth, Inc. v. United States, 74-1 U.S.T.C. ¶ 9360 (N.D. Ala. 1973).

54. See §27.3 in Hopkins, *The Law of Tax-Exempt Organizations*.

55. Form 990, Part I, line 1 (with an option to report *most significant activities*), Part III, line 1(if the mission statement has been approved by the board).

56. See New Form 990, §§1.6(a), 2.1(d), 2.2(a).

57. See §4.6 in Hopkins, *The Law of Tax-Exempt Organizations*.

58. See Chapter 7 in Hopkins, *The Law of Tax-Exempt Organizations*.

59. See Chapter 13 in Hopkins, *The Law of Tax-Exempt Organizations*.

60. See §19.6 in Hopkins, *The Law of Tax-Exempt Organizations*.

61. See §19.15 in Hopkins, *The Law of Tax-Exempt Organizations*.

62. See §19.16 in Hopkins, *The Law of Tax-Exempt Organizations*.

63. See Chapter 15 in Hopkins, *The Law of Tax-Exempt Organizations*.

64. E.g., Reg. §§ 1.501(c)(3)-l(a)(l), 1.501(c)(3)-1(c)(1).

65. E.g., Orange Country Agric. Soc'y, Inc. v. Comm'r, 53 T.C.M. 1602 (1988), aff'd, 893 F.2d 647 (2d Cir. 1990).

66. New Dynamics Found v. United States, 2006-1 U.S.T.C. ¶ 50,286 (U.S. Ct. Fed. Cl. 2006). Also Easter House v. United States, 12 Ct. Cl. 476, 483 (1987), aff'd, 846 F.2d 78 (Fed Cir. 1988), cert. den., 488 U.S. 907 (1988).

67. See Chapter 24 in Hopkins, *The Law of Tax-Exempt Organizations*.

68. Reg. § 1.501(c)(3)-l(c)(l).

69. Aid to Artisans, Inc. v. Comm'r, 71 T.C. 202 (1978).

70. Nonetheless, the courts occasionally stretch this criterion, as illustrated by the decision denying tax-exempt status to a scholarship fund, for violation of the primary purpose test, because its fund-raising activities were conducted in a cocktail lounge and attracted customers to the lounge (P.L.L. Scholarship Fund v. Comm'r, 82 T.C. 196 (1984); also KJ's Fund Raisers, Inc. v. Comm'r, 74 T.C.M. 669 (1997), aff'd, 166 F.3d 1200 (2nd Cir. 1998)). Cf. Hope Charitable Found. v. Ridell, 61-1 U.S.T.C. 5 ¶ 9437 (S.D. Cal. 1961).

71. Better Business Bureau of Washington, DC v. United States, 326 U.S. 279, 283 (1945). Also Universal Church of Jesus Christ, Inc. v. Comm'r, 55 T.C.M. 143 (1988).

72. Rev. Rul. 77-366, 1977-2 C.B. 192.

73. Stevens Bros. Found. v. Comm'r, 324 F.2d 633 (8th Cir. 1963), cert. den., 376 U.S. 969 (1964); Scripture Press Found. v. United States, 285 F.2d 800, 806 (Ct. Cl. 1961), cert. den., 368 U.S. 985 (1962); Fides Publishers Ass'n v. United States, 263 F. Supp. 924, 935 (N.D. Ind. 1967); Edgar v. Comm'r, 56 T.C. 717, 755 (1971); The Media Sports League, Inc. v. Comm'r, 52 T.C.M. 1093 (1986).

74. E.g., Kentucky Bar Found. v. Comm'r, 78 T.C. 921 (1982).

75. World Family Corp. v. Comm'r, 81 T.C. 958 (1983).

76. Orange County Agric. Soc'y, Inc. v. Comm'r, 55 T.C.M. 1602, 1604 (1988), aff'd, 893 F.2d 647 (2nd Cir. 1990).

77. IRS Technical Advice Memorandum (Tech. Adv. Mem.) 200021056.

78. American Inst. for Economic Research Inc. v. United States, 302 F.2d 934 (Ct. Cl. 1962); Edward Orton, Jr., Ceramic Found. v. Comm'r, 56 T.C. 147 (1971); Pulpit Resource v. Comm'r, 70 T.C. 594 (1978); Aid to Artisans, Inc. v. Comm'r, 71 T.C. 202 (1978).

79. See Chapter 24 in Hopkins, *The Law of Tax-Exempt Organizations*.

80. Reg. § 1.501 (c)(3)-l(c)(l).

81. Rev. Rul. 72-369, 1972-2 C.B. 245.

82. Reg. § 1.501(c)(3)-l(c)(l). In one instance, the operational test was found to be unmet because the organization involved, which was organized for the study and promotion of the philately of the Central American republics, operated a mail bid stamps sales service for its members as a substantial activity (Society of Costa Rica Collectors v. Comm'r, 49 T.C.M. 304 (1984)). An organization that is inactive for a significant period of time is likely to have its exempt status revoked by the IRS by application of the operational test (e.g., Priv. Ltr. Rul. 200631028).

83. Reg. §§ 1.501(c)(3)-l(c)(2), 1.501(a)-l(c). Also Wildt's Motorsport Advancement Crusade, Bill v. Comm'r, 56 T.C.M. 1401 (1989); Athenagoras I Christian Union of the World, Inc. v. Comm'r, 55 T.C.M. 781 (1988); Levy Family Tribe Found. v. Comm'r, 69 T.C. 615 (1978). See Chapter 20 in Hopkins, *The Law of Tax-Exempt Organizations*.

84. E.g., The Church of the Visible Intelligence That Governs the Universe v. United States, 83-2 U.S.T.C. ¶ 9726 (Cl. Ct. 1983).

85. Chief Steward of the Ecumenical Temples & the Worldwide Peace Movement & His Successors v. Comm'r, 49 T.C.M. 640, 643 (1985).

86. E.g., Rev. Rul. 64-182, 1964-1 (Part 1) C.B. 186.

87. Reg. § 1.501(c)(3)-l(e)(l).

88. Federation Pharmacy Services, Inc. v. Comm'r, 72 T.C. 687 (1979), aff'd, 625 F.2d 804 (8th Cir. 1980); est of Hawaii v. Comm'r, 71 T.C. 1067 (1979), aff'd, 647 F.2d 170 (9th Cir. 1981).

89. Rev. Rul. 68-26, 1968-1 C.B. 272; Elisian Guild, Inc. v. United States, 412 F.2d 121 (1st Cir. 1969). Cf. Fides Publishers Ass'n v. United States, 263 F. Supp. 924 (N.D. Ind. 1967).

90. See Chapter 24 in Hopkins, *The Law of Tax-Exempt Organizations*.

91. B.S.W. Group, Inc. v. Comm'r, 70 T.C. 352, 356–357 (1978). Also American Campaign Academy v. Comm'r, 92 T.C. 1053 (1989); Goldsboro Art League, Inc. v. Comm'r, 75 T.C. 337 (1980); Aid to Artisans, Inc. v. Comm'r, 71 T.C. 202 (1978); Ohio Teamsters Educ. & Safety Training Fund v. Comm'r, 77 T.C. 189 (1981), aff'd, 692 F.2d 432 (6th Cir. 1982). To determine whether the operational test has been satisfied, the Tax Court wrote that it looks beyond the "four corners of the organization's charter to discover the actual objects motivating the organization" (American Campaign Academy v. Comm'r, 92 T.C. at 1064).

92. General Conference of Free Church of Am. v. Comm'r, 71 T.C. 920 (1979).

93. KJ's Fund Raisers, Inc. v. Comm'r, 74 T.C.M. 669 (1997), aff'd, 166 F.3d 1200 (2d Cir. 1998); Manning Ass'n v. Comm'r, 93 T.C. 596 (1989); Copyright Clearance Center, Inc. v. Comm'r, 79 T.C. 793 (1982).

94. Church by Mail, Inc. v. Comm'r 765 F.2d 1387 (9th Cir. 1985), aff'g, 48 T.C.M. 471 (1984)

95. Reg. § 1.501(c)(3)-l(c)(i).

96. Thus, an organization with the primary activity of influencing legislation was held to not qualify for exemption as a charitable entity (Priv. Ltr. Rul. 200952069)

97. Reg. § 1.501 (c)(3)-l(c)(3)(ii).

98. See § 22.3(d)(iv) in Hopkins, *The Law of Tax-Exempt Organizations*.

99. Reg. § 1.501(c)(3)-l(c)(3)(ii).

100. Reg. § 1.501(c)(3)-l(c)(3)(iii).

101. Reg. § 1.501(c)(3)-l(c)(3)(iv).

102. See § 4.4 in Hopkins, *The Law of Tax-Exempt Organizations*.

103. Monterey Public Parking Corp. v. United States, 481 F.2d 175 (9th Cir. 1973), aff'd, 321 F. Supp. 972 (N.D. Cal. 1970).

104. See § 4.1 in Hopkins, *The Law of Tax-Exempt Organizations*.

105. See Chapter 20 in Hopkins, *The Law of Tax-Exempt Organizations*.

106. Monterey Public Parking Corp. v. United States, 321 F. Supp. 972, 977 (N.D. Cal. 1970).

107. Monterey Public Parking Corp. v. United States, 481 F.2d 175, 177 (9th Cir. 1973). Cf. Rev. Rul. 73-411, 1973-2 C.B. 180.

108. Rev. Rul. 78-86, 1978-1 C.B. 151.

109. Rev. Rul. 77-111, 1977-1 C.B. 144. Also Rev. Rul. 64-108, 1964-1 (Part I) C.B. 189.

110. Rev. Rul. 81-116, 1981-1 C.B. 333. Social welfare organizations are the subject of Chapter 13 in Hopkins, *The Law of Tax-Exempt Organizations*.

111. Rev. Rul. 73-313, 1973-2 C.B. 174.

112. *Id.* at 176, citing In re Estate of Carlson, 358 P.2d 669 (Kan. 1961). Cf. Rev. Rul. 69-266, 1969-1 C.B. 151.

113. Rev. Rul. 72-559, 1972-2 C.B. 247. Also Rev. Rul. 70-640, 1970-2 C.B. 117; Golf Life World Entertainment Golf Championship, Inc. v. United States, 65-1 U.S.T.C. ¶ 9174 (S. D. Cal. 1964). Cf. Rev. Rul. 72-369, 1972-2 C.B. 245.

114. See § 6.3(b) in Hopkins, *The Law of Tax-Exempt Organizations*.

115. Rev. Rul. 64-182, 1964-1 (Part 1) C.B. 186.

116. This technical advice memorandum is reproduced at 4 *Exempt Org. Tax Rev.* (No. 5) 726 (July 1991), and is discussed in detail in Fundraising § 5.15.

117. United Cancer Council, Inc. v. Comm'r, 109 T.C. 326 (1997), rev'd and rem'd, 165 F.3d 1173 (7th Cir. 1999). IRS Exempt Organizations 2009 Annual Report, at 20.

118. Tech. Adv. Mem. 9711003. The IRS concluded, by application of the commensurate test, that the tax-exempt status of four charities should not be revoked because of the small amount of money they grant for charitable purposes (Field Service Advice Mem., 199910007). Also Help the Children v. Comm'r, 28 T.C. 1128 (1957); Rev. Rul. 68-489, 1968-2 C.B. 210.

119. Priv. Ltr. Rul. 200825046.

120. See § 26.7(a)(ii), text accompanied by notes 216–226, in Hopkins, *The Law of Tax-Exempt Organizations*.

121. IRS Exempt Organizations 2009 Annual Report, at 20.

122. *Id.*

123. Aid to Artisanas, Inc. v. Comm'r, 71 T.C. 202, 211 (1978)

124. IRC § 401(a).

125. See § 18.4(i) in Hopkins, *The Law of Tax-Exempt Organizations*.

126. Gen. Couns. Mem. 38283

127. Priv. Ltr. Rul. 8442064

128. See § 4.11 in Hopkins, *The Law of Tax-Exempt Organizations*.

129. See § 8.6 in Hopkins, *The Law of Tax-Exempt Organizations*.

130. Saint Germain Found v. Comm'r, 26 T.C. 648 (1958).

131. *Id.* at 658. Also Elisian Guild, Inc. v. United States, 412 F.2d 121, 124 (1st Cir. 1969), rev'g 292 F. Supp. 219.

132. Scripture Press Found. v. United States, 285 F.2d 800 (Ct. Cl. 1961), cert. den., 368 U.S. 985 (1962).

133. Fides Publishers Ass'n v. United States, 263 F. Supp. 924, 936 (N.D. Ind. 1967).

134. Christian Manner Int'l, Inc. v. Comm'r, 71 T.C. 661 (1979).

135. Pulpit Resource v. Comm'r, 70 T.C. 594, 611 (1978). Also Junaluska Assembly Housing, Inc. v. Comm'r, 86 T.C. 1114 (1986); Industrial Aid for the Blind v. Comm'r, 73 T.C. 96 (1979).

136. Greater United Navajo Dev. Enters., Inc. v. Comm'r, 74 T.C. 69 (1980).

137. Elisian Guild, Inc. v. United States, 412 F.2d 121, 124 (1st Cir. 1969).

138. American Bar Endowment v. United States, 84-1 U.S.T.C. ¶ 9204 (Cl. Ct. 1984).

139. *Id.* at 83, 353.

140. American Bar Endowment v. United States, 761 F.2d 1573 (Fed. Cir. 1985). (This case was resolved by the US Supreme Court, in favor of the government [see § 24.2(b), text accompanied by notes 48–19].) The reference to the "other courts" is to the US Courts of Appeal for the Fourth Circuit (e.g., Carolinas Farm & Power Equip. Dealers v. United States, 699 F.2d 167 (1983)); Fifth Circuit (e.g., Louisiana Credit Union League v. United States, 693 F.2d 525 (1982)); and Sixth Circuit (e.g., Professional Ins. Agents of Mich. v. Comm'r, 726 F.2d 1097 (1984)).

141. The Incorporated Trustees of the Gospel Worker Soc'y v. United States, 510 F. Supp. 374 (D.D.C. 1981), aff'd, 672 F.2d 894 (D.C. Cir. 1981), cert. den., 456 U.S. 944 (1982).

142. American Institute for Economic Research, Inc. v. United States, 302 F.2d 934 (Ct. Cl. 1962). See § 8.6.

## CHAPTER 4

# Evaluating the Charitable Deduction and Proposed Reforms

Roger Colinvaux, Brian Galle, and Eugene Steuerle

Many recent proposals for budget and tax reform would change the value of the charitable contribution deduction. In addition, many other tax policy reforms, such as changes in tax rates, boundaries defining what types of organizations are eligible as donees, and general rules or overall limits on itemized deductions, can affect its value. This report provides context for policymakers who may be considering one or more of these reforms, as well as for other interested observers. We first offer a basic overview of charitable giving and the legal rules for claiming the deduction. Next we discuss the various rationales that have been offered in its support and highlight critiques of the deduction. We then examine various proposed reforms, including caps, floors, credits, and grants, in light of those critiques.

## Rules for the Deduction and Who Benefits from It

The charitable contribution deduction is a long-standing feature of the federal income tax.[1] Enacted in 1917, four years after the income tax, it is linked to tax exemption[2] and has become an important source of support for the charitable sector,[3] and one of the principal subsidies or tax expenditures in the tax code. The Joint Committee on Taxation estimates the deduction's five-year cost as $246.1 billion.[4] Of that number, $25.3 billion is for health, $33.3 billion for education, and the remaining $187.5 [billion] covers other charitable purposes.[5]

## Rules for Claiming the Deduction

### Donors

Individual donors are given an option of claiming a set of itemized deductions, including the charitable deduction, or the standard deduction ($5,950 for singles; $11,900 for joint returns in 2012). Thus, non-itemizers technically do not have a tax incentive to contribute but generally receive an overall deduction of greater value than if they did itemize.[6] Most taxpayers (about 70 percent)[7] take the standard deduction. At

TABLE 4.1. Sources of Contributions to Section 501(c)(3) Organizations, 2010

| | |
|---|---|
| Individuals | $212 billion (73%) |
| Private foundations | $41 billion (14%) |
| Bequests | $23 billion (8%) |
| Corporations | $15 billion (5%) |

*Source:* Giving USA Foundation (2011).

income levels above about $75,000, however, the majority itemize.[8]

Various other limits, such as a maximum charitable deduction of 50 percent of the individual's annual adjusted gross income, apply to the deduction. Tighter percentage limits apply for gifts of capital gain property and for gifts to private foundations.[9] Unlike some other itemized deductions, the charitable deduction is not subject to a particularized floor.[10]

The value of a charitable contribution deduction depends upon the taxpayer's marginal rate of tax. For example, assume a taxpayer in a 25 percent bracket. If the taxpayer makes a qualifying $100 charitable contribution, her taxable income will decline by $100. That, in turn, will reduce her tax by 25 percent times $100, or $25. A similar contribution by a taxpayer with a 15 percent marginal rate would save only $15 in tax.

### Donee Organizations

Organizations eligible to receive deductible charitable contributions, described in section 501(c)(3),[11] serve "religious, charitable, scientific, literary or educational purposes, or to foster national or international amateur sports competition, or for the prevention of cruelty to children or animals."[12] For our purposes, we use "charitable" to mean organizations that qualify under section 501(c)(3). These organizations may not distribute profits to organization insiders, although they may pay reasonable amounts

to their workers, to profit-making firms for services rendered, and for interest on any borrowed money. Thus, an organization can be nonprofit, in the sense of not generating formal returns to shareholders, yet it can provide rents and other returns to both labor and capital. Except for lower percentage limits for gifts to private foundations, the charitable deduction does not distinguish among donee organizations in purpose, function, efficiency, financial health, or sources of revenue.

### Ultimate Beneficiaries

Those who benefit from the work of section 501(c)(3) organizations generally are not taxed on the goods or services they receive.

## Who Gives and Who Benefits from the Deduction?

Charitable giving, of course, is not the exclusive province of individuals or of itemizers. Total charitable giving in 2010 is estimated and reported as $291 billion, less certain contributions made to foundations (Giving USA 2011). Table 4.1 shows the sources of gifts.[13]

## Why the Deduction?

When enacting the charitable contribution deduction in 1917, Congress emphasized that it wanted to ensure that the income tax, particularly at the high World War I levels, would not discourage private giving. Congress was concerned that someone giving away their income might have less money to pay tax—particularly in a system that originally collected tax at the end of the year, rather than through regular withholding. Regardless of the original intention, the deduction tends to be justified today mainly as a subsidy or as an appropriate adjustment to income according to ability to pay.

### Subsidy Theories

Subsidy theories take many forms but generally posit that the deduction is warranted as a way of achieving some widely agreed-upon social good for beneficiaries, either as individuals or part of some collective. In most theories, the deduction helps support the provision of goods and services that would not be supplied sufficiently by the free market.

One type of such market failure derives from so-called "public goods." Public goods are goods that once purchased by one person can be enjoyed at little or no additional cost by many, such as pollution control, basic scientific research, or parkland. These goods may be undersupplied if people fail to contribute and instead free-ride on the contributions of others. The government, of course, can provide such goods, but at times it might also want to encourage individuals to do so. For instance, goods whose benefits cross local governmental borders, such as support for delinquent boys or girls, might not be adequately provided by any one government, but some local group might (with federal fiscal support) be willing to tackle the problem. Other gaps might arise because of constitutional or practical restrictions on what government may do. Governments generally must offer their services equally to all, whereas private individuals may target their assistance more easily. And government, of course, cannot directly support religious worship. Charitable organizations can also create an environment or public sphere in which changes to government behavior are discussed and advocated; government is less likely to criticize itself. Also, there are practical limits on tax collection, partly because of its own set of costs such as for enforcement.

Promotion of the charitable sector may additionally supplement government efforts by developing social welfare organizations to which government can efficiently contract out. For example, charitable organizations may have subject-specific expertise that would be useful to a one-time project. An open debate exists, however, on whether nonprofits perform more cost-effectively than government or other private contractors; it often depends upon the activity or area of the country.

Nonprofits may benefit from volunteer or below-market-cost labor, but these workers may also have poorer training or fewer skills, or require greater supervision to be useful. Some church-related schools seem to recruit quality teachers at lower cost than government; some nonprofit hospitals seem no less expensive or provide no more free care than profit-making or government-operated ones.

Viewed broadly, fostering acts of charity through a charitable deduction may promote a more altruistic, cooperative society and help develop better citizenship. Such gains to society derive not just from the benefits transferred to ultimate donees, but from a contagious effect on the behavior of the donors.

### Ability-to-Pay or Income Measurement Theories

Ability-to-pay theories offer that the deduction is necessary to measure appropriately and fairly the bases for taxation against which taxes are assessed. Equal justice under the law requires equal treatment of those equally situated. In taxation, therefore, a base of taxation should be established so that those with equal ability to pay actually pay equal taxes.

Under an income tax, income is the primary consideration in determining the tax base. For both financial and tax purposes, income is a net concept that excludes money spent in order to earn that income. Exceptions apply when those expenses also convey some personal benefit, such as entertainment. On a similar logic, some costs that reduce the taxpayers' ability to consume are sometimes excluded from the tax base. For example, extraordinary medical expenses are usually deductible (subject to a floor); an individual with $100,000 in income and extraordinary medical expenses of $20,000 can be thought of as having a standard of living more comparable to healthy taxpayers who earn $80,000 than to those earning $100,000.

Under the ability-to-pay rationale, this logic is extended to the charitable contribution deduction, on the theory that such contributions reduce the taxpayers' funds available for personal consumption or payment to the government as tax. A person who gives away earnings arguably has less available to pay taxes, or at least should be treated equally to someone with the same income net of the contributions.[14]

### Sovereignty Explanation

The deduction has also been explained, mainly in the context of religious organizations, as a ceding of "sovereignty." Just as the federal government sometimes cedes sovereignty to state and local governments and Indian tribes, the same ceding of authority may apply to churches, due to separation of church and state (Brody 1998). Although more an argument for exemption than for a deduction, a sovereignty explanation for the deduction could also be seen as a way of setting aside a portion of taxpayer's ability to pay for the support of the other sovereign.[15]

One does not have to choose among a subsidy or ability-to-pay theory, or sovereignty. A deduction might be justified on all these grounds simultaneously.

## Critiques of the Deduction

### Subsidy: Is It Worth the Cost?

Subsidy theories of the deduction have been criticized on cost-effectiveness grounds. How much does it change behavior? Some taxpayers would give the same amount irrespective of the deduction. Some might only respond mildly to the deduction.[16] Thus, the amount of *additional* donations purchased with each dollar of lost government revenue, sometimes known as the "price-elasticity of giving," is an important data point in assessing the efficacy of the deduction.[17]

If each dollar of forgone revenue purchases less than one dollar of giving, arguably the subsidy should be scrapped and replaced with direct spending.[18] That assumes, though, that a dollar of government spending is a direct substitute for charitable activity and the goal of the deduction is simply to encourage the production of the public goods that government would provide. If the goal instead is to encourage some public-good production by the private sector (including some valuable but otherwise undersupplied goods or services the government would not provide), or to encourage individual generosity, then a dollar-by-dollar comparison with government spending may not be the best measure of efficacy. The two sectors can be complementary or adversarial, not just substitutes. For instance, the charitable sector may serve as a catalyst for government action or provide a forum for debate that the government could not easily provide or properly regulate.

In addition, the economic literature measuring responsiveness to charitable deduction incentives is complex, and there is a large dispute as to effectiveness. The research also has gaps. For instance, most studies to date have not accounted for the costs of fundraising. Fundraising costs, of course, diminish the relative efficacy of donations.[19] By the same token, the cost of grants and direct government expenditures often fail to account for the additional direct and indirect costs of taxation.

There are also important subsets of issues that revolve around the design of any incentive. Government incentives would be more powerful if concentrated where responsiveness is expected to be higher. For instance, most taxpayers are likely to give at least some amount to charity. A person may give some fixed amount to a church or pay what she considers her fair "dues" to a charity in which she actively participates; she may be more likely to vary the amount she gives to a special collection that is less related to her involvement with the institution. Suppose a person who gives $1,000 without a charitable deduction would give $1,200 with a charitable deduction for all giving. The incentive has affected the additional $200 of giving but had no effect on the $1,000 that would have been given anyway. This suggests that government incentives would have more effect on giving above some base amount, or for larger or unusual gifts, than for everyday contributions that would be made regardless of encouragement.

Some studies find that higher-income donors are more sensitive to the size of their deduction than others. Other evidence finds that donations to churches and educational organizations appear less sensitive to the amount of the deduction than other gifts. If the goal of the deduction is to increase giving, then one might be most concerned about proposals that would pare it back more among the most responsive givers.

### Ability to Pay and Horizontal Equity: Should the Measure of Taxable Income Be Adjusted for Charitable Contributions?

There also is no consensus on the ability-to-pay justification for the deduction. Some believe as a matter of horizontal equity or "equal treatment of equals" that it is reasonable to adjust taxable income or ability to pay by accounting for donations made, and others do not.

As noted, the Code itself is inconsistent in its treatment of transfers more generally. If one holds strongly to a pure income notion, with few or no exceptions, then a household's ability to pay might be thought to include all the resources it controls, whatever the ultimate use of those resources. Some critics also argue that charitable gifts result in "consumption" benefits or "warm glow" for the giver, such as social recognition and personal satisfaction. Studies of giving tend to confirm that donors are motivated at least in part by "warm glow."

That, in turn, raises the issue of whether such benefits—often referred to as positive externalities—should be added to the tax base. As a general rule, they are not. For instance, the tax code adjusts ability to pay downward for children in the family, even though some suggest that this adjustment should not be allowed because children provide "consumption" benefits to the parent. In some cases, we know that income could be imputed to a person, such as the consumption provided by owning a car, but the tax code still does not attempt to tax it.

Even if one thinks that charitable contributions ought to be treated as income of the ultimate beneficiary, rather than the donor, that beneficiary would not necessarily be poor and subject to no tax (i.e., those who benefit from soup kitchens). Many charitable subsidies go to middle-class or wealthy users of hospitals, universities, or museums. If a tax cannot be assessed on the beneficiaries of such organizations for income received, some may be willing to accept a tax on the donor instead by denying a deduction for charitable contributions.[20]

### Ability to Pay and Vertical Equity: Is the Deduction Unfair or Regressive?

Another ability-to-pay issue refers not to the horizontal (equal treatment of equals) aspect of the deduction, but to its effect on vertical equity or progressivity. One objection sometimes voiced is that the deduction is unfairly regressive because a higher subsidy rate applies to higher-income donors.[21] But regressivity is not inevitable. Marginal tax rates can be adjusted to offset any unwanted distributive effects of the deduction.[22]

For example, suppose in a progressive tax system that there are two high-income taxpayers earning $200,000 each, only one of whom gives to charity, and that the desired degree of progressivity is achieved by collecting $100,000 in total from both of them (25 percent of their combined $400,000 income) whether or not either gives to charity. Let's also assume that no tax is collected from any other person, perhaps because in this world all the others are poorer. Suppose that a charitable deduction is allowed, but the same amount of tax is collected from them. In this case, it is true that the charitable deduction will provide more of an incentive for the high-income taxpayers than for others (who owe no tax and get no deduction). But the tax system is not necessarily any less progressive.

For instance, the tax system might collect $50,000 each from the two high-income taxpayers if it doesn't allow a charitable deduction, or it might allow a charitable deduction and collect $55,000 from the nongiver and $45,000 from the giver. Exactly the same amount is still collected from the higher-income taxpayers. In fact, if the incentive induces more giving, then the lower-income taxpayers come out ahead in this example if they benefit at all from any additional giving the deduction may have inspired. They get the same amount of public services from the government and more from charities.

Ultimately, the ability-to-pay question comes down to whether an adjustment for charitable giving is appropriate for defining equals, not progressivity. Under an ability-to-pay rationale, the deduction does not necessarily reduce progressivity any more than would deductible payments

of alimony: both are simply part of the proper measure of income tax base.

In the end, what is stated as a fairness issue often relates to how the subsidy itself is allocated across charities. A deduction does provide a greater incentive to give for higher- than for lower-income taxpayers. So, also, does a higher standard deduction that by itself increases progressivity but removes charitable incentives for some taxpayers. Thus, both a charitable deduction and a higher standard deduction will bias dollars of subsidy more in the direction of the types of charities higher-income taxpayers favor.[23]

This turns the issue primarily into one of efficiency. Would we get better outcomes if we changed the basic incentive structure? To answer that question, we must delve into many other issues. For instance, the econometric literature tends to find that higher-income individuals, partly because they give more, are more responsive to charitable incentives. Thus, providing them with higher incentives might be more efficient from the perspective of inducing more giving overall.

## Alternative Reforms of the Charitable Deduction

Numerous recent reform proposals would change the tax treatment of charitable contributions. Some proposals are driven by various criticisms of the deduction. For others, budget considerations tend to dominate. In addition, many other tax policy changes indirectly affect charities even more than direct changes. For instance, changes in tax rates may have bigger impacts on charitable organizations than a restructuring of the deduction. Similarly, proposals with comparable revenue scores may have considerably different impacts on charitable giving. It is also possible to increase revenues and simultaneously increase charitable giving.

This section analyzes several recent proposals to reform the charitable contribution deduction or itemized deductions as a whole.

## Caps, Floors, Credits, and Grants

Recent proposals can be grouped loosely into four categories: caps, floors, credits, and grants. Roughly speaking, caps would limit the size of the tax benefit for individual donors, while floors would permit deductions only for total annual giving above a set amount. Credits would delink the value of the tax benefit from the donor's marginal tax rate and instead reduce taxes by a set percentage of total donations for each donor. Credits are also sometimes available to non-itemizers. Grants delink the government subsidy from the donor entirely by paying amounts directly to the donee organizations based on the amount contributed by the donor.

Overall, although floors, caps, and credits can all have similar revenue effects under plausible policy parameters, each has distinctive impact on charitable giving. To the extent that one places emphasis on the subsidy theory for the deduction, then, all else equal, policymakers should favor options that are more "cost effective"—that is, have smaller impacts on charitable giving for any given revenue target. For example, floors are likely to be among the more cost-effective of the proposals. They tend not to affect incentives at the margin, but instead simply provide less of a subsidy for the first dollars of contributions that more likely would be given anyway.[24]

Note, however, that the standard deduction already establishes a floor against itemized deductions more generally; it effectively excludes most taxpayers from the incentive effects of a charitable deduction, but not from getting another tax break in lieu of the deduction. A floor under charitable deductions would move it in the direction of medical expense deductions, which are also subject to their own floor, as well as the standard deduction.

Caps have somewhat the opposite effect of floors in cost-efficacy terms. There is some evidence that wealthier donors are more sensitive to the after-tax cost of donations, implying that a cap would have among the largest negative effects on donations relative to the amount of revenues raised. Caps are often proposed to deliver a system overall that is more progressive by reducing the benefits of higher-income groups.

In many respects, caps do not adhere to any theory of how to treat charitable contributions. They accord neither with a theory that all income should be taxed nor that ability to pay should be adjusted for charitable contributions made. At best they can be thought of as a step toward a credit or an indirect way to increase taxes on richer individuals.[25]

A credit adheres most closely to the notion that equal charitable incentives should be applied to all charitable contributions regardless of the taxpayer's tax rate. As such, it departs significantly from what an ability-to-pay rationale would prescribe. We have already noted that a tax system with a credit is not necessarily more progressive than one with a deduction. Only when converting to a credit with other parts of the tax system (in particular, tax rates) fixed does conversion to a credit necessarily establish greater progressivity.

However, credits are not neutral on all fronts. They create unequal incentives to work for charitable purposes—that is, to make money and donate it to charity. A high-income earner (including a secondary earner in a family) who wants to donate all earnings to charity, for instance, will be less likely to take a job for this purpose than a low-income earner because of these tax effects. Suppose a credit rate is established above the marginal tax rate of the lower-income donor and below the marginal tax rate of the higher-income donor. The former would get a net subsidy when donating income to charity, the latter would get a net penalty.[26]

Direct grants to charities that would be triggered by private donations represent the largest departure from current law of existing proposals, but they do have some precedent here and abroad.

It is unclear whether grants would be as effective as tax subsidies in encouraging donations. If donors are pure altruists who are concerned only with the money they can transfer to charity, and calculate efficiently the exact value of any type of subsidy, then grants or tax subsidies should operate identically. But if donors are "impure" altruists and care also about their own rewards for giving, grants could be less effective, because with grants the donor does not receive a direct tax benefit. Grants paid directly to charities by the government may also simply be harder for donors to notice than the deductions they see when filing their tax returns, and so be less effective even for purely altruistic donors. On the other hand, if taxpayers do not understand the nature of the subsidy, then a grant may get more money to a charity simply because the taxpayer thinks in terms of gross, not net, cost.[27] At least one study implies that grants are more readily seen by taxpayers, who then are more responsive, although the jury is still out on a set of UK grants called Gift Aid.[28]

The importance of the salience and "marketing" of the charitable incentive is also a reason one of us has proposed that taxpayers be allowed a deduction not just for the current calendar year but, like an individual retirement account, up until April 15 or the time of filing for the last calendar year (Steuerle 2011).[29] The simple notion is that people will give more when they directly see the value of the incentive.

Note that grants tend to raise more constitutional or sovereignty issues when dealing with religion. Other types of government grants get around this issue by being only for explicit secular services—for example, the social services provided by Catholic or Lutheran Charities, but not any of their religious activities. It is questionable whether the courts would allow

matching grants that went solely for support of religious worship.

## Other Issues Related to Reform of the Charitable Deduction

In assessing the merit of the charitable deduction and various alternatives, a number of other concerns must be taken into account.

Administrative costs influence the cost-effectiveness of any proposal. Good policy should account for not only the government's own administrative burdens but also the costs of private tax compliance.

Changes to the deduction may also have indirect and significant effects on how people time their charitable contributions and on their volunteer labor. Donors may choose to restructure their support for charity depending on the relative price of each choice.

Various reform proposals could have relatively similar impacts on the federal budget but quite different effects on nonprofits and the tax rules affecting them. Some of these reforms are more consistent with the spirit and the purposes of underlying existing supports for the sector than others. Any reform effort should account for the administrative costs and limitations on what tax authorities can enforce. In the end, the charitable deduction and any reform of it should be judged on the traditional grounds of fairness, effectiveness or efficiency, and simplicity.

## Notes

1. There is also a charitable contribution deduction for estate and gift tax purposes (IRC, sections 2001 through 2801). This report focuses on the income tax deduction.

2. Organizations that qualify for tax exemption under section 501(c)(3) are eligible to receive deductible contributions. See Internal Revenue Service (IRS), "Exemption Requirements—Sec-

tion 501(c)(3) Organizations," http://www.irs.gov /charities/charitable/artide/0,,id=96099,00.html, accessed February 20, 2012.

3. Several other notable tax provisions also affect the nonprofit sector. In addition to tax exemption, section 501(c)(3) charitable organizations may benefit from tax-exempt financing, and section 501(c) (3) status often triggers state-level benefits, such as property-tax and sales-tax exemption, and eligibility to receive deductible contributions in states that provide for a deduction.

4. A tax expenditure estimate is not the same as a revenue estimate, but the tax expenditure estimates provide a good sense of the magnitude of the federal government's support for the charitable sector through the deduction.

5. Joint Committee on Taxation, "Estimates of Federal Tax Expenditures for Fiscal Years 2010–2014," December 15, 2010.

6. Is the itemizer favored over the non-itemizer? While the itemizer gets to take deductions not available to the non-itemizer, the non-itemizer gets bonus deductions not available to the itemizer. Also, non-itemizers do face the incentive but do not give away enough that it applies at the margins at which they operate. The standard deduction is conceived as a way to simplify administration of the tax system, allowing individual taxpayers a generic deduction as a substitute for itemized deductions. No recordkeeping or similar requirements apply.

7. IRS Statistics of Income Division, "SOI Tax Stats," 2009, tables 2.1 and 2.3, http://www.irs.gov /taxstats/indtaxstats/article/0,,id=96981,00.html.

8. IRS Statistics of Income Division, "SOI Tax Stats," 2009, tables 2.1 and 2.3 (showing that itemized deductions make up 66.1 percent of returns for incomes of $75,000–$100,000; 84.7 percent for incomes of $100,000–$200,000, and more than 95 percent of returns for incomes of $200,000 or more. By contrast, at income levels of $50,000–$75,000, itemizers constituted 49.6 percent of returns, decreasing to 37 percent for incomes of $40,000–$50,000, 25.2 percent for incomes of $30,000–$40,000, and continuing to decrease with income.) According to Gerald Auten from the Treasury Department, the share who itemize in 2007 not counting dependent filers is 38 percent. If we exclude those who do not claim a taxpayer exemption in 2009 as an approxi-

mation of dependent filers, then some 34.5 percent would itemize, as opposed to 32.5 percent.

9. Contributions to private foundations are subject to a 30 percent limit, and contributions of capital gain property are subject to a 30 percent limit when given to most charities, but only 20 percent when given to private foundations. Also, there is a 50 percent limit to the total of all charitable contributions made during the year. Any amount in excess of a percentage limit generally may be carried forward and deducted over the subsequent five years. The alternative minimum tax (AMT) indirectly affects the charitable deduction. Although charitable contributions reduce AMT liability, the AMT's disallowance of other itemized deductions somewhat diminishes the usefulness of the charitable deduction. Corporations also may claim the charitable deduction. The corporate deduction may not exceed roughly 10 percent of the corporation's taxable income (with certain adjustments). Like individuals, corporations may carry forward excess contributions for five subsequent years. (IRS, Publication 526, http://www.irs .gov/publications/p526/ar02.html.)

10. As discussed below, a floor excludes amounts beneath it from deductibility. A handful of deductions, "miscellaneous itemized deductions," are subject to a 2 percent floor. Other examples include a 7.5 percent floor for medical expenses and a 10 percent floor for casualty losses. In addition, the charitable deduction has been subject to the overall phaseout of itemized deductions, although that provision has been temporarily repealed. For technical reasons, the phaseout generally does not affect donors' overall incentives. (26 USC § 67–2-percent floor on miscellaneous itemized deductions; 26 USC § 213—Medical, dental, etc., expenses; 26 USC § 165—Losses; http://www .law.cornell.edu/uscode/text/26/67.)

11. Over 1.8 million section 501(c)(3) organizations were registered with the IRS in 2009 (IRS 2009, table 25).

12. Section 170(c) uses the same language as section 501(c)(3) in describing qualifying organizations based on purpose: religious, charitable, scientific, literary or educational purposes, or to foster national or international amateur sports competition, or for the prevention of cruelty to children or animals.

13. This amount includes giving by individuals who are itemizers ($163.56 billion) and by non-itemizers ($42.60 billion; see Giving USA

2011). Because individuals give to private foundations, and foundations later make grants to other charities, the $290 billion figure overstates the total new wealth transferred to the charitable sector.

14. Not all the authors agree on this point. See Galle (2012, 786–787).

15. Sovereignty explanations do not theorize whether or why this is a normatively attractive approach.

16. Although fully inframarginal donors do not respond to changes in the relative cost of giving, the deduction may still somewhat increase their donations by making them a bit wealthier, enabling them to donate more.

17. Ignoring administrative considerations, ability-to-pay adjustments would apply to inframarginal gifts, as well, since the cost of giving is not part of household wealth available to pay federal tax. Administrative considerations, however, generally support the types of floors that apply to other tax base adjustments, such as the miscellaneous itemized deduction.

18. Another comparison might take into account the possibility that direct government spending can crowd out some purely voluntary production that society could have obtained without imposing any tax. Thus, the comparison might be between the amount of charity produced by each dollar of subsidy and the amount of *new* public goods produced by each direct government dollar. Studies find average crowd-out from government spending ranging from zero to $.50 on the dollar. (For example, see Payne 1998.)

19. The Tax Policy Center is currently investigating the relationship between the generosity of the deduction and fundraising costs.

20. Carrying this logic further might suggest that charitable organizations might be taxed on the value of program-related expenditures, as an estimate of the value received by untaxed beneficiaries. Obviously, that is not current law and implies once again that subsidizing charitable actions cannot be removed as a basis for a charitable deduction even if ability-to-pay adjustments are also accepted as reasonable.

21. This disparity may also result in a lower average tax rate for high-earning taxpayers overall.

22. Indeed, these forms of adjustment were part of the policy debate preceding the Treasury's 1984 proposal leading to the Tax Reform Act of 1986. Because the rate schedule was adjusted to achieve the desired degree of overall progressivity, decisions as

to whether to provide deductions, credits, or no tax break at all had no effect on overall progressivity. See Steuerle (2004).

23. At the same time, it may create an even more progressive tax system.

24. If stated as a fixed dollar amount, a floor may have a greater impact (relative to income) on relatively small donors. Designed as a percentage of income, however, a floor tends to reduce taxes less for the wealthy.

25. For additional discussion, see Colinvaux (2011b).

26. Additionally, since volunteer labor is untaxed, and hence is effectively equivalent to a full deduction on the value of labor contributed, shifts to a credit may increase the incentives for high-income households to substitute volunteerism for some paid labor and for low-income households to substitute paid labor for volunteerism.

27. Thus, if one would give $100 to a charity regardless of an incentive, then a taxpayer getting a 25 percent deduction would, on net, be giving $75 ($100 less $25 in tax subsidies) to the charity, and the government would be giving $25. If the government were to provide a 33 percent grant, then the individual giving $75 to charity would still generate $100 for the charity, but the individual giving $100 would end up granting the charity $133.

28. Under a program called Gift Aid, the British government matched 20 percent of a donation (the basic income tax rate). Taxpayers with higher rates still were allowed to claim a reduction in their taxes for whatever amount goes over 20 percent. See Scharf and Smith (2010).

29. See also Galle and Klick (2010), making a similar suggestion for deduction for state and local taxes.

## References

Ackerman, D., and G. Auten. 2006. "Floors, Ceilings, and Opening the Door for a Non-Itemizer Deduction." *National Tax Journal* 59(3): 509–529.

Brody, Evelyn. 1998. "Of Sovereignty and Subsidy: Conceptualizing the Charity Tax Exemption." *Journal of Corporation Law* 23(4): 585–629.

Colinvaux, Roger. 2011a. "Charity in the 21st Century Trending Toward Decay." *Florida Tax Review* 11(1): 45–69.

———. 2011b. "Tax Reform Options: Incentives for Charitable Giving." Testimony before the US Senate Committee on Finance, October 18. Available at http://papers.ssm.com/sol3/papers.cfm?abstract_id=2003955.

Feldstein, Martin, Daniel Feenberg, and Maya MacGuineas. 2011. "Capping Individual Tax Expenditure Benefits." Working Paper 16921. Cambridge, MA: National Bureau of Economic Research. Available at http://www.nber.org/papers/w16921.

Galle, Brian. 2012. "The Role of Charity in a Federal System." *William & Mary Law Review* 53(3): 777–851.

Galle, Brian, and Jonathan Klick. 2010. "Recessions and the Social Safety Net: The Alternative Minimum Tax as a Countercyclical Fiscal Stabilizer." *Stanford Law Review* 63: 242–243.

Giving USA Foundation. 2011. *Giving USA 2011: The Annual Report on Philanthropy for the Year 2010.* Glenview, IL: Giving USA Foundation.

Gravelle, Jane G., and Donald J. Marples. 2010. *Charitable Contributions: The Itemized Deduction Cap and Other FY2011 Budget Options.* Washington, DC: Congressional Research Service.

Internal Revenue Service. 2010. *Databook 2009.* Publication 55B. Washington, DC: Internal Revenue Service. Available at http://www.irs.gov/pub/irs-soi/09databk.pdf.

Payne, A. Abigail. 1998. "Does the Government Crowd-Out Private Donations? New Evidence from a Sample of Non-Profit Firms." *Journal of Public Economics* 69(3): 323–345.

Scharf, Kimberly A., and Sarah Smith. 2010. "The Price Elasticity of Charitable Giving: Does the Form of Tax Relief Matter?" Working paper. Available at http://ssm.com/abstract=1700433.

Seabright, Paul. 2002. "Blood, Bribes, and the Crowding-Out of Altruism by Financial Incentives." Toulouse, FR: Institut d'Économie Industrielle, Université de Toulouse. Available at http://www.altruists.org/static/files/Blood,%20Bribes%20and%20the%20CrowdingOut%20of%20Altruism%20by%20Finandal%20Incentives%20(Paul%20Seabright).pdf.

Sherlock, Molly F., and Jane G. Gravelle. 2009. *An Overview of the Nonprofit and Charitable Sector.* Washington, DC: Congressional Research Service.

Steuerle, C. Eugene. 2004. "Tax Reform: Prospects and Possibilities." Statement before the US House of Representatives Committee on the Budget, October 6. Available at http://www.taxpolicycenter.org/publications/url.cfm?ID=900749.

———. 2011. "The Tax Treatment of Charities & Major Budget Reform." Testimony before the US Senate Committee on Finance, October 18. Available at http://www.urban.org/publications/901460.html.

Wing, Kennard T., Thomas H. Poliak, and Amy Blackwood. 2008. *The Nonprofit Almanac 2008.* Washington, DC: Urban Institute Press.

## CHAPTER 5

# Punctilios and Nonprofit Corporate Governance: A Comprehensive Look at Nonprofit Directors' Fiduciary Duties

## Thomas Lee Hazen and Lisa Love Hazen

## Introduction

Nonprofit organizations generally have a governing board. Members of those governing boards are regarded as fiduciaries. However, this just begins the analysis. As Justice Felix Frankfurter observed in an oft-quoted passage: "[T]o say that a man is a fiduciary only begins analysis; it gives direction to further inquiry. To whom is he a fiduciary? What obligations does he owe as a fiduciary? In what respect has he failed to discharge these obligations?"[1] . . .

Fiduciary relationships are entered into voluntarily and are recognized as placing the fiduciary under a zealous duty of good faith.[2] Fiduciary relationships established by law often are mirrored by relationships established by custom reflecting positive social attributes including "loyalty, civility, self-sacrifice, vocational excellence, and high standards of honesty."[3] The law thus recognizes that a fiduciary relationship

entails a strong duty of the utmost loyalty. This loyalty obligation means that the fiduciary must act solely in the beneficiary's best interests rather than acting in the fiduciary's own interests.[4] . . .

Nonprofit corporations may be established for charitable (sometimes referred to as public benefit corporations) or religious purposes and those nonprofits are generally entitled to tax benefits.[5] . . . This article focuses on the obligations of public benefit or charitable nonprofit directors and does not address mutual benefit entities where the interests are purely private and there is no public mission involved. . . .

## Overview of Nonprofit Governing Board Duties

Nonprofit organizations can be established with either an advisory board or with a governing board. Unlike formal governing boards, advisory boards do not have either statutory authority or

Thomas Lee Hazen and Lisa Love Hazen, "Punctilios and Nonprofit Corporate Governance: A Comprehensive Look at Nonprofit Directors' Fiduciary Duties," 14 *University of Pennsylvania Journal of Business Law* 347 (2012). Reprinted by permission of the University of Pennsylvania.

statutory obligations. In contrast, when a board is established as a formal governing board, board members have fiduciary obligations. Nonprofit corporation acts, following the pattern of business corporation acts, establish a default governing structure that includes a board of directors.[6] Qualification for IRS tax-exempt status is easier if the charitable organization is formed as a nonprofit corporation.[7] Accordingly, it is very common for nonprofits to have a governing board of directors. Nonprofit board duties are generally described as a duty of care, a duty of loyalty, and a duty of good faith.[8] Also, there often is reference to a duty of obedience.[9] While it has been debated as to how many fiduciary duties directors must in fact adhere to, the categorization is less important than the substance.[10]

The duties of nonprofit directors to a large extent parallel the obligations of for-profit directors.[11] The duty of care is basically a negligence standard as it requires directors to act in a manner consistent with reasonably prudent directors under like circumstances.[12] In order to live up to their duty of care, directors must keep themselves informed about the organization's operations.[13] The duty of loyalty is implicated when a board member has a conflict of interest and at a minimum the conflicted board member should not participate in any related decision-making.[14] The duty of good faith is sometimes referred to as a separate obligation but is also a part of the duties of care and loyalty.[15] The duty of obedience is sometimes referred to as a way of describing the board's obligation to remain faithful to the organization's purpose and mission.[16] . . .

The discussion that follows addresses the duties of care (including good faith), loyalty, and obedience.

## Duty of Care

The duty of care for business corporation directors developed as a matter of case law[17] and has since been codified in most business corporation acts.[18] The duty of care includes obligations of keeping informed, remaining attentive, and acting in a manner that the director *reasonably* believes is in the best interest of the corporation.[19] Previously, the law phrased the obligation more in terms of a reasonable person standard so as to judge care according to a reasonable director under like circumstances.[20] Today most statutes speak in terms of a reasonable belief that the director is acting in the best interests of the corporation.[21] This change in language may be more semantic than substantive since both are objective tests based on *reasonableness* and are not limited to the director's subjective good faith belief. The Model Nonprofit Corporation Act retained the prudent person standard until 2008 when it was redrafted to speak in terms of the director's good faith belief of acting in the corporation's best interest.[22] Many state statutes retain the reasonable person standard.[23] In addition, the American Law Institute's draft Principles of Nonprofit Law retains the reasonable person language that sounds more like a traditional negligence standard.[24]

Business corporation directors' duty of care is eased to some extent as it is qualified by the business judgment rule that was developed in case law.[25] The business judgment rule in essence allows the directors to make what turn out to be bad decisions since courts do not view their role as second-guessing the business community with respect to business decisions.[26] The business judgment rule is conditioned on the directors' informing themselves and uninformed directors will not get the rule's protection.[27] . . .

There are limitations on liability for due care violations. However, even in the absence of clear liability, nonprofit directors should be motivated to live up to their statutory responsibilities. For example, there is some evidence that when a nonprofit board is populated with large donors, there is greater efficiency in monitoring management's activities.[28] There is some evidence that this can result in positive outcomes when balanced by management representation on the board.[29] Although having management on nonprofit boards can have positive benefits, the presence of management does not eliminate the need and, if anything, increases the need for independent oversight.[30] . . .

While it is true that the volunteer nature of most nonprofit directors may be a factor in considering liability for mismanagement, it is not a complete bar. Thus, for example, where directors allowed foundation funds to sit in non-interest bearing accounts, the court found this to be a breach of duty.[31] Directors also may be held accountable for allowing mismanagement of assets.[32] It is generally accepted that mere negligence is not sufficient to hold a nonprofit director or officer accountable.[33] . . .

### Business Judgment Rule

Although nonprofit corporations are not focused on business decisions, the business judgment rule is recognized in the nonprofit context. For example, the ALI's Principles of Nonprofit Law provides:

> A governing-board member who makes a business judgment in good faith satisfies § 315 (Duty of Care) if he or she:
>
> a) is not interested, directly or indirectly, in the subject of the business judgment and is otherwise able to exercise independent judgment;
> b) is informed with respect to the subject of the business judgment to the extent he or she reasonably believes to be appropriate under the circumstances; and
> c) reasonably believes that the business judgment is in the best interests of the charity, in light of its stated purposes.[34]

Although not all observers agree that it is appropriate,[35] the business judgment rule is a factor in assessing conduct of nonprofit directors. A key point in this regard is the directors' duty to be informed in making decisions.

## Duty of Loyalty

The duty of loyalty is an important concept in both corporate law and the law of trusts.[36] Among other things, the duty of loyalty addresses situations in which a director has a direct or indirect conflict of interest.[37] In its early stages, the rules relating to directors' obligations of loyalty borrowed heavily from the strict rules governing trustees and agents.[38] The cases often classified corporate directors as trustees and subjected them to strict rules of disqualification of agents contracting with their principal.[39] References to directors as trustees continue in current case law.[40] Whereas the duty of care is often viewed as a matter of process, the duty of loyalty is more about substance, focusing on the director's or officer's motives, purposes, and goals.[41]

The duty of loyalty, among other things, forbids many self-dealing contracts and transactions, which more generally are referred to as conflict-of-interest transactions. A director will not receive the benefit of the business judgment rule if acting out of self-interest and thus not serving the organization's interests.[42] An even more blatant form of loyalty breach arises when the officer or director has usurped a corporate opportunity.[43] Interestingly, in special instances, loyalty violations can even arise when the directors or officers are acting in their good faith belief that they are advancing the corporation's interest.[44] Duty of loyalty and potential conflict of interest situations place directors under a heightened duty of disclosure.[45] For example, a director's duty of loyalty arises when the director, even though financially disinterested, knowingly fails to warn other directors of material facts relevant to a transaction before the board.[46] . . .

Nonprofit corporation law follows the same pattern as the business corporation law. . . .[47]

Similarly, the conflict of interest rules for non-profit corporations follow the pattern of business corporation acts.[48] Thus, a conflict of interest transaction is not voidable due to the relationship creating the conflict if the transaction is approved by a disinterested governing body or if it is proven to be fair to the corporation.[49] In these situations, the burden of proving fairness clearly lies with the person trying to validate the conflict of interest transaction.

Although not necessarily limited to self-dealing transactions, nonprofits must be mindful about not operating too much like a business entity that focuses on profits to its shareholders. . . . The nonprofit corporation can also be used to curtail abuses. Blatant self-dealing will provide a basis for dissolution of a nonprofit corporation.[50] Converting a public benefit nonprofit into a corporation focused on private benefits amounts to a breach of fiduciary duty.[51] Payments by a nonprofit to its officers that purport to be compensation implicate the board as these payments must be approved by the board.[52] In addition to dissolution, the principals who take assets from a nonprofit may be held accountable and held liable in damages.[53]

The corporate opportunity doctrine holds that a corporate fiduciary cannot take for his or her personal benefit an opportunity that should be offered to the corporation.[54] The corporate opportunity doctrine applies to nonprofit corporation directors and managers.[55]

## Good Faith (An Independent Duty?)

There are frequent references in both cases and scholarship to a director's duty of good faith as a third fiduciary duty[56] in addition to the duties of care and loyalty. Even if not viewed as a stand-alone duty, the obligation of good faith is subsumed in the duties of care and loyalty. This is the better view.[57] For example, the Delaware Supreme Court clarified that the duty of good faith is in essence a component of both the duty of care and the duty of loyalty.[58] Good faith is also an important concept when dealing with statutes that permit limitation of liability for due care violations.[59] The current version of the model nonprofit act permits provisions in the articles of incorporation limiting liability for actions by a disinterested director that are taken in good faith.[60] The exculpation provision is not applicable to charitable organizations since their directors are already protected by a liability shield.[61]

A director's duty of good faith also includes disclosure obligations. It has thus been said that nonprofit directors are subject to a duty of candor.[62] Whether good faith is viewed as a separate obligation is not truly significant in measuring directors' duties. Since good faith is clearly included in the duties of due care and loyalty, directors not acting in good faith should be held accountable.

## Duty of Obedience

In addition to the duties of care, loyalty, and good faith, courts and observers speak in terms of a director's duty of obedience with respect to both business corporations and nonprofit corporations.[63] The duty of obedience is especially significant in the case of nonprofit corporations. References to a duty of obedience capture the idea that a director is under an obligation to ensure that the corporation acts within its proper purpose and mission. This obedience can also include honoring a donor's intent in the administration of the organization's assets. . . .

The duty of obedience is a reflection of the age-old *ultra vires* doctrine that prohibits corporate acts beyond the corporation's mission and purpose.[64] The same concept applies with nonprofit corporations.[65] From a practical standpoint the duty of obedience can be seen as a substantive rather than process-oriented view of board obligations.[66] . . . The duty of obedience is also included in guidebooks for nonprofit directors.[67] State attorneys general who have enforcement responsibilities regarding nonprofit corporations also recognize the significance of the duty of obedience in the nonprofit sector.[68] Many charitable nonprofits have a limited mission statement and, if so, this would bear upon the board's duty of obedience with respect to that mission.[69] Similarly, if there are donor restrictions on use of funds,[70] the board needs to assure proper procedures are in place and that there is sufficient transparency to assure obedience to the donor's restrictions.[71] For example, in one case a group of trustees were allowed to challenge a change in the charity's mission and to attempt to enforce the duty of obedience even though the state attorney general was not concerned since the funds were still being used for the public good.[72] The trustees were thus allowed to try to enforce the duty of obedience even though the state attorney general's charge under the statute is primarily to assure that the funds were being used for the public good.

Charitable organizations that disburse donor funds have special obligations. For example, failure to follow the donors' intent can be problematic and form the basis for challenging the charity's operations.[73] The charitable trust doctrine[74] holds that, with restricted gifts, a donor's intent creates trust obligations in managing the trust.[75] The Board's oversight functions can include having a reasonable basis for believing that donor intent is being honored.[76] There has been a debate concerning the extent to which a charity should have to honor the so-called dead hand of a donor's intent.[77] The issues can be quite complex. For example, is the donor's intent no longer consistent with the foundation's goals due to a change in circumstances? Are there other reasons that a board may believe that the donor's intent should yield to the public good or the mission of the foundation? On the other hand, adhering to donor intent is in the public interest to the extent it encourages charitable contributions.[78] Even if the board can de-

cide that the donor's intent should yield to the charity's general purpose, the board's oversight obligation is implicated and they should assure transparency in the charity's decisions. . . .

Nonprofit corporations—especially those with a charitable mission—comprise a public good.[79] If anything, this warrants holding nonprofit directors to higher standards of care and loyalty than in the for-profit sector. On the other hand, while corporate directors of larger companies are generally compensated, nonprofit directors are usually volunteers.[80] It has been suggested that imposing high fiduciary duties on nonprofit directors will deter good people from serving on nonprofit boards.[81] Due to the public benefit from encouraging nonprofit volunteers, most states have volunteer statutes that insulate volunteers (including directors of charitable nonprofit corporations) from liability even more than the exculpatory provisions of the nonprofit statutes. The resulting conundrum is the heightened director duties that are imposed as a result of nonprofit corporation and tax laws are counterbalanced by extreme limitations on liability of nonprofit directors. There are some commentators who maintain that even existing liability provisions go too far, and nonprofit directors should be further immunized.[82] Alternatively they argue that fiduciary duties should be scaled back or eliminated.[83] We disagree. There may be merit in retaining high fiduciary standards combined with the limited liability and immunity provisions that already exist. Although some suggest that the remedies should be expanded,[84] the absence of more robust liability provisions does not necessarily mean that the law's message with respect to oversight obligations is hollow. . . .

## Notes

1. SEC v. Chenery Corp., 318 U.S. 80, 85–86 (1942).

2. See, e.g., Scott Fitzgibbon, "Fiduciary Relationships Are Not Contracts," 82 *Marq. L. Rev.* 303, 304, 308–309 (1999); see also, e.g., Deborah A. De-

Mott, "Beyond Metaphor: An Analysis of Fiduciary Obligation," 1988 *Duke L. J.* 879, 902 (1988) (discussing autonomy as a key assumption of fiduciary relationships).

3. Fitzgibbon, *supra* note 2, at 340.

4. See D. Gordon Smith, "The Critical Resource Theory of Fiduciary Duty," 55 *Vand. L. Rev.* 1399, 1488 (2002).

5. IRC § 501(c) (2011).

6. Revised Model Nonprofit Corp. Act § 8.01(a) (2008).

7. See, e.g., James K. Weeks, "The Not-For-Profit Business Corporation," 19 *Clev. St. L. Rev.* 303, 307 (1970) (suggesting it is easier to obtain a federal tax exemption if the organization is recognized as a charitable entity under state law but also noting that such status is not by itself sufficient).

8. Principles of the Law of Nonprofit Organizations §§ 315 (duty of care), 330 (conflicts of interest) (Tentative Draft No. 1, 2007) (hereinafter "ALI Nonprofit Principles").

9. See, e.g., Queen of Angels Hosp. v. Younger, 136 Cal. Rptr. 36 (Cal. Ct. App. 1977) (dealing with action brought by the state attorney general where a nonprofit breached the duty of obedience in using funds for medical clinics instead of for operating a hospital). See discussion *infra* Part IX in Hazen and Hazen, "Punctilios and Nonprofit Corporate Governance: A Comprehensive Look at Nonprofit Directors' Fiduciary Duties," 14 *U. Pa. J. Bus. L.,* 347 (2012).

10. See, e.g., Julian Velasco, "How Many Fiduciary Duties Are There in Corporate Law?" 83 *So. Cal. L. Rev.* 1231, 1257–1276 (2010) (explaining that the existing debates are largely semantic and that fiduciary duties are too important to be oversimplified into two or three categories). Professor Velasco suggests five paradigms for enforcement that he believes will provide a better framework for analyzing directors' duties. The five paradigms he suggests are: (1) process (gross negligence), (2) conflicts of interest (fairness), (3) bias (reasonableness), (4) misconduct (intent), and (5) substance (waste). *Id.* at 1235.

11. Although this article's focus is on nonprofit directors, it is worth mentioning that even in the wake of corporate governance reforms and heightened accountability, there is still legitimate concern over whether for-profit corporate boards are fulfilling

their obligations in a satisfactory manner. See, e.g., McKinsey & Company, "McKinsey Global Survey Results: Governance Since the Economic Crisis," in *McKinsey Quarterly* 1, 4 (2011) (indicating that (1) 44 percent of respondents indicated that their boards simply review and approve proposed strategies of management, (2) only 25 percent of respondents characterized the overall performance of their boards as excellent or very good, (3) the number of boards that formally evaluate their directors has decreased during the past three years, and (4) only 21 percent of directors purport to completely understand their company's strategy). Our concerns about insufficient accountability of nonprofit directors seem to have application to the for-profit world as well.

12. ALI Nonprofit Principles, *supra* note 9, § 315(b) (describing standard of conduct).

13. *Id.* § 315(a).

14. *Id.* § 330.

15. See, e.g., Clark W. Furlow, "Good Faith, Fiduciary Duties, and the Business Judgment Rule in Delaware," 2009 *Utah L. Rev.* 1061 (2009) (discussing good faith under Delaware corporate law); Leo E. Strine, Jr., Lawrence A. Hamermesh, R. Franklin Balotti, and Jeffrey M. Gorris, "Loyalty's Core Demand: The Defining Role of Good Faith in Corporation Law," 98 *GEO. L. J.* 629, 673–688 (2010) (further discussing good faith under Delaware corporate law as well as "[t]he rise and demise of an independent duty of good faith").

16. See discussion *infra* Part IX in Hazen and Hazen, "Punctilios and Nonprofit Corporate Governance: A Comprehensive Look at Nonprofit Directors' Fiduciary Duties," 14 *U. Pa. J. Bus. L.,* 347 (2012).

17. See, e.g., Bates v. Dresser, 251 U.S. 524 (1920) (noting that directors oversee the operations but are not held directly accountable for day to day management); Hun v. Cary, 82 N.Y. 65 (1880) (holding that a corporate director must act in the same manner as a reasonable person in managing his or her own affairs).

18. See, e.g., Model Bus. Corp. Act § 8.30 (2011) (discussing directors' standard of conduct).

19. See James D. Cox and Thomas Lee Hazen, *Treatise on the Law of Corporations,* § 2:4 (3rd ed. 2010), §§ 10:1, 10:3.

20. *Id.* § 10:3.

21. *Id.*

22. The comments to the 2008 version of the Model Nonprofit Corp. Act explain the change as follows:

In the prior version of the act the duty of care element was included in subsection (a), with text reading: "[a] director shall discharge his duties . . . with the care an ordinarily prudent person in a like position would exercise under similar circumstances." The use of the phrase "ordinarily prudent person" in a basic guideline for director conduct, suggesting caution or circumspection vis-à-vis danger or risk, has long been problematic given the fact that risk-taking decisions are central to the directors' role. When coupled with the exercise of "care," the prior text had a familiar resonance long associated with the field of tort law. See the Official Comment to Section 8.31. The further coupling with the verb "shall discharge" added to the inference that former Section 8.30(a)'s standard of conduct involved a negligence standard, with resultant confusion. In order to facilitate its understanding, and analysis, independent of the other general standards of conduct for directors, the duty of care element has been set forth as a separate standard of conduct in subsection (b).—Model Nonprofit Corp. Act: Official Text with Official Comments and Statutory Cross-References § 8.30 (3d ed. 2008).

23. See, e.g., Cal. Corp. Code § 523l(a) (2011) ("A director shall perform the duties of a director . . . in a manner that director believes to be in the best interests of the corporation and with such care, including reasonable inquiry, as an ordinarily prudent person in a like position would use under similar circumstances"); Minn. Stat. § 317A.251 (2011) ("A director shall discharge the duties of the position of director in good faith, in a manner the director reasonably believes to be in the best interests of the corporation, and with the care an ordinarily prudent person in a like position would exercise under similar circumstances"); N.C. Gen. Stat. § 55A-8-30 (1994) (a director must act "(1) In good faith; (2) With the care an ordinarily prudent person in a like position would exercise under similar circumstances; and (3) In a manner he reasonably believes to be in the best interests of the corporation").

24. With respect to nonprofit directors, the American Law Institute's draft Principles of Nonprofit Law provides:

The duty of care requires each governing-board member—

(a) to become appropriately informed about issues requiring consideration, and to devote appropriate attention to oversight; and

(b) to act with the care that an ordinarily prudent person would reasonably exercise in a like position and under similar circumstances.

—ALI Nonprofit Principles, *supra* note 9, § 315.

25. Cox and Hazen, *supra* note 20, § 10:2.

26. See, e.g., Shlensky v. Wrigley, 237 N.E.2d 776, 780–781 (1968) (refusing to second-guess the directors' judgment not to install lights in Wrigley Field even though every other major league baseball team played night games and revenues for weekday night games were higher than day games).

27. See. e.g., Smith v. Van Gorkom, 488 A.2d 858 (1985) (holding that directors of for-profit corporation could be held accountable for approving sale of company without using due diligence); see also Armenian Assembly of Am., Inc. v. Cafesjian, 772 F. Supp. 2d 20, 103–104 (D.D.C. 2011) (acknowledging the application of the business judgment rule to nonprofit directors but not where the directors have an actual or potential conflict of interest).

28. See, e.g., Jeffrey L. Callen, April Klein, and Daniel Tinkelman, "Board Composition, Committees, and Organizational Efficiency: The Case of Nonprofits," 32 *Nonprofit & Voluntary Sector Q.* 493 (2003) (finding a significant statistical association between the presence of major donors on the board and indicators of organizational efficiency. Although causation was not demonstrated conclusively, the findings are consistent with the suggestion that major donors are likely to monitor nonprofit organizations at least in part through their board membership); see also Eugene F. Fama and Michael C. Jensen, "Separation of Ownership and Control," 26 *J. L. & Econ.* 301, 301–302 (1983).

29. Edward A. Dyl, Howard L. Frant, and Craig A. Stephenson, "Governance and Funds Allocation in United States Medical Research Charities," 16 *Fin. Accountability & Mgmt.* 4 (Nov. 2000).

30. See generally Eric W. Hayden, "Governance Failures Also Occur in the Non-Profit World," 2 *Int'l J. of Bus. Governance & Ethics* 116 (2006) (stating that "governance suffers when boards are dominated by affiliated outsiders or when the allegiance of the

board is not fully committed to the organisation's mission *and* ongoing financial viability").

31. Lynch v. John M. Redfield Found., 88 Cal. Rptr. 86 (Cal. Ct. App. 1970).

32. Vacco v. Diamandopoulos, 715 N.Y.S.2d 269, 270 (N.Y. Sup. Ct. 1998).

33. See, e.g., La. World Exposition v. Fed. Ins. Co., 864 F.2d 1147 (5th Cir. 1989)

34. ALI Nonprofit Principles, *supra* note 9, § 365 (Tentative Draft No. 1, 2007).

35. See, e.g., Denise Ping Lee, Note, "The Business Judgment Rule: Should It Protect Nonprofit Directors?" 103 *Colum. L. Rev.* 925 (2003) (arguing that the current standard for nonprofit directors is too low and urging that courts should not apply the business judgment rule that developed to deal with for-profit corporations to insulate directors from liability for lack of due diligence).

36. See, e.g., Melanie B. Leslie, "Making Non-profits Police Themselves: What Trust Law Can Teach Us About Conflicts of Interest," 85 *Chi-Kent L. Rev.* 551 (2010) (discussing the different standards of fiduciary duties in trust law and corporate law).

37. Cox and Hazen, *supra* note 20, §§ 10:11–10:19.

38. *Id.* § 10:11 (discussing the origins and development of the duty of loyalty).

39. See, e.g., Stack v. Welder, 31 P.2d 436 (Cal. Ct. App. 1934) (discussing the narrow conditions in which a director of a corporation may deal directly with that corporation); N. Confidence Mining & Dev. Co. v. Fitch, 208 P. 328 (Cal. Ct. App. 1922) (holding that a director with an adverse interest in the settlement of a claim could not vote on a resolution of the settlement); Gates v. Plainfield Trust Co., 191 A. 304, 318 (N.J. Ch. 1937) (detailing, among other things, the duties a trustee has to his beneficiaries), aff'd, 194 A. 65 (N.J. 1937); see also Restatement (Second) of Agency §§ 389–393 (1958) (stating the law of agency on the issues of adverse parties and conflicts of interest).

40. On the general topic of determining the roots for corporate fiduciary obligations, see Victor Brudey, "Contract and Fiduciary Duty in Corporate Law," 38 *B.C. L. Rev.* 595 (1997) (proposing a modified contract-based account of a director's fiduciary duty); Deborah A. DeMott, "Breach of Fiduciary Duly: On Justifiable Expectations of Loyalty and

Their Consequences," 48 *Ariz. L. Rev.* 925 (2006) (noting that duty arises from shareholders' justifiable expectations of loyal conduct); Lyman P. Q. Johnson and David Millon, "Recalling Why Corporate Officers Are Fiduciaries," 46 *Wm. & Mary L. Rev.* 1597 (2005) (outlining the history and duties of corporate officers); Park McGinty, "The Twilight of Fiduciary Duties: On the Need for Shareholder Self-Help in an Age of Formalistic Proceduralism," 46 *Emory L. J.* 163 (1997) (arguing that shareholder protections from director self-interest are inadequate, and proposing various means that a stockholder can take to counterbalance director interests); Edward Rock and Michael Wachter, "Dangerous Liaisons: Corporate Law, Trust Law, and Interdoctrinal Legal Transplants," 96 *Nw. U. L. Rev.* 651 (2002) (arguing that loyalty standards within corporate law are more nuanced than in the context of trusts reflecting their differing institutional settings); D. Gordon Smith, "The Critical Resource Theory of Fiduciary Duty," 55 *Vand. L. Rev.* 1399 (2002) (crafting a unified theory of fiduciary duty as a "critical resource theory"); Lynn A. Stout, "On the Proper Motives of Corporate Directors (Or, Why You Don't Want to Invite Homo Economicus to Join Your Board)," 28 *Del. J. Corp. L.* 1 (2003) (discussing the importance of altruistic behavior by board members). For an early consideration of the same topic, see E. Merrick Dodd, Jr., "Is Effective Enforcement of Fiduciary Duties of Corporate Managers Practicable?" 2 *U. Chi. L. Rev.* 194 (1935).

41. Cox and Hazen, *supra* note 20, § 10:11.

42. *Id.* § 10:02.

43. *Id.* § 11:8.

44. Blasius Indus. v. Atlas Corp., 564 A.2d 651, 663 (Del. Ch. 1988) (holding that even though acting in the good faith belief they are serving the corporation's interest, management must demonstrate a compelling justification for action taken for purpose of thwarting the ongoing efforts of a stockholder to exercise its rights of corporate suffrage).

45. See, e.g., Globe Woolen Co. v. Utica Gas & Elec. Co., 121 N.E. 378 (N.Y. 1918) (discussing the duty of loyalty generally and, in particular, the need for full disclosure in conflict of interest transactions).

46. See, e.g., Berkman v. Rust Craft Greeting Cards, Inc., 454 F. Supp. 787 (S.D.N.Y. 1978).

47. Principles of the Law of Nonprofit Orgs. § 330 (Tentative Draft No. 1, 2007); see also Leslie,

*supra* note 36 (calling for heightened rules on nonprofit conflict-of-interest transactions).

48. See Model Nonprofit Corp. Act § 8.60 (2008) (stating that for nonprofit corporations a transaction or contract in which a director is an interested party is not thereby void or voidable).

49. Principles of the Law of Nonprofit Orgs. § 330 (Tentative Draft No. 1, 2007). The draft Principles, which reflect current law, provide:

The governing board may approve a transaction between the charity and a fiduciary, waive the charity's interest in a transaction between another person and a fiduciary, or approve or waive any other conflict of interest of the fiduciary described in § 310(b) if in good faith the board reasonably determines that the transaction with the charity is both fair to and in the best interests of the charity, or that the approval or waiver of the charity's interest in any other conduct is in the best interests of the charity.

*Id.* § 330(a).

In addition, approval by a disinterested governing board or committee is conditioned upon the fiduciary having "made a good-faith disclosure to the decisionmaking body of all relevant material facts, and refrained from seeking to influence the decisionmaking process." *Id.* § 330(b)(1).

50. See Summers v. Cherokee Children & Family Serv., Inc., 112 S.W.3d 486 (Tenn. Ct. App. 2002).

51. *Id.* at 504 ("[A] director's duty of loyalty lies in pursuing or ensuring pursuit of the charitable purpose or public benefit which is the mission of the corporation").

52. Vacco v. Diamandopoulos, 715 N.Y.S.2d 269 (N.Y. Sup. Ct. 1998); State ex rel. Little People's Child Dev. Ctr., Inc. v. Little People's Child Dev. Ctr., Inc., No. M2007-00345-COA-R3-CV, 2009 WL 103509, at *8 (Tenn. Ct. App. Jan. 9, 2009); see also People ex rel. Spitzer v. Grasso, 816 N.Y.S.2d 863 (N.Y. Sup. Ct. 2006) (denying defendant nonprofit CEO's motion to dismiss challenges to executive compensation as excessive). However, on appeal, the New York Court of Appeals found no violation of the New York Nonprofit Corporation Act. People v. Grasso, 893 N.E.2d 105 (2008) (dismissing claims).

53. Little People's Child Dev. Ctr., Inc., 2009 WL 103509; see also Mid-List Press v. Nora, 275 F. Supp. 2d 997 (D. Minn. 2003) (holding director and officer of nonprofit press violated fiduciary duty by misappropriating to himself trade name and ISBN numbers belonging to the nonprofit corporation).

54. Cox and Hazen, *supra* note 20, §§ 11:8–11:10.

55. See Valle v. N. Jersey Auto. Club, 359 A.2d 504 (N.J. Super. Ct. App. Div. 1976); see also Model Nonprofit Corp. Act § 8.70 (2008).

56. See, e.g., Clark W. Furlow, "Good Faith, Fiduciary Duties, and the Business Judgment Rule in Delaware," 2009 *Utah L. Rev.* 1062 (2009) (discussing how good faith relates to directors' duties under Delaware corporate law); Leo E. Strine, Jr., Lawrence A. Hamermesh, R. Franklin Balotti, and Jeffrey M. Gorris, "Loyalty's Core Demand: The Defining Role of Good Faith in Corporation Law," 98 *Geo. L. J.* 629, 673 (2010) (discussing "the rise and demise of an independent duty of good faith").

57. Russell M. Robinson, II, *Robinson on North Carolina Corporation Law* § 14.03 at 14–17 (7th ed., 2010) (The requirement of good faith is listed separately in the statute and has occasionally been cited as a separate duty apart from the duties of due care and loyalty; but it normally operates more as a component of the other two traditional duties, requiring conscientious effort in discharging the duty of care and constituting the very core of the duty of loyalty) (internal citation omitted).

58. Stone v. Ritter, 911 A.2d 362, 370 (Del. 2006). "[A]lthough good faith may be described colloquially as part of a 'triad' of fiduciary duties that includes the duties of care and loyalty . . . [o]nly the latter two duties, where violated, may directly result in liability . . . " (internal citation omitted). The draft ALI Principles applicable to nonprofits discuss the history of good faith in Delaware corporate law as a guide to the meaning of good faith in the context of nonprofits. Principles of the Law of Nonprofit Orgs. § 370 Reporter's Note 15 (Tentative Draft No. 1, 2007).

59. See, e.g., Model Bus. Corp. Act § 2.02(b)(4) (1980) (permitting a clause in the articles of incorporation limiting damages for due care violations).

60. Model Nonprofit Corp. Act § 2.02(c) (2008).

61. *Id.* § 8.31(d).

62. See Armenian Assembly of Am., Inc. v. Cafesjian, 772 F. Supp. 2d 20, 113 (D.D.C. 2011). This ruling echoes the well-established rule with respect to for-profit directors that a breach of duty

does not result in liability absent proof of damages proximately caused by the breach. See, e.g., Barnes v. Andrews, 298 F. 614 (S.D.N.Y. 1924) (providing an illustration of the rule that a lawsuit brought on grounds of a director's negligence must satisfy the element of proximate causation).

63. See, e.g., Alan R. Palmiter, "Duty of Obedience: The Forgotten Duty," 55 *N.Y.L. Sch. L. Rev.* 457 (2010/2011) (discussing the duty of obedience).

64. Cox and Hazen, supra note 20, ch. 4.

65. Carson v. Carson, 88 S.W. 175, 178 (Tenn. 1905) (stating that a "corporation organized for charitable purposes has these purposes and trusts set out in its charter and articles of foundation . . . [b]ut no trusts in such case need be declared, as they are set out in the charter and articles of foundation").

66. Practitioners have described the duty as substantive. See, e.g., David H. Robbins, "New Risks for Hospital Boards: Good Faith Decisions with Bad Outcomes," *Modern Healthcare Magazine* (July 2006) ("[T]he duty of obedience tests the substantive, as opposed to the procedural, quality of decisions by nonprofit boards").

67. See, e.g., Business Law Section of the North Carolina Bar Association and N.C. Center for Nonprofits, *Guidebook for Boards of Directors of North Carolina Nonprofit Corporations* 19, 26, 31 (2d ed., 2003) (referencing the duty of obedience).

68. See, e.g., "Fiduciary Duties of Directors of Charitable Organizations," Office of the [Minn.] Att'y Gen. Lori Swanson, http://www.ag.state .mn.us/charities/fiduciaryduties.asp (last visited June 22, 2011) (discussing nonprofit directors' duties of care, loyalty, and obedience); *A Guide to Non-Profits*, Nev. Dept. of Justice—Office of the Att'y Gen., 9 (2011) (including duty of obedience); *Right from the Start—A Handbook for Not-for-Profit Board Members*, N.Y. Office of the Att'y Gen., 7 (2009) (including the duty of obedience).

69. See, e.g., Shorter C. v. Baptist Convention of Ga., 614 S.E.2d 37, 43 (Ga. 2005) (quoting Manhattan Eye, Ear & Throat Hosp. v. Spitzer, 715 N.Y.S.2d 575 (N.Y. Sup. Ct. 1999)). "It is axiomatic that the board of directors [of a nonprofit] is charged with the duty to ensure that the mission of the charitable corporation is carried out. This duty has been referred to as the 'duty of obedience.' It requires the director of a not-for-profit corporation to 'be faithful to the purposes and goals of the organization,' *since*

*[u]nlike business corporations, whose ultimate objective is to make money, nonprofit corporations are defined by their specific objectives'* . . . ") (emphasis added). The court held that the transfer of nonprofit college assets to a foundation did not constitute a valid dissolution of the nonprofit corporation. *Id.*

70. See, e.g., Susan N. Gary, "The Problems with Donor Intent: Interpretation, Enforcement, and Doing the Right Thing," 85 *Chi.-Kent L. Rev.* 977 (2010) (discussing problems in identifying donor intent); Carrie M. Lovelace and Jeffrey C. Sun, Commentary, "Analyzing the Continuing Relationship Between Universities and Their Donors' Successors," 256 *Ed. L. Rep.* 513 (2010) (discussing the ability of donors' successors to monitor and challenge use of funds); see also Michael J. Hussey, "Avoiding Misuse of Donor Advised Funds," 58 *Clev. St. L. Rev.* 59 (2010) (discussing donor-advised funds).

71. Iris J. Goodwin, "Donor Standing to Enforce Charitable Gifts: Civil Society vs. Donor Empowerment," 58 *Vand. L. Rev.* 1093, 1094 (2005) (discussing the stewardship of donor intent and noting: "[t]he cat is out of the bag: Donors are fast discovering what was once a well-kept secret in the philanthropic sector—that a gift to public charity donated for a specific purpose and restricted to that purpose is often used by the charity for its general operations or applied to other uses not intended by the donor"). Cf. Reid Kress Weisbord, "The Effects of Donor Standing on Philanthropy: Insights from the Psychology of Gift-Giving," 45 *Gonz. L. Rev.* 225 (2009) (discussing impact of donor control of management of funds and suggesting that giving donors standing to sue will not necessarily promote the public policy of the charity); Lisa Loftin, Note, "Protecting the Charitable Investor: A Rationale for Donor Enforcement of Restricted Gifts," 8 *B.U. Pub. INT. L. J.* 361 (1999) (discussing benefits of donor control over use of funds). Just recently, a hospital was required to return a donor's contribution and pay punitive damages for failure to follow the donor's directions. See "Hospital Must Pay Garth Brooks $1 Million," *USA Today*, http://www.usatoday.com/life/people/story /2012–01–24/garth-brooks-hospital-settlement /52783732/1 (Jan. 24, 2012). See also "Ray Charles Foundation Wants $3M Gift Back from Ga. University, Says Arts Center Never Built,"

*Washington Post,* http://www.washingtonpost.com/national/ray-charles-foundation-wants-3m-back-from-ga-college-seeks-building-named-after-late-singer/2012/02/14/gIQAf8zEER_story.html (Feb. 14, 2012) (discussing foundation's attempt to recoup donation due to failure to follow donor's intent).

72. Holt v. Coll. of Osteopathic Physicians and Surgeons, 394 P.2d 932 (Cal. 1964). The attorney general was not the exclusive party to bring suit. *Id.* at 937. The court allowed the plaintiff-trustees to bring suit challenging the change in name and mission of the foundation. *Id.* The attorney general had found that the name change was proper since the funds were still going towards the public good even though the plaintiff-trustees disagreed. *Id.* at 936; see also Dana Brakman Reiser, "Nonprofit Takeovers: Regulating the Market for Mission Control," 2006 *BYU L. Rev.* 1181 (2006) (discussing attempts to change a charity's mission).

73. See, e.g., John K. Eason, "Motive, Duty, and the Management of Restricted Charitable Gifts," 45 *Wake Forest L. Rev.* 123 (2010) (discussing difficulties that can arise in honoring donors' intent with respect to restricted gifts); Gary, *supra* note 72 (same); see also Hussey, *supra* note 72 (same).

74. See, e.g., Evelyn Brody, "Charity Governance: What's Trust Law Got to Do with It?" 80 *Chi.-Kent. L. Rev.* 641, 642 (2005) ("When it comes to enforcing restrictions on gifts—even those made to corporate charities—regulators and courts commonly apply charitable trust doctrines"); see also Restatement (Second) of Trusts § 348 (1959) (stating that "[a] charitable trust is a fiduciary relationship with respect to property arising as a result of a manifestation of an intention to create it, and subjecting the person by whom the property is held to equitable duties to deal with the property for a charitable purpose").

75. See, e.g., Detroit Osteopathic Hosp. v. Johnson, 287 N.W. 466, 471 (Mich. 1939) ("There is no doubt that he and the other donors intended that the use of the property and the contemplated activity of this corporation should be purely eleemosynary and a contribution to the general welfare of the community, and that it should be carried on in a manner not inconsistent with the articles of association and the original by-laws. . . . [T]he original set-up is so clearly a fundamental element of the plan of the orig-

inal founders of this trust that it should be protected and preserved by equity. Especially is this true since jurisdiction over the control and execution of trusts is in general vested in the equity courts. . . . A material change in this provision of the by-laws should be and is perpetually enjoined; and also for the reasons hereinbefore noted defendants' attempted amendment of article V of the articles of association which would materially change the control and execution of this trust, should be and is held to be invalid. . . ."); see also Healy v. Loomis Inst., 128 A. 774 (Conn. 1925) (holding trustees required to follow intent of the will); Hite v. Queen's Hosp., 36 Haw. 250 (Haw. 1942) (approving of the charitable trust doctrine); John K. Eason, "Motive, Duty, and the Management of Restricted Charitable Gifts," 45 *Wake Forest L. Rev.* 123 (2010) (discussing donor intent).

76. Nonprofit corporation acts allow the board to rely on management unless there have been red flags that make reliance questionable. Model Nonprofit Corp. Act § 8.30(f) (2009). It would be good practice for the board or an applicable committee to engage in some independent investigation to reassure themselves of their ability to rely on management.

77. See, e.g., Evelyn Brody, "From the Dead Hand to the Living Dead: The Conundrum of Charitable Donor Standing," 41 *Ga. L. Rev.* 1183 (2007) (referring to the debate over hundreds of years but focusing on the issue of donor standing to enforce donor intent).

78. Ilana H. Eisenstein, Comment, "Keeping Charity in Charitable Trust Law: The Barnes Foundation and the Case for Consideration of Public Interest in Administration of Charitable Trusts," 151 *University of Pennsylvania Law Review* 1747, 1767 (2003) ("Enforcement of donor provisions furthers the general public welfare insofar as it creates a donor-friendly environment, where donors can be confident their wishes will continue to be enforced. . . . [T]he policy . . . encourage[s] donors to continue to dedicate their fortunes to public purposes. Public enforcement also benefits the donor by ensuring that his particularized vision . . . will endure.")

79. See, e.g., Robert S. Lesher, "The Non-Profit Corporation—A Neglected Stepchild Comes of Age," 22 *Bus. Law.* 951 (1967) (discussing nonprofit corporation status) ("The justification [for a higher fiduciary duty] seems to lie in the fact that the assets of the non-profit corporation come in many cases

from public solicitations or contributions and therefore are more like a trust res than corporate capital").

80. There have been some controversial examples of nonprofit director compensation. For example, Massachusetts Blue Cross voluntarily suspended directors' compensation in light of a mounting controversy. See, e.g., Robert Weisman, "Insurer's Board Suspends Own Pay," *Boston Globe* 1 (Mar. 9, 2011) (reporting that Blue Cross and Blue Shield of Massachusetts "voted to suspend their five-figure annual directors' payments").

81. Lesher, *supra* note.

82. See, e.g., Lesher, *supra* note.

83. See, e.g., Rummana Alam, Note, "Not What the Doctors Ordered: Nonprofit Hospitals and the New Corporate Governance Requirements," 2011 *U. Ill. L. Rev.* 229 (2011).

84. See, e.g., Carter G. Bishop, "The Deontological Significance of Nonprofit Corporate Governance Standards: A Fiduciary Duty of Care Without a Remedy," 57 *Cath. U. L. Rev.* 701 (2008) (arguing that the fiduciary duty of care plays an important role in curbing director misbehavior in the nonprofit context, but enforcement mechanisms could be greatly improved); Danne L. Johnson, "Seeking Meaningful Nonprofit Reform in a Post Sarbanes-Oxley World," 54 *St. Louis U. L. J.* 187 (2009) (arguing that reform is needed); see also James Fishman, "Standards of Conduct for Directors of Nonprofit Corporations," 7 *Pace L. Rev.* 389 (1986) (same).

# DAUGHTER DEAREST: NONPROFIT NEPOTISM

*Benjamin S. Bingle and C. Kenneth Meyer*

Dan Grayson felt physically and emotionally spent and was ready for a time-out from his daily office routines. He was a self-identified workaholic with broad experience and knew the responsibilities of his position. He was never given a project that he did not relish doing, but this orientation would soon become problematic. Accordingly, as the number of projects under his purview grew, he became stretched and stressed. Thus, it came as no surprise that he would be waiting with hurried anticipation for the Christmas–New Year break, a week of paid time off.

Generally, Dan enjoyed his position as program director for the Credit Builders Association (CBA), a national 501(c)(3) nonprofit organization that provided training and resources for low-income clients with credit problems. He loved being able to help vulnerable people establish creditworthiness and have a lasting impact on the lives of others in this way. Although national in scope, CBA had a staff of only ten employees—a tight-knit group that Tina Murphy, the CBA executive director, often referred to as "a family."

Dan Grayson did not consider his associates part of his own family, but he did enjoy the cordial and caring working relationships he had established with them. He found the organizational culture of CBA to be inviting, warm, and flexible, but he was not terribly comfortable with its lack of structure and standardization; he preferred organizational formality. For example, although organizational policies governing hiring and procurement (purchasing) were in place, they were essentially "copy-and-pasted" from examples downloaded from the Internet. Though elementary, these policies had been sufficient to pass muster for a national audit that CBA had undergone several years earlier.

The audit required mandatory written policies for the different functions and phases of human resources management, budgeting, and financial administration. However, the executive director and the board of directors did not look at these policies as amounting to much more than "window dressing." In short, as one director quipped, "CBA will comply until we die." It was also noteworthy that organizational decisions were rarely made on the substance of these "boiler-plated" policies.

Dan had five years of experience with the national organization in CBA's Prairie Island office and was the most tenured staff member other than Tina Murphy. The executive director relied on him completely as a trusted and valued coworker and sought out his advice and assistance when making hiring decisions, developing strategic partnership, and confronting organizational difficulties.

Even though he would have preferred a more structured work environment, Dan often laughed to himself about CBA not being policy-bound. When asked for his advice on important matters by

Tina, Dan would sometimes say jokingly, "This isn't in my job description, and it certainly is above my pay level!"

Dan had a few projects to finish before he left for the holidays. First and foremost, he had to prepare the agenda for the upcoming staff meeting at the end of the week. He would be meeting with staff from CBA's other branch offices, and they would present their quarterly progress reports. Then they would have a "holiday lunch," exchange some gifts, and head back to their offices to prepare for the anticipated break. Dan especially was looking forward to "putting his feet up" and taking off some well-deserved time.

The time finally came for the staff meeting, which "went off without a hitch." As Dan and his colleagues were gathering their materials and placing their laptops in the carrying cases inscribed with the CBA acronym, Tina Murphy nervously cleared her throat.

She said, "Excuse me, I have a couple of things I would like to cover that were not on the agenda."

Taken aback, all eyes and attention turned to her as she slowly rose from her chair and began to speak in an authoritative voice. She informed her associates about a commitment she had entered into with Banker's Loan and Trust (BLT) and how excited she was about the new partnership.

She said, "CBA would gain access to new revenue sources and much-needed credit lines. This will enable CBA to help qualified clients get reasonably low interest rates on their loans without meeting the 'normally' expected higher credit scores." Tina did not appear to be conversant with all of the details surrounding the newly formed agreement and did not itemize any of its positive or negative implications. However, she indicated that CBA would be moving ahead with the project because it would open some doors that had been closed and ultimately serve as a good source of unrestricted revenue. Her eyes darting around the conference table, she added that they would need to immediately staff up for the new venture and make a new hire.

Then, to everyone's astonishment, she told the group that she had already made the hiring decision: Mandy Murphy would be joining the staff and heading up the new initiative. While she elaborated, her staff responded with blank stares and stony silence; no words were exchanged, and no one made eye contact. She intoned with a raised voice, "I realize that the decision to hire my daughter may raise questions, but please know that I have thoroughly discussed this appointment with Mandy, and I guarantee you that there will be no conflict of interest. Initially I had some reservations about this hire, but as I talked it over with Mandy it became obvious she was a great candidate and a good fit for the organization. Also, time is a factor if we want to capitalize on the BLT project. To reiterate, and I can't say this more emphatically, there will be no conflict of interest or preferential treatment. As you get acquainted with Mandy, you will come to know that she is a perfect fit with our culture and staff."

As she wound down her remarks, the staff began to fidget nervously with the paperwork they had received during the staff meeting. Tina then asked if there were any thoughts or concerns on the matter. Of course, how could anyone express their concerns or reservations at this juncture? After all, the issue at hand was the hiring of the boss's daughter!

After a period of uncomfortable silence—a quietude that seemed to last for an eternity—Tina thanked them for their attention, wished them a joyful holiday season, and then gleefully closed the matter: "Okay, I just wanted to make sure that everyone was aware of what we have going on. I know Mandy looks forward to working with you. Who's ready for lunch? I'm excited that we will have the opportunity to share some quality time together before we go our separate ways."

Dan carpooled to the restaurant with two of his closest associates, in stark silence. As they waited to be seated, it was obvious that everyone was trying to erase from their minds what they had just heard at the staff meeting. Accordingly, they began to chitchat about their holiday plans and upcoming schedules.

As Dan sat down at the long table set by the restaurant staff, arranging his napkin and adjusting his tie, Tina came over and whispered in his ear, "Just give Mandy a week and she will show you why I hired her for the job. She'll be great!"

Once more, Dan could not believe his ears. Tina had singled him out in front of the entire staff in order to inform him of her daughter's greatness. Dan wondered if Tina actually thought that he was the only staff member who would question Mandy's hiring; if so, she had totally lost her footing in reality.

"What a way to begin a vacation," Dan muttered to himself as he drove back to the office. As he reflected on what had just transpired, he began to feel nauseated. Dan knew that there were no specific state laws against nepotism, but he could not fathom why Tina had approached this hire so differently from past CBA hiring decisions. Tina usually never made a hire without first consulting him. This time the position had not been advertised to ensure a large candidate pool, it had been filled before the funding had been established, and a detailed recruitment and selection process had not been satisfied.

The more Dan assessed what Tina had done the more his nausea turned into psychological disgust. He had a déjà vu moment as he recalled a conversation initiated by Tina six months earlier: she had told him that Mandy had been actively looking for a job the past year, without much luck. Obviously, Dan reasoned further, Tina knew this decision would reverberate throughout the organization. Why else would she have asked him to give Mandy a chance? Had Tina sprung this on the CBA staff right before the holiday lunch and their week off from work as a premeditated strategy? Or was the timing purely coincidental? Would any ill feeling, as Tina presumed, actually subside over time? Then Dan found himself wondering whether Mandy had submitted a résumé. Was she qualified for the task at hand when a position description had not yet been written? And what would happen if the partnership with BLT failed?

Dan knew that all of these questions needed to be probed, but who would risk jeopardizing their relationship with Tina by asking them?

As Dan entered the city limits of his hometown, he thought about the awkwardness of the next staff meeting. He knew that Mandy lived in a city on the East Coast: would she relocate or telecommunicate from a remote office located in her home? Would she be provided with a subsidy for a residential office with a computer, printer, Internet connection, and office supplies? Would CBA authorize air travel for her to attend staff meetings at the home base? Dan thought about the first staff meeting with both Tina and Mandy present. Would this "mother-daughter banquet" have other, possibly even greater, repercussions on the CBA staff, organizational culture, and balance sheet? These questions would eventually be answered, but meanwhile Dan was not only tired but had just had the "wind taken out of his sails."

One last idea occurred to Dan as he pulled into his garage: with the holidays coming up, was there any better way to show love for a daughter than to hire her?

· · ·

Dan Grayson enjoyed his vacation despite all that had transpired earlier in the CBA office, and despite the fact that, as much as he wanted to put the nepotism issue to rest, it seemed to arise as his conversations with visiting friends and family members drifted toward work. When Dan told them about the recent CBA hiring decision, the most common reactions were shock and disbelief. The circumstances surrounding the hiring and the blatant disregard for both the spirit and the letter of Equal Employment Opportunity Act regulations would surely have to be dealt with later.

After the holiday, Dan returned to his office and everything again seemed normal: mountains of paperwork to process, dozens of phone calls and hundreds of emails to answer—some important and some that should have been blocked. One of those emails came from a close colleague with the subject line "Get a load of this!" Attached to the email was a document entitled "Credit Builders Association Conflict of Interest Policy" (as displayed in Exhibit 1).

---

### EXHIBIT 1: CREDIT BUILDERS ASSOCIATION CONFLICT OF INTEREST POLICY

#### Definition: Organizational Conflict of Interest

A conflict of interest arises when a director or employee involved in a decision-making capacity is in the position to benefit, directly or indirectly, from his/her dealings with CBA or entities and/or individuals conducting business with CBA.

Examples of conflicts of interest include, but are not limited to, situations in which a director or employee of CBA:

1. Negotiates or approves a contract, purchase, lease, or other legally binding agreement on behalf of CBA and has a direct or indirect interest in, or receives personal benefit from CBA or the individual providing or receiving the goods or services;
2. Employs, endorses the employment of, or approves the employment of, on behalf of CBA, a person who is an immediate family member of the director or employee; and,
3. Sells products and/or services offered by CBA in competition with CBA.

#### Conflict of Interest Violations

Violations of this policy, including failure to disclose conflicts of interest, may result in termination of a director, executive director, or member of senior management (at the direction of the audit committee) or employee (at the direction of the executive director or chair of the audit committee).

---

Pressed for time, given the backlog of communication he had on his desk, Dan read the attachment quickly and gathered that Tina Murphy's decision to hire her daughter was a direct violation of the CBA policy and was "punishable" with termination. Yet he felt charitable toward his director, since she had never referenced this policy in discussing organizational decisions and might not have known that her new hire violated CBA policy. More problematic and troublesome to Dan was the revelation that the concern over nepotism had spread throughout the office. He knew this was not a good thing.

Fighting the urge, Dan finally opened his Internet browser and typed the words "workplace nepotism" into the search field. He wanted to become more informed about the consequences, legalities, and pros and cons of nepotism. He knew that nepotism had both proponents and detractors in industry and commerce. It was considered one of the many ways in which prospective employees were given preparation to join an organization; along with education, training, internships, apprenticeships, and other means of enhancing vocational aptitude. Nepotism was considered by some an "effective" way to socialize and assimilate prospective employees. Whatever the case, push had come to shove, and Dan and others would have to come to terms with CBA's newest employee.

## Questions and Instructions

1.  Is there any substance to Dan Grayson's questioning of Tina Murphy's hiring decision and the way it was done?
2.  Identify and elaborate on the implications of nepotism, both positive and negative.
3.  Assess the manner in which Tina Murphy announced the new hire. Was her timing premeditated, or was it coincidental that she announced her decision at the holiday staff meeting before a weeklong break?
4.  In consideration of the CBA conflict of interest policy, what responsibilities, if any, do the members of the CBA board of directors share in this case of nepotism?.
5.  Did the conflict of interest policy preclude the hiring of Mandy Murphy? Please explain.
6.  What are some of the considerations that the executive director should have weighed before hiring an immediate family member? Please elaborate. Would you have made a similar decision had you been in Tina Murphy's position? Why or why not?

# CONFLICTING VALUES

*Carol Sipfle and C. Kenneth Meyer*

On With Living (OWL) is a nonprofit organization dedicated to improving the physical and mental health of individuals age sixty-five and older. It is a local chapter of a national organization, the OWL Association, which had been in existence for nearly thirty years. Both the local chapter and the national organizational offer programs and services to help seniors stay healthy and fund research to find ways to prevent, treat, and cure diseases that affect people over sixty-five, such as Alzheimer's disease, diabetes, and heart disease.

Each local chapter is obligated to adhere to the positions of the national organization, and any modification or rejection of the national position is prohibited according to the "statement of relationship" signed by both parties. Any violation of this relationship agreement would result in "disaffiliation from the national organization," which local chapters attempt to avoid at all costs.

One position statement of the national organization took a firm position on stem cell research: "In keeping with our mission, we oppose any restriction or limitation on human stem cell research, provided that appropriate scientific review and ethical and oversight guidelines are in place." Without differentiating between embryonic and adult stem cell research, the position further asserted that the federal government was responsible for defining and monitoring scientific review and ethical and oversight guidelines.

Cora Shipman is the executive director of a local OWL chapter. Her responsibilities are typical for an executive director of a nonprofit organization—strategic planning, financial oversight, selecting and managing staff, fundraising, community relations, and board development. Her work with the organization's board of directors included identifying potential new board members. Upon their appointment to the board, Shipman would orient them to the organization and provide a general overview of the many tasks and responsibilities assumed by board members.

Cora was excited when she learned that Andres Vasquez wanted to serve on the chapter's board of directors. Andres worked as a banker and had the financial acumen that she sought on the board. He was viewed as an up-and-coming leader in the community and was passionate about accomplishing the mission of the organization. Also, he taught a public relations class at a local university and had access to students who could serve as interns or volunteers in supporting the organization's programs. His previous volunteer experience with the chapter made him a qualified candidate for the board of directors.

Andres was quickly nominated and elected to the board of directors. Within six months, he was asked to assume the role of vice president, putting him in line to be the board's next president. Although he was new to the board, things were going well and he has provided many valuable services to the organization. His energy and passion were contagious, and other board members became more involved.

OWL traditionally held several fundraising walks each spring, including one in Andres's community. Andres volunteered to serve on the event planning committee and assist in securing corporate sponsorships. He volunteered to visit a local insurance company and solicit sponsorship for the walk—a solicitation he felt comfortable making because his neighbor, John McNamara, served on the company's charitable giving committee.

Andres and John met over lunch and enjoyed the pleasantries of catching up with each other. When the subject switched to Andres's involvement with OWL and the upcoming walk, John was surprised to learn of Andres's involvement.

John said, "How can you volunteer for an organization that supports stem cell research?" Jokingly, he added, "I thought all good Christian men like you believe life begins with conception. Aren't those stem cells they use for research a human life? Are you comfortable in supporting an organization that destroys those cells for research purposes? And isn't it true that stem cells come from aborted fetuses?"

Andres was shocked and embarrassed and felt ill prepared to respond to John's comments. During his orientation, he had not inquired about the organization's position on stem cell research, nor had Cora mentioned it. In fact, the issue of stem cell research had not crossed his mind.

After ending the lunch hurriedly, he rushed to his office and called Cora. He told her about his conversation with his neighbor and his embarrassment in not being able to provide an informed and definitive response. Cora expressed concern for his embarrassment and provided the clarification that he sought. She once more stated the position of OWL and reminded him that the chapter was bound to the positions of the national office. She further explained that OWL had not actually funded research involving stem cells. She also explained that the policy was in support of its mission and that it allowed the organization to keep all options open for research, both now and in the future. She assured him that no organization obtained stem cells from aborted fetuses. At least for the short term, Andres was satisfied with her response.

However, Andres struggled with this new knowledge over the next week. His personal belief was that life indeed began at the moment of conception. According to his beliefs, stem cells were not simply a collection of cells but a living human being, and to destroy those cells for the purpose of research—even if that research was designed to save lives—was immoral. While he was proud of his association with OWL, he felt like a hypocrite. His personal beliefs were incongruent with the position of an organization he publicly supported and on whose board he gave direction.

The situation intensified over the weekend when a letter to the editor about OWL appeared in the local newspaper. Written by the president of a right-to-life organization, the letter called for a boycott of OWL's upcoming walk. It cited the organization's position on stem cell research and called on the public to stop contributing to OWL and other organizations that approved of this kind of research. After Andres attended church on Sunday, several members of the congregation approached him and asked for his reactions to the letter to the editor.

On Monday morning, Andres called Cora and discussed his beliefs, but also assured her of his commitment to the organization. He proposed a compromise—a solution that he believed would reconcile the conflict between his personal beliefs and the organizational position. He proposed that the OWL board of directors pass a resolution to reject the national position and develop its own position to oppose stem cell research. He envisioned using his public relations knowledge to make this rejection a newsworthy event. He acknowledged that the local chapter would be viewed as a "maverick" in the community by standing up to the more powerful national organization. Andres was also convinced that the maverick position would raise public awareness about the organization and actually increase participation in the upcoming walk.

Cora knew that rejecting a national position statement was both futile and foolhardy and would result in disaffiliation from the national office. It would also mean a loss of valuable national and local support and access to important resources—a price she was not willing to pay because of one board member's personal beliefs. She believed that Andres's opposition to stem cell research was a minority view and that, in reality, "most people" supported this kind of research, which might lead to cures for devastating diseases. She looked to other board members for counsel and learned that most of them rejected Andres's position and proposal. The board cautioned Cora about the consequences of aligning the organization's positions with those of a particular religious group or political party.

Andres soon realized that his compromise would not be supported by the executive director and his fellow board members and withdrew the proposal. Ultimately, he realized the impossibility of reconciling his personal beliefs with the organization's position on stem cell research. He called Cora and resigned from the board of directors. Cora accepted the resignation with mixed feelings. OWL had lost one of its most vocal advocates and promising leaders. Yet she was relieved that her organization would avoid a confrontation with its national office and the serious consequences of disaffiliation. Similarly, she was relieved that the organization's limited human and financial resources could be devoted to serving its mission rather than engaging in a conflict that would result in a no-win outcome.

## Questions and Instructions

1. What criteria should a nonprofit organization utilize in the identification, selection, and appointment of members of the board of directors? Please explain.
2. Contact at least three nonprofit organizations and secure their requirements for membership on their board of directors, trustees, or governors. Present to the class the attributes and characteristics that these organizations use in the appointment process.
3. In OWL's applications for employment, would you recommend that Cora have the human resources department spell out OWL's position on stem cell research on the form? Would opposition to stem cell research be sufficient for disqualification for a position in the organization? Please elaborate.
4. Would it be advisable for Cora to write a rebuttal to the letter to the editor and clarify OWL's position on stem cell research, as well as on attendant issues related to euthanasia and death and dying? If so, please provide an example of what you would write. Alternatively, delineate other actions you would deem appropriate for the executive director to take.

# PART III

# Strategic Leadership*

Interest in leadership has been expressed for centuries. Philosophers, religious figures, politicians, and scientists have all contributed treatises on leadership. In addition, a plethora of do-it-yourself volumes abound. Truly, there are thousands of books on leadership that seemingly offer something for everyone. A short list of titles includes *Leadership A to Z: A Guide for the Appropriately Ambitious, Ultimate Leadership, Leadership Passion, Leadership with a Feminine Cast, Why Leaders Can't Lead, Leadership Is an Art, Leadership: When the Heat's On,* and even, for the deeply discouraged, *Leadership for the Disillusioned.* Some authors have written biographies of famous leaders, while others offer step-by-step approaches that provide the faithful follower with a road map to leadership success. Oh, if it were only that easy!

There is no shortcut to becoming an effective leader. For all that has been written and said, the struggle to recruit, grow, establish, and maintain effective leadership remains a constant concern for all types of organizations, including nonprofits. Chief among these concerns is the ability to recruit good people. Leadership in nonprofit organizations is vested in both a voluntary board of directors (see Part I) and compensated officers, including the executive director[†] and, in larger agencies, a development director, chief financial officer, program managers, and others.

A conservative assumption is that the sector will need "330,000 new senior executives over the next decade."[1] Finding and attracting people to serve in these high-level positions will be a challenge. For example, a survey conducted in 2007 with over 6,000 potential nonprofit leaders showed that although the charity world is expected to require "tens of thousands of new leaders within the next decade," two-thirds of those surveyed said that they did not want to be an executive director or were unsure whether the top spot at a nonprofit organization would be among their goals.[2]

Likewise, the Urban Institute's National Survey of Nonprofit Governance found that the recruitment of new members was a key leadership challenge for nonprofit boards. "Seventy percent of leaders surveyed reported at least some difficulty attracting new members and 20 percent had a lot of difficulty."[3] Part of the problem is that nonprofit compensation levels have lagged behind similarly situated executives in businesses and government agencies. Therefore, turnover is a constant concern. "It is one thing to take a low paying job just out of college to follow your bliss, and another thing entirely to support a family or face retirement on a $40,000 salary, particularly in more urban areas."[4]

---

*Peter M. Nelson contributed substantially to drafting this introductory essay.

†Typically compensated, but in many smaller organizations not compensated.

## Leadership and Management

The study of leadership has typically followed one of two paths. One focuses on the individuals who practice leadership, while the other analyzes the systems that need leaders.[5] "In the first approach, leaders commonly conduct assessments of their organizations and their environments that provide the context, note their constraints and priorities, take stock of their abilities and ultimately act concretely (behaviors) and in patterns (styles). In the second approach, a network or system is analyzed, its needs are diagnosed and ideal leaders styles and behaviors are deduced from that analysis."[6]

Many have sought to distinguish between *leadership* and *management*. Although these two functions and roles overlap substantially, the term *manager* connotes that authority has been formally granted to an individual by an organization. Management involves power—legitimate formal authority—that is granted to the occupant of a position by a higher organizational authority. Responsibility and accountability for the use of organizational resources accompany the power accorded to a manager or director.

In contrast, the term *leader* implies effective use of influence that is independent of the formal authority granted to an individual because of position. Leadership cannot be granted to a person by a higher authority; rather, those who decide to follow bestow it on an individual. Whereas managers and directors have formal authority, leaders have the informal ability to get things done by attracting and influencing followers. Today most believe that effective managers in nonprofit organizations must also be leaders.

Until about 1950, the field of leadership research studied the personal traits and skills of leaders in attempts to determine which were most important. Since then, most of the research has looked at leadership styles, the roles of organizational leaders and other contextual factors, leadership competencies, gender, leader-follower relations, leaders as visionaries, ethical leadership, integrity and stewardship, leadership as collaboration, and the list goes on.[7] Although many unanswered questions remain about leadership, two important practical points stand virtually uncontested: (1) leadership involves a relationship between people in which influence and power are unevenly distributed, formally or informally; and (2), a leader cannot function in isolation. For there to be a leader, there must be followers.[8]

### Ethical Leadership

In "Ethics in Nonprofit Management: Creating a Culture of Integrity," Thomas Jeavons explores the importance of an ethical organizational culture and concludes that responsibility for creating an ethical culture lies at the feet of organizational leaders.[9] Lack of an ethical base ultimately destroys a nonprofit organization—and other organizations around it.

Unfortunately, the problem of unethical behavior has not dwindled since Jeavons's piece first appeared in 1994, and when one nonprofit organization is discovered to be dishonest, other nonprofits suffer: the level of public and regulatory scrutiny of nonprofits has never been higher. Concern about the ethical leadership (or the lack thereof) of nonprofit organizations has moved onto the front pages of newspapers, trade magazines, and professional journals. It is desirable to have an ethical organizational culture not only to avoid legal problems but also as a good business strategy. The study of leadership ethics thus is of high practical importance for nonprofit executives and trustees.

All students of the nonprofit sector are familiar with at least one or two scandals that have hit the front pages and have shaken their heads at the lines that were crossed and the social contracts that were violated. One of these, EduCap Inc., a multibillion-dollar student loan charity, was found by the Internal Revenue Service to have abused its tax-exempt status by charging excessive interest on loans and providing millions in compensation and lavish perks to its CEO and her husband, including use of the organization's $31 million private jet for family and friends.[10] Yet, other difficult but less blatantly unethical situations are also likely to cross the path of a nonprofit leader sooner or later. For example, is it acceptable—ethical—for a nonprofit organization that serves victims of hunger and poverty to create a news story using a composite victim? Do the photographs used in a news story or brochure need to show the real victims or recipients of services? Should a leader in a nonprofit accept large donations for the organization from a polluter if the organization's mission is environmental protection? Most nonprofit organization leaders must eventually deal with and ultimately resolve this type of ethical problem.

## Who Leads a Nonprofit Organization?

Historically, the nonprofit organization literature has placed responsibility for leadership squarely on the board officers, usually the president or chair of the board.[11] Under the traditional leadership model, the executive director (or CEO) is the chief implementer of board policies. From this perspective, to the extent that an executive director plays a central leadership role, it is for purposes of garnering and mobilizing the support necessary to accomplish the board's plans. This traditional model of how nonprofit organization leadership should work faded in the 1980s. For example, Terry McAdam and David Gies argued for "leadership partnerships" between board officers and executive directors, with explicit understandings about mutual expectations.[12] Using a model of organizational life-cycle stages, Michael Ostrowski explained that leadership needs and relationships between a board of trustees and staff are dynamic.[13]

In more current models, leadership in the nonprofit organization is grounded in the executive director. Although the traditional model argued that leadership should reside with the board of directors, in practice it has been shown repeatedly that leadership is exercised significantly by executive directors.[14] In a study of nonprofit organizations in the Kansas City area, Robert Herman and Richard Heimovics concluded:

> We believe that in most established, staffed nonprofit organizations chief executives come to be expected by board members, other staff, and themselves to be finally responsible for the successes and failures of the organization. . . . We discovered that . . . effective executives provided substantially more leadership for their boards than those in the comparison group; that is, they took responsibility for providing board-centered leadership.[15]

Although a handful of authors continue to debate where ultimate leadership resides in a nonprofit organization, most observers today have moved on to an understanding that leadership is usually shared between a few individuals on the board of directors and the executive director. Their newer collaborative models reflect the view that "governance is a team sport."[16] In *Forces for Good: The Six Practices of High-Impact Nonprofits*, Leslie Crutchfield and Heather McLeod Grant assert:

> Strong leadership doesn't only exist at the very top of high-impact nonprofits; rather it extends throughout the organization. CEOs of high-impact nonprofits . . . use their leadership to empower others. And . . . they almost all have large, enduring and engaged boards. They have distributed leadership throughout their organization, and others throughout their larger network of allies and affiliates as well.[17]

As shown in the selection from Barbara Crosby and John Bryson's *Leadership for the Common Good* that is reprinted in this part, the hierarchical organization model with leadership at the top charting the course of action does not capture the complexity of leadership given the preponderance of "wicked problems" that seep across organizational boundaries. Today a nonprofit executive director is but one of many policy actors, and the nonprofit organization is but one of many in a jointly inhabited sea of public problems and concerns. Nonprofit executive directors and managers must be able to navigate convoluted seas and recognize the myriad actors, places, and points where opportunities or dangers may lie at any given time. They also must strive to use shared power to become connected to other effective leaders who can guide their organizations responsibly through those seas.

## Conclusions

Executive directors are managers and—hopefully—organizational leaders who are appointed by the board of trustees, whereas board members are elected to their seats. A board's power to hire and fire the executive director implies that the board is the hierarchical superior, and the logical conclusion is that the board—especially the board president—is the rightful leader in a nonprofit organization. Although it is true that leadership rests in part on the authority that laws give to the board and through it to other positions in an organization, this is not the whole story. Leadership emerges when others willingly follow a person's vision, suggestions, requests, and directives. Leadership can transcend hierarchical superiority and even position-based legal authority. Leadership is created by followers, whereas management is created by authority. Leadership is transitory and fragile, since what is created separate from authority can also leave or be destroyed.

All leaders have a responsibility to help ensure an ethical organizational culture.[18] Lack of an ethical base ultimately destroys a nonprofit organization—and other organizations around it. Unfortunately, the problem of unethical behavior has not dwindled, and the level of public and regulatory scrutiny of nonprofits has never been higher. Concern about ethical leadership (or the lack thereof) of nonprofit organizations has moved onto the front pages of newspapers, trade magazines, and professional journals. Besides the obvious desirability of an ethical organizational culture to avoid legal problems, it also is good business strategy. The study of leadership ethics thus is of high practical importance for nonprofit executives and trustees.

In nonprofit organizations, effective management depends on effective leadership. Newer models of leadership recognize the importance of collaboration, and some models locate leadership in network relationships rather than organizational position. The primary purposes of leadership in nonprofit organizations have always been to help followers engage in activities that advance organizational missions and ensure survival while at the same time creating an organizational culture that respects employees and is centered on ethical values. Any serious attempt to understand the nature of managerial responsibility in the nonprofit sector must consider not only what the manager owes the organization but also what the organization, the sector, and the society owe the manager. "It is a pledge, a promise, a moral pact; and the pact goes both ways."[19]

## Readings Reprinted in Part III

The first reading reprinted in Part III has been retained from the very first edition of *Understanding Nonprofit Organizations* because it continues to stand the test of time. Stephen Block's essay "Executive Director" examines the differences between leaders and managers in for-profit and nonprofit organizations and asks: "How does a person become an executive director?"[20] Block's finding that "executive director applicants comprise candidates with varied backgrounds" continues to hold true today. In a recent study, David Suarez examined the career paths of nonprofit executives and found that "leaders with applied credentials are common in the nonprofit sector including those with advanced degrees in, for example, social work, the arts, counseling, education and a wide variety of others."[21]

Block also explores the competencies required of an effective executive director. Using Henry Mintzberg's model, he explores the ten roles of an executive director within the framework of three sets of behavior: *informational* (monitor, disseminator, spokesperson), *interpersonal* (figurehead, leader, liaison), and *decisional* (entrepreneur, disturbance handler, resource allocator, negotiator).[22] Each role comports with the expectations for executive directors under both old and new models of leadership.

In the second reading, "When No One Is in Charge: The Meaning of Shared Power," Barbara Crosby and John Bryson expose the myth of leadership as "something" situated at the apex of a hierarchical, bureaucratic organization. Models that portray nonprofit leadership as "an individual (president, CEO, director) or small group (board or top management team) that establishes organizational direction, determines guiding policies, and sends directives downward to a group of middle managers" do not describe the reality of nonprofit leadership. "Embedded in this ideal type is the assumption that the organization 'contains' a problem area, or need, and engages in highly rational, expert-based planning and decision making to resolve it." As the authors note, this depiction captures neither the nature of public problems nor the dynamics of the policymaking field. Seldom do nonprofit leaders reach their mission-related goals by confronting an isolated problem using a purely technical solution. Today, as Crosby and Bryan convincingly argue, the nonprofit organization shares power within a field of networked organizations. The methods and resources of sharing may include information, informal or formal coordination, shared power, and shared authority. The network may comprise units, departments, individuals, or organizations, and the organization is part of a variety of external networks that are fluid and chaotic. These organizational and environmental realities affect leadership strategies and require leaders to share space and work collectively with others for common but sometimes conflicting goals. "No single person, group, or individual is 'in charge' of the problem, yet many organizations are affected or have partial responsibility to act. In effect, they have a share of the power that is required for remedying the problem."

One leadership activity that has changed with the shared power paradigm is planning. Strategic planning has become a popular means for nonprofit leaders working with networked stakeholders to clarify common values, establish priorities, and seek to have an impact on the community. The movement has been from long-range planning, which is depicted as "generally considered to assume that current knowledge about future conditions is sufficiently reliable to ensure the plan's reliability over the duration of its implementation," to strategic planning, which "assumes that an organization must respond to an environment that is dynamic and hard to predict."[23] This means of organizational planning is consistent with Crosby and Bryson's depiction of the network playing field.

As with strategic planning (a staple in the nonprofit leadership toolbox for the past two decades), effective leadership today is concerned with building on strengths and tending to weaknesses, as well as with exploiting opportunities and minimizing threats. Leadership includes the responsibility to oversee the internal management of an organization's resources and mission-related goals, but it also requires joint efforts toward outcomes that a cadre of nonprofit leaders (among others) may be pursuing. Taken together, the readings reprinted in Part III shed light on the roles and responsibilities of the executive director and also show that he or she is not an island, but rather part of an archipelago pursuing collective efforts.

## Case Studies in Part III

The first case study, "The Downward Spiral of Founder's Hospital," places the reader in the role of a management consultant to a nonprofit organization that has experienced significant turnover among executive directors. In addition, the hospital is facing financial problems and a loss of confidence among key stakeholders. As the consultant is presented with data and opinions, he must make sense of the organizational, budgetary, and environmental factors that are affecting the success of Founder's Hospital.

In the second case study, "Between a Rock and a Boulder," the executive vice president of a nonprofit association learns the hard way about the "winds of change" that time may usher in when working with governing committees. The reader is asked to consider and explain how decisions approved at one point in time can become "undone" in a moment's notice.

## Notes

1. Thomas J. Tierney, "Understanding the Nonprofit Sector's Leadership Deficit," in *The Jossey-Bass Reader on Nonprofit and Public Leadership,* edited by James L. Perry (San Francisco: Jossey-Bass, 2010), 551–560.

2. Survey participants were drawn from two groups: members of Idealist.org and individuals who participated in workshops and conferences sponsored by CompassPoint. Each group comprised people who had demonstrated an interest in a nonprofit career. See Jennifer C. Berkshire, "Potential Charity Leaders See Top Job as Unappealing, New Survey Reveals," *Chronicle of Philanthropy,* March 6, 2008.

3. Francie Ostrower, "A Better Way to Deal with the Leadership Crisis," *Chronicle of Philanthropy,* May 29, 2008.

4. Leslie Crutchfield and Heather McLeod Grant, "Sustaining Impact," in Perry, *The Jossey-Bass Reader on Nonprofit and Public Leadership,* 451–478.

5. Montgomery Van Wart, "Two Approaches to Leadership," *Public Administration Review* 70, no. 4 (July–August 2010): 650–652.

6. Ibid., 650.

7. Montgomery Van Wart and Lisa A. Dicke, eds., *Administrative Leadership in the Public Sector* (Armonk, NY: M. E. Sharpe, 2008).

8. Fred E. Fiedler and Martin M. Chemers, *Leadership Styles and Effective Management* (Glenview, IL: Scott Foresman, 1974).

9. Thomas H. Jeavons, "Ethics in Nonprofit Management: Creating a Culture of Integrity," in *The Jossey-Bass Handbook of Nonprofit Leadership and Management,* edited by Robert D. Herman (San Francisco: Jossey-Bass, 1994), 184–207.

10. Deborah L. Rhode and Amanda K. Packel, "Ethics and Nonprofits," *Stanford Social Innovation Review* (Summer 2009): 28; Sharyl Attkisson, "Student Loan Charity Under Fire: Is One Education Charity Abusing Their Status with Lavish Travel and Huge Salaries?" *CBS News,* March 2, 2009; Sharyl Attkisson, "Loan Charity's High-Flying Guests Exposed: Educational Nonprofit Under Fire for Transporting Politicians with Money That Could Have Gone to Students," *CBS News,* March 3, 2009.

11. Alfred R. Stern, "Instilling Activism in Trustees," *Harvard Business Review* (January–February 1980): 24–32.

12. Terry W. McAdam and David L. Gies, "Managing Expectations: What Effective Board Members Ought to Expect from Nonprofit Organizations," *Journal of Voluntary Action Research* 14, no. 4 (October–December 1985): 77–88.

13. Michael Ostrowski, "Nonprofit Boards of Directors," in *The Nonprofit Organization: Essential Readings,* edited by David L. Gies, J. Steven Ott, and Jay M. Shafritz (Fort Worth, TX: Harcourt Brace, 1990), 182–189.

14. E. G. Knauft, Renee A. Berger, and Sandra T. Gray, *Profiles of Excellence: Achieving Success in the Nonprofit Sector* (San Francisco: Jossey-Bass, 1991), 9.

15. Robert D. Herman and Richard D. Heimovics, *Executive Leadership in Nonprofit Organizations* (San Francisco: Jossey-Bass, 1991), 55, 57; see also Robert D. Herman and Richard D. Heimovics, "Critical Events

in the Management of Nonprofit Organizations: Initial Evidence," *Nonprofit and Voluntary Sector Quarterly* 18, no. 2 (Summer 1989): 119–131.

16. Doug Eadie, *Extraordinary Board Leadership* (Boston: Jones and Barlett, 2009), 21.

17. Leslie Crutchfield and Heather McLeod Grant, *Forces for Good: The Six Practices of High-Impact Non-profits* (San Francisco: Jossey-Bass/Wiley, 2008), 156.

18. Thomas H. Jeavons, "Ethics in Nonprofit Management: Creating a Culture of Integrity," in Herman, *The Jossey-Bass Handbook of Nonprofit Leadership and Management*, 184–207; see also James H. Svara, *The Ethics Primer for Public Administrators in Government and Nonprofit Organizations* (Burlington, MA: Jones & Bartlett, 2014), 12.

19. Michael O'Neill, "Responsible Management in the Nonprofit Sector," in *The Future of the Nonprofit Sector*, edited by Virginia A. Hodgkinson and Richard W. Lyman (San Francisco: Jossey-Bass, 1989), 272.

20. Stephen R. Block, "Executive Director," in *The International Encyclopedia of Public Policy and Adminis-tration*, edited by Jay M. Shafritz (Boulder, CO: Westview Press, 1998), 832–837.

21. David F. Suarez, "Street Credentials and Management Backgrounds: Careers of Nonprofit Executives in an Evolving Sector," *Nonprofit and Voluntary Sector Quarterly* 39, no. 4 (August 2010): 696–716, 702.

22. Henry Mintzberg, *The Nature of Managerial Work* (New York: Harper & Row, 1973).

23. Michael Allison and Jude Kaye, *Strategic Planning for Nonprofit Organizations: A Practical Guide and Workbook*, 2nd ed. (San Francisco: Wiley, 2005), 7.

## CHAPTER 6

# Executive Director

## STEPHEN R. BLOCK

["E]xecutive director" is] a title that accompanies the management role for the highest-ranking staff position in a private nonprofit organization. In some states, the heads of public agencies are also referred to as executive directors.

Early developments in commerce, followed by improved manufacturing technologies during the Industrial Revolution, led to stronger interests in management techniques during the late 1800s and into the twentieth century. During the same time period that scientific management principles were being advanced, Congress in 1894 created public policy that formally supported tax exemptions for charitable organizations. The development of management as a field of professional practice began to flourish during the first 20 years of the twentieth century. As attention to university programs developed and societies concerned with management practices formed, the importance of senior management positions became significant, not only in business but also in public administration and organizations of the private nonprofit sector.

The title and position of executive director is equivalent to chief executive officer (CEO) or president, both of which are executive management titles generally used in for-profit organizations to designate the foremost decisionmaker who is in charge of operations.

Among private nonprofit organizations, the title of president is often reserved for the highest-ranking volunteer (sometimes called the chief volunteer officer or otherwise known as chairperson of the board of directors). In some nonprofit organizations, however, the corporate title of president is substituted for the title of executive director. In such situations, the highest-ranking volunteer will be referred to as the chairperson of the board of directors.

The relationship between the chairperson, the board of directors, and the executive director position is initially forged through the process of hiring the executive director. In fact, the board of directors has ultimate responsibility for hiring and establishing the compensation of the executive director. The board is also responsible for evaluating the performance of the executive director and rewarding (or terminating, if required) him or her.

Once hired, the executive director may assume many governance and management roles and responsibilities. Though boards of directors can never truly delegate their legal obligations and fiduciary responsibilities, they are known

Originally published in *The International Encyclopedia of Public Policy and Administration,* edited by Jay M. Shafritz. Copyright © 1998 by Jay Shafritz. Reprinted by permission of Westview Press, a member of Perseus Books Group.

to assign (or expect) their executive directors to help them fulfill their roles as effective board members. In some organizations, the role of the executive director is not shaped through the board's articulation of expectations, but rather the position is shaped by the executive director's experiences and know-how. In public sector organizations, the executive director has a responsibility to manage a department. Above all, the focus of the position is to support the policies and direction of the elected official who appointed the executive director.

## How Does a Person Become an Executive Director?

How a person becomes an executive director of a private nonprofit organization may not always follow a clear and logical career path. There is much anecdotal evidence to suggest that many executive directors have been hired on the basis of their programmatic skills and not on their qualifications as executive managers. Laurence J. Peter coined the phrase "the Peter Principle," to identify this type of organizational ascendency into positions beyond one's competency. For example, competent social workers known for outstanding family counseling skills can find themselves hired into executive director positions on the basis of their proven clinical activities. In this example, the social worker may have no training or education in management, no experience with policy implementation, or no other competencies usually required of the executive director position. Consequently, the person is promoted into the highest of management level positions and removed from the one position in which he or she excelled.

More recently, hiring pools of executive director applications comprise candidates with varied backgrounds. Some include individuals with program expertise along with a mix of individuals who have been trained or educated in nonprofit management. Many management oriented candidates seek management expertise through nonprofit management workshops, conferences, and continuing education opportunities, some of which lead to a certificate in nonprofit management from a host college or university. In more recent years, executive director position applicants may include individuals who have earned graduate degrees in nonprofit management or degrees from other disciplines that offer a concentration in nonprofit management, such as those degrees or areas of academic concentration available in the fields of human services, business, or public administration.

Whether individuals have backgrounds emphasizing program capabilities, management skills, or a combination of the two, there does not appear to be a shortage of candidates who willingly express their interest in vacant executive director positions, for a variety of reasons. The size of a nonprofit organization's budget and the complexity of the operations can be factors in attracting an executive director. Salary range and fringe benefits for the executive director position may influence both the size of an applicant pool and the characteristics and competencies of the candidates. For example, one would expect an executive director hired at US$20,000 a year to have competencies different from those of an individual who is paid US$100,000 a year. One might also expect that the larger, more-established nonprofit organization will be able to attract the most experienced and seasoned of executive directors, but the smaller-budgeted organization might be a valuable training ground for the newer and emerging executive manager.

Other important factors that have a bearing on the interest level of qualified applicants include the organization's mission, beliefs, and values; the geographical location of the organization; the reputation of the organization; the status of the board members in the community; the extent of (under-, over-, or balanced) involvement of board members in the organization; and the clarity of the board's expectations of the executive director.

When an organization is searching for a new executive director, it is important to identify clearly the skills and characteristics necessary for leading the organization toward the achievement of its mission and vision. When the board is clear about its organization's direction and purpose, the board has a higher probability of selecting the right person. The most critical factors are a candidate's knowledge about the role of executive director, proven management and human resource skills, and solid (and candid) references.

## What Are Required Competencies for an Executive Director?

The executive director position comprises many multifaceted roles and responsibilities. The effective executive director possesses a range of qualifications that take into account personal characteristics, skills, knowledge, and abilities. Management expert Henry Mintzberg (1973) suggested that the position of an executive manager is organized around ten roles within three sets of behaviors: (1) four decisional roles (entrepreneur, disturbance handler, resource allocator, negotiator); (2) three informational roles (monitor, disseminator, spokesperson); and (3) three interpersonal roles (figurehead, leader, liaison). Mintzberg's concepts have also been applied to managing nonprofit organizations.

Daily work experiences of the nonprofit executive director illustrate the continuum of skills and abilities that are required of the position. Since executive directors tend to be involved in many activities simultaneously, their management focus must continually shift. This shifting can cause a blurring of the boundaries among the various roles categorized as either informational, decisional, or interpersonal, as illustrated in the following scenarios.

1. *Informational.* The executive director monitors the opinions of local stakeholders to determine if there will be any impact on the organization's reputation and its ability to raise private funds. This information is shared (as disseminator) in different formats with key staff and board members in order to plan appropriate responses and fundraising activities. The executive director speaks (spokesperson) before civic groups and corporate funders to explain the mission and direction of the organization.

2. *Interpersonal.* The executive director represents the organization and its board of directors (as figurehead) at important community meetings. At a monthly meeting the executive director (as leader) encourages the staff to work on improving its skills and offers guidance for exploring individual beliefs in comparison with the organization's mission and purpose. The executive director (as liaison) meets with the staff of the mayor's office to determine (as entrepreneur) if local community development funds exist to help finance a volunteer youth program.

3. *Decisional.* In response to a negative article in the local newspaper, the executive director (as disturbance handler) reacts to the external pressures to fend off a public relations crisis. In preparation for drafting the coming year's budget for the board's consideration, the executive director studies the agency's finances (as resource allocator) to shift the revenues among the key priorities and programs of the organization. The executive director also plays a negotiating role among department managers and board members with regard to establishing funding priorities and eliminating some favorite but underfunded projects.

Demands of the executive director position will vary among nonprofit organizations. Regardless of the organizational complexity of the position, the job generally requires some functional ability to shift attention back and forth between internal and external issues. Executive directors are expected to have the skill to assess their organizations' strengths and weaknesses and to analyze the results of the information. The results can be used to develop a purposeful and strategic course of action, such as designing activities to improve or maintain the capability of staff or to protect or enhance the quality of the organization's service delivery system.

The ability to project how current events or emerging trends in the community will positively or adversely impact the nonprofit organization is another critical management trait that is necessary for controlling or influencing outcomes and for planning thoughtful strategic reactions. The executive director is also expected to respond to the pressures of the external environment by developing a network of community supports and collaborative working relationships.

Paying attention to the organization's internal and external environments is just one of many important components of the executive director's job. In fact, there are several essential management tasks in which the results-oriented executive director will participate, lead, or carry out explicitly or implicitly.

The tasks are as follows: *mission development, visioning, goal setting.* The executive director will have an opportunity to assist the board, staff, and other community members in the creation of an organizational mission statement or to annually review and, if necessary, revise the organization's mission statement. The mission statement is a reflection of the needs of the community and represents a collective vision of what the community could strive to become as a result of the efforts of the organization. By exerting leadership, the executive director is in a position to interpret the significance of the mission statements for establishing operational goals and objectives, recommending policy changes, and for motivating staff,

volunteers, and others to believe in the importance of the mission.

### Planning

The executive director plays an instrumental role in working with the board and staff to use the mission statement as a guide for establishing short-term and long-term goals and objectives of the organization and for developing action steps for implementation. The executive director is positioned to communicate to staff the purpose, time lines, and strategies of the plan. Managing the resources of money and people to accomplish the organization's plan and monitoring and developing strategies when obstacles impede progress are also major responsibilities of the executive director. The executive director assists the board of directors with its duties by assuring an evaluation of the plan's progress and reporting its results and, likewise, communicating the need to revise aspects of the plan on an ongoing basis.

### Organizing

In practice, the executive director is responsible for determining what monetary resources and people are needed to accomplish an organization's plan, projects, and program services. Structuring the staffing patterns of the organization and establishing performance standards are other management responsibilities of the executive director.

### Motivating

It is sometimes said that an effective manager is one who is able to get things accomplished through the work of other people. The complexity of motivating individuals either through intrinsic or extrinsic rewards requires an understanding of basic human nature. The effective executive director is one who understands the varying needs of individuals and responds by providing enriching opportunities, which build a sense of spirit and belief in the organization. If the director stimulates an interest in the work of the organization, the staff, board members, and other volunteers will use their energies, knowledge, and skills to achieve accomplishments for the organization and to enhance its service capacity.

## Decisionmaking

Herbert A. Simon once suggested that decisionmaking is synonymous with managing. Decisionmaking is a pervasive management task of the executive director and includes making a choice among varying alternatives and weighing the likely consequences and risks of choosing one alternative over another. The effective executive director is one who uses a model or framework for approaching complex and far-reaching organizational decisions. Of particular importance is the recurring task of seeking and analyzing information through informal and formal communication channels that are internal and external to the organization. Information is a necessary ingredient for recognizing the need to make a decision and for serving as a pertinent database for developing a decision. Savvy executive directors also monitor reactions to their decisions and use the feedback as additional critical bits of data for ongoing decisionmaking.

## Delegating

To be efficient and effective, the executive director must be able to recognize which aspects of his or her work can be scheduled or reorganized for attention during another time period. Also, it is important to identify which portions of the job can be accomplished by assigning responsibility to others within the organization or by making temporary assignments to outside consultants. Appropriate delegation of the execu-

tive director's work assignments to staff requires an understanding of staff's skills and abilities; a sensitivity to its workload demands; a level of trust in staff's ability and willingness to accomplish tasks at a level that will meet or exceed the executive director's own standards; and the capacity to thank staff for helping out, either on temporary or permanently assigned tasks. Even though executive directors can never truly delegate away their organizational management responsibilities, their uses of delegation can help to alleviate the stresses of work overload, which can adversely impact outcomes.

## Coordinating

Executive directors of moderate to large organizations have a management challenge of coordinating the variety of tasks and activities that take place among different specialized departments within an organization. In addition, they need to assure the coordination of work activities that occur up and down the organizational hierarchy. Almost thirty years ago, the term "integration" was introduced, referring to the process of managing the linkages across the formal structures of the organization. Without attending to the function of coordination, departments and staff may work at cross-purposes and thereby waste resources and adversely impact the opportunity for organizational success. The coordination of tasks and activities is also at play in smaller nonprofit organizations; due to smaller size and fewer staff, the executive director may have a greater level of participation in the different activities, thus minimizing the coordination challenges.

## Reporting

The accountability concept of reporting is tied to the idea of lines of responsibilities and a chain of command. Different individuals in the organization are responsible for a variety of outcomes and are responsible to their supervisor for reporting on the progress of achieving assignments, goals, and objectives. The aggregate of all of this information is eventually reported by senior management staff to the executive director, who similarly must report on the organization's progress to the board of directors. The executive director's responsibility is to assure that there is no confusion in the lines of reporting, and that staff have available to them the proper supports and supervision that enable them to do their work and report their outcomes.

### Supervising

The executive director must rely heavily on the capabilities of staff to accomplish the organization's plans; therefore, human resource management is central to an effective organization. In addition to the ability to motivate staff, coordinate activities, and delegate to other personnel, the executive director must have a mechanism of identifying performance outcomes and an acceptable process of supporting or promoting change among staff. The process of supervision is an interactive approach that is centered on developing the abilities of the employee by reflecting on work performance, jointly searching for solutions to work problems, clarifying expectations of the position, clarifying the direction of the organization, assessing the employee's progress in achieving performance objectives, and modeling the values and beliefs of the organization. Supervisors will typically style their supervision of staff based on how executive directors comport themselves in supervisory conferences with senior management staff.

### Managing Finances

All management decisions have some level of impact on an organization's allocation of resources, expenditure of funds, or the need for securing additional money. Technically, a board of directors has a fiduciary responsibility as representatives of the public to assure that there

is an annual budget and a plan to acquire an adequate amount of financial resources for stabilizing the organization and implementing its services. Practically speaking, the management of the daily operations requires that the executive director be the one to provide the oversight for carefully monitoring the level of available cash, the organization's current debt, and its outstanding liabilities and receivables.

Complex or simple managerial decisions require that the executive director be fully aware of the organization's fiscal health. Most responsible executive directors rely on the use of financial management tools and the information they produce for making decisions. The tools include: financial statements, functional expense reports, and cash flow statements. An effective executive director knows how to interpret the financial reports and understands the implications of analysis on the stewardship of the organization's budget and resources. In addition, the executive director analyzes the organization's fiscal health by paying close attention to the effects of rising costs, increased or decreased activities, and the variable impacts from planned or unplanned changes in the organization's internal or external environment—including the organization's available working capital, current ratio, and debt-to-equity ratio.

The executive director also plays an important role in the organization's investment strategies. The executive director advises and supports the board after seeking expert advice on the development investment policy and its execution by locating reasonable investment risks. The executive director can also help the board to be prudent in its decisionmaking by watching the returns on investments and forecasting both the current and future needs of the organization.

### Fund-Raising

Although many fund-raising experts claim that a primary leadership role of the board of directors is to raise sufficient capital for the operations and program, in reality, fund-raising becomes a management responsibility. The executive director should be as concerned, if not more so, for the organization to be financially sound and have the necessary funding to operate programs and pay staff wages and salary.

The executive director may take on a varying level of direct involvement for raising funds or see to it that the fund-raising activities are shared or carried out by specific staff, consultants, or volunteers. An executive director, for example, might secure appointments with community funders and solicit funding, but be accompanied by board members who bring credibility with their volunteer concerns and as examples for other volunteers like themselves who commit unpaid time and energy to the organization's cause.

Though the support and participation of board members is undeniably a critical factor to fund-raising success, the board's ability to be successful is often dependent on the management expertise and involvement of the executive director. The basis for successful fund-raising, for example, is to build off the needs, achievements, and plans of the organization. The short-term or long-term capability of an organization's fund-raising program requires that the organization be in good working order, operating productively and efficiently, both of which are results of effective management. The executive director assures the soundness of the organization's operations and programs through the controls, processes, and systems that he or she manages, making certain they are supported by skillful and knowledgeable staff and, if applicable, a cadre of committed and dedicated volunteers, all of whom are knowledgeable about the organization's mission, vision, and direction.

The basic characteristics of volunteer support require the involvement of the executive director, providing oversight and assurances that the tools of fund-raising are in place. Necessary fund-raising tools include a well-crafted "case statement," a donor or prospect list, an an-

nual report or other significant brochures that illustrate the achievements of the organization, and a plan that has realistic goals with a time frame that is also reasonable. With regard to the implementation of a fund-raising plan, the executive director must also be up-to-date about the efforts of the staff, volunteers, or resource development committee members so that people are working together and not inadvertently at cross-purposes.

Volunteers are very important to fund-raising success; however, if volunteers do not follow through on important assignments or find that their personal lives and occupational demands are interfering with their volunteer commitment, the executive director must be ready to step in. More than one executive director has found him- or herself "jumping in" to salvage a fund-raising project, while publicly giving the credit for the project's success to the volunteers, board, and staff.

## Executive Director's Leadership Role in Relation to the Board's Governance Role

Clarifying the differences between the responsibilities of the board and those of the executive director, Kenneth Dayton stated simply that governance is governance, and not management. It is largely an indisputable custom that the executive director's role is to oversee the day-to-day operations of the organization, as well as to share jointly with the board in matters critical to the strategic direction and survival of the organization. Because the organizational stakes are high, there is good reason to have concern over the ambiguity that sometimes exists between what board members should actually do and what executive directors are expected to do on behalf of the board.

Some authors have suggested that the board–executive director relationship would be more productive if it were conceptualized as a partnership. Research investigations into what constitutes effective governance and executive leadership have led some researchers to suggest that an especially effective executive director is one who takes active responsibility for the accomplishment of the organizational mission and its stewardship by providing substantial "board-centered" leadership for steering the efforts of the board of directors.

This view also asserts that there are several flaws in the traditional governance model. In the traditional model, the executive director is ranked in a subordinate position to the board. The hierarchical relationship would suggest that the executive director's daily work activities are being directed and supervised by the board of directors. Robert Herman and Richard Heimovics (1991) affirm through their research findings what many executive directors have come to believe through practical experience: that the board may legally be in charge, but the work of the organization is accomplished by the leadership demonstrated by the executive director. In this alternative "board-centered" model of governance, the executive director's distinctive leadership skills, information base, and management expertise are used for leading the organization toward the accomplishment of its mission. Furthermore, this model acknowledges that board performance is reliant on the leadership and management skills of the executive director. In this way, the executive director works to promote board participation and to facilitate decisionmaking. In addition, the executive director uses his or her interpersonal skills to craft respectful and productive interaction among the board members. With this approach, the executive director is (justifiably) credited with successful or unsuccessful organizational outcomes.

## References

Bennis, Warren, and Burt Nanus. 1985. *Leaders: The Strategies for Taking Charge.* New York: Harper & Row.

Block, Peter. 1989. *The Empowered Manager: Positive Political Skills at Work.* San Francisco: Jossey-Bass.

Boyatzis, Richard E. 1982. *The Competent Manager: A Model for Effective Performance.* New York: John Wiley & Sons.

Drucker, Peter F. 1990. *Managing the Non-Profit Organization.* Oxford, England: Butterworth-Heinemann.

Heimovics, Richard D., and Robert D. Herman. 1989. "The Salient Management Skills: A Conceptual Framework for a Curriculum for Managers in Nonprofit Organizations." *American Review of Public Administration* 18, no. 2, 119–132.

Herman, Robert D. Herman, and Richard D. Heimovics. 1991. *Executive Leadership in Nonprofit Organizations.* San Francisco: Jossey-Bass.

McCauley, Cynthia D., and Martha W. Hughes, 1993. In Dennis R. Young, Robert M. Hollister, and Virginia A. Hodgkinson, eds., *Governing, Leading, and Managing Nonprofit Organizations.* San Francisco: Jossey-Bass, 155–169.

Mintzberg, Henry. 1973. *The Nature of Managerial Work.* New York: Harper & Row.

Young, Dennis R. 1987. "Executive Leadership in Nonprofit Organizations." In Walter W. Powell, ed., *The Nonprofit Sector: A Research Handbook.* New Haven: Yale University Press, 167–179.

## CHAPTER 7

# When No One Is in Charge: The Meaning of Shared Power

BARBARA C. CROSBY AND JOHN M. BRYSON

Anyone who tries to tackle a public problem or need sooner or later comes face to face with the dynamics of a shared-power world. . . .

Today, anyone who's involved in the fight against AIDS realizes that a host of groups and organizations need to be part of any new initiative to reduce the incidence of the disease or deal with its effects. Anyone who digs deeply into the causes of local unemployment soon finds that causes of the problem (and therefore the solutions) are tied to governmental systems, specific employers, economic institutions, schools, individual experiences and aspirations, and voluntary organizations. Anyone who tries to attack environmental destruction, reform a university, or help a society become more humane likewise soon realizes that many individuals, groups, and organizations have contributed to or are affected by the problem or need at hand, and somehow these individuals, groups, and organizations, as well as many others, will have to be part of any significant beneficial change.

This chapter elaborates our understanding of this complex, no-one-in-charge, shared-power

world. To begin, we describe two contrasting types of organizational structure, planning, and decision making: what might be called an "in-charge" model, and the shared-power model. Then we explain more fully our view of public problems and shared power. We explore the causes and consequences of today's shared-power world and highlight some leadership opportunities and responsibilities in this world. . . .

## Two Types of Organizations, Planning, and Decision Making

An enduring "ideal" organizational structure is the hierarchical pyramid, or bureaucratic model, which might be called the "in-charge organization." At the apex of such an organization resides an individual (president, CEO, director) or small group (board or top management team) that establishes organizational direction, determines guiding policies, and sends directives downward to a group of middle managers, who in turn translate policies and orders into more specific orders that are passed down to the

**FIGURE 7.1.** Hierarchical and Networked
Organizations

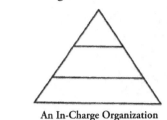

An In-Charge Organization

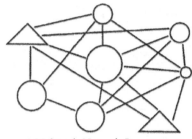

A Single-Node Network Organization

A Multinode Network Organization

and chaotic. . . . See Figure 7.1 for representations of an in-charge organization and of two types of networked organization.

Let's consider the example of US physicians who detected unusually virulent forms of skin cancer and pneumonia among gay patients in their clinics and hospitals in the early 1980s—notably Linda Laubenstein in New York City; Marcus Conant, a dermatologist affiliated with the University of California at San Francisco; and Michael Gottlieb, an immunologist and assistant professor at the University of California at Los Angeles. The physicians soon realized as they talked with local colleagues that other physicians were encountering similar patients, who were dying because no treatments worked. Already Laubenstein, Conant, and Gottlieb were operating within a professional network. They spread their net further, however, as they sought to learn more and alert others to their observations—turning to local public health officials, the national government's Centers for Disease Control, and medical journals. Now the relevant network extended to doctors' offices, clinics, university departments, journals, and public health departments. The network expansion continued, as these and other doctors worked with gay rights activists to help raise money for research into the cause of what appeared to be a new, lethal, sexually transmitted disease. New gay-led organizations emerged to support the people suffering from the new disease and promote needed research and education. The gay press began covering what their writers called the "gay plague."

The network grew even more as evidence emerged that the disease was affecting drug addicts and Haitian New Yorkers, and that it was being transmitted to hemophiliacs through the blood products they received. Now hemophiliac organizations and the blood bank industry were involved. Before long, the physicians became part of local-to-national networks, what Robert Quinn (2000) would call an adhocracy,

large number of lower-level workers. Embedded in this ideal type is the assumption that the organization "contains" a problem area, or need, and engages in highly rational, expert-based planning and decision making to resolve it. . . .

Increasingly, however, this organizational structure is proving inadequate, both as a reflection of how organizations really operate and as a model of the forms most suited for today's interconnected, interdependent world. Thus another ideal type, the networked organization, has emerged. In this view, the organization itself is often a network of units, departments, and individuals; moreover, the organization is part of a variety of external networks that are fluid

FIGURE 7.2. Public Problems in a No-One-in-Charge, Shared-Power World

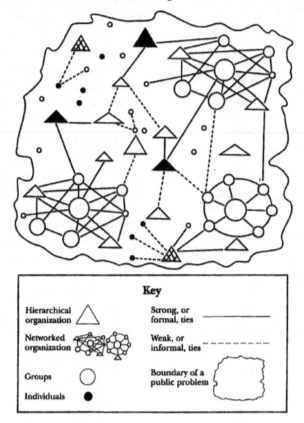

of clinicians, infectious disease researchers, lo-cal elected officials, and gay activists who were putting pressure on members of Congress, top officials in the Reagan administration, and even the president himself to channel resources to-ward the effort to identify the disease and con-trol its spread.

The organizational structure that best fit the developing AIDS crisis is illustrated in Figure 7.2, in which the problem is represented by the amorphous large blob. Within the blob are many individuals, groups, and organizations, represented by the dots, circles, and triangles—in other words, the stakeholders in the problem. (Of course, in the case of the AIDS crisis, the actual picture would be immensely more com-plicated since a tremendous number of people, groups, and organizations were involved.) The

solid and dotted lines between some of the stakeholders represent respectively the formal and informal connections, or networks, among groups and organizations. As time went on, newly created or newly involved groups and or-ganizations would be added to the picture.

Note that the problem spills far beyond the boundary of even the existing networks. No single person, group, or individual is "in charge" of the problem, yet many organiza-tions are affected or have partial responsibility to act. In effect, they have a share of the power that is required for remedying the problem. Of course, this is not to say that all organizations have equal power (they don't) or that power is shared equally (it isn't). The organizations come in various sizes and structures, from large hierarchies to loose networks. In such a shared-power situation, part of the battle is just gaining rough agreement on what the problems are. Indeed, some of the organizations may have radically conflicting aims. The physicians trying to marshal resources to combat AIDS would have encountered some groups and organizations, such as conservative "family values" groups, that they might have wished were not involved. To the conservative groups, the real problem was gay lifestyles. In another example, public health officials who realized that practices at bathhouses frequented by gay men were a major contributor to the rapid spread of the disease faced intense resistance from bathhouse owners against any restrictions on the operation of their businesses. In addition to coping with supportive, neutral, or hostile organizations, change advocates encounter existing networks that may be supportive, neutral, or resistant to their proposed changes. The AIDS crisis developed in the midst of a formidable set of networks, including those of officials in the Reagan administration, scientific and public health associations, groups of bathhouse owners, the gay press, and the blood bank industry. Some of the networks were political alliances, such as those between gay activists and politicians in San Francisco or among some US senators and the right-wing Moral Majority.

To coordinate action and make headway on resolving a complex public problem, the organizations involved need to be aware of the whole problem system and recognize that it has to undergo significant change. The change advocates have to engage in political, issue-oriented, and therefore messy planning and decision making, in which shared goals and mission are being developed as the process moves along. New networks must be created, old ones co-opted or neutralized. These networks range from the highly informal, in which the main activity is information sharing, to more organized shared-power arrangements (which are described more fully in the next section). . . .

## What Do We Mean by Shared Power?

. . . We define *shared power* following Giddens (1979, 90; 1984) and Bryson and Einsweiler (1991, 3) as *actors jointly exercising their capabilities related to a problem in order to further their separate and joint aims.* The actors may be individuals, groups, or organizations working together in order to achieve joint gains or avoid losses. Power sharing requires a common or mutual objective held by two or more actors, whether or not the objective is explicitly stated, agreed upon, or even clearly understood. Yet shared-power arrangements remain a "mixed-motive" situation, in which participants reserve the right of "exit" (Hirschman 1970) to protect their other, unshared objectives. Of course, exit may not be easy or even possible, as when the shared-power arrangements have been mandated by a government body, foundation, or other powerful organization.

Viewed another way, shared-power arrangements exist in the midrange of a continuum of how organizations work on public problems. At one end of the continuum are organizations that hardly relate to each other or are adversaries, dealing with a problem that extends beyond their capabilities. At the other end are organizations merged into a new entity that can handle the problem through merged authority and capabilities. In the midrange are organizations that share information, undertake joint projects, or develop shared-power arrangements such as collaborations or coalitions (see also Himmelman 1996). Particular policy change efforts are likely to involve all the relationship types along the continuum (see Figure 7.3). . . .

## Causes and Consequences of a Shared-Power World

Today's shared-power world arises from a number of interconnected causes and produces many

FIGURE 7.3. Continuum of Organized Sharing

| What Is Shared | Mechanism for Sharing | | | |
|---|---|---|---|---|
| Authority | | | | Merger |
| Power | | | Collaboration | |
| Activities and resources | | Coordination | | |
| Information | Communication | | | |
| Nothing | None | | | |

interconnected consequences. At the outset of the twenty-first century, many wise observers have described the growing interdependence, complexity, and diversity of human societies. . . .

## The Need for Leadership

. . . In our view, potential for effective leadership lies alike with those who do and do not have formal positions of power and authority. Indeed, this view of leadership may be most useful in reminding those with little formal authority how powerful they can be through collaboration (Marris 1996), and in reminding those in a supposedly powerful position just how much they rely on numerous stakeholders for any real power they have. Ours is not a zero-sum view. A shared-power arrangement enhances the power of the participants beyond the sum of their separate capabilities. Moreover, our view is based on an expansive model of what constitutes power. We see power as not just the ability to make and implement decisions (a tra-

ditional view) but also the ability to sanction conduct and, most important, to create and communicate shared meaning. . . .

Leaders who focus on building shared-power arrangements enhance the power of the groups involved by reducing the risk for the participants and by sharing responsibility. If things go well, no person or group gets all the credit, but if things go badly they won't get all the blame either. Second, leaders of a change effort can use a shared-power arrangement simply to manage complexity and interconnectedness—as in a policy network, interorganizational or intergovernmental agreement, federation, business-government partnership, or a variety of other collaborations.

Finally, leaders can change how they view interconnectedness. . . . In *Bowling Alone*, Robert Putnam highlights research that indicates people who have multiple social connections are likely to be healthier and happier than people with few connections (Putnam 2000). He also argues persuasively that rich social networks (social capital) benefit the societies in which they

**TABLE 7.1.**[1] **Tackling Public Problems in a Shared-Power World: Some Definitions**

| | |
|---|---|
| Stakeholders | Individuals, groups, or organizations that are affected by a public problem, have partial responsibility to act on it, or control important resources |
| Shared power | Actors jointly exercising their capabilities related to a problem in order to further their separate and joint aims |
| Shared-power world | Highly networked policy environment in which many individuals, groups, and organizations have partial responsibility to act on public problems, but not enough power to resolve the problems alone; power is fragmented; decision making is messy and seemingly chaotic; shifting coalitions form and dissipate |

are embedded—by, for example, establishing a culture of reciprocity and helping people be more productive.

Using and creating social networks was crucial for the progress that change advocates such as Marcus Conant and Michael Gottlieb were able to make in California during the early years of the AIDS crisis. These and other physicians, public health officials, and gay activists teamed up in 1982 to generate resources for research and for support of AIDS sufferers. Tangible results included creation of the Kaposi's Sarcoma Research and Education Foundation (later the AIDS Foundation); funding from San Francisco's board of supervisors for an AIDS clinic, a nonprofit program supporting people with AIDS, and an education program to be conducted by the new foundation; and funds from the California legislature for AIDS research. Cooperative arrangements among medical researchers also contributed to progress in identifying the AIDS virus. In 1985, when Rock Hudson's death and a growing number of nongay deaths (along with a horrifying level of deaths among gay men) finally made it impossible for citizens and their elected representatives to ignore the disease, the preexisting collaborations among AIDS activists, medical professionals, congressional staff, and others were a foundation for concerted progress on a number of fronts. . . .

Notions of a shared-power world and the desire to revitalize or expand democracy have caused the old image of the leader as the one in charge of a hierarchical organization to diminish considerably. . . . Shared, collaborative, collective, and distributed leadership are recognized and lauded.

Leaders rooted in a networked world may or may not have positions of authority. They inspire and motivate constituents through persuasion, example, and empowerment, not through command and control. They lead up and out rather than down, to borrow imagery from Mark Moore (1995) and Dee Hock (2002). Such leaders foster dialogue with their constituents and the situations in which they find themselves, and they encourage collective action to tackle real problems. Further, they claim and make use of the powers they do have to push for changes in a world often resistant to their demands. As the antislavery leader Frederick Douglass found, leaders must forcefully wield their own power if they expect to overcome entrenched power.

All this does not mean that the in-charge leadership image has disappeared or completely lost its usefulness. The connective or quiet leader sometimes has to make a decision and implement it using whatever powers and controls he or she has. Similarly, leaders who are formally in charge know they often must consult and compromise with other powerful people before acting. In a shared-power situation, however, leadership that encourages the participation of others must be emphasized because only it has the power to inspire and mobilize those others. In the effort to tackle public problems, leadership and power must be consciously shared with a view to eventually creating power-sharing institutions within a regime of mutual gain. As Robert Bellah and his coauthors argue, "The public lives through those institutions that cultivate a constituency of conscience and vision. To achieve the common good, leaders and citizens create and sustain such institutions and use them to change other institutions" (Bellah et al. 1991, 271).

## Summary

If you seek to bring about major social change—whether it be halting the spread of AIDS or improving economic opportunities in your community—you need to understand and act in accordance with the dynamics of today's shared-power world. In this world, public problems such as AIDS or poverty are embedded in a complex system of diverse, interconnected parts. Many individuals, groups, and organizations have some stake in the problem, but no one of them has enough power to resolve it alone.

In such a world, leaders cannot rely on hierarchic bureaucratic models to bring about needed change. Rational planning on its own is ineffective. Instead, leaders must increasingly focus on building and altering shared-power arrangements within and among organizations, and they must engage in political decision making. These strategies should be aimed at developing a widely shared understanding of a public problem and potential solutions, and at building coalitions to support proposed changes and eventually establish a regime of mutual gain. To foster understanding of a complex public problem, leaders should promote an appreciative approach that helps participants delve into multiple causes and consequences of the problem and develop a sense of desired improvements. . . .

## Notes

1 *Note from the editors:* Table 7.1 has been edited for brevity. For the full text table, see Crosby and Bryson, *Leadership for the Common Good,* Exhibit 1.1, p. 22.

## References

Bellah, Robert N., Richard Madsen, William M. Sullivan, Ann Swidler, and Steven M. Tipton. 1991. *The Good Society.* New York: Knopf.

Bryson, John M., and Robert C. Einsweiler. 1991. *Shared Power.* Lanham, MD: University Press of America.

Giddens, Anthony. 1979. *Central Problems in Social Theory: Action, Structure, and Contradiction in Social Analysis.* Berkeley: University of California Press.

———. 1984. *The Constitution of Society.* Berkeley: University of California Press.

Himmelman, Arthur T. 1996. "On the Theory and Practice of Transformational Collaborations: From Social Service to Social Justice." In *Creating Collaborative Advantage,* edited by C. Huxham. Thousand Oaks, CA: Sage.

Hirschman, Albert O. 1970. *Exit, Voice, and Loyalty: Responses to Decline in Firms, Organizations, and States.* Cambridge, MA: Harvard University Press.

Hock, Dee. 2002. "The Art of Chaordic Leadership." In *On Mission and Leadership,* edited by Frances Hesselbein and Rob Johnston. San Francisco: Jossey-Bass.

Marris, Peter. 1996. *The Politics of Uncertainty: Attachment in Private and Public Life.* London: Routledge.

Moore, Mark H. 1995. *Creating Public Value.* Cambridge, MA: Harvard University Press.

Putnam, Robert D. 2000. *Bowling Alone: The Collapse and Revival of American Community.* New York: Simon & Schuster.

Quinn, Robert E. 2000. *Change the World: How Ordinary People Can Accomplish Extra-Ordinary Results.* San Francisco: Jossey-Bass.

# THE DOWNWARD SPIRAL OF FOUNDER'S HOSPITAL

*C. Kenneth Meyer and Alison Lemke*

Frank Jahoda had been a hospital and health care administrator for nearly twenty-five years. He began his career in the field of finance and business administration, but soon was viewed as not only a "quick study" but also as someone who had a talent for asking the right questions. Frank prided himself on being a competent team leader who could size up a problem quickly and turn what was destined to fail into success. Those who worked with him considered him pragmatic and an effective team player and turnaround manager.

Frank loved to demonstrate that there were many routes to success. He believed that listening to and trusting coworkers were two signposts that could not be missed on the journey. He himself felt that his rapid rise through the administrative ranks of a large hospital was part luck and part being at the right place at the right time. Those who knew him well, however, largely discounted his self-deprecation and cited his ability to formulate a vision, communicate it, and build an environment on interpersonal trust. Therefore, when he was hired as a consultant for Founder's Hospital, he came with a set of credentials that were beyond reproach; moreover, his trademark honesty and integrity were embedded in his persona.

Hired as a consultant by Melinda Wise, interim CEO, Frank's job included assessing and objectively reporting on failed board oversight, mismanagement, low physician and staff morale, and declining public confidence in Founder's Hospital. Melinda was an experienced health care provider in her own right, with many years of nursing under her belt at Founder's Hospital and a laudable track record as head nurse in several other regional hospitals.

Frank knew that Founder's, as it was usually called, was facing some difficulties, and he learned from his grapevine connections that things had gone awry. He had a track record of being brought into situations where failure was an ongoing state of affairs, but at Founder's he would reserve judgment until he had spent a week or so interviewing the hospital board of directors, hospital employees, the administrative team, and the physicians, nurses, and allied medical professionals.

In making his rounds, Frank met an allied health care employee who had a calm demeanor and responded to his queries with what he concluded were carefully scripted, independently mature, and objective observations. In the course of his interview, he asked Cheryl Elmore if she would put into her own words a chronological record of what had transpired at Founder's. Frank was not surprised when he received the following statement:

> Hospitals do not operate in a vacuum! Citizens of Pearl Valley are concerned about the recent developments at Founder's Hospital. They learned that a prominent physician group sent a statement

of nonsupport for Harold Alexander, the hospital's CEO, alleging fiscal mismanagement, poor physician/administration relationships, obsolete management practices in the Department of Human Resources and the Office of Accounting, Finance, and Management (OAFM), and ongoing operating losses. The hospital has in rapid succession gone through three failed CEOs: Bill Jones resigned in 2008, Ralph Hays resigned in 2011, and Gary Ward resigned in 2014. All three executives lost the confidence and support of the physicians, but the community was told that they resigned for reasons other than the loss of confidence.

As Frank made his rounds, he probed, listened, and reflected on what he had been told by the many stakeholders. He learned, for instance, that recently some hospital employees had joined forces with the physicians to reiterate the physicians' complaints and grievances through a letter-writing, email, and blogging campaign. By sending their stories to the local newspaper, they had not only gone public but "upped the ante." A careful reading of the letters and emails shows complaints on the following topics:

- Premature and shortsighted management practices among the ranks of the administrative team
- Plummeting employee morale and job satisfaction
- Inhumane treatment of employees by the human resources director
- Precipitous decline in patient care services from increases in nurse-to-patient ratios
- A decline in nursing staffing simultaneous with a dramatic increase in middle-management positions
- Favoritism and cronyism practiced by the board of directors, who were close social friends with the CEO, CFO, and director of human resources
- Long-term permanent hospital employees who felt that they had to submit to administrative prerogatives or face certain retaliation

According to the rumor mill, some board members were bewildered to learn that upper managers were viewed as ruthless in their treatment of employees, although Frank found that all of the recent CEOs seemed to be congenial and nice. He felt it was reasonable to believe that Founder's recent financial difficulties were somewhat related to poor Medicare and Medicaid reimbursements and an increase in the percentage of uninsured patients—problems that apparently were not aired in the administrative meetings with the board.

Upon meeting with the board of directors, Frank wrote in his notebook the following remarks:

Board members who are friends with members of the hospital's administrative team are stunned by the outpouring of dissatisfaction and the complaints that have been published in the newspaper.

Accusations of conflict of interest among board members seem to be somewhat unfair since members state that they are unaware of the widespread unhappiness in the hospital and the local health care community.

Board members have been repeatedly reassured by the two most recent CEOs and by the administrative team that the hospital is basically in fine shape and that the financial problems can be easily fixed. They have also been told that the negativity expressed by a selected few low-performing, disgruntled employees should not be given much credence or veracity, and that these few disaffected employees need to be "weeded out" from the ranks of the valued employees if the hospital is to be successful.

Frank reflected on what he had been told by the various stakeholders and began to put together his report. He wrote the following preliminary statements. Of course, he was just beginning to see the full picture of what was taking place at Founder's Hospital. Reflecting on his interviews, he made the following points that would be used in his final report.

- FH has a solid reputation for being a compassionate, personalized, and competitive center that provides an excellent standard of care.
- FH has a history of investing in new diagnostic and treatment equipment to provide high-quality patient care.
- Several years of patient surveys demonstrate high levels of satisfaction with the physicians, hospital services, and health care employees.
- During the last decade, FH has experienced an increase in the number of uninsured patients and in the number of patients covered by Medicare and Medicaid. Unlike private insurers, both programs have a record of providing inadequate reimbursement based on diagnostic related groups (DRGs), thus producing substantial patient cost-shifting.
- FH has experienced increased competition for hospitalization services from larger, metropolitan hospitals in the regional delivery area.
- Controversy exists among the board members over the compensation package established for the positions of CEO, CFO, and HR director. Founder's Hospital is a 501(c)(3) not-for-profit organization and is housed in a government-owned (municipal) facility; therefore, it is not exempt from publicly revealing the pay for its top executives as reported with the IRS 990 form. Legal counsel has cited the state's attorney general's opinion that since the city, in effect, owns the hospital, but does not give it ongoing operating funds, the hospital is not obligated to release salary information. Bonuses for executives are given at the end of the fiscal year, are based on financial results, and are approved by the board of directors.
- Physicians and the board of directors are developing a new strategic plan.
- The new strategic plan will retain FH's long-standing mission statement: to meet community needs by providing compassionate, personalized health services.
- Perhaps because of their private-sector backgrounds, the CEO and administrative team appear to prioritize meeting the twin goals of growing net revenues and managing expenses in order to remain competitive.
- Salaries for clinical staff are benchmarked below the salaries for similar job classifications in other area hospitals.
- A new information system with costly computer software has been installed. Clinical and nursing staff generally view the new system as cumbersome and time-consuming to use and say that time for direct patient care has decreased and their own job dissatisfaction has increased.
- The patient satisfaction survey for 2011 revealed an "'alarming" decline in the availability of nursing staff, the food quality, room cleanliness, and other important hospital services and amenities.
- Hospital employees and physicians are dissatisfied with the administration of the hospital and have vented their grievances publicly.

Frank completed his interviews with hospital stakeholders and then settled in to write a report on his findings and recommendations. He had ample evidence that the rapid turnover of executives at the highest levels had left its own "DNA" on administrative leadership, oversight, accountability, transparency, and management continuity. Frank understood that emotions had been "rubbed raw" in the physician and health care ranks and that it would take more than a onetime application of a magical "happy lotion" to assuage these disgruntled and alienated feelings. He also understood that his findings would be presented to the board of directors in several weeks and that what he presented would not please all stakeholders. His past consulting experiences had taught him that some would want to know what had gone wrong at the hospital and who was to blame, while others would worry about its survival. And of course, some would want the problems identified and quickly remedied. Realistically, Frank thought to himself, there was no "silver bullet" in his armory that would immediately solve this management scenario and enable Founder's Hospital to heal quickly.

## Questions and Instructions

1.  Did the board of directors exercise adequate and appropriate oversight of their community hospital? Why or why not? Please elaborate. What role should the board play for a public or nonprofit hospital? Please be specific.

2.  What are some internal management issues that are raised in the case study? Did these internal management issues contribute to the difficulties this hospital is now facing? Please explain.

3.  Do you think the emphasis on financial performance, as reflected in the hospital's strategic goals and the bonuses it awarded to executives based on financial performance, is appropriate for a public hospital? Why or why not?

4.  What does it mean to manage a hospital "for the public good" with regard to financial performance and community benefit? Please comment.

# BETWEEN A ROCK AND A BOULDER

### C. Kenneth Meyer and Don Munkers

John Simpson, executive vice president of the Intermountain Ag Processors Association (IAPA), a 501(c)(6) organization, was hired to bring about major changes in the nonprofit organization, which represented agricultural processors of grain in a four-state area. The organization teetered on a budget base that the board said represented a "tightrope" scenario. That is, one tiny slip by Simpson and IAPA would be in serious trouble, since the forces of gravity only went in one direction. Simpson knew that he had been hired with the understanding that if he was successful in turnaround management and met the targeted production goals, he would be "taken care of," as the board president told him during the initial interview.

Simpson relished the chance to prove that there was substance to his "can-do" attitude and viewed the challenge as an opportunity to make a positive difference. He also knew from the "inner circle" of his friends who were closely associated with IAPA board members that it faced more than a troubled financial status—the governance of the organization was also questionable. As Simpson put on the leadership mantle, he soon learned about the temporary executives who had attempted to set IAPA on a course that would bring it financial strength and effective leadership, but who had failed in these efforts.

Rumor had it, Simpson discovered right away, that his predecessors had been friends of the board members and that this "cronyism" had incurred a "bundle" of risks, including loss of respect, lowered expectations, and a tarnished reputation among the IAPA membership.

Simpson had not decided hurriedly or easily to take on the IAPA challenge. He was secure and comfortable in his parent agency at the time, and his preliminary research had revealed that it might be a risky proposition to leave an organization that was strong and stable and swap it for an opportunity with IAPA. Nevertheless, Simpson felt in his heart that he could move the organization forward, and he had confidence in his own ability to set the desired course and navigate any troubled waters that might be encountered. He recalled what he had told the board: "It is not difficult to achieve if there are tangible rewards associated with taking a failing organization and making it 'whole' again."

IAPA had a small staff consisting of only Mary Holmes and himself. Ms. Holmes, as she preferred to be called, was a seasoned veteran with the organization and had the valued experience of having been "on-deck" since the IAPA opened its doors for business in the late 1990s. Indeed, Simpson quickly discovered that she was a treasure trove of organizational facts and historical information and that she knew where all of the "skeletons" were neatly kept in IAPA's "closet." Simpson thought that she would have done a far better job of running the place than the several temporary executives who had preceded him. Ms. Holmes and Simpson hit it off right from the start. He relied on her and trusted her, and both of them were committed to bettering the organization and willing to make needed changes.

As executive vice president, Simpson dedicated most of his time to dealing with the many policy issues that had come before several state legislatures. A steady stream of issues crossed his desk for clarification or resolution, and almost every day he had to reconcile the policy changes that legislators proposed for the field of commodities and the legislative actions they took. As he closely monitored the actions of these legislators he also had to "lobby, lobby, and lobby," as he once put it. Of course, the business of answering email messages and responding to the inquiries of IAPA members was time-consuming as well, but not terribly laborious.

On the other side, Ms. Holmes had her plate full with financial and budgetary matters, and it was a chore for her to plan the annual conference for IAPA, but their roles and accompanying tasks seemed to be fully synchronized. They could both see that the path that Simpson had set for the IAPA was bringing growth, as measured by an increase in membership fees, regained budgetary health, and recouped prestige.

IAPA was governed by a board of directors consisting of twenty-two members drawn from the four states it represented. The organization's governance bylaws provided for the allocation of five directors for each state and two directors elected "at large," although at-large directors needed to be drawn from different states. The board of directors was further defined by a number of executive positions: president, first vice president, second vice president, and secretary-treasurer. These positions were filled from within the board. Owing to its large size, the board met only biannually, and, importantly, during the interim an elected executive board met quarterly to provide governance.

The executive board was empowered by IAPA's constitution and bylaws to act on behalf of the board between the biannual meetings, and it was also the policymaking and governing body of the organization. The full board would customarily ratify whatever the executive board had decided. The executive board consisted of the president, two vice presidents, and the secretary-treasurer of the board, joined by the immediate past president, who acted as the chairperson of the executive board. Thus, routine policymaking and decision-approving activities were made by a small board that met regularly, could be convened with ease, and normally felt confident about the courses of action recommended by the professional staff—John Simpson and Mary Holmes.

Because the organization had grown rapidly and there were many signs of positive organizational change, the executive board and Simpson celebrated their "turnaround." Appreciative of the changing dynamics, the board of directors suggested at their fall meeting that Simpson be authorized to purchase a new vehicle, of his own choosing, for both official business and personal use. The board's discussion of the proposal went well enough, and it was further decided that the personal-use provision be qualified only with the clause "within reason." IAPA would pay for the maintenance of the car, its insurance, and sundry other expenses, including the fuel costs associated with organizational business. In turn, Simpson would be responsible for paying for fuel associated with his own use. The car would be made available to Simpson only; this authorization did not extend to other members of his family.

The rationale for the sponsored car was justifiable enough, especially since Simpson would be given this organizational benefit in lieu of a standard pay increase. The arrangement was perfectly acceptable to Simpson, especially since he had been obligated to use his own car while traveling for the organization and his many trips across the four states had taken a toll on his relatively new and expensive sedan, especially in terms of mileage.

In general, the board seemed amenable to the idea—except for one of the more influential members, Jacob Haggerty, whose initial concern later turned to opposition. Not unlike other decisions, discussion of the issue began to manifest the rule of inverse proportionality—the smaller the issue the more time a board spends on its deliberation. Haggerty questioned the down payment and how much would be expended and then raised major concerns about the type of fuel that would power the vehicle—gasoline, gasoline-ethanol blend, ethanol only, or bio-diesel. It soon became apparent to the other members of the board that Haggerty was not in favor of the car sponsorship in any form, and as a persuasive and influential member, he was eventually able to convince a majority of his colleagues to defeat the new-car motion. Simpson, a consummate gentleman, accepted the board's decision, but by then he had already purchased the car and was faced with a lean year, since there had been no salary increases. The board meeting adjourned, and the next meeting was scheduled to coincide with the annual spring conference.

When the executive board conducted its November meeting, the chair, the immediate past president of IAPA, requested that the purchase of a company vehicle be added to the agenda. Simpson was somewhat surprised by this action, since he had been neither contacted before the meeting nor notified about the added agenda item. As far as he was concerned, the issue had been decided, and it would not be put back on the agenda until the June meeting of the full board.

## Questions and Instructions

1. In your opinion, did the executive board overstep its authority? If so, in what ways? Please be specific.
2. Could Simpson have handled the executive board's addition of the agenda item differently? If so, in what way? Please explain.
3. Would it have been in Simpson's interest to ignore the decision of the executive board to purchase the vehicle? If yes, why? If no, why not?
4. Would it have been wiser for Simpson to delay the purchase of the car until the next board meeting, when the approved motion would have been placed on the agenda for the entire board to approve? What implications, if any, would have been associated with delaying the purchase of the car? Please explain.

# PART IV

# INNOVATION AND CAPACITY

Whether innovations originate within the nonprofit sector or as part of the larger environment is somewhat unimportant. In this country, the free-market business sector, with profits as its driving force, has thrived on innovation arguably more than in any other country in history. Government agencies, too, have sought to be innovative in order to find solutions to complex "wicked problems" and to effectively address political, economic, and social needs. Nonprofit organizations do not exist separate from their environment: the existence, roles, functions, and revenues of nonprofits are affected by changes in these other two sectors as well as by technology and ideology, and the nonprofit culture has always had innovation as one of its goals.[1]

Facebook, Twitter, YouTube, Tumblr, and SharePoint are part and parcel of today's vernacular, and there are thousands of other examples of how technology has changed the way nonprofits get their message out and collaborate with others. For example, the National Marrow Donor Program's "Be the Match" registry uses database and communication technology to gather information about volunteers willing to donate bone marrow and connects them with patients, doctors, and researchers on a scale hard to imagine thirty years ago. Caring Bridge provides free websites that connect people experiencing a significant health challenge to family and friends. The Generation Project sends the gifts of young donors directly to teachers and students in need. Obviously, technological advances are changing the type of work in which nonprofit organizations are engaged and how they accomplish the work they have been doing all along.[2]

"Innovation" has been defined as a multistage process involving leaders, coworkers, and organizational components such as culture and climate.[3] It also refers to a process of turning opportunities into new ideas and putting these into widely used practices.[4] Nonprofits that are creative strive to be close to and in tune with the needs of their service recipients. At the same time, they must also be innovative to successfully meet the needs and wishes of funders and other stakeholders. As an example, nonprofits have been viewed as innovative contracting partners for government agencies seeking to save money. Their flexible service delivery models are attractive, but they also must find ways to produce the accountability reports required by government agencies and other funders. In a 2012 survey conducted by the Urban Institute, the most frequently cited problems with contracting with government "involved governments' complicated and time consuming application and reporting requirements."[5] Paradoxically, the amount of US government money flowing to the human services, the arts, and environmental protection has declined steadily and sometimes dramatically.[6] Moreover, states, counties, and municipalities have not been eager to replace declining federal funds when tax and deficit reductions continue to command high public support.[7]

Although funders' reporting requirements may be daunting, many nonprofits are finding that using data has been an effective way to report to and engage with not only funders but also the larger community. Advances in technology have made it easier for them to do so. See, for example, Beth Kanter and Katie Delahaye Paine's "Measuring the Networked Nonprofit: Using Data to Change the World," reprinted in this part.

## Innovation and Leadership

The leadership arrangements and mechanisms of nonprofits are ideal for creating and supporting innovation. Leadership is chief among the factors that influence creativity and innovation.[8] A nonprofit's board of directors provides shared governance and should bring together people from a variety of backgrounds to ensure a diversity of talent for generating innovative ideas. In addition, board leadership is shared with an executive director who has his or her own distinctive perspectives and talents. Nonprofit staff members and a solid volunteer base can also bring a variety of backgrounds and interests together to help innovation grow and thrive. "In the organizational context, innovation can occur in products, processes, or services. It can be incremental or radical and it can occur at various levels in an organization, from management groups and departments to project teams and even individuals."[9] Of course the number of people involved with an organization does not necessarily ensure innovation. Nonprofits must be on guard against groupthink and other potentially stultifying scenarios. "In the management of the innovation process, destroying poor ideas often is as important as nurturing good ones; in this way, scarce resources can be released and good ideas spotlighted."[10]

## Innovation and Social Entrepreneurship

Nonprofits face a never-ending struggle to find new sources of revenues (see Part V). In many instances, they have faced this challenge by becoming more entrepreneurial in pursuing businesses and businesslike ventures. *Nonprofit entrepreneurship* is "a proactive style of management through which leaders of nonprofit organizations seek to implement change through new organizational and programmatic initiatives."[11] Dennis Young captures three indicators of the importance of entrepreneurship to nonprofit organizations: (1) the rapid growth of the nonprofit sector signals the presence of considerable entrepreneurial activity; (2) many nonprofits have been in existence for only a short period of time, a trend that "reflects the classic mode of nonprofit entrepreneurship—individuals or groups motivated to address a social, health, environmental, or other issue, unsatisfied with existing services and aware of potential resources to support their interests, forming their own organizations"; and (3) many nonprofits were established for the specific purpose of introducing change. Entrepreneurship thus has been a factor in "the sector's ability to transform concern over social issues . . . into new operating programs and services."[12]

To anticipate and respond to Young's indicators, many nonprofit organizations have increased the level of professionalism in their management and put representatives with business backgrounds on their boards. As a result, many nonprofits have become aggressively commercial and compete for business directly with for-profit firms.[13] Changing from an organization focused on operations to an entrepreneurial organization is exciting, but it is also among the most frustrating aspects of contemporary nonprofit management.

On the one hand, [an entrepreneurial organization] offers the excitement of breakthrough think-ing, compelling life stories, and potentially dramatic progress against daunting global problems such as hunger, poverty, and disease. . . . On the other hand, the field offers fewer evidence-based insights on how social entrepreneurs can improve the odds of impact. Given few tools for separat-ing the wheat from the chaff, social entrepreneurs are left with long menus of advice. As a result, they often reinvent the wheel as they struggle to discern lessons from a relatively small number of exemplary peers.[14]

## Commercialization: Blurring the Line Between Businesses and Nonprofits

Nonprofit organizations in many subsectors have ventured into a variety of commercial markets.[15] Figures and percentages differ according to definitions and sources of information, but in 2005 pub-lic charities reported total revenues of $1.1 trillion. Fees from the sale of services and goods, which include tuition payments, hospital patient revenues, and ticket sales, accounted for approximately 70 percent of their revenues. This number also includes large charitable nonprofits such as hospitals and higher education institutions. When these larger institutions are excluded, sources of revenue distributions change substantially. Smaller nonprofit organizations are less dependent on fees for services and more dependent on private contributions and government contracts and grants.[16]

Some are critical of government contracts being awarded to large, politically astute nonprofits that are subsequently portrayed as models of entrepreneurial success, which smaller and less polit-ically connected nonprofits cannot hope to emulate. The *Nonprofit Quarterly* cites nonprofit social entrepreneurialism as just one more example of politically derived government largesse paid to large, influential nonprofits:

To most small local nonprofits . . . the concept of social entrepreneurialism that they hear touted by their funders implies earning income from business related activities. But some of the most highly publicized nonprofit social entrepreneurs promoted as models for the nonprofit sector . . . demonstrate part of their entrepreneurialism by success at the public trough.

Due to size, entrepreneurial aggressiveness, and solid political contacts, part of TFA's [Teach For America's] federal success, for example, is attributable to attracting juicy earmarks, not simply successful competitive grantsmanship.[17]

Despite the obstacles and criticisms, nonprofits are entering into entrepreneurial activities and often are successfully competing directly with for-profit businesses. Nonprofits in the health care subsector, for example, have been competing directly and aggressively with for-profit businesses since the 1970s.[18] Many nonprofit hospitals and clinics own for-profit subsidiaries that provide corporate wellness programs, manage condominium physicians' offices, and operate private health clubs.[19] Nonprofits in the mental health, intellectual challenges, and other fields that serve mostly low-income populations regularly buy and manage companies that operate apartment houses, pet stores, laundries, and other historically low-wage service businesses. "Major museums, such as Chicago's Art Institute, Shedd Aquarium, and the Field Museum of Natural History . . . have begun holding afterhours cocktail parties that compete with local taverns. . . . Revenue is produced through admission fees and drink sales."[20] Although the unrelated business income tax (UBIT) limits nonprofit activity that competes with market-based firms, many commercial ventures have proven enormously successful for nonprofits.

Commercial-type ventures can contribute to the financial health of a nonprofit and provide bene-fits for clients. Entrepreneurial nonprofits, for example, have generated revenues that can be "plowed back" into more or better services, thereby benefiting clients and advancing their mission. They also can create employment opportunities for current and former clients that would not have existed.[21] It is easy to understand why the commercial activities of nonprofit organizations have occasionally caused loud cries of "unfair competition," particularly from small businesses.[22]

Other developments have contributed to the commercialization of the nonprofit sector. First, for-profit businesses have been "invading turf" that historically has "belonged" to the nonprofit sector.[23] For-profit chains have replaced nonprofits as the primary providers of hospital care in the United States. Private emergency medical services (EMS) companies have all but driven nonprofit ambulance squads out of urban and suburban markets and made major inroads in many rural areas. Businesses also have aggressively entered the mental health and substance abuse fields, as well as day care centers, trade and technical schools, and youth and adult corrections. Nonprofits and for-profits thus are competing with each other in fields that used to be each other's "turf"; to compete successfully nonprofits have had to become more businesslike.

Second, the professionalism of nonprofit organization managers has increased dramatically in recent decades. Master's degree programs (and concentrations) in nonprofit organization management have proliferated at a dizzying pace over the past thirty-five years, with correspondingly dramatic increases in the number of students and graduates.[24] And many larger nonprofit organizations recruit business executives who, in a few subsectors, are receiving "Fortune 500" wages.[25]

Third, more business executives and fewer government and nonprofit organization managers sit on boards of trustees than was the case thirty years ago. Overall, boards of trustees have become more business-oriented.[26]

Finally, mutually beneficial venture partnerships between businesses and nonprofits started to become commonplace in the 1990s. Planned giving programs, cause-related marketing ventures, and businesses using higher education research facilities and faculty (rather than investing in their own) are a few examples of the array of these partnerships.

When nonprofits enter commercial ventures, they must carefully follow regulations to avoid or limit UBITs and to preserve their tax-exempt status with the IRS and state taxing authorities. The stakes are higher, however, than worries about UBIT. "The greatest peril is not that nonprofits may ultimately be driven out of the social service marketplace. Rather, the danger is that in their struggle to become more viable competitors in the short term, nonprofit organizations will be forced to compromise the very assets that made them so vital to society in the first place."[27]

Lester Salamon asserts that the nonprofit sector is facing four challenges "of crisis proportions."[28] Each of these challenges by itself represents a serious danger to the sector's ability to survive in its current form. Of Salamon's four categories of challenges—fiscal challenges, economic challenges, effectiveness challenges, and legitimacy challenges—the crisis of legitimacy is the most problematic. The single greatest force behind this crisis is the sector's inability to find or define its role in between the government and business sectors. Citizens and elected officials alike are questioning whether the "commercialized" nonprofit sector should continue to receive favorable tax treatment and preferred contracting status with government. William Ryan asks, "Is the common interest best served when nonprofits aim to compete on for-profit terms?"[29] In the United States, we still have a mental image of a nonprofit as a community-based organization that organizes volunteers to administer to people in need—not as a multi-state conglomerate with a director who earns a six-digit salary.[30] Unless the nonprofit sector is able to (re)define its role in the minds and perceptions of citizens and elected officials, the crisis of legitimacy eventually may disable it. According to one scholar:

> Because government funding has declined precipitously and the reporting requirements have become increasingly onerous, it appears that many nonprofits are abandoning their mission in order

to gain revenues through the market. This could cause nonprofits to win and lose simultaneously. Can nonprofits win contracts and still be responsive to their clients and communities? Can they really compete long-term in markets dominated by for-profit firms? Unlike their for-profit counterparts, if faced with compromising their social missions, nonprofits may conclude that winning isn't everything.[31]

## Readings Reprinted in Part IV

The first reading reprinted in Part IV is "Taking Social Entrepreneurship Seriously" by J. Gregory Dees. The author considers social entrepreneurship as a phenomenon of innovation reflective of the continuing reinvention of the third sector over the past 150 years. Dees outlines the influences that have created historical shifts in how nonprofits seek to advance their missions. His faith in the nonprofit sector as a conduit for creating positive change through entrepreneurialism is cautiously optimistic. Social entrepreneurs "are better positioned to innovate and experiment than government agencies. They have flexibility in how they serve their missions that should allow them to be more efficient and effective. They increase our chances of learning, and they bring private resources to the table." Although there is tremendous interest in entrepreneurialism, the need to evaluate and assess social impacts and create economies of scale is a roadblock to innovation in the sector. Moreover, increased investments of capital will be necessary for significant social impacts to be realized.

The second reading in Part IV is an excerpt from *Measuring the Networked Nonprofit: Using Data to Change the World* by Beth Kanter and Katie Delahaye Paine, who discuss the importance of using data as part of a nonprofit's web-based strategic efforts to reach new markets and achieve mission-related goals. The networked nonprofit is described as a new type of nonprofit organization that leverages the power of social media to expand its network of supporters and thereby greatly increases its capacity and success.[32] The authors argue that measurement is a powerful tool that provides feedback, stimulates ideas, helps with documentation, offers credibility, saves time (since wasted activities can be avoided), and fuels passion for the work.[33] In an era when nonprofits are using social media to appeal to a younger demographic, this medium requires the same care as any other outreach tactic. If appropriately understood, staffed, and funded—all big ifs—social media can serve as an effective way for two-way communications between administrators and employees, citizens, clients, consumers, audiences, and a myriad of other stakeholders. There are no shortcuts when seeking to be innovative. As with all managerial strategies, using social media requires resources and careful attention to the relationships that these tools can help create.

## Case Studies in Part IV

The first case study in Part IV, "Creative Curmudgeonry," introduces the age-old issue of how to manage impediments to change in the workplace. Although generational differences may spur a diversity of ideas and inspire creativity, some organizational managers may also be slow to accept advice about change from newcomers.

In "Introspection, Creativity, and Cloud Computing," the reader is asked to analyze the privacy and accountability issues that are raised in enacting a comprehensive medical record system. In reviewing the case and responding to the managerial questions asked, the reader must decide how to balance the needs of a variety of stakeholders when a new technology is introduced.

## Notes

1. See, for example, Jay M. Shafritz, J. Steven Ott, and Yong Suk Jang, "Theories of Organizations and Environments" and "Theories of Organizations and Society," in Jay M. Shafritz, J. Steven Ott, and Yong Suk Jang, *Classics of Organization Theory*, 8th ed. (Boston: Cengage/Wadsworth, 2016).

2. Kelly M. Hannum, Jennifer Deal, Liz Livingston Howard, Linshuang Lu, Marian N. Ruderman, Sarah Stawiski, Nancie Zane, and Rick Price, *Emerging Leadership in Nonprofit Organizations: Myths, Meaning, and Motivations* (Greensboro, NC: Center for Creative Leadership, 2011).

3. Susanne G. Scott and Reginald A. Bruce, "Determinants of Innovative Behaviour: A Path Model of Individual Innovation in the Workplace," *Academy of Management Journal* 37 (1994): 580–607.

4. Joe Tidd, John Bessant, and Keith Pavitt, *Managing Innovation: Integrating Technological, Market, and Organizational Change*, 2d ed. (Chichester, UK: Wiley, 2001); Adela J. McMurray, Md. Mazharul Islam, James C. Sarros, and Andrew Pirola-Merlo, "Workplace Innovation in a Nonprofit Organization," *Nonprofit Management and Leadership* 23, no. 3 (Spring 2013): 367–388, 370.

5. Sarah L. Pettijohn and Elizabeth T. Boris, "Contracts and Grants Between Human Service Nonprofits and Government: Comparative Analysis," Urban Institute Brief 4, July 2014, http://www.urban.org/UploadedPDF/413189-Contracts-and-Grants-between-Human-Service-Nonprofits-and-Government.pdf.

6. Lester M. Salamon, "Trends and Challenges," in Lester M. Salamon, *America's Nonprofit Sector: A Primer*, 3rd ed., 245–269 (New York: Foundation Center, 2012); see also Virginia A. Hodgkinson and Murray S. Weitzman, *Nonprofit Almanac, 1996–1997: Dimensions of the Independent Sector* (San Francisco: Jossey-Bass, 1996).

7. Heather R. McLeod, "The Devolution Revolution—Are Nonprofits Ready?" *WhoCares* (Fall 1995): 36–42.

8. McMurray et al., "Workplace Innovation in a Nonprofit Organization," 370.

9. David O'Sullivan and Lawrence Dooley, *Applying Innovation* (Thousand Oaks, CA: Sage Publications, 2009), 4.

10. Ibid.

11. Dennis R. Young, "Nonprofit Entrepreneurship," in *The International Encyclopedia of Public Policy and Administration*, edited by Jay M. Shafritz (Boulder, CO: Westview Press, 1998), 1506–1509, 1506.

12. Ibid. 1507.

13. Salamon, "Trends and Challenges."

14. Paul C. Light, "Searching for Social Entrepreneurs: Who They Might Be, Where They Might Be Found, What They Do," in Rachel Mosher-Williams, *Research on Entrepreneurship: Understanding and Contributing to An Emerging Field*, Association for Research on Nonprofit Organizations and Voluntary Action (ARNOVA) Occasional Paper Series 1, no. 3 (Washington, DC: Aspen Institute, 2006), 13–37.

15. Burton A. Weisbrod, "The Future of the Nonprofit Sector: Its Entwining with Private Enterprise and Government," *Journal of Policy Analysis and Management* 16, no. 4 (1997): 541–555.

16. Amy Blackwood, Kennard T. Wing, and Thomas H. Pollak, *The Nonprofit Sector in Brief: Facts and Figures from the Nonprofit Almanac 2008: Public Charities, Giving, and Volunteering* (Washington, DC: Urban Institute).

17. Rick Cohen, "Social Entrepreneurship at the Public Trough," *Nonprofit Quarterly*, February 13, 2009, accessed March 15, 2011, https://nonprofitquarterly.org/policysocial-context/1539-social-entrepreneurialism-at-the-public-trough.html.

18. Since about 1995, however, nonprofit hospitals have been "losing" in the competition.

19. Montague Brown, "Commentary: The Commercialization of America's Voluntary Health Care System," *Health Care Management Review* 21, no. 3 (1996): 13–18; see also Malik Hasan, "Let's End the Nonprofit Charade," *New England Journal of Medicine* 334, no. 16 (April 18, 1996): 1055–1058.

20. Burton A. Weisbrod, "Commercialism and the Road Ahead," in Burton A. Weisbrod, *To Profit or Not to Profit: The Commercial Transformation of the Nonprofit Sector* (Cambridge: Cambridge University Press, 1998), 288.

21. Robert Egger, *Begging for Change: The Dollars and Sense of Making Nonprofits Responsive, Efficient, and Rewarding for All* (New York: HarperCollins, 2004).

22. US Small Business Administration, *Unfair Competition by Nonprofit Organizations with Small Business: An Issue for the 1980s*, 3d ed. (Washington, DC: US Government Printing Office, June 1984); see also James T. Bennett and Thomas J. DiLorenzo, *Unfair Competition: The Profits of Nonprofits* (Lanham, MD: Hamilton Press, 1989).

23. William P. Ryan, "The New Landscape for Nonprofits," *Harvard Business Review* (January–February 1999): 127–136.

24. Naomi B. Wish and Roseanne M. Mirabella, "Educational Impact on Graduate Nonprofit Degree Programs: Perspectives of Multiple Stake Holders," *Nonprofit Management and Leadership* 9, no. 3 (Spring 1999): 329–340.

25. For example, *U.S. News and World Report*'s October 2, 1995, cover story exclaimed: "Tax Exempt! Many nonprofits look and act like normal companies—running businesses, making money. So why aren't they paying Uncle Sam?"

26. Melissa Middleton Stone, "Competing Contexts: The Evolution of a Nonprofit Organization's Governance System in Multiple Environments," *Administration and Society* 28, no. 1 (May 1996): 61–89.

27. Ryan, "The New Landscape for Nonprofits," 128.

28. Salamon, "Trends and Challenges."

29. Ryan, "The New Landscape for Nonprofits," 128.

30. Edward T. Pound, Gary Cohen, and Penny Loeb, "Tax Exempt! Many Nonprofits Look and Act Like Normal Companies—Running Businesses, Making Money. So Why Aren't They Paying Uncle Sam?" *US News & World Report*, October 2, 1995, 36–39, 42–46, 51.

31. Ryan, "The New Landscape for Nonprofits," 136.

32. Beth Kanter and Katie Delahaye Paine, *Measuring the Networked Nonprofit: Using Data to Change the World* (San Francisco: Jossey-Bass, 2012), 7.

33. Ibid., 45; for similar arguments, see "Trends, Fads, and Staying Ahead of the Curve," ch. 5 in *An Executive's Guide to Fundraising Operations*, edited by Christopher M. Cannon (San Francisco: Wiley and Sons, 2011).

## CHAPTER 8

# Taking Social Entrepreneurship Seriously

J. GREGORY DEES

A cursory look at world affairs should convince any thinking and caring person, regardless of political ideology, that we have considerable room for improvement. Despite the tremendous strides in the quality of life that humankind has made in the past two centuries, many persistent problems remain, and new ones have emerged. Rapid economic growth and various experiments with activist governments have not been sufficient to lift a huge portion of the world population out of poverty. Curable and preventable diseases still cause tremendous suffering and claim many lives, particularly among the poor. Access to education and the quality of education vary widely across the globe, even within some developed countries. Slavery and human trafficking are more serious and widespread than most of us care to admit. Violence and conflict abound on personal, tribal, national, regional, and global levels. The earth is warming, polar icecaps are melting, and biodiversity is declining at an unusually high rate, raising serious questions about the impact on future generations, regardless of the cause. The list could go on and on. We may not all agree on our visions for an ideal world, but we can generally agree that the gap between reality and our notions of the ideal is still enormous.

One potentially promising strategy for improvement is to encourage and support social entrepreneurs, individuals, and organizations that bring to social problems the same kind of determination, creativity, and resourcefulness that we find among business entrepreneurs. One prime example is 2006 Nobel Peace Prize winner Muhammad Yunus, who founded the highly successful Grameen Bank in Bangladesh to provide credit to the poor to help them move out of poverty. Two of the 2006 MacArthur Fellowship winners were also leading social entrepreneurs. Victoria Hale founded the Institute for One World Health, a nonprofit pharmaceutical company that develops safe, effective, affordable medicines for developing countries, and Jim Fruchterman is a Silicon Valley engineer who created Benetech to craft technological solutions to social needs, ranging from literacy to human rights and landmine detection.

The concept of "social entrepreneurship" emerged in the 1980s from the work of Bill Drayton at Ashoka, funding social innovators around the world, and Ed Skloot at New Ventures, helping nonprofits explore new sources

Originally published as "Taking Social Entrepreneurship Seriously: Uncertainty, Innovation, and Social Problem Solving," in *SOCIETY* 44, no. 3 (2007). Copyright © 2007 by Springer. Reprinted with kind permission from Springer Science and Business Media.

of income. It has come into its own in the last decade, capturing the imaginations of many thoughtful observers. For instance, David Gergen, Harvard professor and former advisor to four US presidents, has described social entrepreneurs as the "new engines of reform." Numerous universities, including Harvard, Stanford, Columbia, New York University, Oxford, and Duke, have launched centers or major initiatives in this arena. The World Economic Forum has openly embraced social entrepreneurship, and the Forum's founders, Klaus and Hilde Schwab, have created their own Foundation for Social Entrepreneurship. Jeffrey Skoll, eBay's first president, has devoted his foundation to "investing in, connecting, and celebrating social entrepreneurs." Actor and director Robert Redford hosted a Public Broadcasting series in 2005 on the "New Heroes," supported by the Skoll Foundation, to profile successful social entrepreneurs. Major media outlets from the *New York Times* to *The Economist* have run feature articles on this trend. The Manhattan Institute, with which Howard Husock is affiliated, gives an annual Social Entrepreneurship Award. The embrace of this concept cuts across political and national boundaries, with activities and interest cropping up around the world.

Is this attention and excitement warranted? Does social entrepreneurship have the potential to create sustainable and scalable impact in arenas where government efforts have been ineffective? After studying this activity for over a decade, I am convinced that social entrepreneurs, operating outside of the constraints of government, significantly enhance our ability to find and implement effective solutions to social problems. Of course, the real test of any thesis of this sort lies in action and results. My goal in these pages is to convince readers that we should take social entrepreneurship seriously and make the necessary investment of resources, time, and energy to give this idea a serious and sustained test.

## Government as Problem-Solver

To put the current interest in social entrepreneurship in perspective, it is useful to think about human history as a series of experiments in social organization—from family, clan, and tribal structures to the elaborate governmental, corporate, and social structures of today. These experiments can be seen as a response to the question: How should we organize ourselves, publicly and privately, to move closer to the ideals of a good society? This article is not the place to trace the evolution of different forms of social organization, but it is helpful to look back briefly at a particular turning point in late eighteenth-century Europe that had ripple effects around the world.

The major social problem of the day was poverty. Some leading political thinkers, such as Thomas Paine and the Marquis de Condorcet, recognized the ineffectiveness of charity and, in the spirit of the Enlightenment, proposed more scientific and secular state-based alternatives. Charity was largely grounded in the practice of alms giving, typically organized by the church. The term comes from the Latin *caritas,* referring to a sentiment, compassion for others, which was not always a reliable or effective platform for action. It allowed givers to demonstrate their virtue, but charity at best provided temporary relief for the poor. This relief did not always reach all those that could benefit from it, and many feared it exacerbated the very problem at which it was directed, creating dependency and undermining the industriousness of the poor. According to historian Gareth Stedman Jones, in his book *An End to Poverty?,* Paine, Condorcet, and their fellow travelers offered a secular and rational alternative. A republican state could take a scientific approach to administer aid to the poor in a more rigorous, fair, and effective way. Though their particular schemes were not immediately implemented, these thinkers planted the seeds for social democracy and the welfare state.

The Enlightenment positioned government as the main actor in resolving social problems that were not addressed by economic development. Building on the seventeenth-century scientific revolution, and with Newtonian mechanics as the paradigm, it made sense for the state to take on the central role in engineering a solution to poverty. Of course, this shift away from religious, sentimental approaches to poverty was taken to new heights in the late nineteenth and twentieth centuries by Karl Marx and his followers. Over the course of the past two centuries, the world has witnessed a variety of experiments in government-based efforts to tackle poverty, as well as other social and environmental problems. Over this period, a mixed religious and secular civil society continued to evolve and play a complementary role, but the hope for social problem-solving has largely been on government.

While this focus on government as social problem solver led to some notable successes, such as increased access to education and health care for many, the experience also revealed the limits of government as the vehicle for social problem-solving. It has become clear that large-scale, top-down government programs have serious drawbacks.

Government service delivery, including in the relatively successful arenas of education and health care, has been criticized as bureaucratic, ineffective, wasteful, too political, and antithetical to innovation. After two centuries of aggressive experimentation with different forms of government, we have learned, at the very least, that government is a tool that is effective for some kinds of social interventions but not as effective for others. We do not need to enter the ideological debates about the appropriate role and size of government to recognize the potential value of bringing private initiative, ingenuity, and resources to the table.

Through various government efforts to solve social problems, we have learned that with all our scientific knowledge and rational planning,

we still do not know in advance what will work effectively. Thus, progress in the social sphere depends on a process of innovation and experimentation akin to entrepreneurship in the business world. When the Austrian economist Joseph Schumpeter formulated his theory of economic development, he saw entrepreneurs playing a central role. They drove development by "carrying out new combinations." They could modify existing products or services, develop new ones, improve production and marketing processes, find new sources of supply, take existing products into new markets, or create new forms of organization. In so doing, as he later put it, they "reform or revolutionize the pattern of production." And they shift resources into areas of higher yield and productivity, to paraphrase J. B. Say, the eighteenth-century French economist who popularized the term "entrepreneur." To be sure, large firms engage in incremental innovations, but as Carl Schramm and Robert Litan of the Kauffman Foundation recently put it, "Radical breakthroughs tend to be disproportionately developed and brought to market by a single individual or new firm." Social entrepreneurs are needed to play the same innovating role with regard to social needs and problems.

Social and business entrepreneurs uncover or create new opportunities through a process of exploration, innovation, experimentation, and resource mobilization. This is an active, messy, highly decentralized learning process. Decentralization is critical because finding what works depends on having the right knowledge, being able to envision new combinations, and having the freedom to test ideas through action. The necessary knowledge cannot easily be centralized; much of it is local and dispersed among the population. As a result, some people will see opportunities and conceive of promising new combinations that others could not envision. Because of the creative nature of this process, centralizing social problem-solving makes about as much sense as centralizing art production. Finally, since independent entrepreneurs must mobilize resources to continue to pursue their visions, they have to persuade financiers who are putting their money behind the idea and talented employees who are devoting their time and skills that this venture is worthwhile. This selection process provides a discipline, albeit imperfect, that helps narrow the funnel to those ideas that have better chances of working. When it works well, this decentralized process allows bad ideas to fall by the wayside, encourages lessons to be learned, and provides an incentive for continuous improvement of the more promising ones.

Why can't government agencies do this? When compared to government agencies, independent social entrepreneurs have several distinct advantages. They have greater freedom of action and can usually move more quickly than public officials. They can explore a wider range of alternatives, largely because they are not as constrained by bureaucratic rules, legislative mandates, political considerations, and a fixed budget. Social entrepreneurs can tailor their efforts to different communities or markets in ways that would be difficult for government programs. Moreover, independent social entrepreneurs have access to private resources, while private contributions to government are relatively rare. Thus, social entrepreneurs are able to attract voluntary gifts of money, time, and in-kind donations, leveraging public money devoted to the same problem with philanthropy, social investment, or earned income from their business ventures.

The reliance on independent social entrepreneurs also provides society with greater opportunities to learn with less risk. Government programs usually represent relatively large bets on fairly standardized interventions with commitments to a certain course of action that can be very hard to modify once announced. As economists Douglass North and Robert Thomas observed, "government solutions entail the additional cost of being stuck with the decision in the future—that is, withdrawal costs are higher than those related to voluntary organizations." With social entrepreneurs, we have more and smaller bets on varied efforts to tackle the same social problem. When we have high levels of uncertainty about the best approach, diversification and experimentation increase the opportunities for learning and success. Diversification of activity has the added benefit of reducing the costs of failure during this learning process. If some of the small bets fail, the impact will be far less than the failure of a large-scale government program. To the extent that these experiments are privately funded, this learning process does not come at great public expense.

Furthermore, some social innovations are unlikely to be very effective if they are carried out by governmental organizations. The private nature of social ventures can be a distinct advantage. Consider Planned Parenthood, Alcoholics Anonymous, the Sierra Club, Habitat for Humanity, or community foundations. Could these work as well as branches of government? It seems unlikely. Boy and Girl Scouts would certainly take on a very different connotation if the government ran these programs. A rape crisis center might be effective in large part because it is run and staffed by volunteers who have been victims of rape themselves. Would victims of rape trust the center as much if it were government-run? Additionally, in some cases, it is important to work across governmental levels and jurisdictional boundaries. The Nobel Prize–winning organization, *Médecins Sans Frontières* (Doctors Without Borders), captures this notion in its very name. It is much harder for government agencies to work effectively across boundaries. Since many social and environmental issues cut across these boundaries, it makes sense for the organizations tackling them to be organized accordingly. Thus, many innovative approaches to social problems are not only best started outside government, they are best kept outside government.

Social entrepreneurs have an important role to play, whether it is to complement or supplant government efforts. They are better positioned to innovate and experiment than government agencies. They have flexibility in how they serve their missions that should allow them to be more efficient and effective. They increase our chances of learning, and they bring private resources to the table. Unfortunately, until recently they were not taken as seriously as they should be as an important driver of social progress. People tended to focus on government and markets as the main social forces, treating the "third sector" as marginal, rather than as a potential major engine for progress. Yet independent social entrepreneurs have the potential to play the same role in addressing social needs that business entrepreneurs play in what economic Nobel Laureate Edmund Phelps calls "dynamic capitalism." Social entrepreneurship engages the problem-solving skills and local knowledge of many individuals and organizations in search of innovative solutions. As a result, it has some powerful advantages over centralized policy analysis and planning.

## Charity and Problem-Solving

Today's social entrepreneurs do not see themselves as engaged in "charity" in the traditional alms-giving sense. They recognize its limits and weaknesses, as did the Enlightenment critics. Muhammad Yunus (1999) makes the point forcefully: "When we want to help the poor, we usually offer them charity. Most often we use charity to avoid recognizing the problem and finding a solution for it. Charity becomes a way to shrug off our responsibility. Charity is no solution to poverty. Charity only perpetuates poverty by taking the initiative away from the poor. Charity allows us to go ahead with our own lives without worrying about those of the poor. It appeases our consciences."

Other social entrepreneurs may not object as strongly to charity. However, even those who acknowledge a need for temporary relief tend to view their own work as fundamentally different. They aim to create sustainable improvements and are willing to draw on self-interest, as well as compassion, to do it.

Social entrepreneurship represents another step in the continuing reinvention of the "third sector" over the past one hundred and fifty years. The Enlightenment not only brought a shift in political philosophy; it also changed private charitable institutions. Many of them embraced the new rationality, leading to the rise of what historian Gertrude Himmelfarb calls "scientific charity." This shift generated a relative boom of new organizations in the later nineteenth and early twentieth centuries. The movement included new religious charities with more "scientific" approaches, the creation of secular charitable institutions, professionally run philanthropic foundations, and the establishment of new helping professions, such as social work. The Salvation Army, YMCA, Boys and Girls Clubs, and many prominent third-sector organizations and major foundations trace their roots to this era.

Leading social entrepreneurs today are most aptly described as pragmatists. They are focused on achieving sustainable results and will use whatever tools are most likely to work. They embrace innovation, value effective management, and are open to a wide range of operational and business models. They are willing to adapt ideas and tools from business when these will help. They are even willing to use for-profit forms of organization or hybrid structures that include for-profit and nonprofit elements. When it is possible, social entrepreneurs will happily craft market-based solutions that rely only on self-interest, allowing scarce philanthropic or government resources to flow to areas that genuinely need subsidy. If they can find an overlooked market opportunity that also improves social conditions, they will gladly pursue it. Yunus's Grameen Bank is legally a for-profit institution owned by its borrowers and is now financially self-sustaining.

Recognizing that for-profit or hybrid organizations may have an important role in creating better social conditions, some new philanthropists are disregarding old sector boundaries. When Silicon Valley venture capitalists Brook Byers and John Doerr started the New Schools Venture Fund, they decided to use it to fund both nonprofit and for-profit ventures that have the potential to create major improvements in K–12 education. Recently, the giant Internet search company Google decided that instead of creating the typical nonprofit company foundation, it would create its philanthropic arm as a for-profit capable of investing in nonprofit or for-profit ventures with a social purpose, such as more fuel-efficient vehicles. The lines between for-profit and nonprofit are breaking down as social entrepreneurs and entrepreneurial philanthropists look for new ways to tackle a range of social issues from alternative energy to improvements in health care.

Today's social entrepreneurs are building on the tradition of Ben Franklin. When Franklin saw opportunities to improve life for his fellow citizens in Philadelphia, he pursued them in whatever form seemed most sensible. He created for-profit printing and publishing businesses to keep citizens informed, a voluntary firefighting association to protect the homes of members, a subscription-based lending library, and a philanthropically supported academy that became the University of Pennsylvania, just to mention a few examples. For each entrepreneurial venture, Franklin adopted an economic, operating, and legal structure that was suitable given the circumstances. Social entrepreneurs operating today embrace this legacy of pragmatic private initiatives to improve social conditions. They do not see themselves as "charities" or even as "nonprofits," though they often use that legal form of organization. They are entrepreneurs who move comfortably across sector boundaries in search of the best ways to achieve sustainable impact.

## A Supportive Infrastructure

The current boom in social entrepreneurship exists despite a relatively poor understanding of this work. Those who take it up often lack the resources and infrastructure they need to succeed on a significant scale. They are swimming against the current of cultural assumptions and biases. As a society, we have not openly embraced social entrepreneurship, do not appreciate the crucial differences between social entrepreneurship and charity, and have not yet constructed the kinds of cultural and institutional mechanisms social entrepreneurs need to be effective. Though today's social entrepreneurs represent a break from sentimental, alms-giving charity, their work is still inhibited by the old norms and assumptions of alms-giving charity that permeate the sector. Even social entrepreneurs who feel they can adopt a for-profit legal form do not find the kind of support they need to blend social and financial objectives. If we want to capitalize on this current wave of interest and test the potential of social entrepreneurship, we need to create an environment conducive to success. We need to support social entrepreneurs with a more efficient and robust infrastructure, appropriate public policy, and a change in the culture of the social sector.

For social entrepreneurship to flourish, we need public policies that recognize and deliberately harness its potential. These policies should free social entrepreneurs to innovate and experiment, manage the risk of this experimentation, encourage private investors to support this activity, and allow those involved to reap appropriate rewards for their success. Even though Grameen Bank is a private initiative, it is owned in small part by the government of Bangladesh, and it required special legislation so that it could take savings deposits and operate as a formal financial institution. Without these deposits, it would not have been able to grow nearly as rapidly. As social entrepreneurs experiment with new business models, we may need new legal forms of organization, such as the "community interest company" category recently created in the United Kingdom. As philanthropists and other financial backers experiment with the best ways to use their resources to support social entrepreneurs, we may need changes in the legal structures and rules for doing that kind of investing as well.

Capitalism required a culture that allowed for trust and a comfort with transactions beyond family and tribal boundaries, as well as a culture in which profit-making is morally acceptable. Similarly, in the social sector, we need a culture that honors and taps into the altruistic impulses that have fueled charity in the past, but directs those impulses toward impact and performance. We need a culture that accepts failure as essential for learning and that honors effectiveness and efficiency as much as the culture of charity honors sacrifice. We also need a culture that does not make it shameful to earn a decent living serving social purposes. Building the right supports will not be easy, but it is essential if this approach is to achieve its potential.

## Challenges to Moving Forward

By making social entrepreneurs a recognized, strategic element in the process by which we improve social conditions, we have the potential to make headway in arenas that have remained vexing. The worldwide potential for mobilizing socially entrepreneurial behavior, if we were to make a deliberate effort to promote it, is enormous. However, this idea is relatively new, is still experimental, and it may not work as well as proponents (including myself) expect it to, just as activist government did not work as well

as many expected it to. Several issues could be raised, but three stand out as especially important: social impact assessment, the selection-investment processes, and scalability.

Entrepreneurship works well in business because markets tend to reinforce value creation both for customers and for investors. Businesses that do not create sufficient value for these two groups usually whither and fail. The test is whether customers will pay enough to cover the costs of production and to generate an attractive return for investors. An attractive return is one that is comparable to or better than those generated by alternative investments of similar risk. Businesses with strong track records and indications of future potential can grow relatively rapidly because of the size of the financial markets and the ability of these markets to respond quickly. These measures are definitely not foolproof. Even seasoned business investors make serious mistakes. However, customer and financial markets work reasonably well to identify, select, and scale firms that are creating the most customer and investor value. The same cannot be said of social entrepreneurship.

Social impact is difficult to measure in a reliable, timely, and cost-effective fashion—especially for the most ambitious social ventures. How and when do we know that someone has been moved out of poverty in a sustainable way or that a strategy will slow global warming? Signs, symptoms, and leading indicators often must be used to provide clues to whether an intervention is having its intended impact. Many innovations that sound logical and promising fail in practice or produce unintended harms that offset the gains. Even with micro-finance, the innovation for which Yunus won the Nobel Peace Prize, attempts to demonstrate its impact in a rigorous and systematic way have produced mixed and sometimes confusing results. The stories of impact on individuals and their families are plenty and powerful, but methods for systematic evaluation have been a subject of debate. Even when the intended impact can be assessed reliably, it may be difficult to attribute causation without very well controlled studies that are costly and complicated. Children who participate in a voluntary after-school tutoring program may have better graduation rates than their classmates, but this could be driven by other factors, such as educated and motivated parents. Even when causation can be established, comparisons across organizations can be very difficult unless they have a very similar mission, strategy, operating environment, and target population. Even among domestic educational interventions, how do we compare Teach For America, the Gates Foundation's US Libraries initiative, and Edison Schools? This does not mean the situation is hopeless. Innovators are working on this challenge and making some headway, but we need to develop better ways to identify the most promising innovations, sort out the failures, and learn from these experiments. In the meantime, we must operate with greater uncertainty, making our best judgments in light of imperfect data.

Even if we can find methods to measure impact more accurately, we need natural selection processes that direct resources and support to the most promising innovations and away from the failed experiments. Current mechanisms in the social sector are highly imperfect, for at least two reasons. First, performance evaluation is not highly valued in the culture of charity. Charity is about compassion, sacrifice, and temporary relief. It is easy to see if you get food to a hungry person. Your motivations are between you and your God or conscience. Why invest in performance assessment? Better for the money to go for programs. This culture is crumbling, especially among major foundations and new philanthropists, but it still holds more sway than we recognize. The second reason selection is weak is that "investors" in the social sector, particularly philanthropists, are motivated by more than social impact. They allocate their capital for emotive and expres-

sive reasons as well. Some want to thank the hospice that cared for their loved one, not reward the best hospice in the country. Others choose to support Greenpeace instead of the Nature Conservancy, not because of a dispassionate assessment of which organization is doing a better job, but because they identify with the ideology and confrontational tactics of Greenpeace. Still others want to support a needy organization, rather than one that seems to be doing well, even if the latter could create more impact dollar for dollar. As things stand, effective and efficient organizations may not be rewarded with additional resources, while ineffective and inefficient ones may thrive because they have a moving story to tell. Resource flows still depend more on sentiment, popular causes, personal charisma, and marketing skills than on social value creation. We need to move toward selection and investment processes that better align the personal satisfaction of resource providers with the potential for impact.

Social entrepreneurs often find it very hard to scale. When they do scale, the process is usually very slow, particularly when viewed relative to the size and growth of the problems being addressed. Even Habitat for Humanity, one of the greatest growth stories of the social sector, cannot keep up with the need for housing in its target population. This is partly because the infrastructure, policy, and culture needed to support the growth has been lacking. It is also partly because private resources devoted to the social sector have been relatively small compared to the problems being addressed and poorly allocated. The oft-touted intergenerational transfer of wealth that we are experiencing in the United States may help, but this infusion of capital could represent a one-time boom, rather than a sustainable solution. To reduce the need for outside funding, many social entrepreneurs are experimenting with earned income strategies. Developing new business models may help, but even profitable businesses often must tap into outside markets for growth capital. Social ventures tend to have smaller pools to tap into. While many people are at work on innovations in the private funding markets for social entrepreneurs, it is still not clear whether the amount of private capital available will be sufficient and appropriately directed to scale the most promising innovations, raising the question of government involvement.

Government-supported programs can scale rather rapidly, when the political will and funding are present. This is because government has the power to coerce compliance and mobilize resources through taxation. But how do we avoid the problems associated with government programs? We need to learn from prior efforts to combine social entrepreneurship with government support to see how this might be done most effectively. What can we learn from charter school legislation, which opened the door to more education entrepreneurs by providing access to public funding? What can we learn from the rapid spread of hospices throughout the United States after Medicare agreed to reimburse for hospice care? Even some of the paradigms of independent social entrepreneurship, such as Teach For America and Habitat for Humanity, rely on some government funding. In his essay "The Age of Social Transformation," Peter Drucker envisioned a society in which "many social sector organizations will become partners with government" through voucher programs. He noted that these organizations would also be competitors with government, concluding, "The relationship between the two has yet to be worked out—and there is practically no precedent for it." Working this out may be essential to assure the scalability of effective social innovations.

Social entrepreneurship is a promising development that may lead into a new era in which we more effectively harness private initiative, ingenuity, and resources to improve social and environmental conditions. We need to provide the right support, and we need to address fundamental questions.

## References

Drucker, Peter. 1994. "The Age of Social Transformation." *The Atlantic Monthly* 274, no. 5, 53–80.

Yunus, Muhammad. 1999. *Banker to the Poor: Micro-Lending and the Battle Against World Poverty.* New York: Public Affairs.

## Further Readings

Bornstein, David. 2004. *How to Change the World: Social Entrepreneurship and the Power of New Ideas.* New York: Oxford University Press.

Dees, J. Gregory, and Beth Battle Anderson. 2003. "Sector Bending: Blurring the Lines between Nonprofit and For-Profit." *SOCIETY* 40, no. 4 (May–June). Reprinted in Peter Frumkin and Jonathan B. Imber, eds., *In Search of the Nonprofit Sector.* New Brunswick, NJ: Transaction Publishers, 2004.

Jones, Gareth Stedman. 2004. *An End to Poverty? A Historical Debate.* New York: Columbia University Press.

Mosher-Williams, Rachel, ed. 2006. *Research on Social Entrepreneurship: Understanding and Contributing to an Emerging Field.* ARNOVA Occasional Paper Series 1, no. 3.

Nichols, Alex. 2006. *Social Entrepreneurship: New Paradigms of Sustainable Social Change.* New York: Oxford University Press.

## CHAPTER 9

# Measuring the Networked Nonprofit: Using Data to Change the World

## Beth Kanter and Katie Delahaye Paine

## The Keys to Nonprofit Success: Networking and Measurement

Two key processes lead to tremendous success for nonprofits: becoming networked and using measurement. . . .

A *networked nonprofit* is an organization that uses social networks and the technology of social media to greatly extend its reach, capabilities, and effectiveness. *Measurement* is the process of collecting data on your communications results and using the data to learn and improve your programs. An organization with a *data-informed culture* uses data to help make decisions and uses measurement to continuously improve and refine its systems.

Most nonprofit organizations use at least some sort of informal measurement and some form of social media–enabled networking. Many nonprofits are striving to build a data-informed culture and networked mindset. But few organizations use these powerful techniques to their greatest potential. One of these is MomsRising.org, a poster child for

networked nonprofits and nonprofit measurement mavens.

## MomsRising: A Superstar of Networked Nonprofits Knows the Joys of Measurement

Kristin Rowe-Finkbeiner and Joan Blades founded MomsRising in 2006. To design this nonprofit, they combined their experience in grassroots organizing and social media with successful ideas from organizations like Move On, ColorOfChange, League of Conservation Voters, and others. The result was an organization that embraces constant learning from experience and embeds this powerful concept in its organizational culture and processes. It has fueled the organization's growth from zero members in May 2006 to over a million active members—moms, dads, grandparents, aunts, and uncles—today.

MomsRising uses measurement to achieve tremendous success . . . and there are several themes concerning measurement and how it is used. . . .

### Theme 1: "Likes" on Facebook Is Not a Victory—Social Change Is

Proper measurement keeps organizations focused on results rather than the tools they use. . . . MomsRising, for instance, does not simply count "likes" on Facebook. Instead, it uses social change to define its successes and develops metrics accordingly. Its most important goals generally include these:

- Getting policies passed on family-related issues
- Increasing capacity
- Increasing the movement size by increasing membership
- Working with aligned partner organizations
- Garnering attention from all media through creative engagement

For MomsRising, the holy grail of results is getting legislatures to pass family-friendly policies. This requires grabbing the attention of policymakers. As one indicator of progress toward that goal, it counted an invitation to bring mothers to the White House to talk with policymakers about their experience with Medicaid. The White House blogged about the power of people's stories, and MomsRising members blogged about their White House experience, resulting in even greater exposure for their messages. Says Rowe-Finkbeiner, "The after-story is just as important because it will often get picked up by mainstream media outlets like NPR or the Huffington Post."[1]

### Theme 2: Measurement Helps Nonprofits Understand and Improve Their Social Networks

Another theme is that measurement helps nonprofits listen to and engage with their constituents. Measurement enables organizations to assess and improve their relationships with their members and stakeholders. . . .

An important part of MomsRising's decision making is the use of member feedback in the form of stories or comments on social channels or e-mail and in more structured ways such as surveys. Says Rowe-Finkbeiner, "We are in constant dialogue with our members to figure out what works and what doesn't. The data keeps us focused on our mission of building a movement for family economic security, while listening and engaging with our members breathes life into our movement."

### Theme 3: Measurement Means Data for Decisions, Not for Data's Sake

Unfortunately, many organizations see measurement as collecting data to dump on the boardroom table or the executive director's desk. But measurement isn't about justifying one's existence or budget, and it isn't about filling spreadsheets with lots of "just-in-case" data to throw over the fence.

Measurement is about using data to learn to become more effective and more efficient. It's about doing your job better, and helping your organization achieve its mission with fewer resources. It's about reaching more people, and becoming better at saving the world.

### Theme 4: Measurement Makes You Plan for Success

More and more nonprofits are making larger investments in social media: hiring dedicated staff, upgrading Web sites to incorporate social features, and using more powerful professional tools to do the work. Measurement helps you make smarter investments and helps you use those investments in a smarter way. Having a social media measurement plan and approach is no longer an afterthought. It's the smart way to run an organization.

## Theme 5: Good Measurement Is Good Governance

As networked nonprofits become more skilled in their social media practice, their boards and senior management are becoming more knowledgeable about this area. They expect reports showing social media results, and they expect results expressed in the kind of language that measurement provides. In addition, foundations and other funders want credible evaluation reports and demonstrations of impact. Today boards and foundations increasingly include executives from the for-profit world who have come to expect actionable data and standardized measurement systems.

## Theme 6: Data Without Insight Is Just Trivia

The key to MomsRising's success is that it uses data to refine its strategies and tactics. It has achieved its success not by luck or gut instinct but by using measurement to make decisions.

MomsRising holds a weekly staff meeting, nicknamed "Metrics Monday." Prior to this meeting each program and campaign staff person reviews his or her results as part of an explicit process of preparation. The meeting is actually a group conversation about what actions to reinforce, how to refine messages, and what other improvements need to be made. Says Rowe-Finkbeiner, "Our dashboards have multiple views: a high-level view and the ability to drill down into specific campaigns. This informs our discussion."

## Theme 7: Measuring Failure Is Part of the Path to Success

Some experiments bomb. Some projects or ideas seem brilliant at first, but when the results come in the data shows that they simply didn't work. The staff at MomsRising give themselves permission to kill these. To remove the stigma of failure, they do this with humor, calling it a "joyful funeral." To learn from the experience, they reflect on why it didn't work.

## Theme 8: Incremental Success Is Not Failure

Many organizations experiment with social media. Networked nonprofits are expert at setting up and measuring low-risk experiments and pilots. What sets MomsRising apart is that the staff don't do aimless experiments; they set realistic expectations for success and measure along the way.

Some experiments, actions, or issues provide dramatic results. For example, a MomsRising interactive educational video garnered over 12 million views, hundreds of comments, and thousands of new members who signed up or took action. Rowe-Finkbeiner says, "That type of success does not happen every day, but we need to try for that kind of success every day. We can do it only if we decide not to pursue things that don't work." They analyze these game-changing successes to understand how they can be replicated and to make sure they weren't accidents.

## Theme 9: Measurement Is Valuable at Every Level of Functioning

Any nonprofit can learn to use measurement to make its social media more effective. It is not hard to get started and doesn't require expensive software, a graduate degree, or even an aptitude for mathematics. The trick is to start simple and grow from there. . . .

# Seven Vital Characteristics of Networked Nonprofits

Knowing how to use social media well is not just about knowing which button to push or what technological wizardry to employ. The power of a networked approach is its ability to connect people to one another and help build strong, resilient, trusting relationships that lead to real on-the-ground social change. We see seven characteristics as vital in this approach:

1. *Networked nonprofits know their organizations are part of a much larger ecosystem of organizations and individuals that provides valuable resources.* They understand that they don't need to own the to-do list, only the results.

2. *Networked nonprofits know that relationships are the result of all the interactions and conversations they have with their networks.* They are comfortable doing their work transparently. It makes them open to serendipity and new ideas.

3. *Networked nonprofits experiment and learn from experience.* They are masters at experimenting their way into dramatic wins. They don't shy away from failure because it leads them to innovation and success.

4. *Networked nonprofits have data-informed cultures.* They use data to develop strategy, measure success, assess their experiments, and then make decisions on how best to move forward with new strategies.

5. *Networked nonprofits know how to inspire people.* They motivate their networks of support to help shape the organization's programs, share stories in order to raise awareness of social issues, change attitudes and behavior, and organize communities to provide services or advocate for legislation.

6. *Networked nonprofits work differently from other organizations.* They enjoy a social culture that encourages everyone in and outside the organization to participate and spread their mission. They challenge deeply held assumptions about leadership, roles, and structures. They have broken down departmental silos. They are comfortable sharing control or cocreating with their networks—whether that means allowing people to retell the organization's story in their own words or scaling programs.

7. *Networked nonprofits are masters at using social media.* They are adept at using tools that encourage conversations and building relationships between people and between people

and organizations. They are able to scale their efforts quickly, easily, and inexpensively. They are adept at blending tried-and-true methods with new digital tools. . . .

## Becoming a Networked Nonprofit: The Crawl, Walk, Run, Fly Model

Learning to use social media and other emerging technologies and putting the ideas into practice will be successful only if nonprofits take small, incremental, and strategic steps. Our model incorporates four levels of social media practice: crawl, walk, run, and fly. Each level indicates where the organization is with respect to becoming a networked nonprofit.

It is important to note that reaching the highest level of networked nonprofit practice takes months, if not years. Even an organization like MomsRising, which was born as a networked nonprofit and has several years of social media experience, has not won its dramatic victories over night. . . .

Not every nonprofit will go through the levels at the same pace because different organizations have different cultures, capacities, communication objectives, program designs, and target audiences. Moreover, the reality will be messy; an organization might not precisely fit the profile in any specific category. But every organization can take pride in its success at whatever level it has achieved. . . .

[Below,] . . . we set out a crawl, walk, run, fly self-assessment checklist that any organization can use to evaluate where it is in its development as a networked nonprofit.

### Crawl

Organizations in the crawl stage of becoming networked nonprofits are not using social media or emerging technology at all or, if they are using it, are not using it consistently. These organizations lack a robust communications strategy or program plan that can be scaled using a networked approach. Crawlers are not just smaller nonprofits; they include larger institutions that have all the basics in place but lack a social culture or are resisting transforming from a command-and-control style to a more networked mind-set. These nonprofits need to develop a basic communications strategy or program plan. . . . The first measurement step at this level is setting up a listening process and integrating listening on social channels into planning research.

### Walk

Nonprofits at the walk stage (dubbed "the walkers") are using one or more social media tools consistently, but this use isn't linked to a communications strategy, campaign, or program plan. They have in place best practices on tools and techniques as part of the organizational skill set but may need assistance in developing a social media strategy to support short- and long-term SMART (specific, measurable, achievable, realistic, and time) objectives. They may also need help to correctly identify the audiences they need to target.

Walkers have internalized listening and are able to use the data they collect to improve engagement and content best practices. At this stage, leaders may not fully understand social media and networked ways of working. Often the question "What's the value?" surfaces. Nonprofits in the walk stage need to avoid spreading the organization's resources too thin. They should instead focus on one or two social media tools, going deep on tactics, and generating tangible results to demonstrate value.

Walkers must identify low-cost ways to build capacity internally, for example, by using interns or volunteers effectively and integrating social media tasks into existing job descriptions. Staff members should evaluate their job tasks and identify what they don't need to do in order to make time for social media and other emerging technologies, all with support from leaders. They must also enlist the help of their social networks outside their organization.

A nonprofit's social media policy in the walk stage formalizes the value and vision for social media use and networked approach and encourages free agent outsiders to help with implementation. The organization integrates simple measurement techniques and learning as an organizational habit that helps improve practice.

### Run

Nonprofits at the run stage use one or more social media tools and are strategic, identifying key result areas and key performance metrics that drive everything they do. They also have a formal ladder of engagement and know how to measure it. They understand the importance of visualizing their networks and measuring their relationships.

In these organizations, social media are not in a silo or guarded by one person or department. With a social media policy in place and a more social culture, the organization is comfortable with working transparently and working with people outside its organization. . . . They know how to use measurement to identify these influencers. The board is also using social media as part of its governance role.

The main problem at this stage is scaling. To build internal capacity, organizations may need to bring on a half- or full-time staff person who serves as a community manager, building relationships with people on social media or new technology platforms. This social media point person also works internally as a network weaver or trainer to help departments and individuals use social media to support the organization's programs.

These runners effectively integrate social media and emerging technologies such as mobile messaging across all communications channels and know the right combination of measurement tools to evaluate their performance. They have strong capacity in content creation as well as repurposing or remixing across channels and use crowdsourcing to create and spread content. Runners also incorporate social fundraising, knowing that community engagement is as important to measure as dollars raised.

For program strategy, runners use crowdsourcing to help design pilots, generate feedback on an evaluation, or rethink programs. They know how to measure the impact of the crowd. . . . The organization has adequately engaged and built relationships with key influencers—both organizations and individuals. The organization has codified and shared its program work flow and has made all program tools and materials available so its network can assist with implementation.

### Fly

Organizations at the fly stage have mastered everything at the running stage and internalized it. These "flyers" create a culture of public learning for both individuals and the entire organization. They embrace failure and success alike and learn from both. The organization uses data to make decisions, but leaders understand how to lead from the heart as well as the head. The organiza-

tion has documented and shared dramatic results with its stakeholders and peer organizations. Flyers are part of a vibrant network of people and organizations focused on social change.

Organizations in this category have adopted sophisticated measurement techniques, tools, and processes. This may include benchmarking, testing, shared organizational dashboards, and linking results to job compensation for larger institutions. Above all, measurement is not viewed as an afterthought. It is part of an ongoing decision-making process that helps the organization continuously improve its programs.

## Crawl, Walk, Run, Fly Assessment Tool for Networked Nonprofits

This assessment tool lists the ideal best practices for networked nonprofits. Review each practice and self-assess whether you are crawling, walking, running, or flying. Where could you improve current practice?

This assessment tool builds on and adapts the work of Ash Shepherd, who created an integrated communications audit and, with Beth Kanter's encouragement, set up a wiki to share the documents and encourage people to "remix it."[2]

TABLE 9.1.  Crawl, Walk, Run, Fly (CWRF) Assessment Tool

| Practice | Indicator | CWRF Rating |
|---|---|---|
| *Strategy* | | |
| Identifies goals and measurable objectives | Identifies the most important overall results and creates measurable objectives based on those. | |
| Identifies specific target audience | Identifies specific audience target groups, including key stakeholders and influencers. | |
| Identifies success and value | Identifies what success looks like and the value it brings to the organization. | |
| Networked mind-set | Management understands and supports social media and networked approaches as part of the overall communications or program plan. | |

| Practice | Indicator | CWRF Rating |
|---|---|---|
| *Strategy (continued)* | | |
| Social media policy | Has formally identified appropriate personal and organizational use. | |
| Listening and influencer research | Has done research to learn what other organizations are doing and what the conversations are. Has done research to identify influencers and free agents. | |
| Allocates sufficient resources | Understands the capacity to implement by hiring staff or having social media tasks in job description or recruits volunteers. Tracks investment of time against results. | |
| *Implementation* | | |
| Tool selection | Uses best practices on a selective number of social media tools that match audience and capacity to implement. | |
| Engagement | Takes steps to foster online engagement and conversations related to strategic objectives. Has a formal ladder of engagement and uses it to guide strategy and measurement. | |
| Transparency | Works in a transparent way and has measured trust and other factors. | |
| Content | Has an editorial calendar and strategy for linking, producing, and distributing content across social media and other channels. | |
| Network building | Takes steps to foster online community or networked effects, with linkages to other organizations and free agents. | |
| Crowdsourcing | Gets feedback from network on ideas and strategies as appropriate and has a process to measure the value of feedback. | |
| Job description and training | Provides appropriate training to those responsible for implementation. | |
| Involves all staff | Social media are not isolated function. Most, if not all, staff or volunteers have some knowledge or participate as appropriate. | |
| Builds valuable partnerships | Relationships have been made with stakeholders and other organizations to achieve goals. Measures relationships on a regular basis. | |
| Measures, monitors, evaluates | Activities are monitored, measured, and evaluated for improvement. A formal process for reflecting on data and improving is in place. | |

*(continues)*

TABLE 9.1. *(continued)*

| Practice | Indicator | CWRF Rating |
|---|---|---|
| *Integration* | | |
| Website | Strategic linkages and integration between social media and website include link, content, and distribution. | |
| Other social channels | Strategic cross-promotion and integration among social channels. | |
| Print materials | Strategic links between social media and printed materials. | |
| E-mail marketing | Strategic links between social media and e-mailed newsletters. | |
| Mobile | Strategic links between social media and mobile. | |
| Offline | Strategic links between offline activities and social media channels. | |

## Notes

1. In Beth Kanter and Katie Delahaye Paine, *Measuring the Networked Nonprofit* (San Francisco: Jossey-Bass, 2012), 8.

2. "Nonprofit Social Media Audit," http://nonprofitsocialmediaaudit.wikispaces.com/, in Kanter and Paine, *Measuring the Networked Nonprofit,* 279.

# CREATIVE CURMUDGEONRY[1]

*C. Kenneth Meyer, Lance J. Noe, and Stephen Panyan*

Jason Malone, the longtime executive director of Pottawatomie Mental Health Care, Inc. (PMHC), a 501(c)(3) organization, had administered over the years what he affectionately referred to as the "possible and the impossible." As the executive director of PMHC, he felt that he was "in charge," although his position required extensive conversations with a board of directors, his own staff, other nonprofits, and the county government. In personal conversations, he was proud to mention that his degrees were obtained from "CHK—the College of Hard Knocks." Jason was quick to diminish the importance of new theories or trends in management, whether encouraging diversity in the workplace, emphasizing team development, or adopting managerial philosophies that placed a premium on innovativeness. Personal computers had been adopted at PMHC and the organization had a functioning website, but using cell phones or text messaging for work-related business was frowned upon, as was the idea of holding virtual meetings. He would frequently react to suggestions for change that emanated from his staff or others with the formulaic response, "We work in the real world and with real people. We don't need any 'pie in the sky' theorizing around here." Overall, he was a "hard-liner," as he called his managerial style, and the need to integrate theory with practice typically received short shift in his administrative manual.

Today Jason found himself at a roundtable that included his own staff members, a few of his board members, and representatives from area agencies to discuss expanding the array of mental health services offered to the surrounding area. The conversation was polite, as always, and the speech of those voicing their ideas during the meeting and reacting to others was thoughtful and measured in cadence. One new department head at PMHC, Sharon Hernandez, indicated that she had recently returned from a meeting of the National Society of Nonprofit Officials (NSNO), where she attended several presentations on the use of social media and other web-based communications. These, she said, had opened up her mind to new vistas on how to make organizations "more collaborative, more accessible, more responsible, and more transparent." She noted that research presented at the meeting had shown that stakeholders now expect more involvement in decision-making and that this is especially true of younger people.

Jason locked his complete attention on what Hernandez was saying, and the room filled with silence as he looked around, cleared his throat in an authoritative manner, and then said, "I thought I had heard everything up until now—the crazy, the weird, and the zany. But these ideas really take the cake."

The concept of using technologies such as apps, blogs, Facebook, Twitter, Instagram, and web-based communications had just been broached, and Jason found it difficult to envision how these means could possibly have anything to do with the effective, efficient, and fair administration of the organization's mission. He recognized that his staff members, including Sharon Hernandez, were younger workers, but he viewed them as "learners and mentees" rather than as advisers or cogovernors.

Jason did not lead an isolated life untouched by the changes associated with the arrival of the digital age, but he equated most new technologies with passing fads, a loss of managerial control, the introduction of alienation, and a loss of face-to-face interactions. He knew that management had everything to do with either encouraging or impeding change; he himself felt most comfortable and satisfied with the familiar. Jason stated, "We already have a website where our information is posted for the public to read. We can't do every cockamamy thing just because it is being done someplace else. 'Tried and true' is my motto. Most of these new electronic discoveries just bring along problems!"

The meeting seemed to die as those in attendance marched through the remaining agenda items in a routine, standardized, and mundane manner. Items were placed before the group, little discussion was raised, Jason commented, and then he said what would be done. Most assuredly, the message had been sent to the group that if you have a vision of what might be possible, keep it to yourself. "The only good ideas," one department head noted, "belong lock, stock, and barrel to Jason, and he never lets us forget it."

When Jason returned to his office, he knew full well that he had squashed the discussion on using social media or other technological innovations, and that was fine with him. He also soon remembered, however, a speech given by a successful entrepreneur at the Society for Human Resource Management (SHRM), who pointed out that rigidity, apathy, custom, habit, fear of uncertainty, and fear of losing power, status, and control were some of the factors associated with resistance to change, poor organizational performance, and failure to thrive.

This was a very difficult time for Jason. He was, as he often joked with his best friends, at the "twilight of a rather mediocre career," and he knew that, in some sense, the world had passed him by—especially the world of technology, digitization, computerization, and miniaturization. He felt pressured to keep up with his profession, but he also had a rather complicated feeling that the profession had abandoned him and did not really serve his personal outlook, interests, or goals.

As Jason paced around in the comfort of his office, he periodically paused and rearranged some of the material on his office shelves. He wondered when the social media fad would pass. As he pondered the notions that had been put forth by Sharon Hernandez, it became clear to him that the world of work was now quite different from what it had been like when he entered the workforce nearly thirty years earlier. Now Jason mumbled out loud, "How does one go about dealing with a changing workplace, technology, and daily set of management concerns and at the same time meet the needs of our clients and deliver our programs?" He caught himself answering his own question in nearly audible tones and then mused, "Am I obsolete or what?"

Several weeks later, Jason raised his head at the water cooler in the main hallway at Pottawatomie Mental Health Care. He could hear footsteps rapidly coming toward him, and as he looked over his shoulder, he heard Sharon Hernandez call out his name. Abruptly standing up, he quickly turned and asked her how her day was going. Sharon responded by exchanging the obligatory pleasantries, and then she said, "Mr. Malone, have you seen the new study that was recently conducted by the International Management Association on electronic media?" And before he could respond, she enthusiastically reported, "Nearly 48 percent of the organizations surveyed say that stakeholder contact has increased since they initiated social media, and 97 percent finance it with unrestricted funding."

Wowed by her assertiveness, Jason retorted, "Why are you so personally interested in this social media craze? Don't you realize that we are already strapped with the programs we are delivering?

If we go to this 'new way' of conducting business, not only will we need to fund the initiatives, but it will increase the workload and the magnitude of the services we will need to supply. In real terms, the budget just simply can't afford it, even if we could agree that it is a great idea."

## Questions and Instructions

1. What are the implications, from financial to customer service, in moving PMHC toward using social media in the delivery of its messaging, its interactions with stakeholders, and the delivery of its services and products? Please elaborate.
2. What are some of the best examples of nonprofit use of social media by organizations in your area? Can you envision requiring the use of social media for the betterment of organizations such as PMHC? How would such an initiative affect both the management of PMHC and its customer satisfaction levels? Please explain.
3. If you were Sharon Hernandez or a member of the PMHC board of director, would you bring any pressures to bear on Jason Malone? If so, what would you want him to do? Please outline your objectives. If you would be content with maintaining the status quo, please indicate why the status quo would be preferable to change.

## Notes

1. Adapted from E-Government by C. Kenneth Meyer, Lance J. Noe, and Stephen Panyan.

# INTROSPECTION, CREATIVITY, AND CLOUD COMPUTING

### C. Kenneth Meyer and Karen DeMello

Aamer Farina, the leader of IT solutions at New Trinity Health Systems, enjoyed his time at the annual summit for the Healthcare Information and Management Systems Society (HIMSS). Now that the conference was drawing to a close, he chose to enjoy his last night in the exclusive resort hotel where his organization had housed him during his stay. From his executive suite on the sixty-fifth floor, he relished bathing in the yellow-orange sunlight as it slowly but inevitably dipped into the western horizon, leaving only the shadows of the city's tall buildings and skyscrapers. Since he was no fan of height, he was careful as he gingerly tiptoed onto the glass-enclosed balcony to catch a glimpse of the resort workers below.

He never felt more secure than when he had his feet firmly anchored in terra firma, but as he often chuckled to himself, there was always a price to pay for living in the world of exclusivity. Edging ever so gently toward the balcony rail, he grasped it and held on as if he were its sole anchor to the hotel's infrastructure. Then he peered down, and what he saw filled him with a sense of awe and admiration.

At first glance, it seemed to him that a sea of workers was engaged in a beautifully orchestrated and choreographed "kabuki" dance. He watched as the workers folded, stacked, and transported the beach chairs, then stored them away for the night in their designated storage area; in the morning, they would remove the chairs once again and neatly arrange them around the pools for tomorrow's swimmers and sunbathers. As a matter of fact, it would have seemed strange if he had not been able to discern the rhythm of their actions, the near-metric cadence of covering, loading, and transporting the bulky, although lightweight, aluminum-framed beach chairs.

Aamer could see from afar the five pool areas, some symmetrical and others asymmetrical in design, yet all perfectly suited to meet the needs and demands of those engaged in a perfectly befitting relaxation activity. He also saw that not all of the beach chairs had been put away for the night—other chairs and tables had been readied for an evening of poolside music, dance, and dining. With wonder and admiration, he muttered to himself that the management of people is indeed the oldest of all human professions and even simple tasks require the actions and interactions of people.

Searching the innermost recesses of his managerial memory, he reflected on how correct Frederick Winslow Taylor, the father of scientific management, had been when he articulated the principle that there is one best way to do a job. Tonight, as he witnessed the activity below, it seemed to him that even the utterly mundane and repetitive activity of removing beach chairs and replacing them with their complementary furnishings for the evening's gala events had worked efficiently and gone off without a hitch. Indeed, he thought, these workers had been suitably trained to do a specific job and to do it right, time and time again. For Aamer, this was magic in motion beyond belief!

Aamer's evening of relaxation and wonderment would soon be interrupted, however, by his need to plan for an impending counseling session with a valued employee back at New Trinity headquarters—a session that was needed if a sense of normalcy was to return to his own shop. He longed for the days when he had been a technician and had a predictable forty-hour workweek with a defined set of duties and tasks to perform. On the opposite page of his life's ledger, he had done everything required of a professional who was resolved to move into a managerial position. As such, he thought, he had become competent in what he termed the "-ates" of leadership and management: deleg*ate*, orchestr*ate*, evalu*ate*, coordin*ate*, integr*ate*, motiv*ate*, and communic*ate*. When he was in a humorous mood, he would add to the "-ates" list the actions so often practiced by his managerial peers—procrastin*ate*, obfusc*ate*, and litig*ate*.

Now, he decided, his mind had wandered around enough and it was time to return to the task at hand. He genuinely liked working with Heather Holten, one of his senior developers, but she had a wild side that often showed itself as she fantasized about building a comprehensive health care information system. Most of her coworkers deemed her vision wild, or weird, or illogical. Yet what she proposed seemed perfectly rational, sane, logical, and even predictable in her own mind. Heather displayed attributes that Aamer liked to see "bubble out" of everyone on his staff, and he often remarked to his colleagues that smart jobs require the use of the right side of brain, the seat of creativity, entrepreneurialism, productivity, and fantasy.

The evening was drawing to a close, so Aamer left the balcony, closed the sliding-glass door, and returned to the executive desk located in a room adjacent to his hotel living quarters. He felt ready for the counseling session tomorrow morning. He had been in "ticklish" situations before that involved outlier perspectives that were staunchly held by members of the team. But he was ready for the challenge, and with a sly grin he confidently reminded himself of his own record of accomplishment: he held bachelor's and master's degrees in executive management: he had gained nearly twenty years of progressively solid and responsible experience in large, complex organizations; and he had been tested time and time again in following the routine designated by his supervisor and performing difficult assignments quickly and flawlessly. Indeed, his management of a team of five information technicians tasked with developing and implementing a health care tracking and billing system had met the minimum state-of-the-art standards he had set for himself and his organization: accuracy, relevancy, efficiency, effectiveness, reliability, and privacy.

Back at corporate headquarters, Heather Holten anticipated the upcoming meeting with Aamer with some apprehension, knowing she would need to explain the issues and problems she faced in working on the Comprehensive Health Care Management Program (CHCMP). She understood that the tasks she was assigned had not been fully operationalized, but she would stress in the meeting the delicate legal and privacy issues that New Trinity had to get right on its first iteration, with no room for error.

Remembering that she had faced other issues associated with the electrical-chemical revolution, Heather reflected on the gnawing problems associated with the digitalization of electronic medical records (EMR). In graduate school, she recalled, she had read a report by the Institute of Medicine (1991) that predicted that all physicians would be using computers in their practice by 2000, resulting in improved patient care. Although the cost savings had been touted as a major selling point, this overly optimistic projection had not kept up with reality.

She knew that electronic medical records could not be fully implemented without incurring the high costs of also implementing software and middleware technologies to accommodate different programming formats and data conversion requirements. She pondered the issue of how EMR might change health care delivery in one of the largest and most expensive systems in the world, with its rich mixture of hospitals, clinics, and sundry providers, and worried about finding ways in which these different providers could seamlessly adapt to EMR. She questioned why the United States lagged behind the other industrial democracies, such as Germany, England, Switzerland, and Taiwan, in implementing comprehensive EMR systems.

Heather felt certain that her budget could deal with the technological demands at the hospital level, but larger questions loomed on the horizon:

1. Who owns the health data and digitalized data records—the patient, the physician, or the hospitals and clinics? In other words, do the chart entries, write-ups, and observations of nurses, doctors, and other clinical staff belong to the patient or to the provider?

2. Will digitized medical records reduce medical costs, improve clinical outcomes, accelerate medical discoveries, and lead to added data mining and evidentiary-based medicine?

3. Is there an acknowledgment, at least in practice, that patients have a right to copy and control access to their own digitized data, and even to have their health data corrected? If the provider owns the data, is there a way to transfer the right to control data development between different provider locations and different providers?

Aamer Farina and Heather Holten had prepared themselves for their upcoming meeting, but both were unprepared for the range of concerns that would arise from their conversation. Aamer was prepared insofar as he was an experienced, tested, and successful administrator who had been in on the ground floor in developing data management systems. Heather had met her career objectives early in her professional life by being a knowledgeable and technologically and computer-savvy programmer and information specialist. She had also sought to expedite the planning and implementation of the CHCMP by putting considerable thought into the uses and efficacy of cloud computing, especially the associated costs and privacy (security) issues. Now, in the meeting, the overarching issue would be how much autonomy, flexibility, and creativeness Heather would be permitted or encouraged to exercise at New Trinity. Would Aamer motivate, lead, or simply get out of the way?

## Questions and Instructions

1. Describe Aamer Farina's managerial philosophy, citing examples from the case study to support your description. In your opinion, what is the impact of this leadership style on an organization's approach to innovation?

2. Explain the conflict between Aamer and Heather. Which of the two do you believe is most responsible for resolving the conflict? Explain your response.

3. One potential solution to the privacy concerns brought about by EMR involves a technology called "segmentation" or "sequestration," which allows information about sensitive medical issues like reproduction, mental illness, and substance abuse to be accessed by medical professionals only when "medically necessary." How could this privacy feature aid Heather in formulating an argument for a more comprehensive EMR system at New Trinity? What potential objections could Aamer make to this privacy feature?

4. What, in your opinion, is the greatest risk associated with a national electronic medical record system? What are the greatest potential benefits? Do the benefits of such a system outweigh the potential risks? Why or why not?

## Reference

Rothstein, Mark A. 2012. "Currents in Contemporary Bioethics." *Journal of Law, Medicine, and Ethics* 40, no. 2, 394–400. Available at: doi:10.1111/j.1748-720X.2012.00673.x

# PART V

# FUND DEVELOPMENT: GENERATING REVENUES

Nonprofit organizations raise funds in many ways and from many types of sources, but most limit their fundraising activities and sources of funds to those that "fit" their mission and the strengths and skills of their staff and volunteers. Many nonprofit organizations raise most of their funds from private sources—for example, private and corporate foundations, corporate gifts, and contracts for services.[1] Others appeal to the general public through special events, person-to-person and social media community fundraising drives, and direct-mail campaigns. Religious, fraternal, and professional membership organizations approach their members. Many organizations turn to government agencies for grants, contracts, and subsidies, while others raise funds from sales of goods and services to recipients or third-party payers such as private schools and colleges, museum gift shops, client-staffed pet stores, hospitals, and home health agencies.

Fundraising is both an art and a science. Six functions have been identified as essential for fundraising success: research, planning, cultivation, solicitation, stewardship, and evaluation. The implementation of each of these functions is an art form that "takes time, patience, and the motivation to succeed."[2] Research, for example, is needed to identify prospective donors, including individuals, foundations, corporations, and organizations, and to understand the motivations of each as well as the constraints of their environments. In an environment where many nonprofits compete for funds, research also contributes to an understanding of one's own organization and other organizations with similar missions.[3]

## Types of Fundraising Strategies and Sources

Fundraising strategies and sources can be grouped into the following broad categories:

1. Donations from:
    a. Individuals and families, and their trusts
    b. Public and private foundations
2. Grants from:
    a. Corporations
    b. Government agencies (for example, the National Institutes of Health)
    c. Federated funding sources or intermediaries (for example, the United Way)
    d. Foundations (which can be community, corporate, or family foundations)

3. Sales of Goods and Services from:
   a. Contracts with government agencies
      i.   To provide services or goods to clients of government agencies (third-party payment arrangements)
      ii.  To provide goods or services to government agencies
   b. Contracts with corporations to provide services or goods
   c. Sales to individuals
   d. Sales to other nonprofit organizations
4. Fees, Dues, and Pledges from Members
5. Interest and Investment Income

Although most of these broad categories of fundraising activities and sources are self-explanatory, the category titles mask an almost infinite variety of innovative fundraising tactics and arrangements. For example, there are many types of "sales of goods and services" to individuals, including cause-related marketing arrangements through which contractual "win-win partnerships" are formed with businesses. The business uses a nonprofit's name in promotional advertising, and either the nonprofit receives a percentage of the sales or sales increase in exchange.[4] Although cause-related marketing usually generates needed revenues, some have argued that business-sector approaches to nonprofit management and fund development also may undercut the importance of promoting democratic values and philanthropy. As noted by Angela Eikenberry, increasing reliance on fees for services and entrepreneurial fundraising is causing changes across the nonprofit sector, with important social implications. For example, pursuing fee-based revenues as opposed to donor funds changes the skill sets of nonprofit executives and development staff members—and the curriculum in university nonprofit management programs. Likewise, the marketization of the nonprofit sector and the increasingly common depiction of human relations as "transactions" or "market exchanges" challenges the democratic values of discourse and shared decision-making and undermines the notion of philanthropy as "love of mankind."[5]

There are also many varieties of *donations.* With a *charitable remainder trust,* for example, an individual or family makes a gift (usually a large gift), the gift assets are transferred to a trustee, the family receives income on the value of the assets for a number of years, and when the time arrives, the assets and the income they generate are transferred to a preselected nonprofit. In contrast, a *charitable lead trust* permits an individual or family to transfer income-yielding assets to a trust for a specified period during which the income flows to a chosen nonprofit organization. When the period is up, the assets and the income from them are returned to the family.

*Special events* usually combine donations and *sales of goods and services.* Individuals and corporations buy donated goods and services at the event, or they pay more than market value for them. Corporations and sometimes government agencies also may become *event sponsors,* which is another variety of donation.

Within the category "sales of goods and services," some sales are paid for by the recipient and others are paid for or reimbursed by a *third-party payer,* such as an insurance company or a government program.

All varieties of revenue-generating activities have advantages and disadvantages. They require different skills, time commitments, and types of efforts by board members and staff. They often involve multiple arrangements with government agencies or businesses. Different fundraising activities also have varying levels of expected payouts. Thus, some fundraising strategies fit better with different types of nonprofit organizations than others. Many larger nonprofits can devote considerable skilled staff effort, for example, to writing grants or organizing celebrity-studded gala events that smaller nonprofits are not staffed to handle. Nonprofits that serve sympathy-evoking clients and causes can employ fundraising strategies and tap sources that may not be available to nonprofits that serve unpopular causes or stigmatized populations. Nonprofits enjoying high status in a community can require their trustees to make large annual contributions and to solicit donations from their friends and associates. Many nonprofits are not as fortunate, however, and are happy just to fill all the vacant board positions. A request for these trustees to donate or solicit funds would not be well received and might even cause some trustees to resign.

## Trustees and Fundraising

The trustees are at the heart of fundraising in most nonprofits. Numerous studies have shown that larger donations are made "people to people"—more so than "people to organizations" or to causes. When a respected peer who serves on a board asks for a major gift to an organization or cause, we are more likely to reach for our checkbook or credit card.

> To the extent that trustees are active in the community, are givers themselves, and are not afraid to ask for money, the organization will be more successful in the fundraising effort. Furthermore, the fiscal health of the organization depends on the extent to which the trustees feel that the income gap (the difference between what is earned and what is expended) is their responsibility.[6]

## All Fundraising Strategies Have Advantages and Disadvantages

Almost all types of fundraising activities place some restrictions on the nonprofit organization. Corporate partnership arrangements, for example, may prevent the nonprofit from entering into arrangements with other corporations. Acceptance of United Way funding historically has required nonprofits to refrain from soliciting other funding from participating employers (for example, corporate sponsorships of special events). Government contracts to provide services often come with burdensome requirements and may require a nonprofit to accept clients whom it would not ordinarily serve—or to limit the quantity of services provided to some individuals. A nonprofit organization's reliance on government contracts or a corporate marketing program may cause individual donors to divert their gifts to other causes in the belief that the organization does not need their money. Restricted gifts can commit a nonprofit to a long-term program or project that may decline in importance over the years or to a project that requires a substantial amount of additional funding—thereby possibly creating organizational rigidity or draining limited resources.

The decision to pursue a certain funding source also reduces options. Once a nonprofit has committed itself to one or two major fundraising activities in a year, it is locked in. Few nonprofits have enough staff members and volunteers to pursue multiple sources of funding simultaneously. It is important, therefore, to select carefully.

## Recent Trends in Nonprofit Revenue Sources

In 2010, public charities reported total revenues of $1.51 trillion.[7] The mix of revenues and the importance of each type of revenue vary by type of nonprofit organization. For example, for institutions of higher education and hospitals, fees for services—which include tuition payments, hospital patient revenues including Medicare and Medicaid, and ticket sales—accounted for 70.3 percent of all revenues, and public support—including private contributions at 12.3 percent and government grants at 9.0 percent—totaled only 21.3 percent. Investment income accounted for 5.4 percent of revenue, and all other income for 2.9 percent.

When hospitals and institutions of higher education are excluded, however, the mix of revenues changes markedly. Without these two subsectors, fees for services in 2005 represented 53.6 percent of all revenue to public charities. Public support was 40.3 percent (with private contributions at 23.3 percent and government grants at 17 percent). Other income was 3.9 percent and investment income was 2.3 percent.[8]

During the past two decades, many nonprofits have increased their reliance on government contracts as steady sources of revenue, but at the same time the total amount of US government money flowing into the human services, the arts, and environmental protection has declined steadily—and sometimes dramatically. Delays in government payments have also created difficult circumstances for nonprofits.[9] States, counties, and cities have not been anxious to replace the declining funds from Washington, DC, at a time when political pressures for tax reductions and control of deficits enjoy strong public support. Thus, many nonprofits have turned to fees for services and other entrepreneurial activities to support their activities.

The percentage of income that charitable nonprofit organizations receive from government grants varies by subsector, with human services receiving the lion's share. Despite the widespread cutbacks in government funding, government reliance on nonprofits—and thus government as a source of income—has continued to grow in some subsectors, particularly through contracts for services for persons with mental illness, disabilities (including developmental disabilities), chemical dependencies, youth (including gangs), the elderly, families, individuals who need job training, and victims of abuse (including legal services). Government funding also helps to support and coordinate the arts and to provide financial support, for example, to national parks, seashores, and rivers. Massachusetts and New Jersey, for example, provide almost no direct human services because virtually all such services have been contracted out to nonprofits.[10] This growing reliance—or dependence—on government contracts, unfortunately, comes at a time when government funding has been in a long-term decline. The government "downsizing, devolution, and diffusion movement" of the 1990s and early 2000s peaked at a time when individual and corporate donations to nonprofit organizations had been stagnant and, by many measures, declining.[11]

Nonprofits have been under increasing pressure to be more *entrepreneurial*—to pursue alternative sources of revenue—and many have been doing much better at meeting this "charge" than expected (see Part IV). Many have been selling services and products aggressively and often compete for business directly with for-profit firms. Some have become adept at *social entrepreneurship* and are engaging in a wide array of types of enterprises that were unknown in the sector less than a decade ago.[12]

## Readings Reprinted in Part V

The readings in Part V provide a framework for understanding fund development and a review of some of the "nuts and bolts" of managing fund development activities. In addition, a few philosophical concerns and the managerial realities associated with fluctuations and changes in organizations' fund portfolios are discussed.

In the first essay in Part V, "Capacity-Building: Strategies for Successful Fundraising," Michele Cole introduces the wide variety of techniques and strategies used by nonprofits to raise funds and thereby build their capacity to remain viable organizations. Capacity building includes the myriad "activities that nonprofits undertake to enhance their ability to meet mission goals. Fundraising . . . is a key element in capacity-building." The chapter walks us through a wide range of funding approaches, starting from the fundraising plan through potential sources of support, government fundraising, foundation fundraising, annual funds, special events, capital campaigns, legacy fundraising, endowments, and crowdfunding. Cole emphasizes that fundraising must be "an integral function in the management of any nonprofit relying on public support for a significant portion of its revenue."

In the second reading, "Analyzing the Dynamics of Funding: Reliability and Autonomy," Jon Pratt provides a framework for understanding the advantages and challenges associated with different revenue sources, including individual contributions, membership dues, government contracts, United Way allocations, earned income, third-party payers, foundation grants, and blended and diversified revenues. Each source of income has ramifications for autonomy and reliability. Pratt's framework illustrates nicely problems endemic to nonprofits as they seek to ease financial insecurities. For example, nonprofits that rely too heavily on any single type of revenue are at risk of becoming resource-dependent, which can lead to unhealthy goals displacement whereby goals and activities are modified for purposes of satisfying the preferences of key stakeholders, and in particular, those of major donors.[13]

Too often, nonprofits will write grants for activities that foundations are likely to fund instead of seeking funds that fit well with their mission and the needs of their clients. A beggar's mentality, however, is shortsighted. "Since foundations and corporations have varied priorities, we have often tried to be all things to all people, cutting and tailoring our interests and programs to fit those of the donors. In many cases, the result has been dismal. Either we undermined our mission or initiated programs for which we were ill suited."[14]

To the extent that funded activities are not congruent with a nonprofit organization's mission, goals, or vision, mission creep may change the nature and character of the organization. Government contracts, for example, usually have a formalizing effect on nonprofits because they may require contracted nonprofits to professionalize their staffs and bureaucratize their organizations—which reduces administrative autonomy in the nonprofit organizations.

In the final essay in Part V, "Foundations," Elizabeth Boris describes foundations as a revenue source for nonprofit organizations and as nonprofit organizations themselves. *Foundations* are defined as "nonprofit, nongovernmental organizations that promote charitable giving and other public purposes usually by giving grants of money to nonprofit organizations, qualified individuals, and other entities. Under US law, philanthropic foundations must serve the public by being organized and operated exclusively for religious, charitable, scientific, testing for public safety, literary, or educational purposes."[15] Boris explains the differences between public foundations and private foundations and also among the three types of private foundations: independent foundations, operating foundations, and community foundations.

There were few foundations in the United States until the turn of the twentieth century. "Although the foundation as an institution was an innovation," Boris observes, "it evolved from long-standing traditions of secular and religious giving as well as popular reform movements. . . . The early foundations were formed before the adoption of a national income tax. . . . By 1917 Congress enacted a charitable tax deduction for donors, and in 1919 deductions were permitted for charitable gifts made from estates after the death of the donor."

"Foundations" also provides an overview of major achievements and common criticisms of foundations, how government regulates foundations, patterns of governance, grant-making procedures, typical staffing patterns, and foundations worldwide.

## Case Studies in Part V

In the two case studies, "Ethical Considerations in Fundraising" and "The Selling of America," the perennial concerns about balancing financial need with image, continuity, and political support are raised. In "Ethical Considerations in Fundraising," the lure of "easy money" requires the executive director of a nonprofit serving the elderly to consider the relationship that her organization has formed with a longtime donor who has suddenly upped the financial stakes—along with the risks and ethical concerns. After analyzing the case, readers are asked to draft acceptance policies that are consistent with ethical obligations in fund development.

"The Selling of America" situates the reader in the role of a fire chief who must find ways to do more with less as dollars shrink. The chief is presented with an opportunity to pursue grant funding from an area casino, the Lucky Sevens, which is soliciting funding proposals from public and nonprofit organizations. The reader must consider the ramifications of applying for a potentially controversial source of funding and complying with the stipulations that will accompany the grant monies.

## Notes

1. For an excellent overview of the different types of corporate foundations, see Elizabeth T. Boris, "Foundations," in *The International Encyclopedia of Public Policy and Administration*, edited by Jay M. Shafritz (Boulder, CO: Westview Press, 1998), 928–935.

2. Wesley E. Lindahl, *Principles of Fundraising: Theory and Practice* (Sudbury, MA: Jones and Bartlett, 2010), 129.

3. Ibid., 130.

4. Barbara L. Ciconte and Jeanne G. Jacob, *Fundraising Basics: A Complete Guide,* 3rd ed. (Sudbury, MA; Jones and Bartlett, 2009), 3.

5. Angela Eickenberry, "The Modernization and Marketization of Voluntarism," ch. 2 in Angela Eickenberry, *Giving Circles* (Bloomington: Indiana University Press, 2009), 29–43.

6. Thomas Wolf, *Managing a Nonprofit Organization,* updated 21st-century ed. (New York: Free Press, 2012), 242.

7. Katie L. Roeger, Amy S. Blackwood, and Sarah L. Pettijohn, *The Nonprofit Almanac 2012* (Washington, DC: Urban Institute, 2012), 149.

8. Kennard T. Wing, Thomas H. Pollak, and Amy Blackwood, *The Nonprofit Almanac 2008* (Washington, DC: Urban Institute, 2008), 144.

9. Lester M. Salamon, Stephanie L. Geller, and Kasey Spence, "Impact of the 2007–09 Economic Recession on Nonprofit Organizations," Listening Post Project Communique 14 (Baltimore, MD: Johns Hopkins Center for Civil Society Studies, 2009), 5.

10. Steven R. Smith and Michael Lipsky, *Nonprofits for Hire* (Cambridge, MA: Harvard University Press, 1993).

11. J. Steven Ott and Lisa A. Dicke, "Challenges Facing Public Sector Management in an Era of Downsizing, Devolution, Diffusion, Empowerment—and Accountability?" *Public Organization Review* 1, no. 3 (September 2002): 321–339.

12. See, for example, Jay M. Shafritz, J. Steven Ott, and Yong Suk Jang, "Theories of Organizations and Society," ch. 9 in *Classics of Organization Theory,* 8th ed., edited by Jay M. Shafritz, J. Steven Ott, and Yong Suk Jang (Boston: Wadsworth/Cengage, 2016).

13. See, for example, Karen A. Froelich, "Diversification of Revenue Strategies: Evolving Resource Dependence in Nonprofit Organizations," *Nonprofit and Voluntary Sector Quarterly* 28, no. 3 (September 1999): 246–268.

14. Pablo Eisenberg, "Penetrating the Mystique of Philanthropy: Relations Between Fund Raisers and Grant Makers," in *Challenges for Nonprofits and Philanthropy: The Courage to Change,* edited by Stacy Palmer (Medford, MA: Tufts University Press, 2005), 64.

15. Boris, "Foundations," in Shafritz, *The International Encyclopedia of Public Policy and Administration.*

## CHAPTER 10

# Capacity-Building: Strategies for Successful Fundraising

## MICHELE T. COLE

UNESCO's International Institute for Educational Planning (IIEP) has defined *capacity-building* as "the process by which individuals, groups, organizations, institutions and societies increase their abilities to: (a) perform core functions, solve problems, define and achieve objectives; and (b) understand and deal with their development needs in a broad context and in a sustainable manner" (IIEP 2006, 1). Although UNESCO's IIEP context is educational planning, the definition embraces activities that nonprofits undertake to enhance their ability to meet mission goals. Fundraising as part of the overall development effort is a key element in capacity-building. Unlike its counterparts in the for-profit and public sectors, organizations in the nonprofit sector rely on fundraising to support their programs and pursue their missions.

## Capacity-Building

Why is capacity-building important? Nonprofits, eleemosynary, nongovernmental, and voluntary organizations worldwide provide critical services to people and communities. These are organizations that, in Lester Salamon's words, seek "to alleviate want, deliver health care and education, provide social services, and give voice to a multitude of cultural, artistic, religious, ethnic, social, and environmental concerns" (Salamon, Sokolowski, and Associates 2004, xxi). To be effective, organizations need adequate managerial, financial, and relationship-building skills to be able to deliver services and to serve their purposes. Healthy nonprofits contribute to a vibrant third sector and further advance a global civil society. As an investment in sustainability, capacity-building is about the future of these organizations.

McKinsey & Company (2001) presents the seven key elements of effective capacity-building for nonprofits as a pyramid, not unlike the giving pyramid used in describing the gradual progression of successful donor cultivation. In their framework, capacity-building depends on human resources, systems and infrastructure, and organizational structure. On this foundation, organizational skills are built, strategies developed, and aspirations set. The seventh and final element, culture, surrounds the pyramid,

First published in *Understanding Nonprofit Organizations: Governance, Leadership, and Management*, 3rd ed., edited by J. Steven Ott and Lisa A. Dicke (Boulder, CO: Westview Press, 2016).

providing the framework for capacity-building (McKinsey & Company 2001, 36).

As in the capacity-building framework, successful fundraising also depends on appropriate staffing, adequate technical support, and a recognized position within the organizational structure. Upon that foundation, fundraising skills for staff and board may be developed, a fundraising strategy adopted, and goals set. The organization's culture facilitates successful development efforts.

## Fundraising

Fundraising involves building relationships with individuals, with private and public funders, and with the community. As a key element in the organization's development program, fundraising supports and is critical to realizing the goals and objectives of the organization's strategic plan. Kent Dove explains the relationship this way: "No development program can succeed without an effective fundraising operation to provide the necessary resources. But development in the broadest sense includes much more than fundraising" (Dove 2001, 5). A nonprofit's development program is concerned with "institution-raising." Fundraising is concerned with enabling development efforts.

Different fundraising activities are designed to serve different specific purposes and may require specialized staffing and volunteers. For example, special events, particularly for new or small organizations, are thought of more as "friend-raisers" than fundraisers. Organizing charity balls, golf outings, awards dinners, and marathons, among others, is time-intensive, and these events, unless otherwise funded, often cost more than can be recovered by the ticket revenue. Annual funds, on the other hand, can be managed by a small staff supported by adequate record-keeping and marketing tools, but they may take years to mature. Capital campaigns need board leadership and often require

professional fundraising counsel to support staff and board efforts.

All fundraising involves (1) understanding and appreciating the organization that is the subject of the fundraising effort—its culture, as well as the external and internal forces that impact it; (2) possessing or having access to the research skills necessary to identify potential funding sources; (3) cultivating the relationships that are essential to soliciting support; (4) planning and implementing a fundraising strategy that meets the organization's needs; and (5) having systems in place to ensure stewardship of the funds received.

It has been said that fundraising is more an art than a science. Most often, it is a combination of the two. Relationship-building and stewardship require organizational support. Without an underlying management and governance infrastructure, stewardship is difficult at best. Donors, grantors, and regulators expect it. Stewardship is about transparency, accountability, and ethics (Ciconte 2007).

### Some Fundraising Requirements

Who can fundraise? The short answer is that anyone can solicit funding for any cause or purpose. However, a nonprofit organization in the United States cannot ask for donations in support of its programs and mission without meeting certain legal requirements. At this writing, thirty-nine states and the District of Columbia require charitable nonprofits— those classified as 501(c)(3) organizations under the Internal Revenue Code (26 U.S.C. § 501(c))—to register with the state prior to beginning any solicitation. Many states exempt religious entities, nonprofit hospitals, educational institutions, and very small nonprofit organizations from this requirement.

Organizations engaged in Internet and social media fundraising face additional challenges when soliciting in multiple states. Several states require that the solicitation (as well as the acknowledgment) contain a disclosure statement. If the organization contracts with a professional fundraising consultant, some jurisdictions require that the person be registered with that state as well. Note that certain types of fundraising vehicles, such as bingos and raffles, require a license from the municipality in which the activity takes place. In some instances, joint fundraisers, including onetime or recurring solicitations, special events, and campaigns, among others, are considered commercial co-ventures. Commercial co-ventures have additional requirements (National Council of Nonprofits 2014).

Donations to organizations designated as charitable nonprofits qualify for special treatment under the federal income tax code. However, for the taxpayer/donor to be able to deduct the contribution, the charity must comply with the regulations governing receipt and acknowledgment of gifts.

### The Fundraising Process

Most would agree with Wesley Lindahl (2012) that effective fundraising requires research, planning, cultivation, solicitation, stewardship, and evaluation. As noted earlier, an organization's ability to raise sufficient funding to support its programs rests on its ability to identify, cultivate, and solicit appropriate funding. Research helps to identify those sources of support that are most likely to fund the organization and facilitates profiling the potential donor pool for individual gifts. Throughout the fundraising process, it is helpful to remember that the fundraising function is as affected by staff-board relationships as it is by the capacity of the organization to secure the necessary resources.

### Steps to Successful Fundraising

Fundraising is about building relationships and following a process:

1. Know your nonprofit—its long-range plan, mission, goals, and objectives.
2. Prepare a case statement that will persuade donors/funders that your nonprofit deserves their investment.
3. Research potential funding sources.
4. Identify appropriate donors/grantors.
5. Develop a targeted solicitation strategy.
6. Ensure that adequate resources for fundraising are in place.
7. Implement the strategy.
8. Cultivate donors by acknowledging and thanking them and by keeping in touch.
9. Demonstrate stewardship and ethical fundraising by ensuring (and documenting) that the donor's intent is carried out.
10. Evaluate and, as needed, revise strategy.
11. Keep the board informed.

### The Fundraising Plan

Fundraising plans are meant to support an organization's strategic initiatives and are best developed in consort with board, senior staff, and key stakeholders. Here a development audit can be valuable to identify the organization's strengths and weaknesses, as well as its threats and opportunities (similar to an organizational SWOT analysis). The development audit should include a review of the nonprofit's organizational structure, business processes, communication and marketing programs, reputation, donor base and sources of funding, and staff and board competencies. It can be conducted by staff or by outside counsel and is generally recommended before an organization undertakes a major campaign or begins a significant fundraising program. A development audit can point to shortfalls that need to be addressed before proceeding as well as identify unrecognized strengths.

Fundraising plans should also identify who is responsible for which initiative and who will solicit which donors, when, and how. Evaluation is the final piece in the plan. How successful were the solicitation efforts? How well did the funding meet the needs of the organization? Was the donor's intent fulfilled? The last may also belong under the stewardship function, as would compliance with the various funders' reporting and accounting requirements.

## Potential Sources of Support

Although there has been some dissent (McCambridge 2014), the generally accepted wisdom is that nonprofit organizations should diversify their funding to guard against changes in government support, economic downturns, and fickle donors. However, for a small nonprofit with limited staff and a singular mission, diversification may be as difficult as it can be for controversial nonprofits, such as Planned Parenthood. Nor is diversification automatically the response to an organization's need to grow (Foster and Fine 2007). As Paul Lagasse notes, finding new sources of support "is not a turmoil-free proposition" (Lagasse 2013, 25). That said, identifying and cultivating as many appropriate funding streams as possible helps the nonprofit to build capacity—to provide services and fulfill its mission.

What might a diversified portfolio look like? Charitable nonprofits are supported directly by individuals, corporations, foundations, and government agencies and indirectly by the taxpayer by way of local, state, and federal tax exemptions. Nonprofits may charge fees for services, may operate a profit-making entity (and declare the income), and may partner with other nonprofits or with for-profits to operate an enterprise in which they share revenue. Thus, the nonprofit might be 38 percent government-supported. One half of that might be in the form of a sustaining grant that requires annual grant applications and annual reports. The other half might be a mix of county and city funding that requires periodic proposal pre-

sentations to the relevant council or decision-making body. In these cases, the endorsement of a local official may be important in securing the funding. Other nonprofit scenarios include perhaps 20 percent funding through a fee-for-service contract with the region's area office on aging. The original contract (if a reimbursement contract) may only require timely expenditure reports for the funding to continue. The remaining 42 percent could be made up of the annual fund (10 percent), annual and multi-year foundation grants (20 percent), corporate support (5 percent), an annual special event (2 percent), and 5 percent from endowment.

Different fundraising strategies are required for each of these monetary streams. All require a match between the interests and purposes of the funding source and the mission and services of the nonprofit. Fortunately, there are a number of resources available to those seeking support for their nonprofit organizations. At the end of this chapter is an appendix listing the websites of selected fundraising resources. In the next few sections, common sources of funding are discussed.

### Government Fundraising

Grant funding available from federal agencies can be found in the Catalog of Federal Domestic Assistance (CFDA) and the *Federal Register* (for RFPs). Grant opportunities may also be found in newsletters and on websites of organizations that belong to a network of providers or that fall under the umbrella of a national organization. Staff and board members may be sources of information on local grant opportunities. Once a source is identified and its objectives are shown to align with your nonprofit's goals and objectives, it is important to assess your capacity to perform and follow the guidelines for submission. Grant-writing is about demonstrating that what your organization is prepared to do is what the government program needs to have done for the specified amount.

Contracts are often awarded in response to a publicized *request for proposal* (RFP) and are negotiated based on the funder's specifications and the organization's qualifications. In general, the terms and conditions are specific, and a timeline is imposed. If the RFP is biddable, it is important that the nonprofit not underestimate its costs. Most government grants and contracts allow for indirect costs related to the project, such as a percentage of support services (management, accounting, fundraising), overhead, salaries, space, equipment, and utilities. Indirect rates may be set by various government agencies (US Department of Labor 2012). For a research institution, a rate exceeding 50 percent of the grant is not unusual.

### Foundation Fundraising

There are two types of foundations, *private and public.* In the private category, there are *family foundations* such as the Bill and Melinda Gates Foundation, in which the donor-family is often directly involved in grant-making; *corporate foundations,* such as the Bank of America Charitable Foundation, Inc., which, while legally separate from the Bank of America, does receive its income from the bank's operations; and *operating foundations,* such as the Metropolitan Museum of New York, which funds its own programs.

Public foundations include *community foundations,* such as the Cleveland Foundation and the Pittsburgh Foundation. These are publicly supported to make grants to other nonprofits. Other public foundations include *field-specific funds,* such as those related to health care, and *population-specific funds,* such as the Ms. Foundation for Women.

The nonprofit's strategy for seeking foundation funds will depend on the size, location, and purposes of the foundation. Large foundations, including community foundations, generally have staff who serve as gatekeepers. Grant seekers will be expected to follow published guide-lines that outline what types of organizations are eligible for funding, what sorts of projects are desired, and what levels of funding are appropriate. Guidelines will also prescribe how the foundation should be approached. Some will ask for a letter of intent, to be followed by a discussion with the program officer before a formal proposal is invited. Others will set out the guidelines and due dates for proposal submission without the initial inquiry. It is a good idea to contact the foundation program officer before preparing a submission, as that person can provide valuable information and may become the nonprofit's advocate before the foundation's board of trustees. If the foundation is local, the nonprofit's board members or staff may have contacts on the foundation board. Board members and staff who are involved in the solicitation should be kept informed of the submission. Small foundations may have one staff person who handles all contact with potential grant seekers. Others may rely on a trustee to vet the proposals.

Corporate foundation giving is different from family or community foundation giving in the sense that the corporate foundation's interests are most often tied to the company's interests. Corporate foundations tend to focus on the geographic areas where they are located or have staff. In some cases, the corporate foundation's giving is also part of a marketing plan or community outreach program. Consequently, the nonprofit's proposed activity needs to be positioned in a way that clearly advances the company's interests.

In all cases, the first step is to determine if there is a good fit between the foundation and the nonprofit. The Foundation Center is a good source for information on foundations. Large foundations have websites that outline the components of a successful application. As important as foundation and corporate grant-making is for nonprofits, it should be noted that individuals constitute the bulk of private philanthropy. According to *Giving USA,* grants from foundations and corporations represented only 19 percent of total private giving in 2010. Individual gifts and bequests made up 81 percent (Foundation Center, "*Foundations Today* Tutorial").

## The Annual Fund

The annual fund is critical for many nonprofits' development strategy. Typically, the annual fund is built on individual donors' sustained giving. Often presented as a pyramid, the gradual progression of individual cultivation is built on identifying prospects, soliciting first-time donors, transforming those donors into annual givers, and identifying potential major donors. The apex of the fundraising pyramid is planned giving. These last steps, toward major gifts and bequests, rely on personal cultivation. Moving from one level of the pyramid to the next relies on stewardship. How solicitation is managed depends on the type and size of the organization and its staff and board, as well as how valuable the nonprofit is perceived as being to the well-being of the community.

An annual solicitation may be a direct-mail piece and/or, increasingly, a web-based appeal. The annual fund may also include an annual special event as part of its revenue projections. Some nonprofits include recurring government grants in their annual fund strategy. Major donor cultivation that involves face-to-face interaction is not usually included in the annual fund budget.

Developing the annual fund is a gradual process, one that takes years of cultivation and stewardship. Depending on the organization and the contacts its board and staff may or may not have, identifying potential donors can take time. Data-mining companies supply, for a fee, lists of potential donors based on criteria that the nonprofit defines. This is similar to a university's admissions office purchasing lists of potential applicants. Once obtained, staff or volunteers then mail the prepared solicitation

letter or card. The solicitation could also be emailed or placed on the organization's website. Email and Internet-based campaigns avoid one of the major disincentives of direct mail—cost. However, with the exception of disaster or special needs appeals, first-time direct-mail solicitations have a poor return. Citing JWM Business Services, Julie Richards (n.d.) reports that direct mail yields a 0.5–2 percent return. Laurie Beasley (2013) puts the rate of return on direct-mail marketing at 4.4 percent. Direct-mail remains an expensive venture for small nonprofits.

Before soliciting others outside of the organization, major stakeholders (such as board members and other volunteers, staff, and, where appropriate, clients) should be asked to support the organization in which they are investing their time and care. Some funding sources, particularly foundations, require that board contributions be included in the annual fund budget.

As Kim Klein (2011, 21) points out, fundraising is about acquiring donors, not donations; it's about acquiring givers, not gifts. In other words, fundraising is about building relationships:

> Focusing on building a donor base rather than on simply raising money means that sometimes you will undertake a fundraising strategy that does not raise money in the first year, such as direct mail, or that may not raise money for several years, such as legacy giving. . . . You will relate to your donors as individual human beings rather than ATMs that you engage when you want money but whom you otherwise ignore. . . . Plan fundraising for both the short term and the long term.

## Special Event Fundraising

Special events often play a significant role in the nonprofit's relationship-building campaign. As noted before, special events are time-intensive for both staff and volunteers and often do not raise much money. Before undertaking an event, whether it is a five-mile run, a golf outing, a charity ball, or an awards/recognition dinner, the nonprofit needs to determine what it hopes to achieve with the event and then to evaluate the time and resources needed to support it. Some typical steps in special event planning include identifying an oversight committee; assigning responsible staff; establishing a budget; setting a timeline; and recruiting volunteers. Post-event activities include acknowledging volunteers, evaluating the event's success at achieving the goals set, and reporting to the board.

## Capital Campaign Fundraising

Capital campaigns are usually undertaken for major projects, such as building construction and renovation, or for seeding an endowment. They are intensive and time-limited, usually beginning with a silent phase in which the organization tries to raise at least 50 percent of its goal before going public. Capital campaigns are also viewed as vehicles for moving annual fund donors into the major donor category. Unlike the annual fund campaign, a capital campaign generally seeks large onetime gifts to finance a onetime project. Capital campaigns can include solicitations for assets, such as stocks and bonds, real estate, art, insurance policies, and so forth, as well as legacy gifts such as bequests, in addition to gifts of income.

## Legacy Fundraising

Once referred to as deferred giving, *legacy giving* or *planned giving* is that element of the nonprofit's fundraising program that is built on promised future gifts that a donor provides for in his or her will. Legacy gifts are part of a person's estate plan. In most cases, legal counsel should be involved in the planning. It is not appropriate for the nonprofit's legal counsel to also act on behalf of the donor. Planned giving programs

are well developed in the educational realm and for large nonprofits as well as religious institutions. Small nonprofits do not always have the expertise on staff or on the board to mount planned giving programs.

As with all fundraising, understanding the motivations of potential donors is key to a successful solicitation. Does the nonprofit have an established donor base? If so, is there enough information about the donor to determine if a legacy gift is possible? What is the donor's relationship with the nonprofit? Does the nonprofit have the tools in place to affect a legacy program, such as a gift acceptance policy, a will information kit, legal counsel, and other professional resources? Is the board engaged? Can the nonprofit provide the necessary follow-up once the potential donor is identified?

## Fundraising for Endowments

An endowment may be thought of as a permanent savings account for an organization in which money is set aside as principal and a percentage of the income from it is designated for the organization's use on an annual basis (Klein 2011). While subject to market fluctuations, endowments are considered to be a hedge against changes in government support and declines in private giving. Endowments are often part of the organization's capital campaign. If organized as a separate endowment campaign, the fundraising process is similar to that for a capital campaign in that a goal is set, a gift-range table is developed, a realistic timeline is created, solicitation committees are established, and prospects are identified and assigned to volunteers for solicitation. Evaluation of the campaign's progress is ongoing and subject to modification as necessary.

It is important that the endowment be well managed. If the organization does not have the expertise on staff or on the board, it is advisable to contract with a professional manager. Most likely, the financial institution that holds the endowment's assets will have professional advisers. As part of its fiduciary duty to the organization, the board is responsible for the oversight of management of the endowment.

### Crowdfunding

Crowdfunding is a relatively new tool for fundraising. Because its reach is broad and less costly than other fundraising vehicles, crowdfunding is being touted as a valuable resource for nonprofits. Crowdfunding happens because the organization is using an online website to solicit for a cause or a project, or because it has sponsored a "live" crowdfunding event designed to attract large numbers of potential donors. As Joe Garecht (2013) explains, crowdfunding websites allow the charity to set up an online fundraising campaign based around a fundraising page that enables the organization to receive donations directly from that page using the website's credit card processor. The same websites may also allow individuals outside the organization to set up fundraising pages on behalf of a charity and to tie those pages into the charity's campaign page. Note that the nonprofit organization remains responsible for fundraising activities conducted on its behalf.

Online services, such as Fundraise.com, CauseVox, and Fundly, are organized to help nonprofits raise funds. Others, such as Kickstarter and indiegogo, while not exclusively dedicated to nonprofit fundraising, are used by nonprofits to raise money (Garecht 2013). Live crowdfunding, on the other hand, features live events sponsored by the nonprofit itself or by third-party organizations, such as The Funding Network, which specializes in creating live crowdfunding events for charities (Woodruff 2014).

Nonprofits use crowdfunding to expand their reach and raise money and awareness for their causes. Empirical support for the efficacy of crowdfunding for nonprofit fundraising is

lacking; nevertheless, as crowdfunding specialist Devin Thorpe puts it, "While crowdfunding does not constitute a complete development plan, no development plan is complete without crowdfunding" (Woodruff 2014).

At the present time it is unclear how states' fundraising regulations apply to crowdfunding.

## Conclusion

Fundraising for nonprofit organizations is about building capacity in those organizations to secure the resources needed to fulfill their missions. In so doing, critical services are provided to the most vulnerable and art, music, and dance are made available to the public. Nonprofits enrich our lives, help make education more accessible to all, and hold a promise for building a better future. Fundraising is a process that, over time, develops relationships and helps secure for the nonprofit public awareness of its programs and services, thus building its capacity to provide those programs and services. Fundraising therefore is an integral function in the management of any nonprofit relying on public support for a significant portion of its revenue.

## Appendix: Selected Fundraising Resources

There are a number of excellent resources for fundraising tips and techniques, such as the Association of Fundraising Professionals (AFP), The Grantsmanship Center, and The Foundation Center. Foundation Search enables the grant seeker to research foundations by location, type of grant, and average amount. GuideStar is an excellent resource for data on public charities (501[c][3] nonprofits), including foundations. The *Nonprofit Times* and the *Chronicle of Philanthropy* are both good sources for news on what is happening in the third sector. In addition to the CFDA and the *Federal Register,* Grants.gov provides information on federal grant opportunities. Grants.gov also enables the potential grantee to apply for grants online.

The Center on Philanthropy at Indiana University–Purdue University Indianapolis (IUPUI) publishes research on philanthropy-related issues. The Program on Nonprofit Organizations (PONPO) at Yale University is also a good resource for working papers on matters related to nonprofits. The Independent Sector (IS) is a forum for organizations interested in furthering a civil society. IS also advocates on behalf of organizations in the third sector.

## Websites

Association of Fundraising Professionals (AFP): www.afpnet.org

Catalog of Federal Domestic Assistance (CFDA): www.cfda.gov/

Center on Philanthropy: http://www.philanthropy .iupui.edu/

*Chronicle of Philanthropy:* www.philanthropy.com/

*Federal Register:* www.federalregister.gov/

Foundation Search: www.foundationsearch.com

Foundation Center, Foundation Directory Online: fconline.foundationcenter.org/

Grants.gov: http:// www. grants.gov/

Grantsmanship Center: www.tgci.com/about/our -mission

GuideStar: www.guidestar.org

Independent Sector (IS): www.independentsector .org

*Nonprofit Times (NPT):* www.thenonprofittimes .com/

Program on Nonprofit Organizations (PONPO) at Yale University: http://ponpo.som.yale.edu/

## References

Beasley, Laurie. 2013. "Why Direct Mail Still Yields the Lowest Cost-per-Lead and Highest Conversion Rate." *Direct Marketing* (June 13). Available at: http://www.onlinemarketinginstitute.org/blog /2013/06/why-direct-mail-still-yields-the-lowest -cost-per-lead-and-highest-conversion-rate/.

Ciconte, Barbara L. 2007. *Developing Fundraising Policies and Procedures: Best Practices for Accountability and Transparency.* Arlington, VA: AFP Ready Reference Series.

Dove, Kent E. 2001. *Conducting a Successful Fundraising Program: A Comprehensive Guide and Resource.* San Francisco: Jossey-Bass.

Foster, William, and Gail Fine. 2007. "How Nonprofits Get Really Big." *Stanford Social Innovation Review* (Spring): 13–26. Available at: http://www .ssireview.org/articles/entry/how_nonprofits _get_really_big.

Foundation Center. "*Foundations Today* Tutorial." Available at: http://foundationcenter.org /getstarted/tutorials/ft_tutorial/compare.html.

Garecht, Joe. 2013. "How to Use Crowd-Funding Sites to Raise Money for Your Non-Profit." The Fundraising Authority (web log post), February 6. Available at: http://trust.guidestar.org/2013 /02/06/how-to-use-crowd-funding-to-raise -money-for-your-non-profit/.

International Institute for Educational Planning (IIEP). 2006. "Capacity Building." Ch. 3 in IIEP, *Guidebook for Planning Education in Emergencies and Reconstruction.* Paris: IIEP.

Klein, Kim. 2011. *Fundraising for Social Change,* 6th ed. San Francisco: Jossey-Bass.

Lagasse, Paul. 2013. "The Right Mix." *Advancing Philanthropy* (Summer): 20–25. Available at: http://www.benevon.com/documents/press/The -Right-Mix--Advancing-Philanthropy-Summer -2013.pdf.

Lindahl, Wesley E. 2012. "The Fundraising Process." In *Understanding Nonprofit Organizations: Governance, Leadership, and Management,* 2nd ed., edited by J. Steven Ott and Lisa Dicke, 117–126. Boulder, CO: Westview Press.

McCambridge, Ruth. 2014. "To Diversify, or Not to Diversify Revenue—(It's Complicated)." *Nonprofit Quarterly* (July 14). Available at: https:// nonprofitquarterly.org/policysocial-context /24501-to-diversify-or-not-to-diversify-that-is -the-question-but-it-s-complicated.html?utm _source=NPQ+New.

McKinsey & Company. 2001. *Effective Capacity*

*Building in Nonprofit Organizations.* Washington, DC: Venture Philanthropy Partners.

National Council of Nonprofits. 2014. "Laws That Regulate Fundraising." Available at: http://www.councilofnonprofits.org/resources /resources-topic/fundraising/laws-regulate -fundraising.

Richards, Julie. N.d. "What Is the Average Rate of Return on a Direct Mail Campaign?" *Houston Chronicle.* Available at: http://smallbusiness .chron.com/average-rate-return-direct-mail -campaign-23974.html.

Salamon, Lester, S. Wojciech Sokolowski, and Associates. 2004. *Global Civil Society: Dimensions of the Nonprofit Sector.* Bloomfield, CT: Kumarian Press.

US Department of Labor. Division of Cost Determination. 2012. "A Guide for Indirect Cost Rate Determination: Based on the Cost Principles and Procedures Required by OMB Circular A-122 (2 CFR Part 230) for Non-Profit Organizations and by the Federal Acquisition Regulation—Part 31.2 for Commercial Organizations." Washington, DC: US Department of Labor (July). Available at: http://www.dol.gov/oasam/programs/boc /costdeterminationguide/cdg.pdf.

Woodruff, Alexandra. 2014. "What Nonprofits Need to Know About Crowdfunding." New York: National Council on Nonprofits (July 9). Available at: https://www.councilofnonprofits .org/thought-leadership/what-nonprofits-need -know-about-crowdfunding.

## CHAPTER 11

# Analyzing the Dynamics of Funding: Reliability and Autonomy

## JON PRATT

Every nonprofit organization begins with high hopes and aspirations for public benefit, with a mission to make the world a better place. An immediate challenge is how to put these goals into action, and how to finance the organization.

Money is a limited and competitive resource; organizations without a permanent source of funds must do their best to accommodate the preferences and conditions of funding sources. Striking necessary bargains with devils and angels constitutes the defining struggle for nonprofit boards and managers. This existential dilemma is played out in every nonprofit budget and strategic plan: How does the organization raise funds to realize its long-range purpose while also scrambling for its existence?

The way an organization handles decisions about funding sources sets in motion an ongoing chain of consequences, further decisions, and compromises about what the organization will and will not agree to do. Throughout the history of nonprofits, major changes in size, direction, and strategy (and even new names and purposes) are more commonly due to shifts in revenue than to changed intent.

Among the funders of nonprofit activity, attaching conditions and targeted funding are considered valid methods for increasing the accountability and effectiveness of grantees. Whether it is a government agency or a private foundation, the allocators of funds have authority over a finite resource with many requests from the outside. They conclude from previous experience which types of activities are most likely to succeed and seek the "biggest bang for the buck" by focusing and restricting their money to this narrower range of activities.

For nonprofit organizations, not all funding has an equal effect on the bottom line. Complying with the conditions attached to funding—and coping with fluctuations in revenue—imposes direct and indirect costs and occupies the attention of managers and boards. The drawbacks of this situation are self-evident to anyone who has managed a nonprofit organization, but board meetings and financial reports can have the effect of simplifying the problem down to "will we take in enough money to cover expenses?"

Board members, nonprofit employees, and clients (and even other funders) frequently believe that an organization has more latitude over how and when it spends its funds than is actually the case. This limited autonomy squeezes nonprofit managers by putting them in the onerous position of enforcing and defending compliance with funding conditions, sometimes in the face of solid arguments for an alternative course—all the while being criticized that "if they wanted to do it, they could." Or worse still, different parts of the organization disagree about the conditions that exist, the wisdom of compliance, or the likelihood and severity of sanctions, causing internal conflict or even misappropriation.

An organization-wide appreciation of these revenue-source issues is in the interest of the board and staff, informed by an examination of the two major variables: reliability and autonomy. This does not lessen the constraints—but can clear the air so that decision making is based on a common understanding of an organization's available degrees of freedom and the future implications for revenue changes.

## Reliability of Funding

To what extent can an organization predict its revenues year-to-year for budgeting, staffing, and program planning? Is it reasonable to expect a particular funding source will be renewed? This information—projecting and tracking revenue and expenses—is key to managing any enterprise. Boards and nonprofit managers are under a legal mandate to exercise their best judgment concerning what revenue will be available, with serious consequences if they are wrong. The decisions they make will be based on their confidence level regarding the relative stability or volatility of each element of the organization's financial support.

The Reliability-Autonomy Matrix divides twelve common types of nonprofit funding into three levels of reliability: high, medium, and low. This necessarily gross categorization is use-

ful to identify funding sources on a continuum from dependable to speculative, although an individual organization's experiences will vary. (The placement of any specific funding source on the reliability axis can vary considerably based on the organization's relationships, existing commitments, and other constraints influencing the funding source.) The three levels of reliability include:

- *High reliability:* Small to medium-sized individual contributions, endowments, memberships, United Way support, rental income, advertising
- *Medium reliability:* Fees for services, ongoing government contracts, third-party reimbursements, major individual contributions, corporate charitable contributions
- *Low reliability:* Government project grants, foundation grants, corporate sponsorships

## Organizational Autonomy

Dependency theory indicates that the autonomy of nonprofit organizations is directly related to the extent of their reliance on suppliers of funds. From government contracts to foundation grants, organizations know they are signing on to a variety of conditions that are attached to funding, comparable to "if you take the King's shilling you do the King's bidding." These conditions can range from the general targeting of an activity to extremely detailed specifications dictating the ingredients, personnel, time, place, and manner of activity. For the donor, these conditions represent due-diligence assurances that funds will be effectively and responsibly expended, while for the recipient organization, a number of these conditions are unwelcome, burdensome, and counterproductive.

As with the reliability index, the matrix divides eight common types of nonprofit funding into three levels of autonomy: high, medium, and low. This similarly gross categorization distinguishes between conditional and unconditional sources, and an individual organization's situation will vary. (The location of any specific funding source on the autonomy axis can be adjusted based on the organization's relationships, existing commitments, and other constraints influencing the funding source.) The three levels of autonomy include:

- *High autonomy:* Small to medium-sized individual contributions, fees for services, foundation operating grants, endowments, memberships
- *Medium autonomy:* Major individual contributions, corporate charitable contributions
- *Low autonomy:* Third-party reimbursements, government project grants, ongoing government contracts, foundation project grants, United Way support

## Understanding an Organization's Reliability/Autonomy Profile

The revenue situation for any particular organization will have special characteristics and could change over time. The eight revenue archetypes set out some typical situations and management responses (see table 11.1). A closer analysis of a single organization can reveal a greater level of detail and more options . . . based on a frank assessment of their own situation and relationships.

## Management and Governance Implications

The Reliability-Autonomy Matrix is designed to reveal priority issues for board and management attention and indicate strategies needed to handle the relative reliability and independence of its revenues. The profiles and archetypes, themselves, are difficult to shift (e.g., dramatically

increasing autonomy), since most mature organizations have an established mix of funding. Wherever a funding source falls within the matrix, it carries with it a variety of management options, many of which, in turn, increase the complexity of the management task. Increasing the number of sources and transactions is generally a useful strategy to increase organizational autonomy and security—though it demands more administration.

One critical additional variable is the sheer number of funding sources. Most organizations work hard to diversify their sources of funding, both in type and number of sources, in order to reduce funding volatility and lower their risk of catastrophic loss (such as when a major funding source withdraws its support).

Boards of directors expect to be involved in budget planning and monitoring, but in many organizations they are often not aware of the degree of volatility of their funding, or what the organization should do about it.

Organizations with funding that is low in reliability have a variety of possible actions to reduce the uncertainty in their environment:

- Maintain higher cash reserves to fill in gaps and reduce the roller-coaster-budget effect.
- Give greater management and board attention to cash management and financial systems, thus predicting shortfalls and allowing quick decisions.
- Use volunteers, consultants, and temporary employees to increase flexibility of the workforce, and thus reduce dislocation.
- Develop close relationships with organizations in the same subject area to track industry changes, and share information on funding source preferences and behavior.
- Submit multiple applications to offset low-response rates.

Organizations *low in autonomy* have a special set of problems, because although their

## Table 11.1 Eight Nonprofit Revenue Archetypes: A Guide for Managers and Boards

The ability to recognize patterns in any endeavor gives us a valuable leg up. Having those patterns explicitly laid out provides us with a greater capacity to make an informed decision about the course we wish to take in choosing the financing model for our work. Sometimes these models may appear to be predetermined by the field that we are in, but there is often some room for choice about balance and proportion.

| COMMON REVENUE TYPES<br>What is the dominant source of income? | EXAMPLES<br>What kinds of organizations tend to rely on this revenue type as dominant? | REVENUE PROFILE<br>Where does this leave you in terms of reliability and autonomy? |
|---|---|---|
| Individual contributions dominant | Small grassroots organizations working on local issues;<br>Humane and animal-rights organizations;<br>Faith-based programs;<br>Environmental and other national advocacy organizations;<br>Disease-specific organizations. | High reliability;<br>High autonomy |
| Individual or organizational: membership dues dominant | Labor unions;<br>Credit unions;<br>Neighborhood associations. | Medium reliability;<br>High autonomy |
| Government contract dominant | Charter schools;<br>Workforce development groups;<br>Human service agencies. | Medium reliability;<br>Low autonomy |
| United Way dominant | YMCA/YWCA;<br>Boys and Girls Clubs;<br>Boy Scouts/Girl Scouts;<br>Campfire Girls. | Medium reliability;<br>Low autonomy |
| Earned Income dominant, Individual payors | Theaters;<br>Private colleges or universities;<br>Management support organizations. | Medium reliability;<br>High autonomy |
| Third-party payor dominant | Community health centers;<br>Hospitals;<br>Nursing homes. | High reliability;<br>Low autonomy |
| Foundation grant dominant | Advocacy groups;<br>Public-policy centers;<br>Start-up organizations;<br>Arts organizations;<br>Some organizing groups. | Low reliability;<br>Low autonomy |
| Blended/diversified revenues | Advocacy organizations;<br>Community-based organizations. | Medium reliability;<br>Medium autonomy |

The following easy-to-use chart begins a process of clearly and simply laying out some common patterns and the association between them including:

- the predominance of a particular revenue source in a nonprofit;
- the degree of autonomy the nonprofit has;
- the degree to which that source is reliable, and;
- the management challenges and tasks associated with that source.

| MANAGEMENT CHALLENGES What are the special problems or demands associated with this revenue situation? | MANAGEMENT FOCUS What appropriate responses are available to management to cope with these specific management challenges? |
|---|---|
| Need for high recognition, good reputation; Management of multiple-donor relationships; List management; Monitoring of continuous changes in market and market reactions to various solicitation techniques. | Systematic research and analysis; Intensive, frequent communications; Excellent information systems; Storytelling; Development of volunteer base; Perpetual scanning for new donors. |
| High expectations for transparency; Member engagement and interactive communications; Leadership development; Collection of dues; Member politics. | Large representative, democratically elected board; Member interest tracking; Visible commitment to procedural rights of members; Pricing; Well-designed member benefits; Effective conflict-resolution mechanisms and skills. |
| Cash flow issues; Limited capital; Maintenance of political relationships; Compliance with reporting regimen and external standards of demonstrating results; Contracts often lag behind innovations; Tight eligibility requirements; Dependence on categorical, inflexible funding leads to political skewing of mission or programs; Underpriced services produce need for other subsidies; Requires ability to predict, track, and produce outcomes required by funders. | Closely monitor and educate authorizing environment; Negotiate optimal contract terms; Maintain cash reserves; Systems-focused to ensure compliance. |
| Often requires compliance with many conditions including those associated with measurement and reporting; May restrict own donor-development activities; May include fundraising blackout periods. | Close monitoring of changing United Way preferences and conditions; Support public relations of United Way; Responsiveness to information requests. |
| Need for visibility in primary and secondary markets; Maintenance of institutional reputation; Maintaining knowledge of market needs and preferences; Incentive to focus exclusively on "billable hours" or strictly marketable or self-paying activities. | Ethic of excellence; Innovation in products and services; Relentless marketing; Customer research; Competitor analysis; Seek charitable or government funds to subsidize and broaden user base. |
| Highly detailed transaction processing; Quality control; Certification, licensing, and regulatory compliance; Employee motivation and retention. | Tight management systems and chains of command; Standardized treatment, automated transaction; Cross-function employed communications. |
| Sponsor relations and education; Visibility in field; Project development and sequencing; Institutional reputation. | Development expertise; Innovation and anticipation of developments in field; Fundraising and negotiating skills to maximize revenue and minimize adverse grant conditions; Substantial cash reserves. |
| Complexity of revenue streams; Complexity of financial management and reporting; Cash flow; Variable combination of all of the above with specific sources driving management challenges. | Attentive board with understanding of budget; Financial protocols and tracking that makes sense of complexity; Strong strategic-planning processes keyed to financial planning. |

funding sources are definitely willing to transfer funds to them, they want to do this in a particular way. An African proverb says that "if you want to give a man a goat you have to let go of the rope," but of course many funders have perfectly good reasons why they can't completely "let go of the rope."

Boards of directors are less aware of their role in monitoring the restrictions placed on the funds their organizations receive. Low-autonomy organizations must also develop a special set of skills to preserve sufficient maneuvering room:

- Emphasize negotiation skills and develop a persuasive case of what the organization brings to the table (local community knowledge, flexibility, reputation, track record, volunteers, leveraged money, etc.) to equalize exchange and offset unwanted conditions.
- Monitor (via the board) the consonance between the organization's mission and the nature of the projects it is asked to undertake.
- Be prepared to resist and reject incompatible conditions by having a gift-and-grant-acceptance policy.
- Maintain a robust financial system to track and comply with conditions and restrictions on funding and effective segregation of funds. Monitor conditions on funding. Discuss as a board the purpose of funding and contract monitoring.
- Increase the total number of funding sources, even if they are low autonomy, to reduce the degree of control of any one source. An organization with a dozen or more low-autonomy funding sources can mitigate the lack of flexibility by diversifying.

- Take part in policy networks and coalitions to resist or reduce excessive conditions by government funding sources.

One of the easiest types of organizations to manage, and the most satisfying for a board experience, is a high-reliability/high-autonomy organization. These organizations are better able to chart their own course and stay flexible, and have the time and freedom to ask the big questions and make long-term plans. More complex are high-reliability/low-autonomy organizations, which are often large institutions enjoying tight relationships with government or the United Way; they are generally long-term relationships in which funding conditions are accommodated over a long period of time.

The most difficult organizations of all to manage are low-reliability/low-autonomy (a.k.a., Dante's Seventh Circle of Hell). These organizations are stuck in an ongoing loop of project creation, submission, and approval, and have a high need for both negotiation and earnings management, which sometimes are in conflict.

Many organizations are so steeped in their existing funding patterns and relationships that they no longer recognize or think about the nature and limits of their situation. The Reliability-Autonomy Matrix enables boards and managers to take a systemic view of their revenues by providing a framework for examining them in a relevant, strategic context. The value of the Matrix is its ability to help non-profits easily identify funding limitations and flexibility within their organizations, which is central to effective strategic and financial planning.

► **CHAPTER 12**

# Foundations

## Elizabeth T. Boris

[F]oundations are] nonprofit, nongovernmental organizations that promote charitable giving and other public purposes usually by giving grants of money to nonprofit organizations, qualified individuals, and other entities. Under United States law, philanthropic foundations must serve the public by being organized and operated exclusively for religious, charitable, scientific, testing for public safety, literary, or educational purposes. In addition to providing grants, foundations may provide services, make loans, conduct research, hold conferences, publish reports, and undertake other related activities.

Foundations are formed by individuals, families, and business corporations, which usually donate money, property, or other financial assets. These assets form an endowment or principal fund from which interest is derived and used to support expenses and grant making. Some foundations are not endowed, but receive periodic gifts from their donors.

## Public Versus Private Foundations

There are two major types of philanthropic foundations: private foundations (independent, company-sponsored, and operating foundations) and public foundations (community foundations, women's funds, and others). The term "*foundation*," however, is often used by organizations that are not philanthropic grantors, and private foundations may use a variety of terms to describe themselves. In addition to "foundations," they are called "funds" (the Rockefeller Brothers Fund), "corporations" (the Carnegie Corporation of New York), "trusts" (the Lucille P. Markey Charitable Trust), and "endowments" (the Lilly Endowment).

Foundations may be organized in perpetuity or only for a specified time period. When a foundation is terminated, all of its assets must be used for charitable purposes.

In 1992 there were 35,765 foundations, according to the Foundation Center, a nonprofit organization that compiles and publishes information about foundations. The foundation field is highly concentrated. The largest foundations, those with US$50 million or more, are responsible for 66.2 percent of assets and 48 percent of grants. Most foundations are small and do not employ staff. Only about 9,600 have assets of one million dollars or more.

Foundations held assets of approximately $177 billion and made grants of more than

Originally published in *The International Encyclopedia of Public Policy and Administration*, edited by Jay Shafritz. Copyright © 1998 by Jay Shafritz. Reprinted by permission of Westview Press, a member of Perseus Books Group.

$10 billion in 1992. Though significant in impact, this grant making is a modest 8 percent of total charitable giving, estimated to be $124 billion in 1992 by the AAFRC Trust for Philanthropy, an organization that compiles annual estimates of philanthropic giving. Foundations also provide only a small proportion of overall revenues received by nonprofit organizations in the United States, which was estimated at $408 billion in 1989 by the Independent Sector, a national nonprofit membership organization.

### Private Foundations

Private foundations are created by individual or family donors (or by their representatives, if created by a will after death) or by business corporations. Donors select the boards of directors (or trustees), which determine how the foundations' money will be donated or used for charitable purposes. Private foundations provide donors with a maximum of control over the selection of charitable recipients but a more limited charitable income tax deduction than is available for gifts to public charities. Individuals may deduct from their taxable income cash gifts of up to 30 percent of income. All private foundations are regulated by the "private foundation" rules of the US tax code. These rules are designed to ensure that foundations use their resources only for public benefit.

### Public Foundations

Public foundations include community foundations, which are "public charities," the charitable designation that applies to most nonprofit organizations under US law. Public charities are required to have broad public participation both in donations and in governance, and therefore provide less individual control of the assets and grants than private foundations. Public foundations are subject to the less-stringent regulations and more-favorable tax deductibility levels that govern public charities in the United States. For income

tax purposes, donors may deduct the value of cash gifts up to 50 percent of their adjusted income.

Public charities are required to demonstrate their public support by raising a certain specified percentage of their revenues each year from the general public, a requirement called the public support test. No one donor may provide a majority of financial support.

## Characteristics of Philanthropic Foundations

Private and public foundations in the United States have the following characteristics:

- They are governed by boards of directors or trustees which are responsible for their financial integrity and the fulfillment of their charitable missions.
- They make grants or operate programs or institutions that promote charitable purposes.
- They may employ a staff or use volunteers or consultants to conduct their charitable work.
- They receive gifts of money, property, or financial securities that are deductible from the donors' income tax up to certain limits specified by law (if the donor is alive) or gifts that are deductible from estate taxes if the gift is given through a bequest at the donor's death.
- Financial assets (for those that have endowments) are invested in financial securities (stocks, bonds, etc.), and the interest and dividends earned (and sometimes additional gifts from their donors) provide the money to make grants or operate programs to benefit society. Unless prohibited by their bylaws or trust instruments, foundations may also make grants from the principal fund.
- They are independent of government.
- They do not distribute a profit (nonprofit status).
- They are classified as tax exempt organizations under United States law (501(c)(3) organizations) and therefore are not subject to taxes on

their revenues (except that private foundations must pay an excise tax of one or two percent on their investment income).

## Private Foundations

There are three types of private foundations, distinguishable by the source of their assets and the type of work they do.

### Independent Foundations

Independent foundations are created by gifts from an individual, a family, or a group of individuals to provide funding for charitable activities, primarily by making grants. Many prominent American entrepreneurs and their families created foundations: the Ford Foundation, William and Flora Hewlett Foundation, Rockefeller Foundation, David and Lucile Packard Foundation, Charles Stewart Mott Foundation, W. K. Kellogg Foundation, and many others.

Foundations may be operated by the donors or their families, by staff hired for that purpose, or by banks or other entities designated by the donors to act in their behalf. Policy and grant decisions are made by the board of directors or trustees, which usually includes the donors and their families (if they are alive), trusted associates, and other civic, business, and academic leaders who can contribute to the work of the foundations. Many independent foundations, like the Ford Foundation, no longer have family members involved in the foundation. The board of directors is legally responsible for overseeing the finances and operations of the foundation; it also elects new directors.

When an independent foundation is primarily governed and operated by the donor and family members, it is often called a "family foundation." Donors and family members form the board of directors and often operate the foundation without employing a staff. In some family foundations, the family lawyer, trusted friends, and business associates may also be asked to serve on the board. (The Meadows Foundation in Texas is an example of a family foundation that includes family members as staff and board members, although it also employs nonfamily members as staff.)

Recently, some independent foundations were formed as a result of the sale of nonprofit hospitals (or similar charitable entities) to for-profit businesses. Several such sales resulted in the creation of new foundations with hundreds of millions of dollars in assets. Although the foundations are legally independent from the resulting for-profit companies, the foundations usually focus on health or issues related to the original charitable purpose of the former nonprofit organization.

### Operating Foundations

Private foundations may also be organized as operating foundations to conduct research or provide a direct service; for example, they may operate an art museum or a home for the aged. The interest generated by the endowment pays for staffing and administering the program or organization. Operating foundations must use at least 85 percent of their investment income to operate programs. They are permitted to make grants, but only up to 15 percent of their income. (The Kettering Foundation of Ohio is a well-known operating foundation that publishes papers and organizes public issues forums throughout the United States. The Getty Trust operates the Getty Museum in California.)

### Community Foundations

Community foundations are classified as public charities and are formed by a group of individuals to benefit their community or region. An endowment is created from the gifts of many donors, which are pooled, and the interest is used to make grants to nonprofit organizations, individuals, and governments to enhance the quality of life, primarily in their geographical area. Community foundations may have separate funds that are donated by different persons or families or businesses. A donor may name the fund and indicate the types of grants that the fund should make. The community foundation board oversees the foundation, and its staff conducts the grant-making program.

Boards of directors of community foundations (also called trustees or distribution committees) are selected to represent the community. Some members are chosen by certain designated public officials (for example, a judge or civic leader).

## Other Public Foundations

There are several other types of public foundations that receive tax-deductible contributions from individual donors and use the money or the interest generated to make grants for specific types of activities. In the 1980s, groups of women in many cities created women's foundations to raise money and make grants to help meet women's and girls' needs that they felt were being neglected by both philanthropy and governments. There are now more than 60 women's foundations in the United States that raise money to benefit women and girls in their communities. Donors usually contribute to public foundations on a yearly basis, although some, like the Ms. Foundation for Women, have raised an endowment. There are women's funds in Chicago, New York, Colorado, San Francisco, and many other areas.

Members of minority groups have created public foundations to raise money and make grants to meet the needs of their groups. The Seventh Generation Fund was created in 1977 to benefit American Indian tribes in the United States and Canada. Public foundations are at present a small part of United States

philanthropy, but their numbers are increasing rapidly.

Many public foundations make grants to promote social change. Often called alternative funds, they employ nonhierarchical decision-making structures and invite community members or grantees to participate on the grant-making boards or distribution committees. (The Haymarket People's Fund in Boston is a well-known alternative fund.)

## Government Foundations

The National Endowment for the Humanities, the National Endowment for the Arts, the National Science Foundation, and the National Endowment for Democracy are examples of foundations established by the US government. Government-initiated foundations are usually supported by public money. They have independent boards of directors, but their programs often become part of the political debate during the budgeting process. In western European countries, government-supported foundations are often larger and more prominent than privately funded ones.

## History of Philanthropic Foundations

Private foundations were popularized shortly after the turn of the twentieth century when Margaret Olivia Sage (1907), Andrew Carnegie (1911), and John D. Rockefeller (1913) formed their foundations. These new organizations were created as corporations, like the businesses then responsible for generating the private fortunes that would be turned to charitable uses. Unlike the traditional charitable trusts handed down in common law from Elizabethan times, the new corporations were flexible and could more easily change with the times. They were governed by self-perpetuating boards of directors that had the power to make program and investment decisions and the legal responsibility for financial oversight.

At about the same time, Frederick H. Goff developed the concept of a community trust in Cleveland, Ohio. The community trust was designed to avoid the "dead hand" of the donor whose charitable purposes became outmoded after his or her death. By creating a charitable fund in a community trust, a donor permitted a distribution committee representative of the community to ensure that his or her gift always fulfilled a relevant charitable purpose. The idea caught on, and in 1914 the Cleveland Community Trust was formed. Numerous community trusts, later called community foundations, were formed in the following years.

Although the foundation as an institution was an innovation, it evolved from long-standing traditions of secular and religious giving as well as popular reform movements. Andrew Carnegie's *Gospel of Wealth* [1889] (1990) provides the classic rationale for the proper stewardship of wealth. He called upon men of wealth to regard surplus revenues as trust funds that they are duty bound to administer for the benefit of the community.

Philanthropic foundations flourished during the 1920s, when immense fortunes were made and there was unbridled optimism in the ability of reason and science to solve society's problems. Foundations were to be instruments of scientific charity, controlled by those of superior achievement and designed to support efforts to get at the root causes of poverty, hunger, and disease. Education and research were the favored methods.

The early foundations were formed before the adoption of a national income tax, although foundations were among the charitable organizations exempted from paying income taxes in the Revenue Act of 1913. By 1917 Congress enacted a charitable tax deduction for donors, and in 1919 deductions were permitted for chari-

table gifts made from estates after the death of the donor.

Despite the tax incentives, the number of foundations grew slowly, until the 1940s, when high rates of taxation (marginal rates up to 90 percent) and postwar prosperity combined to encourage the creation of a large number of new private foundations. This trend accelerated in the 1950s, slowed somewhat in the 1960s, and declined in the 1970s following the enactment of the Tax Reform Act of 1969, which contained many regulatory provisions that affected foundations. In the mid-1980s the creation of new large foundations reached an all-time high, following the revision of some of the most restrictive provisions of the 1969 law and the creation of huge personal fortunes.

## Achievements

In less than a century, philanthropic foundations have produced a long list of achievements. Major foundations that view their assets as social risk capital have financed breakthroughs in scientific research, the arts, and the humanities, and have built and sustained major nonprofit institutions both in the United States and in other countries. The majority of foundations, with modest resources and ambitions, have quietly contributed to local colleges, hospitals, and service organizations, providing needed resources and helping to improve the quality of life in their communities.

Foundations supported the research that led to the new grains that produced the Green Revolution in Asia; helped to create public television and its best-known show, *Sesame Street;* funded the Flexner Report that caused major reforms in medical education; funded the experiments that led to white lines on the right side of all of US roads; championed population research before it was politically possible for the government to do so; and much more.

## Criticisms

From the beginning foundations received mixed reactions. Even though some welcomed the dedication of surplus wealth to philanthropic purposes, many feared that the concentration of resources in foundations would subvert the public agenda and place too much power in the hands of those who already controlled business and politics. Foundations are faulted for their lack of public accountability, for their elitism, for their arrogance, and for their potential to benefit those who form and run them, rather than the public purposes they are ostensibly designed to serve. Periodic scandals reinforce these fears, although the growth of government, business, and the nonprofit sector over the course of the century has limited the negative impacts that early critics feared.

American culture celebrates individual initiative and daring that leads to financial success, but part of the negative reaction to foundations is a distrust of the donor's motives. In a study reported by John Edie (1987) in *America's Wealthy and the Future of Foundations* [edited by Teresa Odendahl], donors' reasons for creating foundations were found to vary significantly. Some had a deeply felt religious background or a tradition of family social responsibility and concern for the poor, and others had political or ideological beliefs they wished to advance. Some donors desired to create a memorial to themselves or their families. Other donors felt a commitment to a community or pressure from their peers to be philanthropic. Relatively few formed foundations because of tax incentives, although the existence of tax incentives often influenced the size of the contribution to the foundation.

Recently, foundations were faulted for being both too political and too timid. Critics of the left challenge foundations for supporting the status quo and neglecting the needs of the poor, of girls and women, of racial and ethnic minorities, and of the disabled. Critics from the right accuse foundations of encouraging the growth of government programs and undermining the free enterprise system. The failure of many foundations to communicate fully with the public about their work inhibits informed assessments of their impacts. Only a minority of foundations issue annual reports or publications that describe their programs.

## Government Regulation

The Internal Revenue Service oversees the activities of philanthropic foundations and other nonprofit organizations because the national laws governing foundations are in the tax code. The 1969 Tax Reform Act and its subsequent revisions provide the national regulatory framework for US foundations. Foundations must pay fines for violating the law, and a foundation may lose its status as a tax-exempt entity for a serious offense.

Foundations may not control a business, provide monetary benefits to any donors or directors (except for reasonable compensation for services provided), make risky investments with their endowment funds, or accumulate assets without paying a reasonable amount for charitable activities. Private (nonoperating) foundations must make grants and operate programs that, with administrative expenses, amount to at least 5 percent of their assets each year.

Foundations may not try to influence the legislative process directly, except in their own defense, and they may not influence elections, except by providing independent research and analysis to inform the political debate.

At the state level, the attorney general or charities officer reviews a foundation's state information forms (if they are required) and oversees compliance with state charitable regulations. At the federal level, a foundation is required by law to complete a detailed disclosure form (Form 990-PF) every year. These documents include information on a foundation's revenues, expenses, investments, loans, salaries, gifts received, income-producing activities, and other financial and program information. Private foundations are also required to list all of the grants they make each year and to provide information about how to apply for a grant. These information forms (Form 990-PF for private, corporate, and operating foundations, and Form 990 for community foundations) are public documents. Foundations must make these forms available to the public. The Foundation Center (1994a) facilitates access to the disclosure forms by making them available in library collections around the country.

## Foundation Governance

Foundations are governed by boards of directors or by trustees (in foundations that are set up as charitable trusts). Directors and trustees are responsible for the proper management of the foundation's assets and for implementing its grant making and other program goals. The foundation's goals may be spelled out in great detail by the donor, or, as in most large US foundations, the goals may be quite general—to improve the lives of people—which leaves to the discretion of the board the definition and implementation of the foundation's program.

Private foundation boards are self-perpetuating. New members are identified and elected by the existing board. In addition to donors and family members, boards usually include business, professional, educational, and community leaders. The majority of foundation board members are white males; approximately 29 percent of board members are women, and 4 percent are members of racial or ethnic minority groups.

Foundation governance may vary from complete donor control to almost complete staff control. There are four main types of foundation governance that capture the continuum: donor, administrator, director, and presidential. These models are somewhat related to the size and longevity of the foundations. Smaller foun-

dations are more likely to be informally run by the donor and family. Larger ones are usually more professionalized, older, and more likely to be run by staffs than by the families that founded them.

The donor model is prevalent in many family foundations in which the donor and family members operate the foundation without a staff and make all of the decisions themselves. The process is informal and the donor's wishes are paramount.

In the administrator model, the foundation employs an administrative staff person who processes the paperwork, but the policy and program decisions are initiated and decided by the board members. In the director model, the foundation employs an executive director and relies on that person to process the requests and provide information and recommendations for the foundation's policy and grant decisions.

The presidential model gives wide discretion to the foundation's chief executive officer (CEO). This model is usually found in the few large foundations that make hundreds of grants and give away many millions of dollars each year. In these foundations, the board of directors employs an experienced national leader to whom it delegates operating and grant-making authority. The board sets fiscal and program priorities and monitors the foundation's finances and programs. It may also make decisions on very large grants.

## Corporate Governance

In corporate foundations, the boards of directors usually comprise the chief executive officer of the corporation and other high-level managers. Infrequently, directors from outside the company may be asked to serve on the corporate foundation board. The decisionmaking process varies by company. In some companies all grant recommendations are brought before the board for final decisions, but in other companies staffs have greater discretion and can make many small grants on their own authority. With the trend toward decentralization in US business, corporations are increasingly delegating grant-making authority to local managers.

## Grant Making

Foundations make grants primarily to qualified public charities, although they may make grants to almost any type of organization or individual, as long as the purpose of the grant is "charitable" and the grantor monitors the use of the funds. Grants can be made to nonprofit organizations, individuals, corporations, and governments, both nationally and internationally. The majority of foundation grants are made to nonprofit organizations, often colleges and universities, that qualify as tax-exempt charitable organizations under section 501(c)(3) of the US tax code.

Grant-making patterns do not change greatly from year to year. The Foundation Center reports that in 1993, 24 percent of foundation grant dollars supported educational projects; 18 percent funded health-related projects; 15 percent were for human services; 15 percent for arts and humanities; 11 percent for public or society benefit; 5 percent for the environment and animals; 4 percent for science and technology; 4 percent for international affairs; 3 percent for social science; and 2 percent for religion.

In addition to making grants, foundations may undertake a wide range of activities. They often bring people together in conferences or informally to discuss new research, ideas, or problems. They help other organizations do their jobs better by providing them with management assistance or training. Some provide space for service-providing organizations, and others conduct or publish research. Foundations may also make loans and invest in projects that have a charitable purpose.

## Staffing

Most foundations in the United States do not employ staffs. They have limited assets and are operated by the donor(s) or by the board of directors. Some unstaffed foundations employ consultants or other part-time staffs for specific tasks, such as accounting, audits, and legal matters. Corporate foundations are often administered by employees of the sponsoring company.

In the largest 2,500 foundations, program, administrative, and clerical staffs are employed to operate foundations, under the guidance of boards of directors. Fewer than 13,000 men and women work for philanthropic foundations. The staff of a typical foundation may include an executive director who heads the foundation, a program officer who investigates grant requests, and a secretary who does the clerical work. A few very large foundations, like the Ford, Kellogg, and Rockefeller foundations, have a large number of employees and a complex organizational structure.

## Foundations Worldwide

Philanthropic trusts and religious funds are traditionally found in many cultures. Recently, increasing numbers of foundation-like institutions of all recognized types are being created throughout the world. Regulations, sources of support, and grant-making patterns vary, but in most cases, foundations are playing important roles in building and maintaining civil societies. As in the United States, foundations often take the name of the individual donor or family. Prominent international foundations include: Soros, Tatas, Calouste Gulbenkian, Aga Khan, Eugenio Mendoza, Bernard van Leer, Sassakawa, and Nuffield foundations. Organizations like community foundations are also evident in many countries and are becoming more common. These include the Asian Community Trust, the Foundation de France, the Puerto

Rico Community Foundation, and many others. Company-sponsored foundations are also increasing in number; for example, the Toyota Foundation, Suntory Foundation, and the Prasetya Mulya Foundation.

Government-initiated or -supported foundations are prominent in many countries. The Volkswagen Foundation in Germany, the Japan Foundation, and the Bank of Sweden Tercentenary Foundation are examples. These types of foundations fulfill charitable or educational purposes and may be permitted to receive donations.

The European Foundation Center was formed in the 1980s to provide services and advocate on behalf of the growing number of European foundations. That organization now compiles a directory of European foundations. Similar country-specific directories also exist in Germany, the United Kingdom, and elsewhere.

Foundations are proliferating around the world as wealth is created and societal needs become more pressing. Sources of foundation funding vary, but the basic goals are the same: to use private resources and ingenuity to serve the public and to support alternative solutions to pressing social problems.

## References

Boris, Elizabeth, 1989. "Working in Foundations." In Richard Magat, ed., *Philanthropic Giving: Studies in Varieties and Goals.* New York: Oxford University Press.

———. 1992. *Philanthropic Foundations in the United States: An Introduction.* Washington, DC: Council on Foundations.

Carnegie, Andrew. [1889] 1990. "The Gospel of Wealth." In David L. Geis, J. Steven Ott, and Jay M. Shafritz, eds., *The Nonprofit Organization: Essential Readings.* Pacific Grove, CA: Brooks-Cole.

Commission on Foundations and Private Philanthropy. 1970. *Foundations, Private Giving and Public Policy.* Chicago: University of Chicago Press.

Commission on Private Philanthropy and Public Needs, Department of the Treasury. 1975. *Giving in America.* Washington, DC: GPO.

———. 1977. [Department of the Treasury] *Research Papers.* Washington, DC: GPO.

Council on Foundations. 1993. *Foundation Management Report.* Washington, DC: Council on Foundations.

Cuninggim, Merrimon. 1972. *Private Money and Public Service: The Role of Foundations in American Society.* New York: McGraw-Hill.

Edie, John A. 1987. "Congress and Foundations: Historical Summary." In Teresa Odendahl, ed., *America's Wealthy and the Future of Foundations.* New York: Foundation Center.

Foundation Center. 1994a. *The Foundation Directory.* New York: Foundation Center.

———. 1994b. *The Foundation Grants Index.* New York: Foundation Center.

Freeman, D., and the Council on Foundations. 1991. *The Handbook of Private Foundations.* New York: Foundation Center.

Hall, Peter Dobkin. 1989. "The Community Foundation in America." In Richard Magat, ed., *Philanthropic Giving: Studies in Varieties and Goals.* New York: Oxford University Press.

Heimann, Fritz. F., ed. 1973. *The Future of Foundations.* Englewood Cliffs, NJ: Prentice-Hall.

Kaplan, Anne, ed. 1994. *Giving USA 1994: The Annual Report on Philanthropy for the Year 1993.* New York: American Association of Fundraising Counsel.

Karl, Barry D., and Stanley N. Katz. 1981. "The American Private Philanthropic Foundation and the Public Sphere, 1890–1930." *Minerva* 19: 236–270.

———. 1987. "Foundations and Ruling Class Elites." *Daedalus* 116 (Winter): 1–40.

Lagemann, Ellen Condliffe. 1989. *The Politics of Knowledge: The Carnegie Corporation, Philanthropy, and Public Policy.* Middletown, CT: Wesleyan University Press.

Nielsen, Waldemar A. 1972. *The Big Foundations.* New York: Columbia University Press.

———. 1985. *The Golden Donors: A New Anatomy of the Great Foundations.* New York: Dutton.

Odendahl, Teresa, ed. 1987. *America's Wealthy and the Future of Foundations.* New York: Foundation Center.

———. 1990. *Charity Begins at Home: Generosity and Self-Interest Among the Philanthropic Elite.* New York: Basic Books.

Odendahl, Teresa J., and Elizabeth Boris. 1983. "The Grantmaking Process." *Foundation News* 24 (September–October).

Odendahl, Teresa J., Elizabeth Boris, and Arlene K. Daniels. 1985. *Working in Foundations: Career Patterns of Women and Men.* New York: Foundation Center.

Renz, Loren, and Steven Lawrence. 1994. *Foundation Giving: Yearbook of Facts and Figures on Private, Corporate, and Community Foundations.* New York: Foundation Center.

Salamon, Lester. 1991. *Foundation Investment and Payout Performance: An Update.* Washington, DC: Council on Foundations.

US Congress. 1965. *Treasury Department Report on Private Foundations.* 89th Cong., 1st sess., February 2.

# ETHICAL CONSIDERATIONS IN FUNDRAISING

*Carol Sipfle and C. Kenneth Meyer*

Nan Brownstone was excited about a meeting she had just finished with the CEO and chief financial officer of Loving Care, a large statewide nursing home corporation. The purpose of the meeting was to discuss possible funding for Seniors United for Healthy Living and Dignity, Inc. (SUHLD), a nonprofit organization for which Nan worked as executive director. Upon completion of the meeting, one sentence stood out in her mind.

"We'll write you a big check," said Mike Donaldson, CFO, about their potential partnership. As she returned to her car, this statement replayed in Nan's mind as if it were on her iPod's automatic replay.

Once back in her office, Nan reviewed the history between the two organizations and her notes of the meeting. SUHLD had previously solicited Loving Care to sponsor its fundraising events, including golf outings and walkathons. These solicitations were usually for small amounts and were made periodically throughout the year. Now, however, Loving Care was agreeable to receiving one sponsorship proposal per year for a much larger amount, and it was up to Nan to determine the best project. In the final analysis, the type of proposal would determine the amount of the "big check." Nan felt up to the challenge and solicited her staff to work with her to develop a winning proposal.

However, Mr. Donaldson's comment "We'll write you a big check," as it was later revealed, had included three contingencies that caused Nan to feel uneasy. First, Loving Care requested that SUHLD make referrals to its nursing facilities throughout the state in exchange for its financial support. This was problematic, of course, since SUHLD was prohibited by its charter from making endorsements of or direct referrals to nursing facilities. Second, Loving Care requested that, when possible, Nan would advocate for its facilities in the event that it received negative publicity, particularly publicity about poor care of nursing home residents. Third, Nan was asked to continue to promote Loving Care as a sponsor of the golf outings and walkathons even though it would no longer provide financial support for these fundraising events.

Nan had nagging doubts about the appropriateness of such requests and whether they fell outside the boundaries of ethical fundraising. However, she took them under consideration and began developing a proposal for funding, not sure how she would address the three contingencies outlined by Mr. Donaldson. Her efforts came to an abrupt stop one morning after she read in the newspaper an article headlined "Nursing Home CEO Accused of Sexual Abuse." Her worst fears were realized when she read the article and learned that the CEO of Loving Care was accused of sexual harassment by a female employee in the corporate office.

Nan's concerns were now elevated to a new level, and the threefold request from Loving Care began to fall into place and make sense. The allegations blemished the reputation of Loving Care, but Nan wondered if her organization's reputation would also be at risk if the proposal was funded. Perhaps she was making a "mountain out of a molehill," or reading more into the news of the allegations than was justified. After all, these were only allegations and the case involved two individuals, not the entire company. She wondered if the general public would remember the allegations months later, when the proposed sponsorship would be publicized.

In considering the ethics of fundraising in this situation, Nan asked herself whether nonprofit organizations should have guidelines on the types of companies they solicited for sponsorships and contributions. Should SUHLD develop guidelines similar to those religiously followed by funds investing in only socially responsible ventures or organizations? And, she mused, at what point did "a big check" carry too high a price tag for an organization to bear?

## Questions and Instructions

1.  Should nonprofit organizations have guidelines on what types of companies they solicit for sponsorships and contributions? Please explain your answer. If yes, provide at least five general examples of guidelines you think nonprofit organizations could use related to seeking sponsorships and contributions.
2.  Please check with at least three nonprofit organizations to determine if they have any specific guidelines for investment of resources. Report on these guidelines to the class.
3.  Would you still submit a proposal to Loving Care in an effort to receive the "big check"? Please explain the reasoning for your answer.
4.  What guidelines would you put in place concerning quid pro quo exchanges like the one proposed by Mr. Donaldson?
5.  Once an organization's reputation has been tarnished or called into question, how does the organization, whether guilty or not, restore its rightful image and reputation? Please research and provide examples of organizations whose images have been tarnished and how their positive image has been restored.

# THE SELLING OF AMERICA

*Garry L. Frank and C. Kenneth Meyer*

Elwood James became a volunteer firefighter when he turned eighteen. This was a momentous time for Elwood, since he had always been fascinated with fire trucks, ladders, pike poles, and hoses, and he was especially intrigued by the ear-busting sirens that blazed when the big red trucks left the fire barn located across the street from his childhood home. Of course he knew that this youthful dream of being fitted for a helmet and the lettered and numbered turnout gear would have to be set aside for the realities that he now faced as an adult. Now he was properly dressed in a uniform, and he was trained to assist individuals, families, and even animals who faced the terror of fire, accidents, and other adversities.

The image of his local fire department was further emblazoned in his mind by the high respect he felt, like his parents and neighbors, for those who placed their lives in harm's way so that the public might be served. He also enjoyed the pancake feed that the firefighters cooked up each year to raise money so that they could give new toys to children who had lost their possessions in household fires.

Elwood chuckled to himself at the pleasant memory of the wonderment, imagination, and fantasy that characterized the days of his youth when his basic character and attitude toward community service were being formed. But that was then and this was now, and time had changed everything. It was nice to reminisce, but as fire chief in Johnsonville, he had to shoulder the responsibility of managing the fire department that had been the focus of his childhood dreams.

Not unlike other urban municipalities, Johnsonville had almost tapped out the various sources of revenue generation, including a sales tax, users' fees, water and utility usage rates, hotel and motel excise taxes, and the ever-unpopular rise in property taxes. These traditional sources of local funding had been fully exploited, and the residents of Johnsonville wanted to "hold the line" on any added taxation efforts. The city had also gambled on the future and taken on the daunting challenge of attracting new industries and businesses to provide good-paying and secure jobs. To achieve this goal, the city had used tax increment financing (TIF) schemes and tax abatement policies for new construction in underutilized and undeveloped areas of Johnsonville, and it had also reduced water and utility rates for new businesses it succeeded in attracting to the town. However, the revenue generated was not keeping up with the escalating costs of providing government services as the city's infrastructure continued to deteriorate, the existing housing stock aged, and the population became increasingly diverse.

Times were especially challenging for the department as the personnel costs of its small core of full-time firefighters ratcheted upward and the cost of health care increased in double-digit, inflationary jumps. Union negotiators were also determined to see that union members were treated fairly in the upcoming labor-management negotiations. As chief, Elwood also had to cope with the continuing saga of aging equipment, an old and deteriorating stock of houses, and the expensive maintenance associated with a fleet of older ambulances, pumper engines, and ladder trucks. He also had to replace the dated protective clothing and safety masks and the equipment required for the safe handling of hazardous materials and accidents.

Elwood presented his customarily well prepared budget before the city council, whose members, in turn, allocated the usual 2 percent increase in funding for the fire department. He spoke to the council about the state of his department and the rising costs associated with providing fire inspection, fire reduction, and fire suppression in a city where the houses were aging, the population was growing, and the fire risk, as his statistics indicated, was increasing. He knew that he sounded like other department heads and that he would not be able to get money from a "stone." At the end of the council meeting, he returned to the fire station and retreated to his office. It was, he thought, the "worst of times." What novel ideas could he come up with that might liberate his department from its financial exigencies?

As Elwood thumbed through the *New Reporter*—the city's only daily newspaper—he noticed an advertisement from the local gambling facility, Lucky Sevens Resort and Casino, claiming to have had a "bumper" year, with its 98 percent payoff rate for the tables and slots. He laughed about the absurdity of gambling and wondered whether this ad was just an unusual ploy to pay back an average of $98 for every $100 dropped into the machines or laid on the green felt tables. Yet, the advertisement touted that it had paid out over $300 million in winnings during the last fiscal year—a figure that Elwood felt was astonishingly high.

The feature story on Lucky Sevens was soliciting funding proposals from public and community nonprofit organizations that would help address recognized community needs. Elwood remembered the added equipment and training that was required in his department when Lucky Sevens came on-line and thought perhaps this was a chance to get some needed funding for the equipment and training needs he had prioritized and just presented to Johnsonville's city council. The article indicated that all inquiries should be directed to the attention of Marietta Hughes, the chair of the board of directors of Lucky Sevens. He would contact her tomorrow, Elwood thought, and she certainly would be receptive to his department, especially given the good relationship he had with the casino and its recognition that Johnsonville's fire department was encumbered with new expenses associated with the largest gaming facility in the state.

When Elwood called the next day, Marietta Hughes seemed most anxious to inform him about their request for proposal (RFP) and told him that they would be happy to talk about the prospect of granting the department up to $600,000. She added, however, that with funding at a level that high, Lucky Sevens would require that the money be used to purchase a piece of equipment such as a first responders' hazmat truck; fortunately, Elwood had just received a low competitive bid of $550,000 for a fire/hazmat vehicle. Hughes also stated that the new truck would be required to bear the logo of Lucky Sevens Resort and Casino on each door of the cab and on the back of the truck. She said that the logo would be shown with a picture that displayed a winning slot machine—all red sevens—and the accompanying statement, "Sponsored by the Lucky Sevens Resort and Casino." Elwood thanked her for her courtesy, time, and information and said that he would examine the ramifications, if any, of their discussion.

Elwood was anxious to get the financing that would enable him to upgrade his department, but the idea of the gaudy logo and the accompanying statement on a department vehicle bothered him. Not being a novice to the budgetary process, he realized that added funding from the city would not be forthcoming. He also knew that the city council had given all department heads the authorization to pursue outside funding at their discretion, whether from companies, philanthropic organizations, private donations and grants, or governmental sources. At a fall meeting of the International City Managers Associations (ICMA), the topic of extramural funding had been addressed during a panel session, and the overall response had been very positive—especially from the city managers. Elwood knew that a gift from the casino was not prohibited under applicable state and local laws. Yet the idea of an advertisement on a city-owned vehicle was deeply troubling to him, especially since, having grown up seeing only the city logo on the sides of city vehicles, it seemed to him that the city logo should be the only allowable logo.

As he faced this dilemma, he thought of many examples of city public space and equipment being used for advertising—some were corporate ads and others were from nonprofit organizations. He reflected on the appropriateness of corporate advertisements being posted on the parking meters, like miniature billboards, but had to concede that revenue was being generated.

He had seen the advertisements posted on public buses, trams, and commuter cars and thought that the buses wrapped in their colorful "vinyl advertisements" were actually attractive. Of course, he had learned early on in his civics courses that speech is protected by the First Amendment, but should Johnsonville's public property—fire trucks, water towers, city vehicles, police cars, traffic control signals, public parks, civic centers and arenas, ballparks, swimming pools, and schools—become the billboards of the future?

Enumerating examples of such advertising did not ease his decision-making dilemma, for the list seemed to be endless. He wondered if the trend toward advertisement on public property was merely a new type of blight seductively taking over urban spaces. If so, was the Lucky Sevens proposal any different from the commercial advertisements that already appeared on park benches and bus stands? Or even more dramatically, was it any different from the public university's advertisements printed in the media and shown on television? Additionally, what about the advertisements that states and cities used to attract business to enhance their chances for economic development?

Elwood thought about the overall implications of commercial advertising, and particularly of advertisements on his fire equipment. He wondered if it was truly worth it to get a new hazmat truck that also sported the casino's "graffiti." What message would his department be giving to the city, and especially to those who were most adversely affected by gambling—those least able to afford to gamble responsibly?

## Questions and Instructions

1. If you were faced with Chief Elwood James's dilemma, what would you do? What would you find alluring about Marietta Hughes's offer? Or do you find Hughes's proposal repugnant? Please elaborate.

2. Explain why you would either accept or reject the offer from Lucky Sevens. How would you justify your decision? Would your justification be the same if you were making it before the city council or the citizenry? Please explain.

3. Although this case involves a local government entity, nonprofit organizations have also used commercial advertisements as a means to generate revenue. What are the implications of using or featuring commercial messages or logos on a nonprofit organization's printed educational materials, social media, or websites? Justify your answers.

4. Please develop a policy statement that could guide a board of directors in its thinking about the appropriateness of an affiliation with commercial advertising and in its use of such advertising.

# PART VI

# PHILANTHROPY IN ACTION

In the summer of 2014, the ALS Ice Bucket Challenge went viral after celebrities and high-profile corporate leaders joined in.[1] The premise was simple: if someone challenged you, you had twenty-four hours to videotape yourself dumping a bucket of ice water over your head or make a donation to a charity benefiting research into amyotrophic lateral sclerosis (ALS), commonly known as Lou Gehrig's disease. Many participants did both. The August 29 headline on the national ALS Association website shouted the results: "The ALS Association Expresses Sincere Gratitude to Over Three Million Donors. Ice Bucket Challenge Donations Top $100 million in 30 days."[2]

Most charitable organizations can only dream about a windfall of unrestricted revenue. Put into perspective, from July 29 to August 29, 2014, the ALS Association received $100.9 million in donations compared to $2.8 million during the same time period in 2013. The ALS Association's president and CEO, Barbara Newhouse, said, "The word gratitude doesn't do enough to express what we are feeling right now."[3]

"Going viral" involves a chain reaction. When original content is posted on an Internet platform, such as Facebook, and people find the content compelling, many of the original poster's friends reshare the photo or video, then many of their friends see it and reshare it, and the resharing goes on and on until thousands or millions of people have seen it—the vast majority of whom are total strangers to the original poster.[4] Donations from the Ice Bucket Challenge were made by individuals, corporations, and foundations; the ALS Association reported gifts ranging from under $1 to $200,000. Individual gifts were made by celebrities, including the actors Leonardo DiCaprio and David Spade, and by corporate leaders such as the president and CEO of T-Mobile USA, John Legere, and Micky Arison, chairman of Carnival Cruise Lines. Corporations contributing included Wells Fargo, Sprint, the Parsons Foundation, and the New York Yankees.[5]

In thirty days, donations through the Ice Bucket Challenge put the ALS Association's cash budget over five times the amount that it had available in the entire 2014 fiscal year. The organization's financial bonanza from the Ice Bucket Challenge has implications for its board of directors and management teams, who must make solid financial decisions about how to use and invest the money. It also has reinvigorated a spontaneous nationwide discussion about how philanthropy is conceptualized and pursued in the nonprofit sector.

The visibility raised through the Ice Bucket Challenge placed the ALS Association on the radar of CharityWatch (formerly the American Institute of Philanthropy, AIP) and Charity Navigator, which are two "charity watchdogs" that provide charitable donors with information to help them make informed giving decisions.[6] Each uses a scoring system to assign a rating that largely reflects a charity's business acumen and fiscal transparency as reported on its annual IRS Form 990-PF. CharityWatch noted on its website that it "will be monitoring the ALS Association to make sure that it has a reasonable plan or budget to spend the Ice Bucket windfall."[7] Ken Berger, president and CEO of Charity Navigator, said: "There is a concern that gimmicky fundraising appeals perpetuate a lack of discussion around what should be a core issue—a charity's impact and true worthiness of support."[8]

The reasons why a specific piece of content goes viral elude precise human understanding, but in practice almost all efforts to intentionally make something go viral fail.[9] The "lottery stories" of philanthropy-gone-viral are rare.[10] Nonetheless, with Facebook reporting over 6.58 million sites linked to it, people and nonprofit organizations will keep trying.[11] Online fundraising is the fastest-growing fundraising channel. In 2006, $6.8 billion was raised online, and this figure rose to over $22 billion in 2011.[12] Still, for all of the attention it receives, online giving accounted for just 6.4 percent of all charitable giving in 2013.[13]

What makes a charity "worthy" sometimes depends on how well it is able to demonstrate its business capabilities, not simply its philanthropic character. This measure of worthiness has generated concerns that extend far beyond the management of philanthropic activities because it challenges what it means to be a nonprofit. Almost twenty-five years ago, Richard Bush expressed his fear that by focusing on private-sector methods, nonprofit organizations were underappreciating the value of what made them distinctive: participation and membership.[14] Jon Van Til has suggested that many professional nonprofits should be removed from the tax-exempt rolls because they look more like businesses than voluntary organizations: "A lean third sector, consisting only of organizations true to principles of voluntary citizen-driven service and advocacy, would merit both the public privileges and the reputation it must continue to earn."[15] As Lori Brainard and Patricia Siplon note, "The soul of the nonprofit sector seems to be up for grabs."[16] More on the contested notion of "worthy philanthropy" is found in Holona LeAnne Ochs's article reprinted in this part. As she argues, worthiness resting on business acumen or measurable results does not necessarily take into consideration human need.

## Philanthropy

Philanthropy has a long history in the United States.[17] The word "philanthropy" is derived from the Greek for "love of mankind."[18] The Association of Fundraising Professionals defines "philanthropy" as: "(1) the love of humankind, usually expressed by an effort to enhance the well-being of humanity through personal acts of practical kindness or by financial support of a cause or causes, such as a charity (e.g., the American Red Cross), mutual aid or assistance (e.g., service clubs and youth groups), quality of life (e.g., arts, education, and the environment), and religion; and (2) any effort to relieve human misery or suffering, improve the quality of life, encourage aid or assistance, or foster the preservation of values through gifts, service or other voluntary activity, and all of which are external to government involvement or marketplace exchange."[19] Philanthropy differs from charity in that philanthropy is "the giving of money or self to solve social problems. Philanthropy is developmental, an investment in the future, an effort to prevent future occurrences or recurrence of socials ills." Charity is "relieving or alleviating specific instances of suffering, aiding the individual victims of specific social ills. Charity is acts of mercy and compassion."[20]

In analyzing philanthropic gifts, multiple perspectives have been offered to explain motivations for giving, including self-interest, altruism, and social relations as well as government and market failures. Gift-giving has also been conceptualized as a component of social obligation. "The gift is the initiator of reciprocity and finds its purpose neither in self-interest nor in altruism, but rather in creating a system of social relations."[21]

Research is showing that the meaning and practices of philanthropy and cultural and moral choices about giving are in flux. In the foreword to this volume, David Renz identifies five trends affecting nonprofits: demographic shifts that redefine participation, technological advances, growing networks, rising interest in civic engagement and volunteerism, and a blurring of sectoral boundaries among nonprofit organizations, for-profit organizations, and government. In the United States, an unprecedented $45 trillion to $150 trillion in wealth will be transferred over the next five decades, with 50 to 65 percent of this amount coming from households with $1 million or more in net worth. Not surprisingly, this is changing the way fundraisers, charities, and financial professionals should perceive, articulate, and implement their endeavors.[22]

There is work to be done, however. A 2013 study of financial planners and affluent donors conducted by Bank of America's US Trust in partnership with The Philanthropic Initiative found that in discussions of charitable giving, nearly three-quarters of financial advisers initiate the discussion from a technical perspective. Only 35 percent focus on their clients' philanthropic goals or passions.[23] Not surprisingly, only 41 percent of the donors were fully satisfied with these conversations.[24] Donors want to choose the ways in which they become who they want to become and accomplish what they want to do for themselves, their families, and the world around them.[25] In 2013 total estimated US charitable individual giving increased by 4.4 percent, to $335.17 billion.[26] Of this, the largest percentage came from individual giving.

## Giving Practices

In the research report *The 2012 Bank of America Study of High Net Worth Philanthropy,* wealthy donors reported becoming more intentional about their giving. The majority of these donors relied on an impact strategy and focused on particular causes or geographical areas.[27] This intentionality is based in the belief that their gift can make a difference. A rise in media attention to celebrity philanthropy and high-profile business entrepreneurs also reflects keen interest in creating measurable impact. In June 2013, the Forbes 400 Summit on Philanthropy included approximately 150 billionaires or near-billionaires and social entrepreneurs. U2's Bono, Bill Gates, Warren Buffett, UN Secretary-General Ban Ki-moon, Nobel Peace Prize winners Ellen Johnson Sirleaf and Muhammad Yunus, and Robin Hood Foundation founder Paul Tudor Jones were either in attendance or being recognized for their contributions to philanthropy. Forum participants considered topics such as disruptive business models and entrepreneurial solutions to global poverty. Bono, cofounder of ONE and (RED), said, "I've learned just to be an evidence-based activist. Find out what works. Find out what doesn't work. Repeat what works. Stop what doesn't work." According to Mike Perlis, CEO and president of Forbes Media, the Forum concluded "that transparency will be critical in driving growth in impoverished countries and ending corruption."[28]

Although philanthropy is associated with the very wealthy, the vast predominance of offerings still come from average citizens of moderate income. Between 70 and 90 percent of all US households donate to charity in a given year, with the typical household's annual gifts amounting to between $2,000 and $3,000.[29]

## Demonstrating Philanthropy

The ways in which philanthropic action and caring may be demonstrated include individual cash donations, corporate sponsorships, social entrepreneurship and enterprises, or investments of time and talents through volunteering. The type or level of one's donations of cash or property may be influenced by a desire to promote a positive public or corporate image, or it may be based on individual or business-related tax incentives (see Part II). Social characteristics, including personal wealth, education level, age, and gender, affect philanthropic behavior as well. Data from the Bureau of Labor Statistics show that education level is the highest predictor of volunteering, along with gender (being female).[30] Generational differences also affect philanthropic behaviors such as volunteering (see Part IX). Economic upturns, recessions, and political mistrust of government or business corporations can alter philanthropic attitudes. Media attention to charitable causes or disasters, religious teachings, social mores, family values, and professional skill sets may also affect one's participation in philanthropic activities. For example, John Wood left a high-paying position at Microsoft to form a charity to address global illiteracy, as he explains in the personal account reprinted in this part.

## The Transmission of Philanthropic Values

The *2012 Bank of America Study of High Net Worth Philanthropy* showed that most high-net-worth households in 2009 depended on their own family's efforts to educate younger relatives about charitable giving (85 percent), but that by 2011 this had dropped to just 51 percent. Likewise, in 2009 about 45 percent of high-net-worth households indicated that they relied on their church, synagogue, mosque, or other place of worship to transmit charitable values to their children, but this figure dropped to 34 percent in 2011.[31] These declines raise a question: from what sources are younger professionals—say, Millennials (those born in 1982 or later)—receiving their philanthropic cues? Technology is clearly transforming philanthropy, from the ways in which people engage with nonprofit organizations to how organizations market and manage information. Mobile technology is also growing. Nearly half of all emails are now read on mobile devices, and this is changing how organizations use data to drive mission delivery.[32]

Some research evidence shows that young people are more apt to ask, "What is in it for me?" than, "How can I give?"[33] Yet young people who are not actively involved in donating to charities may not have been asked.[34] Countless studies show that young people *are* philanthropically engaged through volunteering. The 2010 Volunteering in America data show that in the United States 11.6 million (21.2 percent) of Millennials volunteered in 2010.[35] These numbers may reflect family values and a commitment to meeting human needs, but they are also likely to reflect a community service opportunity or requirement in high school or college.

The Bureau of Labor Statistics reported a dip, however, in Millennial volunteering 2013, and this has some worried.[36] Unfortunately, there is evidence to suggest that young people may not sustain their volunteering activities.[37] Short-term project volunteering and episodic volunteering are on the rise, which may present managerial challenges for nonprofits that need ongoing or long-term support.[38]

## Influences on Philanthropy

The past several decades have seen a sharp rise in social and corporate philanthropy. Cause marketing is a strategy whereby a promotional partnership between a nonprofit and a for-profit corporation is created. Perhaps the best known of these is the Susan G. Komen for the Cure campaign, which has generated over $200 million. Ochs identifies governance partnerships along a spectrum that ranges from those based on civic logic to those that use market logic.[39] The spectrum includes traditional nonprofits, nonprofits engaged in income-generating activities, social enterprises, socially responsible businesses, corporate social responsibility, and traditional private entities. These organizations may be involved in governance partnerships that include or exclude activities typical of each type.[40] Technology has shaped the ways in which philanthropy is carried out, with volunteering recruitment and online activities serving as ways for organizations to build relations. Professional associations, even those whose mission is primarily business-oriented, are using their networks, connections, expertise, and skills to encourage their memberships and staff members to contribute to the welfare of others through volunteering.[41]

## Conclusion

As the field of philanthropy continues to undergo changes, one constant remains—there are many explanations for giving. Some donors create and give their fortunes to foundations because of deeply held religious beliefs or a tradition of family social responsibility and concern for the poor, while others have political or ideological beliefs they wish to advance. Some give to foundations because they want to try to improve the human condition around the world, and others feel a commitment to give back to a local community or a cause. Some seek to create a memorial to themselves or their families, and others are feeling pressure from their peers to be philanthropic.[42] People in all times and places have felt the need and the desire to help others. Developing strong relationships and trust, however, takes time.[43]

Returning to where we began, a *BBC News Magazine* article asked the question: "How Much Has the Ice Bucket Challenge Achieved?" Nonprofit managers are increasingly pressed to respond to a similar question: philanthropically, what did we achieve? From an economic perspective, the Ice Bucket Challenge resulted in a large sum of money being raised in a short time period. As that money is used for research, the hope is that the Challenge will pay off with the development of ALS prevention strategies or cures and that it will improve the quality of life for people currently afflicted with ALS conditions. The visibility of the ALS Association's charitable activity also raised public visibility for the disease. Google searches for both "ALS" and "Lou Gehrig's disease" in the United States rose sharply during the Ice Bucket Challenge. In August 2014, the ALS Wikipedia page had close to 2.8 million views compared with 1.7 million people who had visited it during the whole of the preceding twelve months.[44] These outcomes are encouraging, but as we have shown, they do not tell the whole story.

Philanthropic activities require money, but money is a means to an end. The value of caring for its own sake can be lost in chasing Facebook "shares" in an effort to get a message to go viral. There is another lesson to be learned from the ALS Ice Bucket Challenge: although there was widespread interest in ALS generated in August 2014, the number of "hits" has not been sustained, and it is unlikely that the ALS Association will be able to maintain a relationship with all of those 3 million donors.

Nonetheless, we do not wish to be naysayers. All nonprofits must compete to find ways to increase their resources if they are to carry out their mission-related activities, and the Internet is one tool among many others for doing so. Relationships are built through many channels, however, and we all have a vested interest in promoting the values of caring, sharing, and love of humankind upon which philanthropy is based.

## Readings Reprinted in Part VI

The first reading, "Philanthropic Social Ventures: A Framework and Profile of the Emerging Field" by Holona LeAnne Ochs, offers an analysis and discussion of philanthropic social ventures. Ochs begins with the assertion that "modern philanthropy is infused with the notion that promoting social wealth yields self-sustaining benefits through innovative practices that create value and maintain their worth. The consequence of which may enhance investments among the underserved." As nonprofits adopt strategies and innovative partnerships that hinge on market strategies, they also have "the potential to further marginalize the interests of those who continue to be undervalued in the market context." Ochs's piece provides a useful continuum for understanding the many forms that may be created through philanthropic partnerships. Her key argument is a reminder to all that philanthropy is based on love of mankind, not market metrics.

The second reading in Part VI is taken from John Wood's book *Leaving Microsoft to Change the World: An Entrepreneur's Odyssey to Educate the World's Children.* In this compilation from Wood's book, the author explains his motivation to leave a solid corporate position at Microsoft to pursue his vision of helping to alleviate global illiteracy. Although Wood's personal story provides a compelling narrative of a man with the courage to change his life's direction, the selections reprinted here also show the value of using professional skills to the benefit of those in need. As Wood discusses his strategy for creating change, it is clear that a business plan is not just "something nice to have," but an expected part of doing business in the field of philanthropy.

Together, the readings in Part VI introduce the reader to discussions regarding professionalism and the adoption of market-based strategies in the nonprofit sector. They also reflect the philanthropic challenges and opportunities that organizations are facing. Nonprofit managers are part of a large set of actors who are attempting to make a difference in the world. These efforts include networks of people and organizations across all boundaries and sectors that have introduced new and competing values for those engaged in philanthropy. Traditional values of caring and giving for the sake of others—as foundational values of philanthropy—must remain strong if they are to be the legacy for philanthropy in the decades to come.

## Case Studies in Part VI

The first case in Part VI, "Growing Support Online One Meal at a Time," offers a discussion of social media and how one organization, The Soup Bowl, is trying to use it to build a base of philanthropic and financial supporters. The reader is asked to analyze the data that The Soup Bowl is gathering via Facebook and offer some conclusions about its usefulness. Social media is just one of many avenues that nonprofit organizations are using to encourage engagement and inspire people to support their missions.

In the second case, "Volunteer and Donor Recruitment on Social Media," a nonprofit organization recognizes that generational differences may affect how it does outreach. One of its strategies is to use social media to sponsor a contest and encourage potential supporters to interact with the organization through fun activities and games. As this nonprofit seeks to be innovative and "in touch" with potential volunteers, the reader is asked to consider whether its tactics are working and also whether they constitute the best use of the nonprofit's time.

## Notes

1. Eddie Scarry, "Ice Bucket Challenge Leads to $100 Million in Donations," Mediaite, August 29, 2014, http://www.mediaite.com/online/ice-bucket-challenge-leads-to-100-million-in-donations/ (accessed October 21, 2014).

2. "The ALS Association Expresses Sincere Gratitude to Over Three Million Donors: Ice Bucket Challenge Donations Top $100 Million in 30 Days," ALS Association, August 29, 2014, http://www.alsa.org/news/media/press-releases/ice-bucket-challenge-082914.html. The ALS Association is a 501(c)(3) charitable nonprofit organization.

3. Ibid.

4. Josh Fredman, "What Does 'Goes Viral' on Facebook Mean?" Demand Media, http://science.opposingviews.com/goes-viral-facebook-mean-3009.html (accessed October 21, 2014).

5. "Individuals, Organizations, and Corporations Respond with Immense Generosity to Ice Bucket Challenge," ALS Association, August 29, 2014, http://www.alsa.org/news/media/press-releases/ice-bucket-challenge-generosity.html.

6. See CharityWatch, "About Us," http://charitywatch.org/aboutaip.html; and Charity Navigator, "Mission," http://www.charitynavigator.org/index.cfm?bay=content.view&cpid=17#.VMk76JUtDIU. "Charity Navigator works to guide intelligent giving. By guiding intelligent giving, we aim to advance a more efficient and responsive philanthropic marketplace, in which givers and the charities they support work in tandem to overcome our nation's and the world's most persistent challenges."

7. CharityWatch, "Ice Bucket Donations Pour into ALS Association," September 2014, http://charitywatch.org/articles/alsicebucketchallenge.html.

8. Ken Berger discussed the ALS Association receiving a large influx of cash in a short period of time on *CBS This Morning*, September 19, 2014, http://www.cbsnews.com/news/ice-bucket-challenge-als-association-how-to-spend-money/.

9. Fredman, "What Does 'Goes Viral' on Facebook Mean?"

10. Mashable, "Crowdsourced Philanthropy—Making Your Cause Go Viral." The Nonprofit Quarterly, July 12, 2012, https://nonprofitquarterly.org/philanthropy/20647-crowdsourced-philanthropymaking-your-cause-go-viral.html.

11. Alexa, "facebook.com," http://www.alexa.com/siteinfo/facebook.com (accessed October 21, 2014).

12. Blackbaud, "Most Generous Online Cities," 2012, https://www.blackbaud.com/files/resources/downloads/2012MostGenerousOnlineCities.pdf.

13. Blackbaud, "Charitable Giving Report: How Nonprofit Fundraising Performed in 2013," https://www.blackbaud.com/nonprofit-resources/charitablegiving.

14. Richard Bush, "Survival of the Nonprofit Spirit in a For-Profit World," *Nonprofit and Voluntary Sector Quarterly* 21 (1992): 391–410. See also Lori A. Brainard and Patricia D. Siplon, "Toward Nonprofit Organization Reform in the Voluntary Spirit: Lessons from the Internet," *Nonprofit and Voluntary Sector Quarterly* 33 (2004): 435.

15. Jon Van Til, *Growing Civil Society: From Nonprofit Sector to Third Space* (Bloomington: Indiana University Press, 2000), 203.

16. Brainard and Siplon, "Toward Nonprofit Organization Reform in the Voluntary Spirit," 436.

17. This introductory essay discusses issues in philanthropy. For more focused discussions, see the introductory essays for Part V ("Fund Development: Generating Revenues") and Part IX ("Managing Volunteers"). For a more complete discussion of philanthropy and its historical roots, see Part II, "The Nonprofit Sector's Historical Evolution, Distinctive Values, and Contributions to Society," in *The Nature of the Nonprofit Sector*, 3rd ed., edited by J. Steven Ott and Lisa A. Dicke (Boulder, CO: Westview Press, 2016). See also Peter Dobkin Hall, "A Historical Overview of Philanthropy, Voluntary Associations, and Nonprofit Organizations in the United States, 1600–2002," in *The Nonprofit Sector*, edited by Walter W. Powell and Richard Steinberg (New Haven, CT: Yale University Press, 2006).

18. Barbara L. Ciconte and Jeanne G. Jacob, *Fundraising Basics: A Complete Guide* (Sudbury, MA: Jones and Bartlett, 2009), 2.

19. From the AFP's online dictionary, cited in ibid., 2.

20. Ott and Dicke, *The Nature of the Nonprofit Sector*, 3rd ed.

21. Marcel Mauss, *The Gift: Forms and Functions of Exchange in Archaic Societies* (1925; reprint, London: Cohen and West, 1966); reprinted in Helmut K. Anheier, *Nonprofit Organizations*, 2nd ed. (New York: Routledge, 2014), 228.

22. Paul G. Schervish, "The Cultural Horizons of Charitable Giving in an Age of Affluence: The Leading Questions of the 21st Century," Boston College Center on Wealth and Philanthropy, http://www.wealthandgiving.org/uploads/Cultural_Horizons.pdf.

23. Doug Donovan, "Wealthy Donors Don't Get Giving Advice They Want," *Chronicle of Philanthropy*, October 9, 2013, http://philanthropy.com/article/Wealthy-Donors-Don-t-Get/142221/. For the study, see The Philanthropic Initiative, "The US Trust Study of the Philanthropic Conversation: Understanding Advisor Approaches and Client Expectations," October 2013, http://newsroom.bankofamerica.com/sites/bankofamerica.newshq.businesswire.com/files/press_kit/additional/US_Trust_Study_of_the_Philanthropic_Conversation_2013.pdf.

24. Donovan, "Wealthy Donors Don't Get Giving Advice They Want," 2.

25. Schervish, "The Cultural Horizons of Charitable Giving in an Age of Affluence."

26. See "2014 Report Highlights" in *Giving USA: The Annual Report on Philanthropy for the Year 2013,* www.givingusareports.org.

27. Center on Philanthropy at Indiana University, *2012 Bank of America Study of High Net Worth Philanthropy: Issues Driving Charitable Activities Among Wealthy Households,* November 2012, http://newsroom .bankofamerica.com/files/press_kit/additional/2012_BAC_Study_of_High_Net_Worth_Philanthropy_0.pdf.

28. "Forbes Hosts Second Annual Forbes 400 Summit on Philanthropy," *Forbes,* June 6, 2013, http://www .forbes.com/sites/forbespr/2013/06/06/forbes-host-second-annual-forbes-400-summit-on-philanthropy/print/.

29. Karl Zinsmeister, "DoNation: Which Americans Give Most to Charity?" *Philanthropy* (Summer 2013), reprinted at Philanthropy Roundtable, http://www.philanthropyroundtable.org/site/print/donation; "2014 Report Highlights," in *Giving USA: The Annual Report on Philanthropy for the Year 2013.*

30. US Department of Labor, Bureau of Labor Statistics, "Volunteering in the United States, 2013," http:// www.bls.gov/news.release/pdf/volun.pdf.

31. Center on Philanthropy at Indiana University, *2012 Bank of America Study of High Net Worth Philanthropy.*

32. Mary Beth Westmoreland, "Five Ways Technology Will Shape the Nonprofit Sector in 2014," Black baud, https://www.blackbaud.com/files/resources/downloads/2014/01.14.NonprofitTechTrends.tipsheet.pdf.

33. H. Goodden, "An Enormous Inter-Generational Transfer of Wealth Is Imminent: How Can Charities Benefit?" *Front and Centre* (Canadian Centre for Philanthropy) 1, no. 3 (1994): 1, 17–18.

34. Rita Kottasz, "How Should Charitable Organisations Motivate Young Professionals to Given Philanthropically?" *International Journal of Nonprofit and Voluntary Sector Marketing* 9, no. 1 (2004): 9–27.

35. Corporation for National and Community Service, Office of Research and Policy Development, *Volunteering in America 2010: National, State, and City Information,* Corporation for National and Community Service, June 2010, http://www.nationalservice.gov/sites/default/files/documents/10_0614_via_final_issue _brief.pdf.

36. Bureau of Labor Statistics, "Economic News Release: Volunteering in the United States, 2013," February 25, 2014, http://www.bls.gov/news.release/volun.nr0.htm.

37. Elena Marta, Chiara Guglielmetti, and Maura Pozzi, "Volunteerism During Young Adulthood: An Italian Investigation into Motivational Patterns," *Voluntas: International Journal of Voluntary and Nonprofit Organizations* 17 (2006): 221–232.

38. Lesley Hustinx and Lucas C.P.M. Meijs, "Re-Embedding Volunteering: In Search of a New Collective Ground," *Voluntary Sector Review* 2 (2011): 5–21; Richard A. Sundeen, Cristina Garcia, and Sally A. Raskoff, "Ethnicity, Acculturation, and Volunteering to Organizations: A Comparison of Africans, Asians, Hispanics, and Whites," *Nonprofit and Voluntary Sector Quarterly* 38 (2009): 929–955.

39. Holona LeAnne Ochs, "Philanthropic Social Ventures: A Framework and Profile of the Emerging Field," *Journal of Public Management and Social Policy* 18, no. 1 (Spring 2012): 3–26.

40. Ibid., 9.

41. Marina Saitgalina and Lisa A. Dicke, "The Role of Professional Associations in Strengthening Civil Society Through Membership Engagement," Paper presented at the annual conference of the Association for Research on Nonprofit and Voluntary Associations, Hartford, CT, November 2013.

42. See Part II, "The Nonprofit Sector's Historical Evolution, Distinctive Values, and Contributions to Society," in Ott and Dicke, *The Nature of the Nonprofit Sector,* 3rd ed.

43. Ruth McCambridge, "Naomi Levine: Insights from a Master of Fundraising," *Nonprofit Quarterly* 70 (Summer 2013).

44. Lucy Townsend, "How Much Has the Ice Bucket Challenge Achieved?" *BBC News Magazine,* September 1, 2014, http://www.bbc.com/news/magazine-29013707.

## CHAPTER 13

# Philanthropic Social Ventures:
# A Framework and Profile of the Emerging Field

## Holona LeAnne Ochs

Recent attention has turned to how to best conceptualize and implement philanthropy in the public interest. Defining who deserves assistance, what kind, and how much is influenced by the charitable. The capacity to differentiate a public and direct the corresponding interest has tremendous potential to affect the opportunities available and shape the access to those opportunities. Moreover, the devolved, contractual nature of the provision of public goods within the current governance context results in increasingly blurry boundaries between the public, private, and nonprofit sectors in social service delivery systems. As a result, the intentions, functions, and enactment of social objectives are expressed in a complex, competitive, and highly variable display of civic engagement. Some describe the shift in public interest orientation in pluralist terms, suggesting a socialization of the private sector; while others are concerned that the shift is essentially a colonization of the public and nonprofit sectors by the private sector that may enhance wealth inequalities.

Where traditional philanthropy has served those who tend to be undervalued, modern philanthropy insists upon assigning economic value to social ends or reconstructing economic value as a means to a social end rather than an end in itself. Modern philanthropy is infused with the notion that promoting social wealth yields self-sustaining benefits through innovative practices that create value and maintain their worth. The consequence of which may enhance investments among the underserved but also has the potential to further marginalize the interests of those who continue to be undervalued in the market context.

In many ways, philanthropic innovation is a developing arena in which the public interest is increasingly contested and entrepreneurial processes are transforming the field. Venture philanthropy refers to the financing of innovative social investments; whereas social entrepreneurship encompasses "the activities and processes undertaken to discover, define, and exploit opportunities in order to enhance social wealth by creating new ventures or managing existing organizations in an innovative manner" (Zahra et al. 2009, 522). Venture philanthropy is a form of social entrepreneurship in itself, and alternatively, social entrepreneurs

Originally published as "Philanthropic Social Ventures: A Framework and Profile of the Emerging Field" by Holona LeAnne Ochs, *Journal of Public Management and Social Policy* 18, no. 1 (Spring 2012). Reprinted with permission.

may be funded by foundations using the venture philanthropy model. The evolution of these innovative social investments and the social entrepreneurs implementing them characterize the worth and consequence of the social wealth created by these endeavors. . . .

## Development of the Practice of Philanthropy in the United States

### *Traditional Philanthropy*

Charitable institutions in the United States emerged in a context in which there was initially a considerable degree of hostility toward private philanthropy. Yet, the progressive realignment of the party system early in the 20th century paved the way for the establishment of the first modern grant making institutions (Hall 2006). The various foundations established by Carnegie and Rockefeller did demonstrate to the American public that wealth may be more than simply predatory and self-serving, but the resistance of political officials during that period suggests concerns regarding the influence of foundations persisted (Hall 2006). And, the threat of the potential for political, economic, and social reform originating outside the democratic process was to some extent perceived as a threat to the legitimacy of government. Shifts in influence and sector boundaries between the public, private, and nonprofit sector continue to be a source of tension over the legitimacy of collective, private, and voluntary action in matters described as the "public interest" in the United States.

Historically, traditional philanthropy was conceived of as serving the following functions in ways that were thought to be consistent with the public interest as it was defined at the time (Prewitt 2006): (1) a redistributive function; (2) a more cost-effective distribution of public goods than the public sector could (or would not) provide and that the private sector had no incentive to provide; (3) a liberal function

in which public goods provision through foundations was seen as imposing the least cost on economic liberty; and/or (4) a pluralist function that afforded the opportunity for the expression of benevolence with the potential to inspire social change. These boundaries began to blur with the first reference associating venture capital and philanthropy by F. Emerson Andrews, who described foundations as the "venture capital of philanthropy" (Andrews 1950). It was again political reform and wealth accumulation that eventually led to a shift in influence and the convergence of practices in philanthropy that are now described as venture philanthropy.

### *"New" Philanthropy*

Broadly speaking, two factors help explain the rise of social entrepreneurship and venture philanthropy: the challenges of the welfare state in the modern global context and increased competition within the nonprofit sector (Perrini and Vurro 2006; Robinson 2006). Nonprofits face the pressures of lower financial reserves, increased competition, and increased pressure to perform. Financial support fell as policy was privatized and decentralized in the welfare state (Perrini and Vurro 2006), resulting in reduced government financial support for nonprofits (Wei-Skillern et al. 2007). Lower marginal tax rates in the Bush era also reduced tax savings and the incentive to give to charities, philanthropies, and other nonprofits; the recent recession also contributes to this trend. At the same time, nonprofits face increased public scrutiny and pressure (Boschee 2006). Greater demands for professionalized services and an increasing emphasis on accountability along with escalating competitive pressure among nonprofits for diminishing sources of funding, particularly where there are service redundancies, place tremendous pressure on the nonprofit sector (Alter 2006). Nonprofit organizations are expected to strengthen their evaluation methods, enhance performance, and broaden strategic alliances with increasingly lower levels of financial support. The broad societal trend toward consumerism and moral individualism in conjunction with the rapidly changing market forces of the new global economy dominated by neoliberal managerial ideals have produced a social economy in which welfare demands are not met by the state but may be met by social entrepreneurs (see Mayo and Moore 2001). Yet, meeting these social expectations relies on exploiting opportunities to create social wealth through mutually beneficial exchange in contexts that have been traditionally undervalued.

Venture philanthropy differs from traditional philanthropy in the following ways:

1. The foundation, philanthropreneur(s), partners, investors, and/or consultants are "highly engaged" with the organizations that they support (Pepin 2005; Raymond 2004) in a relationship conceived of as long-term (Frumkin 2003), usually lasting between 4–7 years, beginning with a one-year planning stage (Wei-Skillern et al. 2007).
2. The outcomes and effectiveness are defined by the foundation's business metric and are often referred to as impact (Frumkin 2003; Nicholls 2006).
3. The focus is on strategic management for the sustainability of the organization (Frumkin 2003), dominated by aggressive revenue generation strategies (Bornstein and Davis 2010).
4. Philanthropic social ventures operate within business models that define an "exit strategy" at the outset (Walker 2004).
5. Venture philanthropy tends to involve a wider range of investments and engage in risk management rather than mitigating risk (Osberg 2006).

It is a relationship presumed to be built on mutually beneficial partnerships as well as one recognizing that social investments are maintained through relationships in which all parties are committed to and accountable for turning problems into opportunities. Venture philanthropy is an approach to philanthropy that borrows heavily from private sector concepts, based on the assumption that development models, efficiency, microfinance techniques, and professionalism are optimal in the private sector and that applying these concepts to traditional philanthropic approaches may enhance the social impact (Raymond 2004). Venture philanthropy attempts to improve the strength and sustainability of nonprofit organizations by facilitating sector collaboration through diversified investments, conferences and networking opportunities, fellowships, technology, and advocacy. . . .

Measuring performance is a critical component of venture philanthropy. Many qualitative performance measures are available for social ventures, such as Triple Bottom Line accounting and the Balanced Score Card. . . . Venture philanthropy often utilizes benchmarking to enhance mission-driven performance by comparing the social enterprise to the best in the chosen social arena (Raymond 2004). . . .

Many venture philanthropists pick out social enterprises based on performance, not need (Walker 2004). Unlike traditional philanthropies in which applications are open or invited, venture philanthropies take a proactive approach and seek out partners (Osberg 2006). The nonprofits that demonstrate a willingness to engage in the venture philanthropy model and have high potential for social impact are the most likely candidates for philanthropic investments. . . .

Critics argue that the venture philanthropy model is structurally inappropriate (Shakely 2003), over-extended (Kramer 1999), does not apply after the dot-com boom (Sievers 1997), or that it tries to impose an economic model on an ethical or moral discipline (DiMaggio 1997). Sievers (2001) raises concerns about the potential for venture philanthropy to redefine the frame of reference of civil society in ways that may not benefit society, resulting from a narrow emphasis on performance indicators, the trade-offs inherent in scalability that contribute to the conceptualization of the community and its corresponding responsibilities, the potential for inordinate influence by highly engaged investors, and the fact that commercializing nonprofit organizations is likely to distort the mission. Venture philanthropists themselves contend that there are several factors a foundation should consider when evaluating whether venture philanthropy is suitable. The following have been outlined in several reports and speeches provided by the Chair of Venture Philanthropy Partners, Mario Morino:

1. The mission of the organization needs to be conducive to leveraging financial resources to foster innovation without compromising the organizational principles.
2. The intellectual resources of the staff and board must be sufficiently diverse, given the financial, technical, experiential, and methodological demands of the issue at hand.
3. The funding capacity needs to be large enough to generate innovation on a scale that is proportionate to the mission over the long-term. . . .

. . . The various claims and concerns about venture philanthropy are based on assumptions about the character of the market rather than direct evidence. Understanding the extent to which venture philanthropy might improve performance and the circumstances within which such performance enhancement might result in a greater social impact requires a framework for mapping the emerging philanthropic landscape (see Frumkin 2003; Moody 2008). . . .

## Theoretical Framework

. . . The following section outlines a typology of the organizations that might receive investments or support from venture philanthropists and illustrates the spectrum of organizational motives. This section also defines the various strategies utilized for leveraging impact in order to understand the different components of the venture philanthropy movement.

### The Hybrid Spectrum of Funding

The venture philanthropy movement diversifies the types of investments that philanthropists might make by expanding the types of organizations that are conceived of as contributing to the development of social wealth. Venture philanthropists may invest in the following types of entities: (1) traditional nonprofits; (2) nonprofits engaged in income generating activities; (3) social enterprises; (4) socially responsible businesses; (5) corporate social responsibility; and/or (6) traditional private entities. Social entrepreneurship refers to the hybrid spectrum of organizations that attempt to balance civic motives and market logic. Because philanthropic social ventures may also involve cross-sector collaborations, public-private partnerships, and/or contracts for social service delivery implemented by the public, private, and/or nonprofit sectors, some venture philanthropists further their objectives by engaging the full spectrum of governance partnerships. These relationships are illustrated in Figure 13.1.

The hybrid spectrum includes nonprofits engaged in income generating activities. Those activities include, but are not necessarily limited to, the following:

- cost recovery mechanisms such as special events, conferences, seminars, and fee-for-service; and/or
- earned income revenue streams such as membership dues, sales of publications and products, and consulting programs.

*Social enterprise, social entrepreneurship,* and *social entrepreneurs* are often used to refer to a

FIGURE 13.1.  Hybrid Spectrum of Governance Partnerships

| HYBRID SPECTRUM | | | | | |
|---|---|---|---|---|---|
| CIVIC LOGIC | | | | | |
| | | | | MARKET LOGIC | |
| Traditional Nonprofit | Nonprofit Engaged in Income Generating Activities | Social Enterprise | Socially Responsible Business | Corporate Social Responsibility | Traditional Private Entity |
| GOVERNANCE PARTNERSHIPS | | | | | |

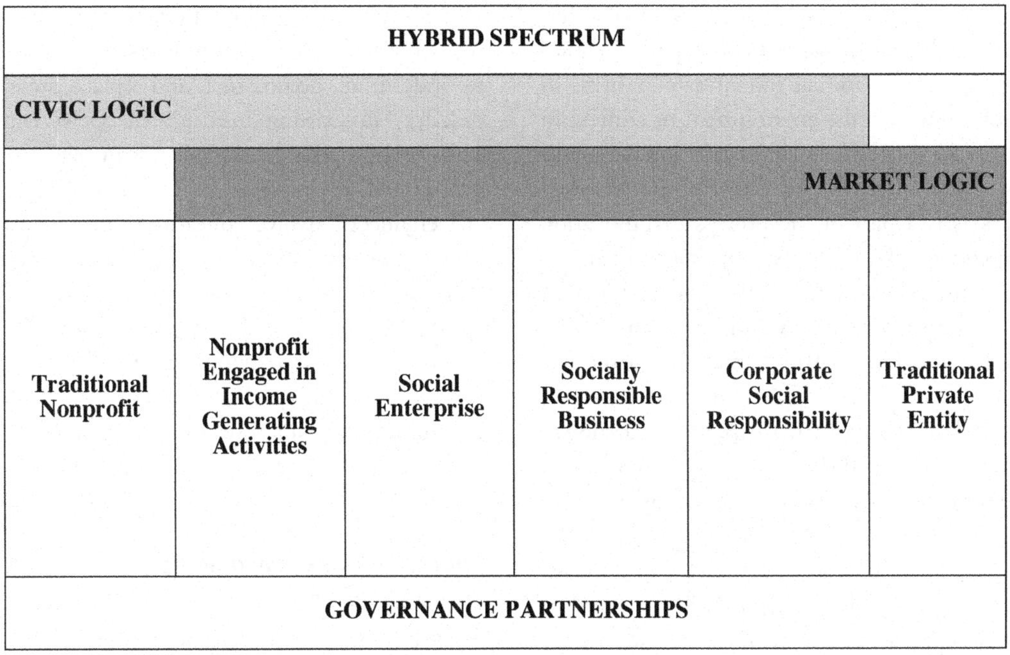

field of research despite the fact that the concepts are distinct and suggest different levels of analysis. In terms of the types of entities that might receive venture philanthropy investments, the social enterprise is the level of focus. The social enterprise is characterized by having a social purpose, an entrepreneurial approach, and an emphasis on stewardship (Fayolle and Matlay 2010). Social enterprises may be structured as departments or affiliates within an organization or as a separate legal entity—either nonprofit or for-profit. Social enterprise is distinct from the socially responsible business in that the latter operates with the dual purpose of generating shareholder profits while contributing to a social good. In the socially responsible business, every decision is anchored in the company's core values. This is distinct from corporate social responsibility in that for-profit businesses operating under the profit motive and also engaging in philanthropy make business decisions apart from the social values supported by their philanthropy.

### Strategies for Leveraging Impact

Zahra et al. (2009) outline a typology of social entrepreneurship, focusing on identifying different types of social entrepreneurs. They propose the following three categories: (1) the social bricoleur; (2) the social constructionist; and (3) the social engineer. Each of these types employs distinct strategic repertoires.

Bricolage is an idea developed by Levi-Straus (1967) that refers to the process of combining and transforming existing resources to innovate and add value. Baker and Nelson (2005) refine this concept by specifying the following conditions: (1) focus on the resources at hand; (2) utilization of existing resources for new purposes; and (3) recombining existing resources for the creation of new economic and social value. The processes, relationships, and interconnections among these networks are the focus of evaluation and the genesis of solution-focused intervention. Bricolage assumes that path creation is possible for rational individuals or firms in interaction with the environment or context in which the individual or firm operates. Generating novel solutions and targeting underserved markets is a part of the process of innovation sometimes referred to as intrapreneurship (see Mair and Martí 2006). Intrapreneurship patterns are theorized to occur in episodes that Corner and Ho (2010) characterize in the following manner: (1) opportunity development; (2) collective action; (3) experience corridors; and (4) spark. These innovative episodes are the critical components of entrepreneurship broadly.

Capitalizing on local markets with minimal or depleted resources that may be accessed at low cost by what is referred to as knowledge spillovers, economic regeneration, and proximity designs . . . describes how bricolage functions (see Fayolle and Matlay 2010). Knowledge spillover occurs when a non-rival mechanism for distributing facts, information, and/or skills that have not previously been accounted for are picked up, stimulating broader improvements (Arrow 1962). Economic regeneration is distinct from economic development in that economic regeneration refers to the reinvestment in industrial or business areas that have suffered decline (Stohr 1990), and proximity designs group related items to maximize gain (Lagendijk and Oinas 2005).

Social constructionists attempt to create social wealth by identifying the inadequacies in existing institutions or organizations and launching ventures to better address those social issues. Constructionists operate at the regional, national, or global level, and they design systemic solutions to address the perceived cause of a broader social problem. Constructionists may fund bricoleurs to build the infrastructure and/or code the operations for the systemic reform. The strategies that

characterize the social constructionist are knowledge transfer and scalable solutions.

Social engineers find fundamental and irreparable flaws in the existing system and seek to undermine, deconstruct, and replace present practices in existing institutions. Social engineers require political capital to legitimize their projects. The strategies that characterize social engineers involve education and advocacy in addition to influencing the policy process through lobbying, resistance/protest, and the media. While all social entrepreneurs are likely to engage in these activities to some degree, social engineers rely on them to build the political capital necessary for collective, collaborative, or voluntary action.

## Characteristics of Philanthropic Social Ventures

There are three distinct but not necessarily mutually exclusive models for engaging venture philanthropy: traditional foundations practicing high-engagement grant making; social value organizations funded by individuals and implemented by a professional staff; and the partnership model in which financial investors become highly engaged with the grantees. These philanthropic models reflect the structure and operations of the foundation as well as symbolize the role the philanthropists envision themselves playing in the generation of social wealth. . . .

Venture philanthropists funding traditional nonprofits are likely to do so with the expectation that the nonprofit begin engaging in more income generating activities as a means to sustainability. This trend is likely to select from the nonprofit sector those "high performing nonprofits" with market potential. . . . It does appear that philanthropic social ventures regularly utilize bricolage strategies. It is common for philanthropic social ventures utilizing constructionist strategies at the global level to also fund local bricoleurs, which is essential to implementing a scalable solution and potentially beneficial to local organizations. Engineering and promoting corporate social responsibility are uncommon strategies among philanthropic social ventures However, these strategies may be more common among other types of changemakers. It is also important to note that some philanthropic social ventures appear to position themselves as a hub for orchestrating change at multiple levels and/or coordinating action among like-minded individuals and organizations.

### Understanding the Legal Environment

With the rapid growth in the number and size of foundations and the greater publicity given to the nonprofit sector, there is increased interest and focus on foundation activities. . . .

The attention of government and the legal sector has resulted in changes along several dimensions as it relates to the practice of modern philanthropy. Supervisory legislation has appeared in many different states, and the IRS has started to police the exemption provisions of the tax laws that govern nonprofits (Fremont-Smith 1965). . . .

Government plays a large role in the realm of philanthropy as a major source of nonprofit revenue as well. Government grants, contracts, and reimbursement from public agencies account for about 36 percent of the sector's revenue (Raymond 2004). Government policy is pivotal in catalyzing new social ventures by defining the laws, regulations, and support given to social enterprises (Mulgan 2006). For example, organizations that solicit contributions nationwide can utilize the Unified Registration Statement, which allows such organizations in 34 states to file a single form in lieu of separate state registration statements.[1] Governments may utilize technology to minimize transaction costs for nonprofit accountability as well, such as the online charitable registration system available in Colorado, Hawaii, and New Mexico (among a handful of other states) or the e-Postcard required by the IRS. Legal environments

that reduce barriers to entry facilitate social entrepreneurship (Mulgan 2006, 82). . . .

Many foundations are now encouraged to perform a voluntary legal audit. This is a decision made by the board to systematically review all legal processes and documents to ensure the minimization of legal risks (Andringa and Engstrom 2002). Because of the changing legal and financial landscape surrounding philanthropy, foundations are being held to higher legal standards and accountability demands. Federal law, IRS regulations, state statutes, and court decisions in recent years have started to remove the traditional hands-off approach. At the same time, donors and employees have become more demanding and litigious (Andringa and Engstrom 2002). . . .

## Conclusion

Venture philanthropy developed within the broad conceptual umbrella of social entrepreneurship due to increasing competition for limited philanthropic dollars, entrepreneurial development, and public demands for greater accountability and efficiency within philanthropic foundations. As the legal environment surrounding philanthropy starts to change, venture philanthropy is in a position to influence this level of change. Venture philanthropy groups differ in number, motivations, characteristics, and pace of evolution by region. Venture philanthropy rapidly evolved and enjoys the most supportive environment within urban areas and California. However, as the venture philanthropy model continues to spread throughout the United States, these regional distinctions are likely to become less pronounced. . . .

## Note

1. This streamlined system developed from a collaborative effort on the part of the charitable

community and the National Association of State Charity Officials (NASCO) and can be downloaded at www.nonprofits.org/library/gov/urs/.

# References

Alter, Sutia Kim. 2006. "Social Enterprise Models and Their Mission and Money Relationships." In *Social Entrepreneurship: New Paradigms of Sustainable Social Change,* edited by Alex Nicholls. New York: Oxford University Press.

Andrews, F. Emerson. 1950. *Philanthropic Giving.* New York: Russell Sage Foundation.

Andringa, Robert C., and Ted W. Engstrom. 2002. *Nonprofit Board Answer Book.* Washington, DC: Board Source.

Arrow, Kenneth. 1962. "Economic Welfare and the Allocation of Resources for Invention." In *The Rate and Direction of Inventive Activity: Economic and Social Factors.* Universities-National Bureau (ed.), UMI (0-87014-304-2), 609–626.

Baker, T., and R. Nelson. 2005. "Creating Something from Nothing: Resource Construction Through Entrepreneurial Bricolage." *Administrative Science Quarterly* 50: 329–366.

Bornstein, David, and Susan Davis. 2010. *Social Entrepreneurship: What Everyone Needs to Know.* Oxford: Oxford University Press.

Boschee, Jerr. 2006. "Social Entrepreneurship: The Promise and the Perils." In *Social Entrepreneurship: New Paradigms of Sustainable Social Change,* edited by Alex Nicholls, 356–390. New York: Oxford University Press.

Corner, Patricia Doyle, and Marcus Ho. 2010. "How Opportunities Develop in Social Entrepreneurship." *Entrepreneurship Theory and Practice* 34: 635–659.

DiMaggio, P. 1997. "Culture and Cognition." *Annual Review of Sociology* 23: 263–287.

Fayolle, Alain, and Harry Matlay. 2010. *Handbook of Research on Social Entrepreneurship.* Northampton, MA: Elgar Publishing.

Fremont-Smith, Marion R. 1965. *Foundations and Government.* Hartford, CT: Connecticut Printers, Inc.

Frumkin, Peter. 2003. "Inside Venture Philanthropy." *Society* (May–June): 7–15.

Hall, Peter Dobkin. 2006. "A Historical Overview of Philanthropy, Voluntary Associations, and Nonprofit Organizations in the United States, 1600–2000." In *The Nonprofit Sector,* edited by Walter W. Powell and Richard Steinberg. New Haven, CT: Yale University Press.

Kramer, Mark R. 1999. "Venture Capital and Philanthropy: A Bad Fit." *The Chronicle of Philanthropy* (April 22): 72–73.

Lagendijk, Arnoud, and Paivi Oinas. 2005. *Proximity, Distance, and Diversity: Issues on Economic Interaction and Local Development.* New York: Ashgate.

Mair, J., and I. Martí. 2006. "Social Entrepreneurship Research: A Source of Explanation, Prediction, and Delight." *Journal of World Business* 41, no. 1, 36.

Mayo, E., and H. Moore. 2001. *The Mutual State.* London: New Economics Foundation.

Moody, Michael. 2008. "Building a Culture: The Construction and Evolution of Venture Philanthropy as a New Organizational Field." *Nonprofit and Voluntary Sector Quarterly* 37, no. 2, 324–352.

Mulgan, Geoff. 2006. "Cultivating the Other Invisible Hand of Social Entrepreneurship: Comparative Advantage, Public Policy, and Future Research Priorities." In *Social Entrepreneurship: New Paradigms of Sustainable Social Change,* edited by Alex Nicholls, 74–98. New York: Oxford University Press.

Nicholls, Alex. 2006. "Introduction." In *Social Entrepreneurship: New Paradigms of Sustainable Social Change,* edited by Alex Nicholls, 1–38. New York: Oxford University Press.

Osberg, Sally. 2006. "Wayfinding Without a Compass: Philanthropy's Changing Landscape and Its Implications for Social Entrepreneurs." In *Social Entrepreneurship: New Paradigms of Sustainable Social Change,* edited by Alex Nicholls, 309–328. New York: Oxford University Press.

Pepin, John. 2005. "Venture Capitalists and Entrepreneurs Become Venture Philanthropists." *International Journal of Nonprofit and Voluntary Sector Marketing* 10, no. 3, 165–173.

Perrini, Francesco, and Clodia Vurro. 2006. *The New Social Entrepreneurship: What Awaits Social Entrepreneurship Ventures,* edited by Francesco Perrini. Northampton, MA: Edward Elgar.

Raymond, Susan U. 2004. *The Future of Philanthropy: Economics, Ethics, and Management.* Hoboken, NJ: John Wiley & Sons, Inc.

Robinson, Jeffrey. 2006. "Navigating Social and Institutional Barriers to Markets: How Social Entrepreneurs Identify and Evaluate Opportunities." In *Social Entrepreneurship,* edited by Johanna Mair, Jeffrey Robinson, and Kai Hockerts, 95–120. New York: Palgrave Macmillan.

Shakely, J. 2003. "The Meta-Foundation: Venture Philanthropy Starts the Next Leg of Its Journey, with a Surprising New Pilot." In *From Grantmaker to Leader: Emerging Strategies for Twenty-First Century Foundations,* edited by F. L. Ellsworth and J. Lumarda, 119–138. New York: John Wiley.

Sievers, Bruce. 1997. "If Pigs Had Wings." *Foundation News and Commentary* (November–December): 44–46.

Stohr, Walter B. 1990. *Global Challenge and Local Response: Initiatives for Economic Regeneration in Contemporary Europe.* London: Mansell.

Walker, Lewis J. 2004. "The Growth of Venture Philanthropy." *On Wall Street* 14, no. 11, 107–108.

Wei-Skillern, Jane, James Austin, Herman Leonard, and Howard Stevenson. 2007. *Entrepreneurship in the Social Sector.* Los Angeles: Sage Publications.

Zahra, S., E. Gedajlovic, D. Neubaum, and J. Shulman. 2009. "A Typology of Social Entrepreneurs: Motives, Search Processes, and Ethical Challenges." *Journal of Business Venturing* 24, no. 5, 519–534.

## CHAPTER 14

# Leaving Microsoft to Change the World: An Entrepreneur's Odyssey to Educate the World's Children

JOHN WOOD

## "Perhaps, Sir, You Will Someday Come Back with Books"

. . . On a normal day I would be ordering another coffee at sundown, preparing for the three or four hours left in my workday as a marketing director at Microsoft. Today was blissfully different—the first of 21 days of trekking in the Himalayas and a break from the treadmill of life in the software industry during the breakneck 1990s. Ahead lay three weeks without e-mail, phone calls, meetings, or a commute. Three weeks where the biggest challenge was walking 200 miles over "donkey trails" with all my gear on my back. On day ten, the trek would reach a Himalayan pass at 18,000 feet. This would be the highest I had ever climbed to in life. The challenging mountain pass and the long break would be a fitting reward for years of nonstop work. . . .

Pasupathi appeared to be in his mid-50s, with thick glasses, weather-beaten dark pants,

a Windbreaker, and a traditional Nepalese *topi* cloth cap. The sun and wind had carved fine lines of wisdom into his face over the years. The Nepalis, I quickly learned, are a friendly and welcoming people, and I struck up conversations with almost everyone.

Pasupathi was eager to tell me about Nepal, so I asked him what he did for a living. "District resource person for Lamjung Province," he explained. He was responsible for finding resources for the 17 schools in this rural province. I noticed his worn-out tennis shoes. In Nepal, that meant that most of the schools were off the main road and far out on the dirt paths I had spent the last seven hours trekking.

I told Pasupathi that I had always loved school as a child and asked whether Nepalese children were eager learners.

"Here in the rural areas we have many smart children," he replied with a rapid-fire assessment. "They are very eager to learn. But we do not have enough schools. We do not have sufficient school supplies. Everyone is poor so we cannot make much investment in education. In this village, we have a primary school, but no secondary school. So after grade five, no more schooling takes place unless the children can walk two hours to the nearest school that teaches grades six and above. But because the people are poor, and they need their children to help with farming, so many of the students stop education too early."

As Pasupathi poured himself tea, he told me more.

"Some days I am very sad for my country. I want the children to get a good education, but I am failing them."

Eager to learn more, I peppered him with questions. I found it hard to imagine a world in which something as random as where you were born could result in lifelong illiteracy. Had I taken my own education for granted?

Pasupathi told me that Nepal's illiteracy rate, at 70 percent, was among the world's highest. This was not the result of apathy on the part of the people, he insisted. They believed in education. The communities and the government were simply too poor to afford enough schools, teachers, and books for their rapidly growing population. His job could be frustrating. Every day he heard about villages that lacked schools, or schools where three children were sharing a textbook. "I am the education resource person, yet I have hardly any resources."

He had many dreams. For example, he wanted to help one village move up from a one-room building in which grades one to five were taught in shifts because the school was crammed into a small space. His enthusiastic voice dropped as he next described the reality of having no budget. All he could do was listen to the requests and hope that one day he could say yes.

Our conversation drew me into his world and incited my curiosity. Here was a potential opportunity to learn about the real Nepal, rather than the trekker's version of the country. I asked where he was headed next. I lucked

out. He was leaving in the morning to visit a school in the village of Bahundanda, which was along the trekking route. It was a three-hour walk up steep hills. I asked if I might join him. He agreed. "I would be proud to show you our school. Please meet me here again at seven for tea."

. . .

I didn't expect to be in the middle of the Himalayas at this point of my life. My notions of a serious adulthood didn't include backpacks and hiking boots. But I was doing more than recapturing my lost adolescence when I went to Nepal.

One factor was exhaustion. I had been working at Microsoft for only seven years, but it felt as if decades had passed. I joined the company shortly after graduate school. The period from 1991 through 1998 was one of tumultuous and exciting growth for the technology industry, and for Microsoft. But the only way to keep up was to work crazy hours. My job had an additional complication. I was a specialist in international markets, and as a result I was always trying to be in seven places at once. It was like a game of Twister played on a global scale. *Be in Johannesburg on Friday and Taiwan on Monday, ready to do presentations, take meetings, and do press interviews.*

The job was financially rewarding but full of high pressure and stress.

It seemed as if my mantra was "You can sleep when you are dead and buried."

Seven years in, though, that nagging question continually popped tip: Is this all there is—longer hours and bigger payoffs? I had adopted the commando lifestyle of a corporate warrior. Vacation was for people who were soft. Real players worked weekends, racked up hundreds of thousands of air miles, and built mini-empires within the expanding global colossus called Microsoft. Complainers simply did not care about the company's future.

I was, however, increasingly aware of the price I was paying. Relationships—starved of my time and attention—fell flat as a result. Family members grumbled when I canceled yet another Christmas reunion. I was a regular last-minute dropout for friends' weddings. Whenever friends proposed an adventure trip, I would usually have an immovable meeting standing in my way. The company could rely on me, but friends and family could not.

I remember a late-night return to my Sydney flat after a ten-day business trip to Thailand and Singapore. "The answering machine must be broken," I thought. "The light is not blinking." I pushed the button anyway. "Beep. You . . . have . . . no . . . new . . . messages," the mechanical voice announced. It might as well have added the word "loser" at the end.

With the software industry doubling every year, and Microsoft fighting to capture market share in every major category, the stakes seemed high enough to justify self-sacrifice. The corporate culture reinforced this mania. It wasn't until I finished a set of meetings with Steve Ballmer, Microsoft's hard-charging, demanding, and voluble second-in-command, that I convinced myself that I had earned a break. Ballmer was in Sydney reviewing our work in Asia. When we finished his business-review meetings, a two-day-long event where Ballmer tended to shout and harangue, a colleague—Ben—suggested we unwind by going to a slide show about trekking in Nepal given by a local adventure travel company.

Seeing those unbelievable mountain ranges squared it away. I was long overdue for a holiday. When the presenter mentioned that the Annapurna Circuit was a "classic trek that takes three weeks, covers two hundred miles, and gets you as far out in the Himalayas as you could imagine," I mentally began booking the time off. Next stop, Nepal. Over a Mongolian hot-pot dinner with Ben, I joked that *maybe* if you went high enough into the Himalayas, you could not hear Steve Ballmer screaming at you.

. . .

Pasupathi introduced the headmaster, who offered a tour. The first-grade classroom spilled over with students. There were 70 in a room that looked as though its capacity was half that. . . . We visited eight classrooms; all were equally packed. As we entered every student stood, without prompting, and yelled, "Good morning, sir," in perfect English. The headmaster next took us to the school library. . . .

I phrased my question in the most polite way possible:

"This is a beautiful library room. Thank you for showing it to me. I have only one question. Where, exactly, are your books?"

The headmaster stepped out of the room and began yelling. A teacher appeared with the one key to the rusty padlock on the cabinet where the books were locked up.

The headmaster explained. Books were considered precious. The school had so few that the teachers did not want to risk the children damaging them. I wondered how a book could impart knowledge if it was locked up, but kept that thought to myself. My heart sank as the school's treasure trove was revealed. A Danielle Steel romance with a couple locked in passionate and semi-clothed embrace on the front cover. A thick Umberto Eco novel written in Italian. The *Lonely Planet Guide to Mongolia*. And what children's library would be complete without *Finnegans Wake?* The books appeared to be backpacker castoffs that would be inaccessible (both physically and intellectually) to the young students.

I asked about the school's enrollment and learned there were 450 students. Four hundred and fifty kids without books. How could this be happening in a world with such an abundance of material goods?

Without prompting, the headmaster then said:

"Yes, I can see that you also realize that this is a very big problem. We wish to inculcate in our students the habit of reading. But that is impossible when this is all we have."

I thought that any educator who used the word *inculcate* in a sentence deserved to have better teaching materials. I wanted to help, but would it be considered condescending if I offered? The headmaster saved me the trouble of thinking this through. His next sentence would forever change the course of my life:

"Perhaps, sir, you will someday come back with books."

. . .

## The Start-Up Years: An Object in Motion Remains in Motion

In December of 1999, I received notice that the IRS had approved charity status for my new organization. Its official name was Books for Nepal.[1]

My immediate thought was "Now what?" I was a corporate refugee who had never worked for a charity in an official capacity. I had always viewed my education projects as a hobby, not a vocation. Although I was eager to get started, I had no idea how to start.

I was so green I sometimes embarrassed myself. An old college friend, Jim, was an experienced philanthropist who sat on the board of his family's foundation. The prior year I had told him of my plans to leave Microsoft and spend more time on my education projects in Nepal. He asked when I would have 501(c)(3) status.

He rolled his eyes as I asked what this meant. He explained that this was the designation my fledgling organization would need for donations to be tax-deductible. I explained that I'd rather keep things simple, avoid bureaucracy, and leave the IRS out of this. Another roll of the eyes, and another lecture. He explained that nobody would donate in a significant way if I could not prove that we were a real organization.

Next, he offered an incentive. Once we had this mysterious 501(c)(3) status, he and his wife, Jen, would write a $10,000 check.

That worked. I called an attorney, who had been recommended by a friend. Christopher

Beck answered on the first ring. "I'm a lawyer, but also a frustrated international relations major who never got to use his degree. You can count on my help. I heard you were in Seattle this week, so how about if we meet at the Starbucks in Belltown? They have comfy chairs, which is good as I'll need several hours of your time."

I hoped we could fast-track the IRS process, and figured that massive amounts of caffeine might be a good place to start. My fledgling organization desperately needed the money.

Dinesh had suggested that we hire a few young Nepalese guys to work full-time on our projects. Our first schools were under construction. More books were coming in from individual donors, and a large publisher had pledged a donation of 25,000 books. Over 100 schools had requested to participate in our library program. Dinesh was willing to hire and manage the new employees, while himself remaining an unpaid consultant.

He said that we could hire local college graduates for about $200 per month. Jim and Jen's money would be more than enough to allow us to build a team in Nepal. It was a tentative start to what would eventually become a perpetual whirlwind of hiring. But even these small steps meant we were becoming a real organization.

Not every potential donor was as friendly, encouraging, and generous as Jim and Jen. I was frequently turned down during the first few years of Books for Nepal's life. This bothered me only slightly. Anyone in a sales career knows that if you're not getting rejected, you're not casting your net widely enough. What did get to me was the condescending manner of some of the people I met during the early years. Had I been less confident, some of these individuals would have dealt crushing blows to my enthusiasm.

One of the first meetings I sought was with the San Francisco–based American Himalayan Foundation (AHF). The American version of

Sir Edmund Hillary's Himalayan Trust, the organization had sponsored numerous projects in Nepal over the previous 25 years, ranging from bridges to hospitals to schools. I had visited some of their schools during my third trip to Nepal and was impressed with their work. I was therefore thrilled when one of their senior directors agreed to a meeting at their well-appointed San Francisco office.

My excitement, alas, was premature. The executive, in her mid-40s and elegantly dressed, was friendly enough upon greeting me. But warning signs soon began flaring. Twice on the way to her office she stopped for conversations with colleagues that lasted for several minutes. She did not bother to introduce me. I assumed she was having a busy day. The skies darkened further when we got to her office. Within two minutes of explaining my goals, I was cut off.

"I am not sure why we should be talking to you. There are hundreds of little groups doing what you do."

"I agree. There are many organizations working in Nepal, and that's a good thing, because the country needs a lot of help. One thing that makes Books for Nepal different is that we have plans to take this project to a pretty massive scale. If I learned one thing at Microsoft, it's to think big. Most charities build one or two schools. I want to build hundreds. There are a lot of charities that have set up a few libraries, but nobody has emulated Andrew Carnegie by setting up several thousand of them in the developing world."

"And what makes you think you have what it takes to do so?" "Good question. To start, I'm ambitious and have a ton of energy. I'm not afraid of hard work. There is a huge network of people I know from my technology days who can all be pitched to donate to the cause. Finally, I am not the least bit shy about asking people for money or favors. For example, I just received word from Carol Sakoian, vice president of international business development of Scholastic, that they are donating twenty-five thousand children's books to our program. She said that this is just the beginning of their support, and that she will introduce me to other publishers."

The executive looked at me with the same indifference with which a cow on the side of the interstate views a passing car. She checked her watch, even though we were only ten minutes into our meeting. Undaunted, I forged on.

"I would think that the news on Scholastic would be of interest. I know that AHF has built forty schools in the Everest region. I have visited a few of them and was impressed. But one thing I noticed was that they have the same problem that most every school in Nepal has—an empty library. So I got to thinking—what if we put some of these new books to good use? My organization could help your schools by setting up forty new school libraries. That, to answer your earlier question, is one of the main reasons I wanted to meet with you."

She made another not-so-surreptitious time check. "I don't know. You'd have to talk to my people about that. Those are all details that I don't follow."

"Great," I naively replied. "With whom should I talk? Are they here in the office today?"

"I'll have to put somebody in touch with you. But for now I really need to get to lunch."

Now it was my turn to check my watch. I forced myself to refrain from making a sly comment that it must be nice to be part of an organization that took lunch at 11:15.

In the nearby neighborhood of North Beach, I licked my wounds at a coffee shop. I hoped that a steaming latte would compensate for the frosty reception in the meeting. The cafe had wireless Internet access, so I pulled out my laptop to write a thank-you e-mail. I felt that I had been treated rudely. But I was a novice. I needed every favor I could get.

I reminded the AHF executive that she'd promised to put me in touch with the officer in charge of the school program in Nepal. I sharply rapped the keyboard as I hit Send. It was obvious that she would not respond.* It was extremely frustrating. I hoped this was not how my new world worked. I was so used to the world of business, where we were constantly in motion and trying to "GSD"—Steve Ballmer's acronym and constant reminder to "get shit done." People leaped onto good ideas because, if they did not, their competitors might. The charity world, more immune from market pressures, apparently did not play by these rules.

I wondered whether this was emblematic of my new status in life. At Microsoft, I had grown used to having calls returned, a staff that would execute my plans, and all the resources I needed. I was now a fish out of water. I felt small and feckless. With no experience in the complex world of international nonprofits, I had a grand vision but few results and even fewer contacts. I felt demoralized and wondered if my transition had been a mistake.

As I gazed out the window at the sidewalk cafes beginning to fill up with their lunch crowds, a New Mail chime sounded on my laptop. Dinesh was working hard as usual. It was 2 a.m. his time. The subject line was irresistible: "Good News from Nepal."

"Dear John, attached are photos of two of our new schools under construction. As you can see, the parents are helping by clearing the land, digging the foundation, and helping to carry the bricks to the building site. The headmasters of the two schools have requested that you be here this fall for the official opening ceremonies. Can you come?"

My heart immediately went from nearly empty to overflowing with optimism. In Dinesh's mail lay a reminder that I could not let the naysayers get me down. The only way to move forward was to focus on the positive. I immediately forwarded photos of the projects to a few dozen friends, in the hope that they might know

someone willing to invest in our dream. Next, I dropped an e-mail to my travel agent to inquire about flights.

Several weeks later I learned about a potential "dream investor"—the Draper Richards Foundation. DRF was born out of a venture capital firm founded and run by legendary venture capitalists Bill Draper and Robin Richards Donohoe. Having hit several home runs with their fund, they had decided to plow some of their winnings into the "social entrepreneur" sector through endowed fellowships. The foundation had just been formed, and little was known about its goals. Two facts, however, stood out clearly—they were looking for organizations in their infancy, and to those they liked they made a three-year pledge of $100,000 per year. Best of all, the money was completely unrestricted—i.e., the chosen "fellow" could do whatever they wanted with it. Most foundation grants came with multiple strings attached, so unrestricted funding, especially a multiyear commitment, looked to me like manna from heaven.

A fellow Kellogg School of Management alumnus made the introduction to DRF's executive director. I was a bit gun-shy after my AHF experience, especially upon walking into DRF's 29th-floor offices with sweeping views of the Bay Bridge. It looked like another AHF-type organization with a five-star office and a zero-star personality.

Jenny, the executive director, immediately put me at ease. She was friendly and encouraging. Rather than immediately asking me questions, she started off by explaining their business philosophy:

"Our niche as a venture capital firm was finding great early-stage businesses. Kana. Hotmail. Tumbleweed," she said, reeling off a quick troika of multimillion-dollar investment wins. "Now we want to take some of that money and

*She never did.

do something similar for the betterment of the world. We are looking to fund early-stage charities. We want our portfolio to be full of young organizations that are going to scale up and change the world. Ideally it will be early enough in their life cycle that a relatively small amount of seed funding will have a huge effect as the organization grows. The key for us is to find people who are natural entrepreneurs."

*Portfolio. Scale. Seed funding. Entrepreneurs.* She was speaking the language of business. I wanted to hug her.

That feeling lasted for about a nanosecond. Next, she told me the bad news:

"I like what your organization does, but you are too far advanced for us. We only like to invest in early-stage ventures."

"But, but, but . . . we are early stage. We're still in our infancy, we're just getting started, we've only taken baby steps," I blurted out, searching desperately and pathetically for more euphemisms for *young*.

"I don't know. You already have a decent number of schools and libraries built. You are talking about expanding beyond Nepal. I think you might be too far along in your life cycle for us."

I put up my best defense—some would refer to it as "pleading."

"Two schools and twelve libraries are total tip-of-the-iceberg," I replied. "And, yes, I am talking about going into other countries, but at this point it's just talk. We can't do anything without the funds. Think of this as being like a great business idea, but one where the entrepreneur can't afford to hire employees yet."

She said nothing, so I continued.

"Look, can I be really honest with you? Every other foundation with which I have spoken has told us that we are too young, and that they only fund organizations that are further along. And now you are telling me that we are too old. Do you know how much this kills me? I feel like a cartoon character who has just gone off the cliff and is running in place in midair. I really

need this funding. We have dozens of communities asking for new schools and libraries, and I don't have the capital to say yes. The way you should look at us is that we are in year two of what will be a multiyear build-out. So we're still comparatively young."

Jenny gave nothing away. She'd let me know if we made it to their next stage of due diligence.

I walked out of their office with a feeling in my gut that was akin to being in love. I wanted so badly for it to work out and was fearful of how it might feel to be rejected.

Two weeks later, on a perfect sunny afternoon, I hung up from a phone call with Sarah Leary, an old friend from my Microsoft years. She had just agreed to endow a school in Nepal to honor her father. An hour's run along the beach would be my celebration. After that, a return to work for what was certain to be a late night. Just as I was grabbing my gym bag, the phone rang again.

"Hi, John. This is Rhonda from Bill Draper's office. Bill heard from Jenny about your work. He would like to come into your office and meet you tomorrow."

Excellent! I told her that I was totally flexible on timing.

"He and Jenny can show up around two. We should probably allocate three hours, as he wants to go through your business plan in detail."

"Yes, our business plan. Excellent. We'll look forward to reviewing it with him. In detail. Thanks."

When a legendary venture capitalist sets aside three hours to review the business plan, any entrepreneur would be nervous. Especially an entrepreneur who doesn't actually *have* a business plan. I mean, there were bits and pieces of a business plan in various locations—in my head, on random sectors of my hard drive, in e-mails that Dinesh had written on his hopes for massive program growth. We had some sketchy notes on our planned expansion into other Asian countries. But we were always in "do" mode and had never taken the time to actually pull everything together into one coherent document. Did I really just agree to meet, in less than 24 hours, with one of the world's foremost venture capitalists?

Realizing how much was on the line, and with the clock ticking, I raced home. I grabbed my sleeping bag, a pillow, and a change of clothes. Returning to the office, I brewed a large pot of coffee. Now was the time for heroes.

With the precision of a fine Swiss watch, Bill and Jenny walked into our cramped office in San Francisco's Presidio National Park at 2:01 p.m. I handed over two copies of a 35-page business plan still warm from the printer.

My first all-nighter since graduate school had been successful. I had slept on the floor from 2 a.m. until 6 a.m. As I listened to the lugubrious foghorn protecting the Golden Gate Bridge, I thought about how my faithful sleeping bag had been with me on that initial trip to Nepal and was now also here during the hard part of putting ethereal dreams into solid reality.

I resumed work at 6 a.m., fueled by the omnipresent fear of failure. I typed frantically, making a mental note to spell-check later. At 1:45 I dashed off to the local YMCA to shower, shave, and don fresh clothes. Screeching into the parking lot, I saw Bill and Jenny pull up in his red Mercedes convertible. I ducked into the office ahead of them. On the printer's output tray sat two thick copies of our business plan. I felt like Reggie Miller sinking a clutch three-pointer with a second on the shot clock.

A large bear of a man, William H. Draper III was perpetually tanned from his daily tennis game. He had large bushy eyebrows, silver hair, a friendly twinkle in his eye, and a fierce intellect. He had recently turned 70 but looked a decade younger. In a camel-hair blazer, crisp white shirt and red silk tie, and with patrician posture, he looked as though he had stepped right off page five of the Brooks Brothers catalogue.

I began by walking Jenny and Bill through our business plan in sequential order. Bill had already flipped ahead to page 17. He wanted to know all about my background, that of our employees, and more about our volunteer fundraisers. "I invest in people. Tell me first about your people, because if you have not gotten that right, then there is no hope for your organization. You mention that you are starting volunteer chapters that raise funds for you. Who are they? Name names."

"This model is built on the knowledge that not every person who wants to change the world is going to quit their job to do so. My goal is to allow anyone, be they an investment banker, a consultant, or a school teacher, to raise funds to help us to get more schools and libraries built. All of them can sneak in an hour during their work day or work at night or weekends to plan fundraising events or campaigns. For example, a group of volunteers here in San Francisco threw an event last fall that raised $35,000. That does not sound like a lot of money. But in Nepal it's enough to construct four schools. This model motivates the volunteers and also the people we invite to the events because they know exactly where their money goes. I have some old friends in Seattle who have offered to do an event next month. The beauty of the model is that we don't have to pay them a dime, so we can keep our fundraising costs low."

"That's excellent—good thinking. I like low overhead," Bill thundered. I breathed a sigh of relief. But it was a quick one, as Bill immediately veered back to page one, on which I had codified our mission statement after several hours of trying to distill my vision for changing the world down to just one sentence: "Our team works in partnership with local communities in the developing world under a coinvestment model to catalyze the creation of new educational infrastructure, including schools, libraries, computer labs, and long-term scholarships for girls."

Bill's stentorian voice boomed, "I like this. Coinvestment makes total sense. You know that I also used to run UNDP [the United Nations Development Program], right? I always thought that the only way these aid programs would work is if the local people were required to also donate labor and small amounts of money. Otherwise the project is just a free gift bestowed by outsiders, and nobody will value it because they have nothing at stake."

I seized on the pause, which I knew would be brief. "I agree. Do you know the quote by Michael Porter from Harvard Business School?" Bill and Jenny nodded no. "He points out that in the entire history of the travel industry, nobody has ever washed a rental car. If they don't feel ownership, they won't do any long-term maintenance. That's the way I feel about our projects."

The random walk through our business plan continued for a few more hours. Bill was voluble, enthusiastic, complimentary, and full of his own anecdotes about international development work. Obviously, the best approach was to give up control of the meeting. Bill would drive.

After several more questions and digressions, Bill said that he was impressed and that he'd look forward to working with us. He suggested that I start thinking about how I'd invest the money. At which point Jenny cut him off: "Bill, we still have a lot of due diligence ahead of us. This is not a done deal. We need to check their references, and I have some more questions that I'd like to ask, and Robin has still not met with them. That can take four to six weeks."

"Not for these guys it won't. They obviously have their act together. But, yes, you can check their references." Behind her back, he winked at me.

On the way out the door, he eyed my bright yellow North Face sleeping bag. Feeling the need to explain, I told him, "On some nights,

when we have important deliverables, this is my home." Bill laughed with the roar of a lion, slapped me on the back, and said, "That's what I like to hear. We want people who aren't afraid of hard work. Too much of the nonprofit sector has a nine-to-five mentality."

At that point, I knew with absolute certainty that the fellowship was mine. I immediately began to envision how much we could do with the increased capital, and how great it would be for our young organization to have this blue-chip stamp of approval.

. . .

## A Postcard from Nepal

Progress in Nepal was happening so quickly that most of my time and energy was consumed.

. . .

For three hours west out of Kathmandu, we were precariously perched on the sides of vertigo-inducing cliffs. We jockeyed for position with diesel-belching Indian buses and trucks bearing the ubiquitous HORN PLEASE signs. We obliged liberally as we weaved through the slower-moving traffic, as though we were a cross between a slalom skier and a honking goose.

Just after 11 a.m. our minibus pulled off the road and into a small courtyard at the school in Benighat. First dozens, then hundreds, of children ran toward us, excitedly yelling, "Namaste." Beyond the children stood a new whitewashed school building. Red ribbons stretched across each of the five classroom doorways. I felt immense pride in my team, and in our work. Each of these kids, and there now appeared to be several hundred of them crowding around us, would have the benefit of a better education. I had truly found my nirvana. All the work back in San Francisco chasing down donations was indeed worth the long nights and the begging.

. . .

Ceremonies in Nepal tend to be joyous. Incense is lit, red *tikka* powder is applied to portraits of the king and queen of Nepal to honor them, and many (sometimes too many) speeches are made. Local politicians orate, the headmaster then has something to say, teachers and parents are not shy about grabbing the stage, Room to Read team members are asked to speak, and the list goes on and on. Broiling in the sun, I reminded myself that the long list of speakers was a positive sign. Obviously, each community member was proud of the new school and felt some degree of ownership.

. . .

As my Nepali language abilities are abysmal, my mind had several opportunities to drift off. I thought about how much my life had changed. Two years ago I had been experiencing my crisis of confidence while working in China. I'd endured tortured introspection about whether there would be "life after Microsoft." And now here I sat in a rural village, as happy as I had even been. I did not have any of the trappings of my old Microsoft life and had not collected a paycheck in over a year. But I felt as though I had found my role in the universe. I looked out at the crowd, and several children smiled and waved at me as soon as we locked eyes. Their faces made every minute of my three-day journey to this remote village in the shadow of the Himalayas worth it.

## Note

1. The name would eventually be changed to Room to Read; John Wood, *Leaving Microsoft to Change the World* (New York: HarperCollins, 2006), 75.

# GROWING SUPPORT ONLINE ONE MEAL AT A TIME

*Alicia Schatteman, Benjamin S. Bingle, and C. Kenneth Meyer*

## Where to Begin?

Laura Schmidt sat in the lobby of the local university's research center, waiting for her appointment with the director of community-based research to begin. She was familiar with the center's services in data collection and analysis for municipal governments, public-sector agencies, and nonprofit organizations. As executive director of The Soup Bowl—a 501(c)(3) whose mission was "to empower the community by serving fresh food with compassion and respect in a restaurant-quality environment to anyone, regardless of situation, background, or ability to pay, while strengthening our community and nourishing hope"—she recognized the need for a formal evaluation of the organization's social media activity. She began mentally preparing for the meeting by reflecting on The Soup Bowl's short history and the important role social media had already played in it.

## Organizational History and Background

The Soup Bowl was founded in 2010 by a group of young adults who had recently returned to their hometown after college. Based in rural Illinois, the idea was prompted by drastic changes in the socioeconomic demographic of the founders' hometown. In response, they collectively decided to start a soup kitchen, but it would be no ordinary soup kitchen. The Soup Bowl was set up as a "community project"—a place where people who needed a nutritious hot meal could get one regardless of their ability to pay, and where community members who had plenty could donate their time, talent, and treasure for the good of others while sitting and sharing a meal with those who had less.

Since 2010, the organization had grown exponentially: it had moved from a donated church kitchen into its own 3,000-square-foot facility with a fully equipped dining room and kitchen, a donated clothing closet, and a community education room. The Soup Bowl had also grown in clientele from serving 300 people per month to 1,200.

In this part of the state, the demographic changes had only increased since The Soup Bowl was created. Racial and ethnic composition was shifting and the elderly population was growing. The number of single-parent households continued to increase, and the county had an overall 32 percent poverty rate. Furthermore, the county had higher-than-average obesity and diabetes rates.

Not surprisingly given the age of the founding members and the board members, a Facebook page for The Soup Bowl was immediately launched when it was formed. The founders, as part of the Millennial generation, were not afraid of risk and embraced all forms of technology, particularly social media, to attract supporters. They used social media and their website to generate excitement about the new organization and capture the attention of younger community members who might not normally have gotten involved with a "soup kitchen." The organization quickly gained a reputation as the "cool" place to volunteer and actually became a hangout spot for youth and young adults from the local high schools and university.

Despite their incredible success using social media to spread awareness and engage a younger audience, The Soup Bowl still had some tremendous challenges, particularly with resource sustainability.

## Back in the Lobby

"Ms. Schmidt," the receptionist said, "please come with me. Dr. Andrews is ready for you." Dr. Andrews had an extensive background in research and evaluation. He managed a large staff of research associates, and Laura felt quite confident in her ability to clarify The Soup Bowl's social media strategy for him.

As an original founder and the current executive director, Laura was well versed in all aspects of the organization. She also happened to be the person responsible for The Soup Bowl's incredible marketing materials, outreach strategy, and social media management. Admittedly, however, she was no expert in fundraising and resource development.

"We've been using social media since day one, but it hasn't translated into revenue," Laura told Dr. Andrews. "We're at the point where we need to increase our focus on bringing in resources."

"How can we help?" asked Dr. Andrews.

"Basically, we'd like you to determine how The Soup Bowl has used Facebook to draw resources into the organization," said Laura. "Have we been effective or not? What might we do differently? Although money is always important, please keep in mind that I would like to know about other resources as well, including volunteers and donations of food or other items."

Dr. Andrews had been jotting down notes throughout the conversation. As he finished writing, he looked up and said, "We've done this type of work before. Here's what I suggest. . . . "

## Evaluating Social Media

The research center used qualitative analysis software to analyze data from The Soup Bowl's Facebook page by seamlessly exporting the information from Facebook and importing it using a website browser extension. A total of 3,071 Facebook posts and 3,542 comments were captured since the page had been created in February 2010.

Of the 3,071 posts, the organization itself had posted 2,665 (87 percent). Of those posts, the word "soup" appeared in 865; the word "thank" appeared in 398; the word "help" appeared in 380; and the word "need" appeared in 338 (see Figure CS 11.1).

Through the analysis, it became clear that The Soup Bowl was doing pretty well at recruiting volunteers and attracting in-kind donations. The main challenge was attracting *financial* resources. The Soup Bowl did not receive any direct government support—a fact they were quite proud of—so all of its operations were sustained mainly by individual donors. The organization had received some corporate sponsorships but had not aggressively pursued foundation or other grant funding owing to limited staff.

FIGURE CS 11.1. Number of Times Keywords Were Used in The Soup Bowl's Facebook Posts

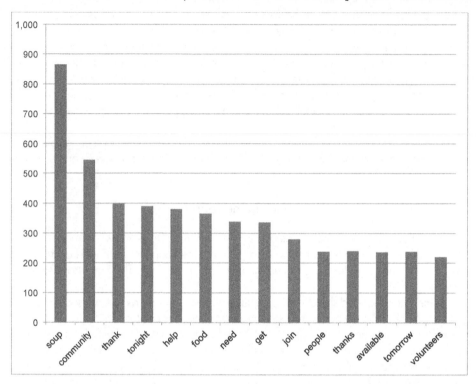

To determine if the Facebook page was specifically addressing resource acquisition, three "nodes" were created based on the three resources of money, volunteers, and donated items (e.g., food, clothing, and equipment). A text search query was conducted to identify instances when the word "donate" was used in Facebook correspondence. Each post was then assigned one of these three nodes:

1.  A post that fit the criteria for "money" asked specifically for a donation, linked to a third-party payment service like PayPal, or asked people to participate in an online poll or event with donating as the main target.
2.  A post that fit the criteria for "volunteer" asked specifically for volunteers or linked to a third-party volunteer sign-up site.
3.  A post that fit the criteria for "things" asked specifically for a resource that was not money or volunteers, or it linked to a third-party e-commerce site such as Amazon.

This analysis yielded somewhat surprising results. It turned out that The Soup Bowl was indeed focusing on money on Facebook. In fact, 18.5 percent of its total posts were categorized in the "money" node. Those in the "volunteer" node made up 17.3 percent of all posts, and posts in the "things" node represented less than 1 percent of total posts (see Figure CS 11.2).

## Next Steps

Laura reviewed the comprehensive report compiled by Dr. Andrews and his team of researchers. She was relieved to have the information on hand, but unsure about how to move forward. She wondered

FIGURE CS 11.2. The Percentage of "Money," "Volunteer," and "Things" Posts on The Soup Bowl's Facebook Page

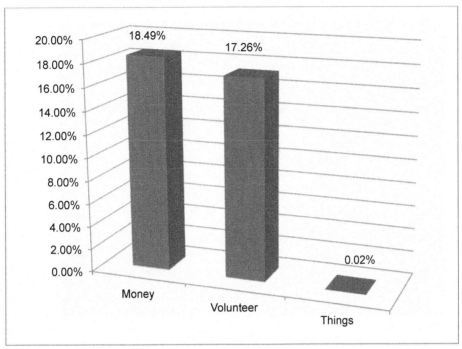

whether she should start focusing even more on money in social media posts or start focusing instead on other ways to raise money. What else could she do to help shore up The Soup Bowl's finances? Despite the wealth of information at her fingertips, Laura was left with more questions than answers after reading the social media evaluation.

## Questions and Instructions

1.  Do you think The Soup Bowl was using its Facebook page effectively to draw resources into the organization? Why or why not? Should it do more posts specifically about money or change its strategy altogether? Please explain your answers.
2.  Do you think that the shifting demographics of the community should influence The Soup Bowl's social media management and its broader outreach efforts? What are some innovative ways that The Soup Bowl could use social media to encourage philanthropy in their community? Please elaborate.
3.  The Soup Bowl staff and board were very proud of not receiving funding from governmental sources and believed that was one reason why people wanted to be involved with the organization. Do you think that The Soup Bowl should seek government funding knowing that it might damage its reputation and status as the cool, independent, youthful organization in town? Please elaborate. Similarly, given what you know about philanthropy and what is identified in your readings, how might the adoption of a business plan affect the image or management activities of The Soup Bowl?

# VOLUNTEER AND DONOR RECRUITMENT ON SOCIAL MEDIA

*Julie Ann Read, Benjamin S. Bingle, and C. Kenneth Meyer*

Sometimes things just do not end up as planned. This lesson was learned the hard way by Hope Center after it implemented a volunteer and donor recruitment campaign on social media.

As a relatively new nonprofit organization, Hope Center was fortunate to have wide-ranging support from a dedicated group of volunteers. Its small yet efficient staff—whose ages spanned from a new college graduate to a recently retired CEO—were well respected for their ability to maximize every single dollar received through donations.

Hope Center was interested in increasing its name recognition, not only in the city in which it was headquartered, but also throughout the broader region. Outreach in the form of volunteer drives, guest speaking engagements, and more had taken place at the local high schools, community colleges, and churches and the area chambers of commerce. The organization had staffed so many booths at festivals, at fairs, and in front of various retail establishments that it was unusual to *not* see the Hope Center logo around town. Unfortunately, all the exposure and dedicated outreach had not resulted in significantly more volunteers or donations. The organization needed a new way to connect with the community and the region.

## Observations

As fate would have it, Bill Perkins, the oldest member of the staff, spent a long weekend with his young-adult grandchildren at a family wedding. The former CEO was floored by how much time his grandchildren devoted to mobile devices. At any given time over the weekend, all five grandchildren could be found on smartphones, tablets, or laptops. As he watched how this generation of young adults interacted with each other and with their devices, he mused that, as connected as he had been to his computer and phone while in charge of his business, it was nothing compared to these "youngsters."

When Bill headed into Hope Center headquarters on Monday morning, he grabbed a cup of coffee and sat down at the desk of Ashley Simmons, the newly graduated college student, to talk about his observations. Ashley confirmed that his grandchildren's behavior was normal, and that her generation did tend to be quite attached to their electronic devices. The coworkers discussed the current trifecta of social media—Facebook, Instagram, and Twitter—and the constant competition inflamed by popular media outlets. As Ashley showed Bill various Facebook postings, Instagram pictures, and tweets posted by her friends, Bill wondered aloud if perhaps Hope Center could capitalize on this by sponsoring a social media contest.

## A Social Media Contest

On the spot, Bill and Ashley created a rough outline of the competition. It would be a two-month online contest where volunteers and friends would be rewarded for their social media posts and their volunteering and donating habits, earning points toward a large prize. A small prize would be awarded for each week's competition, and points would be accumulated for the grand prize. Both Bill and Ashley thought that if they could capture the natural competitiveness of human beings and throw in a great prize at the end, they might be able to garner new friends for the organization while strengthening name recognition in the social media community.

The executive director of Hope Center was impressed with the proposed online competition and was able to secure a promise from a valued donor to purchase a highly anticipated new tablet device as the grand prize for the competition. Local dining establishments donated $10 gift certificates for the weekly prizes. Staff knew that the rules for the competition needed to be short and uncomplicated, and that the competition itself needed to be fun and quirky enough to gain online interest.

The "design" of the competition was set—at different points during each week of the competition, Hope Center would post activities for competitors to complete and then display on social media. This would encourage engagement not only in the physical world but also in the virtual world. It was sure to enliven Hope Center's social media pages.

## Up and Running

It was agreed that the competition would kick off just before registration opened for Hope Center's annual 5-K run. There were a variety of ways to earn points, such as being among the first ten people to register for the run, registering multiple people (bring a friend!), or submitting the funniest photo. Participants were encouraged to take "selfies" at events and post them to Facebook. Hope Center also took photos and posted them on social media so that participants could tag themselves in them. Of course, tagging a photo would earn points for that individual. The posts of the race attendees spiked an increase in new Facebook and Instagram connections. Hope Center staff were thrilled and excited about the possible ways to weave the contest into upcoming programs and events.

The staff was kept busy thinking up these weekly competitions, and Ashley was in charge of posting to social media outlets, tracking point winners, and monitoring content. Sometimes the contest would revolve around responding to a tweet or quiz question on Facebook. Other times it might be more challenging, requiring participants to attend an event and upload photos in order to get points. Each Friday morning the organization posted on all three media sites the name of the person who had won the most points that week, and the winner received one of the donated $10 restaurant certificates. Staff thought the weekly mini-prizes would keep interest in the competition high.

## Flash, but Few Results

The campaign was fun and created a splash among those who participated. Unfortunately, most participants had already been engaged with Hope Center in some way before the contest; very few new people were drawn in. Additionally, tracking point winners each week became quite time-consuming for staff members, and there were instances of inappropriate photos being uploaded to Hope Center social media sites. Finally, most of the newly engaged people were quite young. They might be able to volunteer, but they hardly had the disposable income to be regular Hope Center donors.

At the end of the two-month competition, the number of Hope Center's Facebook "friends" had reached an all-time high, but staff had not noticed an increase in either new volunteers or new donations. As they met to analyze the campaign, they discussed whether the social media competition had been an effective volunteer and donation recruitment tool.

Was it a worthwhile project and a wise use of staff time? Would any of the new "friends" the organization had made on social media remain loyal and active now that the prizes were gone? These questions lingered as the Hope Center staff tried to determine their next move to engage volunteers and donors.

## Questions and Instructions

1. Please discuss some of the positive aspects of Hope Center's social media campaign.
2. Discuss some of the drawbacks and limitations of the campaign.
3. Given what you know about philanthropy, was Hope Center realistic in expecting to see an immediate increase in volunteerism or monetary donations from this contest? Why or why not?
4. How might a social media campaign strengthen a connection to an organization's mission? Identify a nonprofit or public service organization that effectively uses social media to connect their users with their mission. Discuss how they do this and why you consider the selected organization to be effective in this area.
5. Put yourself in the role of a Hope Center staff member. The case ends with a staff meeting where some pressing questions are being discussed. You have been tasked with ensuring that the new "friends" attracted to Hope Center by the contest remain engaged with the organization. Please discuss your plan for cultivating these individuals as long-term volunteers and donors.

# PART VII

# CONTRACTS, PARTNERS, AND COLLABORATIONS

Organizations in the nonprofit, government, and for-profit sectors have distinct features, yet they also share common challenges that create conditions conducive to contracting, partnering, or collaborating. The funding offered by US government agencies through contracts to provide services for persons with mental illness, disabilities (including intellectual challenges), chemical dependencies, youth (including gangs), the elderly, homebound individuals, unstable families, persons who need employment training, and victims of abuse has been a significant driver of contracting partnerships.[1]

The amount of government funding that has flowed to nonprofits to provide these types of services has been enormous. In 2012, for example, public charities reported over $1.65 trillion in total revenues. Of that revenue, 73 percent came from service revenues, which included government fees and contracts. Other estimates suggest that 50 percent of all nonprofit revenues are from dues, fees, and charges that include payments to organizations offering services, such as hospitals, health clinics, and child day-care centers. Another 29 percent of nonprofit revenues come from direct government allocations, including grants and money appropriated for services such as Medicare and Medicaid.[2]

In 2009 sources of revenue for reporting public charities (those with over $25,000 in gross receipts) were as follows:

- Fees for services and goods from private sources: 52 percent
- Fees for services and goods from government: 23 percent
- Government grants: 9 percent
- Private contributions: 14 percent
- Other income: 2 percent

One-third of the 2009 reporting public charities were human services organizations, many of which deliver services under government contracts.[3] Obviously, the flow of revenue from government agencies to nonprofit organizations is huge.[4]

There are many reasons why the nonprofit sector has emerged as the preferred deliverer of many public services.[5] Government agencies seek to lower costs, gain more flexibility, get by with fewer permanent government staff, and be more responsive to clients' needs. Importantly, monitoring contracted nonprofits may have lower "transaction costs"—that is, it may require less effort by government agencies—than monitoring in-house staff or for-profit providers.[6] The decades-long growth in government reliance on nonprofits for the delivery of health and human services also has benefited from a pervasive antigovernment bias,[7] including the widely shared perception that government is incompetent and "cannot be trusted to do much of anything right."[8]

Political conservatives have been strong champions for contracting out services to nonprofits as a key strategy for restructuring welfare programs, downsizing government, and encouraging multiple suppliers of social services, especially in the delivery of services to low-income populations. Interestingly, "this right-wing support is virtually indistinguishable [in its effects] from support from the left, which also advocates a larger role for the voluntary sector, and which has long argued the importance of pluralism, self-help, and mutual help in social service provision."[9]

## Government Requirements: Accountability vs. Burdensome Paperwork

During the Great Society era of the 1970s, the US government embarked on a quest to strengthen the administrative practices of state governments. The "feds" imposed numerous administrative requirements on state governments as conditions for receiving grants, including upgraded personnel systems and practices, budgeting procedures, and financial reporting standards.[10] Although these requirements probably accomplished their stated purpose—improving the administration of grants—in truth the requirements were part of a larger agenda in Washington: to bring the administration of state governments more closely in line with the process and substance of US government policies and practices. Agencies of government at all levels have used the same approach and tactics with nonprofit organizations for the last three decades. Eligibility for contracts and contract awards often has been conditioned upon nonprofits adopting highly burdensome, government-like systems, policies, procedures, practices, and reporting.[11]

In March 2010, for example, the Corporation for National and Community Services issued a "Notice of Federal Funds Availability" for its $1 million Nonprofit Capacity Building Program (NCBP). These federal funds were earmarked for the purpose of helping smaller nonprofits that faced resource hardship challenges. The notice of funding declared that applicants had to demonstrate the ability to fully implement a comprehensive performance management system that included written plans with goals, objectives, target clients, and projected outcomes; indicators for measuring outcomes of service delivery; data sources and data collection procedures for each indicator; and a technology system in place that would track activities, collect data, analyze the data collected, and summarize results.

This program required eligible nonprofits to provide documented evidence that they had improved performance and outcomes on the indicators measured and had used a performance appraisal process where individual performance was linked to organizational performance and feedback was provided. Eligible nonprofits were also required to demonstrate that they had used data to improve service delivery, reward staff performance, and inform management decisions. Stakeholders and funders were to be regularly informed about the impacts of services in the community. The irony of requiring small nonprofits with limited resources and capacity challenges to demonstrate that they were using fully operational, data-driven, performance management systems was not lost on the editors of the *Nonprofit Quarterly:* "So is this a plan to make nonprofits better organized or just more like government?"[12]

## Effects of Government Reporting Requirements on Nonprofit Organizations

Most government reporting requirements are intended to protect the rights of employees, clients, and unserved individuals, to provide accountability for government funds, and to improve the management of records and fiscal resources. Many nonprofit executives and students of nonprofit organizations have been concerned, however, about the overall effects of long-term reliance on government contracts on the governance, leadership, management, and character of the nonprofit sector.[13] In their pioneering book *Nonprofits for Hire*, Steven Rathgeb Smith and Michael Lipsky conclude that the longer a nonprofit relies on government contracts the more it tends to look, think, feel, and act like a small (or not-so-small) government agency.[14] Lester Salamon notes that "involvement with government programs tends to produce an undesirable degree of bureaucratization and professionalization in the recipient agency. . . . Government agencies therefore often involve more red tape, cumbersome application requirements, and regulatory control than is common with other forms of financial support."[15] Others have recognized the possibility of "mission creep": over time nonprofit organizations tend to drift toward programs and activities for clients that governments or others will fund—instead of the programs and activities that they believe their clients need most or that they do best.

There is also fear that nonprofits that have become resource-dependent will lose some of their independence. Smith and Lipsky, for example, argue that government requirements and resource dependence do indeed reduce independence.[16] James Ferris counters that government funding does not necessarily decrease the ability of contracted nonprofits to remain true to their missions or to their community roots.[17] Government contracts provide badly needed resources and thus also can increase the freedom of a contracted nonprofit to act on its mission.

There is little consensus. Nonetheless, there is also little doubt that nonprofits that become dependent on contracts should not only anticipate the benefits but also be alert for potential pitfalls. The standards and requirements imposed on contracted nonprofits by government agencies can be stifling, but the resources provided by government contracts also can fund services and outcomes that could not otherwise be provided or met.[18]

## From Contracts to Networks and Collaborations

The nature of organizational boundaries and relationships has also been changing for reasons unrelated to funding. As Patricia Bromley and John Meyer argue:

> Boundary erosion is not a one sided transformation of nonprofits into more business-like entities . . . [Rather,] many standard features of contemporary organizations, including firms, are neither directly attributable to the pursuit of profits or power, nor structured directly around the pursuit of one specific goal (as in the development of corporate social responsibility movements). Instead, organizations reflect the pursuit of multiple purposes that come from cultural principles endowing human actors (both individual and organizational) with the right, responsibility, and capacity to develop and use scientific approaches (including scientific management) for identifying and solving problems of the natural world and human societies.[19]

More collaborative, problem-solving types of partnerships among nonprofit organizations, government agencies, and businesses can be seen across the country—and around the world. They often have been formed out of necessity to deal with complex, community-wide and society-wide "wicked problems" that cannot be effectively addressed by any single agency.[20] Nonprofits may collaborate, for example, because they serve client populations with overlapping needs or problems stemming from multiple causes. In this type of circumstance, coordination and collaboration produce benefits for the community as well as for the individual organizations. Moreover, the provision of social services often produces positive or negative spillovers into related services.[21] For example, Communities In Schools of North Texas (CISNT), a nonprofit dropout prevention program, collaborates with hunger-relief charities, community back-to-school programs, community health clinics, and drug rehabilitation programs. Since there is no single reason why students drop out of school, CISNT is simply unable to accomplish its mission without service assistances from other organizations. The benefits of collaboration can reduce service provision costs through economies of scale or scope of services.[22] However, collaborating nonprofit organizations may seek funding from the same sources, thereby creating competition among collaborators that may reduce their chances of receiving future funding.[23]

Collaboration among organizations can be highly effective for solving problems, building capacity, reducing redundant and overlapping services, and eliminating waste. Almost inevitably, close working partnerships lead to shared perceptions, values, expectations, and standards, and thus interdependence among organizations grows in many ways. Collaboration is not without challenges, however, as organizations in networks may vie for position and influence: "Power and resources are sources of inter-organizational tension in a competitive environment."[24] As Carol Chetkovich and Frances Kunreuther report in their book *From the Ground Up,*

> social change organizations [regardless of preference to do so] must work with other groups to gain the power or resources needed for mission attainment. Collaboration is not an option for the managers and trustees of these organizations. They *must* collaborate if they are to be effective, survive and sustain themselves. . . . Collaboration is hard, however, in the same way that human relationships can be hard. Often factors not unlike those that support interpersonal cooperation are what make collaboration work.[25]

Forming and sustaining collaborative partnerships can be challenging. Potential problems include the uncertainty of funding streams, differing cultures in the contracting and purchase-of-service agencies, conflicting policies, the distinctive characteristics of grant requirements, and conflicting neighborhood needs.[26] Even with these challenges, however, the governance of partnerships and collaborations is a key mechanism for getting things done in today's complex environment. Although it is difficult and complex, and failure rates can be high, managing in interorganizational networks is a common expectation in nonprofit management today.[27]

## Readings Reprinted in Part VII

The two readings reprinted in Part VII address a variety of issues, opportunities, and problems that most nonprofit managers and board members face when contracting with government agencies or becoming part of a network or a collaboration. Although there are many hurdles to cross, managing joint efforts is necessary to solve community problems.

"A Manager's Guide to Choosing and Using Collaborative Networks" by H. Brinton Milward and Keith Provan presents findings from a report funded through the IBM Center for the Business of Government. Although the reading is targeted at government managers, we include it here because nonprofits are actors—and often the primary actors—in these networks.

Milward and Provan provide a glossary for "networking newcomers" that includes terms such as "networks," "nodes," and "linkages." For example, they present Agranoff's definition of networks as "formal and informal structures, composed of representatives, from governmental and nongovernmental agencies working interdependently to exchange information and/or jointly formulate and implement policies that are usually designed for action through their respective organizations."[28]

Milward and Provan identify the characteristics of four types of networks—service implementation, information diffusion, problem-solving, and community capacity-building—and how the tasks associated with managing each of these vary. "Public managers must understand what type of network they are managing and what its purpose is before they can manage it effectively." Service implementation networks require stability because horizontal relationships are always at risk of fragmentation. Formal information diffusion networks, such as task forces created in the wake of disasters, are contrasted with the emergent information diffusion networks that form when the flow of information from formal networks is too slow to be of use to agency officials. The Community Support Program of the National Institute of Mental Health is an example of a problem-solving network in which nonprofits are key participants that provide information and training to mental health managers. Community-capacity-building networks that exist to establish social capital also include nonprofits as primary participants.

The second reading, "Paradox and Collaboration in Network Management" by Sonia M. Ospina and Angel Saz-Carranza, analyzes the paradox that leaders of networks face in promoting inward work among their network members while also valuing and promoting outward diversity. In their qualitative study of two policy networks dealing with issues that affect immigrants, Ospina and Saz-Carranza found that successful network managers address unity in how decisions are made within a network while recognizing that network diversity proves to be a strategic advantage in helping the networks gain leverage with the external organizations they want to target. The authors also identify useful collaborative practices that leaders in networks use to manage paradoxical demands. Internally, practices aimed at unity include facilitating interactions, cultivating relationships, and promoting openness and participation. Outwardly, in managing diversity successful leaders find ways to maintain credibility, use multilevel working, and cultivate multiple relationships.

## Case Studies in Part VII

The case studies in Part VII highlight the issues that may arise in contracting, grant processes, and collaborative ventures. In the first case, "Printing, Politics, and Personal Preferences," a conflict of interest arises when contracting decisions are based on personal considerations. In the second case, "Show Me the Money," a board of directors appears to invent a nontransparent set of questionably relevant criteria for deciding who represents a worthy partner in a grant funding proposal. In both of these cases, the reader is asked to consider the impacts of decisions made based on information derived from relationships versus those based on rational analysis and written policy.

## Notes

1. See, for example, Steven R. Smith, "Government Financing of Nonprofit Activity," in *Nonprofits and Government: Collaboration and Conflict,* 2nd ed., edited by Elizabeth T. Boris and C. Eugene Steuerle (Washington, DC: Urban Institute Press, 2006); see also Amy Blackwood, Kennard T. Wing, and Thomas H. Pollak, *The Nonprofit Sector in Brief: Facts and Figures on the Nonprofit Almanac 2008: Public Charities, Giving, and Volunteering* (Washington, DC: Urban Institute, 2008).

2. Blackwood et al., *The Nonprofit Sector in Brief.*

3. Katie L. Roeger, Amy Blackwood, and Sarah L. Pettijohn, "Core Files: Public Charities, 2009," in *The Nonprofit Sector in Brief: Public Charities, Giving, and Volunteering, 2011* (Washington, DC: Urban Institute, National Center for Charitable Statistics, 2011).

4. Steven R. Smith and Kirsten Grønbjerg, "Scope and Theory of Government-Nonprofit Relations," in *The Nonprofit Sector: A Research Handbook,* 2nd ed., edited by Walter W. Powell and Richard Steinberg (New Haven, CT: Yale University Press, 2006.)

5. Graeme A. Hodge, *Privatization: An International Review of Performance* (Boulder, CO: Westview Press, 2000); see also Steven R. Smith, "Transforming Public Services: Contracting for Social and Health Services in the US," *Public Administration* 74 (Spring 1996): 113–127.

6. Mary K. Marvel and Howard P. Marvel, "Outsourcing Oversight: A Comparison of Monitoring for In-House and Contracted Services," *Public Administration Review 67*, no. 3 (May–June 2007): 521–530.

7. J. Steven Ott and Lisa A. Dicke, "Important but Largely Unanswered Questions About Accountability in Contracted Public Human Services," *International Journal of Organization Theory and Behavior 3*, nos. 3 and 4 (Summer 2000): 283–317.

8. J. Steven Ott and Jay M. Shafritz, "The Perception of Organizational Incompetence," in *The Enduring Challenges in Public Management*, edited by Arie Halachmi and Geert Bouckaert (San Francisco: Jossey-Bass, 1995), 27–46; and J. Steven Ott and Jay M. Shafritz, "Toward a Definition of Organizational Incompetence: A Neglected Variable in Organization Theory," *Public Administration Review 54*, no. 4 (July–August 1994): 370–377.

9. Josephine Rekart, *Public Funds, Private Provision: The Role of the Voluntary Sector* (Vancouver, BC: UBC Press, 1993), xii.

10. See, for example, Jay M. Shafritz, E. William Russell, and Christopher P. Borick, *Introducing Public Administration*, 8th ed. (New York: Longman, 2013), chs. 2 and 4; and B. Guy Peters, *The Politics of Bureaucracy: An Introduction to Comparative Public Administration*, 6th ed. (London and New York: Routledge, 2010), chs. 7 and 8.

11. US Government Accountability Office (GAO), *Nonprofit Sector: Increasing Numbers and Key Role in Delivering Federal Services*, GAO-07-1084T (Washington, DC: GAO, 2007).

12. "Federal Government to Small and Midsized Nonprofits: If You Ain't Got a Comprehensive Performance Measurement System, You Got Nothing!" *Nonprofit Quarterly*, April 8, 2010, https://nonprofitquarterly.org /policysocial-context/2168-federal-government-to-small-and-mid-sized-nonprofits-if-you-aint-got-a -comprehensive-performance-management-system-you-got-nothing.html.

13. Lester M. Salamon, *Partners in Public Service: Government-Nonprofit Relations in the Modern Welfare State* (Baltimore: Johns Hopkins University Press, 1995), 103–109.

14. Steven R. Smith and Michael Lipsky, *Nonprofits for Hire: The Welfare State in the Age of Contracting* (Cambridge, MA: Harvard University Press, 1993).

15. Salamon, *Partners in Public Service*, 107.

16. Smith and Lipsky, *Nonprofits for Hire*, 97.

17. James M. Ferris, "The Double-Edged Sword of Social Service Contracting," *Nonprofit Management and Leadership 3*, no. 4 (Summer 1993): 363–376.

18. See Seok-Eun Kim, "Balancing Competing Accountability Requirements: Challenges in Performance Improvement of the Nonprofit Human Services Agency," *Public Performance and Management Review 29*, no. 2 (2005): 145–163; and Ott and Dicke, "Important but Largely Unanswered Questions About Accountability and Contracted Public Human Services."

19. Patricia Bromley and John W. Meyer, "'They Are All Organizations': The Cultural Roots of Blurring Between the Nonprofit, Business, and Government Sectors," *Administration and Society*, published online September 4, 2014, DOI: 10.1177/0095399714548268, http://aas.sagepub.com/content/early/2014/09/03 /0095399714548268.full.pdf.

20. Lester M. Salamon and S. Wojciech Sokolowski, eds., *Global Civil Society: Dimensions of the Nonprofit Sector*, vol. 2 (Bloomfield, CT: Kumarian Press, 2004.)

21. Hee Soun Jang, Richard Feiock, and Marina Saitgalina, "Institutional Collective Action Issues in Nonprofit Self-Organized Collaboration," *Administration and Society* (December 2013): 1–27.

22. Ibid.

23. Joseph Galaskiewicz, Wolfgang Bielefeld, and Myron Dowell, "Networks and Organizational Growth: A Study of Community-Based Nonprofits," *Administrative Science Quarterly 51* (2006): 337–380.

24. Carol Chetkovich and Frances Kunreuther, "Collaboration: Mission Driven Partnerships," in Carol Chetkovich and Frances Kunreuther, *From the Ground Up: Grassroots Organizations Making Social Change* (Ithaca, NY: Cornell University Press, 2006), 132–148, 133.

25. Ibid.

26. Elizabeth A. Mulroy, "Community as a Factor in Implementing Interorganizational Partnerships: Issues, Constraints, and Adaptations," *Nonprofit Management and Leadership* 14, no. 1 (Fall 2003): 47–66.

27. Rosemary O'Leary and Lisa Blomgren-Bingham, *A Manager's Guide to Resolving Conflicts in Collaborative Networks* (Arlington, VA: IBM Center for the Business of Government, 2007).

28. Robert Agranoff, "Leveraging Networks: A Guide for Public Managers Working Across Organizations," in *Collaboration: Using Networks and Partnerships,* edited by John M. Kamensky and Thomas J. Burlin (Lanham, MD: Rowman & Littlefield, 2004), 63.

# ▶ CHAPTER 15

# *A Manager's Guide to Choosing and Using Collaborative Networks*

## H. Brinton Milward and Keith G. Provan

In what he calls the "global public management revolution," Don Kettl has identified six common ideas behind the public management revolution: "the search for greater productivity; more public reliance on private markets; a stronger orientation toward service; more decentralization from national to subnational governments; increased capacity to devise and track public policy; and tactics to enhance accountability for results" (Kettl 2005).

Instead of organizing, providing, and managing services on its own, government has increasingly turned to contracting out these services, most often to nonprofit, but sometimes to for-profit, organizations. This increased contracting out of services has meant that public managers at all levels have had to coordinate and oversee the activities of the many organizations that government funds to ensure the smooth provision of multiple services to clients. Thus, government must not only manage its own internal operations but it must also manage multi-organization networks (Goldsmith and Eggers 2004).

These core ideas in the revolution in public management have led public managers to seek alternatives to traditional bureaucratic organizations to provide services to citizens in innovative ways. Two of these ways are *contracting out* services to third parties and relying on *networks of* public, nonprofit, and for-profit organizations, instead of a bureaucratic hierarchy. Contracts may be a way in which two or more organizations are linked, but a set of contractual relationships is not the same as a network (Johnston and Romzek 2000). Networks may be funded by grants, contracts, or fee-for-service arrangements (or a mixture of all three), but they use collaboration as a way of dealing with problems in a coordinated fashion that would be impossible for just one organization. The idea behind contracting is exactly the opposite of collaboration—competition, where two or more organizations are forced to compete for the contract. The network logic is that collaboration is needed to deal with problems that don't fit neatly within the boundaries of a single organization.[1]

Collaborative networks are seen as appropriate devices to tackle public management problems like homelessness, child welfare, and terrorism. Since the problem is bigger than any

---

Originally published online by IBM Center for the Business of Government, 2006 (www.businessofgovernment.org). Reprinted with permission.

organization, collaborating with other organizations is necessary if there is any hope of making progress in effectively managing the problem.

There are many kinds of networks in the world. Each individual is part of a social network that links one to others in a variety of ways—friends, relatives, work colleagues, and so on. Each person is called a "node" in network terminology. Relationships, or linkages, among a group of individuals are commonly referred to as a social network, and the network as a whole is the pattern of linkages among the individuals.[2] In this report, we examine networks of organizations—or what scholars call interorganizational networks—and discuss how managing a network or managing in a network differs from managing an organization.

Like a social network, an interorganizational network consists of linkages among a set of nodes, but instead of people, the nodes are organizations. The term organizational network has many different definitions. Most note that they consist of multiple organizations that are legally autonomous. Relationships (linkages) are based on cooperation and collaboration and, in the public sector, law and funding holds them together:

> [N]etworks of public organizations . . . [involve] formal and informal structures, composed of representatives from governmental and nongovernmental agencies working interdependently to exchange information and/or jointly formulate and implement policies that are usually designed for action through their respective organizations. (Agranoff 2004, 63)

## Public Management Networks: Types and Purpose

The currency of a network is the trust and reciprocity that exist among its members. As Robert Axelrod (1984) famously said, trust and reciprocity "lengthen the shadow of the future" and reward those who choose to cooperate, because people want to work with them again; therefore, the more trust and reciprocity in the network, the greater the ability of the network to accomplish shared goals. The task of network managers is to increase the stock of trust and reciprocity by creating incentives (using resources) and to increase their collaborative skills to build relationships within the network to accomplish network goals, whether it is environmental cleanup, alleviating homelessness, reducing teen pregnancy, or responding to a natural disaster.

Although much is now known about public networks, there is still a great deal of confusion about how they should be managed. One of the main problems is that most of the work on the topic has drawn few distinctions among the types of public networks that exist or the purposes they serve, while assuming that issues of network management are similar for all networks. From our own fieldwork and from our analysis of the literature on networks, however, we have identified four distinct types of public sector networks. Our argument is a contingent one—public managers must understand what type of network they are managing and what its purpose is before they can manage it effectively. The four types of public networks we discuss here are *service implementation networks, information diffusion networks, problem-solving networks,* and *community-capacity-building networks.* The key characteristics of each type of network are summarized in table 15.1.

### Service Implementation Networks

Service implementation networks consist of intergovernmental programs like Temporary Assistance for Needy Families (TANF) and services for those who are seriously mentally ill, the aged, abused and neglected children,

TABLE 15.1. Public Management Networks—Types and Key Characteristics

| Network Type | Key Characteristics |
|---|---|
| **Service Implementation Networks** | • Government funds the service under contract but doesn't directly provide it (frequently health and human services). <br> • Services are jointly produced by two or more organizations. <br> • Collaboration is often between programs of larger organizations. <br> • Horizontal management of service providers is a key task. These can be firms, nonprofits, or government agencies. <br> • A fiscal agent acts as the sole buyer of services. <br> • Key management tasks include encouraging cooperation, negotiating contracts, planning network expansion, etc. |
| **Information Diffusion Networks** | • Horizontal and vertical ties between interdependent government agencies. <br> • Primary focus is sharing information across departmental boundaries. <br> • Commonly used for disaster preparedness and other "high uncertainty" problems. <br> • Key network goal is to shape government's response to problems through better communication and collaboration. <br> • May be either designed or emergent. |
| **Problem-Solving Networks** | • Primary purpose is to help organizational managers set the agenda for policy related to a critical national or regional problem. <br> • Focus is on solving existing complex problems rather than building relationships for future problems. <br> • Often emerges from information diffusion networks. <br> • Relationships may be temporary, to address a specific problem, and then become dormant after the problem is resolved. <br> • May be either designed or emergent. |
| **Community-Capacity-Building Networks** | • Primary goal is to build social capital in community-based settings. <br> • Network purpose is both current and future oriented (i.e., to build the capacity to address future community needs as they arise). <br> • May be created by participants (bottom-up) or by private and government funders (top-down). <br> • Often involves a wide range of agencies with many emergent sub-networks to address different community needs that may arise. |

and the developmentally disabled, which are often funded by federal grants to the states. From the federal and often the state perspective, the task is to manage programs that are lodged in public, private, and nonprofit organizations that actually deliver services directly to clients. The tools in the hands of federal and state managers consist of grants, contracts, rules, and training opportunities that, over time, can help to shape the way a given program is delivered at the local level. For services like this, government effectively becomes the sole buyer of services. Economists refer to this type of market as a *monopsony.*

At the local or state level, managing a service implementation network that actually delivers services is a horizontal management problem involving both assembly and joint production. Using some type of contract or fee-for-service arrangement, the network manager must assemble a set of largely nongovernmental third parties to jointly produce a service like community trauma care or drug and alcohol prevention. The money from each federal or state program usually flows to a lead agency or a network administrative organization, like a mental health authority, whose job it is to arrange for a set of services to be delivered to clients who qualify for the program. Horizontal network management requires a government-designated fiscal agent (like a mental health authority) that issues contracts (sometimes competitively) to specific organizations while urging them to collaborate with one another. Since no one organization delivers all of the services a client is likely to need, collaboration is essential if a client's needs are to be met. Managers of horizontal networks view service integration as their major task as they try to overcome the tendency of networks to fragment, which is why many of the managers we have interviewed think competitive contracting (often in a thin market with few sellers) is an impediment to collaboration. This may be the reason that studies of contracting for social services find that contracting is done no more frequently than required by higher levels of government, and that the same agencies often get the contracts year after year (Smith and Smyth 1996).

### Information Diffusion Networks

Information diffusion networks are a common form of network within any level of government. Whether it is a joint task force on intelligence sharing in the wake of 9/11 or a state task force created in the wake of a child protective

services horror story, the job is the same: Interdependent government organizations need to develop the means to share information across departmental boundaries so that disasters have a better chance of being avoided. Unlike the service implementation network, the product of an interagency task force is to shape government's response to problems through better communication and collaboration rather than more effective service provision, as with the service implementation network. It is the shared information that should lead to improved services produced by each agency. A terrorist watch list that combines the resources of the CIA, FBI, and foreign intelligence agencies allows the State Department consular officer to do a better job of screening out threats to the United States who may apply for a visa in a foreign country.

The National Institutes of Health and some medical foundations have managers whose task it is to manage knowledge that flows from the research that they fund, diffusing information among a set of researchers so that everyone in the program is informed of problems, protocols, and findings. The government of Canada has created networks of excellence in many different areas of health to improve information sharing among networks of doctors, researchers, and healthcare professionals. One of the newest networks is called AllerGen, which brings together allergists, geneticists, and immunologists around the funding of a set of research issues that the government of Canada has deemed critical after seeking advice from the community of practice (Snyder and de Souza Briggs 2004) that has coalesced around the study of the genetic basis of allergic disease.

While AllerGen is a *designed* information diffusion network, there are *emergent* information diffusion networks. Big-city police chiefs in cities like Los Angeles, Washington, DC, Chicago, and Las Vegas have banded together out of frustration with the "slow and sometimes grudging way that federal officials share information about terrorist incidents" (Broder 2005, A12). Spearheaded by William J. Bratton, the [then] Los Angeles police chief, a number of big-city chiefs have instituted their own network to share information about terrorist threats. While acknowledging that the information they receive from the FBI and the Department of Homeland Security is generally of high quality, it is received so slowly that it is rarely actionable. Police chiefs have to deploy officers and cordon off areas in real time if a threat emerges like the London subway or Madrid train bombings, and they view the federal information as more analytical in nature. Federal officials admit that the information they share has to be vetted before it is sent out, which takes time, and the police chiefs want raw, unfiltered information, even if it is later proved to be wrong, since good information received after a terrorist event is worthless.

What is so interesting about this case is that there is a formal, designed network in place where local police chiefs have a place at the table in the Homeland Security Operations Center, whose job is to diffuse information on terrorist threats to police departments all over the country. Chief Bratton is attempting to organize an emergent network in response to perceived weaknesses in this designed network. Bratton is working with the police departments in 10 to 15 US and Canadian cities to share raw data on rapidly emerging terrorist threats. In a twist of irony, the actions of one network serve to create another to remedy the designed network's flaws. Out of this conflict comes a new type of network with a different purpose—a problem-solving network.

## Problem-Solving Networks

Problem-solving networks have several different purposes. When an information diffusion network reaches a certain point, it can morph into a problem-solving network that can help managers set the agenda in regard to policy toward a critical national or regional problem. In a decentralized and devolved political system like the United States has, it can help to shape the implementation of a new policy. After most states deinstitutionalized their mentally ill clients, the Community Support Program of the National Institute of Mental Health proved to be a very effective way of providing information and training to many public and nonprofit mental health managers about how to run a decentralized, community-based mental health system (Weiss 1990).

Problem-solving networks are also used in the case of disasters as a way to quickly solve the ensuing crisis. It can either be designed prior to a problem occurring, like a wildfire incident command system that can be adapted to a variety of settings, or it can emerge in the aftermath of an unanticipated problem. Emergencies of any magnitude are rarely contained within the boundaries of one organization, and public managers have struggled over many years to try to prepare for what [former] Secretary of Defense Donald Rumsfeld calls "known unknowns." This characterization refers to events that we *know* will happen, the only *unknown* being when and where they will happen. Wildfires are an example of a known unknown. In the western United States, generally arid conditions and periodic drought create perfect conditions for seasonal wildfires. Whether started by lightning, a lit cigarette, or a campfire, every summer thousands of acres across the West go up in flames, sometimes threatening major cities like Los Angeles and San Diego.

Given the predictability of wildfires, it makes sense to plan for these occurrences. What has come to be known as the Incident Command System (ICS) was born out of the frustration of the lack of collaboration among agencies and levels of government in the face of these periodic wildfires. Congress required the US Forest Service to design a system to alleviate these problems, and in the 1970s the Forest Service worked with the California Department of Forestry and Fire Protection, Office of Emergency Services, and local police and fire departments in California to coordinate their firefighting efforts. The ICS has proved so successful in fighting wildfires that all federal agencies are required to use it for managing emergencies.

### Community-Capacity-Building Networks

Community-capacity-building networks have become very important in recent years. In the wake of Robert Putnam's pioneering work on social capital, a variety of federal agencies have challenged communities to create partnerships in areas like economic development or the prevention of drug and alcohol abuse (Putnam 1993, 2000). The goal of the network is to build social capital so that communities will be better able to deal with a variety of problems related to education, economic development, crime, and so on. Federal agencies like the Center for Substance Abuse Prevention, which is part of the Substance Abuse and Mental Health Services Administration (SAMHSA) in the Department of Health and Human Services, have given grants to many communities if they will create a prevention partnership organization that will serve as a fiscal agent to coordinate drug and alcohol abuse prevention for youth.

We were involved in one of these grants that created a partnership agency whose job it was to weave together all of the prevention resources in an urban county with a population of just under a million people (Milward and Provan 1998). At the very beginning of the grant, we were hired to map the network of potential partners who were interested in substance abuse prevention. The number of agencies was quite large and included police, school systems, parks and recreation departments, Boys and Girls Clubs, the YMCA, and the YWCA as well as many specific drug and alcohol prevention agencies, some governmental, some nonprofit, and some for-profit. The goal was clear—to increase the level

of community awareness of substance abuse and increase the capacity of the county to decrease the level of youth substance abuse.

This network was both emergent and designed. There had been prior prevention efforts that involved voluntary cooperation, and a group of organizations came together to write the grant proposal, but the Center for Substance Abuse Prevention grant award required that one organization serve as fiscal agent and assume responsibility for network coordination. As an aside, it should be noted that while network researchers often exhibit a bias in favor of emergent networks (Jones, Hesterly, and Borgatti 1997), there is very little evidence to support the assertion that emergent networks are more effective than networks that have been designed or mandated. In this case, a condition of the grant was that the set of substance abuse agencies that submitted the grant would have to create a fiscal agent to receive the funds, promote the cause, manage the network, and monitor its progress through periodic evaluations.

We began our work with the network by conducting meetings with representatives of all of the agencies and getting them to talk about who worked together in regard to substance abuse prevention. We soon found that there were major gaps in the network. The substance abuse agencies operated in one world, the after-school-based programs operated in another, and the police became involved in a crisis or very episodically through programs like DARE in the schools. At a series of meetings with agency representatives, we gave out network questionnaires and asked that the representatives indicate who they had relationships with and the nature of these relationships. Using a network analysis software program,[3] we graphed the relationships so that anyone looking at the results could clearly see which agencies were connected to which other agencies in several different ways—information sharing, referrals, contracts, and joint programming. The response to the analysis was quite interesting. When the network maps were

TABLE 15.2. Management Tasks in Public Networks

| Essential Network Management Tasks | Management of Networks | Management in Networks |
|---|---|---|
| **Management of Accountability** | • Determining who is responsible for which outcomes.<br>• Rewarding and reinforcing compliance with network goals.<br>• Monitoring and responding to network "free riders." | • Monitoring your organization's involvement in the network.<br>• Ensuring that dedicated resources are actually used for network activities.<br>• Ensuring that your organization gets credit for network contributions.<br>• Resisting efforts to "free ride." |
| **Management of Legitimacy** | • Building and maintaining legitimacy of the network concept, network structures, and network involvement.<br>• Attracting positive publicity, resources, new members, tangible successes, etc. | • Demonstrating to others (members, stakeholders) the value of network participation.<br>• Legitimizing the role of the organization among other network members. |
| **Management of Conflict** | • Setting up mechanisms for conflict and dispute resolution.<br>• Acting as a "good faith" broker.<br>• Making decisions that reflect network-level goals and not the specific interests of members. | • Working at the dyad level to avoid and resolve problems with individual network members.<br>• Working inside your organization to act as a "linking pin" to balance organization versus network demands and needs. |
| **Management of Design (Governance Structure)** | • Determining which structural governance forms would be most appropriate for network success.<br>• Implementing and managing the structure.<br>• Recognizing when structure should change based on network and participant needs. | • Working effectively with other network participants and with network-level management, based on the governance structure in place.<br>• Accepting some loss of control over network-level decisions. |
| **Management of Commitment** | • Getting the "buy-in" of participants.<br>• Working with participants to ensure they understand how network success can contribute to the organization's effectiveness.<br>• Ensuring that network resources are distributed equitably to network participants based on network needs.<br>• Ensuring that participants are well informed about network activities. | • Building commitment within the organization to network-level goals.<br>• Institutionalizing network involvement so that support of network goals and participation goes beyond a single person in the organization. |

presented, it verified what leaders of the prevention partnership had been saying—that there were a number of independent networks of substance abuse prevention with little connection between them. In addition, there were some agencies, particularly in the more rural parts of the county, that were completely isolated.

The response to these "network snapshots" was to create a strategic plan to weave the elements of the substance abuse prevention community together much more closely. There was a great deal of discussion about how to bring the isolated agencies to the table and how to bridge the different worlds of substance abuse prevention to create a more coordinated approach to what was clearly a community-wide problem. Seeing the gaps in the networks created a movement to bring the community together around this problem.

## Essential Tasks for Network Managers

No doubt there are countless small things that managers can do to enhance the effectiveness of their network. Rather than getting into these details, we propose what we have found to be five broad and essential tasks that managers must perform if their networks are to be successful. The importance of each task is based both on network research and on our extensive consulting experience. A critical point is that each network management task has both network- and organization-level implications. That is, each task is essential both to the role of the managers *of* networks and to the role of managers operating *in* networks. Effective networks must have both. Managers *of* networks are concerned with the network as a whole. These are typically individuals who are charged with the task of coordinating overall network activities and, in general, ensuring that network-level goals are set, addressed, and attained. The goals and success of organizational members become secondary to the network as a whole. Managers *in* networks

are individuals who represent their organization within the network. They are managers whose primary loyalty is to their organization, but who must work within a network context, addressing both organization- and network-level goals and objectives. These managers have split missions and, sometimes, split loyalties. The essential tasks of both types of managers are explained below and summarized in table 15.2.

## Conclusion

While each type of network (based on purpose) has its own unique characteristics and challenges, all must be managed effectively. To do that, network managers need to accomplish an interrelated series of tasks. Likewise, managers in networks have a challenging set of tasks as well.

To date, most of the literature on networks has focused on discussing their value for addressing complex public problems. Networks have been considered as unique multi-organizational forms that are different from either informal market-based arrangements or formal hierarchy-based organizations. Although the difficulties of networking are often discussed, networks are often thought of as panaceas for problems that cannot be solved by traditional governmental organizations. While networks can be extremely useful for addressing public problems, the reality, of course, is far more complex. In particular, networks are often difficult to form and sustain, and outcomes are not always positive.

What we have argued here is that addressing complex public sector problems effectively is not simply dependent on whether the problem is managed through a hierarchy versus a network. While networks have many advantages over hierarchies, networks can certainly be ineffective and fail. As with organizational hierarchies, effectiveness depends heavily on good management. However, organizational and network management are quite different, and the success of networks in addressing public problems depends on effective network management.

## Notes

1. In the real world, hard and fast distinctions tend to blur at certain points. Collaboration and contracting come together with what economists call "relational contracting," which is contracting that is based on trust and reciprocity (just like networks) rather than a written contract that specifies what both parties' obligations are in great detail. Relational contracts are typically kept in place as long as they serve the interests of both parties rather than being competitively bid with some frequency. They tend to be used for goods and services where price is less important than quality.

2. For an excellent layman's guide to social network analysis, see Duncan J. Watts, *Six Degrees: The Science of a Connected Age* (New York: W. W. Norton and Company, 2003).

3. The network analysis program we used for mapping the network was UCINET, which is available from Analytic Technologies at http://www .analytictech.com.

## References

Agranoff, Robert. 2004. "Leveraging Networks: A Guide for Public Managers Working Across Organizations." In *Collaboration: Using Networks and Partnerships,* edited by John M. Kamensky and Thomas J. Burlin, 61–102. Lanham, MD: Rowman & Littlefield Publishers.

Axelrod, Robert. 1984. *The Evolution of Cooperation.* New York: Basic Books.

Broder, John M. 2005. "Police Chiefs Moving to Share Terror Data." *New York Times,* July 28, A12.

Goldsmith, Stephen, and William D. Eggers. 2004. *Government by Network: The New Shape of the Public Sector.* Washington, DC: The Brookings Institution.

Johnston, Jocelyn M., and Barbara S. Romzek. 2000. *Implementing State Contracts for Social Services: An Assessment of the Kansas Experience.* Washington, DC: IBM Center for the Business of Government.

Jones, Candace, William Hesterly, and Stephen Borgatti. 1997. "A General Theory of Network Governance: Exchange Conditions and Social Mechanisms." *Academy of Management Review* 22: 911–945.

Kettl, Donald F. 2005. *The Global Public Management Revolution,* 2nd ed. Washington, DC: The Brookings Institution.

Milward, H. Brinton, and Keith G. Provan. 1998. "Measuring Network Structure." *Public Administration* 76: 387–407.

Putnam, Robert D. 1993. *Making Democracy Work.* Princeton, NJ: Princeton University Press.

———. 2000. *Bowling Alone.* New York: Touchstone.

Smith, Steven Rathgeb, and Judith Smyth. 1996. "Contracting for Services in a Decentralized System." *Journal of Public Administration Research and Theory* 6, no. 2, 277–296.

Snyder, William M., and Xavier de Souza Briggs. 2004. "Communities of Practice: A New Tool for Government Managers." In *Collaboration: Using Networks and Partnerships,* edited by John M. Kamensky and Thomas J. Burlin, 171–272. Lanham, MD: Rowman & Littlefield Publishers.

Weiss, Janet A. 1990. "Ideas and Inducements in Mental Health Policy." *Journal of Policy Analysis and Management* 9: 178–200.

## CHAPTER 16

# Paradox and Collaboration in Network Management

## Sonia M. Ospina and Angel Saz-Carranza

## Paradox in the Management of Interorganizational Networks

Managing interorganizational networks is an inherently difficult task, whether within the public or private sectors or across them (Human and Provan 2000). They are complex, so the risk of failure is high (Park and Ungson 2001). An estimated 50 percent or more of the efforts to build and sustain business alliances fail (Kelly, Schaan, and Jonacas 2002; Park and Ungson 2001). Although failure rates are not available for public or nonprofit networks, their difficulties are documented (O'Leary and Bingham 2007). For example, interorganizational collaboration often succumbs to what Huxham and Vangen (2000) call "collaborative inertia." Research suggests that these difficulties stem from the complex, dynamic, and ambiguous nature of a key requirement for network success: collaboration (Huxham 2003).

### Interorganizational Action Networks

Our study focuses on a specific type of collaboration, "action networks" (Agranoff 2003). These use interagency adjustments and formally adopt collaborative courses of action, particularly regarding policy advocacy. Action networks are network structures (Keast, Mandell, Brown, and Woolcock 2004) with a formal, centralized network management unit, a coordinating unit or "network administrative organizations" (Milward and Provan 2006). Action networks carry out joint action, as opposed to informal information-sharing networks. Their members pursue at the same time a common objective, and their own independent objectives. They are, by definition, explicitly committed to interorganizational collaboration.

### Ambiguity, Complexity, and Tension in Network Management

Insights from the literature indicate that collaborative efforts often arise to solve complex problems in dynamic social environments (Agranoff and McGuire 2001; Borzel 1998; Castells 2000; Gray 1996; Mandell 2000) and that these efforts are usually complex themselves. We also know that complexity characterizes the nature and management of network features such as membership and size. For example, membership structure is ambiguous and dynamic, given that the same persons may represent different organizations in different arenas (Huxham 2003). There is also ample evidence of the tensions associated with the complexities of setting goals (Huxham 2003; McGuire 2002) and defining success (Provan and Milward 2001). For example, studies suggest that members of interorganizational collaborations may hold diverse views about how to define and measure success (Mizrahi and Rosenthal 2001).

Only recently have scholars explicitly associated these tensions with the paradoxical nature of collaboration in the context of network management (Connelly et al. 2008). The collaboration literature points to an inherent tension in networks: the potential for collaborative advantage depends on the ability of each member organization to bring different resources to the network. This diversity of member resources is a function of the difference in member purpose, which in turn challenges their ability to collaborate (Huxham and Beech 2003). Much can be learned by exploring how effective leaders in the coordinating unit of action networks manage challenges associated with facilitating collaboration in a context full of ambiguity, complexity, and tension.

## Managing Challenges to Collaboration in Networks

Network management studies find that managing an organization *located in a network* requires specialized strategies. These include interacting with other organizations, creating infrastructures for collaboration, attracting and support-

ing potential partners, building and sustaining legitimacy, and capturing resources and support for the network (Agranoff and McGuire 2001; Huxham and Vangen 2000; Keast et al. 2004; Mandell 2000).

These important insights are about managing in a network context, but despite some exceptions (Mandell 2000; Milward and Provan 2006), these studies tend to focus on the behavior of leaders in each member organization of the network rather than on how leaders *at the network level* address similar demands for the whole network as an independent organizational form.

This gap in understanding has been recently addressed by the literature on collaborative governance (Ansell and Gash 2008; Tang and Mazmanian 2008). Of particular relevance is the effort to translate research findings into guidelines to assist public managers in the use and leverage of policy networks and in reducing conflict among network members (Agranoff 2003; Milward and Provan 2006; O'Leary and Bingham 2007). This literature has begun to cast light on the complex nature of collaborative work in a network context, and identifies specific leadership skills, processes, and behaviors required for successful network management. Only a few studies, however, recognize and address paradox as inherent in these issues, and then only tangentially. O'Leary and Bingham, for example, make note of the ubiquitous presence of conflict as a paradoxical factor affecting network management and that particular models of conflict resolution contribute to enhance collaboration. Connelly et al. (2008) identify several paradoxes of collaborative management in networks and suggest that managers must embrace these as they work both within and outside the network. Yet the empirical question of how network managers address the paradoxical demands of this organizational form as they try to develop collaboration at the network level has not been explored.

# Method

This study used narrative inquiry as its primary methodology (Clandinin and Connelly 2000; Ospina and Dodge 2005; Reissman 2002) to answer the research question, How do leaders in successful networks manage collaboration challenges to make things happen? We collected stories about interorganizational collaborative work from interviews with organizational members of two action networks in large urban centers of the United States. Their publicly acknowledged achievement of effective change in the immigration policy domain qualifies them as successful cases of action networks.

## Study Design

The chosen networks represent a theoretically driven sample drawn from 20 organizations participating in a leadership recognition program during 2001 and 2002 (Ospina and Foldy 2009). All were nonprofit, social-change organizations (Chetkovich and Kunreuther 2006) working with particular disadvantaged populations to address systemic inequities, combining strategies of service delivery, organizing, advocacy, and community building. Given the rigor of the program's selection process and criteria, these organizations represent exemplars of success and therefore, suitable sites to explore our research question.[1]

We chose to focus on two similar interorganizational action networks that operated within the policy domain of immigration. Our interest in a topic for which there is scant empirical research indicated an exploratory inquiry that would afford cross-comparisons as well as in-depth exploration of the challenges of collaboration in each particular network context.

The cases are comparable along two key dimensions: policy domain (immigration) and location (large urban centers). Their governing bodies are also similar: a core coordinating unit with an executive director accountable to a board of directors with membership representation. This enhances the comparability of the units of analysis in the study but produces findings that could not be generalized to collaborative work in networks from other policy areas and jurisdictions and with other governing structures.

There are also key differences between the networks. Although they share a federal context, their local and state policy contexts differ. Despite comparable annual budgets ($1.3 million and $1 million, respectively), their funding sources differ slightly.[2] The networks also differ in their size (20 and 150 members), their membership structure, and the complexity and size of the staff working in the coordinating unit (9 and 17). Their age (5 and 15 years) suggests different life-cycle stages, one relatively young and maturing (Rainbow Network) and the other well established (Immigrant Policy Network).

The emphasis on leadership challenges around collaboration for the whole network demanded a primary focus of attention on the networks' coordinating units. Nevertheless, the level of analysis was the network as a whole, which represents the case we are exploring to answer the research question (Ragin 1992).

## Data Collection and Analysis

We collected stories via two rounds of in-depth interview of individuals and groups made during site visits to the offices of both the Immigrant Policy Network and the Rainbow Network, also known as the network coordinating units.[3] Individual leaders from the coordinating unit were interviewed first. Then they joined structured group conversations with selected representatives of stakeholder group members (such as other staff from the coordinating unit, representatives of the board, representatives from network member organizations, clients, finders, allies, and public officials). Interview protocols around relevant dimensions of the network's work elicited stories about how the network had achieved successful milestones as well as instances of conflict, obstacles, and failure. The interviews followed a narrative, interpretive technique, allowing participants to describe their experiences freely and encouraging story telling (Clandinin and Connelly 2000).

Conversational interviews with these stakeholders yielded about 500 pages of transcripts and represent the basic linguistic corpus constructed to engage in narrative analysis (Gaskell and Bauer 2000).[4] These interviews were complemented by additional documentation from the leadership program (such as analytical memos from prior research, participant applications, and other program documents).

Data collection and analysis focused on organizational strategies and activities revealed in the stories, including evidence of challenges to collaboration. We coded in two stages. The stories were first organized in categories from the reviewed literature corresponding to dimensions associated with the nature of interorganizational networks. These included motivation to join, relationships, the scope of work, and successes. Second, "grounded" codes reflecting ways to address the challenges of collaboration emerged from identified stories. Themes like inclusion and participatory process, as well as the need for unity and the value of diversity, emerged from the stories.

Once coded, within-case and cross-case matrices were developed, and the analysis searched for patterns within and across organizations. Then a conceptual interpretation of the results linked the tables to complementary research material, including analytical memos developed in earlier stages of the research program. What emerged as an unexpected but determinant finding to answer our research question was that the network's activities to address the challenges of collaboration responded to the need to manage the paradoxical demands associated with both their inward and outward work.

## The Cases: Work, History, and Accomplishments

Each action network studied supports the immigrant community of a large US city and its surrounding urban area. On the East Coast, the Immigrant Policy Network includes roughly 150 organizations representing most segments of its city's immigrant population. Rainbow Network operates in a large Midwest city, with a diverse membership of 20 immigrant groups. Communities represented range from Mexican, Dominican, Eastern European, and Chinese immigrants to newcomers from other parts of Latin America, as well as Africa, South Asia, and the Middle East.

The central goal shared by the networks is to improve local immigrants' quality of life and to provide a forum for their voices and collective action. Their focus includes civic, community and technical education, advocacy, and policy analysis. They work to influence education, health, and welfare institutions that affect the quality of life of immigrants and consider their local, state, and federal immigration agencies to be key institutional targets.

The seeds from which many of the member organizations and the networks themselves grew were planted when significant changes resulting from the Immigration Reform and Control Act of 1986 (IRCA) altered the demographic landscape of much of the United States, including the urban areas of the studied networks. Three million undocumented workers and their families became eligible for legal status, increasing demand for services and the necessary collaboration among organizations to provide them (Federation for American Immigration Reform 2003; Moran and Petsod 2003). The Immigrant

Policy Network was created in 1987 through the efforts of a small group of immigration reform advocates. The new locally based network of immigrant advocacy organizations offered support for immigrants and new citizens, while responding to IRCA's goal to deter illegal immigration to the United States. In 1996, influenced by the anti-immigrant implications of the 1996 Federal Welfare Reform initiative and in search of a way to make themselves heard, a small collection of immigrant groups in a Midwestern city coalesced around poverty and an unresponsive local Immigration and Naturalization Service (INS) office.[5] In 1998, a foundation grant supporting their search for solutions transformed an ad hoc and reactive collection of groups into the formal and proactive Rainbow Network.

The success of these networks within the dispersed and isolated immigrant communities in two of the largest urban areas of the United States is an achievement in itself, as is their sustainability, the stability of their staff and boards, the size of their budgets, and the strong reputation and public credibility they enjoy.

The networks have received prestigious awards that recognize their work as effective, systemic, strategic, and able to sustain results beyond individual efforts.[6] They also have a record of mission-specific achievements. For example, Immigrant Policy Network enrolled more than 60,000 families in an immigrant voter education and mobilization campaign for the 2000 elections, resulting in the registration of more than 200,000 new voters. Its advocacy campaigns to expand legal services and English classes for immigrants have earned millions of dollars of city and state funding. In the Midwest, Rainbow Network's petition campaign for INS reform collected more than 19,000 signatures, helping to ensure the creation of an Independent Monitoring Board to act as an INS watchdog group. By 2000, approximately 800 documented cases had been sent by the Independent Monitoring Board to members of Congress and the INS, documenting INS backlog and its effect on immigrants and refugees.

The scale of the results achieved by these two networks reflects the success of their leaders' work in managing the interorganizational collaboration essential to attain their network's goals. They serve as excellent sites to study how their leaders manage the paradoxical challenges of collaboration in networks.

## Findings: Addressing Collaboration Challenges by Managing Paradox

In exploring the challenges of collaboration, we distinguished between the inward and outward work of network leaders (Shortell et al. 2002). Inward work refers to the explicit effort to build, nurture, and maintain the network and to coordinate network members, that is, the task of building community. Outward work includes task-oriented behaviors to achieve the network's goals independently or through its members. As leaders tried to make things happen, they were confronted with managing paradoxical realities in both the inward work of collaboration among network members and also in the outward work of influencing target organizations. In this work, they found the means to ensure that both sides of the paradox were honored by addressing demands that appeared contradictory on the surface. In the process, they engaged in effective collaborative management.

Our inductive analysis of how leaders of the Rainbow Network and the Immigrant Policy Network managed competing demands in both their inward and outward work yielded six collaborative practices. An exploration of the implications of the practices for effective network management focused on their direct association to paradox. The collaborative practices represent the means by which the network leaders helped the members find direction, alignment, and commitment to advance their collective work (Drath 2001; McCauley and Van Velsor 2003).

## Managing Paradox to Facilitate Intranetwork Collaboration: Honoring the Competing Demands for Unity and Diversity

Network leaders had to both manage and maintain diversity, as a fundamental characteristic and the starting point of their networks. Leaders had to engage in deliberate work to build community in different ways. A shared "immigrant" identity was not enough to overcome all the differences. Areas of diversity within the member organizations of each network are . . . differences in goals, in ideology, in expected outcomes, in power, in levels of commitment, and in demographic composition or social identity (class, gender, race). These typical differences were amplified by the networks' defining focus and common cause—immigration—with its variety and multiplicity of member organizations responding to the needs of groups distinguished by ethnicity, religion, culture, or linguistics.

Immigrant Policy Network included service providers as well as organizations focusing on organizing or advocacy. Rainbow Network's members were all service providers, but the variety of their specialization ranged from health and aging, to serving the unique needs of individual immigrant communities, to responding to very specific problems such as HIV. Rainbow Network had member organizations with a couple of thousand clients, and others with as many as 20,000 clients a year, whereas Immigrant Policy Network included some organizations that annually had more than 800,000 Latino clients.

The advocacy director at Immigrant Policy Network recognized the potential for conflict, saying, "All of them don't really get along [but] they're all together because there is a strong consensus, you know, on the agenda, as it really brings people together." At Rainbow Network, the training director argued, "There's a lot of

politics . . . and to get everybody to agree [is] not easy." The diverse characteristics, strengths, goals, and resulting priorities of the organizations that constituted the network members made it hard to find the common ground that encouraged collaboration. Leaders' stories emphasized the network's need for a sense of community.

Creatively managing irreconcilable disagreements was one way to clear the way to common ground, as illustrated in this comment from Immigrant Policy Network executive director:

> We sometimes agree not to take positions on certain things, like I know school vouchers came up as part of our education work. . . . And different Board members made presentations, one in favor of us taking a pro-voucher position, another one in favor of us taking an anti-voucher position, and one in favor of us taking no position. And we wound up taking no position, because several of our groups would have walked. It would have really been a "make or break" issue for them, and we just decided that vouchers wasn't an important enough issue on our agenda for us to lose major players of the network over it.

This illustrates the artful management of inward work to promote collaboration: School reform included the contested issue of school vouchers. Ideological differences within the membership threatened the unity of the network as a whole around a key dimension of their school reform agenda. After carefully discussing all possible alternatives, and giving voice to those advocating each position, network members agreed to take no position, thus upholding the ideological diversity while finding unity in the way the decision was made.

Because conflicting views about vouchers did not get resolved, it could be argued that the outcome in this example was not ideal from a consensus-building perspective (Innes and

Booher 1999) or from an interest-based model of conflict resolution (O'Leary and Bingham 2007). After all, not taking action on an issue because of the fear of conflict could be viewed as a solution that has considerable costs. However, the outcome did represent a collective achievement when it is associated with the need to address the paradoxical demands for both unity and diversity. Agreeing to disagree over the issue without losing any member after engaging in the discussion, and clarifying that vouchers was not at the core of the coalition's work, were important sense-making outcomes of the carefully orchestrated process. Ensuring a process that gave equal airtime to each position meant that even those whose position did not win felt sufficient ownership of the outcome to stay. The process ensured that voice and loyalty would trump exit (Hirschman 1970). The final outcome of holding the network together was not a trivial achievement, even if the underlying source of potential conflict was not resolved.

Leaders and representatives in both networks praised organizational diversity and highlighted its importance to their work. Their diversity accounted for the network's strength. Rainbow Network's executive director acknowledged this when he said, "Because . . . what you and you [pointing at representatives of two member organizations] bring to the table . . . is what makes us strong. At least I try to foster that. And so far it has worked. . . . (*laughs*) So I think that if we have to take a magic formula, I think that's it." A cofounder of Immigrant Policy Network explained that internal diversity has "been one of the main reasons why the network has been so effective; and has been increasingly more and more effective . . . because whatever the process has been, we've been able for the most part, to bring so many different groups to the table that don't normally advocate together."

Diversity played a strategic role in helping the networks gain the leverage with the external organizations they wanted to target. The executive director of Immigrant Policy Network illus-trated this when he related, "We have all of these different groups coming, you know, with the shared message on these issues, and then they [actors of the target agency] all scratched their heads saying, 'So, Central American Refugee Center is . . . in on this with UJA and with? . . .' you know, and that's when they realize that they have to pay closer attention."

The need to honor diversity and unity required deliberate and strategic work from leaders in the coordinating unit of the networks. This work was enacted as collaborative practices that helped to manage the network.

## Addressing the Demands of Unity and Diversity

Confronted by the tensions that emerged from the demands for unity and diversity, leaders devised ways to generate the needed unity without threatening the needed diversity. To address paradox in the context of work inside the network, leaders in the network nurtured and facilitated member interaction, they paid attention to personal relationships, and they fostered openness and participatory processes.

### Facilitating Interaction

Members of both networks highlighted the importance of the facilitating role of network leaders in managing member interaction. Setting up a press conference, identifying and proposing immigration-related issues as the source for common work, and setting the structure and processes for interaction are examples of collaborative practices that leaders in the coordinating units used to address the unity and diversity paradox. These tasks signaled to network members that they shared a platform (the network) that embodied unity, or united action. At the same time, network managers were careful to not overshadow organizational members, avoiding a threat to their separate identity, thus guaranteeing the needed internal diversity.

In both cases, the network itself provided a unifying vision to the work of diverse organizations, and their leaders constantly and persuasively reminded network members of the need for interorganizational collaboration. In Rainbow Network, the leader in the network provided structure and took the lead in helping identify and frame the issues. In Immigrant Policy Network, the leader helped get things going and framed the issues appropriately but insisted on letting the members take front-stage in making the case on their own. As a member of Immigrant Policy Network observed about the network manager,

> She never does a press conference by herself. She's always looking for community voices, local community leaders to speak on it and she'll be just doing the emceeing . . . introducing people and just setting up the issues, but still setting up the kind of political framework that we want people to have.

We found that nurturing the process was a critical role for the network leaders—bridging the diversity of the network without reducing it. Rainbow Network members were extremely grateful to have someone constantly following up, setting up the stage, and looking after the small details. But more importantly, through nurturing activities, member organizations received a clear message that they were indispensable. As a member explained,

> It isn't that you were just invited, but I think [the network executive director] really nurtured that well, if you're not here, there is going to be something missing. And it started a trend of feeling like you all needed to contribute in order to make something as successful as it turned out to be.

At Immigrant Policy Network, participants appreciated the executive director's constant attention to the process and to facilitating the roles of organizations' leaders within it. A staff person said: "It is less about [the executive director] being a leader than nurturing other leaders and setting up the processes to nurture them." This, in turn, required cultivating relationships.

### Cultivating Personal Relationships

The value of the personal relationships formed between individual members of network organizations is expressed by a Rainbow Network member:

> The wonderful part of Rainbow Network is that I feel so comfortable calling any of the partner directors and saying, you know, "What do you do?" "How can you help me in this situation I'm struggling in," you know, and also, "What can I do for you?" And I think that's very special.

Nurturing relationships required plenty of energy and work, and the network manager played a key role. As one staff member said to the executive director of Rainbow Network, "And when you get a group that's diverse as we are, staying . . . fairly friendly and really not having a tremendous difference of opinion about who did this and who didn't do that, that's pretty good testimony to your ability to keep us all on track." In the case of Immigrant Policy Network, with more than 150 organizational members to manage, the executive director paid personal attention to each, as a network staff related, "She puts the time into building relationships with local [member] leaders." Attention and engagement through face-to-face conversations or a short personal note sent by mail illustrate this work. The bond created by personalized interaction can be then used as the basis for emotional management in the face of differences, as respect becomes the norm for the individuals involved. This comment by the Rainbow Network executive director points to the consequence of this work:

I think people show a level of respect acknowledging that we very rarely disagree on policies and positions, but we disagree on our strategies. And so you're able to diffuse the conversation and not have to get very . . . (*pause*) it's not as loaded a conversation then, because nobody is attacking somebody else for being a sell-out, or for not being politically, you know, committed, which is where all the emotional stuff comes in. And it's much more of a sort of clear-eye, hard-edge conversation about strategy.

Her approach suggests that the nurture of personal relationships simultaneously demonstrates respect for the need to value differences and the need to maintain unity.

**Promoting Openness and Participation**

Each network devoted substantial resources to ensure the participation of its member organizations in decision making at every level, showing them respect, giving them a sense of their value to the network, and establishing within the membership a relatively balanced distribution of power. . . .

Participation created ownership and a sense of adhesion among network members, thus promoting unity. This inward management task of building community therefore was useful in meeting the demands for unity and diversity. Rainbow Network's director was always "very careful about making sure that every single one of the agencies did take part and felt valued at the time," trying to ensure that they would feel comfortable. A staff member at Immigrant Policy Network commented, "It's been really essential for us to show that we care just as much about the Russian, Korean, Chinese, Haitian and south Asian votes as we do about the Latino vote," and as a consequence, "we've been able to maintain the sense of really, you know, multi-ethnic participation, and our agenda has always been inclusive."

Leaders in both networks made explicit efforts to neutralize the consideration of power in their networks' identity or operation. As a member reflected, "There doesn't feel like a dominance of power in Rainbow Network [so] that one group has more say than the other group." In the case of Immigrant Policy Network, the network manager was able to turn a difference that could produce conflict into a source of strength for the network, thus managing the unity and diversity paradox. She explains, "Instead of trying to take away power or suppress those that are powerful, you just elevate the emerging groups so that they're more on equal grounds. So you don't alienate, you know, some of the more established groups." The inclusive and participatory process kept these heterogeneous organizations together, allowing the added value of their diversity, while generating among them a sense of unity, ownership, and belonging. . . .

## *Managing Paradox to Facilitate External Collaboration: Engaging the Target Agency in Dialogue and Confrontation*

Network member organizations spend considerable energy on outward work aimed at influencing institutional targets. Stories from both networks revealed their relationship with the then Immigration and Naturalization Service (INS) as the primary focus of their external work. . . .

Knowing that an aggressive or confrontational campaign aimed at the federal agency would accomplish little, network leaders found room instead for collaboration with representatives of the INS on strategic issues. The interdependence that developed between the organizations allowed the networks to strategically confront individual representatives or the agency's policies when needed without alienating the INS and ending their dialogue. The advocacy director at Immigrant Policy Network described the engagement strategy of dialogue and confrontation as "Balancing . . . the power that you have and using that to push . . . in a combination of friendly meetings but also public dissing."

Immigrant Policy Network's executive director explained how using dialogue and confrontation helped to balance the ongoing interaction between her organization and its target:

> You're no good to anybody if you're someone's friend all the time. But you're also no good if you're the enemy all the time . . . how do you intelligently and ethically strike the balance between, you know, maintaining relationships being important to people, and at the same time being able to be critical of them, and getting them to do what you want them to do?

In practice, confrontation implied questioning the target agency regarding unacceptable behavior, inhumane policies, or unsatisfactory management of immigration-processing tasks. Rainbow Network would publicly challenge agency representatives by asking them "tough questions" and bringing them "cases" that put the onus on them. However, the coordinator of the Rainbow Network–led Independent Monitoring Board described the Board as "not really anti-INS." Rainbow Network's constant contact with the INS enabled it to build and sustain an informal collaborative relationship. A representative of a Rainbow Network member described this growing interdependence: "[Now the INS's] district director wants to come to our meetings. I think [this] is a sign that, you know, we must be doing something right [so] that he feels it's important to be at these meetings."

### Addressing Confrontation and Dialogue

We identified three collaborative practices that leaders in these networks used so as to manage the paradoxical demands of dialogue and con-

frontation with a powerful target. Leaders addressed paradox in the network's outward work by maintaining the credibility of the network; continuously acting both at the local and national levels; and promoting a multiplicity of personal and institutional relationships.

### Maintaining Credibility

Credibility played an important role in using dialogue and confrontation successfully, in two different ways. First, general credibility made the networks more reliable in the eyes of the target organization. The networks' threats were more powerful during confrontation and their offers for collaboration more convincing during dialogue. Immigrant Policy Network's credibility was established as it upheld its original claim to being politically nonpartisan: ultimately interested in defending its constituents rather than pursuing an electoral agenda. The executive director explained:

> Many other groups have gotten into this work saying they're doing it to be nonpartisan but then they start to get into it and hitch their star to certain [political] candidates, and I think we really found that just saying [to politicians], "No, sorry. You have to really go out and deal with immigrant communities. You have to figure out what it is they want. You know we're not going to broker this. You know you really need to be there and be relevant to them," made much more of the difference in the work.

Second, as the direct voice of immigrants, the credibility of the networks' representation of their constituents established their trustworthiness. A Rainbow Network founder, currently the director of one of its member organizations, described the potential for dialogue as follows: "We've [the Independent Monitoring Board] demonstrated that we have the credibility. . . . In fact, the INS regional local office director . . . has continuously sought out this body to communicate with . . . because he realizes that we're representing the voices of his customers." Credibility was a form of political capital that allowed networks to engage legitimately in confrontation without being discounted as a potential collaborator.

**Multilevel Working**

Network member organizations tended to focus their work and resources within the urban area that was their home. By extending its members' involvement in local issues into state and national contexts, the network's leaders leveraged the efforts of its membership to earn credibility and gain access to levels where policy was made. A Rainbow Network staffer working in the network's community building project noted: "These organizations, with our help, can put pressure in all the government levels . . . county levels, state levels, local levels. . . . So we can do a really good job over there."

Working beyond the local level gave them a view of their problems within a larger context, providing a perspective on their status in various jurisdictional policy arenas. This was especially useful to the networks in their efforts to keep up with the INS's own multilevel presence and operating arenas. The strategic importance of information multiplied when the sources were broadened, as illustrated in the comment of the director of training and legal service at Immigrant Policy Network: "We were the only group that knew what was going on because of our relationship with people in DC."

The depth and quality of information gained through work at multiple levels allowed these networks to combine the engagement strategies of dialogue and confrontation simultaneously at different levels within the same agency. For example, at one point the Immigrant Policy Network collaborated with its district INS to advocate for them in a policy issue involving the INS federal office. In this case, the district office could not resolve the problem of a large backlog of immigration cases affecting the city's

immigrants because of the lack of necessary support from the federal level. The Immigrant Policy Network decided to take up the issue itself, moving the action to the INS commissioner in Washington, DC:

> We could have done the easy thing of protesting down here [but] we wound up being an advocate for the [regional] district [INS office] right up to the level of the INS commissioner . . . we had already done all of our work with the district office to say, you know, "This is not about you, listen carefully to what we say in the media. We're not going to say that you guys are incompetent. . . . This is about the national issue with the backlog."

Confronting federal officials while maintaining dialogue with the district office represents an excellent illustration of how Immigrant Policy Network engaged simultaneously in dialogue and confrontation with the same agency, hence addressing the paradox. In doing so, they were able to build collaborative capacity vis-a-vis INS district representatives. At the same time, they were able to influence INS behavior.

**Cultivating Multiple Relationships**

Having relationships at different layers of an agency and with multiple actors in the environment controlled the risk (using the words of Immigrant Policy Network's executive director) of "burning bridges." The confrontational nature of the work was diffused by the network's credibility and was reinforced by the stability and quality of personal relationships at the operational level. "We always make sure we have good relationships in a few areas [of work relating to the INS] so that we can talk to senior people and we can say some good things about them," explained an Immigrant Policy Network staff member.

Relationships also guaranteed opportunities to reopen the dialogue regardless of the

FIGURE 16.1. The Management of Paradox

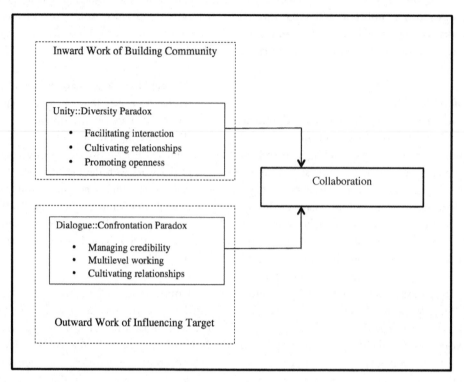

pressures of confrontation. Moreover, personal relationships countered the inconsistency of professional contacts that characterized the INS and many other government organizations and helped the Immigrant Policy Network maintain its relevance in a political environment characterized by internal mobility. Describing the uncertainty associated with a change of commissioner in the INS, the executive director said:

> There we would draw on our relationships with other groups around the country, the other immigration networks, and our partners nationally. Veronica goes to regular meetings down in DC that a lot of the groups have with the INS.

In sum, building credibility, acting at all jurisdictional levels, and cultivating multiple relationships were practices that network leaders used to strategically manage the paradoxical demands of collaboration with target organizations through dialogue while simultaneously engaging them in confrontation when necessary.

## Discussion: Linking Paradox and Collaboration

In our study, paradox is associated with the contradictory demands of the work of networks. . . . Paradox may be defined as "some 'thing' that is constructed by individuals when oppositional tendencies are brought into recognizable proximity through reflection or interaction" (Ford and Backoff 1988, 89). As leaders in the network tried to support the efforts of member organizations to make things happen, and as they supported work to influence the target, they were confronted by contradictory demands inherent in the work of interorganizational management that threatened their ability to collaborate. The nature of these demands required leadership practices that honored both sides of the paradox, while removing obstacles to collaboration. Figure 16.1 helps to summarize our findings and presents the overall logic of our argument.

In answering our research question on how leaders in successful networks manage collaboration challenges to make things happen, we found that leaders devised specific practices that helped them to manage paradoxical demands. The practices were used by network leaders in two contexts of the work where essential collaboration was threatened by conflicting demands: among the network's member organizations, and in the network's complex relationship with target agencies or organizations. Paradox emerged as a key feature of network management and addressing it became a means for network leaders to develop the interorganizational collaboration—inside and outside the network—needed to pursue the networks' goals. . . .

In our study, leaders used six practices in addressing certain paradoxes of network management associated with contexts of either inward or outward work. To address the paradox requiring both unity and diversity within the network, leaders strategically facilitated interaction, cultivated personal relationships, and promoted openness among network participants. To address conflicting demands for confrontation and dialogue with the target, they strategically managed the network's credibility, worked at various levels of action (multilevel), and cultivated multiple external relationships. The inward and outward work was done concurrently rather than sequentially. . . .

Our empirical study opens the door to further exploring the relationships between collaborative management, paradox, and network effectiveness. The theoretical lens that we used to examine our original question—How do leaders in successful networks address collabo-

ration challenges to make things happen?—influenced our use of a research framework that could include collective expressions of leadership. Viewing leadership as a collective achievement (Drath 2001; Ospina and Sorenson 2006) shifted empirical attention from an exclusive focus on leaders' behaviors to how behaviors were associated with collective constructions of leadership that emerged and shaped actions needed to address the complex requirements of organizing, this time in a network context (Drath 2001; Hosking 2007). . . .

As leadership scholars argue, new organizational forms in today's work environment, such as networks, require new understandings and enactments of shared, distributed, and collective leadership (Fletcher and Kaufer 2003).

Finally, the two paradoxes that motivate leaders to find collaborative practices in managing their network appear to be interdependent, in part because network management requires simultaneous attention to inward and outward work. In fact, the collaborative practices seem to support and build on each other. Advancement of the network's agenda depends in large part on the resources its members either pool together or provide separately. It also depends on the members' willingness and capacity to engage together in outward-oriented work. The effectiveness of outward work may depend on the quality of the internal coordination of the network and on the amount of trust developed via inward work.

In the same way, the complexity of work required for the network to attain its external common goals may influence its capacity to engage the complexity of the internal work necessary to sustain collaboration among its members. Lastly, addressing the external paradox of confrontation and dialogue may nurture or hinder the work to address the unity and diversity paradox: confronting an external actor may help unite network members, because outward conflict is related to internal unity. In the same way, disagreements regarding whether to confront or cooperate may turn into disunity within the network. . . .

## Conclusion

Even though they are inherently difficult to manage, networks have become a key organizational form in contemporary society and a popular mechanism of interorganizational governance. The managerial challenges associated with their sustainability and effectiveness are increasingly of interest for both theoretical and practical purposes. . . .

### Declaration of Conflicting Interests

The authors declared no conflicts of interests with respect to the authorship and/or publication of this article.

### Funding

The authors received support from the Ford Foundation and La Caixa Foundation for the research of this article.

## Notes

1. The 20 organizations emerged from a rigorous selection process, beginning with more than 1,000 nominations that were screened by national and regional selection committees. Colleagues or supporters nominated candidates. A national committee selected about 250 top candidates, who were then assessed by a regional selection committee using newly submitted essays from each nominee. They selected 5 primary and 4 secondary regional finalists. The 36 national semifinalists hosted site visits. The national committee reviewed visit reports and by consensus recommended 24 finalists, and 17 to 20 made the final cut. The nominee-to-selected ratio was about 50:1. The research team played no role in the selection process.

2. Immigrant Policy Network depends almost entirely on foundation support and does not accept government funding, while Rainbow Network relies on foundations, government, and corporations. The difference in sources of funding reflects differences in ideology.

3. We use pseudonyms to refer to both networks studied.

4. Gaskell and Bauer (2000) argue that in discourse analysis, a broad range of narrative data is more important than the absolute number of interviews for representativeness.

5. As of March 1, 2003, the former Immigration and Naturalization Service was abolished and its functions incorporated into the US Citizenship and Immigration Services of the US Department of Homeland Security.

6. For example, both received the prestigious Leadership for a Changing World Award in 2001.

## References

Agranoff, R. 2003. *Leveraging Networks: A Guide for Public Managers Working Across Organizations.* Arlington, VA: IBM Endowment for the Business of Government.

Agranoff, R., and M. McGuire. 2001. "Big Questions in Public Network Management." *Journal of Public Administration Research and Theory* 11: 295–327.

Ansell, C., and A. Gash. 2008. "Collaborative Governance in Theory and Practice." *Journal of Public Administration Research and Theory* 18: 543–571.

Borzel, T. A. 1998. "Organizing Babylon: On the Different Conceptions of Policy." *Public Administration Review* 76: 253–274.

Brandenburger, A., and B. Nalebuff. 1996. *Co-opetition.* New York: Doubleday.

Castells, M. 2000. *The Network Society.* Oxford: Blackwell.

Chetkovich, C., and F. Kunreuther. 2006. *From the Ground Up: Grassroots Organizations Making Social Change.* Ithaca, NY: Cornell University Press.

Clandinin, D. J., and F. M. Connelly, eds. 2000. *Narrative Inquiry: Experience and Story in Qualitative Research.* San Francisco: Jossey-Bass.

Connelly, D. R., J. Zhang, and S. Faerman. 2008. "The Paradoxical Nature of Collaboration." In

R. O'Leary and L. B. Bingham, eds., *Big Ideas in Collaborative Public Management,* 17–35. Armonk, NY: M. E. Sharpe.

Drath, W. 2001. *The Deep Blue Sea: Rethinking the Source of Leadership.* San Francisco: Jossey-Bass.

Federation for American Immigration Reform. 2003. *Census Bureau Data.* New York: Author.

Fletcher, J., and K. Kaufer. 2003. "Shared Leadership: Paradox and Possibility." In C. Pearce and J. A. Conger, eds., *Shared Leadership: Reframing the Hows and Whys of Leadership,* 21–47. Thousand Oaks, CA: Sage.

Ford, J. D., and R. W. Backoff. 1988. "Organizational Change In and Out of Dualities and Paradox." In K. S. Cameron and R. E. Quinn, eds., *Paradox and Transformation Toward a Theory of Change in Organization and Management,* 81–121. Cambridge, MA: Ballinger.

Gaskell, G., and M. W. Bauer. 2000. "Towards Public Accountability: Beyond Sampling, Reliability, and Validity." In M. Bauer and G. Gaskell, eds., *Qualitative Researching with Text, Image, and Sound,* 336–350. Thousand Oaks, CA: Sage.

Gray, B. 1996. "Cross-Sectoral Partners: Collaborative Alliances Among Business, Government, and Communities." In C. Huxham, ed., *Creating Collaborative Advantage,* 58–99. London: Sage.

Hirschman, A. O. 1970. *Exit, Voice, and Loyalty: Responses to Decline in Firms, Organizations, and States.* Cambridge, MA: Harvard University Press.

Human, S. E., and K. G. Provan. 2000. "Legitimacy Building in the Evolution of Small-Firm Multilateral Networks: A Comparative Study of Success and Demise." *Administrative Science Quarterly* 45: 327–365.

Huxham, C. 2003. "Theorising Collaboration Practice." *Public Management Review* 5: 401–424.

Huxham, C., and N. Beech. 2003. "Contrary Prescriptions: Recognizing Good Practice Tensions in Management." *Organization Studies* 24: 69–93.

Huxham, C., and S. Vangen. 2000. "Leadership in the Shaping and Implementation of Collaboration Agendas: How Things Happen in a (Not Quite) Joined-Up World." *Academy of Management Journal* 43: 1159–1176.

Innes, J. E., and D. E. Booher. 1999. "Consensus Building as Role Playing and Bricolage: Toward a Theory of Collaborative Planning." *Journal of the American Planning Association* 65: 9–26.

Keast, R. L., M. P. Mandell, K. A. Brown, and G. W. Woolcock. 2004. "Network Structures: Working Differently and Changing Expectations." *Public Administration Review* 64: 363–371.

Kelly, M. J., J. L. Schaan, and H. Jonacas. 2002. "Managing Alliance Relationships: Key Challenges in the Early Stages of Collaboration." *R&D Management* 32: 11–37.

Mandell, M. P. 2000. "A Revised Look at Management in Network Structures." *International Journal of Organization Theory and Behavior* 31: 185–209.

McCauley, C. D., and E. Van Velsor, eds. 2003. *The Center for Creative Leadership Handbook of Leadership Development.* San Francisco: Jossey-Bass.

Milward, H. B., and K. G. Provan. 2006. *A Manager's Guide to Choosing and Using Collaborative Networks.* Arlington, VA: IBM Endowment for the Business of Government.

Mizrahi, T., and B. B. Rosenthal. 2001. "Complexities of Coalition Building: Leaders' Successes, Strategies, Struggles, and Solutions." *Social Work* 46: 63–78.

Moran, T. T., and D. Petsod, eds. 2003. *Newcomers in the American Workplace: Improving Employment Outcomes for Low-Wage Immigrants and Refugees.* Sebastopol, CA: Grantmakers Concerned with Immigrants and Refugees and Neighborhood Funders Group.

O'Leary, R., and L. B. Bingham. 2007. *A Manager's Guide to Resolving Conflicts in Collaborative Networks.* Arlington, VA: IBM Center for the Business of Government.

Ospina, S., and J. Dodge. 2005. "Narrative Inquiry and the Search for Connectedness: Practitioners and Academics Developing Public Administration Scholarship." *Public Administration Review* 65: 409–424.

Ospina, S., and G. Sorenson. 2006. "A Constructionist Lens on Leadership: Charting New Territory. In G. Goethals and G. Sorenson, eds., *In Quest of a General Theory of Leadership,* 188–204. Cheltenham, UK: Edward Elgar.

Park, S. H., and G. Ungson. 2001. "Inter-Firm Rivalry and Managerial Complexity: A Conceptual

Framework of Alliance Failure." *Organization Science* 12: 37–54.

Provan, K. G., and H. B. Milward. 2001. "Do Networks Really Work? A Framework for Evaluating Public-Sector Organizational Networks." *Public Administration Review* 61: 414–424.

Ragin, C. C. 1992. "'Casing' and the Process of Social Inquiry." In H. S. Becker and C. C. Ragin, eds., *What Is a Case? Exploring the Foundations of Social Inquiry,* 217–226. New York: Cambridge University Press.

Reissman, C. K. 2002. "Narrative Analysis." In A. M. Huberman and M. B. Miles, eds., *The Qualitative Researcher's Companion,* 217–270. Thousand Oaks, CA: Sage.

Shortell, S. M., A. P. Zukoski, J. A. Alexander, G. J. Bazzoli, D. A. Conrad, R. Hasnain-Wynia, and F. S. Margolin. 2002. "Evaluating Partnerships for Community Health Improvement: Tracking the Footprints." *Journal of Health, Politics, Policy, and Law* 27: 49–91.

Tang, S. Y., and D. A. Mazmanian. 2008. *An Agenda for the Study of Collaborative Governance.* Working paper. University of Southern California, Los Angeles.

# PRINTING, POLITICS, AND PERSONAL PREFERENCES

*Andrew Zalasky and C. Kenneth Meyer*

Jersey Lake was an affluent community of about 100,000 residents, comfortably nestled in the coastal hills of Humboldt County forty miles north of a major urban center with a population nearing 850,000. The city had recently sold its old community hospital to a newly formed nonprofit called Sunnyside General Hospital (SGH). The sale of the hospital was seen as a triple win for the community. Jersey Lake was able to use the proceeds from the sale of the hospital to endow a community foundation, SGH would modernize the facility and improve patient care, and the city would be able to enter into an agreement with SGH to provide limited discounted or free medical services for city employees.

Gina Baxter, the marketing director at SGH, had served in her position for nearly a decade when Fred Colton joined the hospital as vice president of outreach services. Fred came from an area of the country characterized by stiff competition between health care providers in the search for patients.

He firmly believed in the necessity of establishing a recognizable brand name if SGH was to be successful in the rapidly changing health care market in Humboldt County. During staff meetings, he frequently emphasized the interconnectivity between brand names and products, pointing out that, colloquially, facial tissues and Kleenex, athletic shoes and Nike, lightbulbs and General Electric, and computer software and Microsoft were just as inseparable as bread and butter, peanut butter and jelly, bacon and eggs, or racing and NASCAR. Of course, the staff knew about the powerful phenomenon of brand-name identification in the marketing arena.

Gina did not readily submit to Fred's hard-driving tactics, but reluctantly, although inevitably, she saw the value in strengthening image and awareness—even in the absence of any serious local or regional competition. Upon direction from Fred, and under Gina's leadership, SGH implemented a new general health publication, *HealthWise*, to showcase the wonderful facilities, competent staff, and top-notch physicians they were offering to the Humboldt economic region.

In keeping with SGH's standard operating procedure, Gina used a procurement process to select local printers to produce, prepare for distribution, and mail the new publication, which was sent to approximately 75,000 households in the Humboldt metropolitan statistical area.

Three local companies with established printing, publication, and distribution histories promptly responded to the invitation-to-bid (ITB), which set out the objectives, specifications, and audit requirements that Gina had prepared with the help of SGH's public relations department and media staff in consultation with the department of finance and budgeting. Together they covered the major phases involved in ITB preparation: considering the alternatives to contracting-out; comparing in-house versus private-service delivery; writing the objective and performance indicators; and developing the penalties and incentives. Additionally, they emphasized: the bidder's responsiveness to the ITB proposal; the bidder's fiscal, staff, and facility capacity; the bidder's experience and reputation; and the total cost and cost per unit. They also knew that successful administration of the contract required monitoring it, performing a number of audits—pre-audit to post-audit—and completing a due diligence analysis and report on the firm that received the award.

Interestingly—although predictably, considering their similar size and technological sophistication—the three firms that responded to the ITB submitted almost identical quotes. Polytech Print Shop (PPS) submitted the lowest acceptable bid and was awarded the contract. With the contract complete, Gina and her staff directed their attention and energies toward producing the publication, and based on Fred's recommendation, they outsourced the design work to Cosmos Design, a company that was well known nationally for its fantastic imagination and artistic boldness.

Fred had become familiar with Cosmos Design's graphic and artistic capabilities after conducting a fair amount of business with them over the years he had been employed in a city adjacent to Washington Heights, where Cosmos Design was based. He also had an established professional and social friendship with principals of the firm and knew they could be trusted with meeting all of the contractual obligations. Fred informed Gina that he was confident that Cosmos would deliver a product that stood out and captured the reader's interest and attention. As the project unfolded, Gina found out that Fred had not exaggerated his belief in the company: what he had said about Cosmos Design proved to be true.

The first publication drew rave reviews and exceeded the expectations of SGH's CEO and board of directors. Some local design firms, however, were less than enthused to learn that the publication had been outsourced out of state. The local competition felt that SGH should buy and contract locally whenever possible.

Despite these rumblings, the new publication soon became the centerpiece of an aggressive marketing campaign steered by Gina and carried out by the marketing staff at SGH. There were a number of growing pains in the beginning as the staff became more familiar with issues of copy, design, style, and format. Since the staff was inexperienced with the new designs, it was expected that a few scheduled dates might not be met, and indeed, a few issues did not meet the targeted publication and mailing dates. Although these delays did not draw attention from the regional community, Fred noticed the irregularities and did not like what he saw. As a close supervisor, perhaps even a micro-manager, he brought the scheduling problem to Gina's attention and matter-of-factly told her, "Fix it and get on schedule now!"

As she managed sundry operations and activities, Gina well knew that missing one part of the production cycle had a cascading effect on the other parts, and her anxiety spiraled upward as she began to experience this problem. She was in a real bind, and Fred was not the managerial type who had empathy for those who could not meet established deadlines. On the one hand, she was working with local printers who she acknowledged were not as sophisticated or upscale as those she was working with in Washington Heights. After she told her best copy editor that the local contractors required more lead time than Cosmos Design did, the staff felt added pressure to have the final draft of the publication in the hands of the printer at least one month or more before the distribution date.

The production process was made even more difficult and problematic with Cosmos Design being on the other side of the country. Thus, the marketing staff did not have the luxury and convenience of running the corrected proofs across town for a quick face-to-face consultation. Instead, they had to compile the changes in a document that was emailed to Cosmos Design, which in turn had to decipher and make sense out of the changes, make the needed modifications, additions, and corrections, and email the corrected proof back to SGH. The distance factor usually added two or more days to the production cycle each time changes were noted and made. Gina wondered if Cosmos Design's cutting-age artistry and design work was worth all the problems it caused, especially since she could have sought out reasonably good work produced locally.

Being a steadfast manager, Gina attempted to make the best of a bad situation. As time went on, improvements were regularly made to the publication, and the community continued to express positive feedback. Fred, true to form, continued to maintain a scrupulously close eye on the publication. When the upcoming fall edition, once again, failed to meet the deadline for publication, he became uneasy.

During his weekly meeting with Gina, he told her in no uncertain terms, "We need to talk about *HealthWise*. You are well aware that this publication is once more behind schedule, and that is unacceptable. We raised the performance bar in this organization, and it's vital that you and others meet the timelines we've laid out. You must get a handle on this problem and get it corrected! This type of continued tardiness reflects poorly on SGH and diminishes what I am attempting to establish as a brand name. We simply must meet the expectations we've established among the clientele and community we serve at this hospital. There is no room for failure."

Gina looked directly at Fred and said, "I realize it's a bit behind schedule, but I want to be sure we're doing it the right way now so I don't have to steer the process every time. The delay isn't anything the public will notice, and it won't impact any of the programming we have scheduled up to now."

"That doesn't matter," Fred snapped. "I need to know exactly what the holdup is."

Once more, Gina carefully detailed and explained the publication and production process and all the things that could and often did go wrong, such as the distance factor, the unforeseen delays, the communication problems, staff turnover, and the lead time for printing. Fred listened intently to the scenario that Gina presented and jotted down a number of key words in the small notebook he customarily brought to staff meetings.

To her surprise, Fred then summarily concluded the meeting and said in a strident voice, "The contract with Cosmos Design has worked well. We should explore the need to find a printer who is not in our own backyard. We cannot afford to sacrifice our reputation when it comes to meeting deadlines."

"I can see the benefit in moving the job to someone who can turn it around more quickly," Gina replied. "But we have to keep in mind that politically that might not be a good move. If we move a big job like this out of Humboldt, the local printers will take notice, and we will be faced with a firestorm of controversy."

"We can't worry about what may happen politically," Fred sternly replied. "We have to meet our timelines, and I know Harper Printing can get the job done. They did it for me in my previous job, and we never experienced this comedy of problems that you just articulated. We'll meet this afternoon and put together a new ITB, and we'll see if the local printers can match what Harper Printing can provide."

Upon leaving the meeting and returning to her office, Gina felt a tug-of-war going on in her mind. She knew that Fred was close friends with the lead account representative at Harper Printing, and she knew that the ITB process would result in better pricing and quicker turnaround from Harper than the local contractors. She also had a firm understanding of local politics and had worked with community-based printers for ten years; the fact that they also edited and printed the local papers was worrisome. Aptly, she recalled the admonition of Will Rogers, the humorist and writer who cautioned against picking a fight with someone who buys ink by the barrel. SGH would now find out firsthand if contracting out of state would prove to be mightier than the pen.

## EXHIBIT 1: SUNNYSIDE GENERAL HOSPITAL CONFLICT OF INTEREST POLICY

### Article I: Statement of Policy

Trustees, officers, key employees (administrative staff and department directors), and medical staff members with administrative responsibility to Sunnyside General Hospital (SGH) shall exercise the utmost good faith in all transactions touching upon their duties to SGH. In their dealings with and on behalf of SGH, they shall be held to a strict rule of honesty and fair dealing between themselves and SGH. Acts related to SGH duties of such interested persons shall be for the best interests of SGH. Such persons shall not accept any gifts, favors, or hospitality that might influence their decisions or actions affecting the institution. They shall not use their positions or knowledge gained therein so that a conflict might arise between the interests of SGH and those of the individual.

### Article II: Periodic Reviews

To ensure that SGH operates in an ethical and businesslike manner, periodic reviews shall be conducted by SGH personnel or by outside consultants. The periodic reviews shall be conducted at least annually and, at a minimum, shall include the following subjects:

A. Whether compensation arrangements and benefits are reasonable and are the result of arm's-length negotiation
B. Whether acquisitions of other provider services result in inurement or impermissible private benefit
C. Whether partnership and joint venture arrangements are properly recorded, reflect reasonable payments for goods and services, further SGH's public purposes, and do not result in inurement or impermissible private benefit
D. Whether agreements to provide health care and agreements with other health care providers, employees, and third-party payers further SGH's public purposes and do not result in inurement or impermissible private benefit

## Questions and Instructions

1. Are Fred Colton's recommendations consistent with SGH's conflict of interest policy? Please explain.
2. Should Gina Baxter be concerned about the political fallout if a quicker turnaround is obtained from an outside printer? Please be specific.
3. If Harper Printing does receive the print job, how should Gina communicate the news to the local printers? Should she "massage" the message to try to maintain some semblance of political harmony? If so, how might she do so?

# SHOW ME THE MONEY

*C. Kenneth Meyer and Stacy Gibbs*

Gertrude "Gerty" Madison was astonished when she learned about the demographic statistics of Garmin County and its low per capita income, high unemployment, and high school dropout rate. She was aghast to find that Garmin had an out-county migration rate that was among the state's highest. The county's health indicators, such as its maternal mortality rate (MMR) and infant mortality rate (IMR), were similar to those of many countries in the developing world. Further, she was beginning to develop an intimate knowledge of the county's food security issues as she traveled around and learned that there were no food stores in the county at the scale of a Kroger, a Hy-Vee, or an Aldi grocery store.

Gerty had loved to return from college to visit her relatives who lived in Garmin and spend blissful weekends on the century-old farm that had been homesteaded by her great-grandparents—one that she had often romanticized as characteristic of rural life in general. But as a mature adult, her perspective had shifted and she wondered why Garmin had fallen so far behind adjacent counties on basic indicators of social well-being and quality-of-life measurements. In particular, why did such a low percentage of Garmin's high school graduates go to college and gain higher degrees?

Gerty couldn't believe that her own upper-middle-class upbringing had sheltered her from the plight of her family friends and a large segment of the county. She was ashamed to tell others about her belief that poverty, and its accompanying disarray, is but a mental abstraction. She told her friends at work that rural poverty is no disgrace, but it is inconvenient. And she chuckled with her colleagues about her belief in the variation on the golden rule: those who have the gold, rule.

She also remembered talking to a friend while she was once visiting relatives. Gerty had tried to get a "dipstick reading" on the prevailing economic conditions in Garmin County. Her friend, a trust officer at the community bank, had said, "Gerty, you can't improve on the biblical injunction—the poor will always be with us."

Seeing the concern on Gerty's face, the trust officer of the bank leaned back in her overstuffed burgundy executive chair and explained: "I have been in the banking business for nearly twenty years and have been through some good times and some bad times. I prefer the good times. The economy is really in the dumps right now, and we have tightened our terms for loans to farmers, ranchers, and small businesses. In fact, if you don't need a loan because your balance sheet looks good, we are happy to provide one. On the other hand, if you are in a financial pinch, forget it. We are running a bank, not a charitable foundation."

As Gerty reflected on her impressions of modern-day Garmin County—the robust flurry of anecdotes she had heard as well as the statistics she had consulted—she wondered if she had made the right decision in applying for the executive director position of the Garmin County Development Corporation

(GCDC), a small, nonprofit organization. Gerty had been reserved and tentative when she was actually offered the position, but taking on the executive director responsibilities would be a big step up for her in terms of responsibility and pay. Although a seasoned program manager, she would now have her leadership and administrative skills tested as she worked for an active seventeen-member board of directors.

The GCDC had applied to the state for a gaming license and was granted one for a newly opened riverboat casino. This meant that the Corporation would receive a large portion of the casino's profit each month, thus incurring a considerable fiduciary responsibility that would require careful daily management. As a condition of the licensure, as set forth by state code, GCDC was obligated to distribute this money or return it to the public in the form of grants. Gerty would be in charge of the "whole guacamole," as she told others, and she would have to create policies and procedures for the implementation of the grant program.

Her board of directors was composed entirely of men and was drawn from across the county; it included the mayor and a city council member of Arbor Lake, the largest city in the county; three bank presidents; three owners of real estate agencies; owners of two local insurance agencies; the owners of the two car dealerships; the owner of the local newspaper; two members of the water board; and the manager of the rural electric cooperative. The average tenure on the board was fifteen years. As she sized up the board, Gerty understood that it was a close-knit group and that she was going to have her first experience with a politically savvy and cohesive "good old boys' club."

The board members were very proud of the fact that they were mostly responsible for bringing the casino to the county. They bragged about the projected revenues that might be as high as $40 million a year. Because of their negotiations, the GCDC would receive 1.5 percent of these revenues per year—25 percent of which could be applied toward operations and 75 percent of which the GDCD was required to return to other nonprofit entities in the form of grants.

Every member of the board had his own idea on how the money should be granted out and was very vocal about it. Most importantly, the board members felt a collective ownership and stewardship over the funds it would receive from the casino and wanted a grant process that would be under their close scrutiny and control.

Gerty started creating a grant process by reviewing what other casino license-holders did with their monies. She reasoned that there was no sense in reinventing the wheel. Gerty scouted around and found a model for spending such monies that had been used by a similar-sized group for five years. After several discussions with the executive director of this group, she decided that, with a few modifications, this model could work well for the GCDC. The board created a subcommittee to work with Gerty on a model plan and present it to the full board.

Under the model, grant applications would only be accepted from 501(c)(3) nonprofit organizations or governmental agencies serving a charitable purpose located in Garmin County. It would also require a dollar-for-dollar cash match from the applicant. In other words, for every dollar requested from the grant program, the applicant would have to match it with a dollar of its own funds. A scoring system would be used to rate each application based on selected factors such as projected community impact, contribution to economic development, innovativeness of the project, and the number of people affected. Additionally, there was a maximum award amount of $100,000, and projects awarded had to be completed within twelve months. Applicants who received an award could not apply for another project from GDGC until the awarded project was completed. If an application was denied, the applicant had to wait at least six months before reapplying. Lastly, a subcommittee of the board would review all applications on a monthly basis and make recommendations to the full board for final approval.

Gerty was pleased with the process that she and the subcommittee collectively worked out and excited to present it to the board and begin the grant implementation process. The reaction from the board members, for the most part, was very positive, although they did suggest a few changes to the methods and criteria used in scoring the applications. Finally, after a cordial, if lengthy, discussion, the subcommittee's report was approved by a unanimous vote. It was determined that the board would wait six months to implement the grant program in order to have sufficient funds in reserve for the approved applications.

A year later, with six months of grant applications and awards tucked under her belt, Gerty felt that the grant program was functioning fairly well, although it had needed tweaking in a number of places. The subcommittee was performing well, and the board seemed to accept recommendations without much question. Most applications were for smaller projects that funded youth programs, recreation and parks programs, and beautification projects. Then an application was received from the Arbor Lake Street Department to fund a large portion of a citywide street reconstruction project. The subcommittee, using the scoring system that was in place, scored the application very high. The Arbor Lake city administrator, who wrote the application, had justified the project by emphasizing its impact on Arbor Lake's economic development with the beautification of the city and an increase in property values.

Despite the application's high score, the subcommittee had several problems with approving it. First, they did not think it was appropriate to use grant funds for a tax-supported entity. They also argued that the city received casino revenues as well, so why did the city need GCDC money?

In response, Gerty pointed out that the application fit all of the requirements that had been set forth and published by the board. She also asked the subcommittee to consider that this project would probably not take place without grant funding. Her arguments and justification were not convincing, and the subcommittee sent the application to the full board and asked them to consider the dilemma.

This was Gerty's first setback since becoming the executive director, and she felt a sense of personal defeat as she forwarded the application to the full board with strict instructions to complete the scoring sheet and be prepared to discuss the application at their next meeting.

The intervening month passed rather slowly, and Arbor Lake representatives contacted Gerty several times inquiring on the final disposition of their application for grant money. She was ready to get this political issue behind her and move on to more productive ventures. When the full board convened, Gerty was disappointed and frustrated to learn that the majority of the board, surprisingly, had not completed the scoring sheets. Additionally, most of the discussion centered on opinions instead of the factual information provided by the city administrator in the application. The Arbor Lake mayor and city council member, who were members of the GCDC board, were very vocal about the need for the project and argued vociferously for the approval of the application. They reminded the board of the financial commitment that the Arbor Lake council made each year to the GCDC. The board discussed the many pros and cons associated with the application and went on to approve it with a small majority. Gerty knew that, for the most part, the public would view the board's decision as a good thing, but she also knew that the board had bent to the pressure from Arbor Lake officials and that the approval was not solely based on the merit of the project.

News of the approval quickly spread through the county grapevine and opened the door for an onslaught of similar applications from many of the smaller cities. For instance, the Garmin County Board of Supervisors requested money for road maintenance equipment. The county hospital asked for a new ambulance. One of the smaller city governments in the county requested funds for a city paving project. All of the applications would have to be considered, and the subcommittee once more felt that they had to take all of the requests to the full board and let them decide.

The routine became normal for Gerty, and once more she stressed the importance of following the grant guidelines and using the scoring sheets to justify the board's decisions on the grant applications. She reminded the board of how important it was that they read the proposals and complete the scoring cards on each application prior to meeting as a group. Gerty told the board that they would be held accountable to the public for their decisions on how the grants were approved and that their credibility would be jeopardized if they had no valid justifications for their decisions. She further explained that she would be placed in a delicate and compromised position if the criteria for grant funding were not consistently followed. After all, she stated, she had to explain to some applicants why their applications were denied. She mentioned these concerns to the board because she knew that inconsistent decisions by the board would be talked about and cause great turmoil in the many local jurisdictions.

The next time the full board met, about half of the board members had completed the scoring sheets, but as Gerty quickly discovered, their ratings did not matter. The board members revisited the issue of funding governmental jurisdictions, and the questions and arguments did not differ much from their earlier reservations and concerns. In the end, the full board acted inconsistently in its funding decisions. The applications from the Board of Supervisors for equipment and from the smaller city government for paving funds were rejected. The request for a new ambulance for the county hospital was approved.

The board established a precedent of funding tax-supported entities when it approved the application for the Arbor Lake paving project and when it funded the new ambulance for the county hospital. Gerty knew that it would not take long for the public to figure out the reasoning behind the board's actions. Simply, two members of the GCDC board were from the city of Arbor Lake and three others were also on the county Board of Supervisors. To say that there was a conflict of interest was an understatement. Yet, Gerty was expected to make the board's decision fit the grant scoring and rating criteria.

---

### EXHIBIT 1: GARMIN COUNTY DEVELOPMENT CORPORATION (GCDC) GENERAL GRANT BACKGROUND AND INSTRUCTIONS

#### Garmin County Development Corporation (GCDC) Mission

The Garmin County Development Corporation (GCDC) is a donor-driven public foundation whose purpose is to improve the quality of life in our community through philanthropy.

The GCDC works to improve the quality of life for all by connecting donors with their passions, fostering links between community organizations, and convening local leaders to advance the common good. Increasing our community's connectedness includes building trust, civility, and volunteerism and encouraging informal socializing and civic engagement.

Making community connections builds on our remarkable tendency to reach out to one another and lend a hand to those in need . . . we're simply better together.

#### Leadership and Developmental Grants

Leadership and developmental grants are intended to advance GCDC's agenda and positively impact our communities in Garmin County. The GCDC's Grant-Making Committee is committed to strengthening our community by proactively responding to emerging community needs, trends, and opportunities. Therefore, GCDC allocates a significant portion of its discretionary dollars to fund grants.

##### Eligibility Requirements

Grants are made only to charitable organizations or causes with 501(c)(3) status or to governmental agencies serving a charitable purpose. Geographically, funding is limited to projects that will significantly improve communities in Garmin County. It is strongly recommended that organizations speak with GCDC staff prior to submitting a leadership grant letter of intent.

*Grant Cycle Timeline*

*First cycle:* The letter of intent is due on or before 4:00 PM on April
    4 of the current year.
*Second cycle:* The letter of intent is due on or before 4:00 PM on
    October 3 of the current year.

The GCDC will notify applicants of the status of their proposals within ten
business days after it is received. Proposals that advance in the process will
receive further instructions at that time.

*Documents Required*

Please submit the letter of intent along with the documents listed below:

- A copy of the 501(c)(3) designation letter of organization or fiscal sponsor, unless the organization is a governmental entity
- A projected budget for the project
- A list of the director on the organization's board of directors with
  contact information and email addresses

## Eligible Projects

The GCDC approves grant applications for projects that:

- Advance the initiatives included in the GCDC's leadership
  agenda (see the grant-making guidelines for more information).
- Include an opportunity for GCDC to participate in a "signature"
  program or project within the scope of the entire project.
- Demonstrate significant community impact, are broad and
  wide-reaching in nature, and are inclusive of the entire community.
- Include evidence of a strong statement of community need and
  broad-ranging community support and endorsement, demonstrated by a broad donor base and community buy-in.
- Show evidence of long-term community planning for the project
  and an organizational strategic plan that has been included in
  the project.
- Include a well-developed plan for evaluating success. Grant recipients may be asked to present project results to the GCDC
  Grant-Making Committee.
- Have an achievable plan to sustain the program well beyond the
  grant period.
- Recognize and celebrate our community's diversity and provide
  access for underserved populations. Show planning for outreach
  and accessibility to underserved populations.
- Demonstrate evidence of sufficient planning and organizational
  capacity to suggest a good opportunity for success.
- Show strong probability for leveraged funding from other sources.

In addition, funding will be most favorably considered for those organizations that:

- Build social capital
- Have not received a leadership grant in the prior year
- Have committed to meeting the "Principles and Practices for Charitable Nonprofit Excellence" identified by the State Nonprofit Resource Center

Specific examples of eligible projects include:

- New programs and projects that are the result of an expansion or building project (enhanced programming as a result of a capital project)
- Seed funding for a long-term community betterment project (annual festival)
- Projects that will enhance recreational or community economic development
- Programs or projects that will significantly impact emerging community needs, opportunities, and trends
- Projects that address a critical issue and build community connections and partnerships

The GCDC will not consider:

- Ongoing annual operating expenses
- Grants to individuals
- Sectarian religious programs
- Projects not serving residents of Garmin County

## Questions and Instructions

1. What role, if any, should members of the board play in reviewing grant applications from their own organizations? Please identify two grant-making bodies and contact them to ask for a copy of their conflict of interest policy, if it exists.
2. Do you think the grant program was structured in the most effective manner to address the social capital issues that Gerty discusses at the beginning of the case? Please explain.
3. Should taxpayer-supported organizations be eligible for GCDC grant funding? Would you differentiate between taxpayer-supported nonprofit organizations and local governments? Please explain.
4. Would you suggest any changes in the grant application criteria or scoring process? If so, what changes and why?
5. Do you think the makeup of the GCDC board of directors is sufficient, or would you suggest changes to the makeup of the board?

# PART VIII

# Budgets, Financial Reports, and Management Control

Budgeting, accounting, financial reporting, and management control are the most essential tools for responsible governance, accountability, planning, and management in nonprofit organizations. The budget document is "foremost a tool for maintaining financial accountability . . . a forum for establishing strategic goals and performance expectations . . . [and] a tool for holding administrators accountable for performance expectations."[1] "Budgeting is "a process which matches resources and needs in an organized and repetitive way so those collective choices about what an entity needs to do are properly resourced. Most definitions also emphasize that a budget is an itemized estimate of expected income and operating expenses . . . over a set time period. Budgeting is the process of arriving at such a plan."[2]

A budget is a plan, and the budget process is a planning process about what should happen in the future. The process of preparing budgets has evolved into forums for establishing strategic goals and performance expectations for an organization. "Budgets often represent the most important and consequential policy statements that governments or nonprofit organizations make. Not all strategies and plans have budgetary significance, but enough of them do and public and nonprofit leaders and managers should consider involving themselves deeply in the process of budget making."[3] Thus, "budgets serve as the public record of a community dialogue for improving organizational performance and management oversight. The budget is a tool for holding administrators accountable for performance expectations."[4]

Budgeting matches resources and needs in an organized and repetitive way so that collective choices about what an entity needs to do are properly resourced. "A budget is an itemized estimate of expected income and operating expenses . . . over a set period of time."[5] "In its most complete form, a budget is a compilation of the plans and objectives of management that covers all phases of operations for a specific period of time."[6] Budgets breathe life into mission statements and goals. Mission statements may speak about a wide variety of problems and opportunities that are of concern to the organization, but a budget divides an organization's finite resources among its competing needs and wants—its priorities. Budgets therefore transform an array of noble intentions and high ideals into the ability to act on a select set of problems or opportunities. In this sense, budgeting is an energizing function as well as a definitive governance activity.[7]

Budgeting is the "tool" that boards use to manage the numerous competing visions, requests, and—often—demands of client groups, patrons, donors, staff, trustees, government agencies, and community groups. Executives and boards give energy to their preferred policies and programs by allocating funds to them. Programs or initiatives may be the beneficiaries of increased funding, or they may have their funds reduced or eliminated.

A budget is also an organization's short-term financial road map that identifies planned expenditures and expected revenues. It requires decisions such as whether the organization should borrow or draw down savings to finance a program expansion, or whether it should eliminate a program that is proving less effective than hoped. In a balanced budget, revenues and expenditures are equal. A budget deficit identifies the need to borrow, draw down funds from savings, or increase fundraising. A budget surplus allows funds to be budgeted for new activities, to be set aside for future uses, or to be used to reduce a former year's deficit.

## Budgets as Financial Operating Reports and Management Control

After a budget has been adopted by the board of trustees, it continues to serve two vitally important purposes: (1) as a governance and accountability tool for the board and the executive director; and (2) as a management tool that provides an executive director and the management staff with discretion— the freedom to run the organization with some flexibility, within limits established in the budget.

### Budgets as a Governance and Accountability Tool

Budgets are the basis for an organization's financial operating reports, which almost always contain at least two columns of numbers: budgeted income and expenditures, and actual income and expenditures. When an executive director and the trustees know the shortages and surpluses (the over and under gaps) between budgeted and actual income and expenditures, they can exert management control over operations.

Most boards of trustees spend considerable time reviewing and stewing over financial operating reports because financial accountability is a fundamental governance function. All too often, however, trustees spend too much time on the details of budgets and operating reports rather than on the organization's overall financial status and financial trends and warning signals.

### Budgets as a Source of Management Flexibility

The board should leave "space" for the executive director and staff to make day-to-day management decisions without trustees second-guessing their moves.[8] Program managers should not need to obtain board approval to make routine expenditures. This degree of micromanaging is inefficient, communicates distrust, creates an undesirable working environment for staff, and wastes time. Budgets and financial operating reports give managers the freedom they need to act responsibly within parameters set by budgets at the start of the year and accounted for in financial operating reports as the year progresses. They establish the limits of a manager's discretion to spend certain amounts of money for different categories of expenditures without prior approval.

## Accounting, Financial Reports, Management Control, and Accountability

The primary sources of revenue for nonprofit agencies are (1) private contributions in the form of individual donations, corporate gifts, and foundation grants; (2) public support (government grants);

(3) membership fees; and (4) payments for services (commercial activity) in the form of user fees, government contracts, and the sale of products and services.[9] Each revenue source offers a different set of advantages and disadvantages.[10] Each also requires a nonprofit to be able to manage and account for the funds both legally and ethically (see Part V).

Accounting is the process of recording the financial information that is presented in financial reports. "Because nonprofit organizations enjoy numerous financially lucrative privileges and benefits . . . , they must be able to demonstrate that their fiscal houses are in order. Board members are ultimately responsible for these organizations and must be able to read financial statements and be aware of reporting requirements and fiscal systems."[11] In order to implement an effective budgeting program, an organization must have an efficient financial system in place. This includes accurate financial data, timely and understandable financial statements that meet the organization's needs for information, actual versus budget figures for the period, and an annual audit by an independent certified public accountant (CPA) firm.[12] Murray Dropkin and Allyson Hayden's "Types of Nonprofit Income: Financial and Cash Flow Management Considerations" is reprinted here to help nonprofit officers become fiscally responsible stewards.

Financial reports also inform management and the board about the organization's financial status and the need for corrective actions. Without these, the trustees and management cannot effectively govern. A single system comprising budgets, management, accounting, and evaluation is essential for the health of a nonprofit organization. Despite the importance of such a system, however, "financial analysis and managerial control remain among the most difficult areas for managers and directors [trustees] of nonprofit organizations to conquer."[13]

Few individuals are recruited to serve on boards because of their skills or experience with finances. Particularly in smaller nonprofits, few trustees are educated or experienced in financial analysis or management controls. Accountants and increasingly savvy executive directors are the exceptions. They are often recruited onto boards and to the CEO position in hopes that they will take responsibility for financial information and decisions. If they do, many of the other trustees would gladly leave to them all responsibility for budgets and finances, preferring to devote their time and energy instead to the organization's programs, clients, fundraising, or public relations. Yet this represents a violation of a fundamental board member responsibility. "Attaining a balance between sober financial management and the creation of enlightening services is far from easy."[14]

As we emphasized in Parts I and II, trustees are legally and ethically obliged to account for an organization's actions and assets. They cannot avoid these responsibilities without risking individual and collective liability. Thus, they do not have a choice. A rudimentary understanding of nonprofit financial management is required. Understanding the basics of accounting, budgeting, financial reporting, and management control procedures and systems is a primary instrument of responsible governance and accountability.

## Readings Reprinted in Part VIII

In the first reading, "The Underpinnings of Financial and Fiscal Operations," Dale Swoboda and Georgalu Swoboda explain the importance of maintaining management control and accountability for funds that flow through a nonprofit organization. Although financial subjects may seem dry or boring to those who want to "make a difference" or work hands-on in a community, it is foolish to ignore the importance of finances. Tending to finances, tracking income and expenditures, and setting fiscal and financial goals are tasks as crucial to the success of a nonprofit organization as they are to a business. "No organization can operate without money."[15] In addition to keeping the organization solvent, having a firm grasp on financial matters is essential for nonprofit boards and executives who want to make plans and minimize operational disruptions. "Timely [financial] infor-mation . . . is essential for managers to make choices about services they provide."[16]

Swoboda and Swoboda's framework includes four components—budget, management, account-ing, and evaluation—that are interlocked: neglect in any one of these areas will negatively affect all the others. Moreover, each component must be integrated into a nonprofit organization's strategic plans and day-to-day operations. The strength of Swoboda and Swoboda's analysis is their expla-nation of how finances are directly connected to the viability of a nonprofit organization and its ability to achieve the goals related to its mission.

Murray Dropkin and Allyson Hayden's "Types of Nonprofit Income: Financial and Cash Flow Management Considerations" presents a much-needed discussion of the resource considerations that affect nonprofits and their cash flows. Although there is much in the academic and practitioner literature about grants, contracts, business ventures, and the like, fiscal management issues are usually only touched upon, if they are mentioned at all. Yet contemporary nonprofit executives are expected to be accountable for the proper use of resources and for the results they achieve in using them. This is not possible without sufficient awareness of the many considerations that accompany various streams of funding. In addition, financial pressures create conditions that require nonprofits to become much more creative in their ability to expand their revenue portfolios and, in turn, much savvier in accounting for new revenue streams.

The authors untangle the confusing array of income flows that may be received or earned by a nonprofit and discuss the impacts of each on budgeting and reporting obligations. Nonprofit exec-utives must be able to recognize the implications of these impacts when pursuing various sources of income and consider how information will be documented in the organization's financial reports.

Dropkin and Hayden classify three types of income identified by the Financial Accounting Stan-dards Board (FASB), the body responsible for issuing accounting standings in the United States for nongovernmental entities: unrestricted net assets, temporarily restricted net assets, and permanently restricted net assets. They then systematically consider the implications of the most common donated income and resources received by nonprofits, including grants, donations, gifts and contributions, membership dues, and special fundraising income.

For example, grant income may require matching funds, whether a cash match, an in-kind match, or a combined match. "To avoid violating the grant agreement, organizations must comply with all matching requirements."[17] "In addition, a nonprofit's agreement to provide a program matching share usually becomes an auditable compliance requirement."[18] The authors show that financial planning for grant funding and compliance requires forethought and should not be entered into without consideration of the sources from which matching funds will be obtained.

The authors also provide information about managing earned income, including trade or busi-ness activities, sales of assets, program service fees, income from fees paid by government agencies, and asset-generated income.

## Case Studies in Part VIII

In "Throwing the First E-Stone," a financial officer is embarrassed to find that his practice of "surfing the web" at the office has come to the attention of the board of directors. Is this retaliation for an across-the-board budget cut? The reader is asked to analyze the situation and offer suggestions for dealing with workplace activities that may be viewed as wasteful and inefficient. In the second case, "When the Funding Stops," the reader is asked to consider a variety of options when confronted with an experience that many nonprofit managers will face—trying to manage an organization and "make payroll" when revenue streams do not flow according to plan. For many nonprofit organizations, the scenario in the case presents an all-too-familiar and frustrating set of budgetary circumstances.

# Notes

1. Robert L. Bland, *A Budgeting Guide for Local Government,* 3rd ed. (Washington, DC: International City/County Management Association Press, 2013), 2.

2. Jerry L. McCaffery, "Budgeting," in *The International Encyclopedia of Public Policy and Administration,* edited by Jay M. Shafritz (Boulder, CO: Westview Press, 1998), 294.

3. J. M. Byson, *Strategic Planning for Public and Nonprofit Organizations: A Guide to Strengthening and Sustaining Organizational Achievement,* 4th ed. (San Francisco: Jossey-Bass, 2011), 294.

4. Bland, *A Budgeting Guide for Local Government,* 2.

5. McCaffery, "Budgeting," 294.

6. Blackbaud, "Financial Management of Not-for-Profit Organizations," *Financial Management White Papers* (Charleston, SC: Blackbaud, October 2011), 2.

7. See Part I, "Governance of Nonprofit Organizations."

8. Robert N. Anthony and David W. Young, "The Management Control Function," in *Management Control in Nonprofit Organizations,* 7th ed. (New York: McGraw-Hill/Irwin, 2002).

9. Matthew M. Hodge and Ronald F. Piccolo, "Funding Source, Board Involvement Techniques, and Financial Vulnerability in Nonprofit Organizations," *Nonprofit Management and Leadership* 16, no. 2 (Winter 2005): 171–190, 174.

10. A. C. Brooks, "Public Subsidies and Charitable Giving: Crowding Out, Crowding In, or Both?" *Journal of Policy Analysis and Management* 19, no. 3 (2000): 451–464.

11. Thomas Wolf, "Financial Statements and Fiscal Procedures," in Thomas Wolf, *Managing a Nonprofit Organization,* updated 21st-century ed. (New York: Free Press, 2012), 207–233, 209.

12. Edward J. McMillan, *Not-For-Profit Budgeting and Financial Management,* 4th ed. (Hoboken, NJ: Wiley, 2010), 1.

13. Regina E. Herzlinger and Denise Nitterhouse, "A View from the Top," in *Financial Accounting and Managerial Control for Nonprofit Organizations,* edited by Regina E. Herzlinger and Denise Nitterhouse (Cincinnati: South-Western, 1994), 8.

14. Ibid., 2.

15. Dale Swoboda and Georgalu Swoboda, "The Underpinnings of Financial and Fiscal Operations," in Dale Swoboda and Georgalu Swoboda, *Managing Nonprofit Financial and Fiscal Operations* (Vienna, VA: Management Concepts, 2009), 9–37.

16. Ibid., 14.

17. Murray Dropkin and Allyson Hayden, "Types of Nonprofit Income: Financial and Cash Flow Management Considerations," in Murray Dropkin and Allyson Hayden, *The Cash Flow Management Book for Nonprofits* (San Francisco: Jossey-Bass, 2001), 7–20.

18. Ibid., 11.

## CHAPTER 17

# The Underpinnings of Financial and Fiscal Operations

DALE SWOBODA AND GEORGALU SWOBODA

## The Importance of Financial and Fiscal Administration

Money is vital to all organizations and individuals. Money means a great deal to people. Money is the marker for all things. No organization can operate without money. No organization in the nonprofit sector has ever had enough money to do all of the things it wanted to do and is commissioned to do. What does all this say about the role of nonprofit organization (NPO) finance?

Financial and fiscal administration determines the quality of service that can be provided to a target community. At the end of each fiscal year, the people responsible for financial and fiscal operations determine which areas need to be funded for the next fiscal year, and then the budgeting plan is created accordingly. Financial and fiscal managers try to make sure that an organization anticipates mission success and failure and that it minimizes operational disruptions. Timely information on the status of programs is essential for managers to make choices about services they provide. Financial

and fiscal administration systems provide the means for managing and ultimately delivering those services. Nonprofit financial administration, then, is concerned with how money is raised and spent by board members, volunteers, and professional administrators.

## The Financial and Fiscal Administration Network

Good financial management today means you have to do the following:

- Invest wisely.
- Prepare annual financial statements that routinely receive clean audit opinions.
- Pay your bills on time.
- Collect what is owed you.
- Implement and maintain meaningful management standards.
- Reduce the number of audit findings.
- Ensure that your major internal controls are known and used.

FIGURE 17.1. **The Financial and Fiscal Administration Network**

The Whatcom Council of Nonprofits (2006) offers the following eight best practices for nonprofits in the area of financial management:

- Generating sufficient revenue
- Tying the budget to outcomes
- Maintaining the board-approved budget
- Proper filing of legal financial documents
- Maintaining accurate records according to accepted accounting rules
- Establishing adequate annual internal controls
- Periodic reporting to managers
- Maintaining a diversified funding base[1]

To reach the state of good financial management, an organization should follow an ideal as close as possible and strive to accomplish fiscal and financial administration goals. A financial and fiscal administration network contains the following four major functions that are framed by the strategic plan (see Figure 17.1).

The network is more than technology. It includes all processes, plans, and participants involved in the financial operations of an organization. The interlocking aspects of the four functions are important and can be seen in Figure 17.1. Equally important is how the functions should be integrated. As shown in the figure, theoretically speaking, the strategic plan surrounds the functions and responsibilities of the financial and fiscal administration network. The network consists of several components: a base (strategic plan); four functions/responsibilities (budget, management, accounting, evaluation); and six two-way flow arrows. When a component of the network depicted in Figure 17.1 is deficient or not working well in an organization, it impedes achievement of that organization's goals. The organization works best when all the components of the network are in place and working well.

A strategic plan, of course, is the base upon which the other components of the financial and fiscal network operate. It should drive and explain why the other functions operate as they do. It explains the vision, mission, plans, goals, objectives, and expectations of where an organization wants to be in both the long term and the short term. The annual budget is a reflection of where an organization is being led.

A fiscal year for any organization begins and ends with the budget. The budget is the process where decisions are made, where plans are developed, and where policies are set in motion for a year or for another prescribed period of time. For that year or the prescribed time period, the budget function controls financial decisions and operations. Note in the figure the two-way arrows between the various functions. The budget function links directly to the three other functions, both driving them and responding to them. The budget contains the standards under which the other functions operate.

Managers use budget standards and accounting reports to fulfill the desired outcomes of an organization's mission. Managers need to operate the financial and fiscal system and make sure that the people they supervise operate within the prescriptions of the budget. Managers are also responsible for providing accurate information for the accounting function and the audit/evaluation function. It is a function that cannot be isolated in the way the other functions can. Management is pervasive and is the application—to all functions—of the guidance set out in the strategic plan.

The accounting function provides both control over finances and information about the budget to managers and to auditors. Accounting for and reporting on how dollars are used are especially important in most NPOs, where grants require accounting for special funds that limit the use of money. Accounting information is necessary for auditing and evaluation in order to ensure that accounting was done properly and that the numbers themselves are accurate.

The evaluation function provides assessment in the form of financial and management audits and program evaluation, both of which feed back into the budget and the strategic plan and often lead to adjustments to both the budget and the strategic plan. The evaluation function is where course corrections are identified and developed for consideration in both the present and future periods of time. Managers are subject to audit and evaluation results. They also receive feedback from the results of audits and evaluations. What they learn should guide them as to how to improve management of their budgets.

## How and Where Does the Network Fit Within an Organization?

An NPO must look at its mission and goals, short- and long-term strategic management and planning, and often the organization must make an intelligent estimate of how much funding will be needed (creating budgets to fulfill these needs), always searching for new and better ways of achieving its financial goals. This is obviously an ongoing process.

For-profit organizations operate with the mission to maximize the wealth of their shareholders by selling goods and services for a profit. In this context, financial analysis and planning

for short-term gain is crucial to the organization's success. NPOs, as part of the social and cultural infrastructure, are mission-driven. Responsibility, both cultural and social, and creation of a social infrastructure are of primary concern, and financial planning is therefore centered on financing the organization's needs so it may continue to serve the community.

Keeping careful track of financial resources is such a vital element of successful management that no one questions its necessity, yet the diversion of resources away from direct mission accomplishment in order to support the financial function is extremely hard for members of an organization to accept. Unfortunately, however, the books of an NPO do not keep themselves, and the price of good financial management tools remains steep. Bad things can happen when an organization does not find the time and the means by which to sharpen its financial control.

In many NPOs, the commitment to mission is so pervasive throughout the culture that most staff, except for the accountants and top executives, view financial and fiscal management as a necessary evil that frequently inhibits the realization of greater ideals. And that is only if the staff ever thinks about financial and fiscal management at all. The reality, however, is that to be effective at its mission, an NPO needs to integrate the principles of financial and fiscal management into all aspects of operations.

An effective financial and fiscal administration network will contribute to financial success. One of the great difficulties in organizations is the access to financial information. Modern automated systems notwithstanding, there are numerous horror stories about what can happen when one section of an organization does not communicate with the others. In the worst case, the automated system itself may be the horror if it does not provide adequate communication. In an organization where staff members receive only quarterly reports, which may not be compiled until a month after the quarter has closed, four full months may have passed before a problem (for example, a program with actual revenue far below budgeted projection) can be detected and acted upon. Too great a delay in responding to financial management problems can cost NPOs unnecessary expenses.

Monitoring the budget is roughly the same in both the profit and nonprofit sectors. The difference in the nonprofit sector is often the inflexibility of the use of funds, especially those funds coming from granting organizations. Unused money cannot be transferred easily to other uses. The perspectives of the public, nonprofit, and for-profit sectors differ somewhat in perception and in nomenclature, but the theories, concepts, goals, and even the outcomes are quite similar.

The choice of functional emphasis can have a serious impact on an organization's ability to carry out its mission. For example, for many years, the leaders in an organization focused solely on how money was raised and not how it was spent. Rewards, both symbolic and financial, were based on reaching financial objectives such as fundraising and budget goals. When the board decided to give rewards based on the quality of the programs provided and mission outcomes instead of financial performance, the staff argued for higher budgets that included more money for programs and more money to hire qualified program staff. It is the role of financial and fiscal administrators, through the guidance of the strategic plan, to find an appropriate balance between financial objectives and appropriate spending on mission.

## Value, Risks, and Rewards in Financial and Fiscal Administration

There is a fishbowl factor that all sectors of the economy must be concerned about in managing finances: many stakeholders are watching. In many organizations in the nonprofit sector, there is a need to integrate the various sources of funding sought in order to be able to meet the all-important mission. It is the job of the finan-

cial management system to make sure that the money is taken in and sent out to where it needs to go. As in any other aspect of an organization, professional leadership makes the difference in creating and maintaining an effective finance system. The financial manager is responsible for the overall fiscal functioning of the organization. Organizations either do not exist or, at the least, do not exist efficiently and effectively without an integrated financial and fiscal managerial network that includes accounting, management, and evaluation of financial operations and outcomes. The US Office of Management and Budget has stated that "financial management systems must be in place to process and record financial events effectively and efficiently, and to provide complete, timely, reliable and consistent information for decision makers."[2]

More than likely, an organization without an integrated financial and fiscal administration network would experience significant waste, not meet basic needs, and be in a poor management position that would affect everything from balancing the books to the morale of the organization's personnel. Many NPOs are experiencing these conditions. An integrated financial and fiscal managerial network ensures an organization is free to concentrate on its objectives without finance being a showstopper. When one function is not being addressed adequately, or is even left out, an organization can end up in chaos. Some organizations are lucky and succeed in spite of ignoring or undervaluing one of the four functions of an integrated financial and fiscal administration network. Clearly, you can have all four financial functions in place and value them all, but if one is ignored, it affects all parts of an NPO.

## Board Member Financial and Fiscal Responsibilities

People who serve on NPO boards provide a great service to civil society. They deserve to be honored for the time they spend on behalf of NPOs and the energy they expend, because they do it generally for free. Board members are expected to make an annual contribution to the NPO they oversee or to personally identify or solicit funds for the NPO from outside sources in order to demonstrate their commitment to the organization.[3] This *give, get, or open doors* responsibility is becoming prominent in the nonprofit sector. The board has several fiduciary responsibilities that include:

- Approving comprehensive written financial policies for revenues, purchasing, accounting, investing assets, reserve funds, salaries and benefits, and all financial activities
- Passing a budget that meets the organization's needs and overseeing the budget they approve
- Ensuring that an accurate financial audit occurs

Board members take on a certain amount of financial risk in accepting their roles as directors or officers of the organization, although liability is limited by state laws. Their fiduciary responsibility requires them to exercise diligence toward the financial health of their organizations.

In the case of NPOs, business skill alone does not guarantee effective performance in a nonprofit board. Of what use is business experience on a nonprofit or governmental board? Bottom-line thinking is useful in a business setting, where the demands of the marketplace are predetermined and the board's responsibility is to maximize income and minimize inefficiency. John Carver tells us that in the case of a nonprofit board, however, "the board must substitute for the rigors of the marketplace."[4] It is the board that has the legal and moral responsibility to set the limits and make sure its policies are carried out as they were designed. It is its job to understand the marketplace in which the NPO operates and to know the needs of the clients.[5]

Board members are often chosen for strategic reasons, not necessarily because of their interest in the organization in question. Many are chosen because they may be able to bring in funding, some are chosen because they are powerful in the community, others are selected because they are high-ranking public officials, and still others seek an appointment to a board. Board selection is a very political process.[6]

## Staff Member Financial and Fiscal Responsibilities

Delegation and oversight are demanded of NPO boards. Individual board members can help staff when the time comes, but they cannot be the implementers of their own policies. In most cases, board members have functions and responsibilities outside the NPO. Managers and program people are responsible for implementation of policy. The administration of financial and fiscal functions is especially complex, and board members, who generally come from a cross section of professions, need their NPO director to spend time training them on how the mission, strategic plan, programs, and budgets relate to one another. Regardless of how that is done, an organization's director and the staff he or she supervises are delegated the primary responsibility of carrying out the financial directives and policies of the board. Much of the authority that gets delegated is spelled out in state statutes, incorporation papers, bylaws, and other documents. Where such authority is not clearly understood, or where specific responsibilities need to be clearly spelled out, written policies need to be drawn up. This process begins with the simple yet important financial decision about who may sign a check and for what amount.[7]

## Volunteer Responsibilities

While volunteers are not generally given responsibilities with the revenues and expenditures of the NPOs, they provide services to them and do have a major function. They save the organization money and provide expensive services that NPOs cannot afford to purchase. In 2006, the hourly value of volunteer time was estimated to be at a national average of $19.51, according to *Independent Sector.*[8] Volunteers contribute to the productivity of the nonprofit sector by providing accounting, administrative, fundraising, event management, communications services, and client supervision expertise. It is probably not an exaggeration to say that the nonprofit sector would not have achieved the success it has without the valuable services of volunteers.

## Vital Internal Factors Affecting NPOs

Leadership is probably the key to success for any organization in any sector of the economy. In addition to leadership, there are three other factors, in terms of financial and fiscal administration, that the modern organization must rely on, especially as they apply to the generation of revenues and spending of resources. The factors are *ethics, communication,* and *technology.* Leaders and managers must concentrate on these factors because of several highly scrutinized financial scandals that affected not only corporations like Enron, WorldCom, and others, but also such well-known NPOs as the United Way, the Rainbow Coalition, and the American Red Cross. All of these organizations became subject to scrutiny in the 1990s and the early part of this century for failing to maintain their integrity.

### Ethics

Many NPOs operate under an ethics and accountability code to which board and staff members are expected to subscribe. To operate under a shared understanding of ethics is in the best interests of any organization, and doing so will help any organization meet its mission and goals. It is extremely important for NPO boards

and staff to establish ethical and communication policies and philosophies to establish a system of trust. If done correctly, stakeholders will gain and maintain trust in the organization. NPO staff members must know the chain of command.

An excellent and relevant code of ethical principles is that of the Association of Fundraising Professionals (AFP). AFP members aspire to:

- Practice their profession with integrity, honesty, truthfulness, and adherence to the absolute obligation to safeguard the public trust.
- Act according to the highest standards and visions of their organization, profession, and conscience.
- Put philanthropic mission above personal gain.
- Inspire others through their own sense of dedication and high purpose.
- Improve their professional knowledge and skills, so that their performance will better serve others.
- Demonstrate concern for the interests and well-being of individuals affected by their actions.
- Value the privacy, freedom of choice, and interests of all those affected by their actions.
- Foster cultural diversity and pluralistic values, and treat all people with dignity and respect.
- Affirm, through personal giving, a commitment to philanthropy and its role in society.
- Adhere to the spirit as well as the letter of all applicable laws and regulations.
- Advocate within their organizations adherence to all applicable laws and regulations.
- Avoid even the appearance of any criminal offense or professional misconduct.
- Bring credit to the fundraising profession by their public demeanor.
- Encourage colleagues to embrace and practice these ethical principles and standards of professional practice.
- Be aware of the codes of ethics promulgated by other professional organizations that serve philanthropy.[9]

## Communication

Both external and internal communications are vital to financial success in an organization. While fundraising is clearly more important than many other functions, it should not be the only contact an NPO has with stakeholders. Letting the community know the status of the financial condition can be helpful in fundraising efforts. Nonprofits operate in a fishbowl, so they should strive to be open organizations in order to create appropriate relationships with funding organizations, supporters, clients, and all other stakeholders. Without effective communication to all users, serious problems can ensue. Management too often informs the staff of important commitments and changes after they occur, which results in frustration and resentment. Staff members need to not only be aware of changes prior to implementation, but be made part of the change management whenever possible.

In their book *Financial Management for Nonprofits,* Jae Shim and Joel Siegel write, "Financial information should be recorded, reviewed, summarized, and reported."[10] While information hoarding may be a sort of power ploy, none of us are invincible, and unforeseen events may occur. In the event of an emergency, someone needs to be able to continue the mission of the agency. In such an emergency, or in the event of the unavailability of the person with the information, someone still needs to make decisions and take actions to meet the needs and goals of the agency.

## Technology

Modern technology has become essential to most organizations and is worthy of special attention in this discussion. It is true that some NPOs still operate with technologically disadvantaged systems that cannot transfer data easily and have poor reporting capabilities.[11] Some NPOs are so small and poorly funded that computer technology may be unobtainable. But in order to conduct business effectively and to improve communications, NPOs need to keep up with technological innovations and enhancements. For some nonprofits, technology is not always the priority it ought to be because funds are limited. Overall, NPOs tend to be unsophisticated and unprepared for technological change and advancement, and the so-called digital divide separates organizations as well as people. One useful recommendation is to view information technology not as a cost but as an investment. Organizations should structure information technology systems wisely with a vision that recognizes the following:

- Existing systems
- Implications of updates or changes in information management with consideration of effects on staff, clients, members, and other stakeholders
- Key board members and staff

Simply put, this means that an NPO should do nothing that would unnecessarily hurt existing technology and functional operations. NPOs should share ideas and invest in the necessary training so that the use and application of technology are most effective.

If an NPO has an opportunity to make room in the budget for updated technology, it should do so. If the NPO buys the right equipment and is well prepared to take care of the equipment, there may only be a need for a one-time budget allowance for computers. It may be possible for an NPO to cut back on one program or another for a year while it updates its technological equipment and software. In the end, it is better to be technologically advanced in order to reduce the number of people and the amount of time needed to find information.

## Summary

Financial and fiscal administration was illustrated as a network of four critical functions integrated to ensure that an NPO carries out its mission. This chapter explained the roles and responsibilities of important contributors to an NPO's financial operations, including board members, staff, and volunteers. It also outlined important internal and external factors that affect the outcomes of an NPO as it strives for mission success.

## Notes

1. Whatcom Council of Nonprofits, "Financial Management," *Best Practices for Nonprofits,* 2002, online at http://www.wcnwebsite.org/practices/financial.htm (accessed May 19, 2008).

2. Office of Management and Budget, "Financial Management System," Circular No. A-127, revised version (Washington, DC: Office of Management and Budget, 1993).

3. Fisher Howe, "Nonprofit Accountability: The Board's Fiduciary Responsibility," in *Nonprofit Governance and Management,* ed. Victor Futter (Chicago: American Bar Association, 2002).

4. John Carver, "What Use Is Business Experience on a Nonprofit or Governmental Board?" *Board Leadership* 58 (2001): 2–8.

5. Ibid.

6. L. Stegink, "What Are My Legal Responsibilities?" *Association Management* 57, no. 1 (2005): 84–86.

7. Bruce Collins, "What Every Incoming Director of a Nonprofit Organization Should Know: A Checklist," in *Nonprofit Governance and Management,* ed. Victor Futter (Chicago: American Bar Association, 2002).

8. "Draft Regulations Released for Redesigned Form 990," *Independent Sector,* 2008, online at http://www/independentsector.org (accessed April 28, 2008). Also, "IS Announces New Estimate for Value of Volunteer Time," *Independent Sector,* online at http://www.independentsector.org (accessed May 19, 2008).

9. Association of Fundraising Professionals, *Code of Ethical Principles,* online at http://www.afpnet.org (accessed May 19, 2008).

10. Jae K. Shim and Joel G. Siegel, *Financial Management for Nonprofits: The Complete Guide to Maximizing Resources and Managing Assets* (New York: McGraw-Hill, 1997), 21.

11. Kevin Corder, "Acquiring New Technology: Comparing Nonprofit and Public Sector Agencies," *Administration and Society* 33 (2001): 194.

► CHAPTER 18

# Types of Nonprofit Income: Financial and Cash Flow Management Considerations

Murray Dropkin and Allyson Hayden

The nature of a nonprofit's income is the single most important factor in determining its overall financial management. All organizations, for-profit and nonprofit alike, need cash to operate. The manner in which organizations obtain cash and the form in which cash is received determine how cash flow is managed. In this chapter we provide brief discussions of the different types of income that can be a part of cash flow in nonprofit organizations. It would be highly unusual for your nonprofit to have every type of income we have identified. Most often organizations count on income from one or several sources to support their operations.

Generally, nonprofits either earn income through charging for goods and services or receiving resources (cash and noncash) from government agencies, foundations, businesses, other nonprofits, and private individuals.

In this chapter we identify and discuss the following major topics related to income classification and cash flow:

- Classifying income
- Managing donated income and resources

- Managing earned income
- Managing asset-generated income

## Classifying Income

The types of income received by organizations will determine the approaches that should be used in managing cash flow. The Financial Accounting Standards Board (FASB), which is responsible for issuing accounting standards in the United States for nongovernmental entities, has created three classifications for net assets applicable to nonprofit organizations:

- *Unrestricted Net Assets.* These are defined in FASB Statement of Financial Standards No. 116 as "neither permanently restricted nor temporarily restricted by donor-imposed stipulations."
- *Temporarily Restricted Net Assets.* These are assets for which use is limited to specific purposes or time periods, as specified in contracts, grant agreements, or other written or oral statements.
- *Permanently Restricted Net Assets.* These are assets held in perpetuity for a specific purpose (for

Originally published in *The Cash Flow Management Book for Nonprofits: A Step-by-Step Guide for Managers, Consultants, and Boards* by Murray Dropkin and Allyson Hayden. Copyright © 2001 by John Wiley & Sons, Inc. Reproduced with permission of John Wiley & Sons, Inc.

example, endowments[1]), although the nonprofit can classify income generated from the principal amount as temporarily restricted or unrestricted, depending on donor stipulations. Restrictions on the use of net assets may be conveyed either orally or in writing and may be made:

1. By the individual or organization providing the resources at the time they are given (known as *donor restrictions*)
2. As a result of specific statements or commitments made when the organization originally solicited the contribution

Donor restrictions can only be changed by the organization or individual that made the contribution. Similarly, restrictions placed on contributions by the organization at the time of solicitation may only be changed with the consent of the donor(s). In addition, a nonprofit's board can decide that unrestricted funds may be designated for specific purposes. However, restrictions placed by a board of directors do not change the FASB classification of these funds (termed *board-designated funds*) as unrestricted net assets because the board is free to remove the restrictions at its own discretion.

Contributions that are not specifically designated as temporarily or permanently restricted will be considered unrestricted. Also, the funds received as a result of fundraising campaigns or special events will be considered unrestricted unless the organization had stated that the contribution would be used for a specific purpose when it was solicited. Generally, funds obtained through selling donated or other goods or providing services will be unrestricted unless otherwise stated during sales or solicitation.

Funds provided by government agencies are far more likely to have specific performance requirements than those provided by private individuals or foundations. Although the government has many rules that go along with its funding, such funds are still considered unrestricted net assets by the FASB.

## Managing Donated Income and Resources

Tax-exempt organizations receive money and other resources in a number of ways and from a number of different sources. The characteristics of each of these income streams will require a somewhat different approach to cash flow planning and management. Several of the major categories of contributed income and resources are:

- Grants of various types and from various sources;
- Donations, gifts, and contributions;
- Membership dues, assessments, or other payments from members; and
- Payments made in exchange for the right to attend certain fundraising events (known as *special fundraising income*).

### Grants

**Conditions of Grant**

Nonprofits can receive grants from both private and public sources; in either case, grants are often accompanied by written *grant agreements,* or contracts specifying what the recipient organization must do in return for the funding. The legally binding requirements in most grant agreements (usually known as *conditions of grant*) tend to fall into three broad categories:

1. *Restrictions* on how resources can be used.
2. *Compliance requirements,* which require organizations to comply with specific laws, regulations, and practices in any of a wide range of areas. (See the subsection titled "Government Grants" later in this chapter for some compliance examples.)
3. *Measurable goals or service requirements,* which require nonprofits to achieve specific results or to provide specific quantifiable levels of goods or services to particular groups of individuals (known as *target groups* or *charitable classes*).

Grant agreements can directly (or by reference) require nonprofits to meet a wide range of requirements, including:

- Eligibility standards defining the groups or individuals that must be served under the grant
- Kinds and levels of services or activities the nonprofit must provide
- Additional funds or other resources that must be provided as a matching share to qualify for the grant funds
- Allowable and unallowable expenditures
- Requirements and procedures for making changes in the specific amounts, categories, or line items contained in an approved budget
- Specific hiring, personnel, accounting, cash management, record-keeping, reporting, and auditing requirements
- A wide range of other legally binding requirements that can affect a nonprofit's financial management

### Program Matching Shares

Some grants may be accompanied by grant agreements that require, as a condition of grant, that the recipient organization provide a *program matching share.* This type of grant requirement is also referred to as a *match,* a *program match,* or a *matching share.* (Program matching shares should not be confused with challenge grants, which are defined later in this chapter.) The amount of the program matching share required is usually defined as a percentage of the resources the nonprofit needs to operate the specific program or activity. For example, a funding source or donor that requires a 25 percent program matching share is agreeing to provide 75 percent of the resources needed to support a particular program or activity. The organization is responsible for providing the remaining 25 percent.

Conditions of grant are usually subject to audit either by the specific funding source or as part of the organization's own annual audit. Obviously, specific conditions of grant can directly and indirectly affect almost every aspect

of an organization's financial management system. Therefore, financial managers must carefully read all grant documents and identify all conditions of grant (especially those affecting financial management and flow).

Funding sources may require organizations to meet program matching requirements through one of three methods:

1. A *cash match,* in which the organization must actually provide a specified amount of matching funds (sometimes limited to funds from certain categories or sources)
2. An *in-kind match,* in which an organization can meet matching requirements by receiving in-kind contributions of rental space, equipment, materials, or services, as long as the fair market value of the in-kind goods or services equals the required matching amount
3. A combined cash and in-kind match

The matching requirements of some types of grants will allow organizations to provide program matching shares simply by allocating existing resources to the required purpose. However, some grant agreements will specify that the organization must acquire new funds or resources. In any event, a program matching share is a condition of grant—a contractual obligation—that the organization agrees to meet at the time it receives the support. To avoid violating the grant agreement, organizations must comply with all matching requirements.

In addition, a nonprofit's agreement to provide a program matching share usually becomes an auditable compliance requirement. This means the nonprofit's auditors must determine whether or not the organization actually met the promised program matching requirements and must cite in the audit report any material noncompliance they find.

### Challenge Grants

Challenge grants are grants that have, as a condition of grant, special program matching requirements. In a challenge grant situation, a funding source promises to provide an organization with money once the organization has attracted a specific amount of new support from other outside sources. In other words, the funding source promises to "match" the contributions the organization acquires from other sources.

### Government Grants

Organizations that receive federal funds are subject to requirements beyond those attached to other income streams. Such additional requirements can affect cash flow management, particularly in its reporting and analysis aspects. A number of states have specific rules governing the operation of nonprofit organizations that legally do business in the state or solicit contributions from the state's residents. Depending on the amount of the organization's revenues or assets, states may also require that organizations be audited according to generally accepted auditing standards (GAAS), as issued by the American Institute of Certified Public Accountants (AICPA). Specific funding sources can establish additional audit requirements, which is often the case with federal funds. Receiving federal, state, or local government funds can subject a nonprofit to three sets of auditing requirements in addition to GAAS:

1. The audit requirements set forth in the General Accounting Office's *Government Auditing Standards*
2. The audit requirements spelled out in Office of Management and Budget Circular A-l33
3. Any applicable state, city, or local audit requirements

These three types of audit requirements can affect nonprofit financial and cash flow management in many ways. For example, failure to follow the detailed requirements for record-keeping, auditing, and compliance with a wide range of laws and regulations can lead to sanc-

tions, including discontinuation of cash inflow. In this case, cash flow will be restored only when the requirements set forth in . . . [the] . . . grant agreement are met.

. . .

### Gifts and Contributions

*Gifts* and *contributions* are cash or other assets provided to an organization to support its exempt activities by donors who are eligible to receive little or nothing of direct value in exchange. Gifts and contributions can come from individual, corporate, foundation, or other sources, including bequests. However, if a *tangible benefit* (that is, goods or services) of more than nominal value is offered in return for a contribution, only the amount above the fair market value of the goods or services offered is considered to be a contribution.

Donors can place restrictions on how a nonprofit may use gifts or contributions. They can also make pledges of future support that obligate the nonprofit to do certain things within a specified time period in order to receive the resources pledged.

In order to properly manage cash flow for gift and contribution income, a nonprofit's financial management system must be able to

- Identify the fair market value of any goods or services offered in return for contributions, membership payments, or admission to special fundraising events;
- Identify the expenses involved in generating such payments and determine the total amount of income that qualifies as contributions and that is therefore tax deductible to the donor;
- Provide individual donors who make individual contributions of over $250 with written statements regarding the tax deductibility of their donations; and
- Identify and track individual donations, gifts, and contributions for which use is restricted.

## Noncash Contributions

Organizations may receive two types of noncash contributions from individuals, corporations, or other nonprofits:

1. Property (for example, securities, land, facilities, equipment, materials, or supplies)
2. Services or use of equipment, facilities, or materials owned by others when the service or use is provided free or at reduced cost

Receiving noncash contributions in a form the organization can use to fulfill a purpose reduces the need for the organization to spend cash for that purpose. This will obviously help cash flow. When the contribution is of securities of a publicly traded company, the organization can usually sell the security rapidly and have cash available in a short period of time. Organizations need to have cash flow management policies to properly handle such types of contributions.

Nonprofits must be able to identify, track, and report on each of the various sorts of noncash contributions they receive. Information on income from contributions will be necessary for generating financial statements, documenting the contribution in preparation for the annual audit, completing and submitting the required annual IRS information return, and issuing any required state reports.

## Pledges

*Pledges* are promises to provide future support in the form of cash, securities, land, buildings, use of facilities or utilities, materials, supplies, intangible assets, or services. Pledges can be either conditional or unconditional. *Unconditional pledges* are economic support that donors promise to give with no conditions. *Conditional pledges* are support promised to the nonprofit only if specific conditions are met or come to pass.

Nonprofits must be able to identify, track, and report on individual pledges as either con-

ditional or unconditional. Organizations will have to decide how pledges will be incorporated into cash flow forecasts and make this part of the organization's cash flow policy. If $1 million is pledged for a particular purpose, that money should not go into cash flow projections until the date that the organization is actually working on planning or building that project.

## Membership Dues and Assessments

*Membership dues* or *assessments* are payments that organizations receive from members in exchange for offering them membership privileges. In terms of cash flow management, organizations must be able to perform proper record-keeping and reporting when receiving membership dues.

## Income from Special Fundraising Events

Specific nonprofit fundraising events or activities constitute a substantial portion of some nonprofits' income. Cash flow planning and management for special-event income will include taking the necessary steps to comply with required Internal Revenue Service and financial reporting. Organizations must have financial and cash flow management systems in place to prepare financial reports required to report fundraising event income by event and in total.

## Managing Earned Income

Tax-exempt nonprofits can earn income by providing goods or services for a fee. "Selling" different kinds of goods and services can generate different kinds of *income,* such as:

- Income from trade or business activities
- Income from sales of assets
- Income from program service fees
- Income from fees paid by government agencies (as opposed to grants or awards)

Each of these ways of earning income is discussed in the following subsections.

### Income from Trade or Business Activities

Nonprofits are allowed to generate income by carrying out trade or business activities. Such income falls into three basic categories:

1. *Related business income:* Tax-free income from trade or business activities that are "substantially related" to a nonprofit's exempt purpose
2. *Unrelated business income (UBI):* Income from trade or business activities that are "not substantially related" to a nonprofit's exempt purpose
3. Income that would appear to be UBI but that is actually tax-free because it is excluded from unrelated business income tax (UBIT) under the Internal Revenue Code or specific legislation

Nonprofits that conduct trade or business activities must be able to identify, track, and report on all related, unrelated, and excluded income (as well as applicable expenses).

### Income from Sales of Assets

Nonprofits must be able to track income gains or losses from assets they sell. However, different types of assets are subject to different UBIT treatment and IRS reporting requirements. For example, to complete IRS Form 990 (Return of Organization Exempt from Income Tax), a nonprofit must be able to identify, track, account for, and report separately on income from the sale of at least three different kinds of assets:

1. Income from selling property held as part of a trade or business activity
2. Capital gains from selling investments or other non-inventory property (that is, property not intended for sale as part of a trade or business)

3. Income from selling real or personal property that was donated within the prior two years and for which the donor claimed a federal income tax deduction

### Income from Program Service Fees

A nonprofit can charge fees for services it provides—services that can be either related or unrelated to the organization's exempt purpose. Organizations may receive fees for services directly from the individuals or organizations they serve from third parties who agree to pay all or some of the fees, or from some combination of the two.

When an organization generates fees for services, its financial management system must be able to generate bills and record collections for individual accounts and to track associated income and expenses.

*Program service income* (also called *fee-for-service income*) is primarily income a nonprofit receives in exchange for providing goods or services that further its exempt purpose. Program service revenue can include income from related trade or business activities as well as fees for other services.

Program service income will require organizations to develop financial management systems that are capable of performing all of the necessary billing, collection, data management, reporting, and analysis functions. This type of income stream can be one of the most complex in terms of cash flow planning and management.

### Income from Fees Paid by Government Agencies

A nonprofit can receive fees from a government agency for providing goods or services to the agency. Fees from government agencies only include payments for services, facilities, or products that primarily benefit the government agency, either economically or physically. They do not include government grants or other payments that help a nonprofit provide services or maintain facilities for direct public benefit.

### Service Agreements

Nonprofits may enter into contracts with private and public entities, such as individuals, governmental units, or other nonprofits, to provide services in exchange for money. (These are known as *service agreements, service contracts,* or *performance contracts.*) Such agreements may supply a nonprofit with agreed-on resources either before or after the nonprofit has provided specified goods or services. Under such contracts, the resources supplied are often determined by the specific amount of services the nonprofit provides. For example, Universal Nonprofit has a program that offers comprehensive mental health counseling services to the community. To derive the greatest benefit from the staff and structure of this program, Universal Nonprofit has also negotiated service contracts with other organizations to provide their staffs with employee assistance program services for a fee.

As with grant agreements, any contract can directly (or by reference) commit the nonprofit to meet a wide range of requirements, including standards for eligibility, levels of service, matching resources, accounting, auditing, reporting, and expenditures, as well as other legally binding requirements that can affect a nonprofit's financial management. Some of these legally binding requirements may be restrictions on how resources can be used. Other requirements (*compliance requirements*) may bind the organization to comply with specific laws, regulations, and practices governing hiring, accounting, record-keeping, cash management, and so on.

## Managing Asset-Generated Income

Tax-exempt nonprofits can earn income by using existing assets to produce income, usually through investments. This is because nonprofits are generally allowed to invest money and engage in the same sorts of investment transactions as for-profit entities. In addition to cash investments, such as interest-bearing bank accounts and certificates of deposit (CDs), a nonprofit's investments can also include any noninventory property (that is, property not intended for sale as part of a trade or business), such as stocks, bonds, options to purchase or sell securities, and real estate.

Categories of asset-generated income that affect nonprofit financial management and therefore may require special cash flow management include

- Income from debt-financed assets,
- Interest income,
- Dividend income,
- Gains or losses on investment transactions,
- Gains or losses on disposition of assets,
- Endowment income,[2]
- Rental income from real or personal property,
- Royalty income, and
- Income a nonprofit "parent" receives from a "controlled" taxable subsidiary.

Asset-generated income from any of these sources will have financial and cash flow planning and management requirements that are specific to the source, amount, and restriction status of the assets involved. Also, there will be requirements based on whether or not the income is related to the organization's tax-exempt purpose.

## Notes

1. State laws differ on the definition of an endowment.

2. Some state laws prohibit using endowment funds for certain investments.

# THROWING THE FIRST E-STONE

*C. Kenneth Meyer*

Dean Hall, the new CEO and finance and budget officer of the United Way of Benneville Oak, was shocked to receive an official written reprimand dealing with the "inappropriate use of United Way property." The reprimand noted that he had violated agency policy by using the Internet and email for personal purposes that were not related directly to agency business. Even more shocking and embarrassing was the companion memo that had mysteriously appeared as an attachment to the minutes of the quarterly meeting of the agency's board of directors: it listed the sites he visited, which included news, sports, weather, golf, casino, and travel sites. It also showed that he had ordered items from Amazon, Harry and David Fruit Baskets, Victoria's Secret, and Cabela's Sporting Goods in the previous year.

The memo quoted Butch Hunter, director of information technology and a five-year veteran with the organization: "I have a duty and responsibility to the people who support this agency to inform the board of directors when an employee is in violation of the Internet policy. The computers are not put on their desks for pleasure or self-interest. They are provided by the donors and United Way of Benneville Oak and our region for agency business exclusively. Anyone surfing the net for their own pleasure is using up valuable time and space on our system and wasting the public's money, and that type of activity will not be permitted on my watch!"

Dean suspected that this had something to do with the directive he had been hired to implement when he was taken on by the executive director, which was to cut costs wherever they could be made. The foundation of the directive was to implement a 15 percent across-the-board cut in program and administrative costs, including infrastructure. Butch's plan to purchase a state-of-the-art information system that would handle the increased volume of networking had been cut.

Despite the fact that the memo was true—he did have a habit of checking the news, weather, and sports during his workday—Dean felt outraged. Some of the sites contained information relative to agency business. For example, his time spent on the casino website was in direct response to a request from an area businessman to give him an update on the financial condition of the area's two casinos. Thus, Dean had brought up the website as a starting point. Also, during the crunch time at the end of the fiscal year, Dean did some holiday shopping online from work since he was staying late each evening trying to close the books for the year. At the time it had seemed okay, since he was burning the midnight oil for the agency's sake and there would be no compensatory time given. Now all he could think of was how lucky he was that he had not visited any risqué sites or downloaded "Suzie."

The next day Dean met with the executive director, Sheila Warren, to find out where he stood. By now Dean was angry. "Come on, Sheila, who here doesn't check out the weather or sports or send a personal email from work? This is all about my implementing your policy!"

Sheila was sympathetic, admitting "off the record" that no doubt other staff members had also used agency computers for private matters in an effort to balance their busy workdays and private family lives.

"I don't know what to say," Sheila responded. "Butch has the right to ask for information and monitor the use of the computers and report what he sees as inappropriate uses to a board member, although I would have preferred that he bring it to my attention first. Nonetheless, you were in violation of the policy. My hands are tied," she said, adding with a chuckle, "well, at least you can bet that everyone was busy this morning erasing bookmarks and personal emails as a result of the memo."

Dean didn't grasp the humor that Sheila found in his dilemma.

## Questions and Instructions

1.  Experts report that over $1 billion is "wasted" by employees pursuing personal business on work computers. Is this a problem that needs to be addressed? If so, please indicate how you would begin to compile the information needed to write an effective policy.

2.  Most firms have the technical ability and the legal authority to track employee actions on their office computers. Comment on the situation presented in the case from an ethical and financial perspective. Should budgetary or financial matters affect how an organization monitors its technology use?

3.  All nonprofit agencies must deal with harsh budgetary restrictions from time to time. Do you believe that an across-the-board budget cut is the best way to implement cost-saving decisions? Please explain your answer.

# WHEN THE FUNDING STOPS

*Don Munkers and C. Kenneth Meyer*

The United Operators Association (UOA) was a 501(c)(3) nonprofit organization funded through membership dues and contracts from the parent organization, the American United Operators Association (AUOA). AUOA received appropriated funding from the US government, and these monies were further administered by two national agencies of the federal government—the Environmental Protection Agency (EPA) and the US Department of Agriculture (USDA). In turn, the AUOA entered into contracts with the state chapter of UOA. Overall, the goal of UOA was to provide services in the world of environmental protection as a subcontractor to AUOA, EPA, and USDA. As such, it serviced small rural municipalities throughout the state, thereby not only protecting the environment but also enhancing public health.

The programs delivered by UOA were varied and included the protection of watersheds and aquifers and assistance in the development and implementation of source water protection plans. In total, there were seven programs that linked together services that ranged from providing technical assistance and operator training to actually protecting many sources of drinking water.

The cost reimbursement contracts were based on multiyear contracts and were annually reviewed for renewal purposes. In reality, the contracts were actually "sub-award agreements" between the parent AUOA and the state organization. As part and parcel of the communicated and reinforced organizational culture, employees were "indoctrinated" with the fact that they were employed at the state level. They were not to refer to their employment status at any other level—and it was especially important that they not represent themselves as members of the national organization.

To take care that the fiduciary responsibilities of the UOA were met, the organization required employees to maintain extensive monthly logs with detailed records of their activities as they provided contract-mandated services to the constituents of the state. These technical assistance and financial logs provided the basis or justification for all cost reimbursements made to the state up to, but not exceeding, the total amounted awarded. Expenditures in excess of the contractual agreement approved by the national AUOA were entered into at the expense of the state organization, and any under-expenditures were deducted from the contract for the next year. In addition, one important, but frequently overlooked, section of the contract stipulated that, "if for any reason" the national agency that administered the contract did not pay the parent organization, the state organization would likewise not be reimbursed. However, the state would have to continue to fulfill its work- and service-related obligations under the contract as if they were "fully funded." In essence, the state would have to fulfill its obligation to meet the contractual requirements and perform the necessary work even though, in the final analysis, it might not be entitled to reimbursement for expenses. This cumbersome and uncertain arrangement presented a major problem for the state agency, since the funding was based on the unknown vicissitudes surrounding federal funding of the administering agency. Recently, however, this funding arrangement had changed.

Presently, the state UOA had seven contracts totaling $900,000 under the agreement as previously detailed. This amount, coupled with membership fees, provided a total operating budget of $1.3 million. While each contract specifically outlined the purposes (functions, services, and activities) to which these federal monies might be applied, the regulations governing the utilization of membership dues were much more flexible and made the use of these funds largely subject to the personal judgment calls of the executive director of the state UOA—provided these uses complied with the bylaws of the organization.

For the present fiscal year, an unfortunate set of policies had been put into effect by the administering agencies. Although Congress had appropriated the funding for the programs, the national agencies, while knowing that the funds had been appropriated, failed to allocate them. Two of the programs began experiencing a funding lag at the beginning of the federal budget year. One was the Environmental Training Program (ETP), a program that provided environmental training to address compliance issues connected with national environmental regulation standards. To carry out its mandate of assisting small communities in protecting the environment and public health, this program was delivered through classes given to the municipal employees who had been charged with implementing these standards. The other program assisted small communities in the development of programs to protect watershed areas by assessing and inventorying the potential sources of water contamination. In brief, the needed federal monies were not distributed to the state UOA for an eleven-month period—a long time to be faced with the turbulence of financial uncertainty.

During this period, other programs began to see their funding go into arrears, with delays of up to four months or more in allocation. As the fiscal year progressed, UOA began to experience serious shortfalls in cash flow. It remedied the situation initially by making arrangements with the financial institution that serviced the UOA account. First National Bank simply covered any drafts made on the account, apparently assured by the assumption that "lag-pay" would eventually be forthcoming and that the federal funding was covered by a contractual agreement. The financial officer at First National was fully aware, however, that the contracts could not be used as collateral, as specifically detailed in the terms of the contract.

The national AUOA organization offered to loan the state UOA the non-allocated shortfall at the prime interest rate, plus-1 percent. Detailed financials and authorizations from the UOA board were required monthly, but even though the board submitted these reports monthly, the AUOA always found a reason not to loan the money. Since operations were being covered by the local bank, Orangelo Baldwin, the executive director of the state UOA, upon receiving what she called "sage advice" from Beth Ausman, a veteran employee of the agency, decided to continue funding cash-flow shortages, unabated, through the local bank. While this arrangement presented a financial burden, the state UOA was able, with First National's assistance, to meet its obligations. This arrangement continued until the bulk of the other programs began to fall behind in contributions.

Ted Jacobs, comptroller for the state UOA, called Orangelo and voiced his concern about the basis for funding and reimbursement and wanted to know when the lag-pay would end. He stated, "I find this lag-pay problem to be disruptive to the administration of our programs, especially if I am to convey the confidence normally associated with professional fiduciary responsibility."

Orangelo asked Beth to look into the matter, and she made several telephone calls and emailed her inquiries to the national AUOA asking for ending dates. As they had claimed several times before, they told her that the ending date would be the end of the current week. Beth dutifully passed this information on to Ted, who was patiently waiting for a response. But Ted became irritated when it turned out that his inquiries had once again been answered with false information: the communicated ending date came and went and the agency's claims for reimbursement had yet to be settled.

The problem was exacerbated when First National tired of getting what it called the "runaround" began to "bounce" checks written on the state UOA's account. In an attempt to balance the accounts for UOA, Orangelo had informed all the vendors that they would be paid, but when, through no fault of the UOA's, they were informed that UOA could not meet these obligations, chaos broke out in the organization. As could have been expected, insurance policies were canceled, ordered supplies were not delivered, and critical office equipment was threatened with repossession. Finally, employee payroll was jeopardized. The final threat in a long series of threats had arrived and immediate action was required.

Through the persistent efforts of Ted and Beth, who were in constant consultation with the bank, the payroll was financed. However, travel reimbursements were placed on the back-burner and fringe benefit contributions were not placed in the retirement and pension accounts. For the time being, UOA was still in business. The state UOA staff continued in their efforts to secure an interim loan from the national AUOA to cover obligated expenses. They had sent the required documents via certified mail to the national office in Washington, DC, requesting the required signatures. Delays were more usual than exceptional in dealing with the national office, but this time the staff had tried to convey the real urgency behind its request that the paperwork be promptly processed.

After a week or so had transpired and no word had been received from First National regarding the interim loan, Ted called the principal at the national AUOA and inquired about the status of the loan documentation. The conversation went smoothly enough, but in the end he was told that the papers had not been received. Although Ted was typically cordial in his dealings with the national office, he had reached a point of frustration that was hard to control. He questioned the accuracy of this claim and said that he held a receipt certifying that the document package had been delivered and signed for nearly six days earlier. Three days later, the national AUOA principal called Ted and informed him that the envelope containing the application for the interim loan had been found, and he apologized for what was either the "apparent mix-up" in the US mail or a "misrouting" in the agency.

Completely turned off by the repeated delays in funding and the constant excuses he had received from AUOA over the years, Ted decided that it was time to seek political intervention. As someone who was familiar with the political process and knowledgeable about effective congressional communication, he contacted the office of the state's senior senator and requested that the national agencies responsible for administering the funds be investigated. About a week later, after a member of the senatorial staff contacted the principal parties at the national agencies, the funds began to flow again.

Temporarily, the problem had been fixed, but the state UOA had been severely affected and the damage had already been inflicted. Indeed, at one point in time the federal government owed the state UOA $365,000 for the work it had certified as completed. This represented nearly 40 percent of the total contribution from the contracts, an amount that the UOA could not easily absorb. With the approved and transmitted deposit, however, the state UOA felt that it was back in business and began to refurbish its "tarnished reputation" with its insurer and other service providers.

In discussing the matter with Orangelo, Ted told her what he had done to get the funding dilemma fixed and vowed that, should delays and postponements once again become the "order of the day" in the future, he would not hesitate to contact his congressional delegation and work through them to solve the problem. "It takes powerful people who know the system," he said, "to get the attention of national bureaucrats, and when they are heard, action results." He lamented having had to turn to the political process for action, but the state UOA could not function as a credible agency when it was in a constant state of budgetary crisis—a crisis not of its own making and one that could not be solved with the receipts for membership dues.

Clyde Crimson, chairperson of the UOA board, had been kept informed of the events that led to Ted's call for political help. As Ted reflected on what had transpired, he wondered if the board realized how close the UOA had come to closing its doors. In fact, he wondered, did the board members fully understand the importance of their position on the board during periods of crisis as well as normalcy? And should Orangelo have done a better job of informing them of their overall fiduciary duties and responsibilities, including assistance in identifying supplemental philanthropic, private, and public funding sources? Ted wondered if board members knew how important they were to the agency, especially "when the funding stops."

## Questions and Instructions

1. How would you characterize the funding relationship that existed between the national AUOA and state UOA? Explain.

2. What could be done to resolve the myriad of problems presented in the case, especially the funding mechanism used by the administering agencies? Please elaborate.

3. Do you believe that this type of financial problem is commonly or uncommonly faced by agencies dependent on funding from the national level? Can you provide relevant examples of similar funding problems in your own state? Please discuss.

4. Considerably frustrated by the existing funding process, Ted Jacobs finally resorted to using the political process. What were the implications of his actions, both in the near term and the long term? What were the positive and negative effects of his actions?

5. What role, if any, should Orangelo Baldwin have played in the financial dilemma presented in this case study? What role should a board of directors play when faced with this type of financial exigency?

# PART IX

# MANAGING VOLUNTEERS[*]

Volunteering is an important feature of civil society in countries around the globe, and it represents a distinctive aspect of nonprofit organizations.[1] It is almost impossible to discuss the nonprofit sector without mentioning volunteers, and indeed, in recent years it has been relatively common to hear the nonprofit sector called the "voluntary sector." Because volunteers and nonprofits fit together so closely, many of us mentally connect voluntarism with the nonprofit sector even though many citizens also volunteer with government libraries, fire departments, emergency medical services systems, schools, veterans' hospitals, and numerous other public agencies and programs.[2] In 2011, close to 27 percent of Americans (64 million people) reported volunteering with an organization, and on a typical day 14.6 million Americans volunteered for an average 2.84 hours. Combined, Americans volunteered for an estimated 15.2 billion hours—time worth an estimated $296.2 billion.[3]

## Volunteering and Voluntarism

Ram Cnaan, Femida Handy, and Margaret Wadsworth rightfully argue that *voluntarism* and *volunteer* are "rich concepts" that cannot be explained adequately in a single-sentence definition.[4] They observe that definitions of *volunteer* vary on four key dimensions: the voluntary nature of the act; the nature of the reward; the context or auspices under which the volunteer activity is performed; and who benefits. Each of these dimensions has "steps" that differentiate between volunteers and nonvolunteers. For example, in the dimension of free choice, three key categories emerge: (1) free will (the ability to voluntarily choose), (2) the relative lack of coercion, and (3) the obligation to volunteer. Whereas all definitions would accept free will as relevant in defining a volunteer, pure definitions would not accept the relative lack of coercion, and only the broadest definition would include court-ordered "volunteers" or students in a required service program fulfilling their obligation as volunteers.[5]

Studies of volunteering have escalated over the past decade or two and a variety of theoretical frameworks have emerged to guide the studies. These include sociological theories that focus on individual sociodemographic characteristics such as race, gender, and social class and economic theories that treat volunteerism as a form of unpaid labor motivated by the promise of rewards.

---

[*]The authors would like to thank Peter M. Nelson for his contributions to this introduction.

Psychological studies of motivation may be embedded in a sociological framework that explores the origins of motives in social structures or the economic study of rewards and costs of volunteerism can be embedded in a psychological theory that subjective dispositions, such as empathy, condition the rationality of certain behaviors, or in a sociology theory that factors in circles of friends or memberships in formal organizations as moderators of costs and benefits.[6]

Marc Musick and John Wilson offer five reasons for the growing interest in volunteerism research: (1) volunteers (and nonprofit organizations) are increasingly viewed by political actors as a means for helping government agencies achieve important public policy goals; (2) the growth of identity politics has spawned a wide range of groups that draw heavily on volunteer labor; (3) old modes of civic engagement and associational life have changed and are seen as a threat to the fabric of civil society[7]; (4) traditional notions about what counts as productive labor are being challenged, and volunteering has been absorbed within this broader investigation of how work is being restructured and redefined; and (5) the nonprofit sector is demanding science-based information about volunteering to use for more effective recruitment and retention.[8] Other scholars have been raising questions about the nature of volunteers, the phenomenon of voluntarism, and the cultural and ethnic aspects of volunteerism.[9] Answers to these questions will help unravel the complexities of the nonprofit sector and are vitally important to the trustees and managers of the thousands of nonprofit organizations that rely on volunteers to staff their programs, serve on their boards, and stuff their envelopes.

## Why People Volunteer

Volunteering provides a way to help others in the community and also offers a means for "gaining self-fulfillment, skills, confidence, and a social network."[10] The reasons why people volunteer have long fascinated academic researchers.[11] Explanations include altruistic or values-based motives, social motives, and utilitarian motives. Altruistic or values-based motives include religious beliefs, support for causes, and a desire to help others. Indeed, in a recent study, almost all volunteers (96 percent) reported feeling compassion toward people in need.[12] Those whose motives are social may be looking to extend their social networks, volunteering because friends or colleagues do so, or responding to a variety of other social pressures to volunteer.[13] Utilitarian motives underlie voluntarism by those seeking to enhance their human capital by gaining work experience and job training, developing new skills, exploring career paths, enhancing their résumés, and making useful contacts.[14]

Successful nonprofit organizations must appeal to the motivational needs of volunteers and use their talents appropriately. In his classic piece on motivation, David McClelland identified three need-based motives that affect human activity: the needs for achievement, power, and affiliation.[15] Individuals have varying degrees of need in each of these three areas. In another seminal piece on motivation, Abraham Maslow offered a needs-based hierarchical model.[16] Here, individuals are initially motivated by lower-level needs, but once those are satisfied, they seek to satisfy higher-level needs. Thus, an individual who is struggling to meet the basic physiological needs for food, clothing, and shelter will not be "motivated" by higher-level, more abstract, needs. Maslow believed that most people in our society move among different levels of the needs for safety and security, affiliation, and self-esteem. Recognizing the differences in these motives can assist nonprofit organizations in developing recruiting approaches and also in shaping volunteers' tasks.

Although managers in nonprofit organizations do not need to read McClelland or Maslow to know that people tend to behave in ways that help them satisfy their needs, their failure to understand the importance of tending to these needs may result in preventable turnover among volunteers. Jeffrey Brudney and Lucas Meijs's piece on volunteers as a "renewable resource," reprinted in this part, illustrates the importance of not only recruiting volunteers but also devising strategies to retain them.

## Managing Volunteers

Nonprofits that are thinking about using volunteers need to consider how volunteers would be used and managed. Volunteer labor is not free labor in that managing volunteers consumes considerable staff time, effort, and patience. Add to that the cost of supplies and training, volunteers' possible lack of clarity on organizational expectations, and the unpredictability of staff reactions to their presence. "Problems associated with volunteers' limited time, uncertain motives, and high degree of individual independence can result in debilitating levels of organizational uncertainty."[17]

In a 2007–2008 study of volunteering and giving in the United Kingdom, the most common activities undertaken by regular formal volunteers were organizing or helping to run an activity or event and raising or handling money.[18] A nonprofit organization's needs must be clearly identified for the volunteers, and activities should be assigned that meet the volunteers' primary needs. Which tasks are necessary, and what knowledge, skills, and abilities are required of volunteers to carry out these tasks? What time commitments are necessary? By differentiating among the skills needed and the investments of time required to carry out different types of useful activities, an organization can broaden its volunteer base to accommodate a wider variety of volunteers and target specialized interests and abilities. In recent years, for example, virtual volunteering via online technology and short-term episodic volunteering have both been on the rise.[19] Such opportunities have been especially popular with younger volunteers.

Differentiating among the types of tasks an organization needs to have done makes it easier to create successful matches with volunteers' needs, and it can also help identify areas where existing volunteers may develop new skills and abilities. Developing volunteers requires that an organization (1) know what tasks it needs to have performed and the skills necessary to do so, (2) assess the needs of individual volunteers, and (3) create an organizational process that allows volunteers to grow through strategies such as job enrichment.

## Risk Management and Other Concerns

Nonprofit organizations must consider the risks associated with using volunteers and the nature of the activities that volunteers will perform. Oversight, training, and feedback will be needed to successfully manage volunteers. Policies must be in place that anticipate potential high-risk situations. For example, will volunteers working with the public be able to make discretionary decisions about the type or level of services received? Will performance reviews be conducted, and if so, by whom? Will volunteers be working with vulnerable populations or operating motor vehicles? What background checks are necessary, and what licenses are required for volunteers to be able to legally perform their tasks? An organization's failure to protect vulnerable recipient populations can result in charges of negligent recruiting or negligent hiring.[20] Will volunteers be going into the homes of persons who are elderly or disabled? Should the volunteer be bonded? Will the volunteer be working in dangerous locations, working late at night, or working alone? Will staff members be overseeing the work of volunteers? Is it ever permissible for volunteers to supervise paid staff members? Nonprofit organizations must anticipate and conduct periodic organizational assessments to answer these types of questions.

Many nonprofit organizations carry liability insurance to protect volunteers (including the board of directors) and the organization. For example, volunteers in a local needle exchange program may be at risk of a needle stick from a dirty syringe. Who should pay for the HIV and hepatitis prevention treatment? Who should provide counseling for the volunteers whose lives will change dramatically? Who should pay to treat a volunteer driver who injures her back while assisting elderly patients in and out of an assisted living center's van? If a volunteer is sued while providing services, who will pay for the legal defense of the volunteer, the volunteer director, the executive director, and members of the board of trustees?

Indemnification for volunteers in some form is essential in this litigation-happy society. Often, legal action taken against a volunteer's actions is only a first step. The plaintiff may have little or no desire to take the volunteer's assets, but establishing the legal culpability of the volunteer is a first step toward also establishing the nonprofit organization's responsibility and culpability. This is the doctrine of deep pockets.

Legal liability is an unavoidable part of the volunteer environment in the United States today. The old adage is painfully true: "There are only two types of volunteers (and employees)—those who have been sued and those who are going to be sued." Nonprofit organizations are at least partially responsible for the actions of their volunteers. An attorney who is well versed in tort liability law can be an invaluable resource for an executive director and a board of trustees.

## Recognizing Volunteers

Like paid employees, volunteers appreciate being recognized for their contributions. Many nonprofits and communities sponsor an annual celebration to formally recognize volunteers. Those recognized may be presented with a certificate, plaque, or other acknowledgment of appreciation. Many nonprofit organizations track the number of hours donated by volunteers and proudly announce to the media and the community the time and energy expended by its volunteers.

When a volunteer leaves an organization, it is wise to conduct an exit interview to learn what is working well and what could be changed to improve the experiences of current and future volunteers. Exit interviews can also help the director of volunteers and the executive director detect trends, become aware of general opportunities or problems, and identify problems that could adversely affect the organization if not remedied.

## The Future of Volunteers and Voluntarism

Volunteers will become increasingly important for nonprofits over the upcoming decades for several reasons:

1. Our population will live longer and have more productive years after retirement. Volunteering provides retirees with opportunities to use their skills and feel useful while making a difference.
2. Many higher educational institutions now offer volunteer opportunities—through community service, service learning, internships, and outreach programs—as a way for students to learn to live more fulfilling lives, and some are requiring participation for graduation. Among young volunteers, 44 percent believe that "people working together" can make a great deal of difference in solving local problems.[21]
3. A few government programs are providing a new variety of paid volunteers who may be available to nonprofit organizations. The Corporation for National and Community Service (CNCS) is a federal government agency that engages more than 5 million Americans in service through its core programs, which include Senior Corps, the Social Innovation Fund, and AmeriCorps. The best-known of these, AmeriCorps (founded in 1994), pays stipends and grants to qualified individuals that enable them to provide services through nonprofit organizations while also helping them to finance their college education.[22]

4. More services, skills, and energy from volunteers will be required in the upcoming years because we are in a long-term era of declining government funding for human services and the arts, increasing populations with service needs, and expanded service mandates.[23]

The last reason for increasing voluntarism over the coming years is perhaps the most important: if nonprofit organizations do not provide services for the many vulnerable populations, it is questionable whether other organizations will. More volunteers will be needed than perhaps at any other time in our nation's history. Recognizing this need, studies are on the rise to learn more about attracting various groups to volunteering and creating circumstances and environments that will attract and retain volunteers.[24] Special events such as the once-a-decade 2005 White House Conference on Aging (WHCA) have issued calls for new and more meaningful volunteer opportunities for older Americans.[25] The 2015 WHCA is expected to raise a similar call for volunteering opportunities that will ensure that older Americans remain engaged, active, and vital.[26]

To meet the rising needs for the services of volunteers, nonprofit organizations will need to continue to strengthen their ability to recruit and retain volunteers, match volunteer needs with organizational and community needs, manage volunteers well, develop and implement training programs, and reduce liability risks.

## Readings Reprinted in Part IX

In "What Is Volunteering?" (a chapter from *Volunteers: A Social Profile*), Marc Musick and John Wilson examine the conceptual difficulties and definitional complexities of volunteering.[27] Although most of us have a general idea of what it means to volunteer and seldom question the idea that volunteering is "unpaid work," these authors take us far past simple generalities. Specifically, they seek to provide a way to study the concept scientifically. Such a project is far from easy because "from a scientific point of view, concepts should be both internally consistent and clearly demarcate the phenomenon we want to study from others like it."[28] Musick and Wilson ask questions from the start: "Where does volunteerism end and similar activities such as participating in a voluntary association, social activism, and caring for an elderly relative begin? Do we want to consider helping one's elderly neighbor clear snow from her driveway a volunteer act?"[29]

Using a systematic process that includes a rich review of empirical studies, the authors consider the major definitions and theories used to explain volunteering, including net costs, benefits, self-interest, motivations, social activism, caring, and altruism. It becomes clear that the concept of volunteering is paradoxical on many fronts. For example, depicting volunteerism as "unpaid labor" ignores the many volunteers who receive reimbursement for their time and travel or claim these as charitable gifts on their income tax returns. And as the authors also point out, "AmeriCorps, one of the best-known volunteer programs in the United States, pays its workers." This is true of other stipend-based programs as well, including the foster grandparent program in the United States and the "Good Neighbors" initiative of the UK nonprofit Age Concern. Likewise, while utilitarian researchers do not define volunteering by motives but rather by calculations of net costs and benefits, for other social scientists motives must necessarily be taken into account. "Volunteer work is not simply unpaid labor," the authors point out, "but unpaid labor performed for the correct reason."

In the second reading, "It Ain't Natural: Toward a New (Natural) Resource Conceptualization for Volunteer Management," Jeffrey Brudney and Lucas Meijs present an intriguing argument for viewing volunteers as a natural and renewable resource. A word of caution is offered—volunteer labor is a common-pool resource subject to depletion, as depicted in "the tragedy of the commons."[30] The authors argue that "the volunteer energy-using community must shift from an instrumental to a more sustainable approach."[31] In the words of the 1987 Brundtland Report, a sustainable approach to volunteering, just as with natural resources, must take into account "the needs of the present without compromising the ability of future generations to meet their own needs."[32]

Adopting this approach promises to have significant impacts on how volunteers are viewed, trained, developed, and conceptualized by organizations and communities. Volunteer labor is a relatively fragile shared resource. In essence, a community volunteer endowment must be carefully managed and cultivated. The fruits of volunteer labor must be nurtured for the good of all rather than consumed by any one organization. Thus, stewardship is required of volunteer managers. Roger Lohmann expresses a similar sentiment in his well-known book on nonprofits, *The Commons:* "The endowment of any commons ordinarily consists of its treasures of money, property and marketable goods; its collection of precious, priceless objects; and its repertoires of routines, cults, skills, techniques and other meaningful behavior learned by participants in the commons . . . [and] . . . *passed on to others for the common good* [emphasis added]."[33] It is this message that Brudney and Meijs so skillfully convey.

## Case Studies in Part IX

In the first case study, "Now You See 'Em, Now You Don't: Volunteers and Nonprofits," the challenges of managing a growing volunteer pool take center stage. The case study challenges the reader to analyze how policies may affect outcomes related to retention among groups of volunteers. Managerial concerns also arise in "Turning the Tide: Transitioning from Volunteers to Paid Staff." In this case study, significant growing pains within an organization present a board of directors with some tough decisions that will affect the residents of a community in need.

## Notes

1. Jeffrey L. Brudney and Lucas C.P.M. Meijs, "It Ain't Natural: Toward a New (Natural) Resource Conceptualization for Volunteer Management," *Nonprofit and Voluntary Sector Quarterly* 38, no. 4 (August 2009): 564–581.

2. Jeffrey L. Brudney, *Fostering Volunteer Programs in the Public Sector* (San Francisco: Jossey-Bass, 1990).

3. Amy S. Blackwood, Katie L. Roeger, and Sarah L. Pettijohn, *The Nonprofit Sector in Brief: Public Charities, Giving, and Volunteering* (Washington, DC: Urban Institute, 2012).

4. Ram A. Cnaan, Femida Handy, and Margaret Wadsworth, "Defining Who Is a Volunteer: Conceptual and Empirical Considerations," *Nonprofit and Voluntary Sector Quarterly* 25, no. 3 (September 1996): 364–383.

5. Ibid., 370.

6. John Wilson, "Volunteerism Research: A Review Essay," *Nonprofit and Voluntary Sector Quarterly* 41, no. 2 (2012): 176–212, 178.

7. See Robert D. Putnam, *Bowling Alone: The Collapse and Revival of American Community* (New York: Simon & Schuster, 2000).

8. Marc A. Musick and John Wilson, "What Is Volunteering?" In Marc A. Musick and John Wilson, *Volunteers: A Social Profile* (Indianapolis: Indiana University Press, 2008), 4–6.

9. See, for example, Richard A. Sundeen, Cristina Garcia, and Sally A. Raskoff, "Ethnicity, Acculturation, Volunteering to Organizations: A Comparison of Africans, Asians, Hispanics, and Whites," *Nonprofit and Voluntary Sector Quarterly* 38 (2009): 929–955.

10. *Giving and Volunteering in the US 2001: Findings from a National Survey* (Washington, DC: Independent Sector, 2002), 36.

11. Femida Handy, Ram A. Cnaan, Lesley Hustinx, Chulhee Kang, Jeffrey L. Brudney, Debbie Haski-Leventhal, Kirsten Holmes, Lucas C.P.M. Meijs, Anne Birgitta Pessi, Bhagyashree Ranade, Naoto Yamauchi, and Sinisa Zrinscak, "A Cross-Cultural Examination of Student Volunteering: Is It All About Résumé Building?" *Nonprofit and Voluntary Sector Quarterly* 39, no. 3 (June 2010): 498–523.

12. Ibid., 20.

13. Lorenzo Cappellari and Gilberto Turati, "Volunteer Labour Supply: The Role of Workers' Motivations," *Annals of Public Cooperative Economics* 75 (2004): 619–643.

14. Ram A. Cnaan and Robin S. Goldberg-Glen, "Measuring Motivation to Volunteer in Human Services," *Journal of Applied Behavioral Science* 27 (1991): 269–284.

15. David C. McClelland, *Human Motivation* (New York: Cambridge University Press, 1987).

16. Abraham Maslow, *Motivation and Personality* (New York: Harper & Row, 1954).

17. Jone L. Pearce, "Volunteers at Work," in Jone L. Pearce, *Volunteers: The Organizational Behavior of Unpaid Workers* (London: Routledge, 1993), 3–14.

18. *Communities and Local Government: 2007–08 Citizenship Survey: Volunteering and Charitable Giving Topic Report* (London: Communities and Local Government, 2008), 6.

19. Lesley Hustinx, "I Quit, Therefore I Am? Volunteer Turnover and the Politics of Self-Actualization," *Nonprofit and Voluntary Sector Quarterly* 39, no. 2 (2010): 236–255.

20. Negligent recruiting, hiring, retention, or supervision occurs when the organization knows its responsibility but fails to act to meet that responsibility. A variety of Circuit Court of Appeals and Supreme Court cases have upheld the responsibility of an organization for adhering to proper practices in these areas. See Hartsell v. Duplex Products, Inc. (4th Circuit, 1997); SCI v. Hartford Fire Ins. (11th Circuit, 1998); Burlington Industries, Inc. v. Ellerth, 524 U.S. 742, 754 (1998); and Faragher v. Boca Raton, 524 U.S. 775, 804, n. 4 (1998).

21. Center for Information and Research on Civic Learning and Engagement, *2006 Civic and Political Health of the Nation* (Medford, MA: Tufts University Press, 2006), www.civicyouth.org (accessed June 25, 2010).

22. Corporation for National and Community Service, *AmeriCorps State and National,* www.nationalservice.gov/programs (accessed August 5, 2014).

23. See Part IX, "The Blending and Blurring of the Sectors," in *The Nature of the Nonprofit Sector,* 3rd ed., edited by J. Steven Ott and Lisa A. Dicke (Boulder, CO: Perseus/Westview Press, 2016).

24. Linda S. Hartenian, "Nonprofit Agency Dependence on Direct Service and Indirect Support Volunteers: An Empirical Investigation," *Nonprofit Management and Leadership* 17, no. 2 (Spring 2007): 319–334.

25. Nancy Morrow-Howell, "Civic Engagement at the 2005 White House Conference on Aging," *Public Policy and Aging Report* 16, no. 1 (2006): 13–17.

26. Cecilia Munoz, "On the Horizon: The 2015 White House Conference on Aging," The White House Blog, http://www.whitehouse.gov/blog/2014/07/29/horizon-2015-white-house-conference-aging.

27. Musick and Wilson, "What Is Volunteering?"

28. Ibid., 11.

29. Ibid.

30. Garrett Hardin, "The Tragedy of the Commons," *Science* 162 (1968): 1243–1248.

31. Brudney and Meijs, "It Ain't Natural," 573.

32. Gro Harlem Brundtland, *Report of the World Commission on Environment and Development: Our Common Future* (the Brundtland Report) (Oxford: Oxford University Press, 1987), 39, available at: http://www.un-documents.net/our-common-future.pdf.

33. Roger A. Lohmann, *The Commons: New Perspectives on Nonprofit Organizations and Voluntary Action* (San Francisco: Jossey-Bass, 1992), 18.

## CHAPTER 19

# What Is Volunteering?

## MARC A. MUSICK AND JOHN WILSON

Besides the more obvious forms of one-on-one help, volunteering has been used to refer to mutual aid, as when a group of people work together to achieve a common goal, such as digging a well; organizational participation and self-governance, as when people contribute time to maintaining an organization, such as a religious congregation or a trade union branch; and campaigning and advocacy, as when people contribute their time out of a desire for social change and social justice, such as advocacy on behalf of people with disabilities. As we shall see, it is often quite difficult to decide whether an activity is volunteer work or not. Where does volunteerism end and similar activities such as participating in a voluntary association, social activism, and caring for an elderly relative begin? Do we want to consider helping one's elderly neighbor clear snow from her driveway a volunteer act? Should we treat mentoring teenagers, serving as a guide at the state museum, and preparing posters for the upcoming anti-abortion rally as the same kind of behavior?

Most social scientists—and most of the general public—are realists. They believe that volunteerism does, in fact, possess a self-evident essence. They believe there are clear and identifiable behaviors "out there" that can be described straightforwardly using terms such as "volunteer" and "volunteerism" and that all these behaviors have something in common. Once they are so described and measured, they can be explained through the use of conventional social science methods. Although this might seem to be a simple and straightforward solution to the definitional problem, it largely sidesteps the theoretically problematic status of the nature of volunteering. For example, economists think of volunteer work as unpaid productive labor, in part because it is easier to measure it with empirical indicators. But this tells us nothing about the diverse meanings of volunteer work, nor does it explain why productive labor is, in this case, unpaid.

As part of its 2001 celebration of "The Year of the Volunteer," the United Nations issued a "toolkit" for people planning surveys to gather information on volunteers. Three criteria were used to identify volunteer behavior: it is not undertaken for financial gain; it is undertaken of one's own free will; it brings benefits to a third party as well as to the people who volunteer (Dingle 2001, 11). But even with (or especially with) this rather simple definition, a number of caveats were issued. It was allowed that volunteers *can* be reimbursed (perhaps for expenses), but the amount should not exceed the market value of the work. It was acknowledged that people often volunteer as a result of peer pressure or a feeling of social obligation, but this is not the same as being *required* to do the work or being forced to do the work as a matter of need. Beneficiaries of volunteer work, it was allowed, *can* include friends, neighbors, and complete strangers as well as more abstract causes such as "the environment" or "the arts."

We begin this chapter by drawing a distinction between joining a voluntary association and volunteering. Membership in a voluntary association, especially where the membership is described as "active," can resemble volunteerism and is often associated with it, but it is not the same as volunteering. Then we will consider attempts to derive a social science definition of volunteerism from how that term is used and understood in everyday language. We will see that many people think of volunteers as providing help to others at some cost to themselves. We will consider how helpful it is to think of volunteer work being costly when people's ideas of cost can vary so widely. We will then discuss whether obligation is an essential part of volunteering, followed by a discussion of whether volunteer work is distinctive in its motivation. The bulk of the chapter is devoted to comparing the meaning of volunteering with two cognate sociological categories, social activism and caring. We will argue that there is more overlap between volunteerism and social activism than is ordinarily recognized by social scientists, and that little is to be gained by treating them as distinct phenomena. We will argue that, although caring and volunteering are cognate activities in that one is the provision of help informally and the other the provision of help formally, this distinction between informal and formal is a crucial one. We will also argue against the position that volunteering is simply a formalized method of caring. We will conclude with a discussion of some of the hidden biases of particular ways of thinking about volunteer work.

## Membership Versus Volunteering

Although membership (or even "participation") in voluntary associations and volunteerism are associated, they are not the same thing (Cutler and Danigelis 1993, 150). Indeed, it could be said that people who belong to a voluntary association and limit their involvement to simply attending meetings or otherwise drawing on the benefits of being a member (e.g., playing a tennis game at the tennis club, reading the newsletter) are quintessential "free-loaders" because they consume the "public goods" created by other members of the organization without contributing to their production. Even attending a meeting or rally sponsored or organized by a voluntary association is a questionable measure of volunteerism because behind the stage were people who actually planned, organized, and raised the funds necessary for the event. Surveys that go no further than simply asking if people are "active" members of a voluntary association are not therefore providing much information on volunteer work (Hooghe 2003, 54).

Given the fact that volunteering is often defined as unpaid work for an organization, there is bound to be considerable overlap between membership in voluntary associations and volunteering. The World Values Survey data from 1990–1993 show that the countries with the highest rate of voluntary association memberships are also the countries with the highest rate of people doing "unpaid work for" an organization. Iceland, the Netherlands, and the United States have the highest membership rates and the highest volunteer rates. Nevertheless, in most cases, the volunteer rate (people doing unpaid work for an organization) is about half the membership rate (Torcal and Montero 1999, 172). And many people volunteer who are not members of a voluntary association at all. You do not have to belong to a voluntary association to teach people to read, drive them to the hospital for their doctor's appointments, or answer the telephones during the fundraising campaign of the local public radio station.

## The Net-Cost Definition of Volunteering

When people think of a volunteer, they almost always imagine someone who is making a sacrifice to help another person, an organization, or a cause. In other words, they tend to think of volunteer work in terms of rewards and costs.

The net-cost approach assumes that volunteers provide a service for which they do not get material rewards or, if they do, their costs exceed these rewards. It does not rule out any possibility of volunteers obtaining material benefits, such as job skills or business contacts. Almost all (93 percent) of the volunteers surveyed in the 1997 United Kingdom National Survey of Volunteering saw nothing wrong with people obtaining qualifications (e.g., first aid skills) as a result of their voluntary activity. Not surprisingly, young people (18–24) were twice as likely as older people to approve of this (Smith 1998, 104). As we shall see later, the issue is one of motives. If people volunteer *only* because they want to improve their job skills then it is considered too utilitarian, too calculating, to be considered a real gift of time. Selflessness is therefore an important component of the lay definition of volunteering. We should put the interests of the other person or the group ahead of our own. Although surveys show that volunteers are uncomfortable with the idea of getting paid for what they do, the payment of volunteers is not an anachronism (Frey and Goette 1999, 2).

In the United States it is deemed acceptable for volunteers to have their out-of-pocket expenses, such as travel and meals, defrayed, or they can claim these donations as charitable gifts on their income tax returns. AmeriCorps, one of the best-known volunteer programs in the United States, pays its workers. In return for one year of service, volunteers are awarded an education scholarship, the amount being dou-bled for two years of service. Significantly, the reward here is not cash, which would have been symbolically inappropriate, but credit toward something deemed good by the wider society. At the other end of the life course, Foster Grand-parents are also paid a stipend. The justification in this case is that older people should be encouraged to volunteer to have a more productive and rewarding life of retirement but they, more than younger people, will be deterred by lack of economic resources. In the United Kingdom, the nonprofit organization Age Concern recruits volunteers to act as "Good Neighbors" to look after a number of elderly people in their neighborhood. As with the Foster Grandparents program, the organization assumes that the financial cost of volunteering is an impediment and that stipends can help overcome it.

Finally, we should note that "interests" narrowly defined often play some role in volunteer work. We are more likely to become environmental activists if our backyards are being polluted than we would if our backyards were not threatened. The threat raises the chances we will get involved, although it is by no means a sufficient condition. When Illinois residents were asked in 2000 what it would take to get them more involved in volunteer activities, the most frequently mentioned factor was more free time (25 percent), but a sizeable minority (18 percent) said they would get more involved if they were personally affected by the outcome, if their neighborhood was affected by development, if their jobs demanded some action, or if they would personally benefit from the activity (Profile 2001). In all these cases, volunteers stood to benefit from the work, but this did not disqualify them from volunteer status because they were pursuing a collective good that others would enjoy even if they contributed none of their time. Volunteers often, therefore, pay a premium price for any benefits they reap and, because there are others who will benefit even though they do nothing, interests alone cannot be a sufficient explanation for their behavior.

## Using Motives to Define Volunteering

The net-cost approach tries to be objective about the definition of volunteering. It should be possible for a third party to look at the "volunteer" activities and decide whether the costs exceed the benefits, in which case the designation is appropriate. This is congruent with the utilitarian approach, according to which volunteer work is unpaid productive labor. From the utilitarian perspective, volunteering cannot be defined by its motivation. Motives might explain volunteer work, but they do not define it.

Other social scientists, however, believe that motivation is intrinsic to a definition of volunteer work. It is not simply "unpaid labor" but unpaid labor that is appropriately motivated. Thus, although there is agreement that people can benefit from their volunteer work, they must not volunteer for the purpose of gaining those benefits. They would, presumably, continue to volunteer even if those benefits disappeared. In a focus group convened to discuss the duties of citizenship, a majority of members agreed that volunteering was a good example of virtuous behavior. The group members then debated whether it was possible to judge an act as virtuous without considering the underlying motive. One woman said, "In order to classify someone as good—good citizen, good person—you've got to look at their motives" (Conover et al. 1993, 161). "You have to demonstrate . . . that your heart is in the right place" (Ostrower 2002, 28).

In the public mind, then, volunteer work is not simply unpaid labor but unpaid labor performed for the correct reason. "Good works" are inspired by virtues such as generosity, love, gratitude, loyalty, courage, compassion, and a desire for justice (Martin 1994, 31; Wuthnow 1995, 175). Purity of motivation becomes the template against which individual acts are compared, and volunteer status is denied to those motivated primarily by self-interest (Campbell and Wood 1999, 44). Nonprofit agencies reflect this view, that "real" volunteers have the right motives and respond to the right incentives. For example, emergency squads resist the use of financial incentives (such as tax credits, health benefits, or assistance with continuing education) to attract new volunteers because they worry recruits attracted by an incentive program would not be committed in the same way as "pure" volunteers (Thompson 1993). The core members of the search and rescue organization studied by Lois (2003, 68) denied themselves the reward even of prestige in the community: "One technique of self-denial was to wear pagers on a belt but to turn them in toward the body so that the search and rescue emblem was not visible. By downplaying their group affiliation, members signaled to others that they were not motivated by self-gain."

In summary, a sound argument can be made that motives help define volunteer work and that volunteer work cannot simply be defined as "unpaid labor." But it is no simple matter to agree on the appropriate motivation for volunteer work, and this has persuaded most social scientists to treat motives as exogenous to volunteer work. They do not constitute volunteer work, but they can help explain it.

## Volunteering and Social Activism

To a considerable degree the study of volunteerism has developed independently of the study of social activism. Volunteerism has been most closely associated with studies of voluntary associations and nonprofit organizations, while social activism has been most closely associated with studies of social movements. They have developed as somewhat distinct fields of social science investigation, as if they referred to totally different social phenomena, each requiring its own conceptualization and theorization. In this section we will consider the meaning of volunteerism as distinct from social activism. We will then discuss some of the similarities between the meanings of the two terms.

## Differences

Volunteering and activism are typically contrasted using phrases such as "palliation versus prevention," or "short-term versus long-term solutions to social problems." Volunteering targets people; activism targets structures. Activists care "about solutions that would not depend so completely on each individual's personal feelings of generosity and personal ability to donate money, space, and time but on solutions that would be built into official institutions" (Eliasoph 1998, 175). The activist fights to create and secure funding for shelters, counseling services, health centers, and the like, while the volunteer helps run the places once they are established.

This distinction between changing social conditions and providing services is part of the vernacular language of politics. In *Volunteerism and the Status of Women: A Position Paper,* issued by the Women and Volunteerism Task Force of the National Organization of Women, "change-directed" volunteerism (of which the organization approved) was distinguished from "service-oriented" volunteerism, which "seeks to complement insufficiently funded social services with non-paid labor in order to alleviate social ills. In addition it blunts the pressure for a more equal distribution of the nation's wealth, by muting the unrest which threatens the economic privileges and power of the well-to-do" (quoted in Gold 1979, 21). The organization disapproved of "service-oriented" volunteerism. A distinction between volunteering and activism is also implied—and abetted—by the way in which governments treat voluntary organizations, at least in the United States, where tax-exempt status is granted only to those organizations that refrain from lobbying, issuing propaganda, electioneering, or engaging in any other partisan political activity.

There is much to be said for making these distinctions. Making the coffee after Sunday morning worship service is surely different from knocking on doors in a voter registration drive in the segregated South in the 1960s. We do not think of volunteers when we hear of people being threatened, beaten, jailed, suspended from school or college, fired from their jobs, or having crosses burned on their lawn. The same distinction can be drawn between different types of organizations. Some organizations provide social services; others see their mission as political or social change, their goal being to bring people together into an organization that can exert power.

As people turn their attention away from serving individuals and focus on broader issues of social justice and exploitation, their "vision expands" (Wuthnow 1991, 253). They become aware of the extent of the problem they face or the root causes of the suffering they are trying to alleviate. Vela-McConnell (1999, 173) describes "Brad," a volunteer at a homeless shelter who, as a result of his involvement, became more aware of the structural reasons for homelessness and hunger:

> They say we have enough food to feed the world three times over or something like that, and yet some people can't afford to eat anything. There's something in the very structure and if we tried it so long one way, why wouldn't we at least try it another way because it is not working this way.

For some volunteers, the shift to activism happens when they redefine what they are doing. For example, women who began with the idea of volunteering in a rape crisis center as service provision came to believe that rape had deeper causes and broadened their vision, although they continued doing the same work (Abrahams 1996, 774). People who move from volunteering to activism define commitment in a different way. They no longer think of it in terms of time but in terms of personal investment: commitment means you are willing to "put yourself on the line."

## Similarities

Despite these arguments that volunteer work is different from social activism, an equally persuasive case can be made that they are very similar activities and that "most activists are volunteers" (Ellis and Noyes 1990, 8). First, the volunteer concept includes advocacy, which is a form of service that is very close to social activism. Indeed, the advocacy role of the non-profit sector may be "more important to the nation's social health than the service function the sector also performs" (Salamon 2002, 10). Volunteers can advocate in any number of ways: they can work to identify problems that have been neglected by government agencies and the media; they can develop and promote new positions and policy alternatives; and they can help fund and staff research organizations and foundations dealing with problems such as environmental protection, medical research, or immigration.

A second reason why the two concepts overlap in meaning is that the same activity can be interpreted as one or the other, depending on the social context and the motives and interests of the volunteer. For example, some see acting as an ombudsman in nursing facilities for the aged as helping elderly residents deal with their day-to-day problems of living; others see the same job as one of advocacy and acting to protect the rights of the aged (Keith 2003, 25).

A third reason why the distinction between volunteerism and activism is misleading has to do with the claim that volunteerism is all about service motivated by compassion, whereas activism is all about advocacy motivated by justice. According to this distinction, people become social activists when they are angered by the unfair treatment of others and want to do something about it. Activism is issue-oriented. This description certainly fits many prominent examples of social activism. Admittedly there are many forms of volunteerism, such as being a docent at an art museum, that are not inspired by outrage at how others have been treated. However, the justice motive does not separate activists from volunteers. Much of what we conventionally call volunteering is inspired by a commitment to a cause. A man who volunteers to protect women entering an abortion clinic from protestors stationed outside may be interested less in the individual women than he is in the cause of civil rights. There is nothing in the *nature* of volunteer work that makes it compassionate. "Being emotional is thus a label, a construct. It is not just an internal state" (Groves 2001, 228). People do not necessarily volunteer *because* they are impelled by emotion. The emotional tone of volunteer work emerges as the result of the volunteers' interaction with each other, with the people they are trying to help, and with the public at large. The lesson is that we should be careful about using an emotion—such as compassion—to define volunteering, because the characterization of volunteerism as tinged with emotion is socially constructed.

## Volunteering and Caring

As one kind of unpaid work, volunteering overlaps in meaning with terms such as "helping" and "caring." What is the relation between these concepts?

## Informal Helping

Volunteer work is conventionally defined as being performed on behalf of or in connection with an organization. The organization will define the volunteer role, specify volunteer tasks, set schedules, screen new recruits, train them and manage them, and, if necessary, dismiss them. Volunteer work is a form of bureaucratized help, not to be confused with informal helping, which is unpaid service people provide on a more casual basis, outside of any organizational context, to someone in need.

### Care Work

Care work is normally associated with kin relations. It denotes face-to-face help provided to an individual toward whom one feels some kind of social responsibility: "visiting, managing household tasks, providing transportation, and the direct provision of personal care" (Farkas and Himes 1997, S180). Ellis and Noyes (1990, 5) refer to these as "basic responsibilities"—help that is necessary, unavoidable, required, and generally expected.

There are three ways of distinguishing volunteering from care work. First, caring is usually an outgrowth of already existing social relationships and it is usually quite diffused. Often the caregiver is living with the care receiver and is "on call" all the time. Volunteering, on the other hand, is quite specific, in the sense that the reach of the obligations entailed is strictly controlled and the recipients of help are not necessarily known to or related to the volunteer. Second, the caregiver is likely to think of the role as an inescapable responsibility (Rozario et al. 2004, 436). Care work implies strong obligations, primarily to one's relatives, fictive kin, or other members of the household. In contrast, volunteering is "non-obligatory" (Dekker and Halman 2003, 1). Third, caring carries with it strong expressive components. The emotional tie between the caregiver and the person being cared for is inseparable from the task. Taking care of your elderly parents yourself is very different from paying an aide to do it for you. In contrast, volunteering can be quite instrumental, devoid of emotional or expressive overtones: it is simply unpaid productive labor. It matters not who performs the work as long as it gets done.

We find quite persuasive the arguments that caring and volunteering are distinct activities. However, we must be careful not to exaggerate the differences between them. First, although volunteer work is one way we choose to spend our leisure time, it can also be seen as a duty, something we believe we owe to our community or to a group or organization to which

we belong. This sense of duty moves volunteer work much closer to care work, the difference being that the obligation is owed to a larger social entity rather than to specific others. In short, volunteer work is not always freely chosen. "Voluntary" is not a synonym for "willing." Many people volunteer grudgingly out of a sense of duty or obligation to others they would prefer to avoid. Whether or not the volunteer work is a felt obligation and whether meeting that obligation is pleasurable or not pleasurable is an empirical matter: "It must be determined whether volunteers feel they are engaging in enjoyable and satisfying activity that they have had the option to accept or reject on their own terms" (Stebbins 2004, 4).

## Conclusion

Deciding what should count as volunteer work turns out to be much more difficult than might at first appear. Words such as "volunteering" are folk concepts as well as scientific concepts. They are used by, and have meaning for, people going about their everyday lives. Often their meaning is contested. People do not agree on what should count as volunteering. Sometimes they use words like "volunteering" as labels to pin on people and their actions in order to denigrate them; at other times, these same words are used to indicate approval.

## References

Abrahams, Naomi. 1996. "Negotiating Power, Identity, Family, and Community: Women's Community Participation." *Gender and Society* 10: 768–796.

Campbell, Catherine, and Rachel Wood. 1999. *Social Capital and Health.* London: Health Education Authority.

Conover, Pamela Johnston, Stephen Leonard, and Donald Searing. 1993. "Duty Is a Four-Letter Word: Democratic Citizenship in the Liberal

Polity." In *Reconsidering the Democratic Republic,* ed. George Marcus and Russell Hanson, 147–171. University Park: Pennsylvania State University Press.

Cutler, Stephen, and Nicholas Danigelis. 1993. "Organizational Contexts of Activity." In *Activity and Aging,* ed. John Kelly, 146–163. Newbury Park, CA: Sage.

Dekker, Paul, and Loek Halman. 2003. "Volunteering and Values: An Introduction." In *The Values of Volunteering: A Cross-Cultural Perspective,* ed. Paul Dekker and Loek Halman, 1–18. New York: Kluwer Academic.

Dingle, Alan. 2001. *Measuring Volunteering: A Practical Toolkit.* Washington, DC: Independent Sector.

Eliasoph, Nina. 1998. *Avoiding Politics: How Americans Produce Apathy in Everyday Life.* Cambridge: Cambridge University Press.

Ellis, Susan, and Katherine Noyes. 1990. *By the People: A History of Americans as Volunteers.* San Francisco: Jossey-Bass.

Farkas, Janice, and Christine Himes. 1997. "The Influence of Caregiving and Employment on the Voluntary Activities of Midlife and Older Women." *Journal of Gerontology* 52B: S180–S189.

Frey, Bruno, and Lorenz Goette. 1999. "Does Pay Motivate Volunteers?" Working Paper no. 7. Institute for Empirical Research in Economics, University of Zurich, Switzerland.

Gold, Doris. 1979. *Opposition to Volunteerism: An Annotated Bibliography.* Chicago: CPL Bibliographies.

Groves, Julian. 2001. "Animal Rights and the Politics of Emotion." In *Passionate Politics: Emotions and Social Movements,* ed. Jeff Goodwin, 212–232. Chicago: University of Chicago Press.

Hooghe, Marc. 2003. "Participation in Voluntary Associations and Value Indicators: The Effect of Current and Previous Participation Experiences." *Nonprofit and Voluntary Sector Quarterly* 32: 47–69.

Keith, Pat. 2003. *Doing Good for the Aged: Volunteers in an Ombudsman Program.* Westport, CT: Praeger.

Lois, Jennifer. 2003. *Heroic Efforts: The Emotional Culture of Search and Rescue Volunteers.* New York: New York University Press.

Martin, Mike. 1994. *Virtuous Giving: Philanthropy, Voluntary Service, and Caring.* Bloomington: Indiana University Press.

Ostrower, Francie. 2002. *Trustees of Culture: Power, Wealth, and Status on Elite Art Boards.* Chicago: University of Chicago Press.

Rozario, Philip, Nancy Morrow-Howell, and James Hinterlong. 2004. "Role Enhancement or Role Strain." *Research on Aging* 26: 413–428.

Salamon, Lester. 1997. *Holding the Center: America's Nonprofit Sector at a Crossroads.* New York: Nathan Cummings Foundation.

———. 2002. "The Resilient Sector: The State of Nonprofit America." In *The State of Nonprofit America,* ed. Lester Salamon, 3–64. Washington, DC: Brookings Institution Press.

Smith, Justin Davis. 1998. *The 1997 National Survey of Volunteering.* London: National Centre for Volunteering.

Stebbins, Robert. 2004. "Introduction." In *Volunteering as Leisure/Leisure as Volunteering,* ed. Robert Stebbins, 1–12. Cambridge, MA: CABI Publishing.

Thompson, Alexander. 1993. "Volunteers and Their Communities: A Comparative Analysis of Firefighters." *Nonprofit and Voluntary Sector Quarterly* 22: 155–166.

Torcal, Mariano, and Jose Ramon Montero. 1999. "Facets of Social Capital in New Democracies: The Formation and Consequences of Social Capital in Spain." In *Social Capital and European Democracy,* ed. Jan van Deth, Marco Maraffi, Kenneth Newton, and Paul Whiteley, 167–191. London: Routledge.

Vela-McConnell, James. 1999. *Who Is My Neighbor? Social Affinity in a Modern World.* Albany: State University of New York Press.

Wuthnow, Robert. 1991. *Acts of Compassion: Caring for Others and Helping Ourselves.* Princeton, NJ: Princeton University Press.

———. 1995. *Learning to Care: Elementary Kindness in an Age of Indifference.* New York: Oxford University Press.

► CHAPTER 20

# It Ain't Natural: Toward a New (Natural) Resource Conceptualization for Volunteer Management

JEFFREY L. BRUDNEY AND LUCAS C.P.M. MEIJS

Volunteering is an important feature of civil society all over the world. Salamon and Sokolowski (2001) showed that in 24 countries formal volunteer work contributes an equivalent of 11 million full-time equivalent jobs accounting on average for 65 percent of total nonprofit philanthropic income. Globally, the expectations of what volunteering can achieve seem to rise as, for example, NGOs are seen as important actors to control multinationals (see, for example, van Tulder and van der Zwart 2006). These developments add to growing demands on the volunteer sector for delivering services, campaigning, and maintaining social capital.

At the same time, the practitioner field of volunteering (at least in many Western countries) is awash with stories provoking concern about maintaining, let alone raising, current levels of volunteering. As Merrill (2006) remarks, "While the value of volunteering increases in importance, the time available for volunteering is seen as decreasing" (p. 9). . . . Whether supply has diminished or demand

has increased, some nations, organizations, and policy fields report shortages in volunteers.

This general concern about potential problems in some parts of the volunteer labor market has led to interventions from governments and the voluntary sector internationally. Governments have formulated policies to promote and facilitate volunteering (Davis Smith 2007; Davis Smith and Ellis 2003; van Hal, Meijs, and Steenbergen 2004). Many countries have installed national task forces to guide or safeguard the future of volunteering, such as Commissie Vrijwilligersbeleid, Netherlands (2001–2005); the Commission on the Future of Volunteering, England 2005–2008 (Commission on the Future of Volunteering 2008); Enquete Kommission Zukunft des Bürgerschaftlichen Engagement, Germany (1999–2002); Canada Volunteerism Initiative (part of voluntary sector initiative, 2001); and the government-sponsored National Conferences on Volunteering, Australia.

We propose a new conceptualization of volunteer labor as a renewable resource whose continuation and volume of flow can be affected positively as well as negatively by human intervention. We believe that the new conceptualization opens novel perspectives for researchers and practitioners in the field of volunteering. In this article, we focus on the users of volunteer labor, such as groups, organizations, and associations that enlist volunteers. Accordingly, we develop a new regenerative approach to help manage the volunteer resource in a more sustainable way.

## Early Warning Signs About Sustaining the Volunteer Commons

Problems in sustaining a ready supply of volunteers have surfaced and accelerated over the past decade, albeit more so in some countries and areas than others. Because longitudinal data on volunteering are scarce (Brudney and Gazley 2006), we must draw on less firm, suggestive evidence as well.

In the United States, large annual surveys of volunteering of about 60,000 households are administered by the Bureau of Labor Statistics (BLS). According to the BLS surveys, after holding steady at 28.8 percent of the population from 2003 through 2005, the level of volunteering in the United States fell to 26.7 percent in 2006. The decline continued in 2007, with the percentage of the population who volunteered falling to 26.2 percent. Although about 60.8 million Americans volunteered, both the number of volunteers and the rate of volunteering declined (BLS 2007). Gaps in the supply of volunteers are common in the United States, for example, in mentoring and education (Grantmaker Forum on Community and National Service 2003).

Additional data suggest changes in traditional patterns, if not disaffection, of people in the United States with the prevailing model of volunteering. According to a series of national surveys conducted by the Independent Sector, the average weekly hours spent volunteering dropped markedly over the 1990s. In the first of the surveys conducted in 1987, the average time volunteered amounted to 4.7 hours per week and a total of 244.4 hours per year. Scarcely 10 years later, in the 1998 Independent Sector survey the average volunteer gave only 3.5 hours weekly and 182.0 hours annually—a 25 percent drop (Brudney and Gazley 2006).

Other countries also report downward trends in volunteering. In the Netherlands, 38 percent of nonprofit organizations complain that they cannot find sufficient volunteers; nearly half report that they cannot recruit enough board members, and a shortage of youth leaders plagues sports and recreation programs (Devilee 2005). In Canada, a Web site launched in late 2007 warns of a "Way-Of-Life Wake-Up Call For Canada's Communities," due to decreases in volunteering (Who Cares 2008). Graff and Reed state on the home page of this Web site: "In short, it's [volunteering] declining and it looks like the trend will worsen, possibly significantly."

In addition to decreases in the percentage of volunteers and the amount of volunteer activity, the annual BLS surveys document significant turnover in volunteers. The Corporation for National and Community Service (CNCS) reported that of the estimated 65.4 million people who volunteered in the United States in 2005, 20.9 million did not continue to volunteer in 2006 (CNCS 2007). Thus, a staggering one in three Americans evidently dropped out of volunteering between 2005 and 2006. Other studies document problems in retaining volunteers in other countries (McCurley and Lynch 2005).

Confronted with the sharp attrition in volunteering in the US study, CNCS CEO David Eisner warned,

> This report is a wakeup call for any group that uses volunteers: If you want to keep them, you need to give them serious and meaningful work that affects change in your community; and you have to remember to train, manage,

and thank them the way you would any valued colleague. (CNCS 2007, 1)

## The Traditional Model of Volunteer Management

Research has been dominated by a "workplace" conception of volunteers as part-time employees, giving a few hours each week, and the volunteer program as a "systematic effort to involve volunteers in the work, outputs, and outcomes of an organization" (Brudney and Lee 2008, 638; compare Dunn 1995). Several authors have proposed models to guide these traditional volunteer programs, which form the mainstream of the current, especially practitioner, literature (for example, Ellis 1990; Fisher and Cole 1993; McCurley and Lynch 2005). A review of these models shows that they are quite similar, grounded in a set of core functions that volunteer programs typically perform, including selection, orientation, job design, training, placement, and evaluation. This approach is based largely on a workplace analogy (Davis Smith 1996; Gaskin 2003), expecting that process management principles adapted from business management theory will apply to volunteers (Paull 2002).

## Fissures in the Foundation of Traditional Volunteer Management

At the root of our view of the need to introduce and adopt a new approach to the involvement of volunteers is the preoccupation of the traditional model with recruitment rather than retention. Surveys of managers of volunteer services document that the chief problem they perceive in volunteer-based programs is recruitment. We do not dispute their perception but wish to point out that this finding begs the question of whether the source of the perpetual need for more volunteers resides in failures in volun-

teer program development and management that may be the source of unsteady commitment, high turnover, and urgent recruitment. We would argue that the preoccupation with recruitment distracts attention and resources from the management and retention of volunteers. This lapse provokes an endless cycle of recruitment: If volunteers cannot be retained, new ones must be found to replace them. Alternatively, if continual recruitment works, retaining volunteers becomes less important.

Following the President's Summit for America's Future, a major event held in the United States in 1997 to stimulate volunteering, Brudney (1999) cautioned that the field was consumed with the recruitment of volunteers with little thought or resources dedicated to management and retention of those volunteers on hand. Although the drumbeat continues for more volunteers, much less is heard—or committed—in regard to management and support of existing, or new, volunteers.

Our concern and commitment to a new approach for understanding volunteering and volunteer management stem from what we see as an imprudent use of the volunteer resource. Evidence gathered from several sources suggests that many organizational users of volunteers do not routinely act in a way to sustain the resource. Results of a 1998 national survey of 1,030 Americans demonstrate that two out of five volunteers have stopped volunteering at some point because of one or more shortcomings in the way organizations manage (or fail to manage) volunteers, such as not making good use of volunteers' time or good use of their talents, or not defining volunteer tasks clearly. The study concluded, "Poor volunteer management practices result in more lost volunteers than people losing interest because of changing personal or family needs" (United Parcel Service Foundation 1998, 15). A more recent study finds that for many volunteers dropping out is not a product of a decline in motivation but of failures in bridging the gap between preferred and actual volunteer experiences (Yanay and Yanay 2008).

Data derived from organizational users of volunteers substantiate the complaints of volunteers about lapses in management. A survey of a representative sample of more than 3,000 US charities revealed that not even half of these entities had implemented eight out of nine recommended practices for the management of volunteers to a large degree (the lone exception was regular supervision and communication with volunteers, adopted by 67 percent; Hager and Brudney 2004a, 2004b).

A further sign of the limitations of the traditional model of volunteer management is the frantic search to enlist new types of volunteers, such as corporate volunteers, "done in a day" volunteers, virtual volunteers, stipended volunteers (for example, AmeriCorps members), service learning volunteers, "gap year" volunteers, etc. The dawning and promotion of new forms of civic engagement are hardly a negative development, yet we suspect that the plethora stems equally from fissures in the traditional model in retaining volunteers.

Although the changes observed in volunteering are also a product of larger societal transformations (Hustinx and Lammertyn 2003), we believe that they have been accelerated by the traditional model of volunteer management and its focus on recruitment of volunteers rather than on their support and good management. The introduction of a new approach to volunteer management that broadens the focus beyond recruitment seems both appropriate and useful. We begin by conceiving of volunteer labor as a natural resource.

## Applying the Natural Resource Conceptualization

We offer the proposition that volunteer energy can be understood as a human-made, renewable/recyclable resource that can be grown, and whose

continuation and volume of flow can be influenced by human beings positively as well as negatively. Consuming organizations include nonprofit and government agencies, religious institutions, volunteer centers, associations, social and sports clubs, and civic groups as well as a growing number of private business firms engaged in corporate, employee, and community service programs. All of these organizations vie for the labor of citizens who can produce volunteer energy. Volunteering also faces fierce competition from other greedy institutions such as work, family, and leisure time: "The struggle over their allocation is as much a root fact of social life as is the competition among users of scarce resources in economic affairs" (Coser 1974, 1).

Natural resources are "that part of the stock which has a value as something that can be utilized" (Jones and Hollier 1997, 20–21). Perhaps the most pivotal issue concerning natural resources is their exhaustibility or, positively formulated, their sustainability.... [B]y conceiving of the supply of volunteer energy as a natural resource we hope to alleviate inappropriate harvesting or use of the resource that can weaken its vitality.

## Characterizing Volunteer Energy as a Natural Resource

Natural resources can be renewable or nonrenewable (depletable) (Risvand 2002; Tietenberg 1996, 2006). Depletable or nonrenewable resources are "fixed in supply" (Jones and Hollier 1997, 23). They are called stock resources because "the total supply of the resource is limited in quantity, and each rate of use diminishes some future rate of use" (Risvand 2002, 2). Nonrenewable resources can be easily exhausted (Tietenberg 2006).

Renewable resources, such as cereal grains, fish, forests, and animals, "have a continuing process of renewal and supply in nature" (Risvand 2002, 2). In many cases they "have had a persistent open access status" (Brown 2000, 875) and supply a set amount at constant marginal cost (Tietenberg 1996, 114). With improper use, renewable resources can also be exhausted (Tietenberg 1996). We view volunteer energy as a renewable resource.

Risvand (2002) noted that renewable resources are also called flow resources because it is possible to keep using them so long as production (the flow) continues. Blunden (1985) classified flow resources as "all those items that may be depleted, sustained or increased by the actions of man" (p. 29). For some natural resources, manipulating the flow lies beyond present control, for example, solar/tidal/wind energy (Risvand 2002; Tietenberg 1996). By contrast, the continuation and volume of flow of some renewable resources (such as animals, plants, soil, and groundwater) can be influenced by human beings, a condition which potentially allows not only growth and recycling possibilities but also stagnation and depletion. We view volunteer energy as a flow resource susceptible to human intervention.

The literature on natural resources identifies three types of reserves. Current reserves can yield a profit after extraction at current prices; potential reserves can yield a profit if people are willing to pay a higher price; and the resource endowment is the total amount of the resource available (Tietenberg 1996). Adapted to volunteer energy, the current reserve consists of people who, given current recruitment practices, can be harvested (recruited) efficiently or economically into volunteering. The potential reserve are the people who can be recruited to volunteer but only with markedly higher levels of recruitment or extraction costs. The resource endowment is the theoretical maximum of volunteer energy that might possibly exist.

Conceiving volunteering as a (continuous) flow resource raises the problem of having too much volunteer energy available in the wrong organization (e.g., one that is oversubscribed) or at the wrong time (e.g., on weekends). Just as

with some natural resources (e.g., solar energy), some results of volunteer energy can be stored to be used when needed, although the amounts seem limited relative to the volume of volunteering (e.g., when volunteers prepare mailings or food in advance of a fundraising or other event). Finally, alternatives are crucial to sustain natural resources, as for example, solar energy can prolong the use of fossil fuels. Alternatives are readily available to extend the life cycle of the volunteer resource. For instance, technology can free volunteers from some tasks if considered undesirable by volunteers (e.g., clerical duties), and difficult to fill volunteer assignments can be transferred to paid staff.

Conceiving of volunteer energy as a renewable natural resource in this way raises questions about sustainable use and the risk of depletion. This risk may be alleviated (although not dismissed out of hand) because volunteer energy can be seen as a continuous resource; succeeding generations can be expected to carry on the behavior at some level. In addition, volunteer energy has growth and development potential. Thus, a world without any volunteering is, indeed, hard to imagine. By contrast, anticipating a future with a smaller useable flow of the resource is not only credible but also essential to understand, and address, as portended by the trends and other data presented herein. This realization leads us to consider questions on how to prevent misuse and overuse of the resource as well as how to grow and develop it.

### Volunteer Energy and the Commons

Many natural resources can be or are governed by property rights. Others can be classified as common-pool resources or open access resources (Kula 1992; Ostrom 1990). Ostrom, Gardner, and Walker (1994) provided a general definition. They described a common-pool resource, such as a lake or ocean, an irrigation system, a fishing ground, or the atmosphere, as a natural or human-made resource from which it is difficult to exclude or limit users once the resource is provided, and one person's consumption of units of the resource makes those units unavailable to others.

The concepts of the commons and the tragedy of the commons, as introduced by Gareth Hardin (1968), are familiar to students of nonprofit organizations and volunteerism. What may not be so clear, yet is evident in the definition of Ostrom et al. (1994), is that these ideas can be applied to human and social interaction as well as to the natural and biological world. To our knowledge, though, volunteer energy has not before been likened to a natural resource that is subject to commons problems. Nevertheless, at the level of volunteer hours and also at the level of individual volunteers, volunteer energy is an open access resource that can be used and possibly misused by users, that is, organizations that seek donations of labor.

In fact, we may reasonably speculate that one source of possible stagnation or decline in volunteer energy is the exploitation of the common pool by host organizations. We believe that this problem, as in Hardin's (1968) original formulation, may be exacerbated because volunteer energy is seen as both inexhaustible and inexpensive, a resource to be used as needed by the host organization without much consideration beyond the needs of the present user. As a result, they are caught up in a seemingly endless cycle of recruitment, use, and withdrawal that risks drop-out and burn-out of volunteers and potential stagnation in growth of the total resource. Negative experiences or perceptions on the part of volunteers spill over to affect entry into the field. From this perspective, a failure to pay attention to sustaining the resource contributes to high volunteer attrition rates that diminish the overall condition of the volunteer commons and the prospects of other users.

Hardin (1968) proposed that a common-pool resource could sustain itself over a lengthy period but suddenly and perceptibly veer toward collapse. This story can be told for almost every resource. The open access situation of the common pool only makes the problem more complex to manage (see also Ostrom 1999). As the resource dwindles, users will compete more vigorously to tap the remainder so that the rate of exhaustion can be expected to accelerate. We believe that, as with other common-pool resources, volunteer energy is potentially susceptible to this characterization. Although the supply of volunteer energy may not be in any immediate danger, the signs emanating from studies of volunteer involvement and management raise concerns. It seems appropriate, then, to examine the state of volunteer energy, contemporary practices for management of this resource, and new methods to stimulate and revitalize the volunteer commons.

Table 20.1 summarizes our conceptualization of volunteering as a natural resource. For us, a significant consequence of the analysis is that the volunteer energy-using community must shift from an instrumental to a more sustainable approach. A sustainable approach to volunteering, just as in natural resources, must take into account "the needs of the present without compromising the ability of future generations to meet their own needs" (Brundtland 1987, 24). We conceive of the sustainability of volunteer energy over the long haul as a problem surprisingly similar to the preservation of natural common-pool resources. Borrowing a term from the voluminous literature that treats the regeneration of natural resources, the following section introduces a regenerative approach to guide and redirect the management of volunteer energy.

## A Regenerative Approach to Volunteer Management

Given our conceptualization of volunteer energy as a natural resource, we suggest that a new approach for volunteer management is called

TABLE 20.1. **Volunteer Energy as a Natural Resource**

| Natural Resource Characteristic | Application to Volunteer Energy |
|---|---|
| **Human-made flow** | The amount of volunteer energy (multiplication of people times hours) can be influenced positively or negatively by human intervention |
| **Renewable/recyclable** | If managed in a way to sustain and grow the resource, volunteers tend to volunteer again |
| **Current reserve** | The amount of volunteer energy (multiplication of people times hours) donated at present levels of promotion, recruitment, and incentives (lower extraction costs) |
| **Potential reserve** | The amount of volunteer energy (multiplication of people times hours) that could be donated given greater promotion, recruitment, and incentives (higher extraction costs) |
| **Resource endowment** | The theoretical maximum amount of volunteer energy (multiplication of people times hours) that can be donated |
| **Growable** | Human and program interventions can extend the current reserve of volunteer energy (the number of volunteers and the amount of hours donated) and/or increase the potential reserve |
| **Storage potential** | Limited possibility to store some results of volunteering for later use (for example, when volunteers prepare mailings or food for events) |
| **Alternatives** | Alternatives can extend the lifecycle of the volunteer resource, for example, use of technology and transfer of less popular volunteer assignments to paid staff |
| **Common pool** | Open access to potential volunteers for all organizations results in overemphasis on recruiting without commensurate attention to retaining volunteers |

for to sustain and grow the resource. Table 20.2 presents the new regenerative approach to volunteer management and compares it with the traditional instrumental approach.

First we look at the community. At the center of our analysis is the argument that the nexus of volunteer involvement must be expanded beyond the focal organization to embrace the larger community, including a broad array of stakeholders. The implication is that more parties should be involved than presently in volunteerism, and that these parties should consider not only how

to meet the current needs of the community for volunteers but also how meeting current needs affects the possibility of meeting future needs. In this broader community context, the measure of effectiveness is impact not only on the needs of the community today but also on the possibilities of still having impact tomorrow.

A first party to include in these discussions is the users of volunteers, that is, organizations enlisting their assistance. Among this group, discussion is needed to identify effective ways of involving and managing volunteers seen from the

TABLE 20.2.  **Contrasting Approaches to Volunteer Management**

| Dimension | Traditional Instrumental Volunteer Management | Regenerative Volunteer Management |
|---|---|---|
| **THE COMMUNITY** | | |
| Nexus | Organization-centered | Community-centered |
| Parties involved | Focal organization and its current volunteers, clients, funders, and supporters | All parties to volunteer involvement, including the community of users, volunteers, clients, funders, and supporters |
| Effectiveness | Impact on an organization's current needs | Impact on current organizational needs and on the possibility to have impact on future needs |
| **THE RESOURCE** | | |
| Resource | Instrumental | Recyclable/growable |
| Valuation of volunteering | Replacement value | Life-time value |
| Time horizon/perspective | Single/current assignment or event (short term) | Prolonged interaction (long term) |
| **ORGANIZATIONAL MANAGEMENT** | | |
| Offering of volunteer work | Job description | Combination of availability, assets, and assignments (Meijs & Brudney, 2007) |
| Image | The fit | The negotiation |
| Emphasis | Accomplishments for the organization | Accomplishments for the organization and for the volunteer |

perspective of sustainability and coordination in sharing and co-use of the resource. A second party to include in discussions is funders and local governments. In their funding policies, these entities should not focus exclusively on short-run results or overlook the need for building volunteer management infrastructure (United Parcel Service Foundation 2002). Other parties to involve are agency clients, corporations, educational institutions, and, of course, volunteers and potential volunteers (citizens).

Second, we need to look at the resource itself. A major difference between the new regenerative approach and the traditional instrumental approach lies in the depiction of the goal of volunteer involvement. The major goal of the regenerative approach is to renew and reinvigorate the volunteer resource, that is, to attract people into volunteering and keep them volunteering over the life course. Users of the resource are, then, responsible not only to their organization but also to the larger commons of potential users.

From the perspective of traditional volunteer management, volunteers are a resource that organizations use as needed and replace when necessary through further recruitment. Users may not be overly concerned with volunteer service beyond their own organization; in that sense, volunteer energy is instrumental, or utilized primarily for the purposes of the host organization. From the new point of view, however, we propose that volunteer energy should be seen as recyclable or renewable over the life course so that individuals emerge from host organizations interested in, and prepared for, further volunteer opportunities. We do not mean to imply that the traditional model overlooks the volunteer experience, only that consuming or user organizations generally place greater priority on meeting their own needs than on sustaining and growing the volunteer resource.

As shown in Table 20.2, the valuation of volunteer energy changes as well in the new regenerative approach. In the traditional view, volunteer energy is normally valued at the replacement cost to the organization, such as an accepted wage level or the opportunity cost to the volunteer (Handy and Srinivasan 2004); such estimates are commonly used for organizational and public-policy purposes (e.g., Independent Sector Organization 2008). This view accentuates the instrumental view of volunteers. From our regenerative perspective, volunteer energy is conceived as a life-time valuation of the time and service donated, or, at the least, the value to the organization and to the volunteer as proposed by Brown (1999).

Incorporated into the regenerative approach is the idea of the life-time valuation—and conception—of volunteering. We propose that the value of volunteering be seen as accruing not only to host organizations but also to the volunteers themselves and the larger society, including the enhancement of skills, self-confidence, and civic engagement as well as the transmission of an ethic of service to the next generation. We view volunteer involvement not as a single episode with a single host organization but as an extended, over-time interaction with multiple users (organizations) over the life course.

Third, we move to managing volunteers. With respect to the offering of volunteer work, organizations are traditionally encouraged to prepare job descriptions for volunteer positions that meet organizational needs and to recruit accordingly. In the regenerative approach, volunteer involvement emanates from the assets that volunteers possess, their preferred time availabilities, and the assignments that organizations envision to accommodate them (Meijs and Brudney 2007). Again, in regard to emphasis, the traditional approach is mostly concerned with the work accomplished for the organization, whereas in the regenerative approach the emphasis is on both organizational work and volunteer accomplishment, such as the development of volunteer competencies. Closely related, in the traditional model the image of volunteer work is the fit between the donation of time and organizational requirements. By contrast, in the regenerative approach the image is the negotiation between organization and volunteer to arrive at both realistic and satisfying work assignments that help organizations as well as yield volunteers the types of experiences that will invigorate the commons and renew the resource.

## Conclusion

The conceptualization of volunteer energy as a natural resource draws attention to at least two provocative sets of research questions. First, how can governance be established and maintained at the commons level to ensure the preservation and growth of volunteer energy? Second, what strategies can be used to enrich volunteer management to recycle and grow the volunteer resource?

With respect to the first question, as a preliminary step we might conceive of the role that could be played by community-wide volunteer centers (Brudney and Meijs 2004), the educational system, and/or local governments in maintaining and sustaining the volunteer commons. With regard to the second question, we might consider systematic research on recommended and emerging practices for volunteer management, including attention to differences in methods necessary to accommodate the great diversity of volunteers, programs, and organizational users. The new regenerative approach raises these questions, and more. Attending to them may well help to foster sustainability of the resource of volunteer energy.

## References

Blunden, J. 1985. *Mineral Resources and Their Management: Themes in Resource Management.* London and New York: Longman.

Brown, E. 1999. "Assessing the Value of Volunteer Activity." *Nonprofit and Voluntary Sector Quarterly* 28, no. 1, 3–17.

Brown, G. M. 2000. "Renewable Natural Resource Management and Use Without Markets." *Journal of Economic Literature* 38: 875–914.

Brudney, J. L. 1999. "The Perils of Practice: Reaching the Summit." *Nonprofit Management and Leadership* 9 (Summer): 385–398.

Brudney, J. L., and B. Gazley. 2006. "Moving Ahead or Falling Behind? Volunteer Promotion and Data Collection." *Nonprofit Management and Leadership* 16: 259–276.

Brudney, J. L., and Y. Lee. 2008. "Volunteer Programs." In W. A. Darity Jr., ed., *International Encyclopedia of the Social Sciences,* 2nd ed., 638–641. Detroit, MI: Macmillan.

Brudney, J. L., and L. C.P.M. Meijs. 2004. "Creating Community Payoffs with Winning Volunteer Scenarios." Paper presented at the 2004 Eurofestation, Maastricht, Netherlands (November 9–11).

Brundtland, G. H. 1987. *World Commission on Environment and Development: Our Common Future.* Oxford: Oxford University Press. [Available at: http://www.un-documents.net/our-common -future.pdf.]

Bureau of Labor Statistics (BLS). 2007. *Volunteering in the United States, 2007.* Retrieved February 8, 2008, from http://www.bls.gov/news .release/volun.toc.htm.

Canada Volunteerism Initiative. 2001. [Available at: http://publications.gc.ca/collections/Collection /CH4-54-2001-1E.pdf.]

Commissie Vrijwilligersbeleid, The Netherlands. 2001–2005. Retrieved March 24, 2009, from http://www.movisie.nl/116932/det/home _/vrijwillige_inzet_ /infrastructuur_ondersteuning /wat_doen_overheden/wat_was_de_commissie _vrijwilligersbeleid/.

[The Commission on the Future of Volunteering. January 2008. *Report of the Commission on the Future of Volunteering and Manifesto for Change.* Available at: http://image.guardian.co.uk/sys-files /Society/documents/2008/01/29/Manifesto _final.pdf.]

Corporation for National and Community Service (CNCS). 2007. "New Federal Report Shows Volunteering Strong in America, but 1 in 3 Volunteers Dropped Out in 2006." Retrieved November 1, 2007, from http://www.nationalservice .org/about/newsroom/releases_detail.asp?tbl_pr _id=682.

Coser, L. A. 1974. *Greedy Institutions: Patterns of Undivided Commitment.* New York: Free Press.

Davis Smith, J. 1996. "Should Volunteers Be Managed?" In D. Billis and M. Harris, eds., *Voluntary Agencies: Challenges of Organizations and Management.* London: Macmillan.

———. 2007. "The Inflatable Log: Volunteering, the State and Democracy." In J. Davis Smith and M. Locke, eds., *Volunteering and the Test of Time: Essays for Policy, Organization and Research,* 19–28. London: Institute for Volunteering Research.

Davis Smith, J., and A. Ellis. 2003. "Governments' Best Friend? The State and Volunteering in a Global Context." Paper presented at the 32nd ARNOVA Conference, Denver, CO (November 20–22).

Devilee, J. 2005. *Vrijwilligersorganisaties onderzocht. Over het tekort aan vrijwilligers en de wijze van werving en ondersteuning* [*Voluntary Organizations Studied: About the Shortage of Volunteers and Ways to Recruit and Support Them*]. The Hague, Netherlands: SCP.

Dunn, P. C. 1995. "Volunteer Management." In *Encyclopedia of Social Work,* 19th ed., 2483–2490. Washington, DC: National Association of Social Workers.

Ellis, S. J. 1990. *From the Top Down: The Executive Role in Volunteer Program Success.* Philadelphia: Energize.

Enquete Kommission Zukunft des Bürgerschaftlichen Engagement, Germany. 1999–2002. . . .

Fisher, J. C., and K. M. Cole. 1993. *Leadership and Management of Volunteer Programs: A Guide for Volunteer Administrators.* San Francisco: Jossey-Bass.

Gaskin, K. 2003. *A Choice Blend: What Volunteers Want from Organization and Management.* London: Institute for Volunteering Research. Retrieved September 16, 2008, from http://www.volunteering.org.uk/NR/rdonlyres/C2D97CE0–017F-4BF1–8120–68B08ADD8D26/0/choicblend.pdf.

Grantmaker Forum on Community and National Service. 2003. *The Cost of a Volunteer.* Berkeley, CA: Author. [Available at: http://www.worldvolunteerweb.org/resources/research-reports/national/doc/cost-of-a-volunteer.html.]

Hager, M. A., and J. L. Brudney. 2004a. *Balancing Act: The Challenges and Benefits of Volunteers.* Washington, DC: Urban Institute.

———. 2004b. *Volunteer Management Practices and Retention of Volunteers.* Washington, DC: Urban Institute.

Handy, F., and N. Srinivasan. 2004. "Valuing Volunteers: An Economic Evaluation of the Net Benefits of Hospital Volunteers." *Nonprofit and Voluntary Sector Quarterly* 33, no. 1, 28–54.

Hardin, G. 1968. "The Tragedy of the Commons." *Science* 162: 1243–1248.

Hustinx, L., and F. Lammertyn. 2003. "Collective and Reflexive Styles of Volunteering: A Sociological Modernization Perspective." *Voluntas: International Journal of Voluntary and Nonprofit Organizations* 14: 167–187.

Independent Sector Organization. 2008. *The Value of Volunteer Time.* Retrieved March 6, 2008, from http://www.independentsector.org/programs/research/volunteer_time.html.

Jones, G., and G. Hollier. 1997. *Resources, Society and Environmental Management.* London: Paul Liverpool.

Kula, E. 1992. *Economics of Natural Resources, the Environment and Policies.* London: Chapman & Hall.

McCurley, S., and R. Lynch. 2005. *Keeping Volunteers: A Guide to Retention.* Philadelphia: Energize.

Meijs, L. C.P.M., and J. L. Brudney. 2007. "Winning Volunteer Scenarios: The Soul of a New Machine." *International Journal of Volunteer Administration* 24, no. 6, 68–79.

Merrill, M. V. 2006. "Global Trends and the Challenges for Volunteering." *International Journal of Volunteer Administration* 24, no. 1, 9–14.

Ostrom, E. 1990. *Governing the Commons: The Evolution of Institutions for Collective Action.* New York: Cambridge University Press.

———. 1999. "Coping with Tragedies of the Commons." *Annual Review of Political Science* 2: 493–535.

Ostrom, E., R. Gardner, and J. M. Walker. 1994. *Rules, Games, and Common-Pool Resources.* Ann Arbor: University of Michigan Press.

Paull, M. 2002. "Refraining Volunteer Management: A View from the West." *Australian Journal on Volunteering* 7, no. 1, 21–27.

Risvand, J. 2002. "Natural Resources, Classification and Principles of Optimal Use." Edited by S. Barros. IUFRO Division 6 Meeting Collaboration and Partnership in Forestry, Valdivia, Chile.

Salamon, L. M., and W. Sokolowski. 2001. "Volunteering in Cross-National Perspective: Evidence from 24 Countries." Working Papers of the Johns Hopkins Comparative Nonprofit Sector Project No. 40. Baltimore: The Johns Hopkins Center for Civil Society Studies.

Tietenberg, T. 1996. *Environmental and Natural Resource Economics,* 4th ed. New York: HarperCollins.

———. 2006. *Environmental and Natural Resource Economics,* 7th ed. Boston: Pearson Addison Wesley.

United Parcel Service Foundation. 1998. *Managing Volunteers: A Report from United Parcel Service.* Atlanta, GA: Author.

———. 2002. *A Guide to Investing in Volunteer Resources Management: Improve Your Philanthropic Portfolio.* Atlanta, GA: Author.

Van Hal, T., L.C.P.M. Meijs, and M. Steenbergen. 2004. *Volunteering and Participation on the Agenda: Survey on Volunteering Policies and Partnerships in the European Union.* Utrecht, Netherlands: CIVIQ.

Van Tulder, R., and A. van der Zwart. 2006. *International Business-Society Management: Linking Corporate Responsibility and Globalization.* London: Routledge.

Who Cares. 2008. *A Way-of-Life Wake-up Call for Canada's Communities: The Graff-Reed Conversations.* Available at: http://www.canadawhocares.ca/.

Yanay, G. V., and N. Yanay. 2008. "The Decline of Motivation? From Commitment to Dropping Out of Volunteering." *Nonprofit Management and Leadership* 19, no. 1, 65–78.

# NOW YOU SEE 'EM, NOW YOU DON'T: VOLUNTEERS AND NONPROFITS

*Julie Ann Read, Benjamin S. Bingle, and C. Kenneth Meyer*

Saxeville Community Project (SCP) was the new "darling" of the community, the trendiest place to volunteer and make a difference. A relatively recent nonprofit on the Saxeville scene, SCP had carved out a niche in a relatively short amount of time and was able to mobilize forces in the community to come together for a common cause. Everything appeared to be good—or was it?

## A Small Town with Big-Town Issues

Saxeville was a fairly stable middle-class community with a large hospital, light industry, small family businesses, and close proximity to a growing community college. These assets, along with a strong public school system and affordable housing, made Saxeville an attractive place to live and raise a family. As a matter of fact, families stayed in Saxeville for generations—it was that kind of place.

The face of Saxeville had changed in just a few short years, however, and the image of the town as a stable middle-class community was no longer entirely accurate. In the suffering economy, more and more people had lost their jobs, but Saxeville presented few opportunities to find new work. Some enrolled at the community college to learn new skills and pursue a new career, others took odd jobs to make ends meet, and others fell into deep financial trouble. With the changing demographics came new community needs that demanded attention.

As the economic situation grew worse, people began standing near the local grocery store with signs asking for food, money, or jobs. This was a new sight for many longtime Saxeville residents, and it irked some of the townspeople. Many others, however, tried to help. The principal at the local elementary school posted notices in the school newsletter asking for donations of coats, hats, and mittens for needy students. Church-sponsored food pantries could hardly meet the growing community demand, so pastors implored their members to be generous with canned-food drives. The public library even hosted a toy collection during the holiday season. Yet the number of people without jobs and struggling to make ends meet continued to rise. This caught the attention of a small group of stay-at-home mothers from one of the more upscale neighborhoods in Saxeville. At their weekly book club meetings and regular social gatherings, conversations were dominated by the current state of Saxeville's citizens and the people standing outside the grocery store looking for help.

After many informal conversations, the small group of mothers decided that something needed to be done. That was the beginning of the Saxeville Community Project.

## A Nonprofit Is Born

Once they made the decision to act, the determined group of moms quickly mobilized. They agreed on two primary activities that could be implemented easily: providing food and providing clothing to those in need. Although there were churches and small organizations providing these services, there was no one central location providing both. They chose the name Saxeville Community Project for their one-stop shop because it was broad enough to cover the main areas they wanted to help with (food and clothing) while also providing ample room to expand services if warranted in the future. Additionally, the founding group wanted to make sure the organization's focus was on neighbors helping neighbors—a true *community* effort.

One of the mothers had worked as a graphic designer before she quit work to stay home with her children. She designed a simple but sleek logo that was visually appealing and gave instant cachet to the organization. One member of the group was married to a local businessman who had an empty storefront near the downtown district; he agreed to rent it to the organization for a nominal annual fee. Another member's husband was an attorney who willingly drafted the paperwork to make sure the organization was a registered 501(c)(3) nonprofit, and yet another spouse helped the organization secure insurance. The resourceful group had everything it needed.

## Fast Growth

Once all the basics were in place, the small group of mothers mobilized their friends. Meeting on a Sunday afternoon at the storefront, the group shared their vision with almost forty friends who came to eat a delicious spread of desserts, to mingle, and to learn about the Saxeville Community Project. The group laid out their vision: for community members to come together and provide food and clothing for those in the community who were in need. They also outlined what SCP needed: paint and labor to spruce up the storefront; shelving for the food pantry; and shelves and racks for the clothes closet.

The excitement at the meeting was palpable. Doing good deeds while addressing a major community need was an attractive vision for these longtime residents of Saxeville. Additionally, they had the resources—financial and otherwise—to really help the organization get off to a fast start.

The word spread and people reacted. The SCP storefront became a second home to many of the original group and their friends as they worked diligently to repaint and outfit the space. The storefront was rejuvenated in no time, and the group members started soliciting clothing and nonperishable foods. The Saxeville Community Project was almost ready to open its doors to the community.

The original group, now called "the BOD" (board of directors), used all of their organizational expertise to figure out how many days SCP would be open each week and then to set the work schedules and calculate the number of volunteers needed for staffing. One of the BOD members convinced her computer-savvy teenager to create a website and a simple online volunteer registration form. The group also cajoled their friends to donate clothes and food. The graphic designer mom (now called the SCP marketing coordinator) designed hip outreach materials showcasing the services offered by SCP. Everyone associated with SCP distributed the promotional material at their churches, schools, and neighborhood groups and posted it on every coffee shop bulletin board around town. In addition, those who agreed to volunteer or donate were given a fitted black T-shirt with the striking SCP logo on the front. The T-shirts quickly became sought-after wardrobe additions for young and old alike.

## Grand Opening

The Saxeville Community Project opened its doors on a sunny Saturday in December to much fanfare. Saxeville citizens who found themselves in need of food or clothing felt welcome at SCP, and some came multiple times in the first month. The organization had just opened, and already SCP had a roster of almost fifty people who donated some amount of time to the organization each month.

SCP was a fun place to volunteer. Outgoing and interesting people gathered together in the cool new storefront. It was not an obligation to volunteer, and in fact, going there was more reminiscent of a social gathering. The sounds of music and laughter often wafted out of the SCP headquarters, and volunteers regularly met with each other outside of their allotted time as strong friendships formed. Plus, there were no minimum requirements for volunteering, which made it easy to drift in and out of the organization depending on personal schedules. In its first year of existence, SCP actually had more volunteers than it needed at times, which made it easy for the BOD to decide to open one extra day a week.

## Volunteer Management

As time passed, it became clear to the BOD that a volunteer coordinator would be needed. The number of volunteers had become overwhelming, and more formal processes needed to be developed. One of the moms from the original group had a daughter, Emily Roberts, who had recently graduated from college and had not yet been able to secure a job. She had experience recruiting volunteers as an active member of multiple student groups during college and had served as a volunteer at SCP, so she was familiar with what the job entailed. Even though SCP could not offer much compensation, Emily readily accepted the part-time position.

She hit the ground running by implementing a new policy that required volunteers to attend mandatory orientation training before beginning at SCP. Those who had been involved since the organization opened its doors would also be required to attend. Emily thought this was a reasonable request since the training would enable everyone to work from the same page. At the same time, Emily drafted a policy that introduced a minimum age requirement for volunteers. She had seen some junior high school students who "looked like trouble" hanging around SCP and thought they might be causing some people to steer clear of the organization.

"This decision is justifiable," she argued, "because kids under twenty-one aren't responsible or reliable enough for what we're trying to do at SCP. Plus they're more likely to get hurt or make an inventory error."

These changes were met with a mixed response. Existing volunteers did not want to sit through orientation training for an organization they were already familiar with and might even have been involved in creating. New volunteers were hardly enthused about starting their SCP experience with a boring two-hour training. In fact, some people never returned to actually volunteer after sitting through the orientation. The minimum age restriction was even less popular. Church youth groups, amateur athletic clubs, and teen support groups could no longer volunteer at SCP. In spite of countless inquiring phone calls from the leaders of these groups, Emily held firm. Her resistance was tested, however, when she told many of the original supporters that they could no longer bring their families to volunteer at SCP because many of their children, nieces, and nephews were not twenty-one years old.

## Where Did They Go?

The Saxeville Community Project remained "the place to be" for almost six months after hiring Emily. It was presented with the Community Recognition Award at the chamber of commerce's annual awards banquet, and it received multiple grants to help provide services and pay Emily's salary. Critics complained, however, that SCP received the award and the grants only because the women on the BOD were connected with the chamber and the local community foundation. But the BOD had bigger problems than dealing with unhappy detractors. SCP was losing volunteers.

In the short time since Emily's hire, the number of volunteers had declined by more than 25 percent. She had spent too much time developing policies and conducting orientation trainings to find time to launch her volunteer recruitment strategy. She thought the declining volunteer numbers would rebound once a recruitment initiative got under way.

Emily was the only paid staff member at SCP, meaning that all of its other work was carried out by volunteers. As SCP lost volunteers, BOD members had to devote even more time to the organization because demand for services was still incredibly high. Worse yet, volunteering at SCP had become more like a full-time obligation than the fun, social, and exciting event it used to be.

After working yet another forty-plus-hour week themselves because of the lack of volunteers, the members of the BOD scheduled an ad hoc meeting to discuss what had happened to their community "darling" of an organization and how matters could be improved. Neither Emily nor her mother—a member of the BOD—was invited to the meeting.

## Questions and Instructions

1. Given SCP's strong start, why do you think the number of volunteers declined? Do you think other factors besides Emily's policies contributed to the decline? Please explain your response.

2. What were the demographics of the board of directors and their friends? What impact might those demographics have had on the current issue facing SCP?

3. Emily implemented orientation training and minimum age policies for volunteers. Were these policies unwarranted? Why or why not?

4. What should be included in SCP's volunteer recruitment initiative?

5. The case ends with the board of directors scheduling a meeting to discuss the organization's situation and how it could be improved. What would you recommend to alleviate and improve SCP's situation?

6. The board of directors purposefully did not inform Emily or her mother about the ad hoc meeting to discuss SCP's dilemma. What message did this send? Was it acceptable to exclude them? Why or why not?

# TURNING THE TIDE:
# TRANSITIONING FROM VOLUNTEERS TO PAID STAFF

*Julie Ann Read, Benjamin S. Bingle, and C. Kenneth Meyer*

Long Lake Caring (LLC) quickly became an important community asset during its first five years of existence. It grew from a small, informal group that provided winter coats to those in need to a registered 501(c)(3) organization that stayed open five days a week to provide used clothing to more than 1,000 families each year. As LLC grew, its cadre of volunteers expanded as well.

This growth caused the volunteer coordinator to voice his concerns about LLC's unsustainable model to the board of directors. He told them that by the end of the year his position needed to become a paid position—or he would have to leave.

## Organization Overview

LLC had humble beginnings. Three friends, each of whom attended a different church in the Long Lake area, noticed that young children at the local elementary school lacked adequate coats and hats to protect them from the harsh winter weather. Each woman convinced her church leaders to hold a Thanksgiving coat drive to provide coats for the children in need. Little did the women know that they would collect nearly 500 winter coats (along with hats and gloves) during the first coat drive, and they certainly had no idea how much work it would take to prepare the coats for distribution!

Fortunately, one of the church pastors let the women use a large multipurpose room where they could categorize all the donations based on size and make preparations to distribute the coats. Each of the three women gathered groups of volunteers from her church to host the first Long Lake Coat Fair. In just one afternoon, all of the 500 coats were claimed.

After the initial coat distribution, the volunteers from each church gathered to discuss the event. They noted that the migrant workers who had long shown up in Long Lake each summer to fill low-paying agricultural jobs in the surrounding region had begun in recent years to stay in the area year-round. The volunteers also talked about the impact of the recent economic downturn, which had increased the divide between the "haves" and "have-nots." Both of these factors had contributed to the growing need for affordable clothing—beyond winter coats—in Long Lake. In short, the volunteers decided that the community would benefit significantly from an organization that collected gently used clothing for people in need. Thus was Long Lake Caring born.

## Organization Growth

During the first year, the teams of volunteers planned multiple clothing drives and distributions. Members of the community appreciated having a place to donate excess bedding and clothing, while people in need benefited from the high-quality, affordable items, which helped them stretch their meager budgets to cover other necessary expenses. It was a win-win situation all around.

The second year of operation saw increased cooperation with local businesses. Lee Hopkins, one such businessperson, donated a small building just off the town's main street. The original team of two dozen volunteers agreed to staff the building each Saturday for donation intake and distribution, and the building was also open on Wednesdays so that volunteers could sort and organize the clothing. Volunteers indicated their availability to serve on a sign-up sheet posted in the LLC kitchen, and this very informal system seemed to work quite well for all involved. It was during this time of growth that one person from each of the three churches agreed to serve on the executive board of the organization, and papers were drawn up to officially register the group as a 501(c)(3).

By the end of the second year, however, it became apparent that having the building open to volunteers just one day a week was not enough. Heavy traffic on Saturday mornings became the norm around the LLC building, and volunteers had to park blocks away in order to allow customers to use the facility. In addition, the original group of volunteers was starting to grow weary, especially when faced with the prospect of increased operating hours. A newer member of the volunteer team, Neil Henderson, agreed to become volunteer coordinator, an unpaid position. He was a recently retired banker who enjoyed volunteering at LLC, and he had a keen interest and background in organizational software. With his expertise, he was able to supplement existing software to develop an easy-to-use volunteer registry that was accessible to prospective volunteers online.

As demand for the organization's services grew, so did its need for volunteers. After just three years, LLC was open five days a week and utilizing more than fifty volunteers each week in order to keep the doors open. Meanwhile, Neil continued to tweak the software system to make it more user-friendly. He also introduced both volunteer recruitment and retention programs so that LLC could continue to attract the large numbers needed to ensure that it remained a viable community organization. Volunteer training was added to the mix, and LLC was able to continue staffing the facility five days a week with a trained, reliable network of support.

## Volunteers or Paid Staff?

After another full year of organizing volunteers, Neil's wife commented that he spent as much time at LLC as he had at his full-time job—except without a paycheck. What had begun as an enjoyable, part-time position to occupy his spare time had turned into a full-time job that was a linchpin of the organization. Living on a retirement income was not as easy as Neil and his wife had hoped, but his demanding responsibilities at LLC had made looking for a part-time job nearly impossible. As LLC continued to grow and began to experience a steady flow of both in-kind and monetary donations, Neil wondered if there was room in the budget to pay him a stipend.

Neil voiced his concerns at the next LLC board meeting. In noting that there were other people who also donated a great deal of time to the organization and who were deserving of compensation, he reminded the board of the dangers an all-volunteer staff can pose. He told them that as much as he loved organizing the volunteers, if his position was not paid by the beginning of the next fiscal year, he would be forced to step down.

The board was stunned. Never before had they discussed or considered hiring a paid staff. They had always been an entirely volunteer-run organization, and the organization's success using that model was substantial. Nevertheless, the board recognized the gravity of Neil's proposal and saw that it would soon need to discern whether LLC had outgrown its all-volunteer model. Deliberation continued during the next several board meetings. Most board members conceded that the organization had reached a pivotal point where it needed to begin offering compensation to those in key positions if it was to continue to grow. A few others, however, remained firm in their belief that the organization could move ahead with an all-volunteer staff. They suggested that perhaps it was time to find another person to fill the volunteer coordinator position so that Neil could find a paid position elsewhere.

The tide was turning, and LLC had to decide what to do next. Choosing to hire a paid staff, even a small one, would be a big commitment for Long Lake Caring—and one that would have serious implications for the young organization's future.

## Questions and Instructions

1. Please identify and discuss some factors that should be considered when a nonprofit transitions from a volunteer to a paid staff.
2. How should LLC's board of directors determine which jobs become paid positions? Please explain your response.
3. The organization currently had no stable source of funding, although the annual budget was sound. What did the board of directors need to do to ensure the level of funding required to cover salaries?
4. Identify and discuss some of the benefits and drawbacks of using a volunteer staff. Are volunteers a renewable resource? Please explain.
5. At the end of the case, some board members were in favor of transitioning to paid staff while others wanted to retain the volunteer model. Based on the information available, which option do you think would be best for LLC? Please justify your response.

# PART X

# ACCOUNTABILITY AND EVALUATION

*Accountability* means *answerability* for one's actions or behavior.[1] *Evaluation* is determining the value or effectiveness of an activity for the purpose of decision-making.[2] Both accountability and evaluation present measurement difficulties and reporting challenges for nonprofit organizations. These arise, in part, from internal and external environments characterized by multiple stakeholders and the very real possibility that they cannot all be satisfied. "The problem that we face in the implementation of a performance measurement is not how to build an effective performance measurement system, but for whom we are building that effective system. . . . Often we get so wrapped up in the measuring of performance that we forget to examine the purposes for which we measure."[3]

Thus, the difficult questions for nonprofit organizations begin at the outset: To whom are they accountable? And for what?

## Accountable to Whom?

Within any organization, the primary accountability is up to the organization's higher levels of management, the executive director, and the board of trustees. For nonprofit organizations and the people who work and volunteer in them, however, this is only a limited view of accountability. A nonprofit organization and its volunteers, staff, executives, and board members are accountable to all of the individuals, groups, and organizations they are answerable to—at least for some things and to some extent. Thus, for instance, a performing arts nonprofit is accountable to its many types of paying and nonpaying audiences; to its rising and established performers; to the high schools and universities that provide it with interns; to individual, family, corporate, and nonprofit donors and sponsors; to government grant-making agencies; and to its community, including influential people, elected officials, and the print and electronic media. For a nonprofit organization, accountability truly is *answerability* to the individuals and groups with a stake in the organization and its activities.

## Accountable for What?

People who own stock in corporations regularly scrutinize the fine print in the stock market reports because stockholders want to know how their investments are doing. For a business, trends in its stock price, profits, earning ratios, market penetration, and dividends serve as measures of its organizational performance—its efficiency and effectiveness. Thus, a business can satisfy most of its accountability requirements by regularly publishing data about these performance measures for its shareholders, government regulators, and the general public.

Likewise, publishing data in an open and easily accessible manner allows a nonprofit to demonstrate accountability and its corollary, transparency. *Transparency* is a mechanism to allow the public to scrutinize meaningful information, and it is an expected part of being accountable. When an investigation shows a lack of transparency or dishonest practices by one nonprofit organization, a shadow is cast on other nonprofits as well. The usefulness of transparency is reduced when information overload or overly technical terminology hinders meaningful evaluations. This was the case with Enron in the early 2000s: information was publicly available, but it was indecipherable except by a select few accounting experts.[4] In 2014 a number of foundations and charities established by professional football players were facing heightened scrutiny owing to accusations of fraud or, at best, poor accounting practices.[5] Such publicity draws the attention of the IRS and other stakeholders to the accountability practices of all foundations and charities in the nonprofit sector.

In nonprofit organizations, efficiency—the quantity of resources consumed in the production of services or outputs to the public or its members—should serve as a clear and useful measure of performance. Demonstrating accountability for efficiency does not raise unique problems for most nonprofits. Accountability for effectiveness, however, is a different story; it is far more complex for reasons that cannot be resolved easily. Effectiveness "for what" is relevant beyond programmatic concerns. For example, some nonprofits are increasingly being asked to account for the quality of their capacities. In this vein, a 2007 study of nonprofit accountability focused not on program effectiveness per se but rather on the composition, best practices, and governance capabilities of organizations' boards of directors.[6]

## Effectiveness as Seen Through Whose Eyes?

Effectiveness seldom, if ever, means the same thing to all stakeholders. Effectiveness is not a "thing" but rather a subjective phenomenon that is constructed differently by different constituencies.[7] Effectiveness is defined from the divergent perspectives of many beholders. Each of the many constituencies of an organization shares some goals with others, but each also has its own specific and sometimes changing goals and priorities—and thus also criteria of organizational effectiveness.[8] Because each constituency brings its own interests and expectations into its relationship with a nonprofit organization, some priorities are almost always in competition with others for scarce organizational resources and attention. Thus, nonprofit organizations are webs of fluid interactions, constantly changing interests, and perennially shifting balances of power among coalitions of constituencies.

Nonprofit organizations that house and provide services to troubled youths, adults on parole, and individuals who have been in mental hospitals provide not-uncommon examples. These "halfway house" programs help individuals reintegrate into society, but their presence in a community often causes neighbors to believe that they and their children have been placed at risk ("not in my backyard"). What is effectiveness for these types of programs? What measures should be used to evaluate how successful they are?

How effective is a symphony orchestra that fills its halls for performances but performs only well-known works by long-established composers? If this orchestra offered some performances by up-and-coming local composers that filled only one-third of the hall, would this programming change increase or decrease its effectiveness? Or how would its effectiveness change if the orchestra were to decrease the frequency of its symphony hall performances and initiate instructional activities and performances in elementary and secondary schools across the state? Different stakeholders would have different answers to these questions.

Nonprofit organizations sometimes face difficult decisions about which of several competing constituencies' interests will have priority. When this occurs, the interests of some stakeholders must be set aside either temporarily or permanently. They may decide to "fight" or to withdraw their support from the organization, either of which responses may weaken it.[9] Interestingly, when it comes to effectiveness, sometimes it is not organizational outputs or outcomes that are recognized by stakeholders; instead, a subjective assessment of board effectiveness becomes "the most important determinant of evaluating organizational effectiveness."[10]

## Difficulties in Measuring Effectiveness

Many of the services that nonprofit organizations provide can also be difficult to measure.[11] The mission of most nonprofit organizations is to change the lives of individuals in some way—either to make their lives better or to prevent deterioration in their current quality of life. How, then, should effectiveness be measured in evaluating programs that strive to improve the quality of life for persons with lifelong disabilities or chronic mental illness? How do we measure changes in beliefs, attitudes, and behaviors that are co-produced by the service providers and the recipients of services?[12]

In addition, collecting information to evaluate the effectiveness of programs sometimes requires intrusion into sensitive personal areas.[13] Consider the privacy problems involved, for example, in collecting data to evaluate the effectiveness of a program that is trying to prevent teenage pregnancies. Few of us would accept pregnancy rates—the ultimate outcome measure—as an adequate single measure of effectiveness. We also would want to know at least something about sensitive private behaviors, including frequency and patterns of sexual activity, prevention methods used and not used, STD prevalence, and abortions performed. Even if we were able to collect information, how would we know whether or not the information was accurate, and could we convince others of its accuracy?

Evaluation measurements are less difficult when the important processes, outputs, and/or outcomes can be quantified or observed objectively; for example, it is not difficult to measure how many pregnant women attend prenatal classes, how many contact hours there are between service providers and patients with Alzheimer's disease, or how many people are removed from the welfare rolls during a given year. All too frequently, however, the variables that can be measured are not particularly important. Does anyone truly care how many pregnant mothers attend classes if they do not change their unhealthy lifestyles? How meaningful are measurements of program effectiveness that do not account for the quality of life of those individuals who are removed from the welfare rolls, have nowhere to live except on the streets, and become ineligible for health care services?

Usually it is not especially difficult to measure the quantity of inputs, activities, and outputs for a nonprofit's services, but it is often very difficult to measure the quality of its activities and outputs; moreover, it is also very difficult to measure both the quantity and quality of its outcomes. It is yet more difficult and much more expensive to measure and establish cause-effect relationships between activities and outcomes, especially with co-produced services that do not cause outcomes but only influence them.[14] When changes in behavior or lifestyle are the desired outcome (for example, programs to improve the outcome of pregnancies or to treat individuals with chemical dependencies), the timeliness of measurements often poses additional serious problems. Outcomes can take years or even decades to establish.[15]

Despite the difficulties, evaluation activities are an expected responsibility of nonprofit organizations, and in recent years some evaluation efforts have been facilitated by funders. For example,

United Way of America has worked with local affiliates to help United Way–funded agencies learn to evaluate and report on program and performance outcomes.[16] Three major forces are behind the move:

- Local UWs want to ensure that they can direct money to demonstrably effective programs and demonstrate to donors the results of their financial contributions.
- Measuring outcomes reflects the logical evolution of performance measurement.
- US society, including the government and business sectors, has been in an era since the early 1990s in which results and accountability are expected.

Not surprisingly, there is a connection between the performance evaluations that service providers conduct and their ability to raise funds from outside sources.[17] Obviously, funders of all types want to know whether their investments are paying off and in what ways lives are being improved.

The limited abilities of the populations served by many nonprofits introduce another difficulty, however, when measuring program effectiveness. Many nonprofit programs use some aspects of quality of life or changes in quality of life as indicators of program effectiveness. Evaluators attempt to measure quality of life through surveys administered to recipients of services, the people who know them, or the public. Surveying for quality of life has many difficulties and limitations in and of itself; with recipients of services who have severe cognitive, emotional, or communication challenges, these difficulties are compounded. How should quality of life be determined for people with severe intellectual challenges? Answers to this question require difficult value judgments, not technical solutions. Are the judgments of family members or professionals acceptable as proxy measures? Should we accept the judgment of the professionals who provide services to the clients, or only other professionals who represent supposedly neutral and objective funding agencies or groups that advocate for the clients and their families? Can family members always be trusted to make decisions that are in the best interests of their relative who is a client of the service provider? These questions are far from hypothetical: they reflect some of the difficult realities of being accountable for effectiveness in nonprofit organizations.

## Accountable for What?

Accountability has at least five, often competing, dimensions: hierarchical, legal, professional, political, and moral or ethical.[18] The evaluation methods that are used most commonly today are best able to achieve and verify hierarchical, legal, and political accountability and least able to achieve and verify ethical or moral accountability—the dimension of accountability most directly associated with quality of services. Accountability thus means far more than compliance with contractual, legal, or financial reporting requirements.[19] It also includes responsibility for the moral, professional, and ethical dimensions of service, which means that nonprofits need to be answerable for the quality as well as the quantity of their services.

Accountability problems of this nature and complexity are not limited to nonprofit organizations—they cross sector boundaries. Far too much attention has been paid to traditional or compliance accountability and process accountability, and far too little to managerial accountability (which focuses on the judicious use of public resources), program accountability (which is concerned with the outcomes or results of operations), and social accountability (which attempts to determine the societal impacts of government programs).[20] Likewise, using performance evaluations for the purpose of satisfying the multiple expectations of diverse stakeholders is not a one-size-fits-all proposition. "When different funders use their own approaches, terms, definitions, time frames, and reporting requirements, local agencies are forced to change their procedures for each funder. This harms the agencies and undermines each funder's intentions."[21] To begin to solve this problem requires, at the very least, the time and willingness of all invested stakeholders to compromise.[22]

## Readings Reprinted in Part X

In the first article in this section, "Balancing Competing Accountability Requirements," Seok-Eun Kim discusses and analyzes the challenges of performance improvement for government-funded nonprofit human services agencies. As the title of the article implies, balancing hierarchical, legal, professional, and political accountabilities can create serious managerial challenges for nonprofits. When the expectations and activities associated with upholding accountability in any one of these areas are aligned with those in other areas, it makes the job easier for managers and staff. When expectations diverge, however, accountabilities compete, with some areas being upheld while others are compromised. And when professional and political accountabilities are compromised, the stakes can be very high. Kim notes that legal accountability has taken center stage in the delivery of human services as these agencies seek to uphold the requirements of state regulators. When the activities required to uphold legal accountability rest on the preparation of documentation, however, rather than on activities to promote the quality of care, the results can be life-threatening for clients of these agencies.

Gregory D. Saxton and Chao Guo's "Accountability Online: Understanding the Web-Based Accountability Practices of Nonprofit Organizations" reports on the online accountability practices of 117 community foundations in the United States. Not unexpectedly, nonprofit community foundations with strong financial capacity and highly effective boards of directors are most likely to use the web for accountability purposes.

The understanding of accountability as simply being transparent in reporting financial documents, however, or demonstrating conformity to performance expectations, is fast becoming outdated. As Saxton and Guo show, web-based technology has opened the doors to a more interactive interpretation of accountability, or "being accountable." Web-based accountability practices include not only *disclosure* (transparency in documentation) but also *dialogue*, "which encompasses the solicitation of input from and interactive engagement with core stakeholders."[23] Other research has demonstrated the usefulness of this more interactive approach to accountability and performance expectations. "Submitting information . . . is not the most appropriate way of aligning or realigning matters. . . . Discussion is more important as . . . [it] . . . offers room for an exchange of views. . . . [All] parties in the accountability relationship are likely to benefit from discussion."[24] To the dismay of Saxton and Guo, however, web-based approaches, though they provide an ideal medium for two-way engagement, are the least likely to be used by community foundations.

## Case Studies in Part X

The case studies in Part X present transparency and accountability dilemmas. In the first case study, "An Awareness Campaign Gone Awry," the reader is introduced to an educational project that triggers a public relations nightmare for the nonprofit involved. As the media picks up the story, concerns about the organization's evaluation and oversight processes extend far beyond the scope of the single project highlighted in the case. The efficacy of the organization's entire accountability system is called into question, and the reader is tasked with addressing the managerial choices that must be made.

As circumstances in "Technology and Transparency at the Museum" show, a nonprofit may not be comfortable sharing financial or performance data on the web. Regardless of their comfort level, however, nonprofits are expected to conform to the public's expectations regarding the availability of data, online or otherwise. When expectations are not met, there may be unpleasant or unexpected ramifications.

## Notes

1. Kevin P. Kearns, *Managing for Accountability: Preserving the Public Trust in Public and Nonprofit Organizations* (San Francisco: Jossey-Bass, 1996), 11.

2. Susan C. Paddock, "Evaluation," in *The International Encyclopedia of Public Policy and Administration*, edited by Jay M. Shafritz, 818–823 (Boulder, CO: Westview Press, 1998).

3. Daniel Bromberg, "Performance Measurement: A System with a Purpose or a Purposeless System," *Public Performance and Management Review* 33, no. 2 (December 2009): 214–221, 214.

4. Stuart C. Gilman and Howard Whitton, "When Transparency Becomes the Enemy of Accountability: Reflections from the Field," *PA Times* (2013), http://patimes.org/transparency-enemy-accountability-reflections-field/.

5. John Brothers, "As NFL Suffers Ethical Lapses, Player Charities Also Under Scrutiny," *Nonprofit Quarterly* (October 9, 2014), https://nonprofitquarterly.org/policysocial-context/24954-as-nfl-suffers-ethical-lapses-player-charities-also-under-scrutiny.html.

6. Francie Ostrower, *Nonprofit Governance in the United States: Findings on Performance and Accountability from the First National Representative Study* (Washington, DC: Urban Institute, June 2007).

7. For more information about the "multiple constituency theory" approach to organizations and their effectiveness, see Robert D. Herman and David O. Renz, "Multiple Constituencies and the Social Construction of Nonprofit Organization Effectiveness," *Nonprofit and Voluntary Sector Quarterly* 26, no. 2 (June 1997):185–206; Terry Connolly, Edward J. Conlon, and Stewart Jay Deutsch, "Organizational Effectiveness: A Multiple-Constituency Approach," *Academy of Management Review* 5 (1980): 211–217; and Robert E. Quinn and John Rohrbaugh, "A Competing Values Approach to Organizational Effectiveness," *Public Productivity and Management Review* 2 (1981): 122–140.

8. See, for example, Herman and Renz, "Multiple Constituencies."

9. J. Steven Ott and Lisa A. Dicke, "Organization Theories," in *The Nature of the Nonprofit Sector,* 2nd ed. (Boulder, CO: Westview Press, 2012); and J. Steven Ott, "Perspectives on Organizational Governance: Some Effects on Government-Nonprofit Relations," *Southeastern Political Review* 21, no. 1 (Winter 1993): 3–21.

10. Robert D. Herman and David O. Renz, "Multiple Constituencies and the Social Construction of Nonprofit Organization Effectiveness," *Nonprofit and Voluntary Sector Quarterly* 26, no. 2 (June 1997): 185–206.

11. J. Steven Ott and Lisa A. Dicke, "Important but Largely Unanswered Questions About Accountability in Contracted Public Human Services," *International Journal of Organization Theory and Behavior* 3, nos. 3 and 4 (Summer 2000): 283–317.

12. Bruce B. Clary, "Coproduction," in *The International Encyclopedia of Public Policy and Administration*, edited by Jay M. Shafritz, 531–536 (Boulder, CO: Westview Press, 1998).

13. J. Steven Ott and Lisa A. Dicke, "Challenges Facing Public Sector HRM in an Era of Downsizing, Devolution, Diffusion, and Empowerment . . . and Accountability?" in *Strategic Public Personnel Administration/HRM: Building Human Capital for the 21st Century,* edited by Ali Farazmand (Westport, CT: Greenwood Press, 2007).

14. Edward A. Suchman, *Evaluative Research: Principles and Practice in Public Service and Social Action Programs* (New York: Russell Sage Foundation, 1967).

15. Indirect and/or proxy measures can be used, but these introduce additional measurement difficulties. See Emil J. Posavac and Raymond G. Carey, "Program Evaluation: An Overview," in Emil J. Posavac and Raymond G. Carey, *Program Evaluation: Methods and Case Studies,* 8th ed. (Upper Saddle River, NJ: Prentice-Hall, 2011).

16. Michael Hendricks, Margaret C. Plantz, and Kathleen J. Prichard, "Measuring Outcomes of United Way–Funded Programs: Expectations and Reality," In *Nonprofits and Evaluations: New Directions for Evaluation,* edited by Joanne G. Carman and Kimberly A. Fredericks (San Francisco: Josey-Bass, 2008), 119, 13–35.

17. Joanne G. Carman, "Nonprofits, Funders, and Evaluations: Accountability in Action," *American Review of Public Administration* 39, no. 4 (July 2009): 374–390.

18. See Lisa A. Dicke and J. Steven Ott, "Public Agency Accountability in Human Services Contracting," *Public Productivity and Management Review* 22, no. 4 (June 1999): 502–516; Barbara S. Romzek and Melvin J. Dubnick, "Issues of Accountability in Flexible Personnel Systems," in *New Paradigms for Government,* edited by Patricia W. Ingraham and Barbara S. Romzek (San Francisco: Jossey-Bass, 1994), 263–294.

19. Lester M. Salamon, *Partners in Public Service: Government-Nonprofit Relations in the Modern Welfare State* (Baltimore: Johns Hopkins University Press, 1995).

20. Gene E. Caiden, "The Problem of Ensuring the Public Accountability of Public Officials," in *Public Service Accountability,* edited by Joseph G. Jabbra and O. P. Dwivedi (West Hartford, CT: Kumarian Press, 1988), 23–24.

21. Hendricks et al., "Measuring Outcomes of United Way–Funded Programs," 29.

22. Bromberg, "Performance Measurement."

23. Gregory D. Saxton and Chao Guo, "Accountability Online: Understanding the Web-Based Accountability Practices of Nonprofit Organizations," *Nonprofit and Voluntary Sector Quarterly* 40, no. 2 (2011): 271.

24. Gijs Jan Brandsma and Thomas Schillemans, "The Accountability Cube: Measuring Accountability," *Journal of Public Administration Research and Theory* 23, no. 4 (September 2013): 953–975, 957.

# Balancing Competing Accountability Requirements: Challenges in Performance Improvement of the Nonprofit Human Services Agency

Seok-Eun Kim

Attention to nonprofit accountability surged in the early 1990s when many of the nation's giant charities were rocked by scandals. Since then, confidence in nonprofit agencies has generally increased, especially due to their dedicated work during the September 11 tragedy. However, following September 11, issues of accountability were revived, with criticism directed at the American Red Cross and other charities regarding their questionable handling of emergency relief funds and their alleged financial mismanagement (Independent Sector 2002; Light 2002, 2003).

Assuring accountability of nonprofit human services agencies (NHSAs) such as community mental health centers is necessary but often difficult because these agencies provide vital human services through federal and state grants but function outside the regular government structure in complicated arrangements. Multiple and complex monitoring mechanisms (e.g., financial and program audits, licensures,

annual contract evaluations, codes of ethics, and outcome-based assessments) have been put into place to ensure accountability in the delivery of human services (Dicke 2002; Dicke and Ott 1999; Salamon 1999). However, these accountability mechanisms are often limited because of the complications in accountability relationships among multiple stakeholders, each with different and many times conflicting performance expectations.

This article presents findings from a qualitative analysis of these accountability quandaries and their effect on agency performance in a large community mental health center (hereinafter "the Center") in a southeastern state.

Nonprofit agencies nationwide are struggling to balance the increasing demand for accountability against multiple and often conflicting requirements. The Center, as a typical NHSA operating within multiple and competing accountability relationships, has been subjected to continuous performance challenges despite

Originally published in *Public Performance and Management Review* 29, no. 2 (2005): 145–163. Copyright © 2005 by M. E. Sharpe, Inc. Reprinted with permission.

repeated efforts for organizational reinvention sufficient to address the complex requirements. Using Johnston and Romzek's (1999) four types of accountability system (i.e., hierarchical, legal, professional, and political),[1] I analyze the impact of the accountability quandaries at the Center with the purpose of developing an effective explanation of the consistent performance challenges that face NHSAs generally.

## Challenges of Nonprofit Accountability

The contemporary interest in nonprofit accountability is primarily concerned with answerability to diverse and multiple performance expectations (Kearns 1994; Rubin 1990; Salamon 2002). Satisfying multiple and competing accountability expectations, however, generates tremendous challenges for NHSAs due to the difficulty of defining performance as well as the significant costs involved in both monitoring and keeping records for the purpose of outcome measurement (Behn and Kant 1999; Kettl 1993: Milward, Provan, and Else 1993).

Performance evaluation of nonprofits is also complex due to the conflict between their traditional missions and funding requirements (Alexander, Nank, and Stivers 1999). The pressure for marketization directs nonprofits to compromise their original missions with administrative concerns and revenue generating activities. Furthermore, the different performance expectations held by the multiple constituencies of an NHSA tend to be conflicting and contradictory (i.e., accountability for a particular constituent may collide with accountability for another; Dicke and Ott 1999). For example, funding agencies have increasingly demanded that human services programs be efficient and compliant with specific contractual obligations. Clients, on the other hand, pressure the organization for a higher quality of service, despite increased services' often leading to cost inefficiency in program management. Therefore, determining the

entity to whom the NHSA is accountable is not a simple question of conflicting accountability requirements (Chisolm 1995).

## A Framework for Analyzing Competing Accountability Relationships

I adopt Johnston and Romzek's (1999) framework for analyzing competing accountability mechanisms, which are loosely coupled and often self-contradictory. Legal accountability relationships exist when the agency's performance is externally audited for compliance with contractual obligations that have been specified as a form of legal mandate. Financial and program audits, oversight hearings, and reporting requirements are commonly used for ensuring this type of accountability. Political accountability involves responsiveness to the agency's major constituencies such as clients, the state, advocacy groups, and the community. Professional accountability refers to "deference to expertise and performance standards derived from professional norms and prevailing practices of one's peer or work group" (Johnston and Romzek 1999, 387). Hierarchical accountability requires close supervision from a higher authority, which utilizes a set of performance standards, organizational rules and regulations, and supervisory directives.

The multiple and competing accountability relationships pose significant managerial challenges in NHSAs insofar as the diverse expectations among multiple stakeholders impede the establishment of the single most important effectiveness standard. The absence of the unifying effectiveness standard may be desirable because it is socially constructed through a set of judgments made by various stakeholders (Herman and Renz 1997). However, multiple and often conflicting standards of effectiveness leave a central question of performance accountability: Which type of accountability is superior when one is faced with directions that conflict with legislative mandates or hierarchical control? Members of the professional staff of a nonprofit agency often believe that a moral obligation to their profession might force them to make decisions that potentially conflict with expected legal or formal standards of action. Similarly, compliance with contractual requirements and a set of standard operating procedures could limit professional accountability for the clients' needs. Thus, balancing different accountability requirements has become imperative, as losing that balance necessarily leaves a certain accountability relationship vulnerable.

## Organizational Change at the Center

Since early 1998, the Center has implemented a comprehensive program of organizational change for improving its performance. Initially, the primary purpose of the organizational change was to maintain an annual contract with the state, as the Center was being subjected to a state investigation into certain wrongdoings by its employees and its poor management of a residential facility. However, organizational change has become a patterned practice caused by continued financial pressure from the state and increasing demands for performance accountability. The Center has seriously examined work structures, policies and procedures, and human resources, with the goal of maintaining accountability by improving its performance.

Completely rewritten policies and procedures have established a new organizational structure in which various committees perform oversight functions, and the top management team serves as the final decision-making entity. The new policies and procedures also contain an employee code of ethics, procedures for client complaints, variance reports, quality grievances, and incident reports. To maintain its annual contract with the state, the Center made new investments in a management information system to improve outcome measurement and monitor client information. For example, the state mandated using various outcome measurement tools for measuring clients' symptom improvement between intake and discharge as well as recording their satisfaction with the Center's services.

The Center also began to design standards of practice for compliance with state requirements. Employee work productivity is measured and reported to the state each month using direct service time as a measure of billable work hours.[2] The Department of Continuous Quality Improvement (CQI) launched an internal audit system to ensure accurate documentation of clinical charts and billing statements, as well as to encourage best practices of providing clinical services. As a result of the increased focus on effective service delivery, the emphasis on employee training also gained new impetus. Specific elements of the employee training program include instruction on the organization's mission, values, and work rules and the importance of customer satisfaction, but its overall focus has tended to move toward documentation training to increase paperwork compliance with the state.

Despite the series of organizational changes, the Center still suffered from performance problems that raised constant suspicion over the Center's accountability. For example, the October 2001 audit revealed that the state's Department of Human Resources warned the Center about a lack of clear accountability in the handling of clients' funds at its facility. Furthermore, the Center nearly lost its contract with the state in 2002 due to a host of shortcomings identified by state auditors (Johnson 2003). In early 2003, the Center experienced a budget crisis that forced salary reduction onto individual employees. Why have the comprehensive efforts for organizational change produced such disappointing results?

For the exploratory analysis of the performance challenge, both subjective and objective data were analyzed. A semistructured employee attitude survey conducted in September 2001 evaluated the employees' reactions to the organizational changes. In the four open-ended questions of the survey, 96 out of 191 Center employees, each of whom was consistently employed during the 3-year organizational change period, provided extensive comments about the problems and successes of the change, ideas for future improvement, and the desirable future state of the Center.

Employee responses were supplemented by in-depth interviews conducted during 2001 and 2002 of seven members of the management team and the other five program managers. These interviews provided extensive information about the Center's contractual relationship with the state, financial constraints, and other managerial barriers faced during the organizational changes, as well as the various reporting practices required for compliance with the contractual obligations. Mandated client satisfaction surveys, which are conducted three times a year at the Center, also reinforced the findings from the employee survey. The results from the fiscal year (FY) 2001 to FY 2003 mailed surveys provided extensive information about clients' perception of overall service effectiveness as well as valuable feedback for identifying which types of services most needed managerial intervention for improvement. On average, 853 clients (38 percent) responded to the survey, and 285 clients provided approximately 20 pages of single-spaced comments.

Several types of objective data were also used to cross-validate subjective data, thereby reducing the likelihood of obtaining an inaccurate result. The analysis of the weekly management team meeting minutes from December 2000 to April 2004 provided substantial information about the multiple accountability requirements faced by the Center. The Center's strategic plans from FY 2002 to FY 2004 suggested managerial programs to cope with immediate and future challenges addressed by the complex accountability relationships. A series of contractual

outcome reports, copies of government contracts, financial audit statements, public relations reports, Center policies and procedures, staff turnover reports, and other organizational reports were reviewed and analyzed to add substance to this study.

## Multiple and Competing Accountability Relationships

As a typical nonprofit human services agency, the Center operates under multiple and competing accountability relationships within the democratic systems of governance. Table 21.1 shows the accountability relationships at the Center under the contract with the state.

### Hierarchical Accountability

Since the beginning of the organizational change in 1998, the top management team, which consists of an executive director and 11 program directors, has served as the final point of responsibility for overall Center management. Subordinate to the management team, the Center established various committees (e.g., the oversight committee, finance committee, and legislative committee) to deal with specific management issues in their respective areas of emphasis.

A group of auditors at the CQI department conduct a bimonthly internal audit of selected work units, focusing on documentation of clinical charts and billing statements. The purpose of the internal audit is to maintain accurate clinical records and to ensure that services are provided to individual clients based on an individualized service plan and billed accordingly.

### Legal Accountability

Legal accountability is typically associated with principal and agent relationships, in which a principal (the state funder) directs an agent's

TABLE 21.1. **Multiple and Competing Accountability Relations at the Center**

| *Hierarchical* | *Legal* |
|---|---|
| • Management team | • Annual contract with the state |
| • Monitoring (oversight) committees | • Financial audits by independent auditors |
| • Internal/clinical audits | • Performance audits by submitting outcome measurement reports (monthly, quarterly, annually) |
| | • Quarterly clinical audits from an external auditing agency (American Psychiatric System) |
| | • Accreditation from an external accreditation commission (Commission for Accreditation of Rehabilitation Facilities) |
| | • Monitoring number of state hospital utilizations |

| *Professional* | *Political* |
|---|---|
| • Mission, values, philosophy | • Client satisfaction/client complaints |
| • Code of Ethics | • Community service board |
| • Credit/licensing | • State funding agency |
| • Employee (mandatory) training | • State legislators |
| • Quality improvement/best practices | • Community (e.g., town meetings) |
| | • Advocacy group conferences |
| | • Local media (newspapers, TV, radio) |

(the Center) behavior regarding the agent's compliance with a set of specified performance standards mandated in the annual contract. The demands for legal accountability from the state focused largely on completing financial audits and performance audits.

The performance audits have become the greatest challenge to the Center's management. The performance accountability requirements are so vast and complicated that the Center is forced to allocate substantial resources to meet performance expectations to gain and retain annual funding. Specifically, the Center is required to provide the state with comprehensive

forms of performance outcome data, including (a) monthly clinical assessments to demonstrate clients' symptom improvement; (b) quarterly outcome reports covering all program areas such as mental illness, mental retardation, and alcohol and substance abuse; and (c) yearly contractual outcome reports summarizing all quarterly outcome data, together with the results of the three waves of client satisfaction surveys that are mandated by the state.

In addition to the outcome reporting requirements, the Center is subject to an external clinical audit conducted by the American Psychiatric System (APS), a Maryland-based for-profit health-care company. The state hired the APS to monitor every treatment plan for Medicaid clients at the Center to prevent possible abuse of government funds. The APS also conducts an on-site clinical audit each quarter to ensure that clients are being billed for services received in accordance with their individual service plans and the progress notes.

Another component of external monitoring involves the number of state hospital beds used by clients of the Center. One of the main purposes of mental health care reform in the state was to reduce the amount of time that clients of the Center spent in state hospital treatment centers and to transfer that care over to increasingly available community-based services (State Commission on Mental Health, Mental Retardation, and Substance Abuse Service Delivery 1992, 1996). Since the 1960s, many states have discharged a substantial number of patients with mental disorders from state hospitals, shifting the burden to community care programs by providing budgetary incentives to community mental health centers (Gaynor 1990). For example, community mental health centers can obtain a monetary incentive if they use fewer state hospital beds than they are expected to use in a fiscal year. Excessive use of state hospital beds, however, may cause cuts in funding for the next fiscal year. Therefore, a reduction in the total number of state hospital visits by mental health patients indicates that the Center is performing well and is meeting its contractual obligations with the state.

## Professional Accountability

Professional accountability requires that clinicians provide their services based on accepted professional norms of practice with a level of discretion substantial enough to properly render those services. Due to its direct impact on clients' care, the state provides specific utilization guidelines and service standards for all Center programs. For example, the 2003 provider manual required that all services be furnished under the authorization of licensed professionals such as a physician, licensed psychologist, clinical nurse specialist, or licensed clinical social worker (State Department of Human Resources 2003).

The utilization guidelines and service standards of the state are manifested by the mission statement, values, and philosophies of the Center. Those principles direct the Center's policies and procedures, which govern the standards of conduct of the individual employees. The Center established a code of ethics and a standard of conduct as a general policy, requiring that all employees observe high moral and ethical standards in official relationships and job-related conduct. The Center's employees must also be qualified, competent, and people-oriented in their delivery of services. Mandatory employee training thus serves as the primary way of improving employees' professional standards by helping them to acquire necessary skills and knowledge about work rules, uphold organizational values, and increase their focus on client satisfaction.

Another component of professional accountability is to institute best practices in every area of Center management, such as the establishment of new policies and procedures, the development of new services, the improvement of internal communication, the development of superior disciplinary policies for the staff, and networking with other centers to learn about their best practices.

## Political Accountability

Political accountability exists to the extent that the Center must be responsive to its multiple stakeholders, including clients and their families, the Community Service Board (CSB), the state funder, state legislators, various advocacy groups, and the community as a whole.

Accountability to the state is the Center's greatest challenge insofar as the state, as the major funder, plays a critical role as a monitoring device for Center service planning, program coordinating, the maintenance of an annual contract, and the allocation of resources. In response to pressure from the state and the increasing demand for accountability from the community, the Center began to hold monthly CSB meetings as a major device to check any deviations of the Center from its organizational mission. However, the role of the CSB has been reduced as the authority shifts from the board to the executive director, who exercises greater discretion to be more entrepreneurial and expand the Center's base of support (Smith 2002).

The Center has expanded the functions of its public relations (PR) department to deal effectively with its multiple constituents. The PR department disseminates important news and events of the Center through issues of various newsletters. For example, a monthly newsletter is distributed to all staff members with their paychecks and is mailed to board members, advocates, and state legislators. *Legislative Update,* another monthly newsletter, is distributed to state senators, legislators, and various other government officials. The quarterly CSB community newsletter serves as a public relations tool for clients and their family members, advocates, individuals from other social service agencies, and legislators. The PR department also disseminates news releases regarding positive outcome data of the Center to local newspapers and radio and television stations. Finally, the members of the Center's management team periodically attend conferences held by advocacy groups (e.g., State Mental Health Consumer Network) to share their concern about client rights in the treatment process.

## Managerial Challenges from Competing Accountability Requirements

A series of organizational changes since 1998 has saved the Center from extinction, as it was on the verge of losing its annual contract with the state. Presently, the Center's policies and procedures are functioning, its organizational structures are integrated into a "one-stop shopping" system, and the Center's employees began to be recognized as important resources for the provision of quality mental health services. Before the organizational changes, the Center could be characterized as having had a laissez-faire climate, but that has changed and it has become an organized and performance-oriented service provider.

Despite the intended directions of change, the net results of the constant efforts for performance improvement are not encouraging. Although yearly utilization of state hospital beds has decreased significantly, the Center can hardly claim improved performance because it has merely utilized a subcontractor as a means to reduce consumption of state hospital beds by the Center's clients. Furthermore, the number of client complaints has only been marginally reduced, and the levels of client satisfaction have fluctuated during the organizational change periods. The rates of employee turnover have remained consistent, at an average of 38 percent a year, totaling the loss of almost half of its employees for approximately 3-year periods. A series of warnings from state auditors changed into compliments in early 2002 after the Center undertook serious efforts to improve its performance (Shearer 2002), but recently it has struggled with a financial crisis that has forced a salary reduction on its employees. Why have the Center's changes produced these seemingly mixed but still clearly disappointing results even after its comprehensive efforts to effect a performance improvement? I propose that the answers can be found in the quandaries of competing accountability relationships emanating from the democratic systems of governance.

### Greater Emphasis on Legal Accountability

Maintaining its annual contract with the state by improving organizational performance has always been the top priority of the Center, as the level of funding is increasingly dependent on the evidence of service effectiveness. High pressure for legal accountability from the state, however, has produced a plethora of rules and regulations and a variety of reporting requirements, to the point where the practice of micromanagement—direct and meddlesome control in a detailed manner—has inhibited performance improvement by demoralizing the Center's employees.

The immediate impact of state micromanagement resulted in increased workload due to sizable paperwork and other excessive documentation requirements. For example, a clinician complained, "I want to do less paperwork and have more personal time with clients. Paperwork occupies 60 to 70 percent of my job. This time makes quality and quantity of care less effective." Similarly, another clinician grumbled, "I would like to see better programs for our clients. Our staff is so overloaded with paperwork that the clients of our program are lacking in planned structure and consistency."

The practice of state micromanagement entails two significant management challenges on the part of the Center. First, excessive reporting requirements decrease employee morale significantly. All program managers interviewed agreed that state accreditation requirements and clinical audits from an external organization (i.e., APS) are the primary cause of the demoralization of themselves and of their employees. Over 80 percent of employee survey respondents concurred that their decisions are totally driven in terms of paperwork by Medicaid and APS requirements that make the paper workload unnecessarily onerous. In particular, filling out a six-page clinical record along with specific clinical plans for all services is especially daunting.

Second, decreased employee morale adversely impacts the quality of services and client satisfaction, as demoralization generates consistent high turnover of Center employees. The manager of a children's mental illness program

argued that dissatisfaction with salary is a major factor for employees leaving the Center. However, the heavy workload is an equally important factor leading to perpetually high turnover rates at the Center. This consistent high turnover rate affects quality of services in two ways. First, it demoralizes other employees who remain in the organization, as they are forced to take over the workload of former workers. Second, it reduces the level of client satisfaction due to disruption in the provision of services. The program manager claimed that clients and their families have been complaining about services due to the frequent change of clinicians during their treatment period. A client confirmed, "I would prefer to see the same doctor, not a different one, when I come. I see three or four. I never know which one I will see." Another client agreed, "There are too many changes in staff and others. It stifles one's satisfaction in comfortability with too many changes." In brief, the high turnover rate of employees not only decreases employee morale, but it also decreases the level of client satisfaction by disrupting the continuity of care for clients.

### Hierarchical Pressure for Performance Improvement

An apparent irony of government contracting is that government contractors have been increasingly required to improve their performance while spending fewer financial resources. An immediate lesson of this irony is that the traditional, mission-oriented work culture in nonprofit agencies can no longer meet this reality. For example, nonprofit agencies are increasingly forced to rely on revenue-generating activities (i.e., fundraising) as a way of overcoming consistent budget cutbacks and ever-increasing performance expectations (James 2003; Light 2000; Weisbrod 1997; Young 2002).

By the same token, the Center changes were designed to establish a market-oriented performance culture in response to the state's increasing performance expectations and shrinking financial support. However, this new style of performance culture works against service-oriented Center employees and those clients who believe that nonprofits should not be run in a businesslike way that may distort the central mission of serving clients. This cognitive dissonance against market orientation results in philosophical resistance to the efforts of performance improvement, because service professionals tend to view such efforts as divergent to the quality care of clients (Buntz 1981).

Not surprisingly, over 76 percent of the employee survey respondents complained that the hierarchical pressure for higher work productivity—as measured by direct service time—not only increased their stress levels at work, but also decreased the quality of care. Monitoring of direct service time implies that clinicians should manage their time well by not spending time on nonbillable tasks such as receiving phone calls from clients and their family, which are important aspects of client care. Thus, one clinician complained, "Those making decisions about direct service time do not seem to have a working knowledge of what's involved at the clinical level. Experienced staff are not being allowed to be used in the most effective capacity." Another clinician concurred that the greater emphasis on work productivity is forcing "client care [to become] secondary to productivity."

Employees' philosophical resistance to market-oriented change culminated with the recent financial crisis of the Center that resulted in salary reduction of individual employees. The major cause of the financial crisis was poor documentation of billing for Medicaid clients, which then required the reimbursement of the state for bills that failed to meet the state's reporting requirements. The director of clinical services contended that the root of the financial problem was the lack of a business mentality among employees, who tended to view the fee-based services as a violation of the central mission of rendering services to people

in need, regardless of their ability to pay for the services.

In sum, the hierarchical pressure for performance improvement is a relevant response by the Center to meet its legal accountability. However, the pressure for work productivity discounted the professional accountability of Center employees and created a management-clinician dichotomy in which individual clinicians tend to distrust or even refuse to follow the directions of the Center's management team (Buntz 1981). This internal cacophony is preventing the Center from accomplishing a smooth transition from a traditional mission-oriented culture to a market-oriented performance culture.

## Conclusion

An analysis of the quandaries of competing accountability relationships at the Center reveals that the disappointing results of a series of reforms stem from the efforts to meet legal accountability imposed by the state regulator. A web of requirements from the state regulator has led the Center's management to increase hierarchical control to achieve better work productivity and appropriate documentation of paperwork. However, these pressures for legal and hierarchical accountability are ill-suited, given the nature of the Center's services, which require some professional expertise, discretion, and political responsiveness to its constituencies.

The pressures for legal accountability prevent the Center's employees from fully exercising their professional expertise and discretion, which not only impairs their morale but also negatively affects the quality of care that ultimately makes political accountability susceptible. The nature of the Center's services requires that professional accountability receive at least an equal, if not a higher, level of attention as do legal and hierarchical accountability. However, reality does not seem to follow this proposition, considering that the Center faces continuous budget cuts and ever-increasing performance expectations from the state. Thus, one can expect a continued challenge in nonprofit performance as the balance in competing accountability relationships is skewed due to the domination of any one set of accountability relationships.

Heavy dependence on government funders among NHSAs tends to put greater emphasis on legal accountability while neglecting the professional nature of human services programs. Solving the tension between demands for legal accountability and managerial needs for professional accountability will remain the central challenge in nonprofit management in the future.

## Notes

1. The accountability framework was originally developed by Romzek and Dubnick (1987).

2. The state requires the Center to provide evidence of the work productivity of clinicians using direct service time as a measure of billable work hours. The direct service time can be calculated by the number of service units each clinician actually collected divided by the number of service units each clinician is supposed to collect based on working hours.

## References

Alexander, J., R. Nank, and C. Stivers. 1999. "Implications of Welfare Reform: Do Nonprofit Survival Strategies Threaten Civil Society?" *Nonprofit and Voluntary Sector Quarterly* 28, no. 4, 452–475.

Behn, R. D., and P. A. Kant. 1999. "Strategies for Avoiding the Pitfalls of Performance Contracting." *Public Productivity and Management Review* 22, no. 4, 470–489.

Buntz, C. G. 1981. "Problems and Issues in Human Service Productivity Improvement." *Public Productivity Review* 5, no. 4, 299–320.

Chisolm, L. B. 1995. "Accountability of Nonprofit Organizations and Those Who Control Them: The Legal Framework." *Nonprofit Management and Leadership* 6, no. 2, 141–156.

Dicke, L. A. 2002. "Ensuring Accountability in Human Services Contracting: Can Stewardship Theory Fill the Bill?" *American Review of Public Administration* 32, no. 4, 455–470.

Dicke, L. A., and J. S. Ott. 1999. "Public Agency Accountability in Human Service Contracting." *Public Productivity and Management Review* 22, no. 4, 502–516.

Gaynor, M. 1990. "Incentive Contracting in Mental Health: State and Local Relations." *Administration and Policy in Mental Health* 18, no. 1, 33–42.

Herman, R. D., and D. O. Renz. 1997. "Multiple Constituencies and the Social Construction of Nonprofit Organization Effectiveness." *Nonprofit and Voluntary Sector Quarterly* 26, no. 2, 185–206.

Independent Sector. 2002. *Keeping the Trust: Confidence in Charitable Organizations in an Age of Scrutiny.* Washington, DC (August). Available at: www.independentsector.org/PDFs/trust.pdf (accessed September 2, 2005).

James, E. 2003. "Commercialism and the Mission of Nonprofits." *Society* 40, no. 4, 29–35.

Johnson, J. 2003. "A Community Mental Health Center Aims to Tighten Controls: Scrutiny Again Falls on Agency. *Athens Banner-Herald,* October 12. Available at: www.onlineathens.com/stories/101203/new_20031012070.shtml (accessed October 13, 2003).

Johnston, J. M., and B. S. Romzek. 1999. "Contracting and Accountability in State Medical Reform: Rhetoric, Theories, and Realities." *Public Administration Review* 59, no. 5, 383–399.

Kearns, K. P. 1994. "The Strategic Management of Accountability in Nonprofit Organizations: An Analytical Framework." *Public Administration Review* 54, no. 2, 185–192.

Kettl, D. F. 1993. *Sharing Power.* Washington, DC: Brookings Institution Press.

Light, P. C. 2000. *Making Nonprofits Work: A Report on the Tides of Nonprofit Management Reform.* Washington, DC: Brookings Institution Press.

———. 2002. *Trust in Charitable Organizations.* Policy Brief No. 6 (December). Washington, DC: Brookings Institution Press.

————. 2003. *To Give or Not to Give: The Crisis of Confidence in Charities.* Policy Brief No. 7 (December). Washington, DC: Brookings Institution Press.

Milward, H. B., K. G. Provan, and B. A. Else. 1993. "What Does the 'Hollow State' Look Like?" In B. Bozeman, ed., *Public Management: State of the Art,* 309–322. San Francisco: Jossey-Bass.

Romzek, B. S., and M. J. Dubnick. 1987. "Accountability in the Public Sector: Lessons from the Challenger Tragedy." *Public Administration Review* 47, no. 3, 227–238.

Rubin, H. 1990. "Dimensions of Institutional Ethics: A Framework for Interpreting the Ethical Context of the Nonprofit Sector." In D. Gies, S. Ott, and J. M. Shafritz, eds., *The Nonprofit Sector: Essential Readings,* 211–216. Pacific Grove, CA: Brooks/Cole.

Salamon, L. M. 1999. *America's Nonprofit Sector: A Primer,* 2nd ed. New York: Foundation Center.

————. 2002. *The State of Nonprofit America.* Washington, DC: Brookings Institution Press.

Shearer, L. 2002. "Health Agency Makes the Grade After Problems." *Athens Banner-Herald,* June 12. Available at: www.onlineathens.com/stories/061302/new_20020613031.shtml (accessed June 13, 2002).

Smith, S. R. 2002. "Social Services." In L. M. Salamon, ed., *The State of Nonprofit America,* 149–186. Washington, DC: Brookings Institution Press.

State Commission on Mental Health, Mental Retardation, and Substance Abuse Service Delivery. 1992. *Call for Change: Empowering Consumers, Families, and Communities,* Atlanta.

————. 1996. *Call for Resolve: Fulfilling Our Promise to Consumers, Families, and Communities.* Atlanta.

State Department of Human Resources. 2003. *Medicaid Community Mental Health Center Program Manual.* Atlanta.

Weisbrod, B. A. 1997. "The Future of the Nonprofit Sector: Its Entwining with Private Enterprise and Government." *Journal of Policy Analysis and Management* 16, no. 4, 541–555.

Young, D. R. 2002. "The Influence of Business on Nonprofit Organizations and the Complexity of Nonprofit Accountability: Looking Inside as Well as Outside." *American Review of Public Administration* 32, no. 1, 3–19.

## Notes

1. The accountability framework was originally developed by Romzek and Dubnick (1987).

2. The state requires the Center to provide evidence of the work productivity of clinicians using direct service time as a measure of billable work hours. The direct service time can be calculated by the number of service units each clinician actually collected divided by the number of service units each clinician is supposed to collect based on working hours.

## CHAPTER 22

# Accountability Online: Understanding the Web-Based Accountability Practices of Nonprofit Organizations

## Gregory D. Saxton and Chao Guo

The idea of holding organizations and their leaders accountable for their actions has long been a matter of concern in the nonprofit sector. In recent years, the rapid diffusion of advanced Internet-based technologies among nonprofit organizations has brought with it considerable potential for demonstrating and promoting organizational accountability. How are nonprofit organizations taking advantage of this potential?

And what is driving their use of the Internet as an accountability- and public trust–building tool? In this article, we examine these questions in reporting the results of the first comprehensive study of nonprofit organizations' adoption of Web-based accountability practices.

Our central aims here are, first, to present a framework for conceptualizing and operationalizing Web-based accountability practices and, second, to present and test a theoretical model that can account for variation in these practices. Specifically, building on existing literature, we propose to understand the Web-based account-

ability practices of nonprofit organizations through two key dimensions: (a) disclosure, which concerns the transparent provision of key information on organizational finances and performance, and (b) dialogue, which encompasses the solicitation of input from and interactive engagement with core stakeholders. We then present a theoretical model in which four groups of factors—strategy, capacity, governance, and environment—are posited to affect the extent to which organizations vary in their adoption of Web-based accountability practices along our two dimensions.

In providing a generalized test of Web-based accountability, this article represents an important first step toward understanding the role of information technology in enhancing nonprofit accountability. Using our four-factor model and new data collected through a content analysis of 117 US community foundation[1] Web sites in conjunction with survey and financial data, we demonstrate that organizations vary greatly in the extent to which they adopt Web-based accountability practices along the dimensions of disclosure and dialogue. Though the typical community foundation takes care to disclose at least minimal financial- and performance-related information, many community foundations' Web sites are, it appears, mostly information-only brochureware; they provide few mechanisms to facilitate input from or interactively engage with key stakeholders. The dialogue dimension is hence severely lacking in the typical community foundation. Our multivariate analyses, in turn, provide some support for the validity of the four-factor model we identified, with the governance- and capacity-related factors tending to dominate the results. . . .

## Web-Based Accountability: A Two-Dimensional View

In the most general of terms, we might refer to a nonprofit organization's Web-based accountability practices as any online reporting, feedback, and/or stakeholder input and engagement mechanisms that serve to demonstrate or enhance accountability. . . .

There are both demand and supply forces at work. On the demand side, Internet-based technologies are providing citizens with the increasing ability and interest to gain access to information they deem important.[2] According to a Pew Internet & American Life Project (2008) survey, as of May 2008, 73 percent of Americans use the Internet. More and more people are getting their information from the Web—and in such a way that it is affecting how they volunteer with, give to, and otherwise interact with charitable organizations (e.g., see Gordon, Knock, and Neely 2008). On the supply side, in turn, Internet-based technologies have led to an increased ability of organizations to disclose financial and operational information. Through the use of interactive electronic networking capabilities, the technology also facilitates stakeholder in-

clusion in organizational decision making by lowering participation costs.

In short, with the diffusion of Internet technology, there is both an increased need as well as ability to use the Web to address organizational accountability. . . . We posit that there are two fundamental dimensions to Web-based accountability practices: *disclosure* and *dialogue*.

### Disclosure

. . . [A]n organization's online efforts in the areas of both accountability for finances and accountability for performance essentially amount to demonstrating accountability through the voluntary disclosure of key organizational information.[3] . . .

**Financial Disclosure**

. . . [W]e conceptualize financial disclosure as the extent of financial information a nonprofit organization discloses on its Web site. Such disclosure aims at demonstrating accountability for finances, and in the online environment involves posting such content as budgeting materials, reporting on the utilization of financial resources, and compliance-related documents—including information on administrative fees for funds; fund investment, management, and spending policies; investment philosophies; investment performance and asset growth; audited and unaudited financial reports; Internal Revenue Service (IRS) 990 forms; overhead costs; annual reports; codes of ethics and conflict-of-interest policies; and adherence to best practice standards.

**Performance Disclosure**

. . . [W]e conceptualize performance disclosure as the extent of goal- and outcome-oriented information a nonprofit organization discloses on its Web site. Such disclosure aims at demonstrating accountability for performance, which . . . covers both the organization's mission and its results. Performance disclosure thus involves an organization making available online any information, first, on what it is trying to achieve—such as its mission statement, history, vision, plans, values, and goals—and, second, on what it has achieved in terms of outputs, outcomes, and broader community impacts.

### Dialogue

The second dimension of Web-based accountability concerns mechanisms for stakeholder input and interactive engagement. . . . [W]e refer to this dimension as dialogue. Although preliminary evidence suggests the disclosure element can be critical to organizational outcomes (e.g., Gordon et al. 2008), it is on this second dimension that the Web holds special promise.

#### Solicitation of Stakeholder Input

. . . [D]ialogue includes two related but distinct components. The first refers to the solicitation of stakeholder input, and includes any Web-based mechanism that can tap stakeholders' preferences, needs, and demands in such a way that, ultimately, stakeholders have some degree of say in the organization's decision making regarding policies and programs. In addition to simple feedback forms, discussion lists, and bulletin boards, the recent development and growth of collaborative wikis, online surveying and polling tools, and tagging and social bookmarking projects has opened up new opportunities for intense, decentralized, and highly participatory problem-solving, decision-making, brainstorming, and knowledge-creation efforts. Collectively, the architecture of participation (O'Reilly 2005) in these technologies has dramatically increased organizations' ability to obtain meaningful stakeholder input.

#### Interactive Engagement

Although the first component of dialogue can be seen as the input of stakeholder preferences, this second component can be seen as an output of those preferences in the form of interactive content, tools, and services specifically designed for and targeted at particular stakeholder groups. This component is built on the notion that what best distinguishes second-generation Web technologies is precisely the ability to facilitate intense interactions between actors and, moreover, that highly interactive content targeted at core stakeholders is a key component of an organization's attempts to be accountable to those stakeholders by responding to their preferences.[4] . . .

## Strategy, Capacity, Governance, and Environment: A Model of Web-Based Accountability Practices

We propose that a nonprofit organization's level of Web-based accountability derives from four sets of factors familiar to nonprofit organizational scholars: strategy, capacity, governance, and environment. In particular, an organization's adoption of Web-based accountability practices is a function of (a) the extent to which the organization's strategy is focused on certain stakeholder groups or geographic service areas; (b) the degree to which the organization has the capacity to sustain strategic-level projects, especially with regard to the utilization of information technology; (c) the degree to which the organization is well governed; and (d) the degree to which the external environment is receptive to or demanding of Web-based organizational practices.

In this section, we lay out specific hypotheses about these relationships. It is our assertion that all of these determinants—strategy, capacity, governance, and environment—must be considered when explaining a nonprofit organization's level of Web-based accountability.

### Strategy

The particular strategy that a nonprofit organization develops to accomplish its social mission has important implications for its adoption of Web-based accountability mechanisms. We consider two elements here, the first of which is stakeholder focus. Community foundations' strategies are often categorized according to whether the dominant stakeholder focus is on donor services or community leadership (Graddy and Morgan 2006). . . . The community-focused model emphasizes community leadership, participation in community collaborative initiatives, and raising unrestricted funds to target high-priority needs. The donor-focused model, on the other hand, focuses on fulfilling the charitable interests of individual donors and on managing donor-advised funds. These two models have led to distinct views regarding community foundations' accountability relationships. In line with the community-focused model, the foundation should be accountable to the community where it operates and responsive to the needs and concerns of that community. In line with the donor-focused model, however, the community foundation should be accountable to its donors and facilitate each donor's individual charitable interests.

Taking the important differences between these two models into account, we posit that donor-focused foundations will adopt a higher level of Web-based accountability practices than community-focused foundations because of the stronger influence of and closer monitoring by donors. . . . In recent years, donor-advised funds have grown in popularity as a major funding source for many community foundations (Luke and Feurt 2002). This more restrictive type of funds, while offering hope of accumulating assets at a much faster pace than unrestricted funds, allows donors to have stronger control over the use of funds. It is thus reasonable to expect that a foundation that relies on donor-advised funds is more likely to demonstrate a higher level of online accountability or, conversely, that a foundation with greater amounts of unrestricted funds in its endowment will

have lower levels of Web-based accountability. This leads to our first hypothesis:

*Hypothesis 1:* Online accountability is negatively associated with the percentage of unrestricted funds.

The second strategy-related factor is geographic service area. Each community foundation serves a specific geographic area that often does not overlap with others. In a recent study (Guo and Brown 2006), those foundations serving smaller or more-defined geographic or sociopolitical regions are defined as *specialist* foundations, and those serving larger and more heterogeneous regions as *generalist* foundations. . . . The authors suggest that specialist foundations can make fuller use of local knowledge and experience to connect donors with effective providers. Following this line of reasoning, it seems reasonable to expect that specialist foundations will demonstrate a higher level of online accountability than generalist foundations:

*Hypothesis 2:* Online accountability is negatively associated with the size of geographic service area.

### Capacity

The capacity the organization has to undertake strategically driven initiatives also has implications for the adoption of Web-based accountability practices. One of the most consistently important capacity factors cited in the literature is organizational size. Size is a particularly important determinant of nonprofit accountability. As an organization grows, it becomes more visible and therefore attracts greater attention and scrutiny by multiple external constituencies, such as the state, the media, and the general public (Luoma and Goodstein 1999).

The literature also demonstrates a strong relationship between size and access to technology (Berlinger and Te'eni 1999; McNutt and Boland 1999; Schneider 2003); more importantly, there appears to be a critical connection between wealth and the ability to exploit technology for specifically mission-related purposes (Hackler and Saxton 2007).[5] In effect, size predicts an organization's capacity to employ information technology for strategic functions—such as boosting accountability—as opposed to purely administrative functions. Recent nonprofit research has also found a positive relationship between size and voluntary disclosure (e.g., Behn, DeVries, and Lin 2007; Gordon, Fisher, Malone, and Tower 2002). Accordingly, we submit the following hypothesis:

*Hypothesis 3:* Online accountability is positively associated with organizational size.

We also posit that younger organizations will be more likely to resort to Web-based accountability mechanisms. The literature denotes several reasons for this. First, accounting scholars have argued that there is a greater information asymmetry between insiders and outsiders in new organizations, which spurs younger organizations to greater voluntary disclosure to bridge the gap (e.g., Trabelsi, Labelle, and Dumontier 2008). Management scholars, in turn, are likely to cite organizational age as a factor that increases inertia and weakens discretion (Hambrick and Finkelstein 1987), rendering older organizations less likely to be innovative in the adoption of new technology. This leads us to the following hypothesis:

*Hypothesis 4:* Online accountability is negatively related to organizational age.

### Governance

The upper-echelons perspective (Hambrick and Mason 1984) attributes major influence (in terms of both strategic choices and organizational performance) to organizational leadership. We present propositions for two specific governance characteristics. The first is board performance. In the United States, the law ultimately holds the board of directors accountable for the affairs and conduct of the organization. . . .

Brody (2002) . . . described the role of a nonprofit's board as the "classical model of nonprofit accountability" (p. 476). Given the board's ultimate responsibility for a foundation's mission, direction, and policies (Bothwell 1989), we expect that those organizations with a high-performing board will demonstrate a greater level of online accountability than those with a low-performing board:

*Hypothesis 5:* Online accountability is positively associated with board performance.

Financial stewardship is one of the most important responsibilities of the nonprofit board. It refers to "the degree to which the board scrutinizes finances and the existence of sound financial practices as well as the extent to which the board maintains a degree of objectivity and independence from management" (Gill, Flynn, and Reissing 2005, 278). . . .

. . . [W]e posit it as a direct determinant of an organization's willingness to invest in technology-enabled accountability practices. This leads to the following hypothesis:

*Hypothesis 6:* Online accountability is positively related to financial stewardship.

## Sample and Data Gathering

To investigate the prevalence and determinants of Web-based accountability, we utilize data gathered in September and October of 2005 on 117 US community foundations that had in a previous study (Guo and Brown 2006) completed a questionnaire and follow-up telephone interviews.[6] Our Web site data-gathering method consisted of a multicoder analysis of the complete content on each of the 117 community foundations' Web sites.[7] Our approach was to search for and code any Web site content that conformed to our literature-grounded conceptualizations of financial disclosure,

FIGURE 22.1.  **Generic Model of Causal Factors Determining an Organization's Online Accountability Practices**

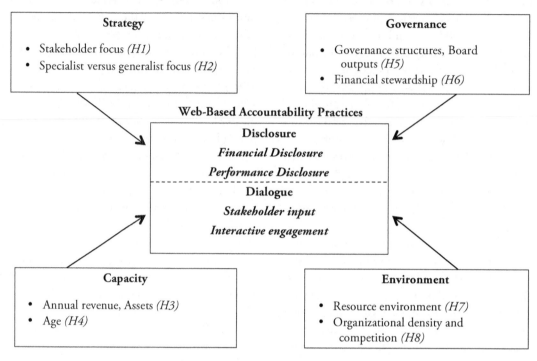

performance disclosure, solicitation of stake-holder input, and interactive engagement.[8] We then combine these data with questionnaire responses data and IRS form 990 data to test our hypotheses.

The average community foundation in our sample was 28 years old in 2005 and had US$58.6 million in assets, of which 24.4 percent were discretionary funds. It generated revenues of US$5.7 million a year, and granted, on average, 9 percent of its assets.[9] Our content analysis showed 113 of the 117 foundations to have meaningful Web sites.[10] In terms of accountability-related content, 92 percent of the organizations made available online at least minimal information relevant to performance-related disclosure, 77 percent had information relevant to financial disclosure, 78 percent had at least simple feedback/stakeholder input mechanisms in place, and 85

percent made available some form of nonstatic interactive engagement mechanism with one or more core stakeholder group.

## Operationalization

We operationalize five dependent variables that conform to our conceptual specifications of Web-based accountability: For the disclosure element, we create indices of both financial- and performance-related disclosure, for the dialogue dimension, we measure both the solicitation of input and the interactive engagement with key stakeholders, and to capture overall effort, we create a composite online accountability index.

In this section, we describe our measurement procedures for these variables before turn-

FIGURE 22.2. **Financial Disclosure**

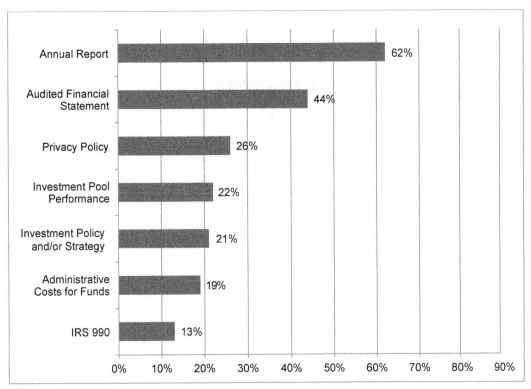

ing to a brief description of our specification of the eight independent variables we use to test our hypotheses.

### Dependent Variables: Measuring Web-Based Accountability

**Financial Disclosure Index (FDI)**

Following the data-gathering approach noted above, for this measure we coded content found anywhere on the site that was targeted at demonstrating financial responsibility. As shown in Figure 22.2, we found seven items that indicate a community foundation's online financial disclosure efforts: annual report, audited financial statement, privacy policy, data on investment pool performance, investment policy and/or strategy, information on administrative costs for funds, and IRS 990 form. . . .

**Performance Disclosure Index (PDI)**

In the area of performance disclosure, we coded any material on the Web site related to the organization's fulfillment of its social mission. In line with our literature review, such disclosure includes any information related to the foundation's mission, or what it is trying to achieve, along with its results, or the outputs, outcomes, and broader community impacts of its grant-making activity.[11] Figure 22.3 shows the eight items we found that indicate community foundations' online performance disclosure in these areas—a mission statement, list of recent grant awards, dollar amounts of individual grants awarded, description of community foundations' general purpose, summaries of funded projects, reporting on program or grant impact, community impact reporting, and grantee success stories. . . .

FIGURE 22.3. **Performance Disclosure**

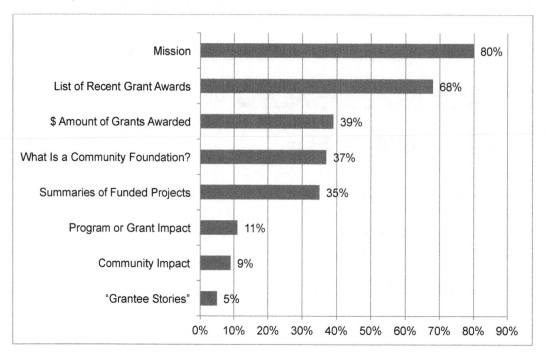

**Solicitation of Stakeholder Input**

With this first component of dialogue, we are interested in how community foundations use Web-based technologies to solicit feedback from their stakeholders, assess their preferences and needs, or engage them in discussions that will help the organization make important program-related decisions. As shown in Figure 22.4, we found a few exemplary practices along this dimension that one or two organizations were using, such as a Nonprofit Listserv or an Interactive Message Center. However, the number of organizations availing themselves of such tools is very low; besides the ubiquitous contact-us links, the great majority of sites had no means of soliciting information on stakeholder concerns. . . .

**Interactive Engagement (Interactivity)**

We are interested here in how community foundations are using the Internet to be responsive to the needs and demands of donors, grant seekers, and the community—their three core stakeholders—through the provision of high-level interactive Web site content. Our framework for evaluating the level of interactive engagement is the information-transaction-interaction hierarchy developed by Saxton, Guo, and Brown (2007). In this framework, an organization that has, for instance, only informational content available for donors cannot have great intensity in its online relationships with this key group. In contrast, an organization that allows online transactions to take place, such as e-donations, newsletter sign-ups, content downloads, or information uploads, has permitted more intense and important interactions with its contributors. And a site that has a variety of interactive,[12] Web 2.0–type content targeted at donors—such as a customizable donor/advisor extranet, interactive blogs, Web-enabled databases, online training, virtual conferences, and social

FIGURE 22.4. **Solicitation of Stakeholder Input**

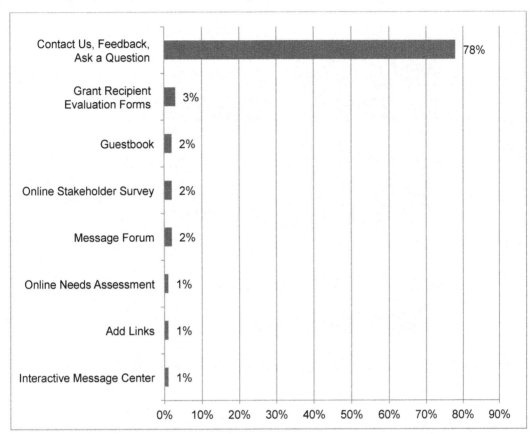

networking applications—will have the most meaningful donor interactions and thus the highest levels of interactive engagement. Based on this hierarchy, Figure 22.5 shows the proportion of foundations with low-level informational content, higher-level transactional content, and highest-level interactive content targeted at donors, grant seekers, and the community, respectively.

To create our measure of interactive engagement, we first assigned each community foundation three provisional scores based on the information shown in the figure. Specifically, with regard to donors, a community foundation received a score of 3 if it provided any donor-related services on its Web site that allow for interaction; it received a score of 2 if it

provided services that allow for transactions but no interactive content; it received a score of 1 if it provided only basic informational content to donors; and it received a score of 0 if it provided no donor-related content. We did the same with regard to grant seekers and the community. Our final composite scale, Interactivity, is then the sum of these three values, such that each community foundation's score can range from a low of 0 to a high of 9.[13]

**Online Accountability Index**

Last, we created a composite index of online accountability by summing each organization's scores on the FDI, PDI, and Interactivity variables. A Cronbach's alpha of .82 indicates a high level of internal consistency.[14]

FIGURE 22.5. **Interactive Engagement with Stakeholders**

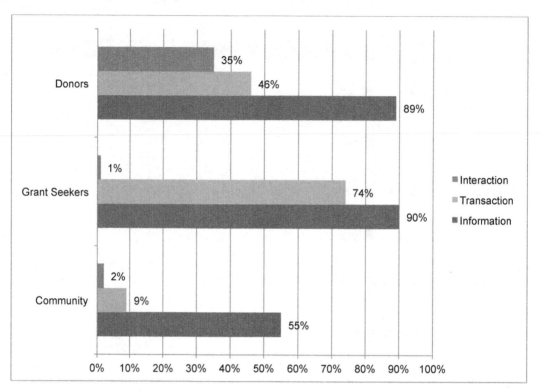

### Independent Variables

As discussed earlier, we operationalize our hypotheses through eight independent variables, two for each of the four factors (strategy, capacity, governance, and environment) in our explanatory model. First, with regard to strategy, Discretionary Income is the natural logarithm of the percentage of permanent unrestricted funds in a foundation's total assets, as reported by the chief executive (Community Foundation CEO survey, Guo and Brown 2006). Size of Service Area, in turn, measures the size of geographical area that a community foundation serves; it is defined as a binary variable with a value of 1 for specialist foundations that serve a small-sized community (i.e., local community such as city or county) and 2 for generalist foundations that serve a medium- to large-sized community (i.e., a regional or statewide foundation). In terms of capacity, we include Asset Size, the natural log of a given foundation's assets from the 2004FY IRS form 990, and Age, the age of the organization in years. To examine governance, we first use our CEO survey data (Guo and Brown 2006) to measure the chief executive's perception of Board Performance on a 1 to 5 scale; this is a composite measure that covers resource acquisition, stewardship, donor service, grant making, marketing, and mission and strategy. We also measure the organization's Net Working Capital as current assets less current liabilities (2004FY IRS form 990); this serves as the proxy for financial stewardship.[15] Last, we measure environment via Community Poverty, the percentage of residents below the poverty line in the foundation's primary county in 2001 (US Census Bureau), and Organizational

Density, the ratio of the number of community foundations in a given state over the state's gross state product.[16]

## Data Analysis and Results

Because the dependent variables in this study involve counts of services and content on a community foundation's Web site, we use a Poisson regression analysis[17] to estimate the following four models:

FDI = $\exp(\beta_0 + \beta_1$ Discretionary Income + $\beta_2$ Size of Service Area + $\beta_3$ Asset Size + $\beta_4$ Age + $\beta_5$ Board Performance + $\beta_6$ Net Working Capital + $\beta_7$ Community Poverty + $\beta_8$ Organizational Density)

PDI = $\exp(\beta_0 + \beta_1$ Discretionary Income + $\beta_2$ Size of Service Area + $\beta_3$ Asset Size + $\beta_4$ Age + $\beta_5$ Board Performance + $\beta_6$ Net Working Capital + $\beta_7$ Community Poverty + $\beta_8$ Organizational Density)

Interactivity = $\exp(\beta_0 + \beta_1$ Discretionary Income + $\beta_2$ Size of Service Area + $\beta_3$ Asset Size + $\beta_4$ Age + $\beta_5$ Board Performance + $\beta_6$ Net Working Capital + $\beta_7$ Community Poverty + $\beta_8$ Organizational Density)

Online Accountability Index = $\exp(\beta_0 + \beta_1$ Discretionary Income + $\beta_2$ Size of Service Area + $\beta_3$ Asset Size + $\beta_4$ Age + $\beta_5$ Board Performance + $\beta_6$ Net Working Capital + $\beta_7$ Community Poverty + $\beta_8$ Organizational Density)

Table 22.1 displays the results of these regression analyses. The coefficients in Models 1 through 4 (with standard errors in parentheses) indicate the effects of each independent variable on the financial disclosure index (FDI), performance disclosure index (PDI), interactive engagement scale (Interactivity), and composite online accountability index, respectively.

To recap, each of the eight independent variables is associated with a specific hypothesis related to one of the four primary factors in our explanatory model. In line with our hypothesis testing, we present our results here briefly factor by factor before discussing the most important implications of these findings in the Conclusions.

First, in Hypotheses 1 and 2, we proposed that two strategy-related variables—the percentage of unrestricted funds and the size of the geographic service area—would be negatively associated with Web-based accountability practices. The regression analyses revealed no significant relationship between either of these variables and the disclosure and dialogue measures of accountability (FDI, PDI, and Interactivity). However, both obtained a strong, negative relationship with the composite measure of accountability, thus providing partial support for our hypotheses.

Next, we created two hypotheses to tap organizational capacity: Hypothesis 3 described a positive relationship between asset size and Web-based accountability practices, whereas Hypothesis 4 posited a negative relationship between age and accountability. The results were mixed. The analyses revealed a strong positive relationship between asset size and all four of the accountability measures; yet, age failed to obtain significance in any of the models.

Hypotheses 5 and 6 then proposed that two governance-related factors—board performance and financial stewardship—were expected to obtain a positive relationship with online accountability. The regression analyses revealed no significant relationship between net working capital, our proxy for financial stewardship, and the disclosure and dialogue measures of Web-based accountability (i.e., FDI, PDI, and Interactivity). Yet, it did obtain a strong negative association with the composite online accountability index. The analyses also revealed a significant, positive relationship between board performance and three of the measures of accountability (FDI, PDI, and the composite index).

Last, in Hypotheses 7 and 8 we posited that community poverty and organizational

TABLE 22.1. **Factors Associated with Online Accountability of Community Foundations: Poisson Regression Analyses**

| Hypothesis | Independent Variable | Hypothesized Direction | Model 1 Financial Disclosure Index (FDI) | Model 2 Performance Disclosure Index (PDI) | Model 3 Interactive Engagement Scale (Interactivity) | Model 4 Composite Online Accountability Index |
|---|---|---|---|---|---|---|
| 1 | Discretionary income | - | -0.03 (0.06) | -0.08 (0.05) | -0.03 (0.04) | -0.05** (0.02) |
| 2 | Size of service area | - | .23 (0.15) | -0.10 (0.13) | -0.17 (0.11) | -0.15*** (0.05) |
| 3 | Asset size | + | 0.29*** (0.06) | 0.15*** (0.05) | 0.13*** (0.04) | 0.17*** (0.02) |
| 4 | Age | - | -0.003 (0.004) | -0.001 (0.003) | -0.001 (0.003) | -0.000 (0.000) |
| 5 | Board performance | + | 0.29** (0.14) | 0.19* (0.12) | 0.12 (0.09) | 0.13*** (0.05) |
| 6 | Net working capital | + | -0.66 (0.47) | -0.46 (0.44) | -0.17 (0.31) | -0.55*** (0.18) |
| 7 | Community poverty | - | -0.01 (0.02) | -0.01 (0.01) | 0.02* (0.01) | -0.00 (0.01) |
| 8 | Organizational density | - | -1.51* (0.80) | -0.36 (0.64) | 0.07 (0.51) | -0.58** (0.27) |
| | Intercept | | -4.42*** (1.07) | -1.65** (0.83) | -1.07 (0.66) | -0.04 (0.34) |
| | $n$ | | 113 | 113 | 113 | 113 |
| | Log likelihood | | -193.82 | -204.34 | -217.67 | -378.32 |
| | $\chi^2$ | | 48.13*** | 23.56*** | 21.37*** | 124.60*** |

*$p < 0.1$. **$p < 0.05$. ***$p < 0.01$. Standard errors are shown in parentheses.

density, our two environment-related measures, would be negatively associated with Web-based accountability practices. Surprisingly, regional poverty was found to be positively associated with the dialogue dimension of accountability (Interactivity) but not with the other accountability measures. However, consistent with our prediction, the analyses revealed a significant and negative relationship between organizational density and both the FDI and the composite index of online accountability.

## Implications and Conclusions

In this article, we have examined the extent to which nonprofit organizations adopt Web-based accountability practices through an analysis of the content of 117 diverse US community foundation Web sites. . . . We believe the spread of interactive second-generation Web technologies has effectively increased organizations' potential for communicating with, strategically engaging, and being responsive to their core constituents.

However, what do our findings suggest about nonprofit organizations' realization of this potential? The strong implication is that community foundations in particular are failing to maximize the opportunity to use the Web to engage stakeholders. For instance, while 78 percent of the community foundations had the most basic contact-us, feedback, or ask-a-question features on their Web sites, only 7 percent of the community foundations in our sample had any higher-level mechanism for the solicitation of stakeholder preferences, needs, and demands—such as an online stakeholder survey, an interactive message forum, an online grant recipient evaluation form, a guestbook, or an online needs assessment. We also found great variability in the extent to which foundations avail themselves of financial accountability mechanisms. . . .

This severe underutilization of the technology deserves further attention—the nonprofit sector may need a resource-rich "accountability entrepreneur" to help nonprofits redefine what is considered good governance with respect to accountability, both on the Web and off. Our findings, however, cast some doubts on whether community foundations are willing and capable of playing this role of accountability entrepreneur, even in the online environment. . . .

Our findings show that capacity, and particularly asset size, stands out as the predominant factor in our model. As with many nonprofit phenomena, resources matter. Moreover, we found that higher levels of community poverty are not generally associated with increased online accountability, except in terms of interactive engagement. On the positive side, we do find that governance in the form of board performance is important. We would like to think that this link between board traits and accountability outputs is causal in nature; practitioners might thus want to look into further institutionalizing the accountability-building function of the board. We also found some evidence that community foundations respond to increases in organizational density by decreasing the amount of financial disclosure. This lends credence to the idea that disclosure is a tool organizations use to boost legitimacy in low-density (i.e., low-legitimacy) industries. . . .

As there is no one typical nonprofit organization, community foundations being no exception, we cannot argue that the same pattern of online accountability practices will necessarily exist in other types of nonprofits. Therefore, caution must be exercised in generalizing the findings of this study to a different industry context. Still, we believe that the two-dimensional view of Web-based accountability and the four broad sets of influencing factors identified in our model should work similarly in the rest of the nonprofit world.

## Notes

1. Community foundations are 501(c)(3) public charities that work to improve the quality of life of a specific geographic community by pooling funds from a wide range of individual, family, and corporate donors and allocating grants to targeted program areas that meet specific local needs. For more on community foundations, see Grønbjerg (2006).

2. An excellent example is the GuideStar Web site, which provides financial and operational information on more than one million nonprofit organizations throughout the United States.

3. The disclosure of financial and performance information has been increasingly identified as an important aspect of nonprofit accountability (e.g., Brody 2002; Melendez 2001).

4. For a complete account of this argument, see Saxton, Guo, and Brown (2007).

5. Similar results have obtained in the for-profit literature, where size has been identified as one of the critical prerequisites or antecedents that enable an

organization to exploit technology for mission-related purposes (e.g., Aral and Weill 2004; Buhalis 1998).

6. The authors of the earlier study (Guo and Brown 2006) began with an original sample of 677 US community foundations, obtained from the Council on Foundations Web site, which essentially represented the population of community foundations in the country. They then contacted chief executives of all 677 community foundations in May and June of 2004. Follow-up e-mails and telephone calls resulted in a final sample of 117, which is a response rate of 17 percent.

7. Several steps were made to ensure the reliability of the analysis. First, we conducted an exhaustive search of the 117 Web sites rather than a limited examination of specific sections of the sites as financial-disclosure items, for example, can be found in a wide variety of differently named Web site sections. Second, in terms of coding, each of the two principal investigators started by analyzing and coding the same 10 community foundation Web sites. This helped standardize the terminology used to code certain generic features (e.g., administrative costs for funds or online stakeholder survey) that were found on multiple sites but under different names. The two principal investigators and a graduate assistant then each coded a third of the remaining sites. Given the comprehensive nature of the examination of the sites and the multicoder review of the initial data-gathering efforts, there were few ambiguous codings at this stage, such as questions about whether an item counted as financial disclosure or performance disclosure. Nevertheless, an additional crucial step was taken to ensure intercoder reliability. Each of the two principal investigators reviewed half of the graduate assistant's sites in addition to half of the other investigator's sites. This step helped discover various minor coding errors and/or discrepancies that were found in less than 10 percent of the sites.

8. Beginning deductively with our theoretically grounded conceptualizations of the types of content implied by the two dimensions of online accountability, we approached the coding process with a fair amount of inductive reasoning in mind, given that we did not know precisely which features (some of which might be unique to the Web) we would find under each of these categories. For instance, we would have no way of knowing a priori that, related to community foundations' solicitation of stake-

holder input, we would find such material as online stakeholder surveys, interactive message forums, or online needs assessments.

9. To check for any potential nonresponse bias, we compared these key characteristics with those of the entire population of 677 community foundations then operating in the United States. We found that the average community foundation in the population at large was 22 years old and had US$43.2 million in assets. It generated revenue of US$5.2 million a year and granted, on average, 8 percent of its assets. In brief, the organizations in our final sample are slightly older and wealthier but overall quite representative of the population at large.

10. Interestingly, two of the foundations had no Web site, and another two had simplistic sites with no meaningful content.

11. It is on this component that community foundations seem to be making better use of Web technologies and providing more imaginative content to their key stakeholders—such as the regularly updated, hyperlinked photo galleries highlighting grant recipient success stories provided by the Lexington Community Foundation of Nebraska or the Madison Community Foundation of Wisconsin. Other organizations, such as the Community Foundation of Jackson Hole, provide copious details of their grant-making activities in a way that is both educational for the general public and instructive to grant-seeking organizations. The organization's Web site also serves a convening function by incorporating a nonprofit community event calendar and information on workshops, talks, and nonprofit executive meet-and-greet sessions. Last, several organizations were using their Web sites to provide extensive assistance in the area of project evaluation and outcome measurement. The Maine Community Foundation, for example, allows grant recipients to submit online a Project Evaluation Report to provide their results and feedback to the foundation on what contributed to the success of their project as well as reasons that made other aspects of their project more difficult or impossible to achieve. The Gulf Coast Community Foundation, meanwhile, provides a free online outcomes-tracking program called Impact Manager that comes bundled with how-to documents, outcome workbooks, links to external sites, online technical assistance documents, frequently asked questions (FAQs), and an online library.

12. As its name suggests, this highest level of content involves some form of interaction—the two-way exchange of ideas, opinions, data, or information between two or more parties.

13. Though a PFA returned a single factor (eigenvalue = 0.64) with a low Cronbach's alpha (.49) score, we decided on theoretical grounds to include the scale in our analyses.

14. A PFA returned a single factor (eigenvalue = 2.06) on which all items load at 0.6 or better.

15. Similar to the current ratio, net working capital is a method of assessing a nonprofit's ability to pay its short-term obligations. For the purpose of measuring financial stewardship, we decided to use net working capital instead of the current ratio because the latter has more missing observations in our sample.

16. We use this ratio instead of the actual number of community foundations to control for the effect of a state's wealth on organizational density.

17. With count variables, the ordinary least squares (OLS) method would tend to result in biased, inefficient, and inconsistent estimates (Long 1997). To deal with this problem, researchers have developed various nonlinear models based on the Poisson and negative binomial distributions. Both analyses were conducted here and produced similar results; since a likelihood ratio test showed that the negative binomial regression model is not a significantly better fit than the Poisson regression model, we only present here the results from the latter. We also ran an ordered logit regression for Interactivity and both an ordered logit and an OLS regression for our composite index. In all cases, there were no changes in sign or significance for any of the variables; thus we do not report the results further.

## References

Aral, S., and P. Weill. 2004. *IT Assets, Organizational Capabilities and Firm Performance: Asset and Capability Specific Complementarities.* MIT Sloan CISR Working Paper No. 343. Boston: Massachusetts Institute of Technology.

Behn, B. K., D. DeVries, and J. Lin. 2007. *Voluntary Disclosure in Nonprofit Organizations: An Exploratory Study.* Retrieved June 15, 2009, from http://ssm.com/abstract=727363.

Berlinger, L. R., and D. Te'eni. 1999. "Leaders' Attitudes and Computer Use in Religious Congregations." *Nonprofit Management and Leadership* 9: 399–412.

Bothwell, R. O. 1989. "Are They Worthy of the Name? A Critic's View." In R. Magat, ed., *An Agile Servant: Community by Community Foundations,* 155–165. New York: Foundation Center.

Brody, E. 2002. "Accountability and Public Trust." In L. M. Salamon, ed., *The State of Nonprofit America,* 471–498. Washington, DC: Brookings Institution.

Buhalis, D. 1998. "Strategic Use of Information Technologies in the Tourism Industry." *Tourism Management* 19: 409–421.

Gill, M., R. J. Flynn, and E. Reissing. 2005. "The Governance Self-Assessment Checklist: An Instrument for Assessing Board Effectiveness." *Nonprofit Management and Leadership* 15: 271–294.

Global Accountability Project Framework. 2005. *London, UK: One World Trust.* Retrieved June 15, 2009, from http://www.oneworldtrust.org/?display=gapframework.

Gordon, T., M. Fisher. D. Malone, and G. Tower. 2002. "A Comparative Empirical Examination of Extent of Disclosure by Private and Public Colleges and Universities in the United States." *Journal of Accounting and Public Policy* 21: 235–275.

Gordon, T. P., C. L. Knock, and D. G. Neely. 2008. *The Role of Rating Agencies in the Market for Charitable Contributions: An Empirical Test.* Working Paper. Moscow: University of Idaho.

Graddy, E. A., and D. L. Morgan. 2006. "Community Foundations, Organizational Strategy, and Public Policy." *Nonprofit and Voluntary Sector Quarterly* 35: 605–630.

Grønbjerg, K. A. 2006. "Foundation Legitimacy at the Community Level: The Case of Community Foundations in the US." In K. Prewitt, M. Dogan, S. Heydemann, and S. Toepler, eds., *Foundations and the Challenge of Legitimacy in Comparative Perspective,* 150–174. New York: Russell Sage Foundation.

Guo, C., and W. A. Brown. 2006. "Community Foundation Performance: Bridging Community Resources and Needs." *Nonprofit and Voluntary Sector Quarterly* 35: 267–287.

Hackler, D., and G. D. Saxton. 2007. "The Strategic Use of Information Technology by Nonprofit Organizations: Increasing Capacity and Untapped Potential." *Public Administration Review* 67: 474–487.

Hambrick, D. C., and S. Finkelstein. 1987. "Managerial Discretion: A Bridge Between Polar Views of Organizational Outcomes." *Research in Organizational Behavior* 9: 369–406.

Hambrick, D. C., and P. A. Mason. 1984. "Upper Echelons: The Organization as a Reflection of Its Top Managers." *Academy of Management Review* 9: 193–206.

Hannan, M. T., and J. Freeman. 1987. "The Ecology of Organizational Founding Rates: The Dynamics of Foundings of American Labor Unions, 1836–1975." *American Journal of Sociology* 92: 910–943.

Luke, J. L., and S. L. Feurt. 2002. *A Flexible and Growing Service to Donors: Donor-Advised Funds in Community Foundations.* Available at Council on Foundations' Web site, www.cof.org.

Luoma, P., and J. Goodstein. 1999. "Stakeholders and Corporate Boards: Institutional Influences on Board Composition and Structure." *Academy of Management Journal* 42: 553–563.

McNutt, J. G., and K. M. Boland. 1999. "Electronic Advocacy by Nonprofit Organizations in Social Welfare Policy." *Nonprofit and Voluntary Sector Quarterly* 28: 432–451.

Melendez, S. E. 2001. "The Nonprofit Sector and Accountability." *New Directions for Philanthropic Fundraising* 31: 121–132.

O'Reilly, T. 2005. *What Is Web 2.0? Design Patterns and Business Models for the Next Generation of Software.* Available from http://www.oreillynet.com.

Pew Internet & American Life Project. 2008. *April 8–May 11, 2008 Tracking Survey.* Available from http://www.pewinternet.org.

Saxton, G. D., C. Guo, and W. A. Brown. 2007. "New Dimensions of Nonprofit Responsiveness: The Application and Promise of Internet-Based Technologies." *Public Performance and Management Review* 31: 144–171.

Schneider, J. A. 2003. "Small, Minority-Based Nonprofits in the Information Age." *Nonprofit Management and Leadership* 13: 383–399.

Trabelsi, S., R. Labelle, and P. Dumontier. 2008. "Incremental Voluntary Disclosure on Corporate Web Sites: Determinants and Consequences." *Journal of Contemporary Accounting and Economics* 4: 120–155.

# AN AWARENESS CAMPAIGN GONE AWRY

*Benjamin S. Bingle, Amanda R. Insalaco, and C. Kenneth Meyer*

Susan Anthony grimaced as the sounds of rapid, heavy footsteps echoed down the corridor. They seemed to be getting closer.

*Not again,* Susan thought. She reluctantly peered around the glowing screen of her computer monitor just as a knock penetrated her office walls.

"Yes?" called Susan, apprehensively.

"Do you have a moment?" inquired a deep, empathetic voice from beyond the closed door. It was the executive director, Michael Henry.

"Oh, please come in," said Susan, with a sigh of relief. She was grateful that the knock at her door wasn't another reporter or angry parent.

## Background

Books for the Bronx, a nonprofit organization based in New York City, advocated for public school children who faced some of the most dilapidated educational facilities in the United States. Susan had enjoyed a successful career in the nonprofit sector, which continued when she joined Books for the Bronx in 2011 as its human resources director. Her responsibilities included overseeing all human resources activities for the small, but growing, organization. Susan also worked closely with Michael, the executive director, and the board of directors to address personnel policies and ensure that an adequate workforce was in place to accomplish organizational goals. In addition, she felt a sense of pride for being involved with Books for the Bronx, a sentiment shared by many of the other employees.

Books for the Bronx was created in 1998 because the poverty encompassing the Bronx borough of New York City had significantly impacted the public school system, resulting in marginal learning environments that, at times, even jeopardized the safety of the children. Books for the Bronx worked to educate policymakers, host informational meetings, raise awareness, and implement programming designed to mitigate the fundamental issue of poverty in the borough. To help fund their efforts while raising awareness, Michael worked tirelessly to give presentations, share informational packets, and disseminate educational materials to politicians and political staff in Washington, DC. Unfortunately, after two years of concentrated effort, these activities had yielded minimal results.

Feeling frustrated and forgotten by the inaction of their representatives, Michael and the board of directors had decided it might be best to diversify their approach. Rather than waiting on funding from the government and relying solely on the same methods of advocacy, Books for the Bronx would embark on an awareness campaign. The centerpiece of this campaign would be a short film to help donors, stakeholders, politicians, and the public at large to visualize the challenges facing the Bronx's public schools. Michael thought that if the organization could reach out to compassionate constituents throughout the United States, they could garner support for their cause, thereby raising the funds needed to help alleviate the dire situation in the Bronx.

## A New Approach

The first step to initiate the public outreach campaign would involve recruiting a highly skilled cinematographer to capture the plight of the children attending public schools in the Bronx. A documentary, after all, would convey to constituents the severity of the dangerous, decaying urban scenes imposed upon Bronx youth in a much more effective way than mere words.

The first step was to recruit and hire a cinematographer, and Susan had been tasked with this responsibility. Michael assured Susan that Books for the Bronx was willing to invest significantly in a well-produced, poignant, and effective documentary in order to reach the widest possible audience. To hire a talented, capable artist, she was instructed to feel free to offer a contract at the top of the pay range typically allowed for the organization's contractors. Initially, Susan was thrilled to be included in the project; however, after weeks of countless interviews, she grew increasingly frustrated by the lackluster qualifications of the applicants. Just when she had almost lost all hope, Jeffrey Madison walked into her office for an interview.

Jeffrey's resumé was very impressive, detailing extensive experience in documentary filmmaking, and his enthusiasm and passion for the project seemed unsurpassed and certainly reassuring. He had even won awards for directing commercials and short films. The extent of Jeffrey's experience did not come without a cost. Although Jeffrey's requested salary actually exceeded the contract amount being offered, Susan and Michael quickly decided that it was a worthwhile expenditure, especially considering their inability to attract other viable candidates.

Michael enthusiastically shared the hiring news with the board of directors and volunteered to manage the project himself. He believed that this video could be just the thing to finally open everyone's eyes to the school problems in the Bronx.

## The Wrong Approach?

Upon hiring Jeffrey, matters almost immediately deteriorated. Although it was clear that Jeffrey was enthusiastic about his art, he was not at all responsive when Michael reached out for status updates, budgetary information, or guidance about the project. When Jeffrey finally responded to the executive director, he seemed agitated, bothered by the request, and uncooperative. During a telephone conversation after filming began, Jeffrey snapped at Michael when he asked Jeffrey to elaborate on what scenes would be included in the film. Jeffrey believed that he was the acclaimed artist and that his vision for the film should prevail and not be second-guessed.

Concerned about his faltering control of the situation, Michael approached Susan for advice. Although they both agreed that the situation was not ideal, they decided to retain faith in Jeffrey's abilities. Besides, they had already invested so much time, money, and resources in the project.

As Susan pointed out, "The film should be completed in just a few more months, and then we can move on from our 'Hollywood diva'!"

Despite the decision, they both remained apprehensive about the project and grew increasingly concerned about the content of the film. After all, Jeffrey had only allowed them to see a few minutes of test footage for the documentary.

## The Rise and Fall of a Viral Video

Nearly three months after the agreed-upon completion date, and $4,500 over budget, Jeffrey had decided the time was right to release his creation. To the dismay of Michael and Susan, the documentary was primarily centered on the filmmaker and his family, who were residents of the Bronx. Though this was a clear distraction from Books for the Bronx and its mission, the initial success of the film was undeniable. It went viral, and in just one week multiple video hosting websites had tallied views in the hundreds of thousands. Donations came flooding in from all over the country as citizens suddenly became aware of the horrors of the Bronx public school system. Although the film was not exactly what Michael and Susan had in mind, it appeared to be effective in raising awareness and money.

Jeffrey reveled in his newfound fame. He was invited for interviews with various radio and television personalities, which only added to his profile and his ego. During public appearances, however, he acted as though he was the formal spokesperson for Books for the Bronx, even though he neither accurately represented the organization nor, frankly, knew much about its work.

In one particularly egregious example, Jeffrey had repeatedly boasted about the amount of money he was paid to complete the video, adding, "It was really a great opportunity to get my name out there and tell the story of a family—my family—and our experiences living in New York City."

Although he did not say exactly how much he had been paid by Books for the Bronx, his words left Michael and Susan increasingly distraught, with no feeling of control over the monster they had created. Their troubles had compounded when complaints from long-standing donors began pouring in, questioning the use of their donations to pay an egomaniac like Jeffrey Madison.

## Media and Public Pressure

The media's attention finally turned from Jeffrey to Books for the Bronx, but not for positive reasons. The press began relentlessly publishing stories about the misuse of funds, lack of internal controls, and poor judgment of the organization's leadership. The media firestorm came to a head when a prominent national newspaper pointedly demanded that Books for the Bronx immediately release its financial statements.

In turn, pressure from the public increased. The comments left on websites hosting the video were no longer about the need to address the dire situation in the Bronx public schools. Instead, people posted comments about this nonprofit "scamming" donors out of their money and the filmmaker "getting rich off the kindness of others." One especially critical comment claimed that Books for the Bronx had done little to actually help the children in Bronx schools and had focused all its time and money solely on raising its own profile. So many telephone, email, and in-person complaints from the public flooded into the organization that little other work was being done. Managing the media and the public outcry had become the primary activity of Books for the Bronx.

With organizational morale in decline and public confidence wavering, the organization felt increasing pressure to justify its existence and use of funds. After a long meeting with the board of directors, Michael instructed that all financial information related to Books for the Bronx be released on its website.

## Transparency and Fallout

Michael understood the need for organizational transparency and normally would have embraced the opportunity to share information with the public. Under these circumstances, however, he and the board of directors were quite reluctant. They knew there was one number that the media and public were after—the amount of Jeffrey Madison's contract.

Once the information became public, the outcry reached a new level. Heightened media attacks called for an audit of Books for the Bronx's entire operation, demanded that the Internal Revenue Service conduct an investigation, called on all donors to halt contributions to the organization, and asked for the resignation of Michael Henry and Susan Anthony.

## Back in the Office

Michael took a seat in a chair opposite Susan's desk and let out a long sigh.

"What a day," said Susan quietly.

Michael clearly had something weighing on his mind and began, in a defeated tone, "How did we get to this point, Susan? I only wanted to increase awareness about what's going on in these schools and raise some money to support the cause." Susan recognized the rhetorical nature of the question as Michael continued: "I'm tired of this whole thing. Ultimately, this all happened on my watch. I was involved with creating the idea, I oversaw the contract, and I had the financials released. I think it's time for me to step aside."

Susan could not believe her ears. Michael was actually thinking about giving in to those calling for his resignation, a possibility to which she had not given even a moment of her time. But that all changed when Michael asked, "When are you planning to submit your resignation letter?"

## Questions and Instructions

1. What are some advantages and disadvantages of hiring employees on a contractual basis? From your own experiences and research, or based on what you know about contract employment, how might Susan Anthony have mitigated some of the issues that developed with the cinematographer?
2. What could Michael and Susan have done differently when they realized there were problems with their contract employee?
3. Is it justifiable to forgo transparency when being transparent may yield larger problems? Please explain your response.
4. The media played an important role in leading the public outrage aimed at Books for the Bronx. How could the organization have better addressed the media attacks? Please explain your response.

# TECHNOLOGY AND TRANSPARENCY AT THE MUSEUM

*Amanda R. Insalaco, Benjamin S. Bingle, and C. Kenneth Meyer*

"How am I going to get all this work done?" Ted Hamilton asked, not expecting an answer in return. He was alone in his second-floor office pondering the coming fiscal year's budget. The sensor on the visitors' center front door released yet another deafening buzz. *The museum simply needs more staff, there is no denying it,* he thought as he scurried downstairs to greet museum guests.

As the executive director of the local historic house museum, it was Ted's duty to impress upon the board the gravity of the museum's need. Surely they would understand. After all, the board had recently initiated a campaign that was thus far successful in increasing admission ticket sales. The only problem: they now had to find the resources necessary to absorb the additional guests! Ted and his small staff were already working nearly seven days a week; clearly this was an unsustainable arrangement.

While Ted acted as host to museum guests in the lobby, his computer monitor dimmed on forgotten windows—Facebook, Twitter, and the museum website remained unattended. Meanwhile, the director of visitor services, Shanna Hernandez, conducted a tour and the programs coordinator, Dan Weber, cleaned bathrooms. The docent who typically volunteered on Tuesday afternoons had called in sick, again.

## Background

The Highside House had been operating as a museum and cultural center for more than fifty years. A prominent component of the arts landscape in the region, the museum frequently served as host to a wide variety of events. Weddings had been held in its gardens, employee trainings in its facilities, and art shows in its vast expanses. Plaques had been carefully placed on the grounds in remembrance of loved ones past. Even the governing board visibly demonstrated the value it placed on the organization. Board members were not reluctant to get their hands dirty, frequently rolling up their sleeves to repair trodden flowerbeds and tend to overgrown terraces.

The Highside House had been donated to the municipal park district by the grandchildren of Ivan and Mary Hinters in the late 1960s. Ivan, originally from modest means, made his fortune in the late nineteenth century raising draft horses on the hundreds of acres surrounding the estate. It was these riches that the Highside House was built upon.

Ivan and Mary had three children, and their youngest daughter and her husband eventually inherited the estate. In their will, they declared that the mansion and land would be donated to the municipal park district. Had the Hinters' descendants not graciously donated the property, it was likely that the historic structures would have been demolished long ago, the land swallowed up by housing developers. Through a unique arrangement, the property and structures were owned by the park district while the items within the structures were owned and managed by a nonprofit, the Highside House Association. The Association also provided the funds necessary for operating expenses.

With just three staff members, the museum maintained a relatively modest operating budget. Collections management and restoration services accounted for a significant portion of the organization's expenses, after salaries and employee benefits. Total annual expenses frequently fell below $200,000, though expenses could be expected to rise when the museum periodically undertook a restoration project.

## Priorities and Challenges

The museum charged a modest fee for its tours, providing senior and student discounts. Other sources of revenue included membership dues and fees for facility rentals. Although the organization's budget was in good health, staff members remained overworked and special exhibits were frequently put on hold, owing to a lack of surplus resources.

The Highside House relied heavily on volunteers to provide tours to the public. They were often expected to manage the museum gift shop as well. Unfortunately, volunteers were at times unable to commit their time; when this happened, staff had to provide these basic services. Frequently overlooked were the standard operational and governance responsibilities. The museum had struggled in years past, for example, to even compile financials for review by the board. As executive director, Ted insisted that staff prioritize direct service to the public over "fancy financial reports."

"After all," said Ted, "the doors stay open, and the public is happy. Why should we concentrate on that stuff when there are tours to give, weddings to book, and exhibits to develop?"

Although museum guests had certainly been pleased in the past, the museum's online reputation had suffered as a result of the disproportionate emphasis on direct service. The website was infrequently updated by overburdened staff, and the number of Facebook followers on the museum page had remained stagnant.

Meanwhile, an online "2-for-1" admission coupon and a targeted marketing campaign had proved successful, resulting in a noticeable increase in tours. Given the steady rise in patrons, Ted could no longer deny the need for additional human resources.

## Online Presence and Transparency

The higher number of guests yielded increased revenue from ticket sales, but also increased attention, some of which was unpopular. Specifically, the online coupon campaign brought unprecedented scrutiny of the organization's online presence—or lack thereof. As more people visited the website, it became clear that having an online presence had never been a priority at the Highside House. Calls began to trickle in inquiring about issues on the website, outdated information, and a lack of solid details related to the museum's finances. Potential donors and members alike asked, "Why isn't your website updated?" and, "How is my donation being used?" and, "Why is there no financial information online?"

In an era when the misuse of funds is commonplace and the best organizations use their websites as avenues for transparency, it appeared that donors and members had finally decided to hold the Highside House accountable. They demanded that more information—including financial data—be made available to the public and that the website be made more professional, appealing, and user-friendly. Embarrassed, Ted reluctantly approached the board.

More staff were needed to ensure that the organization could cater to a culture of transparency. Gradually, the board accepted the severity of the need as well, though some recognized the value of transparency more than others. It was determined that the organization would search for grants to help alleviate the financial strain, shore up operations, stabilize programming, and put the museum in a position to hire additional staff.

Ted located a funding opportunity aimed at providing support for community-based education initiatives. It was a perfect fit! He soon discovered, however, that the funding organization would also insist upon transparency. The museum would have to address five questions:

- Why should grant funds be given to the museum?
- What will the museum do with the grant funding?
- How will results be measured and communicated?
- How will the impact of this grant be shared with the public?
- How will the museum sustain transparent and responsible programming after the grant funding has concluded?

The museum could linger no longer. The pressure from donors, members, potential funders, and even a few board members made it clear that more transparency was necessary.

## The Funding Pursuit

Ted looked at the five primary questions that he was required to answer in the grant application. The first two were pretty straightforward, he thought as he began jotting notes on the grant guidelines and application document. The remaining questions all centered on transparency, measuring results, and sharing results. He had never been forced to think about these matters in such a structured way. "It's much easier to lead a couple tours or recruit some volunteers," Ted muttered. Furthermore, the idea of making financial data widely available still made him, and some board members, uncomfortable. After all, the organization had never even produced an annual report. Instead, all financial reporting was kept in-house and also kept to the bare minimum as required by law.

In the end, the need for financial support overpowered his concerns about financial privacy. Carrying the grant application materials in an overstuffed envelope, he released the package into the mailbox with bated breath and hoped for the best.

## Funding Decision

While waiting for a funding decision, Ted got back to the daily operations of the Highside House. During this time, Ted and his staff did nothing to shore up the website deficiencies. In fact, their only online activity was a few social media posts.

Two months had passed since he submitted the grant proposal, and Ted finally received a letter in the mail from the funding agency. He slowly read through its contents while sitting at his desk. What he read came as a surprise.

The grant allocation committee noted the worthiness of Ted's proposal, but suggested that certain areas of the application were woefully underdeveloped. Namely, the committee thought that Ted had skirted around the transparency clause of the application, using vague descriptions and convoluted wording. Moreover, in their review of applicant websites, the allocation committee had noticed inaccuracies, inconsistencies, and outdated information on the Highside House site. This did not inspire confidence among committee members. The letter said, "As funding partners, the websites of our grantees must not only exemplify their organizational values, but also our own. In essence, our grantees are an extension of us because they carry out the vital programs that we financially support."

Combining these website concerns with its concern about the Highside House's lack of an emphasis on transparency, the committee had decided to deny Ted's grant request this funding cycle. The letter ended, however, on an encouraging note: "The committee is excited by the possibilities you have outlined, and we encourage you to apply for funding again in the future after the Highside House staff has had an opportunity to reevaluate the transparency clause and reinforce its online presence."

Slightly embarrassed, somewhat defeated, and a little insulted, Ted folded the letter and placed it on his desk. Just then, a group of patrons entered the visitors' center and the familiar buzz sound rang out, alerting Ted that it was time to get back to work.

## Questions and Instructions

1.  How much emphasis should nonprofit organizations place on accountability, evaluation, and transparency efforts? Are these vital considerations or are they secondary to programming and services? Please elaborate.

2.  Putting yourself in the place of the executive director, what would you do to make the Highside House more transparent as an organization? How could technology be used to enhance transparency in this case?

3.  How might you persuade a reluctant staff member that it would be advantageous to share the organization's financial information online? Would your strategy change if it was a board member you were attempting to persuade? If so, how?

4.  The push for transparency in this case was primarily externally motivated. Do you think the museum would be likely to embrace and support a transparency initiative under these circumstances? What can an understaffed organization realistically do to meet the accountability expectations of the public or other stakeholders? Is there a need to prioritize accountability expectations under such circumstances? If so, what are the potential costs involved? If not, how would you manage this process?